Rick

BEST OF
EASTERN
EUROPE

2006

Rick Steves & Cameron Hewitt

Rick Steves' ®
BEST OF
EASTERN
EUROPE
2006

AVALON
TRAVEL

CONTENTS

Top Destinations in Eastern Europe

INTRODUCTION

Until 1989, Eastern Europe was a foreboding place—a dark and gloomy corner of the "Evil Empire." But now the obligatory grays and preachy reds of communism live only in history books, museums, and kitschy theme restaurants. Today's Eastern Europe is a traveler's delight, with low prices, friendly locals, lively squares, breathtaking sights, fascinating history, and a sense of pioneer excitement.

This book breaks Eastern Europe into its top big-city, small-town, and back-to-nature destinations. It then gives you all the information and opinions necessary to wring the maximum value out of your limited time and money. If you're planning for a month or less in this region, this book is all you need.

Experiencing Europe's culture, people, and natural wonders economically and hassle-free has been my goal for three decades of traveling, tour guiding, and writing. With this book, I pass on to you all of the lessons I've learned, updated for 2006.

You'll wander among Prague's dreamy, fairytale spires, bask in the energy of Kraków's Main Market Square, and soak with chess players in a Budapest bath. Ponder Europe's most moving Holocaust memorial at Auschwitz. Enjoy nature as you stroll on boardwalks through the Plitvice Lakes' waterfall wonderland or glide across Lake Bled to a church-topped island in the shadow of the Julian Alps. Taste a proud Hungarian vintner's wine and say, "Egészségedre!" (or stick with "Cheers!").

I've been selective, including only the top destinations and sights. For example, Croatia has dozens of island getaways—but Korčula is a cut above the rest.

The best is, of course, only my opinion. But after spending half my adult life researching Europe, I've developed a sixth sense for what travelers enjoy. Just thinking about the places featured in this book makes me want to polka.

This Information Is Accurate and Up-to-Date

This book is updated every year. Most publishers of guidebooks can afford an update only every two or three years (and even then, it's often by e-mail or phone). Since this book is selective, I can update it in person each summer. The prices and hours of sights listed in this book are accurate as of mid-2005—but, especially in fast-changing Eastern Europe, I know you'll understand that guidebooks begin to yellow even before they're printed. Still, if you're traveling with the current edition of this book, I guarantee you're using the most up-to-date information available in print. For any updates, see www.ricksteves.com/update. Also at our Web site, you'll find a valuable list of reports and experiences—good and bad—from fellow travelers who have used this book (www.ricksteves.com/feedback).

Use this year's edition. People who try to save a few bucks by traveling with an old book are not smart. They learn the seriousness of their mistake...in Eastern Europe. Your trip costs about $10 per waking hour. Your time is valuable. This guidebook saves lots of time.

About This Book

Rick Steves' Best of Eastern Europe is a personal tour guide in your pocket. Better yet, it's actually two tour guides in your pocket: The co-author of this book is Cameron Hewitt, who edits guidebooks and leads Eastern Europe tours for my travel company, Rick Steves' Europe Through the Back Door. Inspired by his Polish roots and by the enduring charm of the Eastern European people, Cameron has spent the last five years closely tracking the exciting changes in this part of the world. Together, Cameron and I keep this book up-to-date and accurate. For simplicity, we've shed our respective egos for this book and have become "I."

This book is organized by destination. Each destination is covered as a mini-vacation on its own, filled with exciting sights and convenient, affordable places to stay and eat. In each chapter, you'll find:

Planning Your Time contains a suggested schedule, with thoughts on how to best use your limited time.

Orientation includes tourist information, city transportation, and an easy-to-read map designed to make the text clear and your arrival smooth.

Sights are rated: ▲▲▲—Worth getting up early and skipping breakfast for; ▲▲—Worth getting up early for; ▲—Worth seeing if it's convenient; No rating—Worth knowing about.

Sleeping and **Eating** feature descriptions and contact information for my favorite hotels and restaurants.

Transportation Connections explains how to reach nearby destinations by train, bus, or boat.

Country Introductions give you an overview of each country's culture, customs, history, food, language, and other useful practicalities.

The chapter on **Understanding Yugoslavia,** which sorts out the various countries and conflicts, gives you a good picture of why Yugoslavia was formed, and why it broke up.

The **appendix** is a traveler's tool kit, with telephone tips, a climate chart, and a list of U.S. embassies.

Browse through this book, choose your favorite destinations, and link them up. Then have a great trip! You'll travel like a temporary local, getting the most out of every mile, minute, and dollar. As you travel the route I know and love, I'm happy you'll be meeting some of my favorite Europeans.

PLANNING

Trip Costs

Traveling in Eastern Europe is a great value. Things that natives buy—such as food and transportation—are in line with the local economy (that is, cheap). Hotels can be surprisingly expensive, but if you use my listings to find the best accommodations deals, a trip to these countries is substantially cheaper than visiting Italy, Germany, or France.

Five components make up your trip cost: airfare, surface transportation, room and board, sightseeing/entertainment, and shopping/miscellany. The prices I've listed below are more or less average for all of the destinations in this book. Prices are generally lower in Poland and Slovakia, and higher in Slovenia, Croatia, and Vienna; the Czech Republic and Hungary are in between. Of course, big cities (such as Prague and Budapest) are more expensive than smaller towns (like Český Krumlov and Eger).

Airfare: Don't try to sort through the mess. Get and use a good travel agent. A basic round-trip flight from the United States to Prague should cost $700 to $1,200 (even cheaper in winter), depending on where you fly from and when. Always consider saving time and money in Europe by flying "open jaw" (into one city and out of another). The additional cost of flying into Prague and out of Dubrovnik is almost certainly cheaper than the added expense (and wasted time) of a two-day overland return trip to Prague.

Surface Transportation: For the three-week whirlwind trip described on page 6, allow $300 per person for public

What is "Eastern Europe"?

"Eastern Europe" means different things to different people. To most Americans, Eastern Europe includes any place that was once behind the Iron Curtain, from the former East Germany to Moscow. But people who actually live in many of these countries consider themselves "Central Europeans." (To them, "Eastern Europe" is really eastern: Russia, Ukraine, Belarus, and Romania.)

In this book, I use the term "Eastern Europe" the way most Americans do—to describe the **Czech Republic, Slovakia, Poland, Hungary, Slovenia,** and **Croatia.** I've also thrown in a chapter on **Vienna**. This "gateway city" feels more Western than Eastern, but it has important historical ties to the region, and splices neatly into an Eastern itinerary.

So what do my six core "Eastern European" countries have in common? All of these destinations fell under communist control during the last half of the 20th century. More importantly, for centuries leading up to World War I, they were all part of the Austrian Hapsburg Empire. Before the Hapsburgs, the kings and emperors of these countries also frequently governed their neighbors. And all of these countries (except Hungary) are populated by people of Slavic heritage.

I hope that natives, sticklers, and historians will understand the liberties I've taken with the title of this book. But, after all, would you buy a book called *Rick Steves' Best of the Former Hapsburg Empire*?

transportation (train, bus, and boat tickets). Train travelers will probably save money by simply buying tickets along the way, rather than purchasing a railpass (see "Transportation," page 22). A basic car rental costs about $250 per person per week (based on 2 people splitting the cost of the car, tolls, gas, and insurance). Long-term car rental is cheapest when arranged in advance from the United States, but exorbitant fees for dropping off in a different country can make car rental prohibitively expensive for a multi-country itinerary (see "Car Rental," page 28).

Room and Board: You can thrive in Eastern Europe on an average of $75 a day per person for room and board. A $75-a-day budget per person allows $10 for lunch, $15 for dinner, and $50 for lodging (based on 2 people splitting the cost of a $100 double room that includes breakfast). That's doable. Students and tightwads do it on $40 a day ($20 per bed, $20 for meals).

Sightseeing and Entertainment: Sightseeing is cheap here. Major sights generally cost $3 to $6, with some more expensive sights at around $10. Figure $10 to $25 for splurge experiences (e.g., going to concerts, taking a twilight cruise on the Danube, watching Slovenia's Lipizzaner stallions, or soaking in a Budapest bath). You can hire your own private guide for four hours for about $80–100—a great value when divided among two or more people. An overall average of $20 a day works for most. Don't skimp here. After all, this category is the driving force behind your trip—you came to sightsee, enjoy, and experience Eastern Europe.

Shopping and Miscellany: Figure $1 per postcard, coffee, beer, and ice-cream cone. Shopping can vary in cost from nearly nothing to a small fortune. Good budget travelers find that this category has little to do with assembling a trip full of lifelong and wonderful memories.

When to Go

The "tourist season" runs roughly from May through September.

Summer has its advantages: the best weather, very long days (light until after 21:00), and the busiest schedule of tourist fun.

In spring and fall—May, June, September, and early October—travelers enjoy fewer crowds, milder weather, and the ability to grab a room almost whenever and wherever they like.

Winter travelers find concert season in full swing, with absolutely no tourist crowds (except in always-packed Prague), but some accommodations and sights are either closed or run on a limited schedule. Croatian coastal towns are completely dead in winter. Confirm your sightseeing plans locally, especially when traveling off-season. The weather can be cold and dreary, and night will draw the shades on your sightseeing before dinnertime. You may find the climate chart in the appendix helpful.

Sightseeing Priorities

Depending on the length of your trip, here are my recommended priorities. Assuming you're traveling by public transportation, I've taken geographical proximity into account.

3 days:	Prague
5 days, add:	Budapest
7 days, add:	Kraków and Auschwitz
9 days, add:	Český Krumlov
12 days, add:	Ljubljana and Bled
16 days, add:	Dubrovnik and Split
22 days, add:	Plitvice Lakes, Eger, Korčula

With more time or a special interest, choose among Vienna, Gdańsk, Pomerania, Toruń, Warsaw, the Danube Bend, Zagreb, Slovakia's Spiš Region, and Bratislava.

(The map on page 7 and the 3-week itinerary on page 6 include most of the stops in the first 22 days.)

Eastern Europe: Best Three-Week Trip By Train

Day	Plan	Sleep in
1	Arrive in Prague	Prague
2	Prague	Prague
3	Prague; night train to Kraków	Night train
4	Kraków	Kraków
5	Kraków, day trip to Auschwitz	Kraków
6	Kraków, maybe day trip to Wieliczka Salt Mine; night train to Eger	Night train
7	Eger	Eger
8	Early to Budapest	Budapest
9	Budapest	Budapest
10	Budapest	Budapest
11	To Ljubljana (catch early, direct 8.5-hr train; no handy night-train option)	Ljubljana
12	Ljubljana	Ljubljana
13	To Bled	Bled
14	Day trips around Julian Alps	Bled
15	To Zagreb, sightseeing, then early evening bus to Plitvice Lakes National Park	Plitvice
16	Plitvice hike in morning, then afternoon bus to Split	Split
17	Split	Split
18	Boat to Korčula	Korčula
19	Korčula	Korčula
20	Boat to Dubrovnik	Dubrovnik
21	Dubrovnik	Dubrovnik
22	Dubrovnik and fly home	

This speedy, far-reaching itinerary works best by public transportation. Most of the time, you'll take the train. Exceptions: Bled and Ljubljana are better connected by bus. To get from Bled to Plitvice, take the bus to Ljubljana, the train to Zagreb, then the bus to Plitvice. To get from Plitvice to the coast, take the bus to Split. The Dalmatian Coast destinations are best connected to each other by boat or bus (no trains).

By **car,** this itinerary is exhausting, with lots of long road days. Instead, connect long-distance destinations by night train (e.g., Prague to Kraków, Kraków to Eger/Budapest), then strategically rent cars for a day or two in areas that merit having wheels

Map legend:
- ● = OVERNIGHTS
- • = OTHER STOPS

(e.g., the Czech or Slovenian countryside).

Vienna: The Austrian capital is a likely gateway between Western and Eastern Europe, but it's out of the way for the above itinerary. If you really want to see Vienna, give it two days between Budapest and Ljubljana (It also makes sense if you're going directly between Budapest and Prague).

Travel Smart

Your trip to Europe is like a complex play—easier to follow and really appreciate on a second viewing. While no one does the same trip twice to gain that advantage, reading this book's chapters on your intended destinations before your trip accomplishes much the same thing. As a practical matter (to avoid redundancy), many cultural or historic details are explained for one sight and not repeated for another—even if they would increase your understanding and appreciation of that second sight.

As you read through this book, note days when sights are closed. When setting up your itinerary, anticipate problem days. Most museums throughout Eastern Europe close on Mondays, and they almost always stop admitting people 30 minutes before closing time. Sundays have the same pros and cons as they do for travelers in the United States: Sightseeing attractions are generally open, shops, banks, and markets are closed, and city traffic is light. Rowdy evenings are rare on Sundays. Saturdays in Europe are virtually weekdays with earlier closing hours. Hotels in tourist areas are most crowded on Fridays and Saturdays.

Be sure to mix intense and relaxed periods in your itinerary. Plan ahead for laundry, picnics, and e-mailing home. Every trip (and every traveler) needs at least a few slack days. Pace yourself. Assume you will return.

Reread this book as you travel and visit local tourist information offices. Upon arrival in a new town, lay the groundwork for a smooth departure. Buy a phone card and use it for reservations, reconfirmations, and double-checking hours. Enjoy the hospitality of Eastern Europeans. Slow down and ask questions. Most locals are eager to point you in their idea of the right direction. Wear your money belt, familiarize yourself with the local currency, and learn a simple formula to quickly estimate rough prices in dollars. Keep a notepad in your pocket for organizing your thoughts. Those who expect to travel smart, do.

Attitude Adjustment

Americans approach Eastern Europe expecting grouchy service, crumbling communist infrastructure, and grimy, depressing landscapes. Many Westerners think that independent travel in the East is reckless—or even dangerous. But those who visit are pleasantly surprised at the beauty, friendliness, safety, and ease of travel here. Travel in today's Eastern Europe is nearly as smooth as travel in the West. The natives speak excellent English and are forever scrambling to impress their guests. Any remaining rough edges simply add to the charm and carbonate the experience.

The East-West stuff still fascinates us, but to locals, the Soviet regime is old news, Cold War espionage is the stuff of movies, and oppressive monuments to Stalin are a distant memory. More than a decade and a half after the fall of the Iron Curtain, Eastern Europeans (or, as they prefer to be called, *Central* Europeans) think about communism only when tourists bring it up. Freedom is a generation old, and—for better or for worse—McDonald's, MTV, and mobile phones are every bit as entrenched here as anywhere else in Europe. After joining the European Union in 2004 (everywhere but Croatia), the countries in this book are looking to the future.

RESOURCES

Tourist Offices

In the U.S.

Each country's national tourist office in the United States is a wealth of information. Before your trip, get the free general information packet and request any specifics you may want (such as regional and city maps and festival schedules).

Czech Tourism Office: 1109 Madison Ave., New York, NY 10028, tel. 212/288-0830, fax 212/288-0971, www.czechtourism .com/usa, info-usa@czechtourism.com. To get a weighty information package (1–2 lbs., no advertising), send a check for $4 to cover postage and specify trip dates and places of interest. Basic information and a map are free.

Polish National Tourist Office: 5 Marine View Plaza #208, Hoboken, NJ 07030-5722, tel. 201/420-9910, fax 201/584-9153, www.polandtour.org, pntonyc@polandtour.org. Warsaw and Kraków information, regional brochures, and maps.

Hungarian National Tourist Office: 150 E. 58th St., 33rd floor, New York, NY 10155-3398, tel. 212/355-0240, fax 212/207-4103, www.gotohungary.com, hnto@gotohungary.com. "Routes to your Roots" booklet for those of Hungarian descent, *Budapest Cityguide*, and horseback-riding info.

Slovak Tourist Office: 10 E. 40th St. #3606, New York, NY 10016, www.cometoslovakia.com, info@cometoslovakia.com.

Slovenian Tourist Office: 2929 E. Commercial Blvd. #201, Fort Lauderdale, FL 33308, tel. 954/491-0112, fax 954/771-9841, www.slovenia.info, slotouristboard@kompas.net. *Welcome to Slovenia* brochure, map, information on various regions, hiking, biking, winter travel, and farm stays.

Croatian National Tourist Office: 350 Fifth Ave. #4003, New York, NY 10118, tel. 800-829-4416, fax 212/279-8683, http: //us.croatia.hr, cntony@earthlink.net. Free brochures and maps.

EU Enlargement and the "New Europe"

On May 1, 2004, the Czech Republic, Slovakia, Poland, Hungary, Slovenia, and five other countries joined the European Union. Though EU membership—and investment—should ultimately benefit everybody, old members and new members both had their doubts.

For example, new EU member Poland survived the communist era without having to collectivize its small family farms. But now that they've joined the EU, collectivization is mandatory. Traditional Czech cuisine is also in jeopardy. EU hygiene standards dictate that cooked food can't be served more than two hours old. My Czech friend complained, "This makes many of our best dishes illegal." Czech specialties, often simmered, taste better the next day.

Even when the news is good, it's bad. Slovakia, one of the poorest new EU members, suffers from sky-high unemployment and a rusting armaments industry that was abandoned when the Soviets left. Foreign companies are taking advantage of Slovakia's prime location and cheap labor by building several new car factories—turning Slovakia into what *The New York Times* called "the European Detroit." It's a boost to the economy, sure—but as the poor Slovaks become the exploited workforce of wealthy Europe, is it truly good for Slovakia?

A wise Czech grandmother put it best. In her lifetime, she had lived in a country ruled from Vienna (Hapsburgs), Berlin (Nazis), and Moscow (communists). She said, "Now that we're

Austrian Tourist Office: P.O. Box 1142, New York, NY 10108-1142, tel. 212/944-6880, fax 212/730-4568, www.austria .info, travel@austria.info. Ask for their *Austria Kit* with map. Fine hikes and city information.

In Europe

The local tourist information office is your best first stop in any new city. Try to arrive, or at least telephone, before it closes. In this book, I'll refer to a tourist information office as a **TI**. Throughout Eastern Europe, you'll find TIs are usually well-organized and always have an English-speaking staff. Most local tourist offices in Eastern Europe are run by the government, which means their information isn't colored by a drive for profit.

Unlike in Western Europe, TIs often don't have a room-booking service—though they can almost always give you a list of local hotels, and if they're not too busy, can call around for you to check finally ruled from Prague, why would we want to turn our power over to Brussels?"

For their part, longstanding EU members have been skeptical about taking on more countries. Wealthy nations have already spent huge fortunes to improve the floundering economies of poorer member countries (like Portugal, Greece, and Ireland). Most of the new members expect a similar financial-aid windfall. Also on the financial front, Westerners are fretting about an influx of cheap labor from the East (see "The Polish Plumber Syndrome," page 14). Finally, Western Europeans worry about their political power being diluted. When the 10 new nations joined the EU, the geographical center of Europe shifted from Brussels to Prague. In this "New Europe," Poland or the Czech Republic might emerge with a leading role. The East eagerly embraces the future, intent on distancing itself from its painful recent history, while the West tentatively clings to the past, when its power was at its peak (and French, not English, was the world's language).

As the "New Europe" takes shape, players on both sides will continue to define their new roles and seek compromise. So far, the general consensus in the East is that joining Europe was the right move. In a few years, the Slovenes, Poles, Czechs, and their neighbors will all be working harder than ever and enjoying more coins jangling in their pockets...and those coins will be euros.

on availability. Every town has at least one travel agency with a room-booking service. Even if there's no "fee," you'll pay more for the room than if you book direct, using the listings in this book.

Rick Steves' Guidebooks, Public Television Show, and Radio Show

Rick Steves' Europe Through the Back Door gives you budget-travel skills, such as minimizing jet lag, packing light, planning your itinerary, traveling by car or train, finding rooms, changing money, avoiding rip-offs, buying a mobile phone, hurdling the language barrier, staying healthy, taking great photographs, using a bidet, and much more. The book also includes chapters on 38 of my favorite "Back Doors."

Country Guides: These annually updated books offer you the latest on the top sights and destinations, with tips on how to make your trip efficient and fun. Here are the titles:

Rick Steves' Best of Europe
Rick Steves' Best of
  Eastern Europe
Rick Steves' England
  (new in 2006)
Rick Steves' France
Rick Steves' Germany
  & Austria

Rick Steves' Great Britain
Rick Steves' Ireland
Rick Steves' Italy
Rick Steves' Portugal
Rick Steves' Scandinavia
Rick Steves' Spain
Rick Steves' Switzerland

City and Regional Guides: Updated every year, these focus on Europe's most compelling destinations. Along with specifics on sights, restaurants, hotels, and nightlife, you'll get self-guided, illustrated tours of the outstanding museums and most characteristic neighborhoods.

Rick Steves' Amsterdam,
  Bruges & Brussels
Rick Steves' Florence
  & Tuscany
Rick Steves' London
Rick Steves' Paris

Rick Steves' Prague
  & the Czech Republic
Rick Steves' Provence
  & the French Riviera
Rick Steves' Rome
Rick Steves' Venice

Rick Steves' Phrase Books: This series of practical and budget-oriented series covers German, French, Italian, Portuguese, Spanish, and French/Italian/German. You'll be able to ask the gelato man for a free little taste, chat with your cabbie, and make hotel reservations over the phone.

And More Books: *Rick Steves' Europe 101: History and Art for the Traveler* (with Gene Openshaw) gives you the story of Europe's people, history, and art. Written for smart people who were sleeping in their history and art classes before they knew they were going to Europe, *101* helps Europe's sights come alive.

Rick Steves' Easy Access Europe, geared for travelers with limited mobility, covers London, Paris, Bruges, Amsterdam, and the Rhine River.

Rick Steves' Postcards from Europe, my autobiographical book, packs 25 years of travel anecdotes and insights into the ultimate 2,000-mile European adventure.

My latest book, *Rick Steves' European Christmas,* covers the joys, history, and quirky traditions of the holiday season in seven European countries.

Public Television Show: My series, *Rick Steves' Europe,* keeps churning out shows. Several of the more than 60 episodes feature sights covered in this book.

Radio Show: My new weekly radio show, which combines call-in questions (à la *Car Talk*) and interviews with travel experts, airs on public radio stations. For a schedule of upcoming topics, an archive of past programs, and details on how to call in, see www .ricksteves.com/radio.

Other Guidebooks

Especially if you'll be traveling beyond my recommended destinations, you may want some supplemental information. When you consider the improvements they'll make in your $3,000 vacation, $30 for extra maps and books is money well spent. Especially for several people traveling by car, the weight and expense are negligible. One budget tip can save the price of an extra guidebook.

The Rough Guides, which individually cover the countries in this book, are packed with historical and cultural insight, but are not updated annually (check the publication date). The Lonely Planet guides (also not updated annually) are similar, but are designed more for travelers than for intellectuals. Lonely Planet's fat, far-ranging *Eastern Europe* overview book gives you little to go on for each destination, though their country- and city-specific guides are more thorough.

Students, backpackers, and nightlife-seekers should consider the Let's Go guides (by Harvard students, the best hostel listings, updated annually). Dorling Kindersley publishes snazzy Eyewitness Guides covering Prague, Budapest, Kraków, Warsaw, Poland, Croatia, and Vienna. While pretty to look at, these books weigh a ton and are skimpy on actual content.

In Your Pocket publishes regularly updated magazines on major Eastern European cities (including Prague, Budapest, Kraków, Warsaw, Gdańsk, and Zagreb). These handy guides are especially good for their up-to-date hotel and restaurant recommendations (available locally, usually for a few dollars, but often free; condensed versions available free online at www.inyourpocket.com).

If your exploration of Austria takes you beyond Vienna, consider *Rick Steves' Germany & Austria 2006*. If your Czech travels include destinations outside Prague and Český Krumlov, pick up *Rick Steves' Prague & the Czech Republic 2006*.

More Recommended Reading and Movies

For information on Eastern Europe past and present, consider these books and films:

Non-Fiction Books: Lonnie Johnson's *Central Europe: Enemies, Neighbors, Friends* is the best history overview of the countries in this book. Rebecca West's classic, bricklike *Black Lamb and Grey Falcon* is the definitive travelogue of the Yugoslav lands (written during a journey between the World Wars). For a more recent take, Croatian journalist Slavenka Drakulić has written a trio of insightful essay collections from a woman's perspective:

The Polish Plumber Syndrome

You'll likely enjoy a taste of Eastern European culture on your next trip...to London or Dublin. When Eastern European countries joined the European Union in 2004, three EU members immediately welcomed their new comrades to work without a visa: Great Britain, the Republic of Ireland, and Sweden. This sparked a wave of immigration into these wealthy counties, as Eastern Europeans flocked to the land of plenty to find work. Many ended up in the hospitality industry. A few days before Poland joined the EU, one Kraków hotel manger was already packing his bags. He explained to me, "If I stay here, I can expect only a modest raise every year. But I've got a wife, a kid, and lots of debt. If I move to England, I can get paid in pound sterling instead of złoty for doing the same work—I'll be rich!"

The result has had mixed effects in each region. Those who have moved are enjoying more money and an irreplaceable cross-cultural experience. But Eastern Europe has seen a somewhat alarming "brain drain," as many of its youngest and most westward-thinking residents have rushed away. And in Britain and Ireland, tourists are encountering desk clerks who don't quite speak fluent English.

The other Western European countries are contemplating opening their borders, but it's controversial. One popular symbol, invented by a right-wing French politician in the summer of 2005, was an invading "Polish plumber" who'd put French plumbers out of a job. The Polish tourist board countered with a clever French-language ad featuring an alluring Polish hunk stroking a pipe wrench, saying, "I'm staying in Poland...come visit me!"

This is just one more step in the Europe-wide process of integration. Europeans in their twenties have been dubbed the "Erasmus Generation"—after the Erasmus Student Network, an EU organization that fosters study-abroad opportunities within Europe. As European twentysomethings have grown up accustomed to attending universities in other counties, it seems natural for them to identify as "Europeans" rather than as Spaniards, Slovenes, or Swedes. Multilingualism and international résumés are the norm.

As with all aspects of the EU enlargement, the resettlement of Poles, Czechs, and Hungarians to the bogs of Ireland will most likely ultimately be good for everyone, despite a few growing pains. It's just one more step in the evolution of a truly united Europe.

Café Europa: Life After Communism, The Balkan Express, and *How We Survived Communism and Even Laughed.* Timothy Garton Ash has written several good "eyewitness account" books analyzing the transition in Eastern Europe over the last two decades, including *History of the Present* and *The Magic Lantern.* For information on Eastern European Roma (Gypsies), consider the textbook-style *We Are the Romani People* by Ian Hancock, and the more literary *Bury Me Standing* by Isabel Fonseca. Tina Rosenberg's dense but thought-provoking *The Haunted Land* asks how those who actively supported communism in Eastern Europe should be treated in the post-communist age.

Fiction Books: The most prominent works of Eastern Europe fiction have come from the Czechs. These include *I Served the King of England* (Bohumil Hrabal), *The Unbearable Lightness of Being* (Milan Kundera), and *The Good Soldier Švejk* (Jaroslav Hašek). The Czech existentialist writer Franz Kafka wrote many well-known novels, including *The Trial* and *The Metamorphosis.* Bruce Chatwin's *Utz* is set in communist Prague. James Michener's *Poland* is a hefty look into the history of the Poles. Joseph Roth's *The Radetzky March* details the decline of an aristocratic family in the Austro-Hungarian Empire. *Zlateh the Goat* (Isaac Bashevis Singer) includes seven folktales of Jewish Eastern Europe.

Films: Czech Republic—*Kolya* (1996); *The Trial* (1993); *Kouř* (*Smoke,* 1991); *The Unbearable Lightness of Being* (1988); *The Firemen's Ball* (1967); *Closely Watched Trains* (1966); *The Loves of a Blonde* (1965). Poland—*Karol: A Man Who Became Pope* (2005); *The Pianist* (2002, Oscar winner for Best Director and Best Actor); *Schindler's List* (1993, multiple-Oscar winner); *The Wedding* (1972). Hungary—*Kontroll* (2003); *Csinibaba* (1997); *Time Stands Still* (1981); *The Witness* (1969). Croatia—*How the War Started on My Island* (1996); *Underground* (1995); *Tito and Me* (1992); *When Father Was Away on Business* (1985). Slovenia—*No Man's Land* (2002, Slovenian-produced, but deals with Bosnian war; Oscar winner for Best Foreign Film). The BBC produced a remarkable (but difficult-to-find) six-hour documentary series called *The Death of Yugoslavia,* featuring actual interviews with all of the key players.

Maps

The black-and-white maps in this book, drawn by Dave Hoerlein, are concise and simple. Dave, who is well-traveled in Europe, designed the maps to help you locate recommended places and get to the tourist offices, where you can pick up a more in-depth map (usually free) of the city or region. Better maps are sold at news-stands and bookstores—take a look before you buy to be sure the map has the level of detail you want. For drivers, I'd recommend a

1:200,000- or 1:300,000-scale map for each country. Train travelers can usually manage fine with the freebies they get at the local tourist offices.

PRACTICALITIES

Red Tape: Currently, Americans and Canadians need only a passport, but no visa or shots, to travel in the countries covered in this book. **Borders:** Even though most of these countries are in the EU, you'll still have to show your passport when you cross a border. Americans get needlessly edgy at Eastern European borders, their imaginations fueled by years of Cold War espionage flicks. Scary legends—about greedy, bribe-hungry border guards and passports held hostage—run rampant among travelers.

Relax! Even if any of these stories were once true, they've long since gone the way of the hammer and sickle. Borders, whether by car or by train, are generally a non-event—flash your passport, maybe wait a few minutes, and move on. You'll be quickly checked as many as four times—by the customs and immigration officers of the country you're leaving and, sometimes after continuing ahead a few yards, the one you're entering. On international night trains, you'll likely be woken up at each border (though sometimes your conductor will take your passport overnight to handle the red tape for you).

The procedure at every border is different. Usually, it's just a quick glance at the passport, the clunk of a stamp, and you're on your way. If there is a delay, don't panic. There may be a red-tape backup, or the guards might just be particularly thorough (or grouchy) that day. While I have occasionally seen the offer of a cold beer help speed things along, bribery is generally not necessary—and I've never been asked outright for a bribe (even when I've got a tour bus full of 24 antsy Americans).

The worst thing you can do is get impatient or pushy. The angrier you get, the longer it'll take. A polite smile will speed things along just as fast as a cold beer.

Even as borders fade, when you change countries, you must still change telephone cards, postage stamps, and underpants.

Time: In Europe—and throughout this book—you'll be using the 24-hour clock. After 12:00 noon, keep going—13:00, 14:00, and so on. For anything over 12, subtract 12 and add p.m. (14:00 is 2:00 p.m.) The countries listed in this book are six/nine hours ahead of the East/West Coasts of the United States.

Metric: Get used to metric. A liter is about a quart, four to a gallon. A kilometer is six-tenths of a mile. I figure kilometers to miles by cutting them in half and adding back 10 percent of the original (120 km: 60 + 12 = 72 miles, 300 km: 150 + 30 = 180 miles). For more on metric conversions, see the appendix.

Watt's Up? If you're bringing electrical gear, you'll need a two-prong adapter plug and a converter. Travel appliances often have convenient built-in converters; look for a voltage switch marked 120V (U.S.) and 240V (Europe).

News: Americans keep in touch with the *International Herald Tribune* (published almost daily via satellite throughout Europe). Every Tuesday, the European editions of *Time* and *Newsweek* hit the stands with articles of particular interest to European travelers. Sports addicts can get their fix from *USA Today*. News in English will only be sold where there's enough demand: in big cities and tourist centers. Good Web sites include www.europeantimes.com and http://news.bbc.co.uk.

Museum Tips: Eastern Europe's dusty museums don't quite rank with the Louvre or the Prado. The best attractions here are new, modern museums that chronicle the communist regime and celebrate its demise (like Budapest's House of Terror and Statue Park and Gdańsk's "Roads to Freedom" exhibit at the Solidarity shipyard). But some of the old-fashioned art and history museums are quite good. Generally, you'll follow a confusing, one-way tour route through a maze of rooms with squeaky parquet floors, monitored by grumpy grannies who listlessly point you in the right direction. While many museums label exhibits in English, most don't post full explanations; you'll have to buy a book or borrow laminated translations. In some cases, neither option is available. Audioguides are just catching on.

Discounts: While discounts for sightseeing and transportation are not listed in this book, youths (under 18) and students (only with International Student Identity Cards) sometimes get discounts—but only by asking.

MONEY

Exchange Rates

While none of these countries (except Austria) officially uses the euro yet, it's likely that they eventually all will (Slovenia will be first, probably in January of 2007). Throughout Eastern Europe—especially at hotels—the trend is to quote prices in the local currency for natives, and in euros for tourists. This can be confusing, and I've tried to be as consistent as possible, but I've had no choice but to list euros in some areas. Even if places list prices in euros, they'll happily accept the local currency (and, in fact, might prefer it). Note that if you pay in euros, you'll usually get bad rates and your change back in the local currency.

1 euro (€) = about $1.20
25 Czech crowns (*koruna*, Kč) = about $1
30 Slovak crowns (*koruna*, Sk) = about $1
3.40 Polish złoty (zł, or PLN) = about $1
200 Hungarian forints (Ft, or HUF) = about $1
200 Slovenian tolars (SIT) = about $1
6 Croatian kuna (HRK) = about $1

To roughly convert prices in euros to dollars, add 20 percent: €20 is about $24, €50 is about $60, and so on. To convert prices in Czech crowns into dollars, multiply by four and drop the last two digits (e.g., 1,000 Kč = about $40). For Slovak crowns, divide by three and drop the last digit (e.g., 750 Sk = about $25). To go from Hungarian forints or Slovenian tolars into dollars, divide by two and drop the last two digits (e.g., 10,000 Ft or SIT = about $50). To very roughly convert Polish prices into dollars, divide by three (e.g., 80 zł = about $25). To convert Croatian kuna into dollars, divide by six (e.g., 70 kuna = about $11).

So, that 20-zł Polish woodcarving is about $6, the 5,000-Ft Hungarian dinner is about $25, and the 2,000-Kč taxi ride through Prague is...uh-oh.

Banking

Bring plastic (ATM, credit, or debit cards) along with several hundred dollars in hard cash as an emergency backup. Traveler's checks are a waste of time and money.

The best and easiest way to get local cash is to use the omnipresent bank machines (always open, low fees, and quick processing). The universal word for "cash machine" in all of these countries is *Bankomat*. You'll need a PIN code (numbers only, no letters on European keypads) and your bank card. Before you go, verify with your bank that your card will work, inquire about fees (can be up to $5 per transaction), and alert them that you'll be making withdrawals in Europe; otherwise, the bank may not approve transactions if it perceives unusual spending patterns. Bring two cards in case one gets demagnetized or eaten by a machine.

Bank machines often dispense high-denomination bills, which can be difficult to break (especially at odd hours). My strategy: Request an odd amount of money from the ATM (such as 2,800 Kč instead of 3,000 Kč); or, if that doesn't work, go as soon as possible to a bank to break the big bills.

Visa and MasterCard are more commonly accepted than American Express. Just like at home, credit or debit cards work easily at larger hotels, restaurants, and shops, but smaller businesses prefer payment in local currency.

Damage Control for Lost or Stolen Cards

If you lose your credit, debit, or ATM card, you can stop people from using your card by reporting the loss immediately to the respective global customer-assistance centers. Call these 24-hour U.S. numbers collect: Visa (tel. 410/581-9994), MasterCard (tel. 636/722-7111), and American Express (tel. 336/393-1111).

Have, at a minimum, the following information ready: the name of the financial institution that issued you the card, along with the type of card (classic, platinum, or whatever). Ideally, plan ahead and pack photocopies of your cards— front and back—to expedite their replacement. Providing the following information will allow for a quicker cancellation of your missing card: full card number, whether you are the primary or secondary cardholder, the cardholder's name exactly as printed on the card, billing address, home phone number, circumstances of the loss or theft, and identification verification (your birthdate, your mother's maiden name, or your Social Security number—memorize this, don't carry a copy). If you are the secondary cardholder, you'll also need to provide the primary cardholder's identification verification details. You can generally receive a temporary card within two or three business days in Europe.

If you promptly report your card lost or stolen, you typically won't be responsible for any unauthorized transactions on your account, although many banks charge a liability fee of $50.

Because each country still has its own currency, and you'll likely be crossing several borders throughout your trip, you may wind up with leftover cash from a previous stop. Coins can't be exchanged in other countries, so try to spend them before you cross the border. But bills are easy to convert to the "new" country's currency.

Regular banks have the best rates for changing currency or traveler's checks (except in Poland, where *kantor*s, or money-changing kiosks, generally offer good rates—check several to find the best). Post offices and train stations usually change money if you can't get to a bank.

You should use a money belt (a pouch with a strap that you buckle like a belt and wear under your clothes). Thieves target tourists. A money belt provides peace of mind, allowing you to carry lots of cash safely.

Don't be petty about withdrawing money. Change a week's worth of money, get big bills, stuff them in your money belt, and travel!

Begin Your Trip at www.ricksteves.com

At www.ricksteves.com you'll find a wealth of **free information** on destinations covered in this book, including fresh European travel and tour news every month and helpful "Graffiti Wall" tips from thousands of fellow travelers.

While you're there, the **online Travel Store** is a great place to save money on travel bags and accessories designed by Rick Steves to help you travel smarter and lighter, plus a wide selection of guidebooks, planning maps, and DVDs.

Traveling through Europe by rail is a breeze, but choosing the right railpass for your trip—amidst hundreds of options—can drive you nutty. At www.ricksteves.com, you'll find **Rick Steves' Annual Guide to European Railpasses**—your best way to convert chaos into pure travel energy. Buy your railpass from Rick, and you'll get a bunch of free extras to boot.

Travel agents will tell you about mainstream tours of Europe, but they won't tell you about **Rick Steves' tours.** Rick Steves' Europe Through the Back Door travel company offers more than two dozen itineraries and 300 departures reaching the best destinations in this book...and beyond. You'll enjoy the services of a great guide, a fun bunch of travel partners (with group sizes in the twenties), and plenty of room to spread out in a big, comfy bus. You'll find trips to fit every vacation size, from week-long city getaways to longer cross-country adventures. For details, visit www.ricksteves.com or call 425/771-8303 ext 217.

Tips on Tipping

Tipping in Eastern Europe isn't as automatic and generous as it is in the United States—but for special service, tips are appreciated, if not expected. As in the United States, the proper amount depends on your resources, tipping philosophy, and the circumstance, but some general guidelines apply.

Restaurants: Tipping is an issue only at restaurants that have waiters and waitresses. If you order your food at a counter, don't tip. At Eastern European restaurants that have a waitstaff, service is generally included, although it's common to round up the bill after a good meal (usually 5–10 percent; e.g., for a 380-Kč meal, pay 400 Kč). All too often, American travelers—feeling guilty for paying so little for such a fine meal—are tempted to overtip. But please believe me: It's not necessary. A tip of 10 percent is already overly generous, and 15 percent verges on extravagant.

Taxis: To tip the cabbie, round up about five percent (e.g., for a 750-SIT fare, pay 800 SIT). If the cabbie hauls your bags and zips you to the airport to help you catch your flight, you might want to toss in a little more. But if you feel like you're being driven in circles or otherwise ripped off, skip the tip.

Hotels: I don't tip at hotels, but if you do, give the porter the local equivalent of $0.50 for carrying bags, and, at the end of your stay, leave a dollar's worth of local cash for the maid if the room was kept clean.

Special Services: Tour guides at public sites sometimes hold out their hands for tips after they give their spiels. If I've already paid for the tour, I don't tip extra. In general, if someone in the service industry does a super job for you, a small tip (the equivalent of a dollar) is appropriate...but not required.

When in Doubt, Ask. If you're not sure whether (or how much) to tip for a service, ask your hotelier or the TI; they'll fill you in on how it's done on their turf.

VAT Refunds for Shoppers

Wrapped into the purchase price of your souvenirs is a Value Added Tax (VAT) that varies per country. If you make a purchase of a minimum amount—which also differs per country—at a store that participates in the VAT refund scheme, you're entitled to get most of that tax back (see chart for VAT rates and minimum amounts). Personally, I've never felt that VAT refunds are worth the hassle, but if you do, here's the scoop.

If you're lucky, the merchant will subtract the tax when you make your purchase (this is more likely to occur if the store ships the goods to your home). Otherwise, you'll need to do all this:

Get the Paperwork: Have the merchant completely fill out the necessary refund document, called a "cheque." You'll have to present your passport at the store.

Get Your Stamp at the Border: Process your cheque(s) at your last stop in the country with the customs agent who deals with VAT refunds. It's best to keep your purchases in your carry-on for viewing, but if they're too large or dangerous (such as knives) to carry on, then track down the proper customs agent to inspect them before you check your bag. You're not supposed to use your purchased goods before you leave. If you show up at customs wearing your chic Czech shirt, officials might look the other way—or deny you a refund.

Collect Your Refund: You'll need to return your stamped documents to the retailer or its representative. Many merchants work with a service that has offices at major airports, ports, and border crossings, such as Global Refund (www.globalrefund.com) or Premier Tax Free (www.premiertaxfree.com). These services, which extract a 4 percent fee, usually can refund your money immediately in your currency of choice or credit your card (within 2 billing cycles). If you have to deal directly with the retailer, mail

VAT Rates and Minimum Purchases Required to Qualify for Refunds

Country Of Purchase	Vat Standard Rate*	Minimum in Local Currency	Minimum in U.S. Dollars**
Austria	20%	€75.01	$98
Croatia	18.5%	501 HRK	$90
Czech Republic	19%	1,000 Kč	$45
Hungary	25%	45,000 Ft	$246
Poland	22%	200 zł	$68
Slovakia	19%	5,000 Sk	$175
Slovenia	20%	15,001 SIT	$84

The VAT Standard Rate is charged on the original value of the item, not on the purchase price. Refund percentages will therefore be slightly less than the above rate and may also be subject to commission fees.
** Exchange rate as of 8/5/05
Source: HOTREC (Hotels, Restaurants & Cafes in Europe). Please note that figures are subject to change. For more information, visit www.hotrec.org or www.globalrefund.com.

the store your stamped documents and then wait. It could take months.

Customs Regulations

You can take home $800 in souvenirs per person duty-free. The next $1,000 is taxed at a flat 3 percent. After that, you pay the individual item's duty rate. You can also bring in duty-free a liter of alcohol (slightly more than a standard-sized bottle of wine), a carton of cigarettes, and up to 100 cigars. As for food, anything in cans or sealed jars is acceptable. Skip dried meat, cheeses, and fresh fruits and veggies. (Hungarian paprika is OK as long as it's in a sealed container.) To check customs rules and duty rates, visit www.customs.gov.

TRANSPORTATION

In Eastern Europe, I travel mostly by public transportation. For long distances between big cities (such as Prague to Kraków, Warsaw to Budapest, or Vienna to Dubrovnik), I prefer to take a cheap flight or a night train. For shorter distances (like Gdańsk to Warsaw or Ljubljana to Zagreb), I take a daytime train or bus. In areas with lots of exciting day-trip possibilities, such as the Czech or Slovenian countryside, I rent a car for a day or two—or hire a local

Public Transportation in Eastern Europe

tour guide with a car to drive me around (which can be cheaper than you might think; I recommend several drivers in this book).

If you're debating between public transportation and car rental, consider these factors: Trains and buses are best for single travelers; those who'll be spending more time in big cities; those with an ambitious, multi-country itinerary; and those who don't want to drive in Europe. While a car gives you more freedom—enabling you to search for hotels more easily and carrying your bags for you—trains and buses zip you effortlessly from city to city, usually dropping you in the center, near the tourist office. Cars are great in the countryside, but a worthless headache in places like Prague, Budapest, and Dubrovnik. If you're lacing the big cities together, the last thing you want is a car.

Public Transportation

Trains

Trains are punctual and cover cities well, but frustrating schedules make a few out-of-the-way recommendations difficult—or impossible—to reach (usually the bus will get you there instead; see "Buses," below). For timetables, the first place to check is Germany's excellent all-Europe timetable at http://bahn.hafas.de /bin/query.exe/en. Individual countries have their own train timetable Web sites (for example, Czech train and bus schedules are at www.vlak-bus.cz; Slovak schedules are at www.cp.sk; Hungarian timetables are at www.elvira.hu; for Slovenia, check out www .slo-zeleznice.si; and for Croatia, visit www.hznet.hr). You'll rarely need a reservation, except for night trains.

Night Trains: To cover the long distances between the major destinations in this book, use night trains as often as possible (remember, each night on the train saves a day for sightseeing). Fortunately, most of Eastern Europe's big cities are connected by night trains, even if the timing sometimes isn't ideal (e.g., arrival very early in the morning). The biggest problem night-trainers encounter is being woken up each time they cross a border to show their passports (unless the conductor offers to take your passport to deal with the border checks while you sleep). This can be especially frustrating on the train from Kraków to Eger or Budapest, which goes through Slovakia...and crosses the border twice.

One more thing: No matter how many times you hear "totally true" stories of train cars being "gassed" with a sleep-inducing drug by thieves, it's a legend, most likely invented by travelers who felt foolish for sleeping through a theft. But as on Western European night trains, thefts do occur, so lock the door and secure your belongings (to make it difficult—or at least noisy—for thieves to rip you off). When sleeping on a night train, I wear my money belt.

Railpasses: While railpasses can be a good deal in Western Europe, they usually aren't the best option in the East for two reasons: Point-to-point tickets are cheap and simple here, and most railpasses don't conveniently combine Eastern European countries. For example, with the Eurail Selectpass, you can buy unlimited travel for up to 10 travel days (within a 2-month period) in three adjacent countries; but of the countries in this book, only Hungary, Austria, and Slovenia/Croatia are eligible. Another option is the European East Pass, covering the Czech Republic, Hungary, Poland, Slovakia, and Austria—but not Slovenia or Croatia. The Czech Republic, Hungary, and Austria have their own individual railpasses, valid for trips only within their country. And three different combo-passes combine various countries: one for Austria and the Czech Republic; another for Austria, Slovenia, and Croatia; and another for Hungary, Slovenia, and Croatia. Again, none of these passes is likely to save you much money, but if a pass matches your itinerary, give it a look and crunch the numbers. For all of the options, see the charts on pages 26 and 27, or visit our Railpass Guide online at www.ricksteves.com/rail.

Language Barrier: For tips on buying train tickets from monolingual staff in Eastern European stations, see "Hurdling the Language Barrier" on page 32.

Buses

While the train can get you most places faster than a bus can, there are a few areas where buses are worth considering. For example, Ljubljana and Lake Bled are connected by both train and bus—but the bus station is right in the town center of Bled, while the train station is a few miles away. And a few destinations, including Croatia's Plitvice Lakes National Park and many of the sights in Slovenia's Karst region, are accessible only by bus. In general, the countries in this book have good train coverage—except Slovakia and Croatia, where train lines are limited and buses usually make more sense. In the Czech Republic, it's often a toss-up whether the train or bus is better; I've given specific recommendations for each destination. When in doubt, ask at the local TI which is better on a particular route.

Boats

Once you get to the Croatian coast, boats can be your best option. For details, see "Getting Around the Dalmatian Coast" on page 585.

Cheap Flights

Low-cost airlines have finally arrived in Eastern Europe, allowing you to cheaply connect many of the destinations in this book. One of the biggest Eastern Europe-based budget airlines,

Eastern Europe Railpasses

Prices listed are for 2005. My free *Rick Steves' Guide to European Railpasses* has the latest prices and details (and easy online ordering) at www.ricksteves.com/rail.

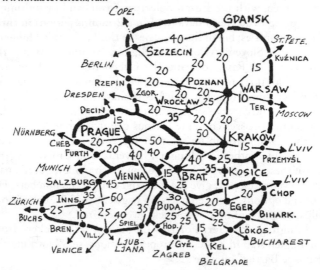

Eastern Europe: The map shows approximate point-to-point one-way 2nd class rail fares in $US. Add up fares for your itinerary to see if a railpass will save you money. First class costs 50% more.

EUROPEAN EAST PASS

	1st Class	2nd Class
Any 5 days in 1 month	$230	$162
Extra rail days (max 5)	28	21

Covers Austria, Czech Republic, Slovakia, Hungary, and Poland. Kids 4-11 half fare; under 4 free.

CZECH FLEXIPASS

	1st Class	2nd Class
Any 3 days in 15	$74	$52
Extra rail days (max 5)	10	7

Kids 4-11 half fare; under 4 free.

HUNGARY FLEXIPASS

	1st Class	2nd Class
Any 5 days out of 15	$79	$52
Extra rail days (max 5)	9	6

Kids 6-14 half fare; Attila and kids under 5 go free.

PRAGUE EXCURSION PASS

	1st Class	2nd Class
Adult	$60	$45
Youth (12-25)	50	40
Child (4-11)	30	23

Good for two train rides within a 7 day period: from any Czech border into Prague, and then from Prague to any border crossing (stops on the way are allowed). This pass is available at EurAide offices in Berlin and Munich or at www.euraide.de/ricksteves, not from Europe Through the Back Door. Kids under 4 free.

Eastern Europe Railpasses

EURAIL SELECTPASSES

This pass covers travel in three adjacent Western European countries such as Germany, Austria & Hungary. Can also choose Slovenia/Croatia as one "country." Please visit www.ricksteves.com/rail or see the railpass guide for four- and five-country options.

	1st Class Selectpass	1st Class Saverpass	2nd Class Youthpass
5 days in 2 months	$370	$316	$241
6 days in 2 months	410	348	267
8 days in 2 months	488	414	317
10 days in 2 months	564	480	367

Saverpass: Price is per person for 2 or more adults traveling together at all times.
Youthpasses: Under age 26 only. Kids 4-11 pay half of First Class or Saver fare; under 4 free.

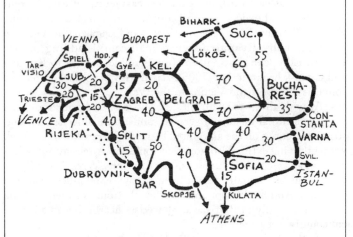

HUNGARY+ROMANIA OR
HUNGARY/SLOVENIA/CROATIA

	1st Class Individual	1st Class Saverpass	2nd Class Youthpass
Any 5 days in 2 months	$200	$170	$140
Any 6 days in 2 months	220	188	159
Any 8 days in 2 months	260	222	189
Any 10 days in 2 months	300	256	209

Saver prices are per person for 2 or more traveling together. Youth passes are for travelers under age 26 and fares vary slightly depending on countries selected. Children 4-11 pay half of First Class or Saver fare; under 4 free.

AUSTRIA+CZECH REPUBLIC OR
AUSTRIA/SLOVENIA/CROATIA

	1st Class Individual	1st Class Saverpass	2nd Class Youthpass
Any 4 days in 2 months	$230	$200	$167
Extra days (max. 6)	35	30	24

Saver prices are per person for 2 or more traveling together. Youth passes are for travelers under age 26. Children 4-11 pay half of First Class or Saver fare; under 4 free.

SkyEurope (www.skyeurope.com), has hubs in Budapest, Kraków, Warsaw, Košice (eastern Slovakia), and Bratislava, with flights to various destinations in both Eastern Europe (including Prague, Dubrovnik, and Split) and Western Europe. **Wizz Air** (www .wizzair.com) has hubs in Budapest, Warsaw, and Katowice (near Kraków), but most of their flights go to Western Europe rather than destinations within Eastern Europe. **Smart Wings** (www .smartwings.net), based in Prague, has flights to Western Europe and to Greece. And LOT, Poland's biggest carrier, has a low-cost subsidiary called **Centralwings** (www.centralwings.com).

Several of the more established budget airlines are expanding their offerings eastward. For example, **easyJet** (www.easyjet.com) connects several major Eastern European cities (including Prague, Kraków, Warsaw, Budapest, Bratislava, and Ljubljana) to Western European hubs. **Ryanair** (www.ryanair.com) is adding several Eastern European destinations (for example, service to Kraków and Gdańsk began in late 2005). **Air Berlin** (www.airberlin.com) connects Budapest and Vienna to the West.

As with all no-frills airlines, be aware of trade-offs for cheap flights: minimal customer service, non-refundable tickets, and strict restrictions on the amount of baggage you're allowed to check without paying extra. Also note that you'll sometimes fly out of less convenient, secondary airports. For example, Wizz Air's flights from "Kraków" actually depart from Katowice, 60 miles away (see page 211). And SkyEurope implies they fly from "Vienna," but the airport is actually in Bratislava, Slovakia—nearby, but in a different country (see page 174).

As the established airlines in Eastern Europe face more competition, they're forced to adapt. For example, the national airlines in both Slovenia (**Adria Airways**, www.adria-airways.com) and Croatia (**Croatia Airlines**, www.croatiaairlines.com) generally offer a handful of super-cheap seats on some of their otherwise expensive flights (for example, €49 1-way from Ljubljana to London or Paris; or €30 from Zagreb to Split or Dubrovnik)—but only to those who book early.

Finally, **Europe by Air** continues to offer their Flight Pass, charging $99 per leg (plus taxes and airport fees) for flights within Europe. They partner with various well-established airlines, providing good coverage for low prices (most useful for Croatia Airlines flights to and from the Dalmatian Coast; tickets can be purchased only in U.S., www.europebyair.com, U.S. tel. 888-321-4737).

Driving

Car Rental

It's cheaper to arrange European car rentals in the United States than in Europe, so check rates with your travel agent or directly with the companies. Rent by the week with unlimited mileage. If you'll be renting for three weeks or more, ask your agent about leasing, which is a scheme to avoid insurance costs and taxes (but you may have to pick up and drop off in Germany or Austria).

Allow about $750 per person (based on 2 people sharing the car) to rent a small economy car for three weeks with unlimited mileage, including gas, parking, and insurance. I normally rent a small, inexpensive model like a Ford Fiesta. You'll pay extra for collision damage waiver (CDW) insurance (described below). Be warned that dropping a car off in a different country—say, picking up in Prague and dropping in Croatia—can be prohibitively expensive (depends on distance, but the fee averages a few hundred dollars, and can exceed $1,000). If you're doing your entire trip by car, find out what the international drop-off fee will be. If it's exorbitant, seriously consider doing a round-trip itinerary instead... or using public transportation. In some cases, it may even be difficult to find a company that will allow you to pick up and drop off in far-apart countries, so you may be forced into using public transportation for at least part of your trip.

For driving in Eastern Europe, it's wise to get an International Driving Permit ahead of time at your local AAA office ($10 plus 2 passport-type photos).

Crossing borders with a rental car into, out of, and within Eastern Europe can be tricky. Though these countries are safe to travel in, some popular destinations (such as Prague) are notorious for sky-high car-theft rates. And, since American companies still think of the former Eastern Bloc as a single unit, the car thieves of Prague make it hard to drive a Western rental even into super-safe Slovenia. You can almost always cross—provided you have the right paperwork. Always state your travel plans up front to the rental company. Some won't allow any of their rental cars to enter Eastern Europe, and some restrict certain types of cars: BMWs, Mercedes, and convertibles. Ask about extra fees—some companies automatically tack on theft and collision coverage for an Eastern European excursion. To avoid hassles at the borders, make sure that you have the car's proof of insurance (often called a "green card") and ask the rental agent if you need any other documentation. For more on borders, see "Borders," page 16.

Collision Damage Waiver

For peace of mind, I spring for the Collision Damage Waiver insurance (CDW, about $15–25 per day), which limits my financial responsibility in case of an accident. Unfortunately, CDW now has a high deductible hovering at about $1,000–1,500. When you pick up your car, many car-rental companies will try to sell you "super CDW" at an additional cost of $7–15 per day to lower the

Driving: Distance and Time

To Gdańsk

Toruń — 220m • 4.5h — Warsaw

Berlin — 180m • 3.75h — Poznań — 190m • 4h

120m • 2.25h

POLAND

365m • 8h
140m • 2.75h
185m • 4h

GERMANY

Dresden
120m • 2.5h

Częstochowa — 80m • 1.5h

390m • 8h

Terezín 40m • 1h

300m • 7h

290m • 5.5h
40m • 1.5h — Kraków
Auschwitz — 80m • 2h
100m • 3h

Prague
25k • .75h
Karlštejn
Castle

40m • 1.25h
Kutná Hora

CZECH REPUBLIC

Zako-pane
45m • 1h

330m • 5.5h

200m • 4h — Poprad

240m • 4.25h

100m • 2.25h

180m • 3.5h

SLOVAKIA

115m • 3.5h

230m • 4h

Český Krumlov

40m • 1h — Bratislava

240m • 5.5h

Eger

380m • 6.25h

Vienna

90m • 2.5h

80m • 2h

90m • 1.5h — Munich

Salzburg

130m • 2.5h — Budapest

Map detail below

175m • 3h

235m • 4h

240m • 4h

AUSTRIA

275m • 5.75h

HUNG.

15m • .5h — Visegrád
Esztergom — 15m • .5h
25m • 1h — Szentendre — 15m • .5h
Budapest

Bled
30m • 1h

SLOV.

220m • 5h

60m • 1.5h

Ljubljana — 90m • 2h — Zagreb

CROATIA

ITALY

Trieste
100m 1.75h

75m 2h

140m 2h

100m 2h

85m • 2h

240m • 4.5h

Rijeka — 90m • 2.5h

Venice

55m 1.5h

Pula

140m • 3h

Plitvice

85m 1.75h

BOSNIA & HERZEGOVINA

Zadar — 90m • 2h — Split

130m • 3h

85m 4h

Korčula — 70m • 2.5h — Dubrovnik

m = miles
h = hours
Note: Your times may vary based on traffic, construction, and road conditions.

deductible to zero. Consider the following alternatives.

Some credit cards offer CDW-type coverage for no charge to their customers. Quiz your credit-card company on the worst-case scenario. You have to choose between the coverages offered by your car-rental company and your credit-card company. This means that if you go with the credit-card coverage, you'll have to decline the CDW offered by the car-rental company. In this situation, some car-rental companies put a hold on your credit card for the amount of the full deductible (which can equal the value of the car). This is bad news if your credit limit is low—particularly if you plan on using that card for other purchases during your trip.

Another alternative is buying CDW insurance from Travel Guard for $9 a day (U.S. tel. 800-826-4919, www.travelguard .com). It's valid throughout Europe, but some car-rental companies refuse to honor it, especially in Italy and the Republic of Ireland. Oddly, residents of some states (including Washington) are not allowed to buy this coverage.

In sum, buying CDW—and the supplemental insurance to buy down the deductible, if you choose— is the easiest but priciest option. Using the coverage that comes with your credit card is cheaper, but can involve more hassle. If you're taking a short trip, an easy solution is to buy Travel Guard's very affordable CDW. For longer trips, leasing is the best way to go.

Driving Tips

During the communist era, Eastern Europe's infrastructure lagged far behind the West's. Now that the Iron Curtain is long gone, superhighways are being rolled out like crazy. The Czech Republic, Hungary, Slovenia, and Croatia all have new expressways, but it's not unusual to find that a still-under-construction expressway ends, requiring a transfer to an older, slower road. Likewise, you'll sometimes discover that a much faster road has been built between major destinations since your three-year-old map was published. (This is another good reason to travel with the most up-to-date maps available and study them before each drive, noting which exits you'll need and which major cities you'll be traveling towards.) New superhighways have just opened between Dresden and Prague (the A17), and from Zagreb to Budapest (to the north) and Zagreb to Split (to the south). As soon as a long-enough section is completed, the roads are opened to the public. Only rarely are backcountry roads the only option (as with part of the trip between Prague and Kraków). These can be bumpy and slow, but they're almost always paved (or, at least, they once were).

Learn the universal road signs (see sidebar). Seat belts are required, and two beers under those belts are enough to land you in jail.

Tolls: In many countries, driving on highways requires a toll sticker (generally available at the border, post offices, gas stations, and sometimes car-rental agencies): **the Czech Republic** (*dálniční známka*, 200 Kč/15 days, 300 Kč/2 months); **Slovakia** (*úhrada*, 100 Sk/15 days); **Hungary** (*autópálya matrica*, 2,300 Ft/10 days, 3,900 Ft/1 month, www.autopalya.hu); and **Austria** (*Vignette*, €8/10 days, €22/2 months). Fines for not having a toll sticker can be stiff. Note that you don't need a toll sticker if you'll be dipping into the country on minor roads—only for major highways. Your rental car may already come

with the necessary sticker; ask. In **Slovenia** and **Croatia**, you'll get a ticket as you enter the freeway, then pay when you get off, based on how far you've traveled. So far, **Poland** is in the process of completing its expressways. Some segments are already open (such as much of the road between Kraków, Wrocław, and the German border). Drivers pay tolls to use completed segments.

Parking: Parking is a costly headache in big cities. You'll pay about $10–15 a day to park safely. Rental-car theft can be a big problem in cities, especially Prague. Ask at your hotel for advice. I keep a pile of coins in my ashtray for parking meters, public phones, and wishing wells.

COMMUNICATING

Hurdling the Language Barrier

The language barrier in Eastern Europe is no bigger than in the West. In fact, I find that it's much easier to communicate in Hungary or Croatia than in Italy or Spain. Immediately after the Iron Curtain fell in 1989, English speakers were rare. But today, you'll find that most people in the tourist industry—and virtually all young people—speak excellent English.

Of course, not *everyone* speaks English. You'll run into the most substantial language barriers in situations when you need to deal with a lesser-educated clerk or service person (train stations

Europe's Best Linguists

Why do Eastern Europeans speak English so well—especially since it wasn't commonly taught in schools before the last 15 years?

Residents of big, powerful Western countries, like Germany or France, might think that foreigners should learn their language. But Eastern Europeans are as practical as Westerners are stubborn. They realize that it's unreasonable to expect an American to learn Hungarian (with only 12 million speakers worldwide), Croatian (5 million), or Slovene (2 million). When only a few million people on the planet speak your language, it's essential to find a common language with the rest of the world—so they learn English early and well. In Croatia, for example, all schoolchildren start learning English in the third grade. (I've had surprisingly eloquent conversations with Croatian grade-schoolers.)

Many times, I've heard a French person and a Hungarian conversing in English—a reminder that as Americans, we're lucky to speak the world's new lingua franca.

and post office counters, maids, museum guards, bakers, and so on). Be reasonable in your expectations. Hungarian museum ticket-sellers are every bit as friendly and multilingual as they are in the United States. Luckily, it's relatively easy to get your point across in these places. I've often bought a train ticket simply by writing out the name of my destination (preferably with the local spelling—for example, "Praha" instead of "Prague"); the time I want to travel (using the 24-hour clock); and, if necessary, the date I want to leave (day first, then month as a Roman numeral, then year). Here's an example of what I'd show a ticket-seller at a train station: "Warszawa–17:30–15.VII.06."

Eastern Europeans, realizing that their language intimidates Americans, often invent easier nicknames for themselves—so Sarka goes by "Sara," András becomes "Andrew," and Jaroslav tells you, "Call me Jerry."

Most of the destinations in this book—the Czech Republic, Slovakia, Poland, Slovenia, and Croatia—speak Slavic languages. Czech, Slovak, Polish, Slovene, and Croatian are closely related to each other and to Russian, and are, to varying degrees, mutually intelligible (though many spellings change—for example, Czech hrad, or "castle," becomes Croatian grad). Slavic languages have simple vocabularies but are highly inflected—that is, the meaning of a sentence depends on complicated endings that are tacked on to the ends of the words (as in Latin).

Slavic words are notorious for their seemingly unpronounce-able, long strings of consonants. Slavic pronunciation can be tricky. In fact, when the first Christian missionaries, Cyril and Methodius, came to Eastern Europe a millennium ago, they invented a whole new alphabet to represent these strange Slavic sounds. The Cyrillic alphabet is still used today in the eastern Slavic countries (such as Serbia and Russia).

Fortunately, the destinations covered in this book all use the same Roman alphabet we do, but they add lots of different diacrit-ics—little markings below and above letters—to represent a wide range of sounds (for example, č, ą, ó, đ, ł). I explain each of these diacritics in this book's various country introductions.

Hungarian is another story altogether—it's completely unre-lated to Slavic languages, German, or English. For more on the challenging Magyar tongue, see page 378.

German is spoken in Vienna. As part of the same language family as English, German sounds noticeably more familiar to American ears than the Slavic languages. Throughout Eastern Europe, German can be a handy second language (especially in Croatia, which is popular among German-speaking tourists). And a few words of Italian can come in handy in Slovenia and Croatia.

Aside from the English pleasantries, there's one word that people throughout Eastern Europe will understand: *Servus* (SEHR-voos)—the old-fashioned international greeting from the days of the Austro-Hungarian Empire. If you draw a blank on how to say hello in the local language, just offer a cheery, "*Servus!*"

Learn the key phrases (see each country introduction) and travel with a phrase book. Consider Lonely Planet's good *Eastern Europe Phrasebook*, which covers all of the destinations in this book (except Vienna).

Don't be afraid to interact with locals. Eastern Europeans can be shy or even brusque—a holdover from the closed communist society—but often a simple smile is the only icebreaker you need to make a new friend. You'll find that doors open a little more quickly when you know a few words of the language. Give it your best shot. The locals will appreciate your efforts.

Telephones

Smart travelers learn the phone system and use it daily to reserve or reconfirm rooms, get tourist information, or phone home.

Types of Phones

You'll encounter various kinds of phones in your European travels.

Pay phones—in booths, free-standing, or fixed to a wall—line the streets of Europe. Most are no longer coin-operated; you have to buy an insertable phone card, or use an international phone card (both options described under "Paying for Calls," below).

Hotel room phones are fairly cheap for local calls, but pricey for international calls, unless you use an international phone card (see below).

American mobile phones work in Europe if they're GSM-enabled, tri-band (or quad-band), and on a calling plan that includes international calls. With a T-Mobile phone, you can roam using your home number, and pay $1–2 per minute for making or receiving calls.

Some travelers buy a **European mobile phone** in Europe. For about $125, you can get a phone that will work in most countries once you pick up the necessary chip (about $30) per country. Or you can buy a cheaper, "locked" phone that only works in the country where you purchased it (about $100, includes $20 worth of calls). If you're interested, stop by any European shop that sells mobile phones; you'll see prominent store window displays. You aren't required to (and shouldn't) buy a monthly contract—buy prepaid calling time instead (as you use it up, buy additional minutes at newsstands or mobile-phone shops). If you're on a budget, skip mobile phones and use international phone cards instead.

Paying for Calls

You can spend a fortune making phone calls in Europe...but why would you? Here's the skinny on different ways to pay, including the best deals.

European Phone Cards come in two types: official phone cards that you insert into a pay phone, and international phone cards that can be used from virtually any phone.

• **Insertable phone cards** can be purchased at post offices, newsstands, or tobacco shops. Simply take the phone off the hook, insert the prepaid card, wait for a dial tone, and dial away. The price of the call (local or international) is automatically deducted while you talk. These cards only work in the country where you buy them (so your Czech phone card is worthless in Poland). Insertable phone cards are a good deal for calling within Europe, but it's cheaper to make your overseas calls with an international phone card.

• **International phone cards** allow you to call home cheap (generally about $0.25/min). Unlike the official phone cards, an international phone card is *not* inserted into the phone. Instead, you dial the toll-free number listed on the card, reaching an automated operator. When prompted, you dial in a scratch-to-reveal code number, also written on the card. Then dial your number. While the cards are a wonderful deal for calling the United States, they can also be used for local and domestic long-distance calls. Since they're not insertable, you can use them from any phone—including the one in your hotel room. These cards are not quite as cheap as similar cards in Western Europe, but they're catching on fast—so rates are sure to drop as more choices become available. (Ah, capitalism.) Look for fliers advertising long-distance rates, or ask about the cards at Internet cafés, newsstands, souvenir shops, and youth hostels. There are many different brands. Simply request an international telephone card, tell the vendor where you'll be making most calls ("to America"), and he'll select the brand with the best deal. Make sure the access number you dial is toll-free, not a local number (or else you'll be paying for a local call *and* deducting time from your calling card). These cards usually work only in the country where you buy them, but some brands work internationally. Buy a lower denomination in case the card is a dud.

Dialing direct from your hotel room without using an international phone card is usually quite expensive for international calls, but it's convenient. Always ask first how much you'll be charged. Keep in mind that you have to pay for local and occasionally even toll-free calls.

Receiving calls in your hotel room is often the cheapest way to keep in touch with the folks back home—especially if your family has an inexpensive way to call you (either a good deal on their long-distance plan, or a prepaid calling card with good rates to Europe). Give them a list of your hotels' phone numbers before you go. As you travel, send your family an e-mail or make a quick payphone call to set up a time for them to call you, and then wait for the ring.

Metered phones are available in phone offices and sometimes in bigger post offices. You can talk all you want, then pay the bill when you leave—but be sure you know the rates before you have a lengthy conversation.

Coin-operated phones, while rare, still exist in some areas. If making a call, have a bunch of coins handy—they go fast.

U.S. Calling Cards (such as the ones offered by AT&T, MCI, or Sprint) are the worst option. You'll nearly always save a lot of money by paying for your call in any of the other ways described above.

How to Dial

Calling from the United States to Europe, or vice versa, is simple—once you break the code. The European calling chart on page 762 will walk you through it. Remember that European time is six/nine hours ahead of the East/West Coasts of the United States.

Making Calls within a European Country: About half of all European countries use area codes; the other half uses a direct-dial system without area codes.

In countries that use area codes (such as Slovakia, Poland, Hungary, Slovenia, Croatia, and Austria), you dial the local number when calling within a city, and you add the area code if calling long distance within the same country. For example, Kraków's area code is 012, and the number of one of my recommended Kraków hotels is 431-0010. To call the hotel within Kraków, dial 431-0010. To call it from Warsaw, dial 012/431-0010. Hungary is a special case: for domestic long distance, you have to dial "06" before the number. For example, to call an Eger hotel, I'd dial 411-711 if I'm calling from within Eger; but from Budapest, I have to dial 06, then 36 (Eger's area code), then 411-711. For more on the confusing Hungarian phone system, see page 368.

To make calls within a country that uses a direct-dial system (such as the Czech Republic), you dial the same number whether you're calling across the country or across the street.

Making International Calls: You always start with the international access code (011 if you're calling from the U.S. or Canada, or 00 from Europe). If you see a phone number that begins with +, you have to replace the + with the international access code.

Once you've dialed the international access code, dial the country code of the country you're calling (see chart in appendix).

What you dial next depends on the phone system of the country you're calling. If the country uses area codes, drop the initial zero of the area code, then dial the rest of the number. To call the Kraków hotel from Prague, dial 00, 48 (Poland's country code), 12/431-0010 (omitting the initial zero in the area code). To call the Czech Republic, which does not use area codes, simply dial the international access code, country code, and phone number (without dropping any digits).

To call my office from Europe, I dial 00 (Europe's international access code), 1 (U.S.A.'s country code), 425 (Edmonds' area code), and 771-8303.

Don't be surprised that in some countries, local phone numbers have different numbers of digits within the same city, or even the same hotel (e.g., a hotel can have a 6-digit phone number, a 7-digit mobile phone number, and an 8-digit fax number).

E-mail and Mail

More and more hotels have e-mail addresses and Web sites (included in this book). I've listed some Internet cafés, but your hotelier or TI can steer you to the nearest Internet access point.

To arrange for mail delivery, reserve a few hotels along your route in advance and give their addresses to friends. Allow 10 days for a letter to arrive. Federal Express makes two-day deliveries—for a price. E-mailing and phoning are so easy that I've dispensed with mail stops all together.

SLEEPING

Much of Eastern Europe simply doesn't have the quaint little family-run pensions and B&Bs that I like to list for other destinations. So, in this book, I've focused my listings on small hotels. I prefer options that are friendly, comfortable, professional-feeling, centrally-located, English-speaking, and family-run. Obviously, a place meeting every criterion is rare, and all of my recommendations fall short of perfection—sometimes miserably. But I've listed the best values for each price category, given the above criteria. I've also thrown in a few hostels, private rooms, and other cheap options for budget travelers.

Prices in Eastern Europe are generally low compared to the West...except for beds. You can uncover some bargains, but I think it's worth paying a little more for comfort and a good location. You can find a central, comfortable double for $100 just about anywhere. Plan on spending $80 to $120 per double in big cities, and $50 to $80 in smaller towns.

While most hotels listed in this book cluster at about $80 to $110 per double, they range from $10 bunks to $200-plus splurges (maximum plumbing and more). The cost is higher in big cities and heavily touristed areas, and lower off the beaten track. Three or four people can save money by requesting one big room. Traveling alone can be expensive: A single room is often only 20 percent cheaper than a double.

Confusingly, some hotels set their rates in euros, then calculate the rate in the local currency when you check out. Others set their rates in the local currency, then convert to euros when you pay. This means that the rates I've listed throughout this book can fluctuate slightly based on the exchange rate. I usually list hotel prices in the local currency. But some hotels prefer to list prices in euros, and in these cases, I've listed the prices they gave me.

For environmental reasons, towels are often replaced in hotels only when you leave them on the floor. In cheaper places, they aren't replaced at all, so hang them up to dry and reuse. The cord that dangles over the tub or shower in big Croatian and Slovenian resort hotels is not a clothesline—you pull it if you've fallen and can't get up.

If asked whether they have non-smoking rooms, most hotels in Eastern Europe will say yes. When pressed, they'll sheepishly admit, "Well, *all* of our rooms are non-smoking"...meaning they air them out after a smoker has stayed there. I've described hotels as "non-smoking" only if they have specially designated rooms for this purpose. Be specific and assertive if you need a strictly non-smoking room.

Sleep Code

I've divided the rooms into three categories, based on the price for a standard double room with bath:

$$$ Higher Priced
$$ Moderately Priced
$ Lower Priced

To save space while giving specific information, I've described my recommended hotels with a standard code. Prices listed are per room, not per person. When a range of prices is listed for a room, the price fluctuates with room size or season. You can assume a hotel takes credit cards unless you see "cash only" in the listing. Unless I note otherwise, the cost of a room includes a buffet breakfast. Virtually all of my recommended accommodations are run by people who speak English; if they don't, I mention it in the listing.

S = Single room (the price for 1 person in a double is often slightly more).
D = Double or twin.
T = Triple (often a double bed with a single bed moved in).
Q = Quad (an extra child's bed is usually cheaper).
b = Private bathroom with toilet and shower or tub.

According to this code, a couple staying at a "Db-2,700 Kč" hotel in Prague would pay a total of 2,700 Czech crowns (about $108) for a double room with a private bathroom. English is spoken, and credit cards are accepted.

Before accepting a room, confirm your understanding of the complete price. Pay your bill the evening before you leave to avoid the time-wasting crowd at the reception desk in the morning. The only tip my recommended hotels would like is a friendly, easygoing guest. And, as always, I appreciate feedback on your hotel experiences.

Private Rooms

A cheap option in Eastern Europe (especially in expensive Croatia) is a room in a private home (*sobe* in Slovenia and Croatia; the German word *Zimmer* works there, too, and throughout Eastern Europe). These places are inexpensive, at least as comfortable as a cheap hotel, and a good way to get some local insight. The boss changes the sheets, so people staying several nights are most desirable—and those who stay less than three nights are often charged a lot more (up to 30 percent). For more on Croatian *sobe*, see page 607.

Hostels

For $10 to $20 a night, travelers of any age can stay at a youth hostel. While official hostels admit nonmembers for an extra fee, it's best to join the club and buy a youth hostel card before you go (call Hostelling International at 202/783-6161 or order online at www.hiayh.org). To increase your options, consider the many independent hostels that don't require a membership card (www.hostels.com). Cheap meals are sometimes available, and kitchen facilities are usually provided for do-it-yourselfers. Expect crowds in the summer, snoring, and lots of youth groups giggling and making rude noises while you try to sleep. Family rooms and doubles are often available on request, but it's basically boys' dorms and girls' dorms. Many hostels are locked up from about 10:00 until 17:00, and a 23:00 curfew is often enforced. Hostelling is ideal for those traveling single: prices are per bed, not per room, and you'll have an instant circle of friends. More and more hostels are getting their business acts together, taking credit card reservations over the phone and leaving sign-in forms on the door for each available room. If you're serious about traveling cheaply, get a card, carry your own sheets, and cook in the members' kitchens.

Making Reservations

It's possible to travel at any time of year without reservations (especially if you arrive early in the day). But given the erratic accommodations values and the quality of the gems I've found for this book, I'd highly recommend that you book rooms ahead as soon as your itinerary is set—or at least call ahead for rooms a day or two in advance as you travel. Even if a hotel clerk says the hotel is fully booked, you can try calling between 9:00 and 10:00 on the day you plan to arrive. That's when the hotel clerk knows who'll be checking out and just which rooms will be available. I've taken great pains to list telephone numbers with long-distance instructions (see "Telephones," above and in the appendix). Use the telephone and the convenient phone cards. Most hotels listed are accustomed to English-only speakers. A hotel receptionist will trust you and hold a room until 16:00 (4:00 p.m.) without a deposit, though some will ask for a credit-card number. Honor (or cancel by phone) your reservations. Long distance is cheap and easy from public phone booths. Don't let these people down—I promised you'd call and cancel if for some reason you won't show up. Don't needlessly confirm rooms through the tourist office; they'll take a commission.

If you know exactly which dates you need and really want a particular place, reserve a room well in advance before you leave home. To reserve from home, e-mail, call, or fax the hotel. Phone and fax costs are reasonable, e-mail is a steal, and simple English is usually fine. To fax, use the form in the appendix (or find it online at www.ricksteves.com/reservation). A two-night stay in August would be "2 nights, 16/8/06 to 18/8/06." (Europeans write the date in this order—day/month/year—and hotel jargon counts your stay from your day of arrival through your day of departure.)

If you e-mail or fax a reservation request and receive a response with rates stating that rooms are available, this is not a confirmation. You must confirm that the rates are fine and that indeed you want the room. You'll often receive a response requesting one night's deposit. A credit-card number and expiration date will usually work. Be sure to fax your card number (rather than e-mail it) to keep it private, safer, and out of cyberspace. If you use your credit card for the deposit, you can pay with your card or cash when you arrive; if you don't show up, you'll be billed for one night. Ask about the cancellation policy when you reserve; sometimes you may have to cancel as much as two weeks ahead to avoid paying a stiff penalty. Reconfirm your reservations several days in advance for safety.

EATING

Eastern European food gets a bum rap. Yes, it can be heavy—but it can also be delicious. This is affordable sightseeing for your palate. Eastern Europe offers good food for very little money—especially if you venture off the main tourist trail.

Slavic cuisine is heavy, hearty, and tasty. Expect lots of meat, potatoes, and cabbage. Still, there's more variety to be had in the East than you might expect. Tune in to the regional and national specialties and customs (see each country's introduction in this book for details).

Ethnic restaurants provide a welcome break from Slavic fare. Seek out vegetarian, Italian, Indian, Chinese, and other similar places. They're especially good in big cities like Budapest or Kraków (I've listed a few tasty options). Hungarian cuisine enjoys some spicy Turkish influence (think paprika), Slovenia and Croatia are as much Italian as they are Slavic (pastas and pizzas), and Croatia also has excellent seafood.

When restaurant-hunting, choose a spot filled with locals, not the place with the big neon signs boasting, "We Speak English and Accept Credit Cards." Incredible deals abound in Eastern Europe, where locals can't afford more than $5 for a fine dinner. Venturing even a block or two off the main drag leads to local, higher-quality food for less than half the price of the tourist-oriented places.

Send Me a Postcard, Drop Me a Line

If you enjoy a successful trip with the help of this book and would like to share your discoveries, please fill out the survey at www.ricksteves.com/feedback or e-mail me at rick@ricksteves.com. I personally read and value all feedback.

Most restaurants tack a menu onto their door for browsers and have an English menu inside. Only a rude waiter will rush you. Good service is relaxed (slow to an American).

When you're in the mood for something halfway between a restaurant and a picnic meal, look for take-out food stands, bakeries (with sandwiches and small pizzas to go), delis with stools or a table, department-store cafeterias, salad bars, or simple little eateries for fast and easy sit-down restaurant food.

The Czech Republic is beer country, with Europe's best and cheapest brew. Poland also has fine beer, but the national drink is *wódka*. Hungary, Slovenia, and Croatia are known for their wines. Each country has its own distinctive liqueur, most of them a variation on *slivovice* (SLEE-voh-veet-seh)—a plum brandy so highly valued that it's the de facto currency of the Carpathian Mountains (often used for bartering with farmers and other mountain folk). Menus list drink size by the tenth of a liter, or deciliter (dl).

TRAVELING AS A TEMPORARY LOCAL

We travel all the way to Europe to enjoy differences—to become temporary locals. You'll experience frustrations. Certain truths that we find "God-given" or "self-evident"—like cold beer, ice in drinks, bottomless cups of coffee, hot showers, cigarette smoke being irritating, and bigger being better—are suddenly not so true. One of the benefits of travel is the eye-opening realization that there are logical, civil, and even better alternatives. A willingness to go local ensures that you'll enjoy a full dose of local hospitality.

Fortunately for you, hospitality is a local forte. The friendliness of the Eastern Europeans seems to have only been enhanced during the communist era: Tangible resources were in short supply, so an open door and a genial conversation were all that people had to offer. For many Eastern Europeans, the chance to chat with an American is still a delightful novelty. Even so, some people—hardened by decades of being spied on by neighbors and standing in line to buy food for their family—seem brusque at first. In my experience, all it takes is a smile and a little effort to befriend these kind, gentle residents of the former "Evil Empire."

If there is a negative aspect to the European image of Americans, we can appear loud, aggressive, impolite, rich, and a bit naive. While Europeans look bemusedly at some of our Yankee excesses—and worriedly at others—they nearly always afford us individual travelers all the warmth we deserve.

While updating this book, I heard over and over again that my readers are considerate and fun to have as guests. Thank you for traveling as temporary locals who are sensitive to the culture. It's fun to follow you in my travels.

Judging from all the positive comments I receive from travelers who have used this book, it's safe to assume you'll enjoy a great, affordable vacation with the finesse of an experienced, independent traveler.

Thanks, and happy travels!

BACK DOOR TRAVEL PHILOSOPHY
From *Rick Steves' Europe Through the Back Door*

Travel is intensified living—maximum thrills per minute and one of the last great sources of legal adventure. Travel is freedom. It's recess, and we need it.

Experiencing the real Europe requires catching it by surprise, going casual..."Through the Back Door."

Affording travel is a matter of priorities. (Make do with the old car.) You can travel—simply, safely, and comfortably—anywhere in Europe for $100 a day plus transportation costs. In many ways, spending more money only builds a thicker wall between you and what you came to see. Europe is a cultural carnival, and, time after time, you'll find that its best acts are free and the best seats are the cheap ones.

A tight budget forces you to travel close to the ground, meeting and communicating with the people, not relying on service with a purchased smile. Never sacrifice sleep, nutrition, safety, or cleanliness in the name of budget. Simply enjoy the local-style alternatives to expensive hotels and restaurants.

Extroverts have more fun. If your trip is low on magic moments, kick yourself and make things happen. If you don't enjoy a place, maybe you don't know enough about it. Seek the truth. Recognize tourist traps. Give a culture the benefit of your open mind. See things as different but not better or worse. Any culture has much to share.

Of course, travel, like the world, is a series of hills and valleys. Be fanatically positive and militantly optimistic. If something's not to your liking, change your liking. Travel is addictive. It can make you a happier American as well as a citizen of the world. Our Earth is home to six billion equally important people. It's humbling to travel and find that people don't envy Americans. They like us, but, with all due respect, they wouldn't trade passports.

Globe-trotting destroys ethnocentricity. It helps you understand and appreciate different cultures. Regrettably, there are forces in our society that want you dumbed down for their convenience. Don't let it happen. Thoughtful travel engages you with the world—more important than ever these days. Travel changes people. It broadens perspectives and teaches new ways to measure quality of life. Many travelers toss aside their hometown blinders. Their prized souvenirs are the strands of different cultures they decide to knit into their own character. The world is a cultural yarn shop. And Back Door travelers are weaving the ultimate tapestry. Come on, join in!

CZECH
REPUBLIC

CZECH REPUBLIC

(Česká Republika)

Despite their difficult 20th-century experience, the Czechs have managed to preserve their history. In Czech towns and villages, you'll find a simple joy of life—a holdover from the days of the Renaissance. The deep spirituality of the Baroque era still shapes the national character. The magic of Prague, the beauty of Český Krumlov, and the lyrical quality of the countryside relieve the heaviness caused by the turmoil that passed through here. Get beyond Prague and explore the country's medieval towns. These rugged woods and hilltop castles will make you feel like you're walking through the garden of your childhood dreams.

Of the Czech Republic's three main regions—Bohemia, Moravia, and small Silesia—the most well-known is Bohemia. It has nothing to do with beatnik bohemians, but with the Celtic tribe of Boheia that inhabited the land before the coming of the Slavs. Home of the Czechs for centuries, Bohemia is circled by a

naturally fortifying ring of mountains and cut down the middle by the Vltava River, with Prague as its capital. The wine-growing region of Moravia (to the east) is more hilly, Slavic, and colorful.

Tourists often conjure up images of Bohemia when they think of the Czech Republic. But the country consists of more than rollicking beer halls and gently rolling landscapes. It's also about dreamy wine cellars and fertile Moravian plains, with the rugged Carpathian Mountains on the horizon. Politically and geologically, Bohemia and Moravia are two distinct regions. The soils and climates in which the hops and wine grapes grow are very different...and so are the two regions' mentalities. The boisterousness of the Czech polka contrasts with the melancholy of the Moravian ballad; the politics of the Prague power-broker is at odds with the spirituality of the Moravian bard.

Only a tiny bit of Silesia—around the town of Opava—is part of the Czech Republic today; the rest of the region is in Germany and Poland. (The Hapsburgs lost traditionally Czech Silesia to Prussia in the 1740s, and 200 years later, Germany in turn ceded it to Poland.) People in Silesia speak a wide variety of dialects that mix Czech, German, and Polish. Perhaps due to their diverse genetics and cultural heritage, women from Silesia are famous for being intelligent and beautiful.

Since 1989, when the Czechs won their independence from Soviet control, more Czechs have been traveling. People are working harder. Roads have been patched up, facades have gotten face-lifts, and neighborhood grocery stores have been pushed out by supermarkets.

Most young Czechs are caught up in the new freedom. Everyone wants to travel—to the practical West to study law, or to the mystical East to learn Egyptian. They want to work for big bucks at a multinational investment bank, or for a meager salary at a non-profit organization based in Chechnya. With so many material dreams suddenly within reach, few Czechs are having children. In the 1990s, the birth rate fell dramatically, but since 2001 it has been slowly rising again.

Yet, even faced with a bright future, some locals maintain a healthy dose of pessimism and are reluctant to dive headlong into the Western rat race. Things still go a little slower here, and people find pleasure in simple things.

Children, adults, and grandparents delight in telling stories. In Czech fairy tales, there are no dwarfs and monsters. To experience the full absurdity and hilarity of Czech culture, you need a child's imagination and the understanding that the best fun comes from being able to laugh at yourself. Czech writers invented the robot, the pistol, and Black Light Theater (an absurd show of illusion, puppetry, mime, and modern dance—see page 120).

The most beloved Czech literary figure is the title character of Jaroslav Hašek's *Good Soldier Švejk*, who frustrates the WWI Austro-Hungarian army he serves in by cleverly playing dumb. Other well-known Czech writers include Václav Havel (a playwright who went on to become Czechoslovakia's first post-communist president; he authored many essays and plays, including *The Garden Party*), Milan Kundera (author of *The Unbearable Lightness of Being*, set during the "Prague Spring" uprising), and Karel Čapek (novelist and playwright who created the robot in the play *R.U.R.*). Most famous of all is the existentialist great Franz Kafka—a Prague Jew who wrote in German about a man who turns into a giant insect *(The Metamorphosis)* and urbanites who are pursued and persecuted for crimes they know nothing about *(The Trial)*.

Ninety percent of the tourists who visit the Czech Republic see only Prague. But if you venture outside the capital, you'll enjoy traditional towns and villages, great prices, a friendly and gentle countryside dotted by nettles and wild poppies, and almost no Western tourists. Since the time of the Hapsburgs, fruit trees have lined the country roads for everyone to share. Take your pick.

Practicalities

Telephones: Dial 112 for emergencies, 158 for police. If an 0800 number doesn't work, replace the 0800 with 822. The basic Český Telecom card works well.

To make phone calls anywhere within the Czech Republic, dial the entire nine-digit number. To call the Czech Republic from another country, first dial the international access code (00 if calling from Europe or 011 from the U.S. or Canada), then 420 (the Czech Republic's country code), then the nine-digit number. To call out of the Czech Republic, dial 00, the country code of the country you're calling (see chart in appendix), the area code if the country's phone system uses area codes (note that sometimes the initial zero is dropped depending on the country), and the local number.

Red Tape: Anyone planning to bring a rental car into the Czech Republic should check with their car-rental company first (see page 28). To drive on Czech highways, you'll need a toll sticker *(dálniční známka)*, sold at borders, post offices, and gas stations (200 Kč/15 days, 300 Kč/2 months).

Transportation: If you have a Eurailpass, note that it doesn't cover the Czech Republic; you'll need to buy train tickets or a Prague Excursion pass for your travels to and from Prague (see page 26).

Czech Republic Almanac

Birth of Two Nations: The nation of Czechoslovakia—formed after World War I, and dominated by the U.S.S.R. after World War II—split on January 1, 1993, into two separate nations: the Czech Republic (Česká Republika) and Slovakia.

Population: 10 million people. About 95 percent are ethnic Czechs, who speak Czech. Unlike some of their neighbors (including the very Catholic Poles and Slovaks), Czechs are inclined to be agnostic: One in four is Roman Catholic, but the majority (60 percent) list their religion as unaffiliated.

Latitude and Longitude: 50°N and 15°E (similar latitude to Vancouver, B.C.)

Area: 31,000 square miles (similar to South Carolina or Maine).

Geography: The Czech Republic is made up of three regions—Bohemia (Čechy), Moravia (Morava), and a small slice of Silesia (Slezsko). The climate is generally cool and cloudy.

Biggest Cities: Prague (the capital, 1.2 million), Brno (380,000), Ostrava (318,000), and Plzeň (165,000).

Economy: The Gross Domestic Product is $172 billion (similar to Indiana). The GDP per capita is $17,000 (less than half that of the average American). Some major money-makers for the country are machine parts, cars and trucks, and beer (including Pilsner Urquell and the original Budweiser—called "Czechvar" in the U.S.). More than a third of trade is with next-door-neighbor Germany. Privatization of formerly government-run industries goes on.

Currency: 25 Czech crowns (*koruna*, Kč) = about $1.

Government: Until 1989, Czechoslovakia was a communist state under Soviet control. Today, the Czech Republic is a vibrant democracy where no single political party dominates. The two-house parliament (of 281 directly elected legislators) selects the president, who appoints the prime minister. The current president, Václav Klaus (a conservative), and his appointed (left-of-center) prime minister, Jiří Paroubek, head a coalition government. The Czech Republic joined the European Union in 2004.

Flag: The Czech flag is red (bottom), white (top), and blue (a triangle along the hoist side).

The Average Czech: The average Czech has 1.2 kids (rising again, after the sharp decline that followed the end of communism), will live 76 years (less if he's a man), and has one television in the house.

Czech History

The Czechs have always been at a crossroads of Europe—between the Slavic and Germanic worlds, between Catholicism and Protestantism, and between the Cold War East and West. As if having foreseen all of this, the mythical founder of Prague—the beautiful princess Libuše—named her city "Praha" (meaning "Threshold" in Czech). Despite these strong external influences, the Czechs have retained their distinct culture...and a dark, ironic sense of humor to keep them laughing through it all.

Charles IV and the Middle Ages

Prague's castle put Bohemia on the map in the ninth century. About a century later, the region was incorporated into the German

Holy Roman Empire. Within a couple hundred years, Prague was one of Europe's largest and most highly cultured cities—even more important than Vienna.

The 14th century was Prague's Golden Age, when Holy Roman Emperor Charles IV ruled from here. Born to a German nobleman and a Czech princess, Charles IV

was a dynamic man on the cusp of the Renaissance. He spoke five languages, counted Petrarch as a friend, imported French architects to make Prague a grand capital, founded the first university north of the Alps, and invigorated the Czech national spirit. (He popularized the legend of the good king Wenceslas to give his people a near mythical, King Arthur–type cultural standard-bearer.) Much of Prague's history and architecture (including the famous Charles Bridge and St. Vitus Cathedral) can be traced to this man's rule. Under Charles IV, the Czech people gained esteem among Europeans.

Jan Hus and Religious Wars

Jan Hus (1369–1415) was a local preacher and professor who got in trouble with the Vatican a hundred years before Martin Luther. Like Luther, Hus preached in the people's language rather than Latin. To add insult to injury, he complained about Church corruption. Tried for heresy and burned in 1415, Hus became both a religious and a national hero. While each age has defined Hus to its liking, the way he challenged authority while staying true to himself has always inspired and rallied the Czech people. (For more on Hus, see the sidebar on page 79).

Inspired by the reformist ideas of Jan Hus, the Czechs rebelled against both the Roman Catholic Church and German political

Notable Czechs

St. Wenceslas (907–935): Bohemian duke who allied the Czechs with the Holy Roman Empire. He went on to become the Czech Republic's patron saint, and was memorialized as a "good king" in the Christmas carol. For more on Wenceslas, see page 94.

Jan Hus (1369–1415): Proto-Protestant Reformer who was burned at the stake (for more on Hus, see below and page 79).

Antonín Dvořák (1841–1904): Inspired by a trip to America, he composed his *New World Symphony*.

Jára Cimrman (c. 1853–1914): Illustrious inventor, explorer, philosopher, and all-around genius. Despite being overwhelmingly voted the "Greatest Czech of All Time" in a recent nationwide poll, he was not awarded the title; for details on the controversy, see page 108.

Alfons Mucha (1860–1939): You probably haven't heard of him, but you might recognize his turn-of-the-century Art Nouveau posters of pretty girls entwined in vines. Visit his museum in Prague (see page 97) and marvel at his marvelous stained-glass window in St. Vitus Cathedral (page 116).

Franz Kafka (1883–1924): While working for a Prague insurance firm, he wrote (in German) *The Metamorphosis, The Trial*, and other psychologically haunting stories and novels.

Milan Kundera (1929–): Author of numerous novels, including *The Unbearable Lightness of Being* (which became a film).

Miloš Forman (1932–): Film director who emigrated from Czechoslovakia to the United States, where he made *One Flew Over the Cuckoo's Nest, Amadeus, The People vs. Larry Flint, Man on the Moon*, and more.

Václav Havel (1936–): The country's first post-Soviet president, who's also known as a playwright and philosopher.

Madeleine Albright (1937–): A Prague-born Czech of Jewish descent whose family fled Czechoslovakia during the Holocaust, Albright went on to become President Bill Clinton's Secretary of State.

Martina Navrátilová (1956–): Tennis star of the 1980s.

control. This burst of independent thought led to a period of religious wars, and ultimately the loss of autonomy to Vienna. Ruled by the Hapsburgs of Austria, Prague stagnated—except during the rule of King Rudolf II (1552–1612), a Holy Roman Emperor. With Rudolph living in Prague, the city again emerged as a cultural and intellectual center. Astronomers Johannes Kepler, Tycho Brahe, and other scientists flourished, and much of the inspiration for

Prague's great art can be attributed to the king's patronage.

Not long after, Prague entered one of its darkest spells. The Thirty Years' War (1618–1648) began in Prague Castle when Czech nobles wanting religious and political autonomy tossed two Catholic/Hapsburg officials out the window of the Prague Castle (one of Prague's many "defenestrations"). The Czech Estates Uprising lasted for two years, ending in a crushing defeat of the Czech army in the Battle of White Mountain (1620), which marked the end of Czech freedom. Twenty-seven leaders of the uprising were executed (today commemorated by crosses on Prague's Old Town Square—see page 81), most of the old Czech nobility was dispossessed, and Protestants had to leave the country or convert to Catholicism. Often called "the first world war" because it engulfed so many nations, the Thirty Years' War was particularly tough on Prague. During this period, its population dropped from 60,000 to 25,000. The result of this war was 300 years of Hapsburg rule from afar, as Prague became a backwater of Vienna.

Czech Nationalist Revival

The end of Prague as a "German" city came gradually. As the Industrial Revolution attracted Czech farmers into the cities, the demographics of the Czech population centers began to shift. Between 1800 and 1900, though it remained part of the Hapsburg Empire, Prague went from being an essentially German town to a predominantly Czech one. Like in the rest of Europe, the 19th century was a time of nationalism, as the age of divine kings and ruling families came to a fitful end. The Czech spirit was stirred by the completion of Prague's St. Vitus Cathedral, the symphonies of Antonín Dvořák, and the operas of Bedřich Smetana performed in the new National Theatre.

After the Hapsburgs' Austro-Hungarian Empire suffered defeat in World War I, their vast holdings broke apart and became independent countries. Among these was a union of Bohemia, Moravia, and Slovakia, the brainchild of a clever politician named Tomáš Garrigue Masaryk (see page 114). The new nation, Czechoslovakia, was proclaimed in 1918, with Prague as its capital.

Troubled 20th Century

Independence lasted only 20 years. In the notorious Munich Agreement of September 1938—much to the dismay of the Czechs and Slovaks—Great Britain and France peacefully ceded to Hitler the so-called "Sudetenland" (a fringe around the edge of Bohemia, populated mainly by people of German descent). It wasn't long before Hitler seized the rest of Czechoslovakia...and the Holocaust began.

For centuries, Prague's cultural make-up consisted of a rich mix of Czech, German, and Jewish people—historically about evenly divided. But only 5 percent of the Jewish population survived the Holocaust. After World War II ended, the three million people of Germanic descent who lived in Czechoslovakia were pushed into Germany. This forced resettlement—which led to the deaths of untold tens of thousands of Germans—was the idea of Czechoslovak President Edvard Beneš, who had been ruling from exile in London throughout the war (see page 152). As a result of both of these policies (the Holocaust and the expulsion of Germans), today's Czech Republic is largely homogenous—about 95 percent Czechs.

Although Prague escaped the bombs of World War II, it went directly from the Nazi frying pan into the communist fire. A local uprising freed the city from the Nazis on May 8, 1945, but the Russians "liberated" them on May 9.

The communist chapter (1948–1989) was grim. The "Prague Spring" uprising—initiated by a young generation of reform-minded communists in 1968—was crushed. The charismatic leader, Alexander Dubček, was exiled (and made a forest ranger in the backwoods), and the years following the unsuccessful revolt were particularly disheartening. In the late 1980s, the communists began constructing Prague's huge TV tower (now the city's tallest structure)—not only to broadcast Czech TV transmissions, but also to jam Western signals. The Metro, built around the same time, was intended for mass transit, but first and foremost it was designed to be a giant fallout shelter for protection against capitalist bombs.

But the Soviet empire crumbled. Czechoslovakia regained its freedom in the student- and artist-powered 1989 "Velvet Revolution" (so called because there were no casualties). Václav Havel, a writer who had been imprisoned by the communist regime, became Czechoslovakia's first post-communist president. In 1993, the Czech and Slovak Republics agreed on the "Velvet Divorce" and became two separate countries (see sidebar on page 166).

Havel ended his second (and, constitutionally, last) five-year term in 2003. While he's still admired by Czechs as a great thinker, writer, and fearless leader of the opposition movement during the communist days, many consider him less successful as a president. Some believe that the split of Czechoslovakia was partly caused by Havel's initial insensitivity to Slovak demands. The current president, Václav Klaus, was the pragmatic author of the economic reforms in the 1990s. Klaus' election in 2003 symbolized a change from revolutionary times, when philosophers became kings, to humdrum politics, when offices are gained by bargaining with the devil (Communist Party votes in the Parliament were the decisive

Czech Sports

Prague's top sports are soccer (that's "football" here) and hockey. Surprisingly, the Czechs are a world power in both.

The Czech **soccer** team reached the finals and semifinals of the last three European Cups. Within the Czech Republic, the two oldest and by far most successful soccer clubs are the bitter Prague rivals, Sparta and Slavia. Slavia has always been the better team, while Sparta has merely harvested more trophies. Sparta's stadium at Letná (behind the metronome ticking above the river) is easier to get to.

The Czech national **hockey** team won four (including 2005) out of last seven world championships (Canada won 2, and Slovakia the remaining 1). Think Jaromír Jágr. There are more than a hundred Czech players in America's NHL.

Sparta and Slavia also have hockey teams, but the rivalry is less jaded, as the teams from smaller towns are more than their equals. Slavia plays in the brand-new, state-of-the-art Sazka Arena built for the 2004 world hockey championships (right at the Českomoravská Metro stop).

Back in the old days, ice hockey was the only battleground on which Czechoslovaks could seek revenge on their Russian oppressors. To this day, the hockey rink is where Czechs are proudest about their nationality. If you are in the country in May (during the hockey championships), join locals cheering their team in front of a giant screen on Prague's Old Town Square and other main squares around the Czech Republic.

Ice hockey is also the most popular sport in Slovakia. To understand the friendly relationship between Czechs and Slovaks after their Velvet Divorce in 1989 (see sidebar on page 166), just walk into any Czech or Slovak pub during the hockey championships. Unless the two teams are playing each other, all Czechs passionately support the Slovak team, and vice versa.

factor in Klaus' election). Another major turning point occurred on May 1, 2004, when the Czech Republic joined the European Union.

Today, while not without its problems, the Czech Republic is enjoying a growing economy and a strong democracy, and Prague has emerged as one of the most popular tourist destinations in Europe.

Czech Food

Czech cuisine is heavy, hearty, and tasty. Expect lots of meat, potatoes, and cabbage. Still, there's more variety than you might expect. Ethnic restaurants provide a welcome break from Slavic

Czech Beer

Czechs are among the world's most enthusiastic beer *(pivo)* drinkers—adults drink about 80 gallons a year. The pub is a place to have fun, complain, discuss art and politics, talk hockey, and chat with locals and visitors alike. The *pivo* that was drunk in the country before the Industrial Revolution was much thicker, providing the main source of nourishment for the peasant folk. As a result, even today it doesn't matter whether you are in a *restaurace* (restaurant), a *hostinec* (pub), or a *hospoda* (bar)—a beer will land on

your table upon the slightest hint to the waiter, and a new pint will automatically appear when the old glass is almost empty. (You must tell the waiter *not* to bring more.) Order beer from the tap *(točené* means "draft," *sudové pivo* means "keg beer"). A *pivo* is large (0.5 liter, or 17 oz); a *malé pivo* is small (0.3 liter, or 10 oz). Men invariably order the large size. *Pivo* for lunch has me sightseeing for the rest of the day on Czech knees.

The Czechs invented lager in Plzeň ("Pilsen" in German). This is the famous Pilsner Urquell, on tap in many local pubs. But be sure to venture beyond Pilsner Urquell. There are plenty of other good Czech beers, including Krušovice, Gambrinus, Staropramen, and Kozel. Budvar, from the town of Budějovice ("Budweis" in German), is popular with Anheuser-Busch's attorneys. (The Czech and the American breweries for years disputed the "Budweiser" brand name. The solution: The Czech Budweiser—actually owned by South Africans—is sold under its own name in Europe, China, and Africa, while in America it markets itself as Czechvar.)

The big degree symbol on bottles does not indicate the percentage of alcohol it contains. Twelve degrees is about 4.2 percent alcohol, 10 degrees is about 3.5 percent alcohol, and 11 and 15 degrees are dark beers.

Each establishment has only one kind of beer on tap; to try a particular brand, look for its sign outside. A typical pub serves only one brand of 10-degree beer, one brand of 12-degree beer, and one brand of dark beer. Czechs do not mix beer with anything, and do not hop from pub to pub (in one night, it is said, you must stay loyal to one woman and to one beer).

fare. Seek out vegetarian, Italian, or Chinese (I've recommended several options).

After a sip of beer, ask for the *jídelní lístek* (menu). *Polévka* (soup) is the most essential part of a meal. The saying goes: "The soup fills you up, the dish plugs it up." Some of the thick soups for a cold day are *zelná* or *zelňačka* (cabbage), *čočková* (lentil), *fazolová* (bean), and *dršťková* (tripe—delicious if fresh, chewy as gum if not). The lighter soups are *hovězí* or *slepičí vývar s nudlemi* (beef or chicken broth with noodles), *pórková* (leek), and *květáková* (cauliflower). *Pečivo* (bread) is either delivered with the soup or you need to ask for it; it's always charged separately depending on how many *rohlíky* (rolls) or slices of *chleba* (yeast bread) you eat.

Main dishes are divided into *hotová jídla* (quick, ready-to-serve standard dishes, in some places available only during lunch hours, 11:30–14:30) and the more specialized *jídla na objednávku* or *minutky* (plates prepared when you order). Even the supposedly quick *hotová jídla* will take longer than fast food you're used to back home.

A Czech restaurant is a social place where people come to relax. Tables are not private. You can ask to join someone and will most likely make some new friends. Instead of worrying about how much sightseeing you're missing during your two-hour lunch, appreciate the opportunity to learn more about Czech culture.

Hotová jídla (ready-to-serve dishes) come with set garnishes. The standard menu across the country includes *smažený řízek s bramborem* (fried pork fillet with potatoes), *svíčková na smetaně s knedlíkem* (beef tenderloin in cream sauce with dumplings), *vepřová s knedlíkem a se zelím* (pork with dumplings and cabbage), *pečená kachna s knedlíkem a se zelím* (roasted duck with dumplings and cabbage), *maďarský guláš s knedlíkem* (the Czech version of Hungarian goulash), and *pečené kuře s bramborem* (roasted chicken with potatoes). In this landlocked country, fish options are limited to *kapr* (carp) and *pstruh* (trout), prepared in a variety of ways and served with potatoes or fries. Vegetarians can go for the delicious *smažený sýr s bramborem* (fried cheese with potatoes) or default for *čočka s vejci* (lentils with fried egg). If you are spending the night out with friends, have a beer and feast on the huge *vepřové koleno s hořčicí a křenem* (pork knuckle with mustard and horseradish sauce) with *chleba* (yeast bread).

The range of the *jídla na objednávku* (meals prepared to order) depends on the chef. You choose your garnishes, which are charged separately.

Šopský salát, like a Greek salad, is usually the best salad option (a mix of tomatoes, cucumbers, peppers, onion, and feta cheese with vinegar and olive oil). The waiter will bring it with the main dish, unless you specify that you want it before.

For *moučník* (dessert), there are *palačinka* (crêpes served with fruit or jam), *lívance* (small pancakes with jam and curd), or *zmrzlinový pohár* (ice-cream sundae). Many restaurants will offer different sorts of *koláče* (pastries) and *štrůdl* (apple strudel), but it's much better to get these directly from a bakery.

No Czech meal is complete without a cup of strong *turecká káva* (Turkish coffee—finely ground coffee that only partly dissolves, leaving "mud" on the bottom, drunk without milk). Although espressos and instant coffees have made headway in the past few years, many Czechs regard them as a threat to their culture.

A good alternative to a beer is *minerálka* (mineral water). These healthy waters have a high mineral content. They're naturally carbonated because they come from the springs in the many Czech spas (Mattoni, the most common brand, is from Carlsbad). If you want plain water, ask for *voda bez bublinek* (water without bubbles).

Bohemia is beer country, with Europe's best and cheapest brew (described in the "Czech Beer" sidebar). Bohemians also like the herb liquor *becherovka*. Moravians prefer wine and *slivovice* (SLEE-voh-veet-seh)—plum brandy. *Medovina* (literally, "honey wine") is mead.

In bars and restaurants, you can go wild with memorable liqueurs, most of which cost about a dollar a shot. Experiment. *Fernet*, a bitter drink made from many herbs, is the leading Czech apéritif. *Absinthe*, made from wormwood and herbs, is a watered-down version of the hallucinogenic drink that's illegal in the United States and much of Europe. It's famous as the muse of many artists (including Henri de Toulouse-Lautrec in Paris more than a century ago). *Becherovka*, made of 13 herbs and 38 percent alcohol, was used to settle upset aristocratic tummies and as an aphrodisiac. This velvety drink remains popular today. *Becherovka* and tonic mixed together is nicknamed *beton* ("concrete"). If you drink three, you'll find out why.

You can stay in a pub as long as you want—no one will bring you an *účet* (bill) until you ask for it: *"Pane vrchní, zaplatím!"* ("Mr. Waiter, now I pay!").

Czech Language

Czech, a Slavic language closely related to its neighbors Polish and Slovak, has little resemblance to Western European languages. These days, English is "modern" and you'll find the language barrier minimal. Among older people, German is a common second language.

An acute accent *(á, é, í, ó, ú, ý)* means you linger on that vowel. The letter *c* always sounds like "ts" (as in "cats"). The little accent *(háček)* above the *č, š,* or *ž* makes it sound like "ch," "sh", or "zh" (as

Key Czech Phrases

English	Czech	Pronounced
Hello. (formal)	*Dobrý den.*	DOH-bree dehn
Hi. / Bye. (informal)	*Ahoj.*	AH-hoy
Do you speak English?	*Mluvíte anglicky?*	MLOO-vee-teh ANG-lits-kee
Yes. / No.	*Ano. / Ne.*	AH-no / neh
Please. / You're welcome. / Can I help you?	*Prosím.*	PROH-zeem
Thank you.	*Děkuji.*	DYACK-quee
I'm sorry. / Excuse me.	*Promiňte.*	PROH-meen-teh
Good.	*Dobře.*	DOHB-zhay
Goodbye.	*Na shledanou.*	nah SKLEH-dah-now
one / two	*jeden / dva*	YAY-dehn / dvah
three / four	*tři / čtyři*	tree / chuh-TEE-ree
five / six	*pět / šest*	pyeht / shehst
seven / eight	*sedm / osm*	SEH-dum / OH-sum
nine / ten	*devět / deset*	DEHV-yeht / DEH-seht
hundred	*sto*	stoh
thousand	*tisíc*	TYEE-seets
How much?	*Kolik?*	KOH-leek
local currency	*koruna (Kč)*	koh-ROO-nah
Where is…?	*Kde je…?*	gday yeh
…the toilet	*…vécé*	vayt-SAY
men	*muži*	MOO-zhee
women	*ženy*	ZHAY-nee
water / coffee	*voda / káva*	VOH-dah / KAH-vah
beer / wine	*pivo / víno*	PEE-voh / VEE-noh
Cheers!	*Na zdraví!*	nah zdrah-VEE
The bill, please.	*Účet, prosím.*	OO-cheht PROH-zeem

in "leisure"), respectively. A *háček* above *ň* makes it sound like "ny" (as in "canyon"), and over *ě* makes it sound like "ye." Czech has one sound that occurs in no other language: *ř* (as in "Dvořák"), which sounds like a cross between a rolled "r" and "zh."

PRAGUE

(Praha)

It's amazing what a decade and a half of freedom can do. Prague has always been historic. Now it's fun, too. No other place in Europe has become so popular so quickly. And for good reason: Prague—the only Central European capital to escape the bombs of the last century's wars—is one of Europe's best-preserved cities. It's filled with sumptuous Art Nouveau facades, offers tons of cheap Mozart and Vivaldi, and brews the best beer in Europe. Beyond its architecture and traditional culture, it's an explosion of pent-up entrepreneurial energy jumping for joy after 40 years of communist rule. Its low prices can cause you to jump for joy, too. Travel in Prague is like travel in Western Europe...15 years ago and for half the price.

Planning Your Time

Prague demands a minimum of two full days (with 3 nights, or 2 nights and a night train). From Budapest, Warsaw, or Kraków, it's a handy night train. From Munich, Berlin, and Vienna, Prague is about a six-hour train ride by day (you also have the option of a longer night train from Munich).

With two days in Prague, I'd spend a morning seeing the castle and a morning in the Jewish Quarter (closed Sat). Use your afternoons for loitering around the Old Town, Charles Bridge, and the Little Quarter, and split your nights between beer halls and live music.

Prague

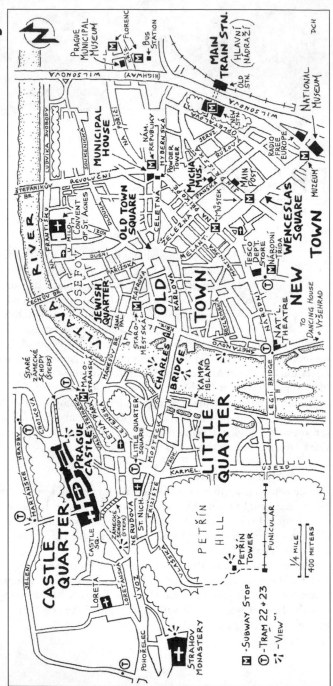

Map labels:
Prague Municipal Museum
Florenc
Bus Station
MAIN TRAIN STN. (HLAVNÍ NÁDRAŽÍ)
OLD STN.
DCH
WILSONOVA (HIGHWAY)
NATIONAL MUSEUM
NEW STN.
RADIO FREE EUROPE
LUDVÍKA SVOBODY
ŠTEFÁNIKŮV BR.
REVOLUČNÍ
MUNICIPAL HOUSE
NA PORIČÍ
SOUKENICKÁ
NÁM. REPUBLIKY
HYBERNSKÁ
OPLETALOVA
JERUZ.
RUZOVA
Powder Tower
MUCHA MUS.
PANSKÁ
MAIN POST
MUZEUM
WENCESLAS SQUARE
NEW TOWN
CELETNA
ŽELEZNÁ
MÚSTEK
NA PŘÍKOPĚ
DLOUHÁ
CONVENT OF ST. AGNES
MILO
SV. FRANTIŠKU
OLD TOWN SQUARE
DUŠNÍ
PAŘÍŽSKÁ
KAPROVA
JEWISH QUARTER
JOSEFOV
ČECHŮV BR.
JANA PAL.
STARO- MĚSTSKÁ
KARLOVA
MELAN.
OLD TOWN
MELANTR.
Tesco Dept. Store
NÁRODNÍ TŘÍDA
TO Dancing House & Vyšehrad
NÁRODNÍ
RIVER
VLTAVA
MANESÚV BR.
KŘIŽOVN.
BETLEM.
SMETANOVO NÁBŘ.
Nat'l. Theatre
CHARLES BRIDGE
KAMPA ISLAND
LEGII BRIDGE
Staré Zámecké Schody (STEPS)
CHOTKOVA
MALO- STRANSKÁ
LETENSKÁ
VLAŠ. PARK
Little Quarter Square
MOSTECKÁ
PROK.
KARMEL.
LITTLE QUARTER
UJEZD
MARIÁNSKÉ HRADBY
PRAGUE CASTLE
Castle Steps
Zámecké Schody (STEPS)
NERUDOVA
ST. NICH.
TRŽIŠTĚ
VLAŠSKÁ
PETŘÍN HILL
PETŘÍN TOWER
FUNICULAR
CASTLE QUARTER
JELENÍ
CASTLE SQ.
LORETÁNSKÁ
ÚVOZ
LORETA
POHOŘELEC
STRAHOV MONASTERY

¼ MILE
400 METERS

M - Subway Stop
T - Tram 22 + 23
ᵛⁱ - View

Prague Landmarks

English	Czech	Pronounced
Main Train Station	Hlavní Nádraží	hlav-nee nah-drah-zhee
Old Town	Staré Město	STAH-reh myehs-toh
Old Town Square	Staroměstské Náměstí	star-roh-myehst-skeh nah-myehs-tee
New Town	Nové Město	noh-vay myehs-toh
Little Quarter	Malá Strana	mah-lah strah-nah
Jewish Quarter	Josefov	yoo-zehf-fohf
Castle Quarter	Hradčany	hrad-chah-nee
Charles Bridge	Karlův Most	kar-loov most
Wenceslas Square	Václavske Náměstí	vaht-slahf-skeh nah-myehs-tee
Vltava River	Vltava	vul-tah-vah

ORIENTATION

Locals call their town "Praha" (PRAH-hah). It's big, with 1.2 million people—but focus on its relatively compact old center during a quick visit. As you wander, take advantage of brown street signs directing you to tourist landmarks.

The Vltava River divides the west side (Castle Quarter and Little Quarter) from the east side (New Town, Old Town, Jewish Quarter, Main Train Station, and most of the recommended hotels). I've arranged my sightseeing, hotel, and restaurant recommendations based on Prague's four towns (see sidebar on page 76).

Prague addresses come with references to a general zone. Praha 1 is in the old center on either side of the river. Praha 2 is in the new city, southeast of Wenceslas Square. Praha 3 and higher indicate a location farther from the center. Virtually everything I list is in Praha 1 (unless noted otherwise).

Tourist Information

TIs are at four key locations: **Main Train Station** (roughly Easter–Oct Mon–Fri 9:00–19:00, Sat–Sun 9:00–16:00—but often closed Sat–Sun; Nov–Easter Mon–Fri 9:00–18:00, Sat 9:00–15:00, closed Sun), **Old Town Square** (Easter–Oct Mon–Fri 9:00–19:00, Sat–Sun 9:00–18:00; Nov–Easter Mon–Fri 9:00–18:00, Sat–Sun 9:00–17:00; tel. 224-482-018), **below Wenceslas Square** at Na Příkopě 20 (Easter–Oct Mon–Fri 9:00–19:00, Sat–Sun 9:00–17:00; Nov–Easter Mon–Fri 9:00–18:00, Sat 9:00–15:00, closed

Rip-Offs in Prague

Prague's new freedom comes with new scams. There's no particular risk of violent crime, but green, rich tourists do get taken by con artists. Simply be on guard, particularly when traveling on trains (thieves thrive on overnight trains), changing money (tellers with bad arithmetic and inexplicable pauses while counting back your change), dealing with taxis (see "Getting Around Prague—By Taxi," page 71), paying in restaurants (see "Eating," page 134), and in seedy neighborhoods (see below).

Anytime you pay for something, make a careful note of how much it costs, how much you're handing over, and how much you expect back. Count your change. Someone selling you a phone card marked 190 Kč might first tell you it's 790 Kč, hoping to pocket the difference. Call the bluff and they'll pretend it never happened.

Plainclothes policemen "looking for counterfeit money" are con artists. Don't show them any cash or your wallet. If you're threatened with an inexplicable fine by a "policeman," conductor, or other official, you can walk away, scare him away by saying you'll need a receipt (which real officials are legally required to provide), or ask a passerby if the fine is legit. On the other hand, do not ignore the plainclothes inspectors on the Metro and trams who have shown you their badges.

Sun; tel. 224-226-087), and the castle side of **Charles Bridge** (Easter–Oct daily 10:00–18:00, closed Nov–Easter). For general tourist information in English, dial 12444 (Mon–Fri 8:00–19:00) or check the TIs' useful Web site: www.pis.cz.

The TIs offer maps, phone cards, a useful transit guide, information on guided walks and bus tours, and bookings for private guides, concerts, hotel rooms, and rooms in private homes. There are several monthly events guides—all of them packed with ads—including *Prague Guide* (29 Kč), *Prague This Month* (free), and *Heart of Europe* (free, summer only).

The English-language weekly *Prague Post* newspaper is handy for entertainment listings and current events (sold cheap at newsstands).

Arrival in Prague

Upon arrival, be sure to buy a city map, with trams and Metro lines marked and tiny sketches of the sights for ease in navigating

Pickpockets can be little children, or adults dressed as professionals or even as tourists. They target Western visitors. Many thieves drape jackets over their arms to disguise busy fingers. Thieves work the crowded and touristy places in teams. They use mobile phones to coordinate their bumps and grinds. Be careful if anyone creates a commotion at the door of a Metro or tram car (especially around the Národní Třída and Vodičkova tram stops, or on the made-for-tourists trams #22 and #23)—it's a smokescreen for theft. Car theft is also a big problem in Prague (many Western European car-rental companies don't allow their rentals to cross the Czech border). Never leave anything valuable in your car—not even in broad daylight on a busy street. The sex clubs on Skořepka Street, just south of Havelská Market, routinely rip off naive tourists and can be dangerous. They're filled mostly with Russian girls and German and Asian guys. Lately this district has become the rage for British "stag" parties (happy to take cheap off-season flights to get to cheap beer and cheap girls). Be warned: Even on the street, aggressive girls can be all over gawkers.

This all sounds intimidating. But Prague is safe. It has its share of petty thieves and con artists, but very little violent crime. Don't be scared—just be alert. You can join in on a local running joke on the pickpockets: a professor of Buddhism from a prestigious American university keeps an empty wallet with a picture of a man giving the finger prominently displayed in his pocket during every Prague visit. So far, he has yet to be robbed. See if you have more luck.

(30–70 Kč, many different brands; sold at kiosks, exchange windows, or tobacco stands). It's a mistake to try doing Prague without a good map—you'll refer to it constantly.

By Train

Most travelers coming from and going to major international destinations us the Main Station (Hlavní Nádraží)—as do travelers going to and from Český Krumlov and many other Czech towns. Other trains use the secondary station (Nádraží Holešovice).

Upon arrival, get money. The stations have ATMs (best rates) and exchange bureaus (rates are generally bad, but can vary—compare by asking at 2 windows what you'll get for $100, but keep in mind that many of the windows are run by the same company). Then buy your map and confirm your departure plans. Consider arranging a room or tour through the AVE travel agency (branches in both stations—see page 124). Anyone arriving on an international train will be met at the tracks by room hustlers, trying to snare tourists for cheap rooms.

Main Station (Hlavní Nádraží): This station's low-ceilinged hall contains a fascinating mix of travelers, kiosks, gamblers, loitering teenagers, and older riffraff. The creepy station ambience is the work of communist architects, who expanded a classy building to make it just big, painting it the compulsory dreary gray with reddish trim. An ATM is near the subway entrance. The station's baggage-storage counter is reportedly safer than the lockers. The Wasteels office can help you figure out train connections, and sells cheap phone cards and tickets for anywhere in Europe (no commission; Mon–Fri 9:00–17:00, Sat 9:00–16:00, closed Sun, tel. 224-641-954, www.wasteels.cz). The information office for Czech Railways (downstairs on the left) is less helpful, and the ticket windows downstairs don't give schedule information. The windows marked *vnitrostátní* sell tickets within the Czech Republic.

If you're killing time here (or for a wistful glimpse of a more genteel age), go upstairs into the Art Nouveau hall. Here, under an elegant dome, you can sip coffee, enjoy music from the 1920s, watch boy prostitutes looking for work, and see new arrivals spilling into the city. The station was originally named for Emperor Franz Josef. Later, it was renamed for President Woodrow Wilson, because his promotion of self-determination led to the creation of the free state of Czechoslovakia in 1918. Look for a commemorative plaque with Wilson's face at the main exit hall from the platforms. Under the communists (who weren't big fans of Wilson), it was bluntly renamed Hlavní Nádraží—literally, "Main Station."

Even though the Main Station is basically downtown, it can be a little tricky to get to your hotel. The biggest challenge is that the **taxi** cabbies at the train station are a gang of no-neck mafia thugs who wait around to charge an arriving tourist five times the regular rate. To get an honest cabbie, I'd walk a few blocks (or ride the Metro one stop), hail one off the street, or call AAA Taxi (tel. 233-113-311). A taxi should get you to your hotel for no more than 200 Kč (see "Getting Around Prague," page 69). A cheaper option—one with far less danger of being ripped off—is to take the **Metro** (inside station, look for the red M with two directions: Háje or Ládví). To get to hotels in the Old Town, catch a Háje-bound train to the Muzeum stop, then transfer to the green line (direction: Dejvická) and get off at either Můstek or Staroměstská; these stops straddle the Old Town. Or, if your hotel is close enough, consider **walking** (Wenceslas Square, a downtown landmark, is about a 10-minute walk away: Turn left out of the station and follow Washingtonova street to the huge National Museum).

Holešovice Station (Nádraží Holešovice): This station, slightly farther from the center, is suburban mellow. The main hall has all the services of the Main Station in a compact area. The friendly, little-frequented café allows you to place cheap international calls through the Internet (7 Kč/min to the U.S., daily 8:00–19:30). Outside the first glass doors, the ATM is on the left, the Czech Railways information office is on the right (daily 9:00–17:00), and the Metro is straight ahead (follow signs toward *Vstup*, which means "entrance"; take it 3 stops to Hlavní Nádraží—the Main Station, or 4 stops to the city-center Muzeum stop). Taxis and trams are outside to the right (allow 200 Kč for a cab to the center).

By Plane

Prague's modern, tidy, low-key **Ruzyně Airport**—a delightful contrast to the old, hulking Main Train Station—is 12 miles (about 30 min) west of the city center. The airport has ATMs (avoid the change desks); desks promoting their transportation service (such as city transit and shuttle buses); kiosks selling city maps and phone cards; and a tourist service with little printed material. Airport info: tel. 220-113-314, operator tel. 220-111-111.

Getting to and from the airport is easy. You have four options:

Dirt cheap: Take bus #119 to the Dejvická Metro station, or #100 to the Zličín Metro station (20 min), then take the Metro into the center (20 Kč, info desk in airport arrival hall).

Cheap: Take the Čedaz minibus shuttle to Náměstí Republiky, across from Kotva department store (daily 5:30–21:30, 2/hr, pay 90 Kč directly to driver, info desk in arrival hall).

Moderate: Take a Čedaz minibus directly to your hotel, with a couple of stops likely en route (360 Kč for a group of up to 4, tel. 220-114-286).

Expensive: Catch a taxi. Cabbies wait at the curb directly in front of the arrival hall. Airport taxi cabbies are honest but expensive. Carefully confirm the complete price before getting in. It's a fixed rate of 600–700 Kč, with no meter.

Helpful Hints

Medical Help: A **24-hour pharmacy** is at Palackého 5 (a block from Wenceslas Square, tel. 224-946-982). There are two state hospitals in the center: the **General Hospital** (U Nemocnice 2, Praha 2, right above Karlovo Náměstí, tel. 224-962-564) and the **Na Františku Hospital** (Na Františku 1, on the embankment next to Hotel InterContinental).

Internet Access: Internet cafés are interspersed through Old and New Towns. Consider **Bohemia Bagel**, with two locations, one in the Jewish Quarter in the Old Town, and the other in the Little Quarter (see page 144). **Káva Káva Káva Coffee**, on the boundary between the Old and New Towns, is in the Platýz courtyard off Národní 37.

Bookstore: Prague has several enjoyable bookshops with English titles. My favorites include **Globe Bookstore** (daily 10:00–24:00, Pštrossova 6, tel. 224-934-203, www.globebookstore.cz), **Anagram Bookshop** (Mon–Sat 10:00–20:00, Sun 10:00–19:00, in the Ungelt courtyard behind Týn Church, Týn 4, tel. 224-895-737, www.anagram.cz), **Big Ben Bookshop** (also in Ungelt courtyard, at Malá Štupartská 5, tel. 224-826-565, www.bigbenbookshop.com), and **V Ráji** (Maiselova 12, next to Maisel Synagogue in the Jewish Quarter, tel. 222-326-925). **Kiwi Map Store,** near Wenceslas Square, has an excellent selection of maps (Mon–Fri 9:00–19:00, Sat 9:00–14:00, closed Sun, Jungmanova Street 23, tel. 224-948-455, www.kiwick.cz).

Laundry: A full-service laundry near most of the recommended hotels is at Karolíny Světlé 10 (200 Kč/8-pound load, wash and dry in 2 hrs, Mon–Fri 7:30–19:00, closed Sat–Sun, 200 yards from Charles Bridge on Old Town side). Or surf the Internet while your undies tumble-dry at Korunní 14 (160 Kč/load wash and dry, Internet-2 Kč/min, daily 8:00–20:00, Praha 2, near Náměstí Míru Metro stop).

Local Help: Magic Praha is a tiny travel service run by hardworking Lída Šteflová. A charming Jill-of-all-trades who takes her clients' needs seriously, she's particularly helpful with accommodations and transfers throughout the Czech Republic, private tours, and side-trips to historic towns (Spálená 21, 1st floor, tel. & fax 224-931-674, mobile 604-207-225, www.magicpraha.cz, magicpraha@magicpraha.cz). **Athos Travel** books rooms (see page 123), rents cars, and has guides for hire (1–5 people-700 Kč/hr—see page 74).

Car Rental: All of the biggies have offices in Prague (check each company's Web site, or ask at the TI). For a local alternative, consider **Alimex**, which features a wide variety of new vehicles plastered with big ads (tel. 233-350-001, toll-free tel. 800-150-170, www.alimexcr.cz). The cheapest model, a Škoda Fabia, is a great value (450 Kč/day with basic insurance, plus 238 Kč/day for full theft and damage insurance; additional fees: 500-Kč tax for airport pickup, 357 Kč for delivery to your hotel; discounts if you book online, smart to reserve up to a week ahead in peak season). They have branches at the airport (daily 8:00–22:00) and near the Holešovice train station (daily 8:00–18:00).

American Express: It's right on Wenceslas Square (foreign exchange daily 9:00–19:00; travel service Mon–Fri 9:00–18:00, Sat 9:00–12:00, closed Sun; Václavské Náměstí 56, tel. 222-800-237). AmEx also has offices on Celetná Street in the

Old Town and on the Old Town Square.

Best Views: Enjoy the "Golden City of a Hundred Spires" during the early evening, when the light is warm and the colors are rich. Good viewpoints include the terrace at the Strahov Monastery (above the castle), the top of St. Vitus Cathedral (at the castle), the top of either tower on Charles Bridge, the Old Town Square clock tower (has an elevator), the Restaurant u Prince Terrace (see page 138), and the steps of the National Museum overlooking Wenceslas Square.

Getting Around Prague

You can walk nearly everywhere. But the Metro is slick, the trams fun, and the taxis quick and easy, once you're initiated. For details, pick up the handy transit guide at the TI. City maps show the tram, bus, and Metro lines.

By Metro and Tram

Affordable and excellent public transit is perhaps the best legacy of the communist era (locals ride all month for 460 Kč). The three-line Metro system is handy and simple, but doesn't always get you right to the tourist sights (landmarks such as the Old Town Square and Prague Castle are several blocks from the nearest Metro stops). The trams take you just about anywhere.

Tickets: The trams and Metro work on the same cheap tickets:

• 20-minute basic ticket with limited transfer options—14 Kč *(základní s omezenou přestupností)*. With this ticket, no transfers are allowed on trams and buses, but on the Metro, you can go up to five stops with one transfer (not valid for night trams or night buses).

• 75-minute transfer ticket with unlimited transfers (*základní přestupní*)—20 Kč.

• 24-hour pass *(jízdenka na 24 hodin)*—80 Kč.

• 3-day pass *(jízdenka na 3 dny)*—220 Kč.

• 7-day pass *(jízdenka na 7 dní)*—280 Kč.

Buy tickets from your hotel, at newsstand kiosks, or from automated machines (select ticket price, then insert coins). For convenience, buy all the tickets you think you'll need—but estimate conservatively. Remember, Prague is a great walking town, so unless you're commuting from a hotel far outside the center, you will likely find that individual tickets work best. Be sure to validate your ticket on the tram, bus, or Metro by sticking it in the machine (which stamps a time on it—watch locals and imitate). Inspectors routinely ambush ticketless riders (including tourists) and fine them 400 Kč on the spot.

Tips: Navigate by signs listing end stations. When you come to your stop, push the yellow button if the doors don't automatically

Prague Metro

open. Although it seems that all Metro doors lead to the neighborhood of Výstup, that's simply the Czech word for "exit." When a tram pulls up to a stop, two different names are announced: first, the name of the stop you're currently at, followed by the name of the stop that's coming up next. Confused tourists, thinking they've heard their stop, are notorious for rushing off the tram one stop too soon. Trams run every five to 10 minutes in the daytime (a schedule is posted at each stop). The Metro closes at midnight, and the nighttime tram routes (identified with white numbers on blue backgrounds at tram stops) run all night in 30-minute intervals. There's more information and a complete route planner at www .dp-praha.cz.

Handy Trams: Trams #22 and #23 are practically made for sightseeing, using the same route to connect the New Town with the Castle Quarter (see tram route marked on color map at beginning of this book). The trams use some of the same stops as the Metro (making it easy to get to—or travel on from—the tram route). Of the many stops these trams make, the most convenient are two in the New Town (Národní Třída Metro stop, between the bottom of Wenceslas Square and the river; and Národní Divadlo, at the National Theatre), one stop in the Little Quarter (Malostranská Metro stop), and four stops above Prague Castle (Královský Letohrádek, Pražský Hrad, Brusnice—on request, and Pohořelec; for details, see "Getting to Prague Castle—By Tram" on page 110).

By Taxi

Prague's taxis—notorious for hyperactive meters—are being tamed. New legislation is in place to curb crooked cabbies, and police will always take your side in an argument. Many cabbies are crooks who consider it a good day's work to take one sucker for a ride. You'll make things difficult for a dishonest cabbie by challenging an unfair fare.

While most hotel receptionists and guidebooks advise avoiding taxis, I find Prague to be a great taxi town and use them routinely. With the local rate, they're cheap (read the rates on the door: drop charge—30 Kč; per-kilometer charge—20-30 Kč; and waiting time per minute—5 Kč). The key is to be sure the cabbie turns on the meter at the #1 tariff (look for the word *sazba*, meaning "tariff," on the meter). Avoid cabs waiting at tourist attractions and train stations. To improve your odds of getting a fair meter rate—which starts only when you take off—call for a cab (or have your hotel or restaurant call one for you). **AAA Taxi** (tel. 233-113-311) and **City Taxi** (tel. 257-257-257) are the most likely to have English-speaking staff and honest cabbies. I also find that hailing a passing taxi usually gets me a decent price.

If a cabbie surprises you at the end with an astronomical fare, simply pay 200 Kč, which should cover you for a long ride anywhere in the center. Then go into your hotel. On the miniscule chance he follows you, the receptionist will back you up.

TOURS

Walking Tours—Prague Walks offers walking tours of the Old Town, the castle, the Jewish Quarter, and more (250–1,000 Kč, 1.5–6 hrs, tel. 222-322-309, fax 261-214-603, mobile 603-271-911, www.praguewalks.com, pwalks@comp.cz). Consider their clever Good Morning Walk, which starts at 8:00 (April–Aug only),

Prague at a Glance

In the Old Town

▲▲▲**Old Town Square** Colorful, magical main square of Old World Prague, with dozens of colorful facades, the dramatic Jan Hus Memorial, looming Týn Church, and fanciful Astronomical Clock. **Hours:** Always open.

▲▲▲**Jewish Quarter** The best Jewish sight in Europe, featuring various synagogues and an evocative cemetery. **Hours:** Sun–Fri 9:00–18:00, closed Sat.

▲▲▲**Charles Bridge** Atmospheric, statue-lined bridge connecting the Old Town to the Little Quarter and Prague Castle. **Hours:** Always open.

Museum of Czech Cubism Exhibit of early-20th-century Czech artistic school, in the Old Town's interesting Black Madonna House. **Hours:** Tue–Sun 10:00–18:00, closed Mon.

Bethlehem Chapel Reconstructed 15th-century chapel with Jan Hus' former pulpit. **Hours:** April–Oct daily 10:00–18:30; Nov–March Tue–Sun 10:00–17:30, closed Mon and during university functions.

Náprstek's Museum of Asian, African, and American Cultures Quirky exhibit with an emphasis on Native Americans (including Sitting Bull's clothes). **Hours:** Tue–Sun 10:00–17:00, closed Mon.

In the New Town

▲▲**Wenceslas Square** Lively boulevard at the heart of modern Prague. **Hours:** Always open.

▲▲**Mucha Museum** Likeable collection of Art Nouveau works by Czech artist Alfons Mucha. **Hours:** Daily 10:00–18:00.

▲**Museum of Communism** The rise and fall of the regime, from start to Velvet finish. **Hours:** Daily 9:00–21:00.

Dancing House Frank Gehry–designed building on the Vltava riverbank, depicting Fred and Ginger. **Hours:** Always viewable.

In the Little Quarter
Torture Museum Prague "goes medieval" in this cheesy and gruesome tourist trap. **Hours:** Daily 10:00–22:00.

Church of St. Nicholas Jesuit centerpiece of Little Quarter Square, with ultimate High Baroque decor and a climbable bell tower. **Hours:** Church—daily 9:00–17:00; tower—April–Oct daily 10:00–18:00, closed Nov–March.

Church of St. Mary the Victorious Pilgrimage church displaying the precious "Infant of Prague." **Hours:** Mon–Sat 10:00–17:30, Sun 13:00–17:00.

Petřín Hill Little Quarter hill with public art, a funicular, a replica of the Eiffel Tower, and the museum of a nonexistent Czech hero. **Hours:** Funicular—daily 8:00–22:00; museum—daily 10:00–22:00.

In the Castle Quarter
▲▲▲**St. Vitus Cathedral** The Czech Republic's most important church, featuring a climbable tower and a striking stained-glass window by Art Nouveau artist Alfons Mucha. **Hours:** Daily April–Oct 9:00–17:00, Nov–March 9:00–16:00—but closed Sunday mornings year-round for Mass.

▲▲**Prague Castle** Traditional seat of Czech rulers, with St. Vitus Cathedral (see above), Old Royal Palace, Basilica of St. George, shop-lined Golden Lane, and lots of crowds. **Hours:** Castle sights—daily April–Oct 9:00–17:00, Nov–March 9:00–16:00; castle grounds—daily 5:00–23:00.

▲**Strahov Monastery and Library** Baroque center of learning, with ornate reading rooms and old-fashioned science exhibits. **Hours:** Daily 9:00–12:00 & 13:00–17:00.

Loreta Church Baroque church featuring what's supposedly the actual house of the Virgin Mary. **Hours:** Tue–Sun 9:00–12:15 & 13:00–16:30, closed Mon.

Toy and Barbie Museum Several centuries of toys, starring an army of Barbies. **Hours:** Daily 9:30–17:30.

before the crowds hit. Several other companies offer good guided walks. For the latest, pick up the walking tour fliers at the TI.

Private Guides—Hiring your own personal guide can be an exceptional value in Prague, especially if you're traveling in a group. Guides meet you wherever you like and tailor the tour to your interests. **Katka Svobodová,** a hardworking guide who knows her stuff and speaks excellent English, enjoys showing individuals and small groups around. She studies anthropology and wrote her thesis on Jewish burial customs (400 Kč or €13 per hour, minimum 3 hrs, tel. 224-818-267, mobile 603-181-300, www .praguewalker.com, katerina@praguewalker.com). **Jana Hronková** knows Hebrew and has a natural style—a welcome change from the more strict professionalism of some of the busier guides (mobile 732-185-180, janahronkova@hotmail.com). **Šárka Pelantová** gets beyond the dates and famous buildings to provide insight into her culture, and is eager to build a walk around your interests (€13/hr, mobile 777-225-205, www.prague-guide.info, saraguide@volny .cz). My readers have also recommended **Renata Blažková** (tel. 222-716-870, mobile 602-353-186, blazer@volny.cz) and **Martin Bělohradský** (martinb@uochb.cas.cz).

Athos Travel's licensed guides can lead you on a general sightseeing tour or fit the walk to your interests: music, Art Nouveau, Jewish life, architecture, Franz Kafka, and more (1–5 people-700 Kč/hr, more than 5 people-800 Kč/hr, arrange tour at least 24 hours in advance, tel. 241-440-571, www.athos.cz, info@athos.cz).

To get beyond Prague, call **Thomas Zahn,** who runs Pathways Guided Travel. Thomas, an American who married into the Czech Republic, specializes in helping Americans of Czech descent find their roots. He also organizes and leads creative, affordable (mostly 1-day and 2-day) excursions from Prague. Hiking, biking, horseback riding, or canoeing, you'll explore the unknown charms of the region with a small group and a committed guide. Explore Thomas' Web site for ways to connect with the rural Czech countryside and experience more than Prague on your visit (tel. 257-940-113, mobile 603-758-983, www.pathfinders.cz).

The **TI** also has plenty of private guides (rates for a 3-hr tour: 1,200 Kč/1 person, 1,400 Kč/2 people, 1,600 Kč/3 people, 2,000 Kč/4 people; desk at Old Town Square TI, arrange and pay in person at least 2 hours in advance, tel. 224-482-562, guides@pis.cz). For a listing of more private guides, see www.guide-prague.cz.

Bus Tours—Cheap big-bus orientation tours provide an efficient, once-over-lightly look at Prague and a convenient way to see the castle. But in a city as walkable as Prague, bus tours should be used only in case of rain, laziness, or both. Several companies have kiosks on Na Příkopě. Premiant City Tours offers 20 different tours, including several overview tours of the city (250 Kč/1 hr,

380 Kč/2 hrs, 750 Kč/3.5 hrs), the Jewish Quarter (700 Kč, 2 hrs), Prague by night, Bohemian glass, Terezín Concentration Camp, Karlštejn Castle, Český Krumlov (1,750 Kč, 10 hrs), and a river cruise. The tours feature live guides and depart from near the bottom of Wenceslas Square at Na Příkopě 23. Get tickets at an AVE travel agency, hotel, on the bus, or at Na Příkopě 23 (tel. 224-946-922, mobile 606-600-123, www.premiant.cz). Tour salespeople are notorious for telling you anything to sell a ticket. Some tours, especially those heading into the countryside, can be in as many as four different languages. Hiring a private guide can be a much better value (see above).

Cruises—Prague isn't great for a boat tour. Still, the hour-long Vltava River cruises, which leave from near the castle end of Charles Bridge about hourly, are scenic and relaxing, though not informative (100 Kč). You can rent a small rowboat or paddleboat on the island by the National Theatre, and float among the swans at your own pace (about 80 Kč/hr, bring photo ID for deposit).

SIGHTS

I've arranged these sights according to which of Prague's four towns you'll find them in (see sidebar): Old Town, New Town, Little Quarter, or Castle Quarter.

The Old Town (Staré Město)

From Prague's dramatic centerpiece, the Old Town Square, sightseeing options fan out in all directions. Get oriented on the square before venturing onward. You can find out about Jewish heritage in the Jewish Quarter (Josefov), a few blocks from the Old Town Square. Closer to the square is Celetná street, which leads to the Museum of Czech Cubism and the landmark Estates Theatre on the way to the New Town. If you're intrigued by Jan Hus, the preacher and martyr, look for his pulpit in the chapel on Bethlehem Square. Where the Old Town meets the river, you'll find one of Prague's most enduring, goosebump-worthy landmarks: the Charles Bridge.

Old Town Square (Staroměstské Náměstí)

The focal point for most visits, Prague's Old Town Square is well worth ▲▲▲. This has been a market square since the 11th century. It became the nucleus of the Old Town (Staré Město) in the 13th century, when its Town Hall was built. Today, the old-time market stalls have been replaced by cafés, touristy horse buggies, and souvenir hawkers. But under this shallow surface the square hides a magic power to evoke the history that has passed through here.

Prague's Four Towns

Until about 1800, Prague was actually four distinct towns with four town squares, all separated by fortified walls. Each town had a unique character, which came from the personality of the people who initially settled it. Today much of Prague's charm survives in the distinct spirit of each of its towns.

Castle Quarter (Hradčany): Since the ninth century, when the first castle was built on the promontory overlooking a ford across the Vltava River, Castle Hill has been occupied by the ruling class. When Christianity arrived in the Czech lands, this hilltop—oriented along an east-west axis—proved a perfect spot for a church and, later, the cathedral (which, according to custom, must be built with the altar pointing east). Finally, the nobles built their representative palaces in proximity to the castle to compete with the Church for influence on the king. Even today, you feel like clip-clopping through this neighborhood in a fancy carriage. The Castle Quarter—which hosts the offices of the president and prime minister—has high art and grand buildings, little commerce, and few pubs.

Little Quarter (Malá Strana): This Baroque town of fine palaces and gardens rose from ashes of a merchant settlement that burned in the 1540s. The Czech and European nobility that settled here took pride in the grand design of their gardens. In the 1990s, after decades of decay, these gardens were carefully restored. While some are open only to the successors of the former nobility—including the Czech Parliament and the American, German, and Polish embassies—many are open to visitors.

Old Town (Staré Město): Charles Bridge connects the Little Quarter with the Old Town. A boomtown since the 10th century, this has long been the busy commercial quarter—filled with merchants, guilds, and natural supporters of Jan Hus (folks who wanted a Czech stamp on their religion). Trace the walls of this town in the modern road plan (the Powder Tower is a remnant of a wall system that completed a fortified ring, half provided by the river). The marshy area closest to the bend—least inhabitable and therefore allotted to the Jewish community—became the ghetto (today's Jewish Quarter, or Josefov).

New Town (Nové Město): The New Town rings the Old Town—cutting a swath from riverbank to riverbank—and is fortified with Prague's outer wall. In the 14th century, the king initiated the creation of this town, tripling the size of what would become Prague. Wenceslas Square was once the horse market of this busy working-class district. Even today, the New Town is

Prague Overview

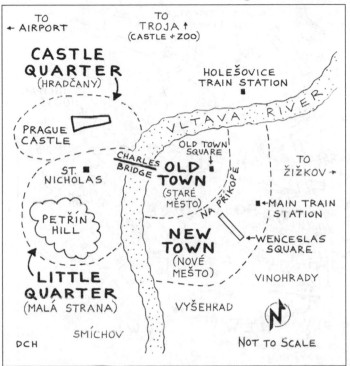

separated from the Old Town by a "moat" (the literal meaning of the street called Na Příkopě). As you cross bustling Na Příkopě, you leave the glass and souvenir shops behind and enter a town of malls and fancy shops that cater to locals and visitors alike.

Cutting through the four towns—from St. Vitus Cathedral down to the Charles Bridge, and then from the bridge to the Powder Tower—is the Royal Way (Královská Cesta), the ancient path of coronation processions. Today this city spine is marred by tacky trinket shops and jammed by tour groups. Use it for orientation only—try to avoid it if you want to see the real Prague.

Prague's Old Town

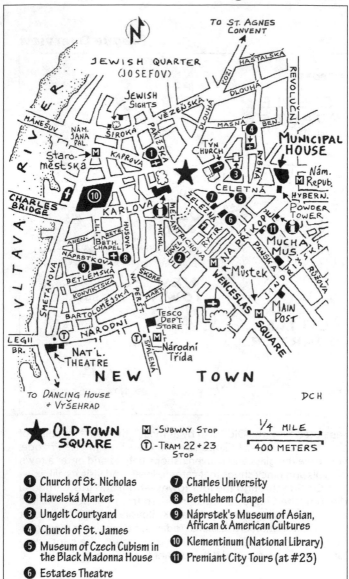

★ OLD TOWN
  SQUARE

Ⓜ – SUBWAY STOP

Ⓣ – TRAM 22 & 23
      STOP

¼ MILE

400 METERS

DCH

❶ Church of St. Nicholas
❷ Havelská Market
❸ Ungelt Courtyard
❹ Church of St. James
❺ Museum of Czech Cubism in
   the Black Madonna House
❻ Estates Theatre

❼ Charles University
❽ Bethlehem Chapel
❾ Náprstek's Museum of Asian,
   African & American Cultures
❿ Klementinum (National Library)
⓫ Premiant City Tours (at #23)

Hus and Luther

The word *catholic* means "universal." The Roman Catholic Church—in many ways the administrative ghost of the Roman Empire—is the only organization to survive from ancient times. For more than a thousand years, it enforced its notion that the Vatican was the sole interpreter of God's word on earth, and the only legitimate way to be a Christian was as a Roman Catholic. Jan Hus (1369–1415) lived and preached a century before Martin Luther. Both were college professors, as well as priests. Both drew huge public crowds as they preached in their university chapels. Both promoted a local religious autonomy. Both helped establish their national languages. (Hus gave the Czechs their unique accent marks to enable the letters to fit the sounds.) And both got in big trouble. While Hus was burned, Luther survived. Living after Gutenberg, Luther was able to spread his message more cheaply and effectively, thanks to the new printing press. Since Luther was high-profile and German, killing him would have caused major political complications. While Hus may have loosened Rome's grip on Christianity, Luther orchestrated the Reformation that finally broke it. Today, both are honored as national heroes as well as religious reformers.

• *Gawk your way to the square's centerpiece, the...*

Jan Hus Memorial: This monument, erected in 1915 (500 years after the Czech reformer's martyrdom by fire), symbolizes the long struggle for Czech freedom (see sidebar above). Walk around the memorial. Jan Hus stands tall between two groups of people: victorious Hussite patriots and Protestants defeated by the Hapsburgs. One of the patriots holds a cup—in the medieval Church, only  priests could drink the wine at Communion. Since the Hussites fought for their right to take both the wine and the bread, the cup is their symbol. Behind Jan Hus, a mother with her children represents the ultimate rebirth of the Czech nation. Because of his bold stance for independence in the way common people worship God, Hus was excommunicated and burned in Germany a century before the age of Martin Luther.

Old Town Square

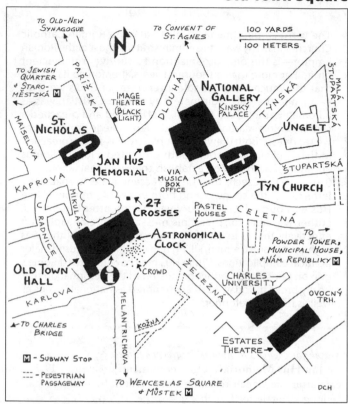

• *Standing by Jan Hus, get oriented with a...*

Spin-Tour: Whirl clockwise to get a look at Prague's diverse architectural styles: Gothic, Renaissance, Baroque, rococo, and Art Nouveau.

Start with the green domes of the Baroque **Church of St. Nicholas**. Originally Catholic, now Hussite, this church is a popular venue for concerts. (There's another green-domed Church of St. Nicholas—also popular for concerts—by the same architect across the Charles Bridge in the Little Quarter.) The Jewish Quarter (Josefov) is a few blocks behind the church, down the uniquely tree-lined Pařížská—literally, "Paris Street." (For more on the Jewish Quarter, see page 84.) Pařížská, an eclectic cancan of mostly Art Nouveau facades, leads to a bluff that once sported a 100-foot-tall stone Stalin. Demolished in 1962 after Khrushchev exposed Stalin's crimes, it was replaced in 1991 by a giant ticking **metronome**—partly to commemorate Prague's centennial exhibition (the 1891 exhibition is remembered by the Little Quarter's

Eiffel-esque Petřín Tower), and partly to send the message that for every power, there's a time to go.

Spin to the right, past the Hus Memorial and the fine yellow Art Nouveau building. The large rococo palace on the right is part of the **National Gallery**; the temporary exhibits here are often the best in town.

To the right, you can't miss the towering, Gothic **Týn Church** (pronounced "teen"), with its fanciful spires flanking a solid-gold effigy of the Virgin Mary. For 200 years after Hus' death, this was Prague's leading Hussite church. Inside, black Baroque altars clash with the simple Gothic style. The narrow lane next to the church has the **Via Musica**, the most convenient ticket office in town (see page 120). Behind the Týn Church is a gorgeously restored medieval courtyard called **Ungelt** (home to a pair of great bookstores—see "Helpful Hints," page 68—and Ebel Coffee House, described on page 144). The row of pastel houses in front of Týn Church has a mixture of Gothic, Renaissance, and Baroque facades. To the right of these buildings, shop-lined **Celetná street** leads to a square called Ovocný Trh (with the Estates Theatre and Museum of Czech Cubism—see page 88), and beyond that, to the Powder Tower and Municipal House in the New Town (see page 89).

Continue spinning right—with more gloriously colorful architecture—until you reach the pointed 250-foot-tall spire, marking the 14th-century **Old Town Hall** (which also encompasses the 5 houses to the left of the tower). Across the square from the Old Town Hall, touristy **Melantrichova street** leads directly to the New Town's Wenceslas Square (see page 92), passing the craft-packed Havelská Market along the way (see page 82). At the far end of the square in front of the Old Town Hall, **Karlova street** twists its touristy way to the Charles Bridge (just follow the crowds; *Karlův Most* signs lead to the bridge).

• *Now wander across the square, towards the Old Town Hall Tower. Embedded in the pavement at the base of the tower (near the snack stand), you'll see...*

Twenty-Seven Crosses: These white inlaid crosses mark the spot where 27 Protestant nobles, merchants, and intellectuals were beheaded in 1621 after rebelling against the Catholic Hapsburgs. The execution ended Czech independence for 300 years—and, for locals, it's still one of the grimmest chapters in their history. Until recently, Czechs walked around this sacred spot, avoiding

Havelská Market

Skinny, tourist-clogged Melantrichova street leads directly from the Old Town Square's Astronomical Clock to the bottom of Wenceslas Square. But even along this most crowded of streets, a genuine bit of Prague remains: the Havelská Market, offering crafts and produce.

The open-air market was set up in the 13th century for the German trading community. Though heavy on souvenirs these days, the market still keeps hungry locals and vagabonds fed cheaply. It's ideal for a healthy snack; merchants are happy to sell a single vegetable or piece of fruit, and you'll find a washing fountain and plenty of inviting benches midway down the street.

The market is also a fun place to browse for crafts. It's a home-grown, home-made kind of place; you'll often be dealing with the actual farmer or artist. The market is open daily from 9:00 to 18:00. It's better on weekdays for produce, but offers more puppets and toys on weekends.

stepping on it, and many would even stop to pay their respects. But today the sacred soil is home to a hot-dog vendor, and few notice the crosses in the pavement. Locals lament this transition: As the commercialized Old Town loses the power to evoke history, people here trample over their own past.

• *Looming behind the crosses is the...*

Old Town Hall: The main TI, to the left of the Astronomical Clock, contains a guides' desk and sells tickets for these two options: zipping up the only tower in town that has an elevator (40 Kč, fine views); or taking a 45-minute tour of the Gothic chapel and Town Hall, which includes a close-up of the inner guts of the Astronomical Clock (including its statues of the 12 apostles; 50 Kč, 2/hr). A gallery inside the Town Hall features fine temporary exhibits (especially photography—check in the office for schedule). Notice the elaborate Renaissance window on the Town Hall house with the pink facade—the railings and the golden inscription *(Praga Caput Regni)* make it one of Prague's most beautiful windows.

• *The part of the Town Hall that visitors are generally most interested in is the iconic...*

Astronomical Clock: Ignore the ridiculous human sales racks, and join the gang for the striking of the hour on the Town Hall clock (daily 8:00–21:00, until 20:00 in winter). As you wait, see if you can figure out how the clock works.

With revolving disks, celestial symbols, and sweeping hands, this clock keeps several versions of time. Two outer rings show the hour: Bohemian time (Gothic numbers, counts from sunset—find the zero, next to 23...supposedly the time of tonight's sunset) and modern time (24 Roman numerals, XII at the top being noon, XII at the bottom being midnight). Five hundred years ago, everything revolved around the earth (the fixed middle background).

To indicate the times of sunrise and sunset, arcing lines and moving spheres combine with the big hand (a sweeping golden sun) and the little hand (the moon showing various stages). Look for the orbits of the sun and moon as they rise through day (the blue zone) and night (the black zone).

If this seems complex to us, it must have been a marvel 500 years ago. Since the clock was heavily damaged during World War II, a lot of what you see today is a reconstruction.

The circle below (added in the 19th century) shows the signs of the zodiac, scenes from the seasons of a rural peasant's life, and a ring of saints' names—one for each day of the year, with a marker showing today's special saint.

Four statues flanking the clock represent the 15th-century outlook on time. A Turk with a mandolin symbolizes hedonism, a Jewish moneylender is greed, and the figure staring into a mirror stands for vanity. All these worldly goals are vain in the face of Death, whose hourglass reminds us that our time may soon run out.

At the top of the hour (don't blink—the show is pretty quick): First, Death tips his hourglass and pulls the cord, ringing the bell;

then the windows open and the 12 apostles parade by, acknowledging the gang of onlookers; then the rooster crows; and then the hour is rung. The hour is often off because of daylight saving time (completely senseless to 15th-century clockmakers). At the top of the next hour, stand under the tower—protected by a line of banner-wielding, powdered-wigged concert salespeople—and watch the tourists.

• *Now that you're oriented, you can use this delightful square as your launchpad for the rest of Prague's Old Town sights.*

Prague's Jewish Quarter (Josefov)

Prague's Jewish Quarter neighborhood and its well-presented, profoundly moving museum tell the story of the Jews of this region. For me, this is the most interesting Jewish sight in Europe (and worth ▲▲▲). The Jewish Quarter is an easy walk from Old Town Square, up delightful Pařížská street (next to the green-domed Church of St. Nicholas).

As the Nazis decimated Jewish communities in the region, Prague's Jews were allowed to collect and archive their treasures here. While the archivists ultimately died in concentration camps, their work survives. Seven sights scattered over a three-block area make up the tourists' Jewish Quarter. Six of the sights—all except the Old-New Synagogue—are called "the Museum," and are treated as one admission. Your ticket comes with a map locating the sights and listing admission appointments—the times you'll be let in if it's very crowded. (Without crowds, ignore the times.) You'll notice plenty of security (stepped up since 9/11).

Cost, Hours, Tours: To visit all seven sights, you'll pay 500 Kč (300 Kč for the 6 sights that make up the Museum and 200 Kč for the Old-New Synagogue; all sights open Sun–Fri 9:00–18:00, closed Sat—the Jewish Sabbath). There are occasional guided walks in English (40 Kč, 2.5 hrs, start at Maisel Synagogue, tel. 222-317-191). Most stops are described in English. The ticket lines at the cemetery and Pinkas Synagogue are longest. You'll likely save time if you buy your ticket at the Maisel Synagogue (the best place to start your visit, anyway).

Maisel Synagogue (Maiselova Synagóga)—This synagogue was built as a private place of worship for the Maisel family during the 16th-century Golden Age of Prague's Jews. Maisel was the financier of the Hapsburg king—and he had lots of money. The synagogue's interior is decorated neo-Gothic. In World War II, it served as a warehouse for the accumulated treasures of decimated Jewish communities that Hitler planned to use for his "Museum of the Extinct Jewish Race." The one-room exhibit (the upstairs "women's gallery" is closed for renovation) shows a thousand years of Jewish history in Bohemia and Moravia. Well-explained in

Prague's Jewish Heritage

The Jewish people of Palestine were dispersed by the Romans 2,000 years ago. Over the centuries, their culture survived in enclaves throughout the world: "The Torah was their sanctuary which no army could destroy." Jews first came to Prague in the 10th century. The main intersection of Josefov (Maiselova and Široká streets) was the meeting point of two medieval trade routes.

During the age of the Crusades in the 12th century, the pope declared that Jews and Christians should not live together. Jews had to wear yellow badges, and their quarter was walled in. It became a ghetto. In the 16th and 17th centuries, Prague had one of the biggest ghettos in Europe, with 11,000 inhabitants. Within its six gates, Prague's Jewish Quarter was a gaggle of 200 wooden buildings. It was said that "Jews nested rather than dwelled."

The "outcasts" of Christianity relied mainly on profits from moneylending (forbidden to Christians) and community solidarity to survive. While their money bought them protection (the kings highly taxed Jewish communities), it was often also a curse. Throughout Europe, when times got tough and Christian debts to the Jewish community mounted, entire Jewish communities were evicted or killed.

In the 1780s, Emperor Josef II, motivated more by economic concerns than by philanthropy, eased much of the discrimination against Jews. In 1848, the walls were torn down, and the neighborhood—named Josefov in honor of the emperor who provided this small measure of tolerance—was incorporated as a district of Old Town.

In 1897, ramshackle Josefov was razed and replaced by a new modern town—the original 31 streets and 220 buildings became 10 streets and 83 buildings. This is what you'll see today: an attractive neighborhood of pretty, mostly Art Nouveau buildings, with a few surviving historic Jewish structures. By the 1930s, Prague's Jewish community was hugely successful, thanks largely to their ability to appreciate talent—a rare quality in the small Central European countries whose citizens, as the great Austrian novelist Robert Musil put it, "were equal in their unwillingness to let one another get ahead."

Of the 120,000 Jews living in the area in 1939, just 10,000 survived the Holocaust to see liberation in 1945. Today only a couple of thousand Jews remain in Prague...but the legacy of their ancestors lives on.

Prague's Jewish Quarter

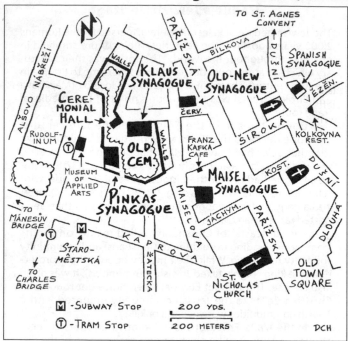

M - SUBWAY STOP
T - TRAM STOP

200 YDS.
200 METERS

DCH

English, the topics covered include the origin of the Star of David, Jewish mysticism, discrimination, and the creation of Prague's ghetto. Notice the eastern wall, with the holy ark containing the scroll of the Torah. The central case shows the silver ornamental Torah crowns that capped the scroll.

Spanish Synagogue (Španělská Synagóga)—This 19th-century, ornate, Moorish-style synagogue continues the history of the Maisel Synagogue, covering the 18th, 19th, and tumultuous 20th centuries. The upstairs is particularly intriguing (with c. 1900 photos of Josefov). The Spanish Synagogue is now used for classical concerts, often featuring the music of Jewish composers such as Felix Mendelssohn and Gustav Mahler (ticket desk just outside at the door). The building also contains the Jewish public library, the only one of its kind in Prague.

Pinkas Synagogue (Pinkasova Synagóga)—A site of Jewish worship for 400 years, today this is a poignant memorial to the victims of the Nazis. The walls are covered with the handwritten names of 77,297 Czech Jews who were sent from here to the gas chambers of Auschwitz and other camps. (You'll hear the somber reading of the names as you ponder this sad sight.) Hometowns are in gold and family names are in red, followed in black by the individual's first name, birthday, and last date known to be alive. Notice that families generally perished together. Extermination camps are listed on the east wall. Climb six steps into the women's gallery. The names in poor condition near the ceiling are from 1959. When the communists moved in, they closed the synagogue and erased everything. With freedom, in 1989, the Pinkas Synagogue was reopened and all the names rewritten. The Synagogue closed briefly in 2003, as flood damage meant the names needed to be rewritten once again.

Upstairs is the **Terezín Children's Art Exhibit**, displaying art drawn by Jewish children who were imprisoned at Terezín Concentration Camp and later perished. Terezín is a powerful day trip from Prague (get details at the TI). But the evocative power of the children's drawings is stronger than all of Terezín.

Old Jewish Cemetery (Starý Židovský Hřbitov)—As you wander among 12,000 evocative tombstones, remember that from 1439 until 1787, this was the only burial ground allowed for the Jews of Prague. Because of limited space, the Jewish belief that the body should not be moved once buried, and the sheer number of graves, tombs were piled atop each other. With its many layers, the cemetery became a small plateau. And as things settled over time, the tombstones got crooked. The Jewish  word for cemetery means "House of Life." Many Jews believe that death is the gateway into the next world. Pebbles on the tombstones are "flowers of the desert," reminiscent of the old days when a rock was placed upon the sand gravesite to keep the body covered. Wedged under some of the pebbles are scraps of paper containing prayers.

Ceremonial Hall (Obřadní Síň)—Leaving the cemetery, you'll find a neo-Romanesque mortuary house built in 1911 for the purification of the dead (on left). It's filled with a worthwhile exhibition, described in English, on Jewish burial traditions. A series of crude but instructive paintings show how the "burial brotherhood" took care of the ill and buried the dead. As all are equal before God, the rich and poor alike were buried in embroidered linen shrouds similar to the one you'll see on display.

Klaus Synagogue (Klauzová Synagóga)—This 17th-century synagogue (also at the exit of the cemetery) is the final wing of a museum devoted to Jewish religious practices. On the ground floor, exhibits explain the Jewish calendar of festivals. The central case displays a Torah (the first 5 books of the Bible) and solid silver pointers used when reading—necessary since the Torah is not to be touched. Upstairs is an exhibit on the rituals of Jewish life (circumcision, bar and bat mitzvah, weddings, kosher eating, and so on).

Old-New Synagogue (Staronová Synagóga)—For more than 700 years, this has been the most important synagogue and the central building in Josefov. Standing like a bomb-hardened bunker, it feels like it has survived plenty of hard times. Stairs take you down to the street level of the 13th century and into the Gothic interior. Built in 1270, it's the oldest synagogue in Central Europe (separate 200-Kč admission includes worthwhile 10-minute tour—ask about it, Sun–Thu 9:30–18:00, Fri 9:30–17:00, closed Sat).

The lobby (where you show your ticket) has two fortified old lockers—where the most heavily taxed community in medieval Prague stored its money in anticipation of the taxman's arrival. As 13th-century Jews were not allowed to build, this was constructed by Christians. The builders were good at four-ribbed vaulting, but since that resulted in a cross, it wouldn't work for a synagogue. Instead, they made the ceiling using clumsy five-ribbed vaulting.

The interior is pure 1300s. The **Shrine of the Ark** in front is the focus of worship. The holiest place in the synagogue, it holds the sacred scrolls of the Torah. The old rabbi's chair to the right remains empty out of respect. The red banner is a copy of the one the Jewish community carried through town during medieval parades. Notice the yellow pointed hat, which the pope ordered all Jewish men to wear in 1215. Twelve is a popular number (e.g., windows) because it symbolizes the 12 tribes of Israel. The horizontal slit-like windows are an 18th-century addition allowing women to view the men-only services.

Along Celetná Street, towards the New Town

Celetná, a pedestrian-only street, is a fine place to do some shopping (see page 122). It's also a convenient and relatively untouristy way to get from the Old Town Square to the New Town (specifically the Powder Tower and Municipal House, described on page 89). Along the way, at the square called Ovocný Trh, you'll find these two sights.

Museum of Czech Cubism in the Black Madonna House (Dům u Černé Matky Boží)—This is my favorite piece of 20th-century architecture in the Old Town. Cubism was a potent force in Prague, as this fascinating museum documents. On three floors, you'll see paintings, furniture, graphics, and architectural drafts by Czech Cubists. On the outside, the architect Gočár (who also designed several successful functionalist structures in the city) managed to scale the Cubist facade to fit with the surrounding buildings. Notice how from the third floor up, the Cubist shapes are much less accentuated, allowing the house to flow with the surrounding roofs. This is an example of what over centuries has been considered the greatest virtue of Prague's architects: the ability to adapt their grandiose plans to the existing context (100 Kč, Tue–Sun 10:00–18:00, closed Mon, Ovocný Trh 19, corner of Celetná and Ovocný Trh, tel. 224-301-003). If you're not interested in touring the museum itself, consider a drink in the similarly decorated upstairs Grand Café Orient (see page 144).

Estates Theatre (Stavovské Divadlo)—Built by a nobleman in 1770s, this classicist building—gently opening its greenish walls into Ovocný Trh—was the prime opera venue in Prague in times when an Austrian prodigy was changing the course of music. Wolfgang Amadeus Mozart premiered *Don Giovanni* in this building, and personally directed many of his works here. Prague's theater-goers would whistle arias from Mozart's works on the streets the morning after they premiered. Today part of the National Theatre group, the Estates Theatre continues to produce *The Marriage of Figaro*, *Don Giovanni* (plays through May 2006), and occasionally *The Magic Flute*. For a more intimate encounter with Mozart, go to Villa Bertramka (see page 121).

By the fountain on the side of the theater, combining Gothic with 1970s red brick, is the central building of **Charles University** (Karlova Univerzita). Small graduation ceremonies are held throughout the year, which is why you'll likely see people with flowers.

If you continue up Celetná, you'll go through the **Powder Tower** and find yourself in front of the Art Nouveau **Municipal House** (described on page 98).

Bethlehem Square (Betlémská Náměstí)

These sights sit on charming, relatively quiet Bethlehem Square (Betlémská Náměstí)—a pleasantly untouristy chunk of Old Town real estate.

Bethlehem Chapel (Betlémská Kaple)—Emperor Charles IV founded the first university in Central Europe, and this was the university's chapel. Around the year 1400, priest and professor Jan Hus preached from the pulpit here (see sidebar on page 79). While meant primarily for students and faculty, Hus' Masses were open to the public. Standing-room-only crowds of more than 3,000 were the norm when he preached. Hus proposed that the congregation should be more involved in worship (e.g., actually drink the wine at Communion) and have better access to the word of God through services and scriptures written in the people's language, not in Latin. The stimulating, controversial ideas debated at the university spread throughout the city and, after Hus' death at the stake, sparked off the bloodiest civil war in Czech history.

Each subsequent age has interpreted Hus to its liking: For the Protestants, Hus was the founder of the first Protestant church (though he was actually an ardent Catholic); for the revolutionaries, this critic of the power of the Church was a proponent of social equality; for the nationalists, this Czech preacher was the defender of the language; and for the communists, Hus was the first communist ideologue.

Today's chapel is a 1950s reconstruction of the original. Try the unbelievably bad acoustics inside—it demonstrates the sloppy work sponsored by the communists (tiny upstairs exhibit and big chapel with English-info sheets available; entry-35 Kč; April–Oct daily 10:00–18:30; Nov–March Tue–Sun 10:00–17:30, closed Mon and during university functions; Betlémská Náměstí, tel. 224-248-595).

Klub Architektů, across from the entry, has a cavernous atmosphere inside, straw-chair seating outside, and good food in both places (see page 137).

At the other end of the square from the chapel is...

Náprstek's Museum of Asian, African, and American Cultures (Náprstkovo Muzeum Asijských, Africkych a Americkych Kultur)—A 19th-century philanthropist named Vojta Náprstek assembled one of Prague's most fascinating collections, focusing on the culture of Native Americans. Look for the actual attire of the Lakota chief Sitting Bull (Tue–Sun 10:00–17:00, closed Mon, Betlémská Náměstí 1, tel. 224-497-500, www.aconet.cz/npm).

Nearby, Karlova street leads to the famous Charles Bridge.

Charles Bridge (Karlův Most)

One of Prague's defining landmarks, and easily worth ▲▲▲, this much-loved bridge offers one of the most pleasant and entertaining 500-yard strolls in Europe. Be on the Charles Bridge at dawn, when it's magical, or any time before 9:00 to have the place to yourself. To get here from the Old Town Square, simply walk down crowded, zigzagging Karlova street (follow *Karlův Most* signs).

At the Old Town end of the bridge, in a little square, is a statue of the bridge's namesake, **Charles IV.** This Holy Roman Emperor (*Karlo Quatro*—the guy on the 100-Kč bill) ruled his vast empire from Prague in the 14th century. He's holding a contract establishing Prague's university, the first in Northern Europe. This statue was erected in 1848 to celebrate the university's 500th birthday. The women around Charles' pedestal symbolize the university's four faculties: the arts, medicine, law, and theology.

Bridges were built on this spot before, as the remnant tower from the Judith Bridge (the smaller of the two bridge towers at the far end) testifies. All were washed away by floods. After a major flood in 1342, Emperor Charles IV decided to commission an entirely new structure rather than repair the old one. Until the 19th century, this was Prague's only bridge crossing the river.

How do you make a bridge last seven centuries? Back in the 1300s, they believed in the magic of time and numbers. The founding stone was laid in 1357, on the 9th of July at 5:31 (it's a palindrome: 135797531). On the Old Town bank, a spot was chosen for the ending of the bridge that lined up perfectly with the tomb of St. Vitus (in the cathedral across the river) and the setting sun at equinox.

This magical spot is now occupied by the **bridge tower,** con-

sidered one of the finest Gothic gates anywhere. Contemplate the fine sculpture on the Old Town side of the tower, showing the 14th-century hierarchy of kings, bishops, and angels. Climb the tower for a fine view...but nothing else (40 Kč, daily 10:00–19:00, as late as 22:00 in summer). The other side of the tower lacks decoration. Instead, a plaque commemorates the Swedish siege of 1648, when the bridge turned into a major battleground and the tower was heavily damaged (but the invading Swedes never made it across).

In the days of the Swedish siege, there were no statues on the bridge—only a **cross,** which you can still see as part of the third sculpture on the right. The gilded Hebrew inscription celebrating Christ was paid by a fine imposed on a Jew for mocking the cross.

The Baroque bronze statue depicting **John of Nepomuk**—a saint of the Czech people—draws a crowd (look for the guy with the 5 golden stars around his head, near the Little Quarter end of the bridge on the right). John of Nepomuk was a 14th-century priest to whom the queen confessed all her sins. According to a 17th-century legend, the king wanted to know his wife's secrets, but Father John dutifully refused to tell. He was tortured and eventually killed by being tossed off the bridge. When he hit the water, five stars appeared. The

shiny plaque at the base of the statue depicts the heave-ho. Devout pilgrims—from Mexico and Moravia alike—touch the engraving to make a wish come true. You get only one chance in life for this wish, so think carefully before you touch the saint. Do not touch the dog, which is said to bring bad luck. Notice the date on the inscription: This oldest statue on the bridge was unveiled in 1683, on the supposed 300th anniversary of the martyr's death. In times when the Czechs were being forcibly converted to Catholicism, John of Nepomuk became the rallying national symbol—"We will convert, but our patron must be Czech." John of Nepomuk was canonized three centuries after his death. You'll find a statue like this one on nearly every square and bridge in the country.

Most of the other Charles Bridge statues date from the late 1600s and early 1700s. Today half of them are replicas—the originals are in city museums, out of the polluted air.

At the far end of Charles Bridge, you reach the **Little Quarter**. For sights in this neighborhood, see page 102.

The New Town (Nové Město)

Enough of pretty, medieval Prague—let's leap into the modern era. The New Town, with Wenceslas Square as its focal point, is today's urban Prague. This part of the city offers bustling boulevards and interesting neighborhoods. The New Town is the best place to view Prague's remarkable Art Nouveau art and architecture and to learn more about its recent communist past.

Wenceslas Square (Václavské Náměstí)

More a broad boulevard than a square (until recently, trams rattled up and down its parklike median strip), this ▲▲ city landmark is named for King Wenceslas—featured both on the 20-Kč coin and the equestrian statue that stands at the top of the boulevard. This square functions as a stage for modern Czech history: The creation of the Czechoslovak state was celebrated here in 1918; in 1968, the Soviets put down huge popular demonstrations here; and, in 1989, more than 300,000 Czechs and Slovaks converged here to claim their freedom.

Starting near the Wenceslas statue at the top (Metro: Muzeum), stroll down the square:

The **National Museum** (Národní Muzeum) stands grandly at the top. While the museum is dull, the building offers a powerful view, and the interior is richly decorated in the Czech Revival neo-Renaissance style that heralded the 19th-century rebirth of the Czech nation (80 Kč, daily May–Sept 10:00–18:00, Oct–April 9:00–17:00, halls of Czech fossils and animals). The light-colored patches in the museum's columns fill holes where Soviet bullets hit during the crackdown against the 1968 "Prague Spring" uprising.

Prague's New Town

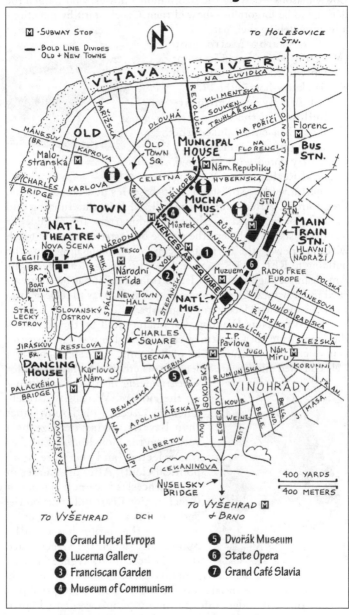

M - Subway Stop

— - Bold Line Divides Old + New Towns

① Grand Hotel Evropa
② Lucerna Gallery
③ Franciscan Garden
④ Museum of Communism
⑤ Dvořák Museum
⑥ State Opera
⑦ Grand Café Slavia

Lowly masons—defying their communist bosses, who wanted the damage to be forgotten—showed their Czech spirit by intentionally mismatching their patches.

The nearby Metro stop (Muzeum) is the crossing point of two Metro lines built with Russian know-how in the 1970s.

The ugly **communist-era building** to the left of the National Museum housed the rubber-stamp Parliament back when they voted with Moscow. A Social Realist statue showing triumphant workers still stands at its base. It's now home to Radio Free Europe. After communism fell, RFE lost its funding and could no longer afford its Munich headquarters. In gratitude for its broadcasts—which kept the people of Eastern Europe in touch with real news—the current Czech government now rents the building to RFE for 1 Kč a year. (As RFE energetically beams its American message deep into Islam from here, it has been threatened recently by al-Qaeda, and a plan is underway to relocate it to an easier-to-defend locale in the suburbs.)

St. Wenceslas (Václav), commemorated by the statue, is the "good king" of Christmas-carol fame. He was the wise and benevolent 10th-century duke of Bohemia. A rare example of a well-educated and literate ruler, he was credited by his people for

Christianizing his nation and lifting up the culture. Wenceslas astutely allied the Czechs with Saxony, rather than Bavaria, giving the Czechs a vote when the Holy Roman Emperor was selected (and therefore more political clout). After his murder in 929, Wenceslas became a symbol of Czech nationalism and statehood—and remains an icon of Czech unity whenever the nation has to rally. Supposedly, when the Czechs face their darkest hour, Wenceslas will come riding out of Blaník Mountain (east of Prague) with an army of knights to rescue the nation. In 1620, when Austria stripped Czechs of their independence, many people went to Blaník Mountain to see whether it had opened up. They did the same at other critical points in their history (in 1938, 1948, and 1968)—but Wenceslas never emerged. Although now safely part of NATO and the EU, Czechs remain realistic: If Wenceslas hasn't come out yet, the worst times must still lie ahead....

Study the statue. Wenceslas is surrounded by the four other Czech patron saints. Notice the focus on books. A small nation without great military power, the Czech Republic chose national heroes who enriched the culture by thinking, rather than fighting. This statue is a popular meeting point. Locals say, "I'll see you under the horse's...tail."

Thirty yards below the big horse is a small garden with a low-key **memorial** "to the victims of communism"—such as Jan Palach. In 1969, a group of patriots decided that an act of self-immolation would stoke the fires of independence. Jan Palach, a philosophy student who loved life, but wanted it with freedom, set himself on fire on the steps of the National Museum for the cause of Czech independence and died a few days later in a hospital ward. Czechs are keen on anniversaries. Huge demonstrations swept the city on the 20th anniversary of Palach's death. These led, 10 months later, to the overthrow of the Czech communist government.

This grand square is a gallery of modern **architectural styles**. As you wander downhill, notice the fun mix, all post-1850: Romantic neo-Gothic, neo-Renaissance, and neo-Baroque from the 19th century; Art Nouveau from around 1900; ugly functionalism from the mid-20th century (the "form follows function" and "ornamentation is a crime" answer to Art Nouveau); Stalin Gothic from the 1950s "communist epoch" (a good example is the Jalta building, halfway downhill on the right); and the glass-and-steel buildings of the 1970s.

Walk a couple of blocks downhill through the real people of Prague (not tourists) to **Grand Hotel Evropa,** with its hard-to-miss, dazzling Art Nouveau exterior and plush café interior full of tourists.

In **November of 1989**, this huge square was filled every evening with more than 300,000 ecstatic Czechs and Slovaks believing freedom was at hand. Assembled on the balcony of the building opposite Grand Hotel Evropa (look for the *Marks & Spencer* sign) were a priest, a rock star (famous for his unconventional style, which constantly unnerved the regime), Alexander Dubček (hero of the 1968 revolt), and Václav Havel (the charismatic playwright, newly released from prison, who was every freedom-loving Czech's Mandela). Through a sound system provided by the rock star, Havel's voice boomed over the gathered masses, announcing the resignation of the Politburo and saying that the Republic of Czechoslovakia's freedom was imminent. Picture that cold November evening, with thousands of Czechs jingling their keychains in solidarity, chanting at the government, "It's time to go now!" (To quell this revolt, government tanks could have given it the Tiananmen Square treatment—which spilled lots of patriotic blood in China just 6 months earlier. Locals believe Gorbachev must have made a phone call recommending that blood not be shed over this.) For more on the events leading up to this climactic rally, see "Národní Třída and the Velvet Revolution" on page 100.

Immediately opposite Grand Hotel Evropa is the **Lucerna Gallery** (use entry marked *Divadlo Rokoko* and walk straight in). This is a grand mall from the 1930s, with shops, theaters, a ballroom in the basement, and the fine Lucerna Café upstairs. You'll see a sculpture—called *Wenceslas Riding an Upside-Down Horse*—hanging like a swing from a glass dome. David Černý, who created the statue in 1999, is the Czech Republic's most original contemporary artist. Always aspiring to provoke controversy, Černý has painted a legendary Russian tank pink, attached crawling babies to the rocket-like Žižkov TV tower, defecated inside the National Gallery to protest the policies of its director, and sunk a shark-like Saddam Hussein inside an aquarium for a 2005 exhibition. The Lucerna building (which also includes luxury apartments and offices) was built and until recently owned by Václav Havel's family. Inside are also a **Ticketpro box office** (with all available tickets, daily 9:30–18:00), a lavish 1930s Prague cinema (which shows artsy films in Czech with English subtitles, or vice versa, 110 Kč), and the popular **Lucerna Music Bar** in the basement (disco themes, 100 Kč, nightly from 21:00—see page 122).

Directly across busy Vodičkova street (with a handy tram stop) is the Světozor mall. Inside you'll find the **World of Fruit Bar Světozor;** it's every local's favorite ice-cream joint. True to its name, the bar tops its ice cream with every species of fruit. They sell cakes and milkshakes, too. Ask at the counter for an English menu.

Farther down the mall on the left is the entrance to a peaceful **Franciscan Garden** (Františkánská Zahrada). Its white benches and spreading rosebushes are a universe away from the fast beat of the city that throbs behind the buildings surrounding the garden.

Back on Wenceslas Square, if you're in the mood for a mellow hippie teahouse, consider a break at **Dobrá Čajovna** (literally, "Good Teahouse") near the bottom of the square at #14. Or, if you'd like an old-time wine bar, pop into the plain **Šenk Vrbovec** (nearby at #10); it comes with a whiff of the communist days, embracing the faintest bits of genteel culture from an age when refinement was sacrificed for the good of the working class.

They serve traditional drinks, Czech keg wine, Moravian wines (listed on blackboard outside), *becherovka* (the 13-herb liqueur), and—only in autumn—*burčák* (this young wine tastes like grape juice halfway to wine).

The bottom of Wenceslas Square is called **Můstek**, which means "Bridge"; a bridge used to cross a moat here, allowing entrance into the Old Town (you can still see the original Old Town entrance down in the Metro station).

Running to the right from the bottom of Wenceslas Square is the street called **Na Příkopě** (meaning "On the Moat"). This busy boulevard follows the line of the Old Town wall, leading to one of the wall's former gates, the Powder Tower. Along the way, it passes the Museum of Communism (see page 99) and several of Prague's top Art Nouveau sights (see below). City tour buses (see page 74) leave from along this street, which offers plenty of shopping temptations (such as these two malls: Slovanský Dům at Na Příkopě 22, and Černá Růže at Na Příkopě 12, next door to Mosers, with a crystal showroom upstairs).

Na Příkopě: Art Noveau Prague

Stroll up Na Příkopě to take in two of Prague's best Art Nouveau sights. The first one is on the street called Panská (turn right up the first street you reach as you walk up Na Příkopě from Wenceslas Square); the second is two blocks farther up Na Příkopě, next to the big, Gothic Powder Tower.

▲▲**Mucha Museum**—This is one of Europe's most enjoyable little museums. I find the art of Alfons Mucha (MOO-kah, 1860–1939) insistently likeable. See the crucifixion scene he painted as an eight-year-old boy. Read how this popular Czech artist's posters, filled with Czech symbols and expressing his people's ideals and aspirations, were patriotic banners that aroused the national spirit. And check out the photographs of his models. With the help of this abundant supply of slinky models, Mucha was a founding father of the Art Nouveau movement. Prague isn't much on museums, but, if you're into Art Nouveau, this one is great. Partly overseen by Mucha's grandson, it's two blocks off Wenceslas Square and wonderfully displayed on one comfortable floor (120 Kč, daily 10:00–18:00, Panská 7, tel. 224-233-355, www.mucha.cz). While the exhibit is well-described in English, the 30-Kč English brochure on the art is a good supplement. The included 30-minute video is definitely worthwhile (in English, ask for the starting time upon entry); it describes the main project of Mucha's life—the *Slavic Epic*, now on display in the village of Moravský Krumlov (in the eastern Czech Republic).

Coming back to Na Příkopě and continuing toward the Powder Tower, notice the neo-Renaissance **Živnostenská Banka**

Art Nouveau

Prague is the best Art Nouveau town in Europe, with fun-loving facades gracing streets all over town. Art Nouveau, born in Paris, is "nouveau" because it wasn't inspired by Rome. It's neo-nothing...a fresh answer to all the revival styles of the later 19th century and an organic response to the Eiffel Tower art of the Industrial Age. The style liberated the artist in each architect. Notice the unique curves and motifs on each Art Nouveau facade, which express originality. Artists such as Alfons Mucha believed that the style should include all facets of daily life. They designed everything from buildings and furniture to typefaces and cigarette packs.

Prague's three top Art Nouveau architects are Jan Koula, Josef Fanta, and a guy (Osvald Polivka) whose last name means "soup" in Czech (think "Cola, Fanta, and Soup"—easy to remember and impress your local friends).

Prague's Art Nouveau highlights include the facades lining the streets of the Jewish Quarter, the Mucha window in St. Vitus Cathedral, and Grand Hotel Evropa on Wenceslas Square. The top two places for Art Nouveau fans are the Mucha Museum and the Municipal House.

building on the corner of Nekázanka. It houses a modern bank with classy 19th-century ambience (enter and peek into the main hall upstairs).

At the end of Na Příkopě, you'll arrive at the...

▲**Municipal House (Obecní Dům)**—The Municipal House is the "pearl of Czech Art Nouveau" (built 1905–1911). It features Prague's largest concert hall, a great Art Nouveau café, and two other restaurants. Pop in and wander around the lobby of the concert hall. Walk through to the ticket office on the ground floor. Most days, there are guided tours through the Municipal House that show

you all the halls worth seeing. Then choose your place for a meal or drink (for suggestions, see page 139).

Standing in front of the Municipal House, you can survey four different styles of architecture. First, enjoy the pure Art Nouveau of the Municipal House itself. Featuring a goddess-like Praha presiding over a land of peace and high culture, the *Homage to Prague* mosaic on the building's striking facade stoked cultural pride and nationalist

---

Prague: Pre-1989

It's hard to imagine the gray and bleak Prague of the communist era. Before 1989, the city was a wistful jumble of possibility. Cobbled lanes were shadowed by sooty, crusty buildings. Timbers—strung across the lanes like laundry lines—held crumbling buildings apart. Consumer goods were plain and uniform, stacked like Legos on the thin shelves in shops where customers waited in line for a tin of ham or a bottle of ersatz Coke. The Charles Bridge was as black as its statues, with no commerce except for a few shady characters trying to change money. Hotels had two price schedules: one for people of the Warsaw Pact nations and another (6 to 8 times as expensive) for capitalists. This made the run-down, Soviet-style hotels as expensive as fine Western ones. At the train station, frightened but desperate characters would meet arriving foreigners to rent them a room in their flat, in order to get enough hard Western cash to buy batteries or Levis at one of the hard-currency stores.

---

sentiment. Across the street, the classical fixer-upper from 1815 was the customs house (soon to be renovated). The stark national bank building (Česká Národní Banka) is textbook functionalism from the 1930s. And the big, black Powder Tower (not worth touring inside) was the Gothic gate of the town wall, built to house the city's gunpowder. The decoration on the tower, portraying Czech kings, is the best 15th-century sculpture in town. If you go through the tower, you'll reach Celetná street, which leads past a few sights to the Old Town Square (see page 75).

Národní Třída: Communist Prague

From Můstek at the bottom of Wenceslas Square, you can head west (in the opposite direction from Na Příkopě and the Art Nouveau sights) for an interesting stroll through urban Prague to the National Theatre and the Vltava River. Before starting the walk, consider dropping into the Museum of Communism, a few steps down Na Příkopě (on the right).

▲**Museum of Communism**—This museum traces the story of communism in Prague: the origins, dream, reality, and nightmare; the cult of personality; and finally, the Velvet Revolution. Along the way, it gives a fascinating review of the Czech Republic's 40-year stint with Soviet economics. You'll find propaganda posters, busts of communist All-Stars (Marx, Lenin, Stalin), a photograph of the massive stone Stalin that overlooked Prague until 1962, and re-created slices of communist life—from a bland store counter to a typical classroom (with a poem on the chalkboard extolling the virtues of the tractor). Don't miss the 20-minute video (which plays continuously) showing how the Czech people chafed under the big red yoke from the 1950s through 1989 (180 Kč, daily 9:00–21:00, Na Příkopě 10, above a McDonald's and next to a casino—Lenin would turn over in his grave, tel. 224-212-966, www.museumofcommunism.com).

Now head for the river (with your back to Wenceslas Square, go left down 28 Října to Národní Třída). Along the way, Národní Třída has a story to tell.

Národní Třída and the Velvet Revolution—Národní Třída, the street that connects Wenceslas Square with the National Theatre and the river, is a busy thoroughfare running through the heart of urban Prague. In 1989, this unassuming boulevard played host to the first salvo of a Velvet Revolution that would topple the communist regime.

Make your way down Národní Třída until you hit the tram tracks (just beyond the Tesco department store). On the left, look for the photo of Bill Clinton playing saxophone, with Václav Havel on the side (this is the entrance to Reduta, Prague's best jazz club—see page 120). Just beyond that, you'll come to a short corridor with white arches. Inside this arcade is a simple memorial to the hundreds of students injured here by the police on November 17, 1989. That afternoon, 30,000 students gathered in Prague's New Town to commemorate the 50th anniversary of the suppression of student protests by the Nazis, which had led to the closing of Czech universities through the end of World War II. The 1989 demonstration—initially planned by the Communist Youth as a celebration of the communist victory over fascism—spontaneously turned into a protest *against* the communist regime. "You are just like the Nazis!" shouted the students. The demonstration was planned to end in the National Cemetery at Vyšehrad (the hill just south of the New Town). But when the planned events concluded in Vyšehrad, the students decided to march on towards Wenceslas Square to make history.

As they worked their way north along the Vltava River towards the New Town's main square, the students were careful to keep their demonstration peaceful. Any hint of violence, the demonstrators knew, would incite brutal police retaliation. In fact, as the evening went on, the absence of police became conspicuous. (In the 1980s, the police never missed a chance to participate in any demonstration...preferably outnumbering the demonstrators). At about 20:00, as the students marched down this very stretch of street towards Wenceslas Square, three rows of policemen suddenly blocked the demonstration at the corner of Národní and Spálená streets. A few minutes later, military vehicles with fences on their bumpers (having crossed the bridge by the National

Theatre) appeared behind the marching students. This new set of cops compressed the demonstrators into the stretch of Národní Třída between Voršilská and Spálená. The end of Mikulandská street was also blocked, and policemen were hiding inside every house entry. The students were trapped.

At 21:30, the "Red Hats" (a special anti-riot commando force known for its brutality) arrived. The Red Hats lined up on both sides of this corridor. To get out, the trapped students had to run through the passageway as they were beaten from the left and right. Police trucks ferried students around the corner to the headquarters of the secret police (on Bartolomějská) for interrogation.

The next day, university students throughout Czechoslovakia decided to strike. Actors from theaters in Prague and Bratislava joined the student protest. Two days later, the students' parents—shocked by the attacks on their children—marched into Wenceslas Square. The wave of peaceful demonstrations sparked by the events of November 17, 1989, ended later that year on December 29 with the election of Václav Havel as the president of a free Czechoslovakia.

Along the Vltava River

I've listed these sights from north to south, beginning at the grand, neo-Renaissance National Theatre, which is five blocks south of Charles Bridge and stands along the riverbank at the end of Národní Třída.

National Theatre (Národní Divadlo)—Opened in 1883 with Smetana's opera *Libuše*, this theater was the first truly Czech venue in Prague. From the very start, it was nicknamed the "Cradle of Czech Culture." The building is a key symbol of the Czech national revival that began in the late 18th century. In 1800, "Prag" was predominantly German. The Industrial Revolution brought Czechs from the countryside into the city, their new urban identity defined by patriotic teachers and priests. By 1883, most of the city spoke Czech, and the opening of this theater represented the birth of the modern Czech nation. It remains an important national icon: The state annually pours more subsidies into this theater than into all of Czech film production. It's the most beautiful venue in town for opera or ballet, often with world-class singers on stage (see page 121).

Next door (just inland, on Národní Třída) is the boxy, glassy facade of the **Nová Scéna**. This "New National Theatre" building, dating from 1983 (the 100th anniversary of the original National Theatre building), reflects the bold and stark communist aesthetic.

Across the street from the National Theatre is the former haunt of Prague's intelligentsia, **Grand Café Slavia,** a Viennese-style coffeehouse fine for a meal or drink with a view of the river.

Just south of the National Theatre in the Vltava, you'll find...

Prague's Islands—From the National Theatre, the Legions' Bridge (Most Legií) leads across the island called **Střelecký Ostrov.** Covered with chestnut trees, this island boasts Prague's best beach (on the sandy tip that points north to Charles Bridge). You might see fisherman pulling out trout from a river that's now much cleaner than it used to be. Bring a swimsuit and take a dip just a stone's throw from Europe's most beloved bridge. In summer, the island hosts open-air movies (most in English or with English subtitles, nightly mid-July–early Sept at around 21:00, www.strelak.cz).

In the mood for boating instead of swimming? On the next island down, **Slovanský Ostrov,** you can rent a paddleboat (bring a picture ID as deposit). You'll also find a 19th-century palace that houses the fancy Restaurant Žofín (see page 140).

A 10-minute walk (or one stop on tram #17) from the National Theatre, beyond the islands, is Jirásek Bridge (Jiráskův Most), where you'll find the...

Dancing House (Tančící Dům)—If ever a building could get your toes tapping, it would be this one, nicknamed "Fred and Ginger" by American architecture buffs. This metallic samba is the work of Frank Gehry (who designed the equally striking Guggenheim Museum in Bilbao, Spain, and Seattle's Experience Music Project). Eight-legged Ginger's wispy dress and Fred's metal mesh head are easy to spot. The building's top-floor restaurant, La Perle de Prague, is a fine place for an upscale meal (see page 140).

The Little Quarter (Malá Strana)

This charming neighborhood, huddled under the castle on the west bank of the river, is low on blockbuster sights but high on ambience. The most enjoyable approach from the Old Town is across the Charles Bridge. From the end of the bridge (TI in tower), Mostecká street leads two blocks up to the Little Quarter Square (Malostranské Náměstí) and the huge Church of St. Nicholas. But before you head up there, consider a detour to Kampa Island (all described below).

Between Charles Bridge and Little Quarter Square

Kampa Island—One hundred yards before the castle end of the Charles Bridge, stairs on the left lead down to the main square

Prague's Little Quarter

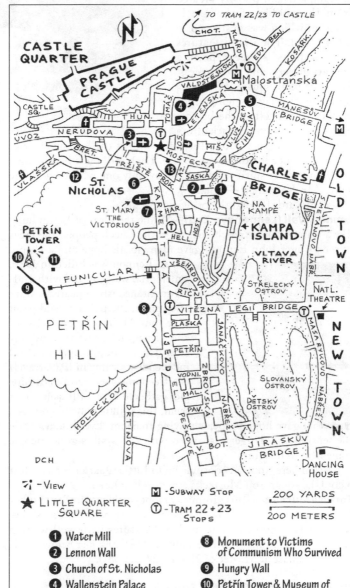

Legend:

⌐ – VIEW

★ LITTLE QUARTER SQUARE

Ⓜ – SUBWAY STOP

Ⓣ – TRAM 22 + 23 STOPS

200 YARDS

200 METERS

DCH

❶ Water Mill

❷ Lennon Wall

❸ Church of St. Nicholas

❹ Wallenstein Palace

❺ Wallenstein Garden

❻ Vrtba Garden

❼ Church of St. Mary the Victorious

❽ Monument to Victims of Communism Who Survived

❾ Hungry Wall

❿ Petřín Tower & Museum of Jára Cimrman

⓫ Mirror Maze

⓬ U. S. Embassy

⓭ Torture Museum

of Kampa Island (mostly created from the rubble of the Little Quarter, which was destroyed in a 1540 fire). The island features relaxing pubs, a breezy park, a new art gallery, and river access. From the main square, Hroznová lane (on the right) leads to a bridge. To the left of the bridge, notice the high-water marks from the flood of August 2002. The water mill is the last survivor of many that once lined the canal here. Each mill once had its own protective water spirit *(vodník)*. Today only one wheel—and one spirit (Mr. Kabourek)—remain.

Fifty yards beyond the bridge is the...

Lennon Wall (Lennonova Zed')—While the ideas of Lenin hung like a water-soaked trench coat upon the Czech people, the ideas of rock singer John Lennon gave many locals hope and a vision.

When Lennon was killed in 1980, a memorial wall covered with graffiti spontaneously appeared. Night after night, the police would paint over the "All You Need Is Love" and "Imagine" graffiti. And day after day, it would reappear. Until independence came in 1989, travelers, freedom-lovers, and local hippies gathered here. Silly as it might seem, this wall is remembered as a place that gave hope to locals craving freedom. Even today, while the tension and danger associated with this wall is gone, people come here to imagine.

From here, you can continue up to Little Quarter Square. Just before the square, on Mostecká street, is Prague's...

Torture Museum—This gimmicky moneymaker is similar to other European torture museums, but is interesting nevertheless, showing models of 60 gruesome medieval tortures with well-written English descriptions (120 Kč, daily 10:00–22:00, just below Little Quarter Square at Mostecká 21, tel. 224-215-581).

On or near Little Quarter Square (Malostranské Náměstí)

The focal point of this neighborhood, Little Quarter Square (Malostranské Náměstí), is dominated by the huge Church of St. Nicholas.

Church of St. Nicholas (Kostel Sv. Mikuláše)—When the Jesuits came to Prague in the 18th century, they found the perfect piece of real estate for their church and its associated school—right on Little Quarter Square. The church (built 1703–1760) is the best example of High Baroque in town (50 Kč, daily 9:00–17:00, opens at 8:30 for prayer). It's giddy with curves and illusions. The altar features a lavish gold-plated Nicholas flanked by the two top Jesuits: St. Ignatius Loyola and St. Francis Xavier.

For a good look at the city and the church's 250-foot dome, climb the **bell tower** (30 Kč, April–Oct daily 10:00–18:00, closed Nov–March, tower entrance is outside the right transept). The Little Quarter residents prized their ancient church bells, which they believed carried the soul of their neighborhood. So before the Jesuits were given permission to build, they had to promise the Little Quarter councilmen that the bell tower standing in the middle of the square would remain untouched, or that a new one would be built. The new bell tower had to be as prominent as the church's dome. That's why this tower can be seen before the dome from any of the streets approaching the square—and why it offers such commanding views over the Little Quarter.

The church is also a **concert** venue in evenings; 400-Kč tickets are generally on sale at the door (www.psalterium.cz).

From here, you can hike 10 minutes uphill to the castle (and 5 more min to the Strahov Monastery). For information on these sights, see "The Castle Quarter" on page 106. If you're walking up to the castle, consider going via...

Nerudova Street—This steep, cobbled street, leading from Little Quarter Square to the castle, is named for Jan Neruda, a gifted 19th-century journalist (and somewhat less talented fiction writer). It's lined with old buildings still sporting the characteristic doorway signs (e.g., the lion, 3 violinists, house of the golden sun) that once served as street addresses. They represent the family name, the occupation, or the various passions of the people who once inhabited the houses. In 1777, in order to collect taxes more effectively, Hapsburg empress Maria Theresa decreed that numbers be used instead of these quaint house names. The surviving signs are carefully restored and protected by law. This neighborhood is filled with old noble palaces, now generally used as foreign embassies and offices of the Czech parliament.

South of Little Quarter Square, to Petřín Hill

Karmelitská street, leading south (along the tram tracks) from Little Quarter Square, is home to these sights.

Church of St. Mary the Victorious (Kostel Panny Marie Vítězné)—This otherwise ordinary Carmelite church displays

Prague's most precious jewel, the Infant of Prague (Pražské Jezulátko). Brought to the Czech lands during the Hapsburg era by a Spanish noblewoman who came to marry a Czech nobleman, the Infant has become a focus of worship and miracle tales in Prague and Spanish-speaking countries. South Americans come on pilgrimage to Prague just to see this one statue (free, Mon–Sat 10:00–17:30, Sun 13:00–17:00, Karmelitská 9, www.pragjesu.com).

Continue a few more blocks down Karmelitská to the south end of the Little Quarter (where the street is called Újezd, roughly across the Legions' Bridge from the National Theatre). Here you find yourself at the base of...

Petřín Hill—This hill, topped by a replica of the Eiffel Tower, features several offbeat sights.

The figures walking down the steps in the hillside make up the **Monument to Victims of Communism Who Survived**. These figures are gradually atrophied by the totalitarian regime. They do not die, but gradually disappear. To the left of the monument is the **Hungry Wall**, the 14th-century Charles IV's equivalent of FDR's work-for-food projects. On the right is the base of a handy **funicular**—hop on to reach Petřín Tower (uses 20-Kč tram/Metro ticket, runs daily, every 10–15 min from 8:00–22:00).

The summit of Petřín Hill is considered the best place in Prague to take your date for a romantic city view. Built for an exhibition in 1891, the 200-foot-tall **Petřín Tower** is a fifth the height of its Parisian big brother built two years earlier. But, thanks to this hill, the top of the tower sits at the same elevation as the real Eiffel Tower. You can take the spiral stairs (on the left) leading up to several rooms with painted coats of arms and no English explanations, or better, climb the 400 steps for amazing views over the city.

In the basement of the tower is the funniest sight in Prague, the **Museum of Jára Cimrman, Genius Who Did Not Become Famous**. The museum traces Cimrman's (fictional life), including pictures and descriptions of the thinker's overlooked inventions (50 Kč, daily 10:00–22:00). For more on the mysterious Cimrman, see the sidebar on page 108.

The **mirror maze** next door is nothing special, but fun to quickly wander through since you're already here (50 Kč, daily 10:00–22:00).

The Castle Quarter (Hradčany)

Looming above Prague, dominating its skyline, is the Castle Quarter. Prague Castle and its surrounding sights are packed with Czech history as well as with tourists. In addition to the castle itself, I enjoy visiting the nearby Strahov Monastery—with a fun old library and beautiful views over all of Prague.

Prague's Castle Quarter

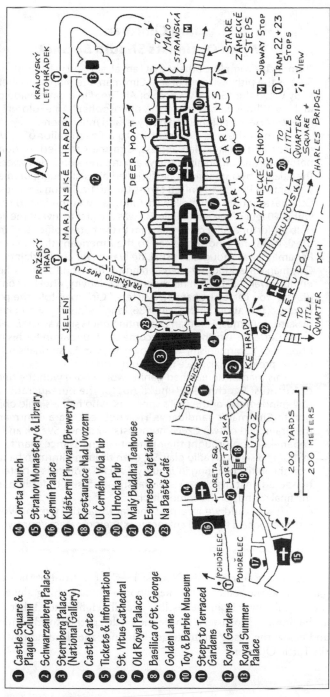

1 Castle Square & Plague Column
2 Schwarzenberg Palace
3 Sternberg Palace (National Gallery)
4 Castle Gate
5 Tickets & Information
6 St. Vitus Cathedral
7 Old Royal Palace
8 Basilica of St. George
9 Golden Lane
10 Toy & Barbie Museum
11 Steps to Terraced Gardens
12 Royal Gardens
13 Royal Summer Palace
14 Loreta Church
15 Strahov Monastery & Library
16 Černín Palace
17 Klášterní Pivovar (Brewery)
18 Restaurace Nad Úvozem
19 U Černého Vola Pub
20 U Hrocha Pub
21 Malý Buddha Teahouse
22 Espresso Kajetánka
23 Na Baště Café

M - Subway Stop
T - Tram 22 + 23 Stops
🔆 - View

200 YARDS
200 METERS

Jára Cimrman:
When Optimists Should Be Shot

"I am such a complete atheist that I am afraid God will punish me." Such is the pithy wisdom of Jára Cimrman, the man overwhelmingly voted the "Greatest Czech of All Time" in a nationwide poll in 2005. Who is Jára Cimrman? A philosopher? An explorer? An inventor? He is all of these things, yes, and much more.

Born in the mid-19th century to a Czech tailor of Jewish descent and an Austrian actress, Cimrman studied in Vienna before starting off on his journeys around the world. He traversed the Atlantic by a steamboat he designed himself, taught drama to peasants in Peru, and drifted across the Arctic Sea on an iceberg. Other astounding feats followed. Cimrman was the first to come within 20 feet of the North Pole. He was the first to invent the light bulb (unfortunately, Edison beat him to the patent office by 5 minutes). It was he who suggested to the Americans the idea for a Panama Canal, though, as usual, he was never credited. Indeed, Cimrman surreptitiously advised many of the world's greats: Eiffel on his tower, Einstein on his theories of relativity, Chekhov on his plays. ("You can't just have *two* sisters," Cimrman told the playwright. "How about three?") In 1886, long before the world knew of Sartre or Camus, Cimrman was writing tracts such as *The Essence of the Existence*, which would become the foundation for his philosophy of "Cimrmanism," also known as "Non-Existentialism." (Its central premise: "Existence cannot not exist.")

This man of unmatched genius would have won the honor of "Greatest Czech of All Time" if not for the bureaucratic narrow-mindedness of the poll's sponsors, who had a single objection to Cimrman's candidacy: "He's not real." Jára Cimrman is the brainchild of two Czech humorists—Zdeněk Svěrák and Jiří Šebánek—who brought their patriotic Renaissance man to life in 1967 in a satirical radio play. So, even though Cimrman handily won the initial balloting in January, Czech TV officials—blatantly biased against his non-existentialism—refused to let him into the final rounds of the competition.

How should we interpret the fact that the Czechs would rather choose a fictional character as their greatest countryman

Castle Square (Hradčanské Náměstí)—right in front of the castle gates—is at the center of this neighborhood. Stretching along the promontory away from the castle is a regal neighborhood that ends at the Strahov Monastery. Above the castle are the Royal Gardens, and below the castle are more gardens and lanes leading down to the Little Quarter.

over any of their flesh-and-blood national heroes—say, Charles IV (the 14th-century Holy Roman Emperor who established Prague as the cultural and intellectual capital of Europe), Jan Hus (the 15th-century religious reformer who challenged the legitimacy of the Catholic Church), Comenius (the 17th-century educator and writer considered one of the fathers of modern education), or Martina Navrátilová (someone who plays a sport with bright green balls)? The more cynically inclined—many Czechs among them—might point out that the Czech people have largely stayed behind their mountains for the past millennia, with little interest in, or influence on, happenings elsewhere in the world. Perhaps Cimrman is so beloved because he embodies that most prickly of ironies: a Czech who was greater than all the world's greats, but who for some hiccup of chance has never been recognized for his achievements.

Personally, I like to think that the vote for Cimrman says something about the country's rousing enthusiasm for blowing raspberries in the face of authority. Throughout its history—from the times of the Czech kings who used crafty diplomacy to keep the German menace at bay, to the days of Jan Hus and his questioning of the very legitimacy of any ruler's power, to the flashes of anti-communist revolt that at last sparked the Velvet Revolution in 1989—the Czechs have maintained a healthy disrespect for those who would tell them what is best or how to live their lives. Other countries soberly choose their "Greatest" from musty tomes of history, but the Czechs won't play this silly game. Their vote for a fictional personage, says Cimrman's co-creator Svěrák, says two things about the Czech nation: "That it is skeptical about those who are major figures and those who are supposedly 'the Greatest.' And that the only certainty that has saved the nation many times throughout history is its humor."

Cimrman would agree. A man of greatness, he was always a bit skeptical of those who saw themselves as great, or who marched forward under the banner of greatness. As Cimrman liked to say, "There are moments when optimists should be shot."

Getting to Prague Castle

If you're not up for a hike, the tram offers a sweat-free ride to the castle.

By Foot: Begin in the Little Quarter (see page 102), just across Charles Bridge from the Old Town. Hikers can follow the main cobbled road (Mostecká) from Charles Bridge to Little Quarter Square, marked by the huge, green-domed Church of St. Nicholas. (The nearest Metro stop is Malostranská, from which Valdštejnská street leads down to Little Quarter Square.) From Little Quarter Square, hike uphill along Nerudova street (described on page 105). After about 10 minutes, a steep lane on the right leads to the castle. (If you continue straight, Nerudova becomes Úvoz and climbs to the Strahov Monastery.)

By Tram: Trams #22 and #23 take you up to the castle. While you can catch the tram in various places, these three stops are particularly convenient: at the Národní Třída Metro stop (between Wenceslas Square and the National Theatre in the New Town); in front of the National Theatre (Národní Divadlo, on the riverbank in the New Town); and at Malostranská (the Metro stop in the Little Quarter). After rattling up the hill, these trams make three stops near the castle: Get off at **Královský Letohrádek** for the scenic approach to the castle (through the Royal Gardens—see below); or stay on one more stop to get off at **Pražský Hrad** (most direct but least interesting—simply walk along U Prašného Mostu over the bridge into Castle Square); or go yet one more stop to **Pohořelec** to visit the Strahov Monastery (from the stop, go uphill and through the gate toward the twin spires) before hiking down to the castle. Note that between Pražský Hrad and Pohořelec, the tram might make a stop at Brusnice (on request only).

Planning Your Time: When you're choosing which of the castle's three tram stops to get off at, consider the time of day. The castle is plagued with crowds. If visiting in the morning, use the Pražský Hrad tram stop for the quickest commute to the castle. Be at the door of St. Vitus Cathedral when it opens at 9:00 (just 10–15 minutes later, it's swamped with tour groups). See the castle sights quickly, then move on to the Strahov Monastery. I'd avoid the castle entirely mid-morning, but by mid-afternoon, the tour groups are napping and the grounds are (relatively) uncrowded. If going in the afternoon, take the tram to the Pohořelec stop, see the Strahov Monastery, then wander down to the castle.

Above the Castle, near the Královský Letohrádek Tram Stop

These sights, above Prague Castle, are only worth visiting if you get off tram #22 or #23 at Královský Letohrádek (the palace is across the street from this stop).

Royal Summer Palace (Královský Letohrádek)—This love gift is like a Czech Taj Mahal, given by Emperor Ferdinand I to his beloved Queen Anne. It's the finest Renaissance building in town. You can't go inside, but the building's detailed reliefs are worth a close look. In good Renaissance style, they're based on classical, rather than Christian, stories. The one depicted here is Virgil's *The Aeneid*. The fountain in front of the palace features the most elaborate bronzework in the country. (If you stick your head under the bottom of the fountain, you'll find out why it's called the "Singing Fountain.")

From here, you can reach the cathedral by strolling through the...

Royal Gardens (Královská Zahrada)—Once the private grounds and residence (you'll see the building) of the communist presidents, these were opened to the public with the coming of freedom under Václav Havel (April–Oct daily 10:00–18:00, closed Nov–March). Walk through these gardens (with fine views of St. Vitus Cathedral) to the gate, which leads you over the moat and into Castle Square.

Strahov Monastery and Library

Twin Baroque domes high above the castle mark the Strahov Monastery and Library (Strahovský Klášter Premonstrátů a Strahovská Knihovna; a 15-min hike uphill from Little Quarter, or a 5-min walk from castle). Worth ▲, this complex is best reached from the Pohořelec stop on tram #22 or #23 (from the stop, go uphill 200 yards and through the gate into the monastery grounds). After seeing the monastery, hike down to the castle.

Monastery: The monastery had a booming economy of its own in its heyday, with vineyards and the biggest beer hall in town (still open). Its main church, dedicated to the Assumption of St. Mary, is an originally Romanesque structure decorated by the monks in textbook Baroque (usually closed, but look through the window inside the front door to see its interior).

Library: The adjacent library offers a peek at how enlightened thinkers in the 18th century influenced learning (60 Kč, daily 9:00–12:00 & 13:00–17:00). Cases in the library gift shop show off illuminated manuscripts. Some are in old Czech, but these are rare. Because the Enlightenment believed in the universality of knowledge, there was little place for vernaculars—therefore, there are few books in the Czech language. Two rooms are filled with 17th-century books under elaborately painted ceilings. The theme of the first and bigger hall is philosophy, with the history of man's pursuit of knowledge painted on the ceiling. The other hall focuses on theology. Notice the gilded locked case containing the *libri prohibiti* (prohibited books) at the end of the room. Only the abbot had the key, and you had to have his blessing to read these books—by writers such as Nicolas Copernicus and Jan Hus, even including the French encyclopedia. As the Age of Enlightenment began to take hold in Europe in the end of 18th century, monasteries still controlled the books. The hallway connecting these two library rooms was filled with cases illustrating the new practical approach to natural sciences. Find the baby dodo bird (which became extinct in the 17th century).

Nearby Views: Just downhill from the monastery and through the gate, the views from the **monastery garden** are among the best in Prague. From the public perch below the tables, you can see St. Vitus Cathedral (the heart of the castle complex), the green dome of the Church of St. Nicholas (marking the center of the Little Quarter), the two dark towers fortifying the Charles Bridge, and the fanciful black spires of the Týn Church (marking the Old Town Square). On the horizon is the modern **Žižkov TV and radio tower** (conveniently marking the liveliest nightlife zone in town—see page 122). Begun in the 1980s, it was meant to jam Radio Free Europe's broadcast from Munich. By the time it was finished, Radio Free Europe's headquarters had actually moved to Prague.

To reach the castle from Strahov Monastery, take Loretánská (the upper road, passing Loreta Square—see below); this is more interesting than going on the lower road, Úvoz, which takes you steeply downhill, below Castle Square.

On Loreta Square,
between Strahov Monastery and Castle Square

Loreta Square (Loretánské Náměstí) is on Loretánská street, between the Strahov Monastery and Castle Square. As you wander this road, you'll pass several mansions and palaces, and an important pilgrimage church.

Loreta Church—This church has been a hit with pilgrims for centuries, thanks to its dazzling bell tower, peaceful yet plush cloister, sparkling treasury, and much-venerated "Holy House" (90 Kč, Tue–Sun 9:00–12:15 & 13:00–16:30, closed Mon).

The central **Santa Casa** (Holy House) was considered by some pilgrims to be part of Mary's home in Nazareth. Because many pilgrims returning from the Holy Land docked at the Italian port of Loreto, it's called the Loreta Shrine. The Santa Casa is the "little Bethlehem" of Prague. It is the traditional departure point for Czech pilgrims setting out on the long, arduous journey to Europe's most important pilgrimage site, Santiago de Compostela, in northwest Spain.

The small Baroque church behind the Santa Casa is one of the most beautiful in Prague. The frescoes on the ceilings of the ambulatory illustrate a prayer to St. Mary. The Santa Casa itself, with only a few 15th-century frescoes and an old statue of Mary, might seem like a bit of a letdown, but consider that you're entering the holiest spot in the country for generations of believers. Upstairs, the highlight is a room full of jeweled worship aids in the treasury (well-described in English). Behind vault doors, you'll squint at a monstrance (Communion wafer holder) from 1699, with over 6,000 diamonds. Enjoy the short carillon concert at the top of the hour; from the lawn in front of the main entrance, you can see the racks of bells being clanged.

Castle Square (Hradčanské Náměstí)

This is the central square of the Castle Quarter. Enjoy the awesome city view and the two entertaining bands that play regularly at the gate. (If the Prague Castle Orchestra is playing, say hello to friendly, mustachioed Josef, and consider getting the group's terrific CD—see page 121.) A tranquil café called Espresso Kajetánka hides a few steps down, immediately to the right as you face the castle (see page 142). From here, stairs lead into the Little Quarter.

Castle Square was a kind of medieval Pennsylvania Avenue—the king, the most powerful noblemen, and the archbishop lived here. Look uphill from the gate. The Renaissance **Schwarzenberg Palace** (on the left, with the big rectangles scratched on the wall, now under renovation) was where the Rožmberks "humbly" stayed when they were in town from their Český Krumlov estates. The Schwarzenberg family inherited the Krumlov estates and aristocratic prominence in Bohemia, and stayed in the palace until the 20th century.

The archbishop still lives in the yellow rococo **palace** across the square (with the 3 white goose necks in the red field—the coat of arms of Prague's archbishops).

Through the portal on the left-hand side of the palace, a lane leads to the **Sternberg Palace** (Šternberský Palác), filled with the National Gallery's skippable collection of European paintings—mostly minor works by Albrecht Dürer, Peter Paul Rubens, Rembrandt, and El Greco (100 Kč, Tue–Sun 10:00–18:00, closed Mon).

The Baroque sculpture in the middle of the square is a **plague column**, erected as a token of gratitude to the saints who saved the population from the epidemic, and an integral part of the main square of any Hapsburg town.

The statue marked *TGM* honors **Tomáš Garrigue Masaryk** (1850–1937), a university prof and a pal of Woodrow Wilson. At the end of World War I, Masaryk united the Czechs and the Slovaks into one nation and became its first president (see sidebar on page 114).

Prague Castle (Pražský Hrad)

For more than a thousand years, Czech leaders have ruled from Prague Castle. Today Prague's Castle is, by some measures, the biggest on earth. A visit here is worth ▲▲. Four stops matter, and all are explained here: St. Vitus Cathedral, Old Royal Palace, Basilica of St. George, and the Golden Lane.

Tomáš Garrigue Masaryk
(1850–1937)

Masaryk was the George Washington of Czechoslovakia. He founded the first democracy in Eastern Europe at the end of World War I, uniting the Czechs and the Slovaks to create Czechoslovakia. Like Václav Havel 70 years later, Masaryk was a politician whose vision extended far beyond the mountains enclosing the Bohemian basin.

Masaryk was born into a poor servant family in southern Moravia. After finishing high school, the village boy set off to attend university in Vienna. Masaryk earned his Ph.D. in sociology just in time for the opening of the Czech-language university in Prague. By that time, he was already married to an American music student named Charlotta Garrigue, who came from a prominent New York family. Charlotta opened the doors of America's high society to Masaryk. Among the American friends he made was a young Princeton professor named Woodrow Wilson.

Masaryk was greatly impressed with America, and his admiration for its democratic system became the core of his gradually evolving political creed. He traveled the world and went to Vienna to serve in the parliament. By the time World War I broke out in 1914, Masaryk was 64 years old and—his friends

Hours: Castle sights are open daily April–Oct 9:00–17:00, Nov–March 9:00–16:00, last entry 15 min before closing; the grounds are open daily 5:00–23:00. St. Vitus Cathedral is closed Sunday mornings for Mass. Be warned that St. Vitus Cathedral can be unexpectedly closed due to special services—consider calling ahead to confirm. Tel. 224-373-368 or 224-372-434, www .hrad.cz.

Tickets: You can choose from four different types of tickets.

Route A costs 350 Kč and includes everything: the cathedral sights (apse, crypt, and tower—note that just looking around the front part of the cathedral is free), Old Royal Palace, Basilica of St. George, Powder Tower, Golden Lane (during peak sightseeing hours—it's free in the morning and evening), and an exhibition on the castle's building history. For the thorough visit described below, opt for Route A.

thought—ready for retirement. But while most other Czech politicians stayed in Prague and supported the Hapsburg Empire, Masaryk went abroad in protest and formed a highly original plan: to create an independent, democratic republic of Czechs and Slovaks. Masaryk and his supporters recruited an army of 100,000 Czechs and Slovak soldiers willing to fight with the Allies against the Hapsburgs...establishing a strong case to put on his friend Woodrow Wilson's Oval Office desk.

On the morning of October 28, 1918, news of the unofficial capitulation of the Hapsburgs reached Prague. Local supporters of Masaryk's idea quickly took control of the city and proclaimed the free republic. As the people of Prague tore down double-headed eagles (a symbol of the Hapsburgs), Czechoslovakia was born.

On November 11, 1918, four years after he had left the country as a political nobody, Masaryk arrived in Prague as the greatest Czech hero since the revolutionary priest Jan Hus. The dignified old man rode through the masses of cheering Czechs on a white horse. He told the jubilant crowd, "Now go home—the work has only started." Throughout the 1920s and 1930s, Masaryk was Europe's most vocal defender of democratic ideals against the rising tide of totalitarian ideologies.

In 2001, the U.S. government honored Masaryk's dedication to democracy by erecting a monument to him in Washington, D.C.—he is one of only three foreign leaders (along with Gandhi and Churchill) to have a statue in the American capital.

Route B (220 Kč) includes the cathedral sights and Old Royal Palace.

Route C (50 Kč) gets you into the Golden Lane only, and **Route D** (50 Kč) into the Basilica of St. George only. If you want to save time and money, take Route D—tour the Basilica of St. George, wander the grounds, and explore the front half of the cathedral and peek into the tomb of Prince Wenceslas (this part of cathedral is free).

Tours: Hour-long tours in English depart from the main ticket office about three times a day, but cover only the cathedral and Old Royal Palace (80 Kč; reserve a week in advance if you want a private guide-400 Kč for up to 5 people, then 80 Kč per additional person, tel. 224-373-368). If you rent the worthwhile **audioguide** (200 Kč/2 hrs, 250 Kč/3 hrs), you won't be able to exit the castle from the bottom since you need to backtrack uphill to return the audioguide where you got it.

Crowd-Beating Tips: Huge throngs of tourists turn the castle grounds into a sea of people during peak times (9:15–15:00). St. Vitus Cathedral is the most crowded part of the castle complex. If visiting in the morning, ideally be at the cathedral entrance promptly at 9:00, when the doors open. For 10 minutes, you'll have the sacred space for yourself (after about 9:15, tour guides shouting over each other turn the church into a hawkers' square). Late afternoon is least crowded.

Castle Gate and Courtyards—Begin at Castle Square. From

here, survey the castle—the tip of a 1,500-foot-long series of courtyards, churches, and palaces. The guard changes on the hour (5:00–23:00), with the most ceremony at noon.

Walk under the fighting giants, under an arch, through the passageway, and into the courtyard. The modern green awning with the golden winged cat (just past the ticket office) marks the offices of the Czech president.

As you walk through another passageway, you'll find yourself facing...

▲▲▲St. Vitus Cathedral (Katedrála Sv. Víta)—The Roman Catholic cathedral symbolizes the Czech spirit—it contains the tombs and relics of the most important local saints and kings, including the first three Hapsburg kings.

Before entering, check out the **facade**. What's up with the guys in suits carved into the facade below the big round window? They're the architects and builders who finished the church. Started in 1344, construction was stalled by wars and plagues. But, fueled by the 19th-century rise of Czech nationalism, Prague's top church was finished in 1929 for the 1,000th anniversary of the death of St. Wenceslas. While it looks all Gothic, it's actually two distinct halves: modern neo-Gothic and the original 14th-century Gothic. For 400 years, a temporary wall sealed off the unfinished cathedral.

Go inside and find the third **stained-glass window** on the left. This masterful 1931 Art Nouveau window is by Czech artist Alfons Mucha (if you like this, you'll love the Mucha Museum in the New Town—see page 97). Notice Mucha's stirring nationalism: Methodius and Cyril (leaders in

Slavic-style Christianity) are top and center. Cyril is baptizing the mythic, lanky, long-haired Czech man. In the center is a kneeling boy and a prophesying elder—that's young St. Wenceslas and his grandmother, St. Ludmila. In addition to being specific historical figures, these characters are also symbolic: The old woman, with closed eyes, stands for the past and memory, while the young boy, with a penetrating stare, represents the hope and future of a nation. Notice how master designer Mucha draws your attention to these two figures through the use of colors—the dark blue on the outside gradually turns into green, then yellow, and finally the gold of the woman and the crimson of the boy in the center. In Mucha's color language, blue stands for the past, gold for the mythic, and red for the future. Besides all the meaning, Mucha's art is simply a joy to behold.

Show your ticket and circulate around the **apse.** You'll pass a carved wood relief of Prague in 1620, depicting the victorious Hapsburg armies entering the castle after the Battle of White Mountain, while the Protestant king Frederic escapes over the Charles Bridge (before it had any statues). The second part of this Counter-Reformation wood relief, on the other side from the altar, captures the "barbaric" Protestant nobles destroying the Catholic icons in the cathedral after the Prague defeat.

A fancy roped-off chapel (right transept) houses the **tomb of St. Wenceslas,** surrounded by precious 14th-century murals showing scenes of his life (see description on page 94), and a locked door leading to the crown jewels. The Czech kings used to be crowned right here in front of the coffin, draped in red.

You can climb 287 steps up the **spire** for one of the best views of the whole city (included in Route A or B ticket, or pay 20 Kč at the cathedral ticket window, April–Oct daily except Sun morning, 9:00–17:00, last entry 16:15, closes at 16:00 in winter).

Back Outside the Cathedral: Leaving the cathedral, turn left (past the public WC). The **obelisk** was erected in 1928—a single piece of granite celebrating the 10th anniversary of the establishment of Czechoslovakia. It was originally much taller, but broke in transit—an inauspicious start for a nation destined to last only 70 years. Up in the fat, green tower of the cathedral is the Czech Republic's biggest bell, nicknamed "Zikmund." In June of 2002, it cracked—and two months later, the worst flood in recorded history hit the city. As a nation sandwiched between great powers, Czechs are

deeply superstitious. Often feeling unable to influence the course of their own history, they helplessly look at events as we might look at the weather and other natural phenomena–trying to figure out what fate has in store for them next.

Find the 14th-century **mosaic** of the Last Judgment outside on the right transept. It was commissioned Italian-style by King Charles IV, who was modern, cosmopolitan, and ahead of his time. Jesus oversees the action, as some go to heaven and some go to hell. The Czech king and queen kneel directly below Jesus and the six patron saints. On coronation day, they would walk under this arch, which would remind them (and their subjects) that even those holding great power are not above God's judgment. The royal crown and national jewels are kept in a chamber (see the grilled windows) above this entryway, which was the cathedral's main entry for centuries when the church was incomplete.

Across the square and 20 yards to the right, a door leads to the...

Old Royal Palace (Starý Královský Palác)—This was the seat of the Bohemian princes starting in the 12th century. While exten-

sively rebuilt, the **large hall** is late Gothic, designed as a multi-purpose hall for the old nobility. It's big enough for jousts—even the staircase was designed to let a mounted soldier gallop in. It was filled with market stalls, giving nobles a chance to shop without actually going into town. In the 1400s, the nobility met here to elect their king. This tradition survived until modern times, as the parliament crowded into this room until the late 1990s to elect the Czechoslovak (and later Czech) president. The last two elections happened in another, far more lavish hall in the castle. Look up at the flower-shaped, vaulted ceiling—much more elaborate than the simple cross ceiling in the cathedral.

On the right, enter the two small Renaissance rooms known as the **"Czech Office."** From these rooms, two governors used to oversee the Czech lands for the Hapsburgs in Vienna. In 1618, angry Czech Protestant nobles poured into these rooms and threw the two Catholic governors out of the window, sparking the Thirty Year's War. This was the second of Prague's many "defenestrations" (see the pictures) a uniquely Czech solution to political discord, where offending politicians are literally tossed out of a window. The two governors landed—fittingly—in a pile of horse manure... so despite the height, they suffered only broken arms.

Look down on the chapel from the end, and go out on the

balcony for a fine Prague view. Is that Paris' Eiffel Tower in the distance? No, it's Petřín Tower—a fine place for a relaxing day at the park, offering sweeping views over Prague (see page 106).

Across from the palace exit is the...

Basilica of St. George (Bazilika Sv. Jiří)—Step into the beautifully lit Basilica of St. George to see Prague's best-preserved Romanesque church. St. Wenceslas' mother, St. Ludmila, was reburied here in 973. The first Bohemian convent was established here near the palace.

Today, the **convent** next door houses the National Gallery's Collection of Old Masters, featuring the best Czech paintings from the Mannerist and Baroque periods (100 Kč, Tue–Sun 10:00–18:00, closed Mon).

Continue walking downhill through the castle grounds. Turn left on the first street, which leads into the...

Golden Lane (Zlatá Ulička)—During the day, this street of old buildings, which originally housed goldsmiths, is jammed with tourists and lined with overpriced gift shops. Franz Kafka lived briefly at #22. There's a deli/bistro at the top and a convenient public WC at the bottom. In the morning and at night, the tiny street is free, empty, and romantic.

Toy and Barbie Museum (Muzeum Hraček)—At the bottom of the castle complex, just after leaving the Golden Lane, a long, wooden staircase leads to two entertaining floors of old toys and dolls thoughtfully described in English. You'll see a century of teddy bears, 19th-century model train sets, and an incredible Barbie collection (the entire top floor). Find the buxom 1959 first edition, and you'll understand why these capitalistic sirens of material discontent weren't allowed here until 1989 (50 Kč, not included in any castle tickets, daily 9:30–17:30).

After Your Castle Visit: Tourists squirt slowly through a fortified door at the bottom end of the castle. From there, you can follow the steep lane directly back to the riverbank (and the Malostranská Metro station).

Or you can take a hard right and stroll through the long, delightful park. Along the way, notice the modernist design of the **Na Valech Garden**, which was carried out by the "court architect" of the 1920s, Jože Plečnik of Slovenia (see page 512).

Halfway through the long park is a viewpoint overlooking **terraced gardens**; you can zigzag down through these gardens into the Little Quarter (120 Kč, April–Oct daily 10:00–18:00, closed Nov–March).

If you continue through the park all the way to Castle Square, you'll find two more options: a staircase leading down into the Little Quarter, or a cobbled street taking you to historic Nerudova street (described on page 105).

ENTERTAINMENT

Prague booms with live and inexpensive theater, classical, jazz, and pop entertainment. Everything's listed in several monthly cultural events programs (free at TI) and in the *Prague Post* newspaper.

You'll be tempted to gather fliers as you wander through the town. Don't bother. To really understand all your options (the street Mozarts are pushing only their concerts), drop by the **Via Musica** box office at Týn Church on the Old Town Square. The event schedule posted on their wall clearly shows everything that's playing today and tomorrow, including tourist concerts, Black Light Theater, and marionette shows, with photos of each venue and a map locating everything (daily 10:00–19:00, tel. 224-826-969).

Ticketpro, at Rytířská 31 (between the Havelská Market and the Estates Theatre), sells tickets for the serious concert venues and most music clubs (daily 8:00–12:00 & 12:30–16:30; also has a booth in the Tourist Center at Rytířská 12, daily 9:00–20:00).

Black Light Theater—A kind of mime/modern dance variety show, Black Light Theater has no language barrier and is, for many, more entertaining than a classical concert. Unique to Prague (though somewhat comparable to the Canadian Cirque du Soleil), Black Light Theater originated in the 1960s as a playful and mystifying theater of the absurd. The two main venues are **Ta Fantastika** (*Aspects of Alice* at 21:30, more poetic, more puppets, traditional, a little artistic nudity, 620 Kč, reserved seating, near east end of Charles Bridge at Karlova 8, tel. 222-221-366, www.tafantastika .cz) and **Image Theatre** (more mime and absurd—"it's precisely the fact that we are all so different that unites us," shows at 18:00 and 20:00, 450 Kč, open seating—arrive early to grab a good spot, just off Old Town Square at Pařížská 4, tel. 222-314-448, www .imagetheatre.cz). Shows last about 90 minutes. Avoid the first four rows, which get you so close that it ruins the illusion. The other black light theaters advertising around town aren't as good.

Tourist Concerts—Each day, six or eight classical concerts designed for tourists fill delightful Old World halls and churches with music of the crowd-pleasing sort: Vivaldi, Best of Mozart, Most Famous Arias, and works by the famous Czech composer Antonín Dvořák. Concerts typically cost 400–1,000 Kč, start anywhere from 13:00 to 21:00, and last one hour. Common venues are two buildings on Little Quarter Square (the Church of

St. Nicholas and the Prague Academy of Music in Liechtenstein Palace); in the Klementinum's Chapel of Mirrors; at the Old Town Square (in a different Church of St. Nicholas); and in the stunning Smetana Hall in the Municipal House (see page 98). The artists vary from excellent to amateur.

A sure bet is the jam session held every Monday at 17:00 at **St. Martin in the Wall**, where Prague's best professional musicians gather to tune in and chat with each other (400 Kč, Martinská Street, just north of Tesco building in the Old Town).

Prague Castle Orchestra–One of Prague's most entertaining acts performs regularly on Castle Square. This trio–Josef on flute, Radek on accordion, and passionate Jarda on bass–plays a lively Czech mélange of Smetana, swing, old folk tunes, and 1920s cabaret songs. Look for them if you're visiting the castle (see page 113) and consider picking up their fun CD. They're also available for private functions (pay them 2,000 Kč apiece for a 45-min performance, mobile 603-552-448, josekocurek@volny.cz).

Serious Concerts–True music-lovers should consider Prague's top symphonic venue, the **Rudolfinum** (featuring the Prague Philharmonic, on Palachovo Náměstí, in Jewish Quarter on the Old Town side of Mánes Bridge). Concerts in the large Dvořák Hall or the small Suk Hall usually start at 19:30 (also afternoons on weekends). The ticket office is on the right side, under the stairs (250–1,000 Kč, open until few minutes before the show starts).

The **National Theatre** (Národní Divadlo, on the New Town side of Legií Bridge)—with a must-see neo Renaissance interior (see page 101)—is best for opera and ballet (shows from 19:00, 300–1,000 Kč, tel. 224-912-673, www.nationaltheatre.cz). The **Estates Theatre** (Stavovské Divadlo) is where Mozart premiered and personally directed many of his most beloved works (see page 89). *Don Giovanni*, *The Marriage of Figaro*, and *The Magic Flute* are on the program a couple of times each month (shows from 20:00, 800–1,400 Kč, between the Old Town Square and the New Town on a square called Ovocný Trh, tel. 224-214-339, www.estatestheatre.cz). The ticket office for both of these theaters is in the little square (Ovocný Trh) behind the Estates Theatre.

The **State Opera** (Státní Opera) focuses on Verdi (shows at 19:00 or 20:00, 400–1,200 Kč, buy tickets at the theater, on 5. Května—the busy street between the Main Train Station and Wenceslas Square, tel. 224-227-693, www.opera.cz).

During his frequent visits to Prague, Mozart stayed with his friends in the beautiful, small, neo-classicist **Villa Bertramka**, now the Mozart Museum. Surrounded by a peaceful garden, the villa preserves the time when the Salzburg prodigy felt more appreciated in Prague than in Austria. Intimate concerts are held some afternoons and evenings, either in the garden or the small concert hall (110 Kč, daily April–Oct 9:30–18:00, Nov–March 9:30–17:00, Mozartova 169, Praha 5; from Metro: Anděl, it's a 10-min walk—head to Hotel Mövenpick and then go up alley behind hotel; tel. 257-317-465, www.bertramka.cz).

World-class musicians are in town during the **Prague Spring** (mid-May through the beginning of June, www.festival.cz) and **Prague Autumn** (mid-Sept through mid-Oct, www.pragueautumn .cz) music festivals.

For any of these concerts, locals dress up, but many tourists wear casual clothes—as long as you don't show up in sneakers and ripped jeans, you'll be fine.

Music Clubs—Young locals keep Prague's many music clubs in business. Most clubs are neighborhood institutions with decades of tradition, generally holding only 100–200 people. You can buy tickets at the club, or, for most places, at the Ticketpro offices (see above). In the Old Town, consider **Roxy,** with live bands and experimental DJs (concerts start at 20:00, disco at 22:00, cover from 100 Kč, Mon free, easy to book online and pick up tickets at the door, a few blocks from Old Town Square at Dlouhá 33, tel. 224-826-296, www.roxy.cz). In the New Town, **Lucerna Music Bar** is popular for disco nights (Fri and Sat are the "1980s Party"). Young and trendy, the Lucerna has cheap prices, and even older tourists mix in easily (music nightly from 21:00, about 100-Kč cover, at the bottom of Wenceslas Square, in the basement of Lucerna Gallery, Vodičkova 36, tel. 224-217-108). Just up Národní street, the small **Reduta Jazz Club** will launch you straight into the 1960s classic jazz scene (live jazz nightly from 21:00, on Národní Street next to Café Louvre). On the Little Quarter Square, the mellow **Malostranská Beseda** was known in the communist era for playing host to underground rock bands; today it's the only club in the center with daily live performances, enjoyed by an older-than-average crowd (shows from 20:30, about 150-Kč cover, Malostranské Náměstí 21, tel. 257-532-092). The hip **Žižkov** neighborhood, below the Žižkov TV tower (Metro: Jiřího z Poděbrad), has Prague's highest concentration of cool pubs. One of the best is Palác Akropolis, which is *the* home of Czech independent music (advance ticket sales at café, Mon–Fri 10:00–24:00, Sat–Sun 16:00–24:00, corner of Kubelíkova and Fibichova, tel. 296-330-913, www.palacakropolis.cz).

SHOPPING

Prague's entire Old Town seems designed to bring out the shopper in visitors. Puppets, glass, and ceramics are traditional. Shop your way from the Old Town Square up Celetná to the Powder Tower, then along Na Příkopě to the bottom of Wenceslas Square.

Celetná is lined with big stores selling all the traditional Czech goodies. Celetná Crystal, about midway down the street, offers the largest selection of affordable crystal. You can get the glass safely shipped home directly from the shop (for purchases of more than 1,000 Kč, you can get a refund of the VAT tax—see page 21).

Na Příkopě has a couple of good modern malls. The best is Slovanský Dům (Na Příkopě 22), where you wander deep past a 10-screen multiplex into a world of classy restaurants and designer shops surrounding a peaceful, parklike inner courtyard. Another modern mall is Černá Růže (Na Příkopě 12). Next door is Mosers, which has a museum-like crystal showroom upstairs.

My readers highly praise **České Kožené Zboží**, a leather store with products exclusively from Czech craftsmen (Mon–Fri 10:00–18:00, Sat 10:00–14:00, closed Sat, Truhlářská 10, from Municipal House go 2 blocks toward the river along Revoluční street and then turn right, mobile 603-787-175).

SLEEPING

Peak time is during the months of April, May, June, September, and October. During Christmas and Easter, the prices are a bit higher still. July and August are not too bad. I've listed peak-time prices. If you're traveling in July or August, you'll find rates generally 15 percent lower, and during November–March, 30 percent lower.

Room-Booking Services

Prague is awash with fancy rooms on the push list; private, small-time operators with rooms to rent in their apartments; and roving agents eager to book you a bed and earn a commission. You can save about 30 percent by showing up in Prague without a reservation and finding accommodations upon arrival. It is, however, a hustle, and you will not necessarily get your choice. If you're driving, you'll see booking agencies as you enter town. Generally, if you book at one of these, your host can come and lead you to their place.

Athos Travel, run by Filip Antoš, will find the right room for you from among 140 properties (ranging from hostels to 5-star hotels), 90 percent of which are in the historical center. To book a room, call them or use their handy Web site, which allows you to search for a room based on various criteria (best to arrange in advance during peak season, can also help with last-minute booking off-season, tel. 241-440-571, fax 241-441-697, www.athos.cz, info@athos.cz).

Sleep Code

(25 Kč = about $1, country code: 420)
S = Single, **D** = Double/Twin, **T** = Triple, **Q** = Quad, **b** = bathroom, **s** = shower only. Unless otherwise noted, credit cards are accepted and breakfast is included. Everyone listed here speaks English.

To help you sort easily through these listings, I've divided the rooms into three categories based on the price for a standard double room with bath:

$$\$\$\$$$ **Higher Priced**—Most rooms 4,000 Kč or more.
  $$\$\$$$ **Moderately Priced**—Most rooms between
                      3,000–4,000 Kč.
    $$\$$$ **Lower Priced**—Most rooms 3,000 Kč or less.

AVE, at the Main Train Station (Hlavní Nádraží), is a less personable but still helpful booking service (daily 6:00–23:00, tel. 251-551-011, fax 251-555-156, www.avetravel.cz, ave@avetravel.cz). With the tracks at your back, walk down to the orange ceiling and past the "Meeting Point" (don't go downstairs)—their office is in the left corner by the exit to the rip-off taxis. AVE has several other offices—at Holešovice Train Station, the airport, Wenceslas Square, and Old Town Square. Their display board shows discounted hotels. They have a slew of hotels and small pensions available ($80/2,000-Kč pension doubles in old center, $40/1,000-Kč doubles a Metro ride away). You can reserve by e-mail (using your credit card as a deposit) or just show up at the office and request a room. Many of AVE's rooms are not very convenient to the center; be clear on the location before you make your choice. They sell taxi vouchers for those who want the convenience of a ride from the station's taxi stand, though they cost double the fair rate.

For a more personal touch, contact Lída at **Magic Praha** for help with accommodations (Spálená 21, 1st floor, tel. & fax 224-931-674, mobile 604-207-225, www.magicpraha.cz, magicpraha@magicpraha.cz; see "Helpful Hints," page 68).

Central Prague

You'll pay a premium to sleep in the heart of romantic old Prague—but many travelers figure it's worth the expense. I've listed my hotels by neighborhood (see "Prague's Four Towns," page 76). All of these listings are in the very central Praha 1 district.

Old Town Hotels and Pensions

You'll pay higher prices to stay in the Old Town, but for many travelers, the convenience is worth the expense. These places are all within a 10-minute walk of the Old Town Square.

$$$ Hotel Central is a sentimental favorite—I stayed there in the communist days. Like the rest of Prague, it's now changing with the times: Its 69 rooms have been renovated, leaving it fresh and bright. It's well-run, and the location—three blocks east of the Old Town Square—is excellent (Sb-3,990 Kč, Db-4,650 Kč, Tb-5,150 Kč, 5 percent discount with cash, ask for a "Rick Steves discount" with your e-mail request in 2006, elevator, Rybná 8, Metro: Náměstí Republiky, tel. 224-812-041, fax 222-328-404, central@orfea.cz).

$$$ Cloister Inn is well located, with 75 modern rooms. The exterior is more concrete than charm—the building used to be shared by a convent and a secret-police prison—but inside, it's newly redone and plenty comfortable (Sb-4,000 Kč, Db-4,200 Kč, Tb-4,700 Kč, elevator, free Internet in lobby, Konviktská 14, tel. 224-211-020, fax 224-210-800, www.cloister-inn.com, cloister@cloister-inn.com).

$$ Hotel Haštal, on a quiet, hidden square in the Old Town, was a popular hotel back in the 1920s. Renovated and re-opened in 2002, it's decorated with Art Nouveau posters that complement the neighborhood's vibrant circa-1900 architecture (Sb-2,900 Kč, Db-3,600 Kč, extra bed-550 Kč, 20 percent discount when booking online, thin walls, Haštalská 16, tel. 222-314-335, www.hastal .com, info@hastal.com). The hotel's small restaurant has excellent beer and food—try the beefsteak with bleu-cheese sauce, or the lunch specials (popular with a local crowd).

$$ Dům u Krále Jiřího (literally, "House by King George") is situated in a 14th-century palace that once belonged to the Hussite king. More rooms are gradually being added, as the owners buy and refurbish more of the surrounding apartments, fitting stylishly furnished rooms into historic spaces. The upper floors have romantic views over the crooked roofs of the Old Town, while some of the lower-floor rooms open into a private courtyard (Sb-1,950 Kč, Db-3,100 Kč, extra bed-1,000 Kč, Liliová 10, tel. 221-466-100, www.kinggeorge.cz).

$$ Pension u Medvídků has 31 comfortably renovated rooms in a big, rustic, medieval shell with dark wood furniture. Upstairs, you'll find lots of beams to smack into (Sb-2,300 Kč, Db-3,500 Kč, Tb-4,500 Kč, extra bed-500 Kč, "historical" rooms 10 percent more, apartment 20 percent more, Internet in lobby, Na Perštýně 7, tel. 224-211-916, fax 224-220-930, www.umedvidku.cz, info@umedvidku.cz). The pension runs a popular beer-hall restaurant that has live music most Fridays and Saturdays until 23:00.

$$ Hotel u Klenotníka, with 11 modern, comfortable rooms in a plain building, is three blocks off the Old Town Square

Hotels in Prague's Old Town

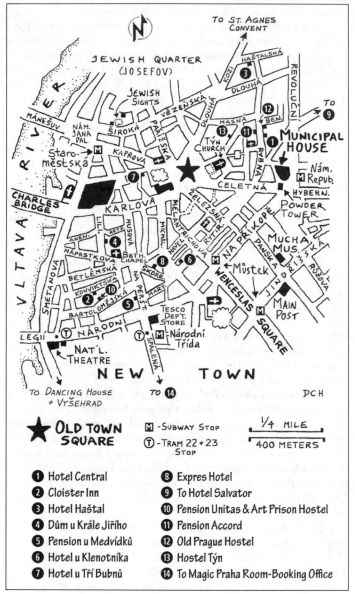

★ OLD TOWN SQUARE

Ⓜ - SUBWAY STOP

Ⓣ - TRAM 22 + 23 STOP

¼ MILE

400 METERS

❶ Hotel Central
❷ Cloister Inn
❸ Hotel Haštal
❹ Dům u Krále Jiřího
❺ Pension u Medvídků
❻ Hotel u Klenotníka
❼ Hotel u Tří Bubnů

❽ Expres Hotel
❾ To Hotel Salvator
❿ Pension Unitas & Art Prison Hostel
⓫ Pension Accord
⓬ Old Prague Hostel
⓭ Hostel Týn
⓮ To Magic Praha Room-Booking Office

(Sb-2,500 Kč, Db-3,300–3,800 Kč, Tb-4,500 Kč, 10 percent off when booking direct with this book in 2006, Rytířská 3, tel. 224-211-699, fax 224-221-025, www.uklenotnika.cz, info@uklenotnika.cz).

$$ Hotel u Tří Bubnů (literally, "Three Drums") fills one of the oldest buildings in town, 50 yards toward the river from the Old Town Square. Its 18 rooms are spacious, with high ceilings and wooden beams (Db-3,900 Kč, extra bed-1,000 Kč, U Radnice 8, tel. 224-214-855, fax 224-236-100, www.utribubnu.cz, utribubnu@volny.cz).

$$ Expres Hotel rents 29 simple rooms and brings a continental breakfast to your room (S-1,000 Kč, Sb-3,000 Kč, D-1,400 Kč, Db-3,200 Kč, Tb-3,600 Kč, 5 percent discount with cash, elevator, Skořepka 5, tel. 224-211-801, fax 224-223-309, www.pragueexpreshotel.cz, info@pragueexpreshotel.cz). While a good value, it's in a red light zone and comes with late-night music from nearby clubs on weekends.

$$ Hotel Salvator rents 30 comfortable rooms on a quiet street above a fun South American restaurant (D-2,100 Kč, Db-3,100 Kč, Qb-4,200 Kč, extra bed-500 Kč, elevator, Truhlářská 10, 3 min from Metro: Náměstí Republiky, tel. 222-312-234, fax 222-316-355, www.salvator.cz, hotel@salvator.cz).

$ Pension Unitas rents 35 small, tidy, youth hostel–type rooms with plain, minimalist furnishings and no sinks (S-1,260 Kč, D-1,580 Kč, T-1,900 Kč, Q-2,200 Kč, T and Q are cramped with bunks in D-sized rooms, easy reservations without a deposit, non-smoking, quiet hours 22:00–7:00, Bartolomějská 9, tel. 224-221-802, fax 224-217-555, www.unitas.cz, unitas@unitas.cz). They run a fine little youth hostel in the former prison downstairs (see "Old Town Hostels," below).

$ Pension Accord, which opened in an apartment building in 2005, offers simple, clean rooms. Since they're new, this place is still figuring things out: Breakfast is served in a nearby restaurant, which doesn't open until 9:00 (as an alternative, eat in the friendly neighborhood bakery shop U Lucerny next door, or ask hotel clerk to have food brought to your room). Still, given the location, the value is unbeatable (Sb-2,200 Kč, Db-2,900 Kč, Tb-3,500 Kč, extra bed-600 Kč, Rybná 9, tel. 222-328-816, fax. 222-324-406, www.accordprague.com, info@accordprague.com).

Old Town Hostels

$ Old Prague Hostel, open since just 2005, is a small and very friendly place on the second and third floors of an apartment building on a back alley near the Powder Tower. The spacious rooms were once apartment bedrooms, so it feels less institutional than most hostels. The TV lounge/breakfast room was once the living room (S-1,180 Kč, D-1,360 Kč, bunk in 3–8-person room-440–530 Kč; includes breakfast, sheets, towels, and lockers; reserve ahead, Benediktská 2, tel. 224-829-058, fax 224-829-060, www.oldpraguehostel.com, oldpraguehostel@seznam.cz).

$ Hostel Týn, hidden in a silent courtyard two blocks from the Old Town Square, is the ultimate find. The management is aware of its value, so they don't bother being too friendly (D-1,100 Kč, T-450 Kč per person, bunk in 4–5-bed room-400 Kč, reserve ahead, Týnská 19, tel. 224-828-519, mobile 776-122-057, www.hostel -tyn.web2001.cz, backpacker@razdva.cz).

$ Art Prison Hostel fills a former prison in the basement of Pension Unitas (see above). With tiny, high windows and no plumbing, the rooms are stark—but not as stark as when Václav Havel did time here (64 beds, S-1,100 Kč, D-1,260 Kč, bunk in 4–5-bed cell-370–510 Kč, includes sheets and breakfast, easy reservations without deposit if arriving by 17:00, no curfew, non-smoking, shared modern facilities, lockers, Bartolomějská 9, tel. 224-221-802, www.unitas.cz, unitas@unitas.cz).

In the New Town, on Wenceslas Square
To locate these hotels, see the map on page 132.

$$$ Hotel Adria, with a prime Wenceslas Square location, cool Art Nouveau facade, and 88 completely modern and business-class rooms, is your big-time, four-star, central splurge (Sb-3,900 Kč, Db-4,650 Kč, these prices only if you reserve online, air-con, elevator, minibars...the works, Václavské Náměstí 26, tel. 221-081-111, fax 221-081-300, www.adria.cz, accom@adria.cz).

$$ Grand Hotel Evropa is in a class by itself. This landmark hotel, famous for its wonderful 1903 Art Nouveau facade, is the centerpiece of Wenceslas Square. But someone pulled the plug on the hotel about 50 years ago, and it's a mess. It offers haunting beauty in all of its public spaces, 92 dreary and ramshackle rooms, and a weary staff. They're waiting for a billion-crown investor to come along and rescue the place, but for now, they offer some of the cheapest rooms on Wenceslas Square (S-1,600 Kč, Sb-3,000 Kč, D-2,600 Kč, Db-4,000 Kč, T-3,100 Kč, Tb-5,000 Kč; some rooms have been very slightly refurbished, some remain in unre-furbished old style, they cost the same either way; every room is different, elevator, Václavské Náměstí 25, tel. 224-228-117, fax 224-224-544, www.evropahotel.cz, info@evropahotel.cz).

In the Little Quarter
$$$ Dům u Velké Boty (literally, "House at the Big Boot"), in front of the German Embassy, is the quintessential family hotel in Prague. Each room is uniquely decorated, most in the taste-ful Biedermeier style of the 19th century (tiny S-1,800 Kč, two D rooms that share a bathroom-3,000 Kč each, Db-4,160 Kč,

Hotels and Restaurants in the Little Quarter

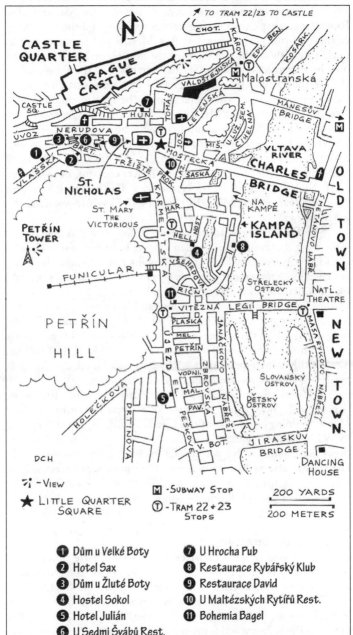

- ① Dům u Velké Boty
- ② Hotel Sax
- ③ Dům u Žluté Boty
- ④ Hostel Sokol
- ⑤ Hotel Julián
- ⑥ U Sedmi Švábů Rest.
- ⑦ U Hrocha Pub
- ⑧ Restaurace Rybářský Klub
- ⑨ Restaurace David
- ⑩ U Maltézských Rytířů Rest.
- ⑪ Bohemia Bagel

extra bed-500 Kč, lavish breakfast-200 Kč extra, Vlašská 30, tel. 257-532-088, www.dumuvelkeboty.cz). The owners, Mr. and Mrs. Rippl, treat every one of their guests as a friend, and the wellspring of their stories never runs dry. Ask Mrs. Rippl about her great uncle (the bishop who once owned the house), or Mr. Rippl about how he served soup to East Germans arriving in the thousands at the German Embassy in October 1989 to obtain exit visas out of the Communist Bloc. There's no sign on the house—find it by the splendid geraniums that Mr. Rippl nurtures in the windows.

$$$ Hotel Sax, on a quiet corner a block below the Little Quarter action, will delight the artsy yuppie with its 22 rooms, fruity atrium, and modern, stylish decor (Sb-4,100 Kč, Db-4,400 Kč, Db suite-5,100 Kč, extra bed-1,000 Kč, elevator, near Church of St. Nicholas, 1 block below Nerudova at Jánský Vršek 3, reserve long in advance, tel. 257-531-268, fax 257-534-101, www.sax.cz, hotel@sax.cz).

$$$ Dům u Žluté Boty (literally, "House at the Yellow Boot") is the most charming small hotel in Prague, hiding on a small lane in the Little Quarter. Each of its seven rooms has a completely different feel: Some preserve the 16th-century wooden ceilings, some feel like mountain lodges, and others are a bit marred by an insensitive 1970s adaptation. The manager's husband is a distinguished artist whose paintings (for sale) embellish the dining room and halls. The only drawback of this hotel is its thin walls—you'll know exactly what your neighbors are arguing about (Sb-3,800 Kč, Db-4,300 Kč, Tb-5,000 Kč, extra bed-900 Kč, Jánský Vršek 11, tel. 257-532-269, fax 257-534-134, www.zlutabota.cz, hotel@zlutabota.cz).

$ Hostel Sokol, plain and institutional, with 100 beds, is peacefully located just off parklike Kampa Island in the Tryš House buildings (the seat of the Czech Sokol Organization). Big WWI hospital–style rooms are lined with single beds and lockers (8–14 per room, 350 Kč per bed, D-900 Kč, cash only, no breakfast, easy to reserve by phone or e-mail without deposit, open 24/7, members' kitchen, Nosticova 2, tel. 257-007-397, fax 257-007-340, hostel@sokol-cos.cz). From the Main Train Station, ride tram #9 to Újezd. From the Holešovice station, take tram #12 to Újezd.

In the Castle Quarter

$$$ Residence Domus Henrici, just above Castle Square, is a quiet retreat that charges—and gets—top prices for its eight smartly appointed rooms, some of which include good views (Ds-5,100 Kč, Db-5,600–6,200 Kč depending on size, extra bed-900 Kč, less off-season, pleasant terrace, Loretánská 11, tel. 220-511-369, fax 220-511-502, www.domus-henrici.cz, henrici@hidden-places .com). This is a five-minute walk above the castle gate in a quiet, elegant area.

Away from the Center

Moving just outside central Prague saves you money—and gets you away from the tourists and into some more workaday residential neighborhoods. The following listings (great values compared to the downtown hotels listed above) are all within a five- to 15-minute tram or Metro ride from the center.

Beyond Wenceslas Square

These hotels are in urban neighborhoods on the outer fringe of the New Town, northeast of Wenceslas Square, but still within several minutes' walk of the sightseeing zone.

$$$ Hotel Sieber, with 20 rooms, is a quality, four-star, business-class hotel in an upscale residential neighborhood near the former royal vineyards (Vinohrady). They do a good job of being homey and welcoming (Sb-4,480 Kč, Db-4,780 Kč, extra bed-990 Kč, 4th night free, 30 percent discount for last-minute reservations, air-con, elevator, 3-min walk to Metro: Jiřího z Poděbrad, or tram #11, Slezská 55, Praha 3, tel. 224-250-025, fax 224-250-027, www.sieber.cz, reservations@sieber.cz).

$$ Hotel Anna, with 24 bright, pastel, and classically charming rooms, is a bit closer in—just 10 minutes by foot east of Wenceslas Square (Sb-2,400 Kč, Db-3,300 Kč, Tb-4,000 Kč, non-smoking rooms, elevator, Budečská 17, Praha 2, Metro: Náměstí Míru, tel. 222-513-111, fax 222-515-158, www.hotelanna .cz, reception@hotelanna.cz). The hotel runs a cheaper but similarly pleasant annex, the Dependence, two blocks away (Sb-1,860 Kč, Db-2,560 Kč, no elevator but all rooms on the 1st floor, reception and breakfast at main hotel).

$$ Hotel Luník, with 35 rooms, is dignified and no-nonsense, but friendly. It's out of the medieval faux-rustic world in a normal, pleasant business district. It's two Metro stops from the Main Train Station (Metro: I. P. Pavlova) or a 10-minute walk south of Wenceslas Square (Sb-2,400 Kč, Db-3,300 Kč, Tb-3,800 Kč, extra bed-500 Kč, 10 percent discount if you reserve online, some street noise, elevator, Londýnská 50, Praha 2, tel. 224-253-974, fax 224-253-986, www.hotel-lunik.cz, recepce@hotel-lunik.cz).

$$ Hotel 16, a stately little place with an intriguing Art Nouveau façade, high ceilings, and a clean, sleek interior, rents 14 fine rooms (Sb-2,600 Kč, Db-3,500 Kč, Db suite-4,000 Kč, Tb-4,700 Kč, back/quiet rooms face the garden, front/noisier rooms face the street, air-con, elevator, 10-min walk south of Wenceslas Square, Metro: I. P. Pavlova, Kateřinská 16, Praha 2, tel. 224-920-636, fax 224-920-626, www.hotel16.cz, hotel16@hotel16.cz).

$ Hostel Elf is close to the Main Train Station and Florenc bus station (a 10-min walk from each). It's fun-loving, ramshackle, and covered with noisy, self-inflicted graffiti. They offer cheap,

Hotels and Restaurants in the New Town

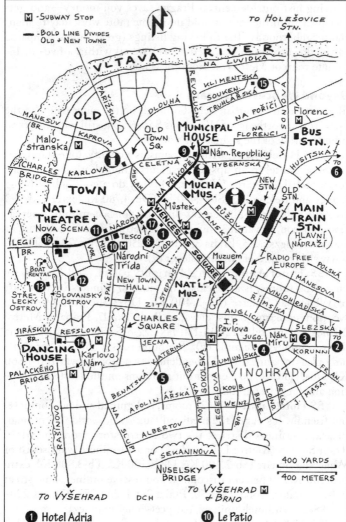

1 Hotel Adria
2 To Hotel Sieber
3 Hotel Anna
4 Hotel Luník
5 Hotel 16
6 To Hostel Elf
7 Grand Hotel Evropa
8 Restaurace u Pinkasů
9 Kavárna Obecní Dům, Francouzská
    Rest. & Plzeňská Rest.
10 Le Patio
11 Čínská Rest. Lee's Garden
12 Hospoda u Nováka
13 Restaurant Žofín
14 La Perle de Prague
15 Rest. Club Des Vins
    Červená Tabulka
16 Grand Café Slavia
17 Dobrá Čajovna Teahouse &
    Šenk Vrbovec Wine Bar

basic beds, a helpful staff, and lots of creative services—kitchen, free luggage room, laundry, no lockout, free tea, cheap beer, a terrace, and lockers (dorm beds-260–340 Kč, D-820 Kč, includes sheets and breakfast, Husitská 11, Praha 3, tel. 222-540-963, www .hostelelf.com, info@hostelelf.com).

South of the Charles Bridge, near the Vltava River

These hotels are listed from north to south.

$$ Hotel Julián, an oasis of professional, predictable decency in a quiet, untouristy neighborhood, is just south of the Little Quarter on the castle side of the river. Its 32 spacious, fresh, well-furnished rooms and big, homey public spaces hide behind a noble neoclassical facade. The staff is friendly and helpful (Sb-3,680 Kč, Db-3,980 Kč, Db suite-4,800 Kč, extra bed-900 Kč, discount for booking online, 5 percent discount off best quoted rate with this book in 2006, free tea and coffee in room, elevator, Internet in lobby, parking lot, Elišky Peškové 11, Praha 5, reservation tel. 257-311-150, reception tel. 257-311-145, fax 257-311-149, www.julian.cz, casjul@vol.cz). Free lockers and a shower are available for those needing to check out early but stay until late (e.g., for an overnight train). Mike's Chauffeur Service, based here, is reliable and affordable (see page 145).

$ Dům u Šemíka, a friendly hotel named for a heroic mythical horse, offers 25 rooms in a residential neighborhood just below Vyšehrad Castle, a 10-minute tram ride south of the Old Town (Sb 2,150 Kč, Db 2,700 Kč, apartment 2,950–5,300 Kč depending on size, extra bed-790 Kč; from the center, take tram #18 to Albertov, then walk 2 blocks uphill; or take tram #7 to Výtoň, go under rail bridge, and walk 3 blocks uphill to Vratislavova 36; Praha 2, tel. 224-920-736, fax 224-911-602, www.usemika.cz, usemika@usemika.cz).

$ Guest House Lída, with 12 homey and spacious rooms, fills a big house in a quiet residential area farther inland, a 15-minute tram ride from the center. Jan and Jiří Prouza, who run the place, are a wealth of information and know how to make people feel at home (Sb-1,380 Kč, small Db-1,440 Kč, Db-1,760 Kč, Tb-2,110 Kč, cash only, family rooms, top-floor family suite with kitchenette, garage parking-200 Kč/day, Metro: Pražského Povstání; exit Metro and turn left on Lomnicka between the Metro station and big blue-glass ČSOB building, follow Lomnicka for 500 yards, then turn left on Lopatecka, go uphill and ring bell at Lopatecká #26, no sign outside; Praha 4, tel. & fax 261-214-766, http://sweb. cz/pensionlida, lidabb@seznam.cz). The Prouza brothers also rent four apartments across the river, equally far away (Db-1,500 Kč, Tb-1,920 Kč, Qb-2,100 Kč).

EATING

A big part of Prague's charm is found in wandering aimlessly through the city's winding old quarters, marveling at the architecture, watching the people, and sniffing out fun restaurants. You can eat well here for very little money. What you'd pay for a basic meal in Vienna or Munich will get you a feast in Prague. In addition to meat-and-potatoes Czech cuisine (see "Czech Food," page 55), you'll find trendy, student-oriented bars and lots of fine ethnic eateries. For ambience, the options include traditional, dark Czech beer halls; elegant Art Nouveau dining rooms; or hip and modern.

Watch out for scams. Many restaurants put more care into ripping off green tourists (and even locals) than in their cooking. Tourists are routinely served cheaper meals than what they ordered, given a menu with a "personalized" price list, charged extra for things they didn't get, or shortchanged. Be wary of waiters padding the tab. Avoid any menu without clear and explicit prices. Speak Czech. Even saying "Hello" in Czech (see phrases on page 59) will get you better service. Carefully examine your itemized bill and understand each line (a 10 percent service charge is sometimes added—in that case, there's no need to tip extra). Tax is always included in the price, so it shouldn't be tacked on later. Part with very large bills only if necessary, and deliberately count your change. Never let your credit card out of your sight. Make it a habit to get cash from an ATM to pay for your meals—you will make waiters infinitely happier. Remember, there are two parallel worlds in Prague: the tourist town and the real city. Generally, if you walk two minutes away from the tourist flow, you'll find better value, ambience, and service.

I've listed these eateries by neighborhood (see "Prague's Four Towns," page 76). The most options—and highest prices—are in the Old Town. If you want a memorable splurge, see "Dining with Style" on page 140. For a light meal, consider one of Prague's many memorable cafés (see "Cafés in the Old Town" on page 144).

In the Old Town

With the inevitable closing of cheap student pubs (replaced by shops and hotels that make more money), it's getting difficult to find a truly Czech pub in the historic city center. Most Czechs no longer go to "traditional" eateries, preferring the cosmopolitan taste of the world to the mundane taste of sauerkraut.

To meet Czechs, head to a trendy bar in the Old Town (see page 137), the New Town (page 139), or in Žižkov and Vinohrady (see page 143).

Prague Restaurants

★ **OLD TOWN SQUARE**

Ⓜ - SUBWAY STOP

Ⓣ - TRAM 22 & 23 STOP

¼ MILE / 400 METERS

❶ Plzeňská Rest. u Dvou Koček
❷ Restaurace u Provaznice
❸ U Medvídků Beerhall
❹ Česká Kuchyně
❺ Havelská Market
❻ Restaurace Mlejnice
❼ Country Life Vegetarian Rest.
❽ Kozička Bar
❾ Klub Architektů
❿ Restaurace u Betlémské Kaple
⓫ Beas Rest.

⓬ Dahab
⓭ Molly Malone's Irish Pub
⓮ Restaurant u Prince Terrace
⓯ Orange Moon
⓰ U Zlatého Tygra Pub
⓱ Grand Café Slavia
⓲ Grand Café Orient
⓳ Café Montmartre
⓴ Ebel Coffee House
㉑ Bohemia Bagel

Characteristically Czech Places

Ancient institutions with "authentic" Czech ambience have become touristy—but they're still great fun and a good value.

Plzeňská Restaurace u Dvou Koček (literally, "By the Two Cats") is a typical Czech pub with cheap, no-nonsense, hearty Czech food and beer, and—once upon a time—a local crowd. Sandwiched between the two red light district streets, the restaurant has a name that's a bit ambiguous (200 Kč for 3 courses and beer, serving original Pilsner Urquell with accordion music nightly until 23:00, under an arcade, facing a tiny square between Perlová and Skořepka Streets).

Restaurace u Pinkasů, with a menu that reads like a 19th-century newspaper, is a Prague institution (founded in 1843). Recent renovation has added convenience to past glory, while tactfully preserving traditional spaces. In the summer, sit in the garden behind the building in the shade of the Gothic arches of the St. Mary of the Snows Church. The cellar, spanned by Renaissance vaults, prepares excellent smoked meats (restaurant—daily 9:00–24:00, cellar—16:00–4:00 in the morning, tucked in a courtyard near the bottom of Wenceslas Square, on border between Old and New Towns, see location on map on page 132, Jungmannovo Náměstí 16, tel. 221-111-150).

Restaurace u Provaznice (literally, "By the Ropemaker's Wife") has all the Czech classics peppered with the story of a once-upon-a-time-faithful wife. (Check the menu for details of the gory story.) Natives congregate here for the best "pig leg" in town (daily 11:00–24:00, a block into the Old Town from the bottom of Wenceslas Square at Provaznická 3, tel. 224-232-528).

U Medvídků, which started out as a brewery in 1466, is now a flagship beerhall of the Czech Budweiser. The ambience of the one large room is bright, noisy, and a bit smoky (daily 11:30–23:00, a block toward Wenceslas Square from Bethlehem Square at Na Perštýně 7, tel. 224-211-916). The small beer bar next to the restaurant (daily 16:00–3:00 in the morning) is used by university students during emergencies—such as after most other pubs have closed.

Česká Kuchyně (literally, "Czech Kitchen") is a blue-collar cafeteria serving steamy old Czech cuisine to a local clientele. There's no English inside, so—if you want apple charlotte, but not tripe soup—be sure to review the small English menu in the window outside before entering. Note the numbers of the dishes you'd like that correspond to the Czech menu you'll see inside. Pick up your tally sheet as you enter, grab a tray, point liberally to whatever you'd like, and keep the paper to pay as you exit. It's extremely cheap...unless you lose your paper (daily 9:00–20:00, across from Havelská Market at Havelská 23, tel. 224-235-574).

Havelská Market, surrounded by colorful little eateries, offers picnic fixings (see page 82).

Hip Restaurants and Bars

Restaurace Mlejnice is a fun little pub strewn with farm implements and happy eaters, tucked away just out of the tourist crush two blocks from the Old Town Square (order carefully and understand your itemized bill, daily 11:00–24:00, between Melantrichova and Železná at Kožná 14, reservations smart in evening, tel. 224-228-635).

Country Life Vegetarian Restaurant is a bright, easy, non-smoking cafeteria with a well-displayed buffet of salads and hot veggie dishes. It's midway between the Old Town Square and the bottom of Wenceslas Square. They're serious about their vegetarianism, serving only plant-based, unprocessed, and unrefined food (Mon–Thu 8:30–19:00, Fri 8:30–18:00, Sun 11:00–18:00, closed Sat, through courtyard at Melantrichova 15/Michalská 18, tel. 224-213-366).

Kozička Bar, hiding in a brick-walled modern cellar, is popular with local yuppies drawn here by the Krušovice beer and late opening hours. They also have good food that ranges from Czech beef tongue to pasta and exotic fish (Mon–Fri 12:00–4:00 in the morning, Sat 18:00–4:00 in the morning, Sun 18:00–3:00 in the morning, Kozí 1, tel. 224-818-308).

On Bethlehem Square (Betlémské Náměstí): **Klub Architektů** is a modern student hangout with a medieval cellar serving cheap vegetarian meals, hearty salads, and a few "gourmet entrées" next to Bethlehem Chapel (daily, Betlémské Náměstí 169, tel. 224-401-214). **Restaurace u Betlémské Kaple**, on the other side of the chapel, has light wooden decor, a cheap lunch menu, and fish specialties that attract natives and visitors in search of a good Czech bite for Czech prices (daily 11:00–23:00, Betlémské Náměstí 2, tel. 222-221-639).

Ethnic Eateries on or near Dlouhá Street

Dlouhá, the wide street leading away from the Old Town Square behind the Jan Hus monument (left of Týn Church), is lined with ethnic restaurants catering mostly to local yuppies. Within the space of a couple of blocks, you can eat your way around the world. These places are all within a few steps of Dlouhá street.

Beas is a cheap vegetarian restaurant ruled by a Punjabi chef who concocts bland *thalis* (mixed platters) in the style of North Indian plains and *dosas* of the south Indian variety. Tucked away in a courtyard behind the Týn Church, this place is popular with university students (Mon–Sat 9:30–20:00, Sun 10:00–18:00, Týnská 19).

Orange Moon specializes in Thai curries, but you'll also find dishes from Burma and India served in a space delightfully decorated with artwork from Southeast Asia. This restaurant attracts a mixture of locals, expats, and occasionally tourists (daily 11:30–23:30, reservations recommended, Rámová 5, tel. 222-325-119).

Dahab has a cheap Moroccan buffet in the front, and a dim hall with metal chandeliers and comfy chairs in the back. This popular hang-out specializes in couscous, teas, and Turkish coffee. Try their goat cheese, chicken couscous, and the "Moroccan whisky" mint tea. There's belly dancing every Friday night (daily 12:00–24:00, Dlouhá 33, tel. 224-827-375).

Dining with an Old Town Square View

Restaurant u Prince Terrace, in the five-star U Prince Hotel facing the Astronomical Clock, is designed for foreign tourists. A sleek elevator takes you to its rooftop, where every possible inch is used to serve good food (fish, Czech, and international) to its guests. The view is arguably the best in town—especially at sunset, when a reservation is smart. The menu is a fun but overpriced mix, with photos to make ordering easy (daily until 24:00, brusque staff, Staroměstské Náměstí 29, tel. 224-213-807).

In the Jewish Quarter

To locate the first two eateries, see the map on page 86.

Kolkovna is big and woody, yet modern, serving a fun mix of Czech and international cuisine—ribs, salads, cheese plates, and good beer (daily 11:00–24:00, across from Spanish Synagogue at V Kolkovně 8, tel. 224-819-701, www.kolkovna.cz). Kolkovna is now a chain, with branches on Republic Square (Restaurant Celnice, daily 11:00–2:00 in the morning, near Náměstí Republiky at V Celnici 4), and near the castle, at the viewpoint by Strahov Monastery (Restaurant Bellavista, daily 10:00–24:00, Strahovské Nádvoří 1).

Franz Kafka Café is a handy spot to break up a demanding tour of the Jewish Quarter with a snack or drink (daily 10:00–21:00, a block from the cemetery at Široká 12).

Molly Malone's Irish Pub has been the expat and local favorite for Guinness ever since the Velvet Revolution enabled the Celts to return to one of their homelands. Worn wooden floors, dingy walls, and the Irish manager transport you right into the heart of blue-collar Dublin (which is, after all, a popular place for young Czechs to find jobs in the high-tech industry). Hidden in a forgotten corner of the Jewish Quarter, Molly Malone's is a destination for those who have adopted Prague, and are not just passing through (Sun–Thu 11:00–1:00 in the morning, Fri–Sat 11:00–2:00 in the morning, U Obecního Dvora 4, tel. 224-818-851). There's another, less local-feeling location opposite the Irish and American embassies in the Little Quarter (Tržiště 4).

In the New Town
Art Nouveau Splendor in the Municipal House
For locations, see the map on page 132.

The **Municipal House** (Obecní Dům), the sumptuous Art Nouveau concert hall, has three special restaurants: a café, a French restaurant, and a beer cellar (Náměstí Republiky 5). The dressy café, **Kavárna Obecní Dům,** is drenched in chandeliered, Art Nouveau elegance (light, pricey meals and drinks with great atmosphere and bad service, 250-Kč hot meal special daily, open daily 7:30–23:00, live piano or jazz trio 16:00–20:00, tel. 222-002-763). **Francouzská Restaurace,** the fine and formal French restaurant, is in the next wing (700- to 1,000-Kč meals, daily 12:00–16:00 & 18:00–23:00, tel. 222-002-777). **Plzeňská Restaurace,** downstairs, brags it's the most beautiful Art Nouveau pub in Europe (cheap meals, great atmosphere, daily 11:30–23:00, tel. 222-002-780).

Trendy Eateries on or near Národní Třída
Along Národní Třída, the street linking Wenceslas Square with the National Theatre and the Vltava River, you'll find fun, memorable restaurants. For locations, see the map on page 132.

At **Le Patio,** the first thing you'll notice are the many lanterns suspended from the ceiling—and the big ship moored out back (okay, just its hulking facade). Le Patio has a hip, continental feel to it, but for a place that also sells furniture (head straight back and down the stairs), they definitely need comfier dining chairs. The food is French with some Czech highlights, and actually worth the high prices you'll pay. Plunk down 150 Kč for some freshly squeezed juice that will send a shiver down your tongue. The atmosphere is as pleasant and carefully designed as the dishes (daily 8:00–23:00, Národní 22, tel. 224-934-375). There's another location in the Old Town, at Haštalská 18 (tel. 224-819-767).

Čínská Restaurace Lee's Garden combines red carpet, darkwood furniture, and excellent food into the best Chinese value in the area. With prices at traditional Czech eateries shooting up due to tourist demand, once-upon-a-time exotic and expensive Chinese food is becoming the thrifty local's favorite. They also sell swords, knives, and sport guns on the first floor (daily 10:30–22:30, on 2nd floor above Chinese shop at Národní 23, tel. 224-221-888).

Hospoda u Nováka, behind the Nová Scéna (the glass annex next door to the National Theatre), takes the treatment of its "patients" seriously—notice the regulars' beer taps filed into the wooden case to the right of the door as "medication taken" reports. A red-and-white sign above the bar (reading "Border area, entry strictly prohibited") is reminiscent of the 1980s, when these plac-ards, spaced every 20 yards, lined the Czech barbed-wire side of the Iron Curtain. Nostalgic of the communist era, in which pubs were close-knit communities where regulars escaped from the depression of daily life, U Nováka is a bright and smoky paradise where you can happily curse whatever regime you happen to live under—just like the natives have always done. The waiter will eventually bring the English menu that consists of well-executed Czech classics, but doesn't list the cheap daily specials (daily 10:00–23:00, V Jirchářích 2, tel. 224-930-639).

Dining with Style

In Prague, a fancy candlelit dinner with fine wines and connois-seur dishes costs more than most locals can afford—but it's still a bargain in comparison to similar restaurants in Paris or Dallas. Even here, they're willing to accept credit cards, but prefer cash. Remember that ATMs are everywhere. My first two listings are south of the sightseeing action; the last one is tucked away north-east of the Old Town. For locations, see the map on page 132.

Restaurant Žofín is a Prague institution, taking you back to the era of waltzing elegance. Nicknamed for Franz Josef's mother, Sofia, it shares a circa-1880 palace with a famous ballroom on a small island south of Charles Bridge (mostly traditional 3-course *menus* range from simple/310 Kč to gourmet/990 Kč, huge and reasonable wine list, plain garden tables or sumptuous reserve-in-advance indoor tables, Slovanský Island, reach island by bridge south of National Theatre, tel. 224-934-548).

La Perle de Prague fills the seventh and eighth floors of Frank Gehry's wild and modern Dancing House building with Prague's high society and top-end visitors enjoying a fine river view and gourmet French cuisine. It's white-tablecloth dressy, and offers terrace seating in good weather. While few tables are actually by the window, be sure to enjoy a pre-dinner drink or sip your last glass of wine upstairs, next to Fred Astaire's wire-mesh head, on the roof terrace (500-Kč business lunch, 900-Kč dinner *menu*, daily 12:00–14:00 & 19:00–22:30, reservations required to even get in the elevator, 15-min walk south of Charles Bridge, Tancící Dům, Rašínovo Nábřeží 80, tel. 221-984-160, www.laperle.cz).

Restaurant Club Des Vins Červená Tabulka (literally, "Red Chalkboard") is in a low, beautifully reconstructed town house in a quiet neighborhood that exists outside of the tourist circus. Sit indoors, next to a 1930s motorcycle, or outdoors, in a court-yard under a wooden staircase and balcony. The delicate dishes, served on ironed tablecloths, cater to Prague's yuppies. The wines are excellent and great value (daily 11:30–23:00; from Municipal House, go up Revoluční and turn right on Truhlářská, which you'll follow to Petrské Náměstí—restaurant is up the street across the square at Lodecká 4; tel. 224-810-401).

In the Little Quarter

These characteristic eateries are handy for a bite before or after your Prague Castle visit. My first three listings are nicely affordable; the last two are splurges. For locations, see the map on page 129.

U Sedmi Švábů (literally, "By the Seven Roaches") is a cool medieval den a world apart from the tacky theme restaurants around town. Since America was not yet discovered in the Middle Ages, you won't find any corn, potatoes, or tomatoes on the menu. The salty yellow things that come with the Krušovice beer are chickpeas. Carnivores thrive here: Try the skewered meats *(špíz u Sedmi Švábů)*, flaming beef *(flambák)*, or pork knuckle (daily 11:00–23:00, Janský Vršek 14, tel. 257-531-455).

U Hrocha (literally, "By the Hippo"), a very authentic little pub packed with beer-drinkers and smoke, serves simple, traditional meals—basically meat starters with bread. Just below the castle near Little Quarter Square, it's actually the haunt of many members of Parliament—located just around the corner (daily 12:00–23:00, chalkboard lists daily meals in English, Thunovská 10).

Restaurace Rybářský Klub, on Kampa Island, is run by the Society of Czech Fishermen and serves the widest and tastiest selection of freshwater fish in Prague at reasonable prices. Dine on fish cream soup, pike, trout, carp, or catfish under the imaginative artwork of Little Quarter painter Mr. Kuba (3-course meal for around 300 Kč, daily 12:00–23:00, U Sovových Mlýnů 1, tel. 257-534-200).

Restaurace David, with two little 18th-century rooms hiding on a small cobblestone street opposite the American Embassy in the Little Quarter, is the best place in town for an elegant meal. The exquisite cuisine—a mix of Czech and European styles, ranging from game to roasted duck and liver—is served in the most artistic of arrangements, and the waiters move around with the grace of the 19th century (most meals 600–1,000 Kč, open daily, reservations highly recommended, Tržiště 21, tel. 257-533-109).

U Maltézských Rytířů (literally, "By the Maltese Knights"— named after the nearby church and monastery) dates back a millennium...and the cavernous basement sure smells like it. But the cuisine is top-notch, whether pheasant or fish, and for 500 Kč you'll get a full meal to round out your midsection. If you're into history, you'll also like the wall tapestries and ancient iconography relating to knightly orders of ages past. The candlelit non-smoking section down below (way below) can be romantic, but avoid it if you're very claustrophobic (daily 13:00–23:00, Prokopská 10, tel. 257-530-075, www.umaltezskychrytiru.cz).

In the Castle Quarter

To locate the following restaurants, see the map on page 107.

Klášterní Pivovar (literally, "Monastery Brewery") was founded by an abbot in 1628. The brewery closed down in 1907, but it finally re-opened in 2004 after meticulous restoration in two large rooms and a pleasant courtyard. The wooden decor and circa-1900 newspaper clippings (including Hapsburg emperor Franz Josef's "Proclamation to My Nations," announcing the beginning of the First World War), bring you to the heart of best in Czech pub dining. Beer cheese served on toasted black-yeast bread is a must starter for any meal here. Both locally brewed beer and Czech Budweiser flows through the piping (daily 10:00–22:00, Strahovské Nádvoří 301, tel. 233-353-155, www.klasterni-pivovar.cz). It's directly across from the entrance to the Strahov library (not to be confused with the enormous, group-oriented Klášterní Restaurace next door).

Restaurace Nad Úvozem is hidden in the middle of a staircase that connects Loretánská and Úvoz streets. This secret spot, which boasts super views of Petřín Hill and the Little Quarter, offers excellent food for surprisingly low prices given its location. Try the roast beef in plum sauce. The service is slower when the restaurant is full, as the kitchen has limited space (daily 12:00–21:00; as you go down Loretánská watch for pans, scoops, and spoons hanging on chains on your right at #15; tel. 220-511-532). To discourage pub-goers from mingling with diners, the beer here is terribly overpriced (69 Kč). Instead, have a Kozel (traditional "goat" brand with excellent darks) before or after lunch in the dingy pub called **U Černého Vola** (literally, "By the Black Ox"), located two houses above the staircase (no sign outside, sniff for cigarette smoke and look for the only house on the block without an arcade, daily 10:00–22:00, no English menu).

Malý Buddha (literally, "Little Buddha") serves delightful food—especially vegetarian—and takes its theme seriously. You'll step into a mellow, low-lit escape of bamboo and peace to be served by people with perfect complexions and almost no pulse (Tue–Sun 13:00–22:30, closed Mon, non-smoking, between the castle and Strahov Monastery at Úvoz 46, tel. 220-513-894).

Cafés near the Castle: **Espresso Kajetánka,** just off Castle Square, is the best place to finish up a castle visit. To escape the sun and the bustle of tour groups, go down the staircase to the outside seating in a serene garden, or inside the bird room (all kinds of flying species painted on the walls). The views from below are as good as from the benches on top. The restroom is in the basement, 70 seventy winding steps below the level of the Castle Square (daily 10:00–20:00, Ke Hradu, tel. 257-533-735). **Na Baště Café**, more convenient but not as scenic, is in a garden through the gate to the left of the main castle entry. The outdoor seating, among Jože

Plečnik's ramparts and obelisks, is the castle at its most peaceful.

Rubbing Elbows with Hip Locals
Away from the Center, in Vinohrady and Žižkov

Café Medúza (literally, "Jellyfish"), an authentic between-the-world-wars café with plush sofas and pictures of 1930s movie stars, draws a crowd of dreamy young Czechs enjoying coffee, cigarettes, dark Svijany beer, and cheap lunch specials (Mon–Fri 11:00–1:00 in the morning, Sat–Sun 12:00–1:00 in the morning, Belgická 17, Metro: Náměstí Míru; from Metro stop, walk a bit down and look for Belgická on your left; tel. 222-515-107).

At **Hlučná Samota** (literally, "Too Loud a Solitude"), the wooden floor and brick walls are dedicated to the great Czech writer Bohumil Hrabal. Though he never visited here, Hrabal would surely be delighted by some of the most beautiful wait-resses in Prague, as well as the rich mix of Czech and Italian cuisine (including honey duck, spinach salmon, and Prague's own Staropramen beer to wash it all down). An outdoor lunch—under the shade of linden trees on a quiet, circa-1900 Zagreb Street—can easily stretch into an all-afternoon affair (daily 11:00–23:00, Záhřebská 14, tel. 222-522-839, www.hlucnasamota.cz).

Restaurace u Sadu, on Škroupa square below the Žižkov TV Tower, is popular with young Czechs in the summer. An outdoor lunch on this quiet square under a futuristic monument must be one of the most atmospheric eating options in Prague (daily 10:00–2:00 in the morning, Škroupovo Náměstí 5, tel. 222-727-072). The restaurant up in the TV tower itself is expensive, but gives you Neil Armstrong's perspective on Prague.

Hospůdka nad Viktorkou, named for this neighborhood's soccer team, is around the corner on Bořivojova Street. This quint-essential blue-collar Žižkov pub features occasional live perfor-mances by local bands, a warm glass terrace in the winter, and a little courtyard with a shady canopy of chestnut trees in the sum-mer. Sipping a beer while chatting with the natives in this purest of Prague institutions, you'll feel like you've really found the true Prague (daily 12:00–24:00, Bořivojova 79, tel. 222-722-557).

Drinks
Beer

For many, *pivo* (beer) is the top Czech tourist attraction. Two classic pubs for enjoying a Pilsner are **U Zlatého Tygra** (literally, "By the Golden Tiger"), just south of Karlova on Husova (daily 15:00–23:00, often jam-packed) and **Hostinec u Pinkasů** (open daily), in the dead-end alley just off the bottom of Wenceslas Square. While you're sipping your brew, read the "Czech Beer" sidebar on page 56.

Cafés in the Old Town

These places—dripping with history—are as much about the ambience as they are about the coffee. Most cafés also serve sweets and light meals.

Grand Café Slavia, across from the National Theatre (facing the Legií Bridge on Národní street), is a fixture in Prague, famous as a hangout for its literary elite. Today, it's a bit tired, with an Art Deco interior, lousy piano entertainment, and celebrity photos on the wall. But its cheap and fun menu, filled with interesting traditional dishes (meals, sweets, coffees, liqueurs—including absinthe for 55 Kč), make it a fun stop (daily 8:00–23:00, sit nearest the river). Notice the *Drinker of Absinthe* painting on the wall (and on the menu)—with the iconic Czech writer struggling with reality.

Grand Café Orient, upstairs in the Black Madonna House (which also houses the Museum of Czech Cubism—see page 88), opened in 2005 after major renovations. With Cubist decor toned to dark green, this stylish space full of air and light is a surprisingly good value, with prices pitched to the local's pocket (Mon–Fri 9:00–22:00, Sat–Sun 10:00–22:00, Ovocný Trh 19—at the corner of Celetná near the Powder Tower, tel. 224-224-240).

Café Montmartre, on a small street parallel to Karlova, combines Parisian ambience with unbeatable Czech prices. Dreamy Czech minds have found their asylum here after Slavia (see above) and other long-time favorites have either closed down or got stuck in their grand past. The main room is perfect for discussing philosophy, while the intimate room behind the courtyard is where you recite poetry to your date (Mon–Fri 10:00–23:00, Sat–Sun 12:00–23:00, Řetězová 7, tel. 222-221-244).

Ebel Coffee House, in the Ungelt courtyard behind the Týn Church, prides itself on the wide assortment of fresh coffee grounds (from every coffee-growing country in the world), and a colorful decor that delights the mind as much as the caffeine does. The Jumbo Latte is double the size of Starbucks' *venti*. Adopting the successful franchise' model, Ebel has opened five other branches in Prague, all of them catering primarily to tourists. But only the Ungelt location has a carefree atmosphere—the others feel cramped (daily 9:00–22:00, Týn 1, tel. 224-895-788).

Bohemia Bagel is hardly authentic—exasperated Czechs insist that bagels have nothing to do with Bohemia. Owned by an American, this trendy café caters mostly to youthful tourists, with good sandwiches (100–125 Kč), a little garden out back, and Internet access (1.50 Kč/min; daily 7:00–24:00; 2 locations: in the Old Town at Masná 2, tel. 224-812-560; and in the Little Quarter at Újezd 16, tel. 257-310-529).

TRANSPORTATION CONNECTIONS

Getting to Prague: Centrally located Prague is a logical gateway between Western and Eastern Europe. If you're coming from the West and using a Eurailpass, you must purchase tickets to cover the portion of the journey from the Czech border into Prague (buy at station before you board train for Prague). Or supplement your pass with a Prague Excursion Pass, giving you passage from any Czech border station into Prague and back to any border station within seven days (first class-€50, second class-€40, youth second class-€30). EurAide, a travel agency with offices in Berlin and Munich, also sells these passes for a bit less from their American office (U.S. tel. 941/480-1555, fax 941/480-1522, www.euraide .de/ricksteves). From the East, Prague has convenient night-train connections with Budapest, Kraków, and Warsaw (see below).

You'll find handy Czech train and bus schedules at www .vlak-bus.cz. Train info tel. 221-111-122 (little English spoken). Remember that for all train connections, it's important to confirm which of Prague's stations to use (see "Arrival in Prague—By Train," page 65).

From Prague by Train to: Český Krumlov (8/day, 1/day direct, 4 hrs), **Budapest** (4/day direct, including 1 night train, 7–9.5 hrs), **Kraków** (1 direct night train/day, 8.5 hrs; otherwise transfer in Katowice, Wrocław, or Ostrava-Svinov, 8–11 hrs), **Warsaw** (2/day direct, including 1 night train, 9–12 hrs; or 1/day, 9 hrs, with transfer in Ostrava-Svinov), **Berlin** (5/day, 5 hrs), **Vienna** (3/day, 5 hrs), **Munich** (3/day with changes, 6 hrs; 1 direct night train), **Frankfurt** (4 direct/day, 6 hrs).

By Bus to: Terezín (hrly, 1 hr), **Český Krumlov** (7/day, 3.5 hrs, from Florenc station; an easy direct 3-hr bus leaves at about 9:00).

By Car with a Driver: Mike's Chauffeur Service is a reliable family-run company with fair and fixed rates around town and beyond. Friendly Mike's motto is, "We go the extra mile for you" (round-trip fares with waiting time included, guaranteed through 2006 with this book: Český Krumlov-3,500 Kč, Terezín-1,700 Kč, Karlštcjn-1,500 Kč, minivan with plenty of room for up to 4 people, minibus also available, tel. 241-768-231, mobile 602-224-893, www.mike-chauffeur.cz, mike.chauffeur@cmail.cz). On the way to Krumlov, Mike will stop at no extra charge at Hluboká Castle or České Budějovice, where the original Bud beer is made. Mike offers a "Panoramic Transfer to Vienna" for 7,000 Kč (depart Prague at 8:00, arrive Český Krumlov at 10:00, stay up to 6 hrs, 1-hr scenic Czech riverside-and-village drive, then a 2-hr autobahn ride to your Vienna hotel, maximum 4 people). Mike also offers a similar "Panoramic Transfer to Budapest" for 10,000 Kč (2 hrs to Český Krumlov, then 1-hr scenic drive to Linz, followed by 5–6 hrs on expressway to Budapest).

ČESKÝ KRUMLOV

Lassoed by its river and dominated by its castle, this enchanting town feels lost in a time warp. While Český Krumlov is the Czech Republic's answer to Germany's Rothenburg, it has yet to be turned into a medieval theme park. When you see its awe-inspiring castle, delightful Old Town of shops and cobbled lanes, characteristic little restaurants, and easy canoeing options, you'll understand why having fun is a slam dunk here.

Český Krumlov (CHESS-key KROOM-loff) means roughly "Czech Bend in the River." Calling it "Český" for short sounds silly to Czech-speakers (since dozens of Czech town names begin with "Český"). "Krumlov" for short is okay.

Since Krumlov is the second-most-visited town (1.5 million visits annually) in the Czech Republic, there's enough tourism to make things colorful and easy—but not so much that it tramples the place's charm. This town of 15,000 attracts a young, bohemian crowd, drawn here for its simple beauty and cheap living.

Planning Your Time

Because the castle and theater can be visited only with a guide (and English tours are offered just a few times a day), serious sightseers should call the castle to reserve these tours first thing, and then build their day around these times. (Those who hate planning ahead on vacation can join a Czech tour anytime with an English information sheet.)

A paddle down the river to Zlatá Koruna is a highlight (4 hours, see "Canoeing and Rafting the Vltava," page 155), and a hike up to the mountain Kleť takes you into the heart of Czech woods (5 hours round-trip, see "Hiking," page 156). Other sights

Český Krumlov

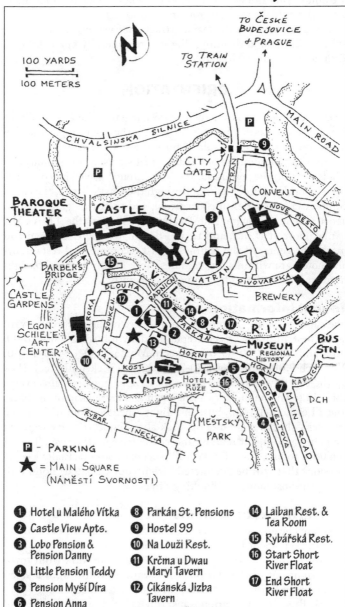

100 YARDS
100 METERS

TO ČESKÉ
BUDEJOVICE
& PRAGUE

TO TRAIN
STATION

CHVALSINSKA SILNICE

MAIN ROAD

CITY
GATE

CONVENT

NOVE MESTO

BAROQUE
THEATER

CASTLE

LATRAN

PIVOVARSKÁ

BREWERY

BARBER'S
BRIDGE

CASTLE
GARDENS

EGON
SCHIELE
ART
CENTER

DLOUHA

SIROKA

SOUKEN

RADNICNI

VLTAVA RIVER

PARKAN

MUSEUM
OF REGIONAL
HISTORY

BUS
STN.

HORNI

KAPLICKA

KAJ.

KOST.

ST. VITUS

HORNI

HOTEL
RŮŽE

HORNI

ROOSEVELTOVA

DCH

MAIN ROAD

RYBAR.

LINECKA

MEŠTSKÝ
PARK

P – PARKING

★ = MAIN SQUARE
(NÁMĚSTÍ SVORNOSTI)

❶ Hotel u Malého Vítka
❷ Castle View Apts.
❸ Lobo Pension &
   Pension Danny
❹ Little Pension Teddy
❺ Pension Myší Díra
❻ Pension Anna
❼ Pension Landauer

❽ Parkán St. Pensions
❾ Hostel 99
❿ Na Louzi Rest.
⓫ Krčma u Dwau
   Maryi Tavern
⓬ Cikánská Jizba
   Tavern
⓭ Krčma v Šatlavské
   Restaurant

⓮ Laiban Rest. &
   Tea Room
⓯ Rybářská Rest.
⓰ Start Short
   River Float
⓱ End Short
   River Float

are quick visits and worthwhile only if you have a particular interest (Egon Schiele, puppets, torture, and so on).

The town itself is the major attraction. Evenings are for atmospheric dining and drinking. Sights are generally open 10:00 to 17:00 and closed on Monday.

ORIENTATION

Český Krumlov is extremely easy to navigate. The twisty Vltava River, which makes a perfect S through the town, ropes the Old Town into a tight peninsula. Above the Old Town is the Castle Town. Český Krumlov's one main street starts at the isthmus and heads through the peninsula. It winds through town and continues across a bridge before snaking through the Castle Town, the castle complex (a long series of courtyards), and the castle gardens high above. The main square, Náměstí Svornosti—with the TI, ATMs, banks (close at 17:00), and taxis—dominates the Old Town and marks the center of the peninsula. All recommended restaurants and hotels are within a few minutes' walk of this square. No sight in town is more than a five-minute stroll away.

Tourist Information

The eager-to-please TI on the main square recently won an award as the best TI in the Czech Republic (daily July–Aug 9:00–20:00, June and Sept 9:00–19:00, March–May and Oct 9:00–18:00, Nov–Feb 9:00–17:00, tel. 380-704-622, www.ckrumlov.cz). Pick up the free city map. The 129-Kč *City Guide* book explains everything in town and includes a fine town and castle map in the back. The TI can check train, bus, and flight schedules, and will change traveler's checks at a fair rate. Ask about concerts, city walking tours in English, car rentals, and canoe trips on the river. The TI can book rooms, but it'll take a 10 percent deposit (actually a commission) that will be "deducted" from your (inflated) hotel bill. Save your host money by booking direct.

Arrival in Český Krumlov

Taxis are cheap; don't hesitate to take one into the center from the train station (about 100 Kč) or bus station (around 60 Kč).

By Train: The train station is a 15-minute walk from town (turn right out of the station, then walk downhill onto a steep cobbled path leading to an overpass into the town center).

By Bus: The bus station is just three blocks away from the Old Town (from the bus station lot, drop down to main road and turn left, then turn right at Potraviny grocery store to reach the center).

Helpful Hints

Internet Access: Fine Internet cafés are all over town and in many of the accommodations. The TI on the main square has several fast, cheap, stand-up stations good for a quick e-mail check.

Laundry: Pension Lobo runs a small self-service launderette under the castle (100 Kč/load, daily, Latrán 73).

Festivals: Locals drink oceans of beer and celebrate their medieval roots at big events such as the **Celebration of the Rose** (Slavnosti Růže), where blacksmiths mint ancient coins, jugglers swallow fire, mead flows generously, and pigs are roasted on open fires (mid-June). The summer also brings a top-notch jazz and alternative music festival to town, performed in pubs, cafés, and the castle gardens (mid-Aug). During the **St. Wenceslas celebrations,** the square becomes a medieval market and the streets come alive with theater and music (late Sept). Reserve a hotel well in advance if you'll be in town for these events.

TOURS

Walking Tours—The TI offers worthwhile guided 90-minute historic town walking tours in English (225 Kč, daily July–Sept at 10:00 and 12:00, meet in front of TI on main square—just show up and buy ticket from guide, minimum 2 people). Or you can do a tour yourself with an audioguide (rent at TI for 60 Kč/hr).

Also consider the one-hour **brewing history tour,** which takes you into the Eggenberg brewery (150 Kč, daily July–Sept at 12:00, meet in front of the TI).

Private Guides—Jiří (George) Václavíček is a local teacher who enjoys showing visitors around during his off-hours (afternoons, evenings, and weekends). Jiří—a gentle and caring man who seems to fit mellow Český Krumlov perfectly—is a joy to share this town with. He's happy to work for as little as an hour (€10/hr, tel. 380-726-813, mobile 603-927-995, jiri.vaclavicek@seznam.cz). Jiří also runs a small pension in the Old Town (see page 157). Another guide service provides private tours for 250 Kč per hour (you name the place and time, mobile 723-069-561).

SIGHTS

Old Town

These sights are listed in the order you'll reach them as you wander along the main street through the Old Town.

Museum of Regional History— This small museum gives you a quick look at regional costumes, tools, and traditions. Ask for the simple English translation that also includes a lengthy history of

Český Krumlov History

With the natural moat provided by the sharp bend in the Vltava, it's no wonder this has been a choice spot for eons. Celtic tribes first settled here a century before Christ. Then came German tribes. The Slavic tribes arrived in the ninth century. The Rožmberks—Bohemia's top noble family—ran the city from 1302 to 1602. In many ways, the 16th century was the town's Golden Age, when Český Krumlov hosted an important Jesuit college. The Hapsburgs bought the region in 1602, ushering in a more Germanic period.

The rich mix of Gothic, Renaissance, and Baroque buildings is easy to under-appreciate. As you wander, look up... notice the surviving details in the stonework. Step into shops and snoop into back lanes and tiny squares. Gothic buildings curve with the winding streets. Many precious Gothic and Renaissance frescoes were whitewashed in Baroque times (when the colorful trimmings of earlier times were way out of style). Today these precious frescoes are being rediscovered and restored.

With its rich German heritage, it was easy for Hitler to claim that this region—the Sudetenland—was rightfully part of Germany. In 1938, the infamous Munich Agreement made it his. After the war, in a kind of ethnic cleansing approved by the Potsdam Treaty, three million Germans in Czech lands were sent west to Germany. Emptied of its German citizenry, Český Krumlov turned into a ghost town inhabited mostly by thieves and Roma (Gypsies). Picture Roma squatters with their fires in the stately noble homes that line the town's main square.

In 1945, Americans liberated the town. But, in the post-WWII world as planned by Stalin, FDR, and Churchill, the border of the Soviet and American spheres of influence fell about here. While the communist government established order, the period from 1945 to 1989 was a smelly time capsule. The town was infamously polluted. Its now-pristine river was foamy from the paper mill just upstream. The hills around the town were marred with blocks of prefabricated concrete. The people who moved in never fully identified with the town; in Europe, a place without ancestors is without life-giving roots. The bleak years of communism here paradoxically provided a cocoon to preserve the town. There was no money, so little changed, apart from a build-up of grime.

Today, with its new prosperity, Krumlov is emerging as a fairy-tale town. Movie producers consider it ideal for films. Much of *Mission: Impossible,* starring Tom Cruise, was filmed right here.

Krumlov. Start on the second floor, where you'll see old paintings, a glimpse of noble life, and a ceramic model of Český Krumlov in 1800. The first floor comes with fine folk costumes and domestic art and a Bronze Age exhibit. The postcards in the hallway offer a fun look at Český Krumlov in the old days. Inside you'll also find the census from 1850, when 75 percent of the town's inhabitants were German. In 1945, the percentage was about the same...until most were expelled (50 Kč, daily 10:00–18:00, Horní 152).

Hotel Růže—Located across the street from the Museum of Regional History, this former Jesuit college hides a beautiful Renaissance courtyard. Pop inside to see a couple of bronze busts. The one on the right, dedicated by the Czech freedom fighters, commemorates the first Czechoslovak president, Tomáš Garrigue Masaryk (in office 1918–1934; see sidebar on page 114). The bust on the left recalls Masaryk's successor, Edvard Beneš (in office 1934–1948; see sidebar on page 152).

Church of St. Vitus—Český Krumlov's main church was built as a bastion of Catholicism in the 15th century, when the Roman Catholic Church was fighting the Hussites. The 17th-century Baroque high altar, showing St. Vitus and the Virgin Mary, is capped with St. Wenceslas. He's the patron saint of the Czech people, long considered their ambassador in heaven. The canopy now in the back—featuring a Rožmberk atop a horse—was once at the high altar. Too egotistical for Jesuits, it was moved to the rear of the nave (daily 10:00–19:00, Sunday Mass at 9:30).

Main Square (Náměstí Svornosti)—Lined by Renaissance and Baroque homes of burghers, the main square has a grand charm. There's continuity here. Lékárna, with the fine, red, Baroque facade on the lower corner of the square, is still a pharmacy, as it has been since 1620. McDonald's tried three times to get a spot here but was turned away. The Town Hall flies the Czech flag and the town flag, which shows the rose symbol of the Rožmberk family, who ruled the town for 300 years.

Imagine the history this square has seen: In the 1620s, the ris-

ing tide of Lutheran Protestantism threatened Catholic Europe. As Krumlov was a seat of Jesuit power and learning, the intellectuals of the Roman church burned 5,000 books on this square. Later, when there was a bad harvest, locals blamed witches—and burned them, too. Every so often, terrible plagues rolled through the countryside. In a village nearby, all but two residents were killed by a plague.

Edvard Beneš and the German Question

Czechoslovakia was created in 1918, when the vast, multiethnic Hapsburg Empire broke into smaller nations after losing World War I. The principle that gave countries such as Poland, Czechoslovakia, and Romania independence was called "self-determination": Each nation had the right to its own state within the area where its people were in the majority. But the peoples of Eastern Europe had mixed over the centuries, making it impossible to create functioning states based purely on ethnicity. In the case of Czechoslovakia, the borders were drawn along historical rather than ethnic boundaries. While the country was predominantly Slavic, there were also areas with overwhelmingly German and Hungarian majorities. One of these areas—a fringe around the western part of the country, mostly populated by Germans—was known as the Sudetenland.

At first, the coexistence of Slavs and Germans in the new republic worked fine. German parties were important power brokers and participated in almost every coalition government. Hitler's rise to power, however, led to the growth of German nationalism even outside Germany. Soon 70 percent of Germans in Czechoslovakia voted for the Nazis. In September 1938, the Munich Agreement ceded the Sudetenland to Germany—and the Czech minority had to leave.

Czechoslovak President Edvard Beneš (in office 1934–1948) led the Czechoslovak exile government in London during the war. Like most Czechs and Slovaks, Beneš believed that after the hard feelings produced by the Munich Agreement, peaceful coexistence of Slavs and Germans in a single state was impossible. His postwar solution: move the Sudeten Germans to Germany, much as the Czechs had been forced out of the Sudetenland before. Through skillful

But the plague stopped before devastating the people of Český Krumlov, and in 1715—as a thanks to God—they built the plague monument that marks the center of the square today. Much later, in 1938, Hitler stood right here before a backdrop of long Nazi banners to celebrate the annexation of the Sudetenland. And in 1968, Russian tanks spun their angry treads on these same cobblestones to intimidate locals who were demanding freedom. Today, thankfully, this square is part of an unprecedented peace and prosperity for the Czech people.

Torture Museum—This is just a lame haunted house: dark, with sound effects, cheap modern models, and prints showing off the cruel and unusual punishments of medieval times (80 Kč, daily 9:00–20:00, English descriptions, facing the main square).

diplomacy, Beneš got the Allies to sign on to this idea.

Shortly after the end of the war, three million people of German ancestry were forced to leave their homes. Millions of Germanic people in Poland, Romania, Ukraine, and elsewhere met with a similar fate. Many of these families had been living in these areas for centuries. The methods employed to expel them included murder, rape, and plunder.

In 1945, Český Krumlov lost 75 percent of its population, and Czechs moved into vacated German homes. Having easily acquired the property, the new residents never took much care of the houses. Within a few years, the once-prosperous Sudetenland was reduced to shabby towns and uncultivated fields—a decaying, godforsaken country. After 1989, displaced Sudeten Germans—the majority of whom live in Bavaria—demanded that the Czechoslovak government apologize for the violent way in which the expulsion was carried out. Some challenged the legality of the decrees, and for a time the issue threatened otherwise good Czech-German relations.

Although no longer such a hot-button diplomatic issue, the so-called Beneš Decrees remain divisive in Czech politics. While liberals consider the laws unjust, many others—especially the older generations—see them as fair revenge for the behavior of the Sudeten Germans prior to the war. In the former Sudetenland, where Czech landowners worry that the Germans will try to claim back their property, Beneš is a hugely popular figure. His bust in Český Krumlov's Hotel Růže is one of the first memorials to Beneš in the country. The bridge behind the Old Town has been named for Beneš since the 1990s. The main square—the center of a thriving German community 70 years ago—is now ironically called "National Unity Square."

Egon Schiele Art Center—This classy contemporary art gallery has top-notch temporary exhibits, generally featuring 20th-century Czech artists. The top-floor permanent collection celebrates the Viennese artist Egon Schiele (pronounced "Sheila," like the woman's name), who once spent a few weeks here during a secret love affair. A friend of Gustav Klimt and an important figure in the Secessionist movement in Vienna, Schiele lived a short life, from 1890 to 1918. His cutting-edge lifestyle and harsh and graphic nudes didn't always fit the conservative, small-town style of Český Krumlov, but townsfolk are happy enough to charge you to see some of his edgy art today (180 Kč, daily 10:00–18:00, Široká 70, tel. 380-704-011).

Barber's Bridge (Lazebnicky Most)—This wooden bridge, decorated with 19th-century statues, connects the Old Town and the Castle Town. In the center stands a statue of St. John of Nepomuk, who's also depicted in a prominent statue on Prague's Charles Bridge (see page 90). Among other responsibilities, he's the protector against floods. In the great floods of August 2002, the angry river submerged the bridge and swept away the banisters...but the bridge survived.

Krumlov Castle (Krumlovský Zámek)

No Czech town is complete without a castle—and now that the nobles are gone, their mansions are now open to us common folk. The Krumlov Castle complex, worth ▲▲, includes bear pits, the castle itself, a rare Baroque theater, and groomed gardens.

Round Tower (Zámecká Věž)—The strikingly colorful round tower marks the location of the first castle, built here to guard the medieval river crossing. With its 16th-century Renaissance paint job colorfully restored, it looks exotic, featuring fancy astrological decor, terra-cotta symbols of the zodiac, and a fine arcade. Climb its 162 steps for a great view (30 Kč, daily 9:00–18:00, last entry 17:30).

Bear Pits—At the site of the castle drawbridge, the bear pits hold a family of European brown bears, as it has since the Rožmberks started this tradition in the 16th century. Bears implied a long and noble family lineage.

Castle—The immense castle is a series of courtyards with shops, contemporary art galleries, and tourist services. You'll get a glimpse of the places where the Rožmberks, Eggenbergs, and Schwarzenbergs dined, studied, worked, prayed, entertained, and slept. Imagine being an aristocratic guest here, riding the dukes' assembly line of fine living: You'd promenade through a long series of elegant spaces and dine in the sumptuous dining hall before enjoying a concert in the Hall of Mirrors, which leads directly to the theater (described on page 155). After the play, you'd go out into the château garden for a fireworks finale.

Hours: June–Aug Tue–Sun 9:00–12:00 & 13:00–18:00, spring and fall until 17:00, closed Mon and Nov–March.

Visiting the Castle: To see the inside, you have to choose between two different one-hour tours: Tour I (160 Kč, Gothic and Renaissance objects—of most general interest) and Tour II (140 Kč, 19th-century castle life, Baroque art, and tapestries). Most tours are in Czech, and English tours come with an extra cost and a longer wait. (Visit the richly decorated Renaissance court-yard—the 3rd one—while you're killing time.) The information on the English tour, mostly given by students working a summer job, comes straight from an English information sheet you can pick up yourself at the ticket office. If you're pressed for time or would rather go at your own pace, ask for the sheet and join a Czech-language tour. If you decide to take the English tour, chat up the guides as you go to divert them from their typical spiel. No pictures are allowed in the castle. Tel. 380-704-721.

▲▲**Baroque Theater (Zámecké Divadlo)**—Europe once had several hundred fine Baroque theaters. Using candles for light and fireworks for special effects, most burned down. Today only two survive in good shape and are open to tourists: one at Stockholm's Drottningholm Palace, and one here, at this castle. Along with a look at the precious theater itself and a video of it in action, you'll see lots of surviving theater gear: a dozen or so painted sets, hundreds of costumes, and original special effects and sound-making machinery. Scenes could be changed in 10 seconds. (Fireworks blinded the audience, and when the smoke cleared it was a new scene.) Unfortunately, the number of visitors is strictly regulated, and there are only three English tours a day—often sold out in advance. Call 380-704-721 to establish English-language tour times and reserve a space; getting a ticket is generally a frustrating experience (180 Kč, 45-min tours daily May–Oct only, departures at 10:00, 11:00, 13:00, 14:00, 15:00, and 16:00).

Castle Gardens—This 2,300-foot-long garden crowns the castle complex. It was laid out in the 17th century, when the noble family would light it with 22,000 oil lamps, torches, and candles for special occasions. The lower part is geometrical and symmetrical—French-style. The upper is rougher—English-style (free, May–Sept daily 8:00–19:00, April and Oct daily 8:00–17:00, closed Nov–March).

The Church of the Annunciation of St. Mary—In 1350, the town began building this church and its attached convent. Today, you can walk under the Gothic vaults and peek into Baroque chapels where monks once meditated (30 Kč).

ACTIVITIES

▲▲▲**Canoeing and Rafting the Vltava**—Český Krumlov lies in the middle of a popular boating valley. Make time to paddle around the town or through Bohemian forests and villages of the nearby countryside.

The easiest half-hour experience is to float around the city's peninsula, starting and ending at opposite sides of the tiny isthmus. (Heck, you can do it twice.) Longer trips involve a minibus

transfer. If you're starting upriver from Krumlov (direction: Rožmberk), you'll go faster with more whitewater, but the river parallels a road so it's a little less idyllic. Going downstream from Krumlov (direction: České Budějovice), you'll have more pastoral scenery and less excitement. You can choose among destinations that take one to eight hours of floating and paddling (lots of work involved, even though you're going downstream). At a set time and place, the minibus will meet you. You'll encounter plenty of inviting pubs and cafés for breaks along the way. Plan on getting wet. There's a little whitewater, but the river is so shallow that if you tip, you simply stand up and climb back in. (When that happens, pull the canoe out to the bank to empty it, since you'll never manage to pour the water out while still in the river.)

Choose from a kayak, a canoe (fastest, less work, more likely to tip), or an inflatable raft (harder rowing, slower, but very stable). Rates vary from 300 Kč for the 30-minute canoe or raft trip around the town; to 700 Kč for a three-hour, 15-km (9-mile) float; to 1,000 Kč for a 35-km (22-mile), all-day trip. Prices are per boat (2–6 people) and include a map and transportation to or from the start and end points. Several companies offer this lively activity. Perhaps the handiest are **Půjčovna Lodí Maleček Boat Rental** (open long hours daily April–Oct, closed Nov–March; they also run the recommended Pension Myší Díra—see "Sleeping," below, Rooseveltova 28, tel. 337-712-508, lode@malecek.cz) and the slightly less expensive **Cestovní Agentura Vltava** (daily April–Oct 9:00–18:00, closed Nov–March, in the Pension Vltava at Kájovská 62, tel. 380-711-988, www.ckvltava.cz). Vltava also rents mountain bikes for 320 Kč per day.

Slupenec Horseback Riding Club—Head about a mile out of town for horseback rides and lessons (Tue–Sun 10:00–18:00, closed Mon, 1 hour outdoors or in the ring-250 Kč, all-day ride-1,800 Kč, helmets provided, Slupenec 1, tel. 380-711-052, www.jk-slupenec .cz, René Srncová).

Hiking—Start at the trailhead by the bear pits below the castle. Red-and-white trail markers will take you on an easy six-mile hike around the neighboring slopes and villages. The green and yellow stripes mark a five-mile hiking trail up the Kleť mountain—with an 1,800-foot altitude gain. At the top, you'll find the oldest observation tower in the country (now a leading center for discovering new planets). On clear days, you can see the Alps (observatory tours July–Aug, Tue–Sun every hour 10:30–15:30, 30 Kč, www .hvezdarna.klet.cz).

SLEEPING

Krumlov is filled with small, good, family-run pensions offering doubles with baths from 1,000–1,500 Kč and hostel beds for 300 Kč. Summer weekends and festivals are busiest and most expensive (see page 149); reserve ahead when possible. Hotels speak some English and accept credit cards; pensions rarely do either. While you can find a room upon arrival here, it's better to book at least a few days ahead if you want to stay in the heart of town.

In the Old Town

$$$ **Hotel u Malého Vítka**, right in the old center, consists of a tangle of Gothic vaults and staircases connecting comfy, woodsy rooms. As some standard doubles are much bigger than others and all are the same price, it's worth requesting a larger standard room. The deluxe rooms—unless you're dying for a whirlpool tub—aren't worth the higher cost (standard Db-1,600 Kč, bigger deluxe Db-2,400 Kč, Radniční 27, tel. & fax 380-711-925, www.vitekhotel.cz, vitekhotel@email.cz).

$$$ **Castle View Apartments,** run by local guide Jiří Václavíček (see "Tours," page 149), offers seven apartments, all with kitchenettes and many with views (apartments 1,500–5,400 Kč depending on size, view, and season; 140 Šatlavská Street, tel 380-726-813, www.castleview.cz, info@castleview.cz).

Hostel

$ **Hostel 99,** one of several hostels in the Old Town, is closest to the train station and has a pleasant, mellow feel. Its fine picnic-table terrace looks out on the Old Town, and the gentle sound of the river gurgles outside your window. It caters to its guests, offering free inner tubes for river floats, rental bikes, and a free keg of beer each Wednesday. The adjacent Hospoda 99 restaurant serves good, cheap soups, salads, and meals (55 beds in 6- to 10-bed rooms-300 Kč, D-700 Kč, T-900 Kč, use the lockers, no curfew or lockout, a 10-min downhill walk from train station or 2 bus stops to Spicak, Vezni 99, tel. & fax 380-712-812, www.hostel99.com, hostel99@hotmail.com).

At the Base of the Castle

A quiet, cobbled pedestrian street (Latrán) runs below the castle just over the bridge from the Old Town. It's a 10-minute walk downhill from the train station. Lined with characteristic shops, the street has a couple of fine little family-run, eight-room pensions.

Sleep Code

(25 Kč = about $1, country code: 420)
S = Single, **D** = Double/Twin, **T** = Triple, **Q** = Quad, **b** = bathroom, **s** = shower only. Unless otherwise noted, credit cards are accepted and prices include breakfast.

To help you sort easily through these listings, I've divided the rooms into three categories based on the price for a standard double room with bath:

$$$ **Higher Priced**—Most rooms 1,300 Kč or more.
$$ **Moderately Priced**—Most rooms between
                  1,000–1,300 Kč.
$ **Lower Priced**—Most rooms 1,000 Kč or less.

$ Lobo Pension fills a modern, efficient, concrete building with fresh, spacious rooms (Sb-700 Kč, Db-1,000 Kč, Tb-1,400 Kč, includes parking, Latrán 73, tel. & fax 380-713-153, www .pensionlobo.cz).

$ Pension Danny is a little funkier, with homier rooms and a tangled floor plan above a restaurant (Db-890 Kč, apartment Db-1,190 Kč, breakfast in room, Latrán 72, tel. 380-712-710, www .pensiondanny.cz).

Between the Bus Station and the Old Town
Pensions on Rooseveltova

Rooseveltova street, midway between the bus station and the Old Town (a 4-minute walk from either), is lined with pleasant eight-room places, each with easy free parking.

$$$ Little Pension Teddy has several riverview rooms sharing a common balcony (Db-1,500 Kč, Tb-1,950 Kč, cash only, Rooseveltova 38, tel. 380-711-595, www.teddy.cz, info@teddy.cz).

$$ Pension Myší Díra (literally, "Mouse Hole") hides eight sleek, spacious, bright, and woody Bohemian contemporary rooms overlooking the Vltava River just outside the Old Town. The reception, which closes at 20:00, also runs a tourist service and rents river boats (Db-1,000–1,690 Kč, bigger deluxe riverview Db-1,200–1,990 Kč, prices depend on day and season, Fri–Sat most expensive, breakfast in your room, 28 Rooseveltova, tel. 380-712-853, fax 380-711-900, www.malecek.cz).

$$ Pension Anna is well-run, with cozy rooms and a restful little garden (Db-1,250 Kč, 1,550-Kč apartment Db is a great deal, Rooseveltova 41, tel. & fax 380-711-692, pension.anna@quick.cz).

$$ Pension Landauer, with small and simple but comfortable rooms, is a fair value (Sb-700 Kč, Db-1,200 Kč, cash only, Rooseveltova 32, tel. & fax 380-711-790).

Cheap Pensions on Parkán

Parkán street, which runs along the river below the square, has a row of pensions with one or two rooms each. These places have a family feel and are cheap (all rated $), charging about 1,000 Kč for two people: **U Vltavy** (Parkán 107, tel. 380-716-396, mobile 603-338-008), **Miroslava Janotová** (Parkán 115, tel. 380-714-805), and **Sladová Hana** (Parkán 125, tel. 602-363-049). For more rooms, visit www.ckrumlov.cz.

EATING

Na Louži seems to be everyone's favorite little Czech bistro, with 40 seats in one 1930s-style room decorated with funky old advertisements. They serve inexpensive, tasty Czech cuisine and the hometown Eggenberg beer. If you've always wanted to play the piano for an appreciative Czech crowd in a colorful little tavern... do it here (daily, Kájovská 66, tel. 337-711-280).

Krčma u Dwau Maryi (literally, "Tavern of the Two Marys") is a characteristic old place with idyllic riverside picnic tables, serving traditional Czech cuisine and drinks (daily 11:00–23:00, Parkán 104, tel. 337-717-228). The fascinating menu explains the history of the house and makes a good case that the food of the poor medieval Bohemians was tasty and varied. Buck up for buckwheat, millet, greasy meat, or the poor-man's porridge.

Cikánská Jizba is a Roma (Gypsy) tavern filling one den-like, barrel-vaulted room. Krumlov has a big Roma history, and even today 1,000 Roma people live on the edge of town. While this little 40-seat restaurant won't win any cuisine awards, the typical Roma food is served under a mystic-feeling Gothic vault, and you never know what festive and musical activities will erupt (daily, 2 blocks toward castle from main square at Dlouhá 31, tel. 380-717-585).

Krčma v Šatlavské is an old prison gone cozy, with an open fire, big wooden tables under a rustic old medieval vault, and tables outdoors on the pedestrian lane. It's great for a late drink or game cooked on an open spit. *Medovina* is the hot honey wine (daily 12:00–24:00, on Šatlavská, follow lane leading uphill from TI on main square, tel. 608-973-797).

Laiban is the modern vegetarian answer to the carnivorous Middle Ages. Sit back in comfy straw chairs or head out onto the river terrace, and lighten up your pork-loaded diet with soy goulash or Mútábúr soup (daily 11:00–23:00, Parkán 105). The Krumlov Buddha dwells in the attached tea room (Tajemná Čajovna).

Rybářská Restaurace (literally, "Fisherman's Restaurant") doesn't look particularly inviting from outside, but don't get discouraged. This is *the* place in town to taste freshwater fish you've never heard of (and never will again). Try eel, perch, shad, carp, trout, and more (daily 11:00–22:00, on the island by the mill wheel).

TRANSPORTATION CONNECTIONS

Virtually all train rides to and from Český Krumlov require a transfer in the city of České Budějovice, a transit hub just to the north. České Budějovice's bus and train stations are next to each other.

From Český Krumlov by Train to: České Budějovice (6/day, 1 hr), **Prague** (8/day, change usually required, 4 hrs—bus is faster, cheaper, and easier), **Vienna** (4/day, 6–7 hrs, up to 3 changes), **Budapest** (4/day with at least 1 change, 11 hrs).

From Český Krumlov by Bus to: Prague (140 Kč, 7/day, 3.5 hrs; 2 departures a day—11:35 and 16:45—can be reserved and paid for at TI, or simply buy tickets from driver), **Vienna** (the Travellers' Hostel offers a direct bus service to Vienna 3 times weekly in summer: Mon, Wed, and Fri at 14:00; 900 Kč, 4 hrs, tel. 380-711-345, www.travellers.cz). The Český Krumlov bus station, a five-minute walk out of town, is just a big parking lot with numbered stalls for various buses.

By Private Car: If money is no object, hiring a private car can be efficient, especially to Budapest (the TI has referrals).

SLOVAKIA

SLOVAKIA

(Slovensko)

Slovakia is the West Virginia of Central Europe—poor, relatively undeveloped, but spectacularly beautiful in its own rustic way. Sitting quietly in the very center of Central Europe, wedged between stronger and more prosperous nations (the Czech Republic, Hungary, and Poland), Slovakia has been brutally disfigured by the communists, then overshadowed by the Czechs. But make no mistake: Even though their nation is just more than a decade old, Slovaks have their own distinct nation, language, and capital. Now independent, the Slovaks are striving to define their own nation and pull their country up to Western standards.

Slovakia is far more ethnically diverse than neighboring countries (like the Czech Republic, Hungary, and Poland). Among Slovakia's large minority groups are Hungarians (about 10 percent of the population), many of whom still cling to the century-old glory days when this was called Upper Hungary and ruled from Budapest. Many Slovaks resent the cultural chauvinism of Hungarians, and still harbor hard feelings towards their

Slovakia Almanac

Official Name: Slovenská Republika, though locals call it Slovensko. The nation is the eastern half of the former Czechoslovakia (split in 1993).

Population: 5.4 million people. The majority are native Slovaks who are Roman Catholic and speak Slovak. But one in 10 has Hungarian roots, and an estimated one in 10 is Roma (Gypsy).

Latitude and Longitude: 48°N and 20°E (similar latitude to Paris or Vancouver, B.C.).

Area: 19,000 square miles (the size of Massachusetts and New Hampshire put together).

Geography: The northeastern half of Slovakia features the beautiful rolling hills and spiky, jagged peaks of the Carpathian Mountains, while the southwestern half is quite flat—a continuation of the Hungarian Plain. The climate is generally cool and cloudy.

Biggest Cities: Only two cities have more than 100,000 inhabitants: Bratislava in the west (the capital, 430,000) and Košice in the east (235,000).

Economy: The Gross Domestic Product is $79 billion (less than half that of the Czech Republic), and the GDP per capita is $14,500 (less than the average Czech and roughly half that of the average German). Despite a recent economic upturn, unemployment hovers at about 15 percent.

former oppressors. Another large group—very loosely estimated at 10 percent of the population—are the Roma (Gypsies; see page 184). Rounding out the cultural cocktail are Czechs, Ruthenians (Carpathian Mountain peasants of Ukrainian origin), and a smattering of Germans.

While the Czechs take pride in a marked agnosticism, the Slovaks tend to be more devout Catholics—more like their other neighbors, the Poles. In fact, there are many other commonalities between the Poles and the Slovaks—including their strong agricultural (rather than industrial) heritage before communism, and many linguistic similarities.

Traditionally an agricultural region, Slovakia was heavily industrialized by the Soviets. Rusting factories now stand where fertile farmlands once were. Gradually, the Slovaks are rebuilding their ailing economy, often with the help of Western investors.

Currency: 30 Slovak koruna (Sk) = about $1.

Government: President Ivan Gašparovič heads a government not dominated by any single political party. In September of 2006, Slovaks vote for their party of choice to select 150 new legislators to the single-house parliament. Slovakia joined the European Union in 2004.

Flag: Horizontal bands of white, blue, and red with a shield

bearing a "patriarchal cross" (with 2 crossbars instead of 1) atop three humps. The three humps represent three historic mountain ranges of Slovakia: Mátra (now in northern Hungary, near Eger), Fatra, and Tatra. The double-barred cross represents St. Stephen (István) of Hungary, commemorating the many centuries that Slovakia was part of Hungary.

Slovaks You May Recognize: Andy Warhol (American Pop Artist, born to Slovak immigrants), Martina Hingis (Swiss tennis player born in Slovakia), Štefan Banič (emigrated to America and invented the parachute).

There are two schools of thought on Slovakia. Some people love the country for its stark natural beauty and because it's an exciting cultural detour off the prettified tourist mainstream. Slovakia gives more adventurous travelers the opportunity to feel the pulse of a nation that's still struggling to transition into democracy—and yet is stable and safe enough to be comfortable. These people enjoy hiking along Slovakia's glorious mountain trails, driving through its humble villages, interacting with its kind and simple people, and pondering the blemish that communism has left on its pastoral landscape.

Other people can't wait to leave Slovakia, turned off by its drab industrial skeletons, relative poverty, and dearth of must-see sights compared to the rest of Eastern Europe. Most tourists blitzing through pretty-as-a-postcard Eastern Europe want to spend more time elsewhere...and should.

What is clear is that Slovakia is not your standard European country. With lots of pleasant surprises, Slovakia is worth a peek for hardy travelers in that first category. The country's capital, Bratislava, is perfectly situated at the western tip of the country,

It's Not You, It's Me: The Velvet Divorce

In the autumn of 1989, hundreds of thousands of Czechs and Slovaks streamed into Prague to demonstrate on Wenceslas Square. Their "Velvet Revolution" succeeded, and Czechoslovakia's communist regime peacefully excused itself.

The Czechs and Slovaks were forced to redefine their roles in the post-communist world. Ever since they had joined with the Czechs in 1918, the Slovaks felt like second-class citizens within their own nation. Prague was unmistakably the political, economic, and cultural capital of Czechoslovakia. And the Czechs, for their part, resented the financial burden of their poorer neighbors to the east. With their new freedom, the Czechs found themselves with a 10 percent unemployment rate...compared to 20 or 30 percent unemployment in the Slovak lands. In this new world of flux, long-standing tensions came to a head.

The dissolution of Czechoslovakia began over a hyphen, as the Slovaks wanted to rename the country Czecho-Slovakia. Ideally, this symbolic move would come with a redistribution of powers: two capitals, two UN reps, but one national bank and a single currency. The Slovaks were also less enthusiastic about abandoning the communist society altogether, since the Soviet regime had fundamentally changed their agricultural-based economy to a heavily industrialized one that depended on a socialist element for survival.

The Czechs rebuffed the Slovaks' requests—the Slovaks were just being silly, and should just keep quiet and enjoy the ample coattails the Czechs were providing. The first post-communist president of Czechoslovakia, the Czech Václav Havel, made matters worse when he took a rare trip to the Slovak half of his country in 1990. In a fit of terrible judgment, Havel promised he'd close the ugly, polluting Soviet factories in Slovakia... neglecting the fact that many Slovaks still depended on these factories. Havel left in disgrace and visited the Slovak lands only twice more in the next two and a half years.

In June 1992, the Slovak nationalist candidate, Vladimír Mečiar, fared surprisingly well in the elections—proving that the Slovaks were serious about secession. At the ballot box, the Slovaks decisively sent the message: "We want to separate!" The Czechs said, incredulously, "Really?" Then, "Okay!"

Though public opinion in both halves of the country opposed separation (the people never actually voted on the split), the politicians soon agreed on the terms. The Velvet Divorce was official on January 1, 1993, and the Slovaks finally had their own capital (Bratislava), currency (Slovak koruna), and head of state (Mečiar). The Slovaks let loose a yelp of excitement, the Czechs emitted a sigh of relief...and mapmakers everywhere swore silently.

right on the train line between Budapest and Vienna. Meanwhile, up in the north—not far from the Polish border—is the most beautiful part of this mountainous nation: the rolling hills of the Spiš Region and jagged peaks of the High Tatras.

Practicalities

Telephones: Insertable telephone cards, sold at newsstands and kiosks everywhere, get you access to the modern public phones.

When calling locally, dial the number without the area code. To make a long-distance call within the country, start with the area code (which begins with 0). To call a Slovak number from abroad, dial the international access number (00 if calling from Europe, 011 from the U.S. or Canada), followed by 421 (Slovakia's country code), then the area code (without the initial 0) and the number. To call out of Slovakia, dial 00, the country code of the country you're calling (see chart in appendix), the area code if applicable (you may need to drop initial zero), and the local number.

Information: For more in-depth information about Slovakia, pick up a copy of *Spectacular Slovakia*, an excellent annual magazine produced by the English-language newspaper in Bratislava.(www .spectacularslovakia.sk).

Slovak History

Even though it's more recently associated with the Czech Republic, Slovakia was for centuries ruled from Budapest and known as Upper Hungary. While the Ottoman Turks occupied most of Hungary in the 16th and 17th centuries, the Hungarians moved their capital to Bratislava. But even throughout the long era of Hungarian domination, most people living in Slovakia were Slavs.

Czechoslovakia was formed at the end of World War I, when the Austro-Hungarian Empire was splitting into pieces. During this flurry of new nation-building, a small country of 10 million Czechs or five million Slovaks was unlikely to survive. These two Slavic peoples decided it was best to unite, allowing them to balance the many Germans and Hungarians that lived in the same region. The union was logical enough—especially in the eyes of Tomáš Masaryk, Czechoslovakia's first president (and a buddy of Woodrow Wilson's from Princeton). Masaryk was from the border of the two regions and spoke a dialect that mixed elements of Czech and Slovak. Czechoslovakia was born.

The Czechs and the Slovaks were constantly reminded that they were countrymen in name only. In a prelude to World War II, these two peoples were again split along the cultural fault that always divided them: Today's Czech Republic was absorbed into Germany, while much of the Slovak land went to Nazi-allied Hungary.

During the communist era, the regime decided to convert the Slovak economy from a low-key agricultural model to a base of heavy industry. But the industry was centrally planned for communist purposes (relying on raw materials imported from elsewhere within the Eastern Bloc)—so it made sense only as a cog in the communist machine. Many of Slovakia's factories built heavy arms, making the country the biggest producer of tanks in the world. Slovakia became one of the ugliest and most polluted corners of Eastern Europe. The Slovak environment—and economy—are still recovering.

When the wave of uprisings spread across Eastern Europe in 1989, Czechoslovakia peacefully achieved its own freedom with the Velvet Revolution. But then the Slovaks wanted their own nation, capital, and parliament. On January 1, 1993, Czechoslovakia amicably split into two nations: the Czech and Slovak Republics (see sidebar). While this has proved beneficial for the Czechs, many Slovaks—now over their initial excitement—will tell you that the split was probably a mistake.

After the so-called Velvet Divorce, the first president of Slovakia was a former boxer named Vladimír Mečiar, whose authoritarian rule was not much better than the communists'. Mečiar was frequently accursed of corruption (including pulling issues off the ballot when they seemed to be going against him), and people suspect he was involved in the kidnapping, torture, and humiliation of one of his political opponent's sons in 1995. He was also notorious for making offensive statements about his country's substantial Hungarian and Roma minorities. Mečiar drew criticism from neighboring Eastern and Western European nations, as well as the United States. He was finally defeated at the polls in 2000, but—like a bad penny—he keeps turning up, nearly winning elections in 2002 and 2004.

Though Mečiar remains a factor in the political landscape, support for him seems to be dwindling, and Slovakia's political situation is improving. Slovakia joined the Czech Republic, Poland, Hungary, and Slovenia in becoming EU members in May of 2004—a monumental step forward. Still, the Slovaks are slow to embrace these changes. In the EU parliamentary elections held a few months after they joined, Slovakia had the lowest voter turnout of the 25 EU nations.

While many cynics argue that Slovaks earned their EU membership only on the coattails of their onetime countrymen, the Czechs, others point to Slovakia's increasingly strong economy. Although Slovakia is among the poorest EU countries, things are looking up—low costs and an unbeatable location have attracted many foreign automakers to build plants here, leading *The New York Times* to dub Slovakia "the European Detroit."

Key Slovak Phrases

English	Slovak	Pronounced
Hello. (formal)	*Dobrý deň.*	DOH-bree dyehn
Hi. / Bye. (informal)	*Ahoj.*	AH-hoy
Do you speak English?	*Hovoríte po anglicky?*	hoh-VOH-ree-teh poh ANG-lits-kee
Yes. / No.	*Áno. / Nie.*	AH-no / nyeh
Please. / You're welcome. / Can I help you?	*Prosím.*	PROH-seem
Thank you.	*Ďakujem.*	DYAH-koo-yehm
I'm sorry. / Excuse me.	*Prepáčte.*	preh-PAHCH-teh
Good.	*Dobro.*	DOH-broh
Goodbye.	*Do videnia.*	doh vih-DAY-neeah
one / two	*jeden / dva*	YAY-dehn / dvah
three / four	*tri / štyri*	tree / SHTEE-ree
five / six	*päť / šesť*	peht / shehst
seven / eight	*sedem / osem*	SEH-dyehm / OH-sehm
nine / ten	*deväť / desať*	DYEH-veht / DYEH-saht
hundred	*sto*	stoh
thousand	*tisíc*	TYEE-seets
How much?	*Koľko?*	KOHL-koh
local currency	*koruna (Sk)*	koh-ROO-nah
Where is...?	*Kde je...?*	gday yeh
...the toilet	*...záchod*	ZAH-khohd
men	*muži*	MOO-zhee
women	*ženy*	ZHAY-nee
water / coffee	*voda / káva*	VOH-dah / KAH-vah
beer / wine	*pivo / víno*	PEE-voh / VEE-noh
Cheers!	*Na zdravie!*	nah ZDRAH-vyeh
the bill	*účet*	OO-cheht

While their path has not always been smooth, Slovaks are looking to the future with optimism about their role in a united Europe.

Slovak Food

Slovak cuisine is similar to Czech cuisine—with lots of starches and gravy, and plenty of pork, cabbage, and potatoes (see "Czech Food," page 55). If there's anything distinctive about Slovak food, it's the slight Hungarian influences—Slovaks use more paprika than their Czech cousins. Slovakia also has a strong tradition of grilling pickled meats. Also keep an eye out for Slovakia's national dish, *bryndzové halušky* (small potato dumplings with sheep's cheese and bits of bacon). Like the Czechs, the Slovaks produce fine beer *(pivo)*. One good brand is Zlatý Bažant (literally, "Golden Pheasant").

Slovak Language

Many people assume Slovak is virtually the same as Czech. To be sure, there are similarities—but they're hardly identical.

Slovak is handy as a sort of a lingua franca of Slavic tongues. Czechs can understand Poles, but not Slovenes; Poles can understand Croatians, but not Czechs. But Slovak speakers generally find they can understand—and be understood in—any of these languages.

Slovak's similarity to Czech was exaggerated during the 75 years that they shared a country. Soccer games would be broadcast with two commentators—one spoke Czech, and the other spoke Slovak. Anyone growing up in this era grew comfortable using the languages interchangeably. But today's teenagers—who have only spoken exclusively Czech or Slovak—find they have trouble understanding each other.

BRATISLAVA

For centuries, Bratislava—known as "Pressburg" to its German inhabitants—was a complex and beautiful city, with deep roots in many different cultures: Slovak, German/Austrian, Hungarian, Jewish, Romanian, and Roma (Gypsy). The Hungarians used the city—which they called "Poszony"—as their capital during the century and a half that Buda and Pest were occupied by Turkish invaders. Later, Bratislava was one of Hapsburg empress Maria Theresa's favorite places. Everyone from Hans Christian Andersen to Casanova sang the wonders of this bustling burg on the Danube. When Czechoslovakia was formed at the end of World War I, the city shed its German and Hungarian names, proudly taking the new Slavic name "Bratislava."

But in the 20th century, Bratislava became the textbook example of a historic city whose multilayered charm and delicate cultural fabric were destroyed and shrouded in gray by the communist regime. The communists were more proud of their ultramodern suspension bridge, New Bridge (Most SNP), than of the historic Jewish quarter they razed to make way for it. Now the bridge and its highway slice through the center of the Old Town, and the heavy traffic rattles the stained-glass windows of St. Martin's Cathedral as it rumbles past.

Today's Bratislava is gradually coming back to life—more slowly, perhaps, and less confidently than Prague or Kraków. The city is blessed with a charming-enough, increasingly rejuvenated Old Town and a priceless location on the Danube (and the tourist circuit) smack-dab between Budapest and Vienna. The outdoor cafés hum with life on a summer day, and the youthful city is looking to the future. Though it's unlikely that the Slovak capital will ever become the "next Prague," travelers are sure to rediscover its charms in the coming years and put it squarely back on the list of worthwhile visits.

Planning Your Time

On my list of priorities, time spent in Budapest and Vienna is more precious. But if you're passing through and you're curious, Bratislava merits a quick sightseeing sprint. Head straight for the Old Town, wander through to the river, and—if time allows—hike up to the castle.

I've listed no hotels in Bratislava; beds are better (and often cheaper) in nearby Vienna and Budapest.

ORIENTATION

(area code: 02)
Bratislava, with nearly half a million residents, is Slovakia's capital and biggest city. It has a small, colorful Old Town (Staré Mesto) surrounded by the ugly communist sprawl of the New Town and suburbs. The Old Town and the castle above it are the only parts of Bratislava worth visiting.

Bratislava's grim Stalinist vibe isn't all bad. It offers an opportunity for a cultural scavenger hunt deep into the guts of apartment-block neighborhoods, where the average Josefs of the "Evil Empire"—from here to Vladivostok—eked out their lives. Across the river from the Old Town, the suburb called Petržalka is gloomy and harrowing, in a *1984*-comes-to-life sort of way.

Beware: Bratislavans in the tourist zone sometimes try to short-change and otherwise rip off their city's visitors as brazenly as their Prague cousins do. Check your bill and count your change carefully.

Tourist Information

The TI, called the Bratislava Culture and Information Centre, has two branches in the heart of the city. There's a small window in the **train station** (June–Sept Mon–Fri 8:00–19:30, Sat–Sun 8:00–16:30; Oct–May Mon–Fri 8:30–17:00, closed Sat–Sun, tel. 02/5249-5906), and the **main branch** is across the square from the back of the Old Town Hall on Primaciálne Námestie (June–Sept Mon–Fri 8:30–19:00, Sat 9:00–17:00, Sun 9:30–16:00; Oct–May Mon–Fri 8:30–18:00, Sat 9:00–14:00, closed Sun; Klobučnícka 2, tel. 02/5443-3715, www.bkis.sk and www.bratislava.sk). Pick up the free map and browse their strange assortment of brochures; they can also help you find a room for a modest fee.

The main TI shares an office with the Bratislava **tour guide association** (tel. 02/5443-4059, guides@bkis.sk). They offer a

Bratislava

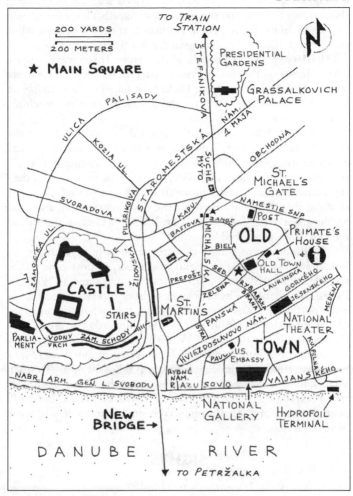

one-hour Old Town walking tour in English every day at 14:00 (400 Sk, 2 people minimum, call ahead to confirm). You can also hire your own local guide, but (strangely) it costs twice as much as hiring a guide in Prague or Kraków (1,200 Sk/hr).

An excellent (but unofficial) Web site about Bratislava's public transportation is www.imhd.sk.

Arrival in Bratislava

By Train: Bratislava's Main Train Station, called Bratislava Hlavná Stanica, is about a half mile north of the Old Town. As you emerge from the tracks, an ATM and the TI are to your left, and the luggage check desk is to your right (look for *úschovňa batožín*; there are no lockers, and the check desk usually closes for 30-min lunch and dinner breaks; try to confirm that they'll be there when you get back if you'll be rushing to catch a train).

It's an easy 15-minute walk to the center. If you want to shave a few minutes off the trip, you can go part of the way by **tram** (from main hall, with tracks at your back, look for signs to *električky* on left; take escalator down, buy a "basic ticket" from the machine, and hop on tram #1).

To **walk**, leave through the front door and head past the buses to the busy street. Take the overpass across the street, and continue straight on Štefánikova. After about 10 minutes, you'll pass the nicely manicured presidential gardens on your left, then the Grassalkovich Palace, Slovakia's "White House." Continue straight, then bear right through the busy intersection, and head for the green onion dome. This is St. Michael's Gate, at the start of the Old Town (described below).

By Plane: Some budget carriers—especially SkyEurope—fly into Bratislava Airport (Letisko Bratislava, airport code: BTS, www.letiskobratislava.sk). This airport is marketed as "Vienna-Bratislava" (thanks to its proximity to both capitals). Located six miles northeast of downtown Bratislava, the airport is named for Milan Rastislav Štefánik, who worked towards the creation of Czechoslovakia at the end of World War I. The airport has easy bus connections into Bratislava's Main Train Station (bus #61, 6/hr in peak time, 3/hr in slow times, trip takes 30 min). To reach Vienna, there are several buses (€10–15, trip takes about 90 min), or take a taxi (figure €60–90, depending on whether you use a Slovak or an Austrian cab). SkyEurope's Web site has more details: www.skyeurope.com.

SIGHTS

On a short visit, it's enough to simply wander the Old Town, enjoy a drink at an outdoor café, and soak in Slovakia. If you need more diversion than that, you can hike up to the castle. More low-impact sightseeing options include a pair of dusty, sleepy museums in the heart of the Old Town (described below). If you're interested in museums beyond the ones I mention, check out www.snm.sk.

Old Town Wander—Bratislava's mostly traffic-free Old Town is peppered with cute, colorful Baroque buildings. Once

Bratislava's Statues

As you wander the Old Town, keep an eye out for whimsical statues—like the nosy admiral watching over the bench in the Main Square. The most famous—a guy dubbed Čumil ("the Peeper"), grinning at passersby from a manhole—is a block down from the Main Square, at the intersection of Panská and Rybárska. Others to look for are a sneaky paparazzo and a jovial chap doffing his top hat (named Schöner Náci).

dreary, this area is slowly coming back to life. From the station, you'll come through the onion-domed **St. Michael's Gate** (Michalská Brána), the last remaining tower of the city wall. From here, stroll down Michalská street, lined with lively, vibrant cafés (with relaxing outdoor tables in the summer).

Two blocks down, the name of this main drag changes to Ventúrska, and the café scene continues. When the street jogs right, turn left, along Zelená, and head for the **Main Square** (Hlavné Námestie)—the bustling centerpiece of Old World Bratislava.

At the top of the Main Square is the **Old Town Hall** (Stará Radnica). This place, constantly added on to over the centuries, is a mish-mash of architectural styles. It houses a ho-hum **City History Museum** (Mestské Múzeum), with a climbable tower and a torture (a.k.a. "feudal justice") museum in the basement (50 Sk, Tue–Fri 10:00–17:00, Sat–Sun 11:00–18:00, closed Mon, www .muzeumbratislava.sk).

On the other side of the Old Town Hall is Bratislava's most interesting museum, the **Primate's House** (Primaciálny Palác, 40 Sk, Tue–Fri 10:00–17:00, Sat–Sun 11:00–18:00, closed Mon). This grand mansion, gradually expanded and glorified over several centuries by a series of archbishops who lived here, features fancy apartments, a Mirror Hall for concerts and meetings, a striking marble chapel, and a series of six English tapestries. It's hardly world-class, but Bratislavans are very proud of this place.

Backtrack to the Main Square. If you leave this square at the bottom (on Rybárska Brána), you'll reach the long, skinny square called **Hviezdoslavovo Námestie**—another part of Bratislava that has undergone much-needed rejuvenation recently, with sharp landscaping and cobbles upon cobbles of lazy cafés. At the east end of the square is the impressive, silver-topped Slovak National Theater (Slovenské Národné Divadlo), a reminder that Bratislava has long had a strong theatrical tradition.

From here, it's just a block to the Danube—passing the Slovak National Gallery, for those fascinated by Slovak art (big green building)—and a good look at the communists' pride and joy, the

New Bridge (Nový Most, a.k.a. Most SNP). As with many Soviet-era landmarks around Eastern Europe, the locals aren't crazy about this structure—not only for the questionable starship *Enterprise* design, but also because of the oppressive regime it represents.

If you follow the Danube towards the bridge, before long you'll spot big **St. Martin's Cathedral** (Dóm Sv. Martina) on the right.

This historic church isn't looking too sharp these days—and the highway thundering a few feet in front of its door (courtesy of the Soviets) doesn't help matters. If it were any closer, the off-ramp would go through the nave. Sad as it is now, the cathedral has been party to some pretty important history. Remember that while Buda and Pest were occupied by Turks for a century and a half, Bratislava was the capital of Hungary. Many Hungarian kings and queens were crowned in this church. A replica of the Hungarian crown still tops the steeple.

If you walk under the highway, then start climbing the stairs marked *Zámocké Schody*, you'll wind up at...

Bratislava Castle (Bratislavský Hrad)—This imposing fortress, nicknamed the "upside-down table," is the city's most prominent landmark. The castle saw its fin-est days when Hapsburg empress Maria Theresa took a liking to Bratislava in the 18th century, and decided she wanted to have a nice place to hold court here. But M.T.'s castle burned to the ground in an 1811 fire, and it was left as a ruin for a century and a half—not reconstructed until 1953. The com-

munist rebuild—especially inside the courtyard, which feels like a prison exercise yard—is drab and uninviting. The castle houses a few dull museums (history, musical instruments) and the chance to toss a coin down an incredibly deep well (280 feet before you hear the plop—the same distance as to the Danube; find entrance at far left corner as you enter main courtyard). But the best reason to visit the castle is for the views—especially of the New Bridge and the endless communist apartment blocks of the Petržalka suburb across the river.

By the way, the huge, pointy monument back towards the train station is **Slavín**, where more than 6,800 Soviet soldiers who fought to liberate Bratislava from the Nazis are buried. A nearby church had to take down its steeple so as not to draw attention from the huge Soviet soldier on top of the monument.

TRANSPORTATION CONNECTIONS

From Bratislava by Train to: Vienna (about hrly, 1 hr), **Budapest** (4/day direct, 2.25–4 hrs), **Prague** (3/day direct, 4.25–5.5 hrs).

You can also connect to both Vienna and Budapest by **boat** (see page 451).

THE SPIŠ REGION

The most beautiful part of Slovakia is the mountainous north-central region, comprising the jagged High Tatras and the Spiš region. The dramatic Carpathian Mountains slice through Central Europe here, dividing the Poles and Czechs in the north from the Hungarians and Yugoslavs in the south. With these Carpathian peaks as a backdrop, this region offers fine high-mountain scenery, easy river-rafting trips with a fun-loving guide through a breathtaking gorge, a classic, Old World walled town with one of Europe's finest Gothic altarpieces, a glimpse at Slovakia's complicated ethnic mix, and treacherous but legendary hiking trails in a place so pretty, they call it "paradise."

Planning Your Time

The Spiš Region is a handy place for drivers to break up the long journey between Kraków and Hungary—Levoča is worth an overnight to recharge and get a taste of rural Slovakia. But unless you have a special interest, don't go out of your way to reach this area. Train travelers or those on a speedy itinerary should skip it (sleep through Slovakia on the night train, and wake up in Eger or Budapest).

Getting to the Spiš Region

Seeing this area is a real headache without a car. You'll take the bus to get to Levoča. If you're going between Kraków and Hungary (Eger or Budapest), the train line veers around Levoča far to the east, through Košice. From Košice, trains will get you to Prešov or Spišská Nová Ves, and the bus will take you the rest of the way to Levoča. From the west, buses run between Bratislava and Levoča

The Spiš Region

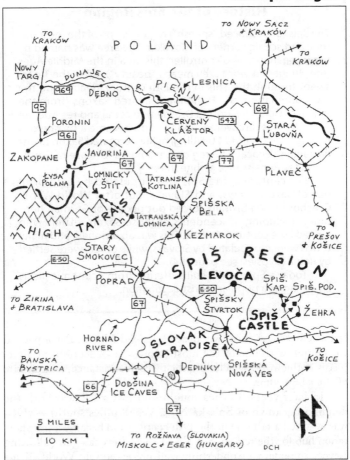

(though it's often faster to take the train to Poprad, then bus to Levoča). For specific schedules, see www.cp.sk.

Levoča

It's not a stretch to call Levoča (LEH-voh-chah) Slovakia's finest small town—with a mostly intact medieval wall, a main square ringed by striking Renaissance facades, and one of the greatest Gothic altarpieces in all of Europe.

Levoča boomed in the Middle Ages, when trade between Hungary and Poland brought abundant merchant traffic through its gates. In the 15th century, the town's centerpiece was built: St.

History of the Spiš Region

The Spiš (pronounced "speesh") region is one of the most historic and scenic corners of Slovakia. The area was named by the Hungarians, who controlled this area in the Middle Ages (the Hungarian word *szép* means "beauty"). After the Tatars swept through the Spiš in the 13th century, decimating the local population, the Hungarians invited Saxons (from the region of Germany around Dresden) to come and resettle the land. Ore was discovered, and the Spiš became a prosperous mining region, with 24 bustling, richly decorated Saxon towns (including Levoča). The region became a showcase of Gothic and, later, Renaissance architecture.

For centuries, the Spiš was populated by a colorful mix of Saxons, Jews, and Slovaks. But after World War II, Czechoslovakia brutally forced out people of German heritage—including descendents of those Saxon settlers who arrived here centuries before. Spiš was abandoned, and many towns were repopulated by Slovaks, while others were settled by Roma (Gypsies; see page 184).

Today's Spiš, while still suffering from economic ills, is emerging as a popular tourist destination.

James Church. A local woodcarver named Master Pavol packed the church with one of the most impressive collections of altarpieces in the world—including the pièce de résistance, an exquisite 60-foot-high altar.

In later years, Levoča fought and lost a PR war with the neighboring town of Spišská Nová Ves (8 miles south)—which was awarded a rail line in the 19th century and became a transportation hub for the region. S.N.V.'s loss was Levoča's gain, allowing Levoča to remain a wonderfully well-preserved Old World village of 10,000. If all of this makes Levoča feel off the beaten track, so much the better.

ORIENTATION

(area code: 053)
Levoča is small—you can walk from one end of the walled burg to the other in 15 minutes—and all roads lead to the town's main square, which is named for the important woodcarver, Master Pavol (Námestie Majstra Pavla).

The **TI**, like most everything else of interest, is on the main square (tel. 053/451-3763, www.levoca.sk). You can hire your own **local guide** for 500 Sk per hour. This is a cheap way to maximize your sightseeing time...and get to know a local (TI can help you arrange).

SIGHTS AND ACTIVITIES

▲**Church of St. James (Chrám Sv. Jakuba)**—This huge Gothic church, dominating Levoča's main square, contains 11 ornately decorated altars—including the tallest wooden altarpiece in the world.

The church dates from the 14th century. In the late 15th century, neighboring VIPs visited here. The greatest Hungarian king, Mátyás Corvinus, came in 1474 (for more on Corvinus, see sidebar on page 402). Two decades later, representatives of Poland's powerful Jagiellonian dynasty visited. These important visits—both commemorated inside the church—are a reminder that Slovakia has long been at a crossroads of Eastern Europe.

In the early 16th century, the great sculptor Master Pavol left his mark on the church. Master Pavol's unique, almost cartoonish style features figures with too-big heads, strangely weepy eyes, and honest-to-goodness personalities. Pavol's masterpiece is the church's single most impressive sight: the 60-foot-tall **main altar**, carved out of linden wood and bathed in gold paint. The large central figures represent Mary and the Baby Jesus, flanked by St. James (the church's namesake, on left) and St. John the Evangelist (on right). The four panels surrounding these figures depict scenes from James' and John's lives and deaths. Beneath them is a depiction of the Last Supper. Unusual in Gothic art, each apostle has his own individual features (based on the local merchants who financed the work). With this and his other carvings, Master Pavol was knocking on the door of the Renaissance.

The nave is lined with several other altarpieces—some by Master Pavol, some by others. At the front of the right nave (right-hand corner), look for the altar depicting the **Passion of Christ**, carved for the 1474 visit of Hungarian King Mátyás Corvinus. Jesus looks like Mátyás, Mary resembles his Italian wife, and the altar was supposed to bring the couple good luck in having a child.

To the left as you view the main altar, notice the interesting medieval **frescoes** on the wall (splotchy from a bad 19th-century renovation job). The frescoes on the left depict the life of St. Dorothy. On the right are two strips. The upper strip shows a couple performing good deeds (feeding the hungry, visiting prisoners, burying the dead, and so on). In the lower strip, they sit on animals representing the mortal sins.

As you leave, at the back of the left nave, look for Master Pavol's statue of **Mary**. When the Counter-Reformation swept Europe in the 16th century, locals hid statues such as Mary (who was tucked away in the Town Hall) to protect them from iconoclasts—Catholics who destroyed religious symbols to unclutter their communion with God. Two centuries later, the long-forgotten statues were miraculously discovered, and brought back to the church...for you to enjoy.

Cost, Tours, Hours: The cost is 50 Sk, and you can visit only at appointed times. The specific times are posted on the door of the church office, across the street from the church entrance (on the north side of the church, facing the top of the square). You'll be accompanied by a guide, but you don't have to listen to her spiel (usually Slovak only—but ask for English). Use the above information to appreciate the church, or find the talking box in the back of the nave and insert a coin for English. The church is open July–Aug Tue–Sat 9:00–17:00, Sun 13:00–17:00, Mon 11:00–17:00 (tours every 30 min); Sept–Oct and Easter–June Tue–Sat 8:30–16:00, Sun 13:00–16:00, Mon 11:30–16:00 (tours roughly hourly, though not always at the top of the hour); Nov–Easter Tue–Sat 8:30–16:00, closed Sun–Mon (tours roughly hourly). Tel. 053/451-2347, mobile 0907-521-673, www.chramsvjakuba.sk.

House of Master Pavol—The biggest downside of the Church of St. James is that you can see the breathtaking altarpieces only from a distance, so you can't get a sense of what made Pavol the Master. At this museum, replicas of the statues allow you to look at Pavol's creations right in their big, weepy eyes (30 Sk, daily 9:00–17:00, tel. 053/451-2786).

Levoča Town Hall (Radnica v Levoči)—The huge, Renaissance-style building behind the Church of St. James used to be the town hall; now it's a museum of the town and region's history and colorful folk cultures. You'll watch a movie in English before wandering though a grand, wood-carved meeting hall (with a beautifully painted ceiling) and rooms of maps of historic Levoča and the Spiš region (30 Sk,

skimpy English information, daily 9:00–17:00, tel. 053/451-2786).

When Central Europe's presidents came to Levoča in 1998, they met in this building. Someone decided there weren't enough bathrooms, so they started to put more in the passage that connects the main building and the belfry. When construction began, they discovered fine sgraffito wall decorations under the plaster. They were uncovered, restored...and now adorn the new bathrooms (not open to the public).

Mariánska Hora—This humble church, overlooking Levoča from a perch on a nearby hill, has been an important site for pilgrimages for centuries. Every year, on the first weekend of July, hundreds of thousands of Slovaks flock to the hill from the surrounding countryside—many walking as far as 30 miles to get here. In 1995, Pope John Paul II made a pilgrimage here, saying Mass in front of some 650,000 people.

Near Levoča

Spiš Castle (Spišský Hrad)—Just a few miles from Levoča lies one of Europe's largest castles. Spiš Castle watches over the region from high on a bluff, overlooking a desolate terrain. Though there have been castles on this strategic spot for as long as there have been people here, the current version was built during the 15th century. Since its destruction in 1781, the castle has remained as the evocative ruins you see today.

The interior is tourable, though anyone you ask will tell you it's pretty dull in there (100 Sk, daily May–Sept 8:30–19:00, Oct 8:30–18:00, last entry 45 min before closing, closed Nov–April, tel. 053/454-1336, www.spisskyhrad.sk). Even if there's not much to see inside, views of the castle from the surrounding countryside are majestic.

Spiš Castle is the centerpiece of a cluster of interesting sights. The town just below the castle is **Spišské Podhradie** (literally, "Under the Spiš Castle"). On a ridge opposite Spiš Castle is **Spišská Kapitula**, the site of the Spiš region's cathedral, surrounded by a modest village and an imposing 14th-century wall. And tucked behind Spiš Castle is **Žehra**, a village with a simple, onion-domed church that contains some 13th- to 15th-century wall paintings.

Getting There: From Levoča, take the main road (E50) east. After 7.5 miles, you'll see the first turnoff, which takes you scenically past Spišská Kapitula and through Spišské Podhradie (park near town and hike all the way up, or cut through town back to the main road and wind around to the 2nd exit). To get to the castle more directly, stay on past the first exit and go another two miles, where there'll be another turnoff to the right leading up to the parking lot behind the castle.

Slovak Paradise (Slovenský Raj)—Outdoors enthusiasts from all over Central Europe flock to this national park, and for good reason—it offers some of the most enjoyable hikes this side of the Plitvice Lakes (see page 664). The Slovak Paradise is known for its seemingly treacherous trails—one oft-photographed stretch features ladders laid at sharp uphill angles, spanning a gaping gorge. The faint of heart should steer clear of these more challenging

The "Gypsy Question"

Eastern Europe is home to a silent population—mostly in Romania, Bulgaria, Hungary, and this part of Slovakia—of millions of dark-skinned people who speak an Indian dialect and live according to their own rules. Whether roaming the countryside in caravans, squatting in dilapidated apartment blocks, conning tourists in big cities, or attempting to integrate with their white neighbors, these people are a world apart.

The most common name for Europe's overlooked culture, "Gypsy," is a holdover from the time when these people were thought to have come from Egypt. While the term isn't overtly offensive to most, it's both geographically mistaken and politically incorrect. It's also taken on a negative connotation—as with the ethnic slur, "I've been gypped!" Instead of these outdated names, today's most widely accepted term for these people is "Roma" (though for ease of understanding, I've occasionally used the more familiar "Gypsy" elsewhere in this book).

The Roma most likely originated in today's India. In fact, the language still spoken by about two-thirds of today's European Roma—called Romany—is related to contemporary Indian languages. The Roma migrated into Europe through the Ottoman Empire (today's Turkey), arriving in the Balkan Peninsula in the 1300s. Under the Ottomans, the Roma weren't allowed into towns, but were still treated relatively well. Traditionally, Roma earned their livelihood as entertainers (fortune telling, music and dancing, horse shows, dancing bears); as thieves; and as metalworkers (which is why they tended to concentrate in mining areas, like Slovakia and Kosovo).

Roma were initially not allowed to enter Austrian territory, but as the Hapsburgs recaptured lands once controlled by the Ottomans (like Slovakia and Hungary), they permitted the Roma already living there to stay. In the 18th and 19th centuries, as "Gypsy music" funneled into the theaters of Vienna and Budapest, a romantic image of Europe's Roma emerged. Many people's image of the Roma date from this era: a happy-go-lucky nomadic lifestyle; intoxicating music, with dancers swirling around a campfire; mystical, or even magical, powers over white Europeans, as if by an occult hand; and beautiful, alluring, sultry women. But white Europe's image of the Roma also had a sinister side. Even today, Europeans and Americans alike might warn their children, "If you don't behave, I'll sell you to the Gypsies!" This widespread bigotry culminated in the Holocaust—when half a million Roma people were murdered in Nazi concentration camps.

Today's Roma are Europe's forgotten population—estimates range from 6 to 12 million throughout the Continent. Unemployment among the Roma hovers at about 70 percent. While only 3 percent of the Hungarian population is Roma, nearly two out of every three male prison inmates is a Roma.

Roma are subject to a pervasive prejudice unparalleled in today's Europe. Local news anchors—hardly fair or balanced—pointedly scapegoat the Roma for problems. A small town in the Czech Republic tried to build a wall between its wealthy neighborhood and the Roma ghetto—until the European Parliament forced them to stop. Schools are sometimes carefully segregated, with signs reading, "Whites Only."

It's easy for us to criticize Eastern Europeans for their seemingly closed-minded attitudes. But to be fair, the Roma's poor reputation is at least partly deserved. Many Roma do turn to thievery for survival. It's downright foolish not to be a little suspicious of a Roma person hanging out in a tourist zone. And the Roma population puts an enormous strain on the already overtaxed social welfare networks in these countries. To an Eastern European trying to make his way in today's world, the Roma are a problem.

Still, the situation is tragic. Attempts at cooperation are often unsuccessful. The Roma—whose culture is inherently nomadic and independent—generally aren't inclined to settle down and integrate. Roma who do find jobs and send their kids to school often find themselves shunned both by their fellow Roma, and by the white Europeans they're trying to integrate with. The communists attempted to force integration, splitting some apartment buildings between Roma and Slavic people. The Slavs moved out as soon as the regime fell.

So far, the Roma haven't produced a Martin Luther King, Jr., to mobilize the culture and demand equal rights—and many experts think they likely never will. The greatest "crossover" success stories are musicians and artists, with no political aspirations. But the white European community is beginning to take note. The Decade of Roma Inclusion—launched in 2005 by Hungarian-American businessman George Soros—is an initiative being undertaken by eight Eastern European countries to better address the human rights of their Roma citizens (www.romadecade.org).

Despite the best efforts of many well-intentioned people, the so-called "Gypsy Question" in Eastern Europe still doesn't have a satisfactory answer. Hopefully the Roma will find a place in the new, united Europe.

hikes; in other parts of the park, you'll find trails suitable for any hiker (www.slovenskyraj.sk). Spišská Nová Ves is the handiest gateway, on the northeastern fringe of the park (and with a convenient train station).

River Rafting in the Pieniny—A few miles north of Levoča, at the border with Poland, is the Pieniny region (www.pieniny.sk). Here, the Dunajec River flows through a dramatic gorge in the shadows of sheer limestone cliffs, with Poland on one bank and Slovakia on the other—like a set from *The Lord of the Rings.*

The best way to experience the Pieniny is on a boat cruise. You'll board a *plt'*—a strange, pontoon-type raft made up of five canoe-like skiffs lashed together and bridged with long benches—and ply the waters of the Dunajec River. Your lively conductor is dressed in the traditional costume of the Góral folk who populate this region. The trip is generally smooth—no whitewater to speak of—and offers a lazy chance to enjoy the scenery.

Rafting trips go roughly from early May through late October, weather permitting (daily 8:30–17:00, until 15:00 Sept–Oct, about 250 Sk per person, last about 1 hr). The best stretch of river is the 5.5-mile-long, U-shaped canyon that begins near the town of **Červený Kláštor** (literally, "Red Cloister"—this old building is near the town itself), and ends at the town of **Lesnica**. Hop on at a raft landing—marked as *prístav plt'í* on signs and maps. When you reach Lesnica, catch the bus back to your starting point...or hike the three miles back to Červený Kláštor.

SLEEPING

All of the presidents of Central European countries converged on Levoča for a conference in 1998, and you'll see photos of many of them decorating the few proud hotels in town. All of these hotels are right on the main square, Námestie Majstra Pavla.

$$ Hotel Satel is a plush, swanky place that caters to tour groups. Its 23 frou-frou rooms are all pastel pinks, spread around a beautifully restored inner courtyard (Sb-€50, Db-€75, 40 percent cheaper Oct–April, breakfast-€4, elevator to some rooms, Námestie Majstra Pavla 55, tel. 053/451-2943, fax 053/451-4486, www.satel-slovakia.sk, satelle@satel-slovakia.sk).

$ Arkada Hotel is nondescript and also popular with tours. Its 32 rooms don't have much style (Sb-€30, Db-€45, lavish suite-€50, 10 percent cheaper Oct–April, extra bed-€10, breakfast-€4, Námestie Majstra Pavla 26, tel. 053/451-2372, fax 053/451-2255, www.arkada.sk, arkada@stonline.sk).

$ Hotel Barbakan, near the top of the main square, is traditional-feeling. Though its 15 rooms are dark, it's a decent option for the price (Sb-€33, Db-€44, suite-€52, 10 percent cheaper

---

Sleep Code

(30 Sk = about $1, €1 = about $1.20, country code: 421, area code: 053)
S = Single, **D** = Double/Twin, **T** = Triple, **Q** = Quad, **b** = bathroom, **s** = shower only. Credit cards are accepted and English is spoken at each place. For the convenience of their international guests, Levoča's hotels generally quote prices in euros.

   To help you sort easily through these listings, I've divided the rooms into three categories, based on the price for a standard double room with bath:

   $$ Higher Priced—Most rooms €50 or more.
   $ Lower Priced—Most rooms less than €50.

Oct–April, extra bed-€11, breakfast-€4, lots of stairs with no elevator, Košická 15, tel. 053/451-4310, fax 053/451-3609, www.barbakan.sk, recepcia.hot@barbakan.sk).

EATING

Hotel Satel and **Hotel Barbakan**, listed above, both have restaurants. But **Reštaurácia u 3 Apoštolov** ("Three Apostles"), also right on the square, is a cut above, serving tasty Slovak cuisine. The decor is nothing special, but the food is delicious and cheap: pungent garlic soup, excellent trout, and the tasty "Apostle Specialty"—sautéed beef and vegetables in a spicy sauce, wrapped in a potato pancake (main dishes about 150 Sk, long hours daily, Námestie Majstra Pavla 11, tel. 053/451-2302).

The High Tatras
(Vysoké Tatry)

While not technically in the Spiš region, Slovakia's most breathtaking mountain range is nearby. The High Tatras mountain range is small but mighty—dramatic, 9,000-foot peaks spiking up from the plains, covering an area of only about 100 square miles. This is the northernmost leg of the Carpathians, which stretch across the heart of Eastern Europe all the way to Romania. The Tatras boast long, tranquil valleys, emerald mountain lakes, roaring waterfalls, and high mountain flora and fauna—including chamois, marmots, roebucks, stags, boars, bears, otters, and eagles. These cut-glass peaks have quickly become legendary among hardy, in-the-know travelers for their remarkably inexpensive hiking and skiing opportunities.

The High Tatras make up the Polish-Slovak border. Without a car, the most accessible approach is from the Polish resort town of **Zakopane** (an easy bus or train connection from Kraków). But for more rugged beauty, head to the southern part of the range, in Slovakia.

The mid-sized city of **Poprad**—not in the mountains, but sitting quietly on a plain about 10 miles from the range—is the most convenient launchpad for venturing into Slovakia's High Tatras. Along the base of the High Tatras are various modest resort towns (including the biggest, Starý Smokovec). There's no shortage of scenic hikes all over the region (good maps and guidebooks available locally). The best no-sweat high-altitude option is to take the **cable car** from the resort village of Tatranská Lomnica up to the viewpoint at Lomnický Štít (8,640 feet; popular and crowded, so visit early).

By car, take road 537 along the base of the High Tatras to connect the various towns. By public transportation, you'll commute by electric trains *(električky)* from Poprad into Starý Smokovec. (There are also direct, one-hour buses from Levoča to Starý Smokovec.) From Starý Smokovec, you can continue by electric train on to Tatranská Lomnica and other villages. Each town has its share of simple resort-type hotels, but serious hikers enjoy staying in the High Tatras' many *chaty* (mountain huts). For more details on the High Tatras, visit www.tanap.sk or www.tatry.net. *Spectacular Slovakia* magazine, mentioned on page 167, also has good coverage of the High Tatras (www.spectacularslovakia.sk).

POLAND

POLAND

(Polska)

Americans who think of Poland as run-down—full of rusting factories, smoggy cities, and gloomy natives—are speechless when they step into Kraków's vibrant main square, Gdańsk's colorful pedestrian drag, or Warsaw's lively Old Town. While parts of the country are still cleaning up the industrial mess left by the Soviets, Poland also has some breathtaking medieval cities that show off its warm and welcoming people, dynamic history, and unique cultural fabric.

The Poles are a proud people—as moved by their spectacular failures as by their successes. Their quiet elegance has been

tempered by generations of abuse by foreign powers. The Poles place a lot of importance on honor, and you'll find fewer scams and con artists here than in other countries.

In a way, there are two Polands: Lively, cosmopolitan urban centers, and hundreds of tiny farm villages in the countryside. City-dwellers often talk about the "simple people" of Poland—those descended from generations of farmers, working the same plots for centuries and living an uncomplicated, traditional lifestyle. This large contingent of old-fashioned, salt-of-the-earth folks—who like things the way they are—is a major reason why Poland was so hesitant to join the European Union (see page 201).

Poland is the poorest of the countries that joined the European Union in 2004. While the most important tourist centers have been prettied up admirably, you only need venture a few blocks, or drive through the countryside, to see unmistakable signs of poverty. It's the little things that aren't quite up to Western snuff: parks with patches of mud instead of grass; an overabundance of litter and graffiti; rusting infrastructure (railings, canopies of train stations); and a general sense of chaos and unpredictability. These finer points are expensive to cultivate—unnecessary niceties that the Poles simply can't afford yet. But with the Poles' ambitious spirit and new EU investment, it shouldn't be long before Poland looks more First World than Third.

Poland is one of Europe's most devoutly Catholic countries. Catholicism defines these people, holding them together through times when they had little else. Squeezed between Protestant Germany (originally Prussia) and Orthodox Russia, Poland wasn't even a country for generations (1795–1918). Its Catholicism helped keep it alive. In the last century, while "under communism" (as that age is referred to), Poles found their religion a source of strength as well as rebellion—they could express dissent by going to church. Some of Poland's best sights are churches, usually filled with locals praying silently. While these church interiors are worth a visit, be especially careful to show the proper respect (maintain silence, keep a low profile, and snap pictures only discreetly).

Visitors are surprised at how much of Poland's story is a Jewish story. Before World War II, 80 percent of the world's Jews lived in Poland. Warsaw was the world's second-largest Jewish city, after New York, with 380,000 Jews (out of a total population of 1.2 million). Poland was a magnet for Jews because of its relatively welcoming policies. Still, Jews were forbidden from owning land; that's why they settled mostly in the cities. Before the war, along with its huge Jewish minority, the country had an exhilarating ethnic mix—including Germans, Russians, Ukrainians, and Lithuanians. A third of Poland spoke no Polish. But World War II (and a later Soviet policy of sending troublemaking Jews to Israel)

Poland Almanac

Official Name: Rzeczpospolita Polska (Republic of Poland), or Polska for short.

Snapshot History: This thousand-year-old country has been dominated by foreigners for much of the last two centuries, finally achieving true independence (from the Soviet Union) in 1989.

Population: 39 million people, slightly more than California. About 97 percent are ethnically Polish, Polish-speaking, and—at least nominally—Roman Catholic. Three out of every four Poles is a practicing Catholic. The population is younger and better educated than most (aging) European countries, with an average age of 35 (Germany's is 42).

Latitude and Longitude: 52°N and 20°E (similar latitude to Berlin, London, and Edmonton, Alberta).

Area: 122,000 square miles, the same as New Mexico (or Illinois and Iowa put together).

Geography: Because of its overall flatness, Poland has been a corridor for invading armies since its infancy. The Vistula River (678 miles) runs south-to-north up the middle of the country, passing through Kraków and Warsaw, and emptying into the Baltic Sea at Gdańsk. Poland's climate is generally cool and rainy—40,000 storks love it.

Biggest Cities: Warsaw (the capital, 1.6 million), Łódź (790,000), and Kraków (735,000).

Economy: The Gross Domestic Product is $463 billion (a little more than the state of Ohio), but the GDP per capita is $12,000—less than a third what the average Ohioan makes. The 1990s saw an aggressive—and very successful—transition from state-run socialism to privately-owned capitalism. Still, Poland's traditional potato-and-pig farming society is behind the times, with 16 percent of the country's workers producing less than 3 percent of its GDP. One in five Poles is unemployed, and nearly one in five lives in poverty. Poland's entry into the European Union in 2004 brought substantial financial aid that should improve things.

Currency: 1 złoty (zł, or PLN) = 100 groszy (gr) = about 30 cents; 3.40 zł = about $1.

ended that. Today, 97 percent of the country speaks Polish, and only a few thousand Polish Jews remain.

Poland is historically extremely pro-American. Of course, their big neighbors (Russia and Germany) have been their historic enemies. And when Hitler invaded in 1939, the Poles felt let down by their supposed European friends (France and Britain), who declared war on Germany but provided virtually no military

Real Estate: A typical, one-bedroom apartment in Warsaw (250 square feet) rents for roughly $600 a month.

Government: Poland's president selects the prime minister and Cabinet, with legislators' approval. They govern along with a two-house legislature (Sejm and Senat) of 560 seats. In October of 2005, Lech Kaczyński was elected president. Kaczyński's party—called "Law and Justice," and headed by his twin brother, Jarosław—is more conservative than previous administrations. Its success seems to decisively bring the left-of-center days of Lech Wałęsa and Solidarity to an end.

Flag: The upper half is white, and the lower half is red—the traditional colors of Poland. Poetic Poles claim the white represents honor, and the red represents the enormous amounts of blood spilled by the Poles to honor their nation. The flag sometimes includes a coat of arms with a crowned eagle (representing Polish sovereignty). Under Poland's many oppressors (including the Soviets), the crown was removed from the emblem, and its talons were trimmed. On regaining its independence, Poland coronated its eagle once more.

The Average Pole: Despite new prosperity, the average Pole spends just 4 percent of what a German spends on personal consumption. One in four Poles uses the Internet, and the average Pole will live to age 75 (unless you're a man). The average woman gets married at 24 and will have 1.39 children.

Not-so-Average Poles: Despite the many "Polack jokes" you've heard (and maybe repeated), you actually know many famous Polish intellectuals—you just don't realize they're Polish. The "Dumb Polack" Hall of Fame includes Karol Wojtyła (Pope John Paul II), Mikołaj Kopernik (Nicolas Copernicus), composer Fryderyk Chopin, scientist Marie Curie (née Skłodowska), writer Teodor Józef Korzeniowski (better known as Joseph Conrad, author of *Heart of Darkness*), filmmaker Roman Polański *(Chinatown, The Pianist)*, politician Lech Wałęsa...and one of this book's co-authors.

support. America has always been regarded as the big ally from across the ocean. In 1989, when Poland finally won its freedom, many Poles only half-joked that they should apply to become the 51st state of the United States.

On my first visit to Poland, I had a poor impression of Poles, who seemed brusque and often elbowed ahead of me in line. I've since learned that all it takes is a smile and a cheerful greeting—preferably in Polish—to break through the thick skin that helped these kind people survive the difficult communist times. With a friendly hello *(Dzień dobry!)*, you'll turn any grouch into a new friend.

Practicalities

Train Station Lingo: "PKP" is the abbreviation for Polish National Railways ("PKS" is for buses). In larger towns with several train stations, you'll usually use the one called Główny (meaning "Main"—except in Warsaw, where it's Centralna). Underneath the stations are often mazes of walkways—lined with market stalls—that lead to platforms *(peron)* and exits *(wyjście)*. Most stations have several platforms, each of which has two tracks (tor). Departures are generally listed by the peron, so keep your eye on both tracks for your train. Arrivals are *przyjazdy*, and departures are *odjazdy*. Left-luggage counters or lockers are marked *przechowalnia bagażu*. *Kasy* are ticket windows. "Information" windows are more often than not staffed by monolingual grouches. Smile sweetly, write down your destination and time, and hang on to your patience. To get into town, follow signs for *wyjście do centrum* or *wyjście do miasta*.

Museum Tips: Virtually every museum in Poland is closed on Monday. The ticket window for any museum closes a half hour before the museum's closing time, and this last-entry deadline is strictly enforced. Poland's museums are notorious for constantly tweaking their opening times (especially in Kraków). I've tried to list the correct hours, but be aware that it's virtually impossible to predict—try to confirm locally if you have your heart set on a particular place.

Restroom Signage: To confuse tourists, the Poles have devised a secret way of marking their WCs. You'll see doors marked with *męska* (men) and *damska* (women)—but even more often, you'll simply see a triangle (for men) or a circle (for women). Likewise, a sign with a triangle, a circle, and an arrow is directing you to the closest WCs.

Pay to Pee: To irritate tourists, Polish bathrooms often charge a small fee. Sometimes you'll even be charged at a restaurant where you're paying to dine. Sadly, many American visitors let this minor inconvenience interfere with their enjoyment of the trip. My advice: You don't have to like it, but get used to it—it's a hassle, but it's cheap (usually 1–2 zł).

Telephones: Insertable telephone cards, sold at newsstands and kiosks everywhere, get you access to the modern public phones. Cheap international phone cards for calling the United States have only recently begun to appear (often sold at Internet cafés or youth hostels; see page 35 for details).

Top 10 Dates that Changed Poland

A.D. 966—The Polish king, Mieszko I, is baptized a Christian, symbolically uniting the Polish people and founding the nation.

1385—The Polish queen marries a Lithuanian duke, starting the two-century reign of the Jagiełło family.

1410—Poland defeats the Teutonic Knights at the Battle of Grunwald, part of a Golden Age of territorial expansion and cultural achievement.

1572—The last Jagiellonian king dies, soon replaced by bickering nobles and foreign kings. Poland declines.

1795—In the last of three partitions, the country is divvied up by its more-powerful neighbors: Russia, Prussia, and Austria.

1918—Following World War I, Poland gets back its land and sovereignty.

1939—Gdańsk (then called Danzig) is invaded by Nazi Germany, starting World War II. At war's end, the country is "liberated" (i.e., occupied) by the Soviet Union.

1980—Lech Wałęsa leads a successful strike, demanding more freedom from the communist regime.

1989—The Berlin Wall falls, and Poland soon gains independence under its first president...Lech Wałęsa.

2004—Poland joins the European Union, pedaling fast to catch up to its more-prosperous neighbors.

In an emergency, dial 112; to summon the police, call 997. Remember these prefixes: 0800 is toll-free, and 0700 is expensive (like phone sex). Many Poles use mobile phones (which come with 060 and 050 prefixes).

When calling locally, simply dial the seven-digit number. To call long distance within the country, start with the area code (which begins with 0). To call Poland from another country, dial the international access number (00 if you're calling from Europe, or 011 from the U.S. and Canada), followed by 48 (Poland's country code), then the area code (without the initial 0) and the seven-digit number. To call out of Poland, dial 00, the country code of the country you're calling (see chart in appendix), the area code if applicable (may need to drop initial zero), and the local number (see page 761 for details).

Polish History

Poland is flat. Take a look at a topographical map of Europe, and you can see the Poles' historical dilemma: The path of least resistance from northern Europe to Russia is right through Poland. Over the years, many invaders—from Napoleon to Hitler—have taken advantage of Poland's strategic location. The country is nicknamed "God's playground" for the many wars that have rumbled through its territory. Poland has been invaded

by Soviets, Germans, French, Austrians, Russians, Prussians, Swedes, Teutonic Knights, Tatars, Bohemians, Magyars—and, about 1,300 years ago, Poles.

Medieval Greatness

The first Poles were a tribe called the Polonians ("people of the plains"), a Slavic band that showed up in these parts in the 8th century. In 966, Mieszko I, Duke of the Polonian tribe, adopted Christianity and founded the Piast dynasty (which would last for more than 400 years). Poland was born.

Poland struggled with two different invaders in the 13th century: the Tatars (Mongols who ravaged the south) and the Teutonic Knights (Germans who conquered the north—see page 348). But despite these challenges, Poland persevered. The last king of the Piast dynasty was also the greatest: Kazimierz the Great, who famously "found a Poland made of wood and left one made of brick and stone"—bringing Poland (and its capital, Kraków) to international prominence (see page 218). The progressive Kazimierz also invited Europe's much-persecuted Jews to settle here, establishing Poland as a haven for the Jewish people—which it would remain until the Nazis arrived.

Kazimierz the Great died at the end of the 14th century without a male heir. His grand-niece, Jadwiga, became queen and married Lithuanian Prince Władysław Jagiełło, uniting their countries against a common enemy, the Teutonic Knights. Their marriage marked the beginning of the Jagiellonian dynasty and set the stage for Poland's Golden Age. With territory spanning from the Baltic Sea to the Black Sea, Poland flourished.

Foreign Kings and Partitions

When the Jagiellonians died out in 1572, political power shifted to the nobles. Poland became a nation governed by its wealthiest 10 percent—the *szlachta*, or nobility, who elected a series of foreign kings. Many of these kings made bad diplomatic decisions and squandered the country's resources. To make matters worse, the Polish Parliament *(Sejm)* introduced the concept of *liberum*

Polish Artists

Though Poland has produced world-renowned scientists, musicians, and writers, the country isn't known for its artists. Polish museums greet foreign visitors with fine artwork by unfamiliar names. If you're planning to visit any museums in Poland, there are two artists worth remembering: **Jan Matejko,** a 19th-century positivist who painted grand historical epics (see page 287); and one of his students, **Stanisław Wyspiański**, a painter and playwright who led the charge of the Młoda Polska movement (the Polish answer to Art Nouveau—see page 221) in the early 1900s.

veto, whereby any measure could be vetoed by a single member of parliament. This policy—which effectively demanded unanimous approval for any law to be passed—paralyzed the *Sejm*'s waning power.

By the late 18th century, Poland was floundering—and surrounded by three land-hungry empires (Russia, Prussia, and Austria). Over the course of less than 25 years, these countries divided Poland's territory among themselves in a series of three partitions. In 1795, "Poland" (nicknamed "the cake of kings"—to be sliced and eaten at will) disappeared from Europe's maps, not to return until 1918.

Even though Poland was gone, the Poles wouldn't go quietly. As the partitions were taking place, Polish soldier Tadeusz Kościuszko (a hero of the American Revolution) returned home to lead an unsuccessful military resistance against the Russians. After another failed uprising against Russia in 1830, many of Poland's top artists and writers fled to Paris—including pianist Fryderyk Chopin and Romantic poet Adam Mickiewicz (whose statue adorns Kraków's main square and Warsaw's Royal Way). These Polish artists tried to preserve the nation's spirit with music and words; those who remained in Poland continued to fight with swords and fists. By the end of the 19th century, the image of the Pole as a tireless, romantic insurgent emerged.

At the end of World War I, Poland finally regained its independence—but the peace didn't last long.

Saddle on a Cow: World War II and Communism

On September 1, 1939, Hitler began World War II by attacking the Baltic port city of Gdańsk. With six million deaths in the next six years, Poland suffered the worst per-capita WWII losses of any nation. At the war's end, Poland's borders were shifted significantly westward—forcing the resettlement of millions of

The Heritage of Communism

While Poland has been free, democratic, and capitalist since 1989, even young adults carry lots of psychological baggage from living under communism. Although the young generally embrace the fast new affluence with enthusiasm, many older people tend to be nostalgic about that slower-paced time that came with more security. And even young professionals, with so much energy and hope now, don't condemn everything about that stretch of history. A friend who was 13 in 1989 recalled those days this way:

"My childhood is filled with happy memories. Under communism, life was family-oriented. Careers didn't matter. There was no way to get rich, no reason to rush, so we had time. People always had time.

"But there were also shortages—many things were 'in deficit.' Sometimes my uncle would bring us several toilet paper rolls, held together with a string—absolutely the best gift anyone could give. I remember my mother and father had to 'organize' for special events...somehow find a good sausage and some Coca-Cola.

"Boys in my neighborhood collected pop cans. Since drinks were very limited in Poland, cans from other countries represented a world of opportunities beyond our borders. Parents could buy their children these cans on the black market, and the few families who were allowed to travel returned home with a treasure-trove of cans. One boy up the street from me went to Italy, and proudly brought home a Pepsi can. All of the boys in the neighborhood wanted to see it—it was a huge status symbol. But a month later, communism ended, you could buy whatever you wanted, and everyone's can collections were worthless.

"We had real chocolate only for Christmas. The rest of the year, for treats we got something called 'chocolate-like product'—it was sweet, dark, and smelled vaguely of chocolate. And we had oranges from Cuba for Christmas, too. Everybody was excited when the newspapers announced, 'The boat with the oranges from Cuba is just five days from Poland.' We waited with excitement all year for chocolate and those oranges. The smell of Christmas was so special. Now we have that smell every day. Still, my happiest Christmases were under communism."

Germans, Poles, and Ukrainians, resulting in Poland's becoming one of Eastern Europe's most ethnically homogenous countries (97 percent Polish).

Poland was arguably hit harder by the Soviet regime than the other countries in this book. As conditions worsened in the 1970s, food shortages were the norm. Stores were marked by long lines stretching around the block. Poles were issued ration coupons for food staples, and cashiers clipped off a corner when a purchase was made...assuming, of course, the item was in stock. It often wasn't. One Pole, born in 1973, told me that his mother used to joke that he was one-third Polish, one-third salmon (a local product), and one-third mango juice (from Egypt, traded by the government for Polish cars).

Everything was out of order and out of stock. A working telephone booth was cause for celebration. Visitors to Poland came back with poignant anecdotes. On returning home, one traveler was asked if he learned any Polish. "Yes!" he said. "I know the word for 'elevator.'" In fact, the word he had learned meant "out of order." In the waning days of communism, an American businessman went to a Polish restaurant with an extensive menu. He chose carefully, only to be told the item wasn't available. So, he chose again, and discovered this, too, was unavailable. After going through this a few more times, he grew frustrated. "Do you have *anything*?" "Sorry, sir. Only pierogi and borscht."

The little absurdities of communist life—which today seem almost comical—made every day a struggle. For years, every elderly woman in Poland had hair the same strange magenta color. There was only one color of dye available, so the choice was simple: Let your hair grow out (and look clownishly half red and half white), or line up and go red.

During these difficult times, the Poles often rose up—staging major protests in 1956, 1968, 1970, and 1976. Stalin famously noted that introducing communism to the Poles was like putting a saddle on a cow.

When an anti-communist Polish cardinal named Karol Wojtyła was elected Pope in 1978, it was a sign to his countrymen that change was in the air. (For more on Pope John Paul II, see page 224.) In 1980, Lech Wałęsa, an electrician at the shipyards in Gdańsk, became the leader of the Solidarity movement, the first workers' union in communist Eastern Europe. After an initial 18-day strike at the Gdańsk shipyards, the communist regime gave in, legalizing Solidarity (for more on Solidarity, see page 326).

But the union grew too powerful, and the communists felt their control slipping away. On Sunday, December 13, 1981, Poland's head of state, General Wojciech Jaruzelski, declared martial law in order to "forestall Soviet intervention." (Whether the

Polish Jokes

Through the dreary communist times, the Poles managed to keep their sense of humor. A popular target of jokes was the riot police, or ZOMO. Here are just a few of the things Poles said about these unpopular cops:

- It's better to have a sister who's a whore than a brother in the ZOMO.
- ZOMO police are hired based on the 90-90 principle: They have to weigh at least 90 kilograms (200 pounds), and their I.Q. must be less than 90.
- ZOMO would be dispatched in teams of three: one who could read, one who could write, and a third to protect those other two smart guys.
- A ZOMO policeman was sitting on the curb, crying. Someone came up to him and asked what was wrong. "I lost my dog!" he said. "No matter," the person replied. "He's a smart police dog. I'm sure he can find his way back to the station." "Yes," the ZOMO said. "But without him, *I* can't!"

The communists gave their people no options at elections: If you voted, you voted for the regime. Poles liked to joke that in some ways, this made communists like God—who created Eve, then said to Adam, "Now choose a wife." The communists could run a pig as a candidate, and it would still win. A popular symbol of dissent became a pig painted with the words, "Vote Red."

There were even jokes about jokes. Under communism, Poles noted that there was a government-sponsored prize for the funniest political joke: 15 years in prison.

Soviets actually would have intervened remains a hotly debated issue.) Tanks ominously rolled through the streets of Poland on that snowy December morning, and the Poles were terrified.

Martial law would last until 1983. Each Pole has his or her own chilling memories of this frightening time. During riots, the people would flock into churches—the only place they would be safe from the ZOMO, or riot police. But Solidarity struggled on, going underground and becoming a united movement of all demographics, 10 million members strong (more than a quarter of the population).

In July 1989, the ruling Communist Party agreed to hold open elections (reserving 65 percent of representatives for themselves). Their goal was to appease Solidarity, but the plan backfired: Communists didn't win a single seat. These elections helped spark the chain reaction across Eastern Europe that eventually tore down the Iron Curtain. Lech Wałęsa, a shipyard electrician from Gdańsk, became Poland's first post-communist president. (For more on Lech Wałęsa, see page 326.)

Poland in the 21st Century: The European Union

When 10 new countries joined the European Union in May 2004, Poland was the most ambivalent of the bunch. After centuries of being under other empires' authority, the Poles were hardly eager to relinquish some of their hard-fought autonomy to Brussels. Many Poles see the EU as an unstoppable monster, but believe that to survive in the modern Europe, their country had to join. They expect things to get worse (higher prices, a loss of traditional lifestyles) before they get better. Though their adjustment to the EU has been fitful, most Poles believe it will be good for the next generation.

While other countries were planning their fireworks displays to celebrate EU enlargement on May 1, 2004, Poland was seized by a strange sort of mass hysteria. The country buzzed with rumors of increased prices. When the news reported that sugar would be subject to a higher tax rate, there was a run on the stores, as the Poles bought up as much sugar as they could stockpile. The result? A shortage of sugar...and higher prices, even before May 1. (Sounds silly, sure. But remember the days after September 11, 2001, when U.S. stores ran out of tarp, duct tape, and bottled water.)

Poland is by far the most populous of the new EU members, with 39 million people (about the same as Spain, or two-thirds the size of Germany). This makes Poland the fifth-largest of the 25 EU member states—giving it serious political clout, which it has already asserted in shaping a new EU constitution. As the EU learns to live with its new Eastern European comrades, Poland looks poised to take a leading role in the "New Europe."

Polish Food

Polish food is hearty and tasty. Since it's north of the Carpathian Mountains, Poland's weather tends to be chilly, which limits the kinds of fruits and vegetables that flourish here. Like other northern European countries (such as Russia or Scandinavia), dominant staples include potatoes, dill, berries, and bread. Much of what you might think of as Jewish food turns up on Polish menus (gefilte fish, potato pancakes, chicken soup, and so forth)—not necessarily because either group influenced the other, but because they lived in the same area for centuries under the same climatic and culinary influences.

Polish soups are a highlight. The most typical are *żurek* and *barszcz*. *Żurek* is a light-colored soup made from a sourdough base, usually containing a hard-boiled egg and pieces of *kiełbasa* (sausage). *Barszcz*, better known to Americans as borscht, is

Bar Mleczny (Milk Bar)

Eating at a *bar mleczny* is an essential Polish sightseeing experience. These super-cheap cafeterias, which you'll see all over the country, are an incredibly cheap way to get a good meal... and, with the right attitude, a fun cultural experience.

In the communist era, the government subsidized the food at milk bars, allowing lowly workers to enjoy a meal out. The tradition continues, and today, Poland still foots the bill for most of your milk-bar meal. Prices are astoundingly low— my bill usually comes to about $3—and, while communist-era fare was gross, today's milk-bar cuisine is usually quite tasty.

Milk bars usually offer many of the traditional tastes listed in this section. Common items are soups (like *żurek* and *barszcz*), a variety of cabbage-based salads, *kotlet* (fried pork chops), pierogi (like ravioli, with various fillings), and *naleśniki* (pancakes). You'll often see glasses of juice and (of course) milk, but most milk bars also stock bottles of water and Coke.

The service is aimed at locals—no English menu and a confusing ordering system. Every milk bar is a little different, but here's the general procedure: Head to the counter, wait to be acknowledged, and point to what you want. Handy vocabulary: *to* (sounds like "toe") means "that"; *i* (pronounced "ee") means "and."

If the milk-bar lady asks you any questions, you have three options: nod stupidly until she just gives you something; repeat one of the things she just said (assuming she's asked you to choose between two options, like meat or cheese in your pierogi); or hope that a kindly English-speaking Pole in line will leap to your rescue. If nothing else, ordering at a milk bar is an adventure in gestures. Smiling seems to slightly extend the patience of milk-bar staffers.

Once your tray is all loaded up, pay the cashier, do a double-take when you realize how cheap your bill is, then find a table. After the meal, it's generally polite, if not expected, to bus your dishes (watch locals and imitate).

a savory beet soup. There are various types of borscht: the clear *barszcz czerwony* (red borscht), and *Barszcz ukraiński* (Ukrainian borscht)—which is similar but has vegetables mixed in (usually cabbage, beans, and carrots). *Biały barszcz*, or white borscht, has no beets at all. In summer, you can try *chłodnik*, a cold beet soup.

Another familiar Polish dish is pierogi. These ravioli-like dumplings come with various fillings. The most traditional are minced meat, sauerkraut, mushroom, cheese, and blueberry, but many restaurants experiment with more exotic fillings. Pierogi are often served with specks of fatty bacon to add flavor. Pierogi are a budget traveler's dream: Restaurants serving them are everywhere, and they're generally cheap, filling, and tasty.

Bigos is a tasty sauerkraut stew cooked with meat, mushrooms, and whatever's in the pantry. *Gołąbki* is cabbage leaves stuffed with minced meat and rice in a tomato sauce. *Kotlet schabowy* (fried pork chops)—once painfully scarce in communist Poland—remain a local favorite to this day. *Kaczka* (duck) is popular, as is fish: Look for *pstrąg* (trout), *karp* (carp, beware of bones), and *węgorz* (eel). Poles eat lots of potatoes, which are served with nearly every meal.

Poland has excellent pastries. A *piekarnia* is a bakery specializing in breads. But if you really want something special, look for a *cukiernia* (pastry shop). The classic Polish treat is *pączki*, glazed jelly doughnuts. They can have different fillings, but most typical is a wild-rose jam. *Szarlotka* is apple cake—sometimes made with chunks of apples (especially in season), sometimes with apple filling. *Sernik* is cheesecake, and *makowiec* is poppy-seed cake. *Winebreda* is an especially gooey Danish. *Babeczka* is like a cupcake filled with pudding. You may see *jabłko w cieście*—slices of apple cooked in dough, then glazed. *Napoleonka* is a French-style treat with layers of crispy wafers and custard.

The bagel-like rings you'll see on the street, *obwarzanki*, are fresh, tasty, and cheap. *Lody* (ice cream) is popular. The most beloved traditional candy is *ptasie mleczko* (birds' milk), which is like a semi-sour marshmallow covered with chocolate.

Thirsty? *Woda* is water, *woda mineralna* is bottled water (*gazowana* is with gas/carbonation, *niegazowana* is without), *kawa* is coffee, *herbata* is tea, *sok* is juice, and *mleko* is milk. Żywiec and Okocim are the best-known brands of *piwo* (beer). *Wódka* (vodka) is a Polish staple—the name is actually derived from the Polish word for "water." Żubrówka, the most famous brand of vodka, comes with a blade of grass from the bison reserves in eastern Poland (look for the bottle with the bison). The bison "flavor" the grass...then the grass flavors the vodka. Poles often mix Żubrówka with apple juice. For "Cheers!" say, *"Na zdrowie!"* (think "nice driving").

Unusual drinks to try if you have the chance are *kwas* (a cold, fizzy, Ukrainian-style non-alcoholic beverage made from day-old rye bread) and *kompot* (a hot drink made from stewed berries). Poles are unusually fond of carrot juice (often cut with fruit juice); Kubuś is the most popular brand.

"Bon appétit" is *"Smacznego."* To pay, ask for the *rachunek* (rah-KHOO-nehk) or say, *"Płacę"* (PWOTS-eh, "I'll pay").

Polish Language

Polish is closely related to its neighboring Slavic languages (Slovak and Czech), with the biggest difference being that Polish has

Key Polish Phrases

English	Polish	Pronounced
Hello. (formal)	*Dzień dobry.*	jehn DOH-bree
Hi. / Bye. (informal)	*Cześć.*	cheshch
Do you speak English? (asked of a man)	*Czy Pan mówi po angielsku?*	chee pahn MOO-vee poh ahn-GYEHL-skoo
Do you speak English? (asked of a woman)	*Czy Pani mówi po angielsku?*	chee PAH-nee MOO-vee poh ahn-GYEHL-skoo
Yes. / No.	*Tak. / Nie.*	tahk / nyeh
Please. / You're welcome. / Can I help you?	*Proszę.*	PROH-sheh
Thank you.	*Dziękuję.*	jehn-KOO-yeh
I'm sorry. / . Excuse me	*Przepraszam.*	pzheh-PRAH-shahm
Good.	*Dobrze.*	DOHB-zheh
Goodbye.	*Do widzenia.*	doh veed-ZAY-nyah
one / two	*jeden / dwa*	YEH-dehn / dvah
three / four	*trzy / cztery*	tzhee / chuh-TEH-ree
five / six	*pięć / sześć*	pyench / sheshch
seven / eight	*siedem / osiem*	SYEH-dehm / OH-shehm
nine / ten	*dziewięć / dziesięć*	JEH-vyench / JEH-shench
hundred	*sto*	stoh
thousand	*tysiąc*	TEE-shanch
How much?	*Ile?*	EE-leh
local currency	*złoty (zł)*	ZWOH-tee
Where is...?	*Gdzie jest...?*	gdzeh yehst
...the toilet	*...toaleta*	toh-ah-LEH-tah
men	*męska*	MEHN-skah
women	*damska*	DAHM-skah
water / coffee	*woda / kawa*	VOH-dah / KAH-vah
beer / wine	*piwo / wino*	PEE-voh / VEE-noh
Cheers!	*Na zdrowie!*	nah ZDROH-vyeh
the bill	*rachunek*	rah-KHOO-nehk

lots of fricatives (hissing sounds—"sh" and "ch"—often in close proximity). Consider the opening line of Poland's most famous tongue-twisting nursery rhyme: *W Szczebrzeszynie chrząszcz brzmi w trzcinie* ("In Szczebrzeszyn, a beetle is heard in the reeds"—pronounced vuh shih-chehb-zheh-shee-nyeh khzhahshch bzh-mee vuh tzhuh-cheen-yeh...or something like that).

Polish intimidates Americans with long, difficult-to-pronounce words. But if you take your time and sound things out, you'll quickly develop an ear for it. First of all, the stress is always on the next-to-last syllable. The letter *c* always sounds like "ts" (as in "cats"). The letter combinations *ć, ci,* and *cz* all sound like "ch"; *ś, si,* and *sz* all sound like "sh"; and *ź, ż, zi,* and *rz* all sound like "zh" (as in "leisure"). The letter *ń* and the combination *ni* sound like "ny" (as in "canyon").

Some Polish vowels have a nasalized sound, like in French. If you see *ę* or *ą*, pronounce them as "en" or "an."

One of the trickiest changes to get used to: *w* sounds like "v," and *ł* sounds like "w." So, "Lech Wałęsa" isn't pronounced "lehk wah-LEH-sah," as Dan Rather used to say—but "lehkh vah-WEHN-sah."

As you're tracking down addresses, these words will help: *miasto* (town), *plac* (square), *rynek* (big market square), *ulica* (road), *aleja* (avenue), and *most* (bridge).

KRAKÓW

Kraków is the Boston of Poland: a beautiful, old-fashioned city buzzing with history, enjoyable sights, tourists, and college students. Even though the country's capital moved from here to Warsaw 400 years ago, Kraków remains Poland's cultural and intellectual center. Of all of the Eastern European cities laying claim to the boast "the next Prague," Kraków is for real. Now's the time to visit: just as the tourist infrastructure ramps up, but before it's swamped with crowds.

Kraków grew wealthy from trade in the late 10th and early 11th centuries. Traders who passed through were required to stop here for a few days and sell their wares at a reduced cost. Local merchants turned around and sold those goods with big price hikes...and Kraków thrived. In 1038, it became Poland's capital.

Tatars invaded in 1241, leaving the city in ruins. Krakovians took this opportunity to rebuild their streets in a near-perfect grid, a striking contrast to the narrow, mazelike lanes of most medieval towns. The destruction also paved the way for the spectacular Main Market Square—still Kraków's best attraction.

King Kazimierz the Great sparked Kraków's Golden Age in the 14th century (see page 218). In 1364, he established the university that still defines the city (and counts Copernicus and Pope John Paul II among its alumni).

But Kraków's power waned as Poland's political center shifted to Warsaw. In 1596, the capital officially moved north. At the end of the 18th century, three neighboring powers—Russia, Prussia, and Austria—partitioned Poland, annexing all of its territory and dividing it among themselves. Warsaw ended up as a satellite of oppressive Moscow, and Kraków became a poor provincial

Kraków

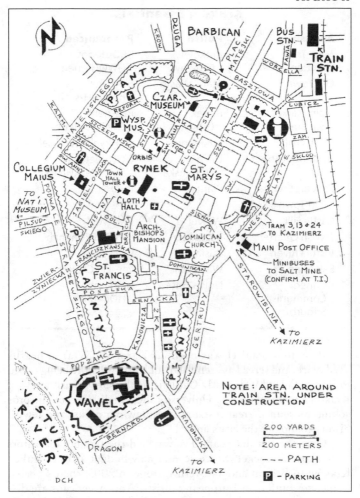

NOTE: AREA AROUND TRAIN STN. UNDER CONSTRUCTION

200 YARDS
200 METERS
--- PATH
P - PARKING

backwater of Vienna. But despite Kraków's reduced prominence, Austria's comparatively liberal climate helped turn the city into a haven for intellectuals and progressives (including a young revolutionary thinker from Russia named Vladimir Lenin).

Kraków emerged from World War II virtually unscathed. But when the communists took over, they decided to give intellectual (and potentially dissident) Kraków an injection of good Soviet values—in the form of heavy industry. They built Nowa Huta, an enormous steelworks and planned town for workers, on Kraków's outskirts—dooming the city to decades of smog. Thankfully, Kraków is now much cleaner than it was 15 years ago.

Kraków Essentials

English	Polish	Pronounced
Main Train Station	Kraków Główny	KROCK-oof GWOHV-nee
Old Town	Stare Miasto	STAH-reh mee-AH-stoh
Main Market Square	Rynek Główny	REE-nehk GWOHV-nee
Cloth Hall	Sukiennice	soo-kyeh-NEET-seh
Floriańska Street	Ulica Floriańska	OOH-leet-suh floh-ree-AHN-skah
Park around the Old Town	Planty	PLAHN-tee
Castle Hill	Wawel	VAH-vehl
Jewish Quarter	Kazimierz	kah-ZHEE-mehzh
Vistula River	Wisła	VEES-wah
Salt Mine	Wieliczka	vee-LEECH-kah
Planned Communist Suburb	Nowa Huta	NOH-vah HOO-tah

Pope John Paul II was born (as Karol Wojtyła) in nearby Wadowice, and served as archbishop of Kraków before being called to Rome. Poland is devoutly Catholic; make sure to visit a few of Kraków's many churches. University life, small but thought-provoking museums, great restaurants, sprawling parks, and Jewish history round out the city's appeal.

Over the last few years, I've watched the number of visitors to Kraków skyrocket. Since several new budget airlines linked Kraków to Britain and Western Europe in 2005, there's been a tremendous influx of European tourists. And Americans are discovering it, too. The city has come to life at a speed paralleled only by Prague's transition a decade ago. Yet despite its overwhelming popularity, competition keeps prices delightfully low.

Planning Your Time

Kraków and its important side-trips deserve at least two full days on the busiest itinerary. Most people can easily fill three days. The city's sights are quickly exhausted, but more than any town in Europe, Kraków is made for aimless strolling.

Ideally, spend two full days in Kraków itself, plus a visit to Auschwitz (either as a side-trip on the 3rd day, or en route to or from Kraków). In a pinch, spend one day sightseeing in Kraków, another at Auschwitz, and two evenings on the Main Market Square.

With only one full day in Kraków, follow this plan: Take my self-guided walk of Krakow's Royal Way to cover the city's core. Visit any Old Town museums that interest you (Wyspiański Museum, Gallery of 19th-Century Polish Art, Czartoryski Museum, Jagiellonian University Museum), and have lunch on or near the Main Market Square. Spend the afternoon at Wawel Castle (note that many castle sights close at 15:00). Savor the Square over dinner or a drink, or enjoy traditional Jewish music and cuisine in Kazimierz.

With more time in Kraków, explore Kazimierz, the former Jewish Quarter—a must for those interested in Jewish heritage, and illuminating for anyone. Or, if you're intrigued by the architecture of the communist era, head for the Nowa Huta suburb.

Auschwitz, an essential side-trip, requires the better part of a day for a round-trip visit (see next chapter). If you have more time, nearby Wieliczka Salt Mine makes another good day trip. It's conceivably possible to fit Auschwitz and Wieliczka into the same day, especially with an early start and a local driver—but it's far more reasonable to do them on separate days.

ORIENTATION

(area code: 012)
Kraków (KROCK-oof, sometimes spelled "Cracow" in English) is mercifully compact, flat, and easy to navigate. While the urban sprawl is big (with about 735,000 people), the tourist's Kraków feels small. You can walk from the northern edge of the Old Town to the southern edge (Wawel Hill) in about 15 minutes.

A greenbelt called the Planty rings the Old Town (Stare Miasto) where the walls and moat once stood. Most sights—and almost all recommended hotels and restaurants—are in the Old Town (inside the Planty). In the center of the Old Town lies the Main Market Square (Rynek Główny), with the Cloth Hall in the middle and St. Mary's Church at the corner. From the Main Market Square, the Main Train Station is a 10-minute walk to the northeast; Kazimierz (the old Jewish quarter) is a 20-minute walk to the southeast; and Wawel Hill is a 10-minute walk south, just beyond the Planty. Here you'll find a historic castle, museums, and Poland's national church. Just beyond Wawel is the Vistula River.

Tourist Information

Kraków has several TIs, which are all open sporadic hours based on demand. The handiest for travelers are in the **Planty** park, between the Main Train Station and Main Market Square (daily June–Sept

9:00–19:00, Oct–May 9:00–17:00, in round, green-roofed kiosk at ulica Szpitalna 25, tel. 012/432-0110); just north of the Main Market Square, on **ulica Św. Jana** (June–Sept daily 10:00–18:00; Oct–May Mon–Sat 10:00–18:00, closed Sun; at #2, tel. 012/421-7787); and in the **Town Hall Tower** right on the Main Market Square (daily June–Sept 9:00–19:00, Oct–May 9:00–17:00, tel. 012/433-7310). Other, less convenient offices are in **Kazimierz** (ulica Józefa 7, tel. 012/422-0471), **Nowa Huta** (os. Centrum B9, tel. 012/685-5900), and the **airport** (tel. 012/285-5341). The Web site for all TIs is www.krakow.pl.

At any TI, ask what's new in fast-changing Kraków, browse the brochures, and pick up the free one-page map and the Kraków Tourist Information booklet. I'd skip the **Kraków Tourist Card**, which covers public transportation in Kraków, admission to several city museums, and moderate discounts to outlying sights and tours (45 zł/2 days, 65 zł/3 days). Since public transportation is mostly unnecessary and museums are so cheap, this card doesn't make sense for most visitors.

The TI on ulica Św. Jana specializes in cultural events. They can tell you what's on in Kraków, book tickets for some concerts (no extra fee), and tell you how to get tickets for others. The monthly *Karnet* cultural events book lists everything (4 zł, mostly Polish with some English, also online at www.karnet.bci.pl).

Arrival in Kraków

By Train: Kraków's Main Train Station (called "Kraków Główny") is just northeast of the Old Town. The area around the station will likely be in the midst of a massive construction project through late 2006. When finished, this new complex will consist of a super-modern shopping mall (Galeria Krakówska) and brand-new train and bus stations. But the project has been on-again, off-again for years, and nobody knows when—or if—it will be completed.

On arrival, follow signs into the center *(wyjście do centrum)*—the walk to the Main Market Square takes about 10 minutes. As you exit the station, signs will direct you to the left, through a construction zone and towards a pedestrian underpass that goes beneath the busy ring road (once down there, bear right). When you emerge in the Planty park, you'll see the round TI kiosk on your left. The Main Market Square is a few blocks straight ahead. Somewhere near the station, you should come across a taxi stand (the fair metered rate to downtown is a reasonable 10–15 zł).

By Car: Check with your hotel. The most central parking lot is on ulica Szczepańska, a block west of the Main Market Square.

By Plane: The small, modern **John Paul II Kraków-Balice Airport** is 10 miles west of the center. Bus #192 takes you to the train station and the edge of the Old Town (3.10 zł, 40 min), or you can catch a cab (around 50 zł). Airport info: tel. 012/285-5120, www.lotniski-balice.pl.

Note that many budget flights—including those on Wizz Air, SkyEurope, Centralwings, easyJet, and Ryanair—use the **International Airport Katowice in Pyrzowice** (Międzynarodowy Port Lotniczy Katowice w Pyrzowicach, www.gtl.com.pl). This airport is in the city of Katowice, about 50 miles west of Kraków. A few direct buses each day run between Katowice Airport and Kraków's Main Train Station (50 zł, about 4/day, trip takes 1.75 hrs, www.axet.com.pl). You can also take the bus from Katowice Airport into the Katowice train station, then take the train to Kraków (hrly, 1.5 hrs). Wizz Air's Web site is useful for figuring out your connection: www.wizzair.com.

Helpful Hints

Sightseeing Schedules: Most museums are closed Monday, and many are free one day a week (which tends to change from year to year). Hours at museums tend to change frequently; carefully confirm the opening times of sights at the TI.

Internet Access: Kraków's many Internet cafés—it seems there's one on every corner—charge around 1 zł for 15 min. **Internet Klub Garinet** is convenient (daily until 24:00, on the Royal Way just a block north of the Main Market Square at ulica Floriańska 10).

Post Office: In peak season, a small postal wagon sells stamps in the middle of the Main Market Square. The main post office (Poczta Główna) is at the intersection of Starowiślna and the Westerplatte ring road, a few blocks east of the Main Market Square.

Bookstore: For used English books, try **Massolit Books,** just west of the Old Town (Sun–Thu 10:00–20:00, Fri–Sat 10:00–22:00, ulica Felicjanek 4, tel. 012/432-4150).

Laundry: Doing laundry in Kraków is frustrating. There's no good self-service launderette in the center, unless you're staying at a hostel. Your hotel can do your wash, but it's expensive. If you must have something laundered, a central option is **Betty Clean** (about 9 zł per shirt, 12 zł for pants, takes 24 hours, pay 50 percent more for express 3-hr service, Mon–Fri 7:30–19:30, Sat 8:00–15:30, closed Sun, just outside the Planty at ulica Zwierzyniecka 6, tel. 012/423-0848).

Travel Agencies: Orbis, at the top of the Main Market Square, books bus tours, changes money, and sells train tickets (May–Sept Mon–Fri 9:00–19:00, Sat 9:00–15:00, closed Sun, closes 1 hour earlier Oct–April, Rynek Główny 41, www.orbis.krakow .pl, tel. 012/619-2449). The agency posts a handy complete train schedule in their window. Buy your train tickets in this central location (no fee, English spoken) to avoid the trip to the station.

Also on the Square—right in the Cloth Hall—is **MCIT** (Małopolskie Centrum Informacji Turystycznej), which sells maps and guidebooks, books tours, arranges transportation and car rentals, and has a room-finding service (generally open summer Mon–Fri 8:00–20:00, Sat–Sun 9:00–16:00; winter Mon–Fri 9:00–17:00, Sat 9:00–14:00, closed Sun; in middle of Cloth Hall facing St. Mary's Church at Rynek Główny 1–3, tel. 012/421-7706, www.mcit.pl).

Getting Around Kraków

Kraków's top sights and best hotels are easily accessible by foot. You'll only need wheels if you're going to the Kazimierz Jewish quarter or the Nowa Huta suburbs.

By Public Transit: Trams and buses zip around Kraków's urban sprawl. While most trams are new and modern, a few rickety old trams with big windows (dubbed "aquariums" by locals) also rattle around the city.

The trams you're most likely to use are #4 to Nowa Huta, and #3, #13, and #24 to Kazimierz. The same tickets are used for both trams and buses, and can be purchased at kiosks marked *RUCH*, or—for 0.50 zł extra—from the driver. There are three kinds of tickets: A *bilet jednoprzejazdowy* (basic single ticket, no transfers) costs 2.50 zł at a kiosk. Technically, if you're using this cheap ticket, you have to buy a separate ticket for your bag (or risk a fine). So you might as well get a *bilet godzinny*—good for an hour, and allowing transfers and luggage (3.10 zł). Always validate your ticket when you board the bus or tram.

There are also longer-term tickets for 24 hours (10.40 zł), 48 hours (18.80 zł), and 72 hours (25 zł). These must be validated the first time you use them, and can only be purchased at special MPK ticket booths (the handiest is in the Planty near the TI).

By Taxi: Just as in other big Eastern European cities, only take cabs that are clearly marked with a company logo and telephone number. Kraków taxis start at 5 zł and charge 2–3 zł per kilometer. Rides are very short and generally run less than 10 zł. You're more likely to get the fair metered rate by calling or hailing a cab, rather than taking one waiting at tourist spots. To call a cab, try **Radio Taxi** (tel. 012/919 or toll-free 0800-500-919).

By Buggy: Romantic, horse-drawn buggies trot around Kraków from the Main Market Square. The going rate is about 70 zł for a 30-minute tour, but prices are slushy. Ask three drivers, and go with the cheapest offer.

By Bike: Wypożyczalnia Rowerów Rent-a-Bike, half a block off the Main Market Square, is run by easygoing Michał Bisping. Biking the Planty park and along the riverside promenades gives

your trip a great extra dimension and gets you out of the pret-
tied-up Old Town to see a slice of untouristy Kraków (4 zł/hr, 30
zł/day, April–Oct daily 9:00–dusk, closed Nov–March, ulica Św.
Anny 4, mobile 0501-745-986, www.bikes-rental.prv.pl).

TOURS

Local Guides—Kraków has several affordable guides. I've enjoyed
working with two in particular, both of whom have cars (for driving you to Auschwitz or on other day trips, or for taking you into
the countryside to help you track down your Polish roots): **Marta
Chmielowska** (250 zł/half-day, 300 zł with her car, full day just
a little more, mobile 0603-668-008, martachm@op.pl) and **Anna
Gega** (by foot: 250 zł/4 hrs, 350 zł/day; by car: 300 zł/4 hrs, 400
zł/day; tel. 012/411-2523, mobile 0604-151-293, leadertour@wp.pl).
Crazy Guides—This irreverent company offers tours to the communist suburb of Nowa Huta and other outlying sights. For details,
see page 243.
Bus Tours—Various tour companies run bus-plus-walking itineraries (each of them around 120 zł), including a general city overview (3 hrs), Auschwitz (6 hrs), Wieliczka Salt Mine (4 hrs), and
other regional side-trips. Get information at the TI.
Golf-Cart Tours—Several golf-cart companies based on the Main
Market Square offer tours (50 zł for half-hour tour of Old Town,
80 zł for hour-long tour, plus 25 zł per person for headphone commentary).
Walking Tours—There are walking tours in English daily April
through October (70 zł, doesn't include admissions, 4.5 hours;
leaves at 10:00 from MCIT office on the Main Market Square,
route includes Kraków Old Town, then break, then Kazimierz
Jewish quarter). But four people can actually hire their own excellent local guide for less money (see above).

SIGHTS

Krakow's Royal Way Walk

Most of Kraków's major sights are conveniently connected by this
self-guided walking tour. This route is known as the "Royal Way,"
because the king used to follow this same path when he returned
to Kraków after a journey. After the capital moved to Warsaw,
most kings were still coronated and buried in Wawel Cathedral at
the far end of town—and they followed this same route for both
occasions. You could sprint through this three-part walk in an
hour (less than a mile altogether), but it's much more fun if you
take it slow.

Kraków at a Glance

Be Warned: Kraków's museum hours tend to fluctuate. If you want to be sure to get into a certain sight, confirm the hours in advance.

▲▲▲**Main Market Square** Stunning heart of Kraków and a people magnet any time of day. **Hours:** Always open.

▲▲**Planty** Once a moat, now a scenic park encircling the city. **Hours:** Always open.

▲▲**St. Mary's Church** Landmark church with extraordinary wood-carved Gothic altarpiece. **Hours:** Mon–Sat 11:30–18:00, Sun 14:00–18:00.

▲▲**Cloth Hall** Fourteenth-century market hall with 21st-century souvenirs. **Hours:** Summer Mon–Fri 9:00–18:00, Sat–Sun 9:00–15:00, sometimes later; winter Mon–Fri 9:00–16:00, Sat–Sun 9:00–15:00.

▲▲**St. Francis' Basilica** Lovely Gothic church with some of Poland's best Art Nouveau. **Hours:** Open long hours daily.

▲▲**Wawel Cathedral** Poland's splendid national church, with tons of tombs, a crypt, and a climbable tower. **Hours:** Ticket sales for crypt and tower May–Sept Mon–Sat 9:00–17:15, Sun 12:15–17:15; Oct–April Mon–Sat 9:00–15:45, Sun 12:15–15:45.

▲▲**Wawel Castle Grounds** Historic hilltop with views, castle, cathedral, courtyard with chakras, and a passel of museums. **Hours:** Grounds open daily May–Sept 6:00–20:00, Oct–April 6:00–17:00.

▲▲**Jewish Cemeteries** Two touching burial sites—the New

Royal Way Walk Part 1: Barbican to Main Market Square

Begin the walk at the north end of the Old Town, at the barbican.

▲**Barbican (Barbakan), Florian Gate (Brama Floriańska), and City Walls**—Tatars invaded Kraków three times in the 13th century. After the first attack destroyed the city in 1241, Krakovians built this wall. The original rampart had 47 watchtowers and eight gates. The big, round defensive fort standing outside the wall is a barbican. Structures like this provided extra fortification to weak sections. Imagine how it looked in 1500, when this barbican stood outside the town moat with a long bridge leading to the Florian Gate—the city's main entryway.

(post-1800) and Old (1552–1800)—in Kazimierz. **Hours:** Old Cemetery—May–Oct Sun–Fri 9:00–18:00, Nov–April until 16:00, always closed Sat, New Cemetery—Sun–Fri 8:00–18:00, until 16:00 in winter, closed Sat.

▲**Czartoryski Museum** Varied collection, with European paintings (da Vinci and Rembrandt) and Polish armor, handicrafts, and decorative arts. **Hours:** Generally open Tue–Sat 10:00–16:00, Sun 10:00–15:00, closed Mon, open until 19:00 some evenings in summer, shorter hours Nov–April.

▲**Gallery of 19th-Century Polish Art** Easy-to-appreciate works by Poland's finest painters, little known outside of the country. **Hours:** Generally Tue–Sat 10:00–16:00, Sun 10:00–15:00, closed Mon, open later some evenings in summer, shorter hours Nov–April.

▲**Wyspiański Museum** Art by the talented leader of the Młoda Polska Art Nouveau movement. **Hours:** Generally open Tue–Sun 10:00–16:00, closed Mon, open later some evenings in summer, shorter hours Nov–May.

▲**Isaac Synagogue** Kazimierz house of worship showing evocative historical movies of the Jewish Quarter. **Hours:** Sun–Fri 9:00–19:00, July–Aug until 20:00, closed Sat, closes at sundown on winter Fri—as early as 15:00 in Dec.

▲**Polish Folk Museum** Traditional rural Polish life on display—an open-air museum moved inside. **Hours:** May–Sept Mon and Wed–Fri 10:00–17:00, Sat–Sun 10:00–14:00, closed Tue; Oct–April Mon 10:00–18:00, Wed–Fri 10:00–15:00, Sat–Sun 10:00–14:00, closed Tue.

• *Before you step through the gate yourself, look to the left and right of the barbican to see the...*

▲▲**Planty**—By the 19th century, Kraków's no-longer-necessary city wall had fallen into disrepair. Krakovians decided to tear down what remained, fill in the moat, and plant trees. Today, the Planty is a beautiful park that stretches for 2.5 miles around the entire perimeter of Kraków's Old Town.

• *Go through the gate into the Old Town.*

▲▲**Floriańska Street (Ulica Floriańska)**—You're standing at the head of Kraków's historic (and now touristic) gamut. On the inside of the city wall, you'll see a makeshift **art gallery**, where starving students hawk the works they've painted at the Academy of Fine Arts (across the busy street from the barbican). Portraits, still lifes, landscapes, local scenes, nudes...this might just be Kraków's best collection of art. If you were to detour along the gallery (to the left as you face the gate), in a block you'd arrive at another fine collection—the eclectic Czartoryski Museum, home to a rare Leonardo da Vinci oil painting (see "Museums," page 231).

Walking down Floriańska Street, you can't miss the **McDonald's** on the left. When renovating this building, they discovered a Gothic cellar—so they excavated it and added seating. Today, you can super-size your ambience by dining on a Big Mac and fries under a medieval McVault.

Cukiarnia Jama Michalika (farther down on left at #45)—a dark, atmospheric café popular with locals for its coffee and pastries—began in 1895 as a simple bakery in a claustrophobic back room. A brothel upstairs scared off respectable types, so the owner attracted students by creating a cabaret act called "The Green Balloon." To this day, the cabaret—political satire set to music—still runs (in Polish only). Around the turn of the 20th century, this was a hangout of the Młoda Polska (Young Poland) movement—the Polish answer to Art Nouveau (see page 221). The walls are papered with sketches from poor artists who couldn't pay their tabs. (Poke around inside, and see how many green balloons you can spot. Consider having a snack or meal here—see page 252.)

Two blocks ahead on the left (at #3, 50 yards before the big church), you'll see **Jazz Club U Muniaka.** In the 1950s, Janusz Muniak was one of the first Polish jazzmen. Now he owns this place, and jams regularly here in a cool cellar surrounded by jazzy art (10- to 20-zł cover, open nightly 19:00–1:00 in the morning, live music nightly at 21:30, cheap drinks after that, best music Thu–Sat, www.umuniaka.krakow.pl). If you hang around the bar before the show, you might find yourself sitting next to Janusz himself, smoking his pipe...and getting ready to smoke on the saxophone.

• *Continue into the Main Market Square, where you'll run into...*

▲▲**St. Mary's Church (Kościół Mariacki)**—A church has stood on this spot for 800 years. The original church was destroyed by the first Tatar invasion in 1241, but all subsequent versions—including the current one—have been built on the same foundation. You can look down the sides to see how the Main Market Square has risen about seven feet over the centuries.

How many church towers does St. Mary's have? Technically, the answer is one. The shorter tower belongs to the church; the taller one is a municipal watchtower, from which you'll hear a bugler playing the hourly *hejnał* song. During that first Tatar

invasion, so the story goes, a watch-
man in the tower saw the enemy
approaching and sounded the alarm.
Before he could finish the tune, an
arrow pierced his throat—which
is why, even today, the *hejnał* stops
subito partway through. Today's
buglers—12 in all—are firemen first,
musicians second. Each one works
a 24-hour shift up there, playing
the *hejnał* on the hour, every hour
(broadcast on national Polish radio
at noon). In July and August, you can
climb up and meet them (Wed and Sat).

The church's front door is open 14 hours a day and free to those
who come to pray. Tourists use the door around the right side (4
zł, Mon–Sat 11:30–18:00, Sun 14:00–18:00). The rusty neck-stock
(behind the tourists' left door) was used for public humiliation
until the 1700s.

Inside, you're drawn to one of the most impressive medieval
woodcarvings in existence—the exquisite, three-part Gothic
altarpiece by German Veit Stoss (Wit Stwosz in Polish). Carved
in 12 years and completed in 1489, it's packed with emotion rare
in Gothic art. Stoss used oak for the structural parts and linden
trunks for the figures. When the altar doors are closed, you see
scenes from the lives of Mary and Jesus. The open altar depicts the
Dormition (death) of the Virgin. The artist catches the apostles
(11, without Judas) around Mary, reacting in the seconds after she
collapses. Mary is depicted in three stages: dying, being escorted
to heaven by Jesus, and (at the very top) being crowned in heaven
(flanked by 2 Polish saints—Adalbert and Stanisław). The six
scenes on the sides are: the Annunciation, birth of Jesus, visit by
the Three Magi, Jesus' Resurrection, his Ascension, and Mary
becoming the mother of the apostles at Pentecost. The altar is open
daily between noon and 18:00. Try to be here by 11:45 for the ceremonial opening or at 18:00 for the closing.

There's more to St. Mary's than the altar. While you're admiring this church's art, notice the flowery neo-Gothic painting covering the choir walls. Stare up into the starry, starry blue ceiling.
As you wander around, realize that the church was renovated a
century ago by three Polish geniuses from two very different
artistic generations: the venerable positivist Jan Matejko and his
Art Nouveau students, Stanisław Wyspiański and Józef Mehoffer
(we'll learn more about these two later on our walk). The huge silver bird under the organ loft in back is the crowned eagle—symbol
of Poland.

Kazimierz the Great
(1333–1370)

Out of the centuries of Polish kings, only one earned the nickname "great," and he's the only one worth remembering: Kazimierz the Great.

K. the G., who ruled Poland from Kraków in the 14th century, was one of those larger-than-life medieval kings who left his mark on all fronts—from war to diplomacy, art patronage to womanizing. His scribes bragged that Kazimierz "found a Poland made of wood, and left one made of brick and stone." He put Kraków on the map as a major European capital. He founded many villages (some of which still bear his name) and replaced wooden structures with stone ones (such as Kraków's Cloth Hall). He also established the Kraków Academy (today's Jagiellonian University), the second-oldest university in Central Europe.

Most of all, Kazimierz is remembered as a progressive, tolerant king. In the 14th century, other nations were deporting—or even interning—their Jewish subjects, who were commonly scapegoated for anything that went wrong. But the enlightened and kindly Kazimierz actively encouraged Jews to come to Poland by granting them special privileges, often related to banking and trade—establishing the country as a safe haven for Jews in Europe.

Kazimierz the Great was the last of Poland's long-lived Piast dynasty. Although he left no male heir—at least, no legitimate one—Kazimierz's advances set the stage for Poland's Golden Age (14th–16th centuries). After his death, Poland united with Lithuania (against the common threat of the Teutonic Knights), the Jagiellonian dynasty was born, and Poland became one of Europe's mightiest medieval powers.

▲▲▲Main Market Square (Rynek Główny)—Kraków's marvelous square, one of Europe's most gasp-worthy public spaces, bustles with street musicians, colorful flower stalls, cotton-candy vendors, loitering teenagers, businesspeople commuting by foot, gawking tourists, and the lusty coos of pigeons. This Square is where Kraków lives. On my last visit, local teens practiced break-dancing moves at one end of the Square while activist types protested Poland's EU membership at the other.

The Square was established in the 13th century, when the city had to be rebuilt after being flattened by the Tatars. At that time, the Square was the biggest in medieval Europe. It was illegal to sell anything on the street, so everything had to be sold here on the Main Market Square. It was divided into smaller markets, such as the butcher stalls, the ironworkers' tents, and the Cloth Hall (see below).

The statue in the middle of the Square is of Romantic poet **Adam Mickiewicz** (1789–1855). His epic masterpiece, *Pan Tadeusz*, is still regarded as one of the greatest works in Polish, and Mickiewicz is considered the "Polish Shakespeare." A wistful, nostalgic tale of Polish-Lithuanian nobility, *Pan Tadeusz* stirred patriotism in a Poland that had been dismantled by surrounding empires.

Near the end of the Square, you'll see the tiny **Church of St. Adalbert,** the oldest church in Kraków (10th century). This Romanesque structure predates the Square. Like St. Mary's (described above), it seems to be at an angle because it's aligned east–west, as was the custom when it was built. (In other words, the churches aren't crooked—the Square is.)

Drinks are cheap at cafés on the Square (most around 10 zł). Find a spot where you like the view and the chairs, then sit and sip. Enjoy the folk band. Tip them, and you can photograph their traditional Kraków garb up close. (A big tip gets you *The Star-Spangled Banner.*)

As the Square buzzes around you, imagine this place before 1989. There were no outdoor cafés, no touristy souvenir stands, and no salesmen hawking cotton candy. The communist government shut down all but a handful of the businesses (keeping open, for instance, the Cloth Hall, which was a tourist arcade with shops, much like today). They didn't want people to congregate here—they should be at home, resting, because "a rested worker is a productive worker." The buildings were covered with soot from the nearby Lenin Steelworks in Nowa Huta. (The communists denied the pollution, and when the student "Green Brigades" staged a demonstration in this Square to raise awareness in the 1970s, they were immediately arrested.)

Now imagine the Square just a short time ago, during Pope John Paul II's illness and death in the spring of 2005. News trucks sat anxiously around the perimeter of the Square, and TV cameramen jockeyed for position on temporary platforms. After the Pope died, huge banners—red and white (for Poland) and yellow and white (for the Vatican), both with black bands—were draped from the towers of St. Mary's Church. An enormous photograph of the Pope was displayed from the top of the Town Hall Tower, and makeshift memorials filled window displays around the city. On April 4, two nights after the Pope died, a memorial service took

place at a soccer stadium south of the Old Town. Throughout the day, Kraków's students—communicating by e-mail and mobile phone text messages—coordinated a huge, spontaneous memorial parade. As the sun set, tens of thousands of young Krakovians marched silently into one end of this Square, around the Cloth Hall, and out the other end, towards the stadium.

• *The huge, yellow building right in the middle of the Square is the...*

▲▲**Cloth Hall (Sukiennice)**—In the Middle Ages, this was the place that cloth-sellers had their market stalls. Kazimierz the Great turned the Cloth Hall into a permanent structure in the 14th century. In 1555, it burned down, and was replaced by the current building. The letter *S* (above the entryway) stands for King Sigismund the Old, who commissioned this version of the hall. As Sigismund fancied all things Italian (including women—he

married an Italian princess), this structure is in the Italianate Renaissance style. We'll see more works by Sigismund's imported Italian architects at Wawel Castle.

The Cloth Hall is still a functioning market—mostly souvenirs, including wood carvings, chess sets, jewelry, painted boxes, and trinkets (summer Mon–Fri 9:00–18:00, Sat–Sun 9:00–15:00, sometimes later; winter Mon–Fri 9:00–16:00, Sat–Sun 9:00–15:00). Cloth Hall prices are slightly inflated, but still cheap by American standards. You're paying a little extra for the convenience and the atmosphere, but locals insist they buy gifts here, too. Upstairs in the Cloth Hall is the very good Gallery of 19th-Century Polish Art (see page 233). WCs and telephones are at each end.

• *Browse through the Cloth Hall passageway. As you emerge into the other half of the Square, the big tower on your left is the...*

Town Hall Tower—This is all that remains of a Town Hall building from the 14th century—when Kraków was the powerful capital of Poland. After the 18th-century partitions of Poland, Kraków's prominence took a nosedive. By the 19th century, Kraków was Nowheresville. As the town's importance crumbled, so did its Town Hall. Krakovians tore down everything but this tower, nearly 200 feet tall. It's climbable, with 117 steps, a museum on Kraków history, and good views down over the Square (5 zł, May–Oct daily 10:30–14:00 & 14:30–18:00, closed off-season). The tower also houses a TI.

• *There are plenty of diversions to keep you busy here on the Square (including some good restaurants; see "Eating," page 251). When you're ready to continue down the Royal Way, follow Part 2 of the walk (below).*

Młoda Polska (Young Poland)

Polish art in the late 19th century was ruled by positivism, a school with a very literal, straightforward focus on Polish history (Jan Matejko led the charge; see page 287). But when the new generation of Kraków's artists came into their own in the early 1900s, they decided that the old school was exactly that. The students of Jan Matejko experimented with more wistful, creative interpretations of Polish history. They returned to Romanticism, with a renewed appreciation of folklore and country culture. Polish peasant life was held up as idyllic and beautiful. Though moved by the same spirit and goals as the previous generation—evoking Polish patriotism at a time when their country was being occupied—these new artists used very different methods. Rather than earnest and literal (an 18th-century Polish war hero on horseback), the new art was playful and highly symbolic (the artist frolicking in a magical garden in the Polish countryside). This movement became known as Młoda Polska (Young Poland)—Art Nouveau with a Polish accent.

Stanisław Wyspiański (vees-PAYN-skee, 1869–1907) was the leader of Młoda Polska. He produced beautiful artwork, from simple drawings to the stirring stained-glass images in Kraków's St. Francis' Basilica. The versatile Wyspiański was also an accomplished stage designer and writer. His patriotic play *The Wedding*—about the wedding of a big-city artist to a peasant girl—is regarded as one of Poland's finest dramas. The largest collection of Wyspiański's art is in Kraków's Wyspiański Museum, but you'll also see examples in Kraków's St. Francis' Basilica and Warsaw's National Museum.

Józef Mehoffer (may-HOH-fehr), Wyspiański's good friend and rival, was another great Młoda Polska artist. See his work in Kraków's St. Francis' Basilica and at the artist's former residence; and in Warsaw, at the National Museum.

Other names to look for include **Jacek Malczewski** (mahl-CHEHV-skee), who specialized in self-portraits, and **Olga Boznańska** (bohz-NAHN-skah), the movement's only prominent female artist. Both are featured in Warsaw's National Museum.

Royal Way Walk Part 2:
Main Market Square to Wawel Castle

After the king passed through the grand Main Market Square, he'd continue on to his castle. We'll take a one-block detour from his route to introduce you to one of Kraków's best churches. Leave on the street in the middle of the bottom of the Square. Ulica Bracka leads one long block (and across the busy Franciszkańska street) directly to the side door of a big red-brick church. Go ye.

▲▲**St. Francis' Basilica (Bazylika Św. Franciszka)**—This beautiful Gothic church, which was Pope John Paul II's home church while he was archbishop of Kraków, features some of Poland's best Art Nouveau *in situ* (in the setting for which it was intended). After an 1850 fire, it was redecorated by members of the Młoda Polska (Young Poland) movement—the Polish version of Art Nouveau. It features brilliant works by the two men at the forefront of this movement: Stanisław Wyspiański and Józef Mehoffer. These two talented and fiercely competitive Krakovians were friends who apprenticed together under Poland's greatest painter, Jan Matejko. The glorious decorations of this church are the result of this great rivalry run amok. (For more Wyspiański or Mehoffer, visit their museums—see "Museums," page 231.)

Highlights include:

1. Paintings and stained-glass windows by **Stanisław Wyspiański.** The windows over the high altar represent the Blessed Salomea (the church's foundress, buried in a side chapel) and St. Francis (the church's namesake). The window in the rear of the nave is *God the Father Let It Be*, Wyspiański's finest masterpiece. The colors beneath the Creator change from yellows and oranges (fire) to soothing blues (water), depending on the light. Wyspiański was supposedly inspired by Michelangelo's vision of God in the Sistine Chapel. Wyspiański also painted the delightful floral designs decorating the walls of the nave. (For more on the artist, see page 234.)

2. The chapel on the left side of the nave (as you face the altar) contains some evocative Stations of the Cross. This is the response to Wyspiański's work by **Józef Mehoffer.** The centerpiece of the room is a replica of the Shroud of Turin—which, since it touched the original shroud, is also considered a holy relic.

3. The modern painting (with an orange background, midway up the nave on the right as you face the altar) depicts **St. Maksymilian Kolbe,** the Catholic priest who traded his own life to save a fellow inmate at Auschwitz (see his story on page 264).

4. As you face the back door (below Wypiański's stained-glass window), find the **silver plate** labeled "Jan Pawał II" on the second pew from the last (on right); this was Pope John Paul II's favorite place to pray when he was bishop here.

• *Stepping outside (through the door you entered), look left. The light-yellow building (100 yards away) is the...*

Archbishop's Palace—This building (specifically, the window over the stone entryway) was Pope John Paul II's residence when he was the archbishop of Kraków. After he became Pope, it remained his home-away-from-Rome for visits to his hometown. On his last visit to Kraków in 2002, the ailing Pope went to bed, while thousands of Krakovians—sensing they may never see him again—called to him from the street below. Finally, to the delight of his countrymen, he appeared in this window once more. Three years later, when the Pope's health worsened, this street filled again with his supporters. For days, somber locals focused their vigil on this same window, their eyes fixed on a black crucifix that had been placed here. At 21:37 on the night of April 2, 2005, the Pope passed away in Rome. Ten thousand Krakovians were in this street, under this window, listening to a Mass broadcast on loudspeakers from the church. When the priest announced the Pope's death, every single person simultaneously fell to their knees in silence. For the next several days, thousands of the faithful continued to stand in this street, staring intently at the window where they last saw the man they considered to be the greatest Pole.

• *Now turn right, walk along the side of the church, cross the little square, and turn right again down Grodzka at the light purple building. You're back on the Royal Way proper. After two blocks, on the right (at #45), you'll see a...*

Milk Bar (Bar Mleczny)—These government-subsidized cafeterias are the locals' choice for a quick, cheap, filling, lowbrow lunch. Prices are deliriously cheap (soup costs less than a złoty), and the food isn't bad. For more on milk bars, see page 202.

• *Just a block ahead—after passing another milk bar (Bar Grodzki)—the square on your right is...*

Mary Magdalene Square (Plac Św. Marii Magdaleny)—In the Middle Ages, Kraków was known as "Small Rome" for its many churches. Today, there are 142 churches and monasteries within the city limits (32 in the Old Town alone), more per square mile than anywhere outside Rome. You can see several of them from this spot: The nearest, with the picturesque white facade and red dome, is the **Church of Saints Peter and Paul** (Kraków's 1st Baroque church). The next one down, with the twin towers, is the Romanesque **St. Andrew's.** According to legend, a spring inside this church provided water to citizens who holed up here during Tatar invasions in the 13th century. If you look farther down the street, you can see three more churches. And the courtyard next to you used to be a church, too—it burned in 1855, and only its footprint survives.

• *Go through the square (admiring the sculpture on the column that won Kraków's distinguished "ugliest statue" award in 2002), and turn left down...*

Kanonicza Street (Ulica Kanonicza)—With so many churches around here, the clergy had to live somewhere. Many lived on this well-preserved street. Continue left down Kanonicza. As you walk, look for the cardinal hats over three different doorways. Find the yellow house (#19) on the right near the end of the street. The top window over the doorway is where a priest named Karol Wojtyła

Karol Wojtyła (1920–2005):
The Life and Death of the Greatest Pole

Karol Wojtyła was born to a humble family in the town of Wadowice (near Kraków) on May 18, 1920. Karol's mother died when he was a young boy. When he was older, he moved with his father to Kraków to study philosophy and drama at Jagiellonian University. Young Karol was gregarious and athletic—an avid skier, hiker, swimmer, and soccer goalie. During the Nazi occupation in World War II, he was forced to work in a quarry. In defiance of the oppressive Nazis, he secretly studied theology and appeared in illegal underground theatrical productions. When the war ended, he resumed his studies, this time at the theology faculty.

After graduating in 1947, Wojtyła rose through the ranks of the Catholic Church hierarchy. By 1964, he was archbishop of Kraków, and just three years later, he became the youngest cardinal ever in the Roman Catholic Church. Throughout the 1960s, he fought an ongoing battle with the regime when they refused to allow the construction of a church in the Kraków suburb of Nowa Huta. After years of saying Mass for huge crowds in open fields, Wojtyła finally convinced the communists to allow the construction of the Lord's Ark Church in 1977 (see page 245). A year later, just as Poland was facing its darkest hour, Karol Wojtyła was called to the papacy—the first non-Italian pope in more than four centuries.

Imagine you're Polish in the 1970s. Your country was devastated by World War II, and has struggled under an oppressive regime ever since. Food shortages are epidemic. Lines stretch around the block even to buy a measly scrap of bread. You're not allowed to speak your mind, you're not allowed to travel, and—it seems—you're not allowed even to hope. Then someone who speaks your language—someone you've admired your entire life, and one of the only people you've seen successfully stand up to the regime—becomes one of the world's most influential people. A Pole like you is the leader of a billion Catholics. He makes you believe that the impossible can happen. He says to you again and again: *"Nie lękajcie się"*—"Have no fear." And you begin to believe it.

In addition to encouraging his countrymen, the Pope had a knack for challenging the communists. He'd push at them strongly enough to get his point across, but not going so far as to jeopardize the stature of the Church in Poland. Gentle, pointed wordplay was his specialty. The inspirational role he played in the lives of Lech Wałęsa and the other leaders of Solidarity gave them the courage to stand up to the communists (for more on Solidarity, see page 326). Many people (including Mikhail Gorbachev) credit Pope John Paul II for the collapse of Eastern European communism.

Well after the fall of the Berlin Wall, Pope John Paul II's failing health and conservative policies caused him to lose stature in worldwide public opinion. But approval of the Pope never waned in Poland. His countrymen saw John Paul II both as the greatest hero of their people...and as a member of the family, like a kindly old grandfather.

When Pope John Paul II died on April 2, 2005, the mourning in Poland was profound. Though the world had long anticipated the Pope's passing, it created an overwhelming wave of grief that flooded the country for weeks. Musical performances of all kinds were cancelled for a week after his death, and the irreverent MTV-style music channel simply went off the air out of respect. Kraków's two soccer teams, Cracovia and Vistula, are hated rivals. But two nights after the Pope died, Cracovia hosted a memorial service in their stadium, and went out of their way to invite the Vistula fans. Over 100,000 people showed up, spilling into a nearby field. "I'm a Vistula fan," one young Krakovian told me that night. "I hate Cracovia. But tonight, I'm going to their stadium for the first time in my life. Maybe this is a good thing—it's bringing everyone together."

Karol Wojtyła has already been fast-tracked for sainthood. Out of 265 popes, only two have been given the title "great." There's already talk in Rome of increasing that number to three—and someday soon we may speak of this remarkable soul as "John Paul the Great." His countrymen already do.

lived for 10 years after World War II—long before he became Pope John Paul II.

• *At the end of Kanonicza street, a ramp leads up to the most important piece of ground in all of Poland.*

Royal Way Walk Part 3: Wawel Hill

Wawel (VAH-vehl), a symbol of Polish royalty and independence, is sacred territory to every Polish person. A castle has stood here since the beginning of recorded history. Today, Wawel—awash in tourists—is the most visited sight in the country. Crowds and a ridiculously complex admissions system for the hill's many historic sights can be exasperating. Thankfully, for most non-Polish visitors, a stroll through the cathedral and around the castle grounds requires no tickets, and—with the help of the following self-guided commentary—is enough. The many museums on Wawel (described below) are mildly interesting, but can be skipped (grounds open daily May–Sept 6:00–20:00, Oct–April 6:00–17:00).

Walk up the long ramp to the castle entry. When Kraków was part of the Hapsburg Empire in the 19th century, the Austrians turned this castle complex into a fortress—destroying much of its delicate beauty. When Poland regained its independence after World War I, the castle was returned to its former glory. The bricks you see on your left as you climb the ramp bear the names of Poles from around the world who donated to the cause.

The jaunty equestrian statue ahead is **Tadeusz Kościuszko** (1746–1817)—whom American History buffs might remember learning about in school. Kościuszko was a hero of the American Revolution and helped design West Point before returning to Poland to fight bravely but unsuccessfully against the Russians (during the partitions that would divide Poland's territory among 3 neighboring powers).

• *Hiking through the gate next to Kościuszko, you pass the ticket office (see "Tickets and Reservations," page 231) and, as you crest the hill, you'll see to your left...*

▲▲**Wawel Cathedral**—Poland's national church is its Westminster Abbey. While the history buried here is pretty murky to most Americans, to Poles, this church is *the* national mausoleum. It holds the tombs of nearly all of Poland's most important rulers and greatest historical figures.

Exterior: Go around to the far side of the cathedral to take in its profile. This uniquely eclectic church is the product of centuries of haphazard additions...yet somehow, it works. It began as a simple, stripped-down Romanesque church in the 12th century. (The white base of the nearest tower is original; you can see a model of the complete, basic structure in the "Lost Wawel" exhibit described below.) Kazimierz the Great and his predecessors gradually surrounded the cathedral with some 20 Gothic chapels, which were further modified over the centuries. To the right of the tall tower are two particularly interesting domed chapels. The gold one is the Renaissance Sigismund's Chapel, housing memorials to the Jagiellonian kings. The green one (which looks the same—but is a copy, built 150 years later) is home to the Swedish Waza dynasty. As time went on, more additions were grafted on, making this beautiful church a happy hodgepodge of styles.

Go back around and face the front entry for more architectonic silliness. You see Gothic chapels flanking the door, a Renaissance ceiling, lavish Baroque decoration over the door, and big bones (thought to come from extinct animals). Years ago, these were taken for the bones of giants and put here for protection. It's said that as long as they hang here, the cathedral will stand. The door is the original from the 14th century, with fine wrought-iron work. The *K* with the crown stands for Kazimierz the Great. The black marble frame is made of Kraków stone from nearby quarries.

For a quick peek at the interior, step inside. (If you want to visit the other interior sights described below—a crypt and a tower climb to a big bell—first buy a 10-zł ticket in the building across the street.)

Interior: The cathedral interior is slathered in Baroque memorials and tombs. The silver tomb under a canopy in the center is that of St. Stanisław (dating from the 15th century, and inspired by the one in St. Peter's at the Vatican). Circling around to the right (behind the main altar, with a dog at her feet), you'll find the sarcophagus of St. Jadwiga, the 14th-century "Queen of Poland," who helped Christianize Lithuania, fought the Teutonic Knights, and was sainted by Pope John Paul II in 1997. All the flowers here prove she's popular with Poles today. Across from Jadwiga, the 16th-century Sigismund Chapel—with its silver altar—is considered by Poles to be the finest Renaissance chapel north of the Alps. Farther back on the left is The Great One—Kazimierz, of course (look for *Kazimierz Wielki*). Poke into the choir for a look at the high altar. For 200 years, the colorful chair on the right has been the seat of Kraków's archbishops, including Karol Wojtyła, who served here for 14 years before becoming pope. Near the main door (on the left as you face outside), peek into the Gothic chapel with its Russian Orthodox–style 15th-century frescoes.

For most visitors, that's everything worth seeing in the cathedral. But if you're a fan of big bells and the tombs of VIPs (Very

Important Poles), you can see—with a ticket—the...

Bell, Crypt, and Tombs: Claustrophobic wooden stairs lead up to the 11-ton **Sigismund Bell** and pleasant views of the steeples and spires of Kraków. Then, descend into the little **crypt** (housing Adam Mickiewicz—the Romantic poet whose statue dominates the Main Market Square). Finally, when you're ready to leave (since you'll exit back out into the courtyard), head through the chapel in the back-right corner to find the door down to the **royal tombs**. The first room houses Poland's greatest war heroes: Kościuszko (of American Revolution fame), Jan III Sobieski (who successfully defended Vienna from the Turks; in the simple black coffin with the gold inscription "J III S"), Sikorski, Poniatowski, and so on. Then you'll wander through several rooms of second-tier Polish kings, queens, and their kids. Marshal Józef Piłsudski, the WWI hero who ruled Poland from 1926 to 1935, has the last grave (in the room on the right, just before you exit). His tomb was moved here so the rowdy soldiers who came to pay their respects wouldn't disturb the others.

Cost and Hours: While most of the cathedral is free, you'll need a ticket to climb down through the royal tombs or up the tower to see the bell (10 zł, tickets sold across from entrance, May–Sept Mon–Sat 9:00–17:15, Sun 12:15–17:15; Oct–April Mon–Sat 9:00–15:45, Sun 12:15–15:45).

Cathedral Museum—This small museum, with various holy robes and replicas of what's buried with the kings, plus the Sigismund Bell's original clapper, is nearby (5 zł, Tue–Sun 10:00–15:00, closed Mon).

• *When you're finished in the cathedral, stroll around the...*

▲▲**Wawel Castle Grounds**—This hill has seen lots of changes over the years. Kazimierz the Great turned a small fortress into a mighty Gothic castle in the 14th century. Today, you'll see the cathedral and a castle complex, but little remains of Kazimierz's grand fortress, which burned to the ground in 1499. In the grassy field across from the cathedral, you'll see the foundations of two Gothic churches that were destroyed when the Austrians took over Wawel in the 19th century and needed a parade ground for their troops.

Behind the cathedral, a grand green entryway leads into the palace **courtyard.** When Kazimierz's castle burned down, this courtyard was rebuilt in the Italian Renaissance style. The dark, ivy-covered side later served as the headquarters of the notorious Nazi governor of German-occupied Poland, Hans Frank. (He

was tried and executed in Nürnberg after the war.) The entrances to most Wawel museums are here, and some believe that you'll find something even more special: chakra.

Adherents to the Hindu concept of **chakra** believe that a powerful energy field connects all living things. Mirroring the seven chakra points on the body (from head to groin), there are seven points on the surface of the earth where this energy is most concentrated: Delhi, Delphi, Jerusalem, Mecca, Rome, Velehrad... and Wawel Hill—specifically over there in the corner (immediately to your left as you enter the courtyard). Look for peaceful people (here or elsewhere on the castle grounds) with their eyes closed. One thing's for sure: They're not thinking of Kazimierz the Great. The smudge marks on the wall are from people pressing up against this corner, trying to absorb some good vibes from this chakra spot.

The Wawel administration seems creeped out by all this. They've done what they can to discourage this ritual, but believers still gravitate from far and wide to hug the wall. Give it a try...and let the Force be with you. (Just for fun, ask a Wawel tour guide about the chakra, and watch her squirm—they're forbidden to talk about it.)

If you plan to visit some of the castle museums, now's the time (see "Wawel Castle Museums," on next page). But if you're looking for a scenic wrap-up to this royal ramble, leave the courtyard the way you came in, and keep going straight toward the opening in the wall. You'll be rewarded with a beautiful view over the Vistula River and Kraków's outskirts. Directly below you, along the riverbank, is a fire-belching monument to the **dragon** that was instrumental in the founding of Kraków...

Once upon a time, a prince named Krak founded a town on Wawel Hill. It was the perfect location—except for the fire-breathing dragon who lived in the caves under the hill and terrorized the town. Prince Krak had to feed the dragon all of the town's livestock to keep the monster from going after the townspeople. But Krak, with the help of a clever shoemaker, came up with a plan. They stuffed a sheep's skin with sulfur and left it outside the dragon's cave. The dragon swallowed it, and before long, developed a terrible case of heartburn. To put the fire out, the dragon started drinking water from the Vistula. He kept drinking and drinking until he finally exploded. The town was saved, and Kraków thrived.

Our walking tour is finished. If you want to head down to see the Vistula and the dragon close up, take a shortcut through the nearby **Dragon's Den** (Smocza Jama). It's just a 135-step spiral staircase and a few underground caverns—worthwhile only as a quick way to get from the top of Wawel down to the banks of the

Vistula (3 zł, April–Oct daily 10:00–17:00, closed Nov–March, enter around corner from bookstore on courtyard overlooking river).

Wawel Castle Museums—There are five museums and exhibits in Wawel Castle (not including the cathedral and Cathedral Museum). Each has its own admission (ranging from 6–18 zł, slightly cheaper off-season; hours for all museums, unless otherwise noted: April–Oct Sun 10:00–15:00, Mon 9:30–12:00, Tue and Fri 9:30–16:00, Wed–Thu and Sat 9:30–15:00; Nov–March Sun 10:00–15:00, Tue–Sat 9:30–15:00, closed Mon, tel. 012/422-5155 ext. 219, www.wawel.krakow.pl). Notice that in the high season (April–Oct), visiting on Monday has both advantages (Royal State Rooms, Crown Treasury and Armory, and Lost Wawel are all free) and disadvantages (Royal Private Apartments and Oriental Art are closed, and the rest closes at 12:00). Off-season (Nov–March), everything is closed on Monday—except, mysteriously, the Lost Wawel exhibit.

The **Royal State Rooms** (Komnaty Królewskie), while precious to Poles, are mediocre by European standards (free on Mon April–Oct, free on Sun Nov–March, enter through courtyard). Still, this is the best of the Wawel museums. First you'll wander through some ho-hum halls to get to the Throne Room, with 30 carved heads in the ceiling. According to legend, one of these heads got mouthy when the king was trying to pass judgment—so its mouth has been covered to keep it quiet. Then you'll walk along the outdoor gallery (enjoying views down into the courtyard) before heading upstairs. These top-floor rooms are best, with remarkably decorated wooden ceilings, gorgeous "leather tooled" walls, and 16th-century Brussels tapestries (140 of the original series of 300 survive). Wandering these halls (with their period furnishings), you get a feeling for the 16th- and 17th-century glory days of Poland, when it was a leading power in Eastern Europe. The Senate Room, with its throne and fine tapestries, is the climax.

The **Royal Private Apartments** (Prywatne Apartamenty Królewskie) are more of the same, and the only part of the complex that must be visited with a guided tour (enter through courtyard; April–Oct closed Mon, English-language tours Tue–Sun at 10:50, 12:00, 13:10, and 14:20, often more; Nov–March closed Sun-Mon, English-language tours Tue–Sat at 12:00, usually plus others).

The **Crown Treasury and Armory** (Skarbiec i Zbrojownia) is a decent collection of swords, saddles, and shields; ornately decorated muskets and crossbows; and cannons in the basement (free on Mon April–Oct, closed Sun–Mon Nov–March, enter through courtyard).

The small **Oriental Art** (Sztuka Wschodu) exhibit displays swords, carpets, vases, and remarkable Turkish tents (upstairs, next to the Senate Room) used by the Ottomans during the 1683 Battle of Vienna. These are trophies of Jan III Sobieski, the Polish king who led a pan-European army to victory in that battle (tickets sold at the door, closed Mon April–Oct, closed Sun–Mon Nov–March, enter through courtyard, don't miss entry on your way back downstairs from Royal State Rooms).

The **Lost Wawel** (Wawel Zaginiony) exhibit traces the history of this hill and its various churches and castles. The one-way route leads through excavations of a 10th-century church, and exhibits include a model of the cathedral in its original Romanesque form (much simpler, before all the colorful, bulbous domes, chapels, and towers were added). There's also a replica of the entire castle complex in the 18th century (pre-Austrian razing). A display shows fascinating decorative tiles from 16th-century stoves that once heated the place, and some medieval artifacts (free on Mon April–Oct, free on Sun Nov–March; Nov–March open Mon but closed Tue, enter near snack bar across from side of cathedral).

Tickets and Reservations: Tickets are sold at several points around the Wawel grounds (most convenient at top of long entry ramp, shorter lines inside bookstore around corner from Dragon's Den). Tickets are limited for the Royal State Rooms, Crown Treasury and Armory, and Royal Private Apartments (which can be visited only with a tour). Boards show how many tickets for each of these are still available today. Tickets come with an assigned entry time (though you can usually sneak in before your scheduled appointment). In the summer, ticket lines can be long, and sights can sell out by midday. You can reserve tickets ahead for the tour of the Royal Private Apartments (no fee) and the Royal State Rooms and the Crown Armory and Treasury (16-zł reservation fee; tel. 012/422-1697). Frankly, the sights aren't worth all the fuss—if they're sold out, you're not missing much.

Museums

Kraków's **National Museum** (Muzeum Narodowe) is made up of a series of small but interesting museums scattered throughout the city. Oddly enough, the main branch (Gmach Główny) is the least worth visiting, with 20th-century Polish art and temporary exhibits (9 zł, more for special exhibits, aleja 3 Maja 1). I've listed the best of the National Museum's branches below, followed by the Jagiellonian University Museum.

Be warned: It seems to be the inexplicable policy of the National Museum to completely overhaul the opening hours of its various branches about every six months. All of the museums below (except the Jagiellonian University Museum) are generally open Tue–Sat 10:00–16:00, Sun 10:00–15:00, closed Mon. Some evenings—especially in summer—these museums may be open later (until 19:00). Hours can be shorter (until 15:30) November through April. Some museums are free one day a week (usually Sun).

▲Czartoryski Museum (Muzeum Czartoryskich)—This eclectic collection, displaying armor, handicrafts, decorative arts, and paintings, is one of Kraków's best-known (and most overrated) museums. While it's mostly just dull historical bric-a-brac, two world-class paintings—a da Vinci and a Rembrandt—make it worth ▲▲ for art-lovers (8 zł, more for special exhibits, decent 5-zł audioguide helps make things meaningful, generally open Tue–Sat 10:00–16:00, Sun 10:00–15:00, closed Mon, open until 19:00 some evenings in summer, shorter hours Nov–April, last entry 30 min before closing, no photos allowed, 2 blocks north of the Main Market Square at ulica Św. Jana 19, tel. 012/422-5566). Be warned that its major attractions are often not displayed (on loan to other museums), and this disappointing fact isn't well advertised before you buy your ticket. Try to confirm the paintings are actually there before you enter.

Inspired by Poland's 1791 constitution (Europe's first), Princess Izabela Czartoryska began collecting bits of Polish history and culture. She fled with the collection to Paris after the 1830 insurrection, and 45 years later, her grandson returned it to its present Kraków location. When he ran out of room, he bought part of the monastery across the street, joining the buildings with a fancy passageway. The Nazis took the collection to Germany, and although most of it has been returned, some pieces are still missing.

Buy your ticket and walk up to the second floor. You'll wander through rooms of armor (the ceremonial Turkish tent—from the 1683 siege of Vienna—and feathered Hussar armor are impressive), tapestries, treasury items, majolica, Meissen porcelain figures, and paintings.

The third floor is devoted to European art. After a few halls of also-rans, you'll come to the museum's prize possessions. First is *Lady with an Ermine*, by Leonardo da Vinci. This small (21" x 16"), simple portrait of a teenage girl is one of the most influential paintings in art history and a rare surviving work by one of history's greatest minds. The girl is likely Cecilia Gallerani, the young mistress of the Duke of Milan, Leonardo's employer. The ermine (white during winter) suggests several overlapping meanings: a pun on Cecilia's name, a symbol of chastity (thus praising her questioned virtue), and a naughty reference to the Duke's nickname, "Ermellino"—notice that his mistress is sensually, um, "stroking the ermine"...

Painted before the *Mona Lisa*, the portrait was immediately recognized as revolutionary. Cecilia turns to look off-camera at someone, catching her in an unguarded moment, a behind-the-scenes look unheard of in the days of the posed, front-facing formal portrait. Her simple gestures and faraway gaze speak volumes about her inner thoughts and personality. Leonardo tweaks the generic Renaissance "pyramid" composition by turning it to three-quarters angle and softening it with curved lines—from her eyes, down her cheek and sloping shoulders, then doubling back across her folded arms.

Lady with an Ermine is one of only three surviving oil paintings by Leonardo. It's better preserved than her famous cousin in Paris *(Mona Lisa)*, and—many think—simply more beautiful. Can we be sure it's really by the enigmatic Leonardo? Well, recently they found the master's fingerprint—literally—pressed into the paint.

On the wall opposite the lady and her ermine, notice the empty frame with a print of a Rembrandt portrait inside. This is one of the pieces the Nazis didn't give back.

In the next room is the museum's other highlight, Rembrandt's **Landscape with the Good Samaritan**. This small, remarkably detailed painting depicts the popular parable. On the right, see the Samaritan help the wounded man onto his horse (as a little boy watches). To the left, much farther down the road (just beyond the waterfall), find the two tiny figures walking—the priest and the Levite who passed the injured man by.

Back on the second floor and across the passageway, in the former monastery, is the rest of the collection: more armor (with some beautifully ornate saddles), Czartoryski family portraits, and ancient art.

▲**Gallery of 19th-Century Polish Art (Galeria Sztuki Polskiej XIX Wieku)**—This enjoyable collection is surprisingly classy for a museum above a market hall. If you like Polish art, you'll love it. If you don't know anything about Polish art, you'll be pleasantly surprised (8 zł, paintings labeled in English, good 40-zł English guidebook, skip the poorly produced 5-zł audioguide, generally open Tue–Sat 10:00–16:00, Sun 10:00–15:00, closed Mon, open later some evenings in summer, shorter hours Nov–April; upstairs in big, yellow Cloth Hall on Main Market Square—enter on east side, facing St. Mary's; tel. 012/422-1166).

While you probably won't recognize any of the names in here, some of these paintings are just plain good. The biggest works are by the historical painter Jan Matejko (for more on Matejko, see page 287). One of Matejko's paintings depicts Tadeusz Kościuszko—a hero of the American Revolution, now back in his native Poland fighting the Russians—doffing his hat after his unlikely victory at the battle at Racławice. Another Matejko painting shows the last Grand Master of the fearsome Teutonic Knights swearing allegiance to the Polish king in 1525. This historic ceremony took place in the Main Market Square of the capital at the time,

Kraków. Notice this very Cloth Hall in the background, and in the upper right-hand corner, look for the spires of St. Mary's Church. Matejko has painted his own face on one of his favorite historical figures, the jester Stańczyk (at the foot of the throne; for more on Stańczyk, see page 290).

Other excellent, but more obscure, painters are also represented. Find Józef Chełmoński's energy-charged *Four-in-Hand* (depicting a Ukrainian horseman giving a lift to a pipe-smoking nobleman) and misty *Cranes*. And my favorite: Władysław Podkowiński's gripping *Frenzy,* with a pale, sensuous woman clutching an all-fired-up black stallion. The painting caused a frenzy indeed at its 1894 unveiling—leading the unbalanced artist to attack his creation with a knife.

▲**Wyspiański Museum (Muzeum Wyspiańskiego)**—If you enjoyed Stanisław Wyspiański's stained glass and wall paintings in St. Francis' Basilica, visit the museum that collects his work. Housed in a renovated mansion, this museum traces the personal history and artistic development of the Młoda Polska poster boy (7 zł, dry 5-zł English audioguide basically repeats the good English descriptions posted in most rooms, generally open Tue–Sun 10:00–16:00, closed Mon, open later some evenings in summer, shorter hours Nov–May, 1 block west of the Main Market Square at ulica Szczepańska 11, tel. 012/292-8183).

You'll begin by climbing the stairs to view some of Wyspiański's precocious childhood sketchbooks, then move on to see works from his youthful collaboration with his teacher Jan Matejko and his friend Józef Mehoffer as they renovated St. Mary's Church (with designs for beautiful stained-glass windows). One of the museum's highlights is the design for the dramatic stained-glass *Apollo,* which hangs in the House of the Medical Society. Also on this floor are portraits and self-portraits, the costumes and plans for sets Wyspiański designed for his own plays, and copies of Wyspiański's printed works (which he also designed himself).

On your way up to the next floor, you'll see the designs for Wyspiański's masterpiece, *God the Father Let It Be,* from St. Francis' Basilica. Once upstairs, head for the model of the elaborate acropolis Wyspiański planned for the top of Wawel Hill, with a domed palace, an amphitheater, and a circus maximus. Filling another room are portraits of Wyspiański's family—including his daughter Helenka just waking up, and his wife breast-feeding their son Staś. Helenka circles around to get good views of both of them, appearing twice in the painting. You'll end with a display of Wyspiański's serene landscapes.

More National Museum Branches—You can also check out the museum of Wyspiański's friend and rival, the **Józef Mehoffer House** (Dom Józefa Mehoffera, 6 zł, ulica Krupnicza 26, tel. 012/421-1143), and the former residence of their mentor, the **Jan Matejko House** (Dom Jana Matejki, 6 zł, ulica Floriańska 41, tel. 012/422-5926). Both are usually open the same hours as the Wyspiański Museum.

Jagiellonian University Museum: Collegium Maius—Kraków had the second university in Central Europe (after Prague), boasting over the centuries such illustrious grads as Copernicus and Pope John Paul II. This city is still very much a university town, and Jagiellonian University proudly leads tours of its historic oldest building, the 15th-century Collegium Maius (1 block west of the Main Market Square at ulica Jagiellońska 15, www.uj.edu.pl /muzeum). Tour groups routinely duck into the building's Gothic courtyard for free. To visit the interior, you'll choose between two different guided tours. The shorter 30-minute route includes the library, refectory, treasury, assembly hall, and an exhibit of Copernicus' original instruments (12 zł, free on Sat, only some in English, leaves every 20 min Mon–Fri 10:00–14:20, Thu until 17:20, Sat until 13:20, none Sun). The one-hour deluxe version adds some medieval sculptures, a Rubens, a Rembrandt, some old scientific instruments, and Chopin's piano (16 zł, usually in English, Mon–Fri at 13:00, none Sat–Sun). It's always smart to call ahead to find out when the shorter tour is scheduled in English, and to reserve for either tour (tel. 012/663-1521). The shorter tour is especially popular and books up long in advance, particularly on Saturdays, when it's free.

Aside from the courtyard, the only part of the Colleguim Maius you can see without a tour is an interactive exhibit that allows you to tinker with replicas of old scientific tools (7 zł, free on Sat, open Mon–Sat 10:00–14:30, closed Sun).

Kazimierz (Jewish Quarter)

The neighborhood of Kazimierz (kah-ZHEE-mezh), 20 minutes by foot southeast of Kraków's Old Town, is the historic heart of Kraków's once-thriving Jewish community. After years of neglect, the district is today being rediscovered by Krakovians and tourists alike. With a smattering of new, mostly Jewish-themed restaurants and hotels, it's accessible to travelers, but still retains its local flavor.

Visitors expecting a polished, touristy scene like Prague's Jewish Quarter will be surprised...and maybe disappointed. This is basically a local-feeling neighborhood with a handful of Jewish cemeteries, synagogues, and restaurants, and often a few pensive Israeli tour groups wandering the streets. But for me, the lack of crowds makes it an even more evocative experience than the Prague alternative.

Getting to Kazimierz: It's about a 20-minute **walk** from the Old Town. From the Main Market Square, walk down ulica

Kazimierz

1 Hotel Astoria

2 Karmel Pensjonat

3 El-jot Art Center Rooms

4 Tournet Guest House

5 Restauracja Samoobsługowa Polakowski

6 Jarden Bookshop & Restauracja Arka Noego

7 Klezmer-Hois Restaurant

8 Ariel Restaurant

9 Pierożki U Vincenta

10 Bagel Mama

Sienna (near St. Mary's Church). At the fork, bear right through the Planty park. At the intersection with the busy Westerplatte ring road, you'll continue straight ahead (bear right at fork) down busy Starowiślna for 15 more minutes. To hop the **tram,** go to the stop on the left-hand side of ulica Sienna (at the intersection with Westerplatte, across the street from the Poczta Główna, or Main Post Office). Catch tram #3, #13, or #24 and go two stops to Miodowa. Walking or by tram, at the intersection of Starowiślna and Miodowa, you'll see a small park across the street and to the right. To reach the heart of Kazimierz—ulica Szeroka—cut through this park. To get back into the Old Town, catch tram #3, #13, or #24 from the intersection of Starowiślna and Miodowa and go two stops back to the Poczta Główna stop.

Jewish Kraków

After King Kazimierz the Great encouraged Jews to come to Poland in the 14th century (see page 218), a large Jewish community settled in and around Kraków. According to legend, Kazimierz (the king) established Kazimierz (the village) for his favorite girlfriend—a Jewish woman named Ester—just southeast of the city walls. (If you have a 50-zł note, take a look at it: that's Kazimierz the Great on the front, and on the back is his capital, Cracovia, and the most important town he founded, Casmirus.)

It's a cute legend, but the village of Kazimierz didn't really become a Jewish enclave until much later. By the end of the 15th century, there were large Jewish populations in both Kazimierz and in Kraków. Kraków's Jewish community and the university students clashed, and when a destructive fire broke out in 1495, the Jews were blamed. The king at the time (not Kazimierz the Great) forced all of Kraków's Jews to move to Kazimierz.

Kazimierz was an autonomous community, with its own Town Hall, market square, and city walls (though many Jews still commuted into Kraków's Square to do business). The Christian (west) and Jewish (east) neighborhoods were also separated by a wall. But by 1800, the walls came down, Kazimierz became part of Kraków, and the Jewish community flourished.

By the start of World War II, 65,000 Jews lived in Kraków (mostly in Kazimierz)—making up more than a quarter of the city's population. When the Nazis arrived, they immediately sent most of Kraków's Jews to the ghetto in the eastern Polish city of Lublin. Soon after, they forced Kraków's remaining 15,000 Jews into a walled ghetto at Podgórze, across the river. The Jews' cemeteries were defiled, and their buildings ransacked and destroyed. In 1942, the Nazis began transporting Kraków's Jews to death camps. Many others were worked to death in the Podgórze ghetto. Only a few thousand Kraków Jews survived the war.

Today's Kraków has only about 200 Jewish residents. Kazimierz still has an empty feeling, but the neighborhood has enjoyed a renaissance of Jewish culture, following the popularity of *Schindler's List* (which was filmed partly in Kazimierz). Look for handwritten letters from Steven Spielberg and the cast in local restaurants (such as Ariel) and hotels. These have more recently been joined by autographs from *The Pianist* director Roman Polański. While few Jews live here now, the spirit of the Jewish tradition lives on in the many synagogues, as well as in the soulful cemeteries.

Orientation: Start your visit to Kazimierz on **ulica Szeroka,** which is more of a long, parking-lot square than a street, surrounded by Jewish restaurants, hotels, and synagogues. Check in at the **Jarden Bookshop** at the top of the square (Mon–Fri 9:00–18:00, Sat–Sun 10:00–18:00, ulica Szeroka 2, tel. 012/421-7166, www.jarden.pl, jarden@jarden.pl). It serves as a tourist information center for the neighborhood, and sells a wide variety of books on Kazimierz and Jewish culture in the region (including a good 4.50-zł Kazimierz map and well-illustrated 18-zł *Jewish Kraków* guidebook). They also run several tours: Jewish Kazimierz overview (35 zł, 2 hrs, walking tour), Kazimierz and the WWII ghetto (45 zł, 3 hrs, walking, the best overview), *Schindler's List* sights (65 zł, 2 hrs, by car), and Auschwitz-Birkenau (110 zł, 6 hrs, by car). Call to reserve ahead, as tours are by appointment only. Tours will run if a minimum of three people sign up, but pairs or singles can join an already scheduled tour.

If you visit on Saturday, you'll find only the Old Synagogue museum open. For hotel and restaurant suggestions, see page 250 of "Sleeping" and page 253 of "Eating." Some recommended restaurants offer live traditional Jewish music nightly in summer.

▲▲**Jewish Cemeteries**—Kazimierz has two Jewish cemeteries, far less touristy and, to me, at least as powerful as the famous one in Prague.

The small **Old Cemetery** (Stary Cmentarz) was used to bury members of the Jewish community from 1552 to 1800. It has been renovated—so in a way, it actually feels "newer" than the New Cemetery. After the New Cemetery (described below) was opened in the 1800, this cemetery gradually fell into disrepair. What remained was further desecrated by the Nazis during World War II. In the 1950s, it was discovered, excavated, and put back together

as you see here. Shattered gravestones form a mosaic wall around the perimeter. As in all Jewish cemeteries, you may see small stones stacked on the graves (originally placed over desert graves to cover the body and prevent animals from disturbing it). Behind the little synagogue to the left, the tallest tombstone next to the tree belonged to Moses Isserle (a.k.a. Remu'h), an important 16th-century rabbi. He is believed to be a miracle worker, and his grave was one of the only ones that remained standing after World War II. The knee-high metal receptacle nearby is for written prayers (5 zł, May–Oct Sun–Fri 9:00–18:00, Nov–April until 16:00, always closed Sat, enter through Remu'h Synagogue at ulica Szeroka 40).

The much larger **New Cemetery** (Nowy Cmentarz) has graves of those who died after 1800. Nazis vandalized this cemetery, selling many of its gravestones to stonecutters, and using others as pavement in their concentration camps. Today, many of the gravestones have since been returned to their original positions. Other headstones could not be replaced, and were used to create the moving mosaic wall and Holocaust monument (on the right as you enter). Most gravestones are in one of three languages: Hebrew (generally the oldest, especially if there's no other language); Yiddish (which looks like German); and Polish (from Jews who assimilated into the Polish community). The earliest graves are simple stones, while later ones imitate graves in Polish Catholic cemeteries—larger, more elaborate, and with a long stone jutting out to cover the body. Notice that some new-looking graves have old dates. These were most likely put here well after the Holocaust (or even after communism) by relatives of the dead (free, Sun–Fri 8:00–18:00, until 16:00 in winter, closed Sat, tricky to find—go under railway bridge at east end of ulica Miodowa, jog left as you emerge, cemetery is to your right, enter through gate at #55).

▲**Isaac Synagogue (Synagoga Isaaka)**—This is Kraków's most accessible sight for learning more about the Kazimierz Jewish community. The synagogue, Kraków's biggest, was built in the 17th century. During a recent renovation, they discovered giant wall paintings of prayers (for worshippers who couldn't afford to buy books). In a side room is a powerful display of photographs, and a continuously running 98-minute loop of six different films about the Jewish heritage of Kazimierz (mostly silent, others in Hebrew, Polish, Yiddish, and English). Two of the most important films (lasting a total of 7 min)—showing the town before the Nazis came, and then the forced transition to the Podgórze ghetto—play continuously in the main hall (7 zł, Sun–Fri 9:00–19:00, July–Aug until 20:00, closed Sat, closes at sundown on winter Fri—as early as 15:00 in Dec, a block west of ulica Szeroka at ulica Kupa 18, tel. 012/430-5577).

Other Synagogues—Two synagogues sit right on Kazimierz's main square, ulica Szeroka. The **Old Synagogue** (Stara Synagoga), the oldest surviving Jewish building in Poland, is now a three-room museum on local Jewish culture, with English descriptions (7 zł, free on Mon, mid-April–mid-Oct Mon 10:00–14:00, Tue–Sun 10:00–17:00; mid-Oct–mid-April Mon 10:00–14:00, Wed–Thu and Sat–Sun 9:00–16:00, Fri 10:00–17:00, closed Tue, ulica Szeroka 24). **Remu'h Synagogue,** from 1553, has been carefully renovated and is the only active synagogue in Kraków (included in 5-zł entry fee for New Cemetery, Sun–Fri 9:00–18:00, until 16:00 Nov–April, always closed Sat, ulica Szeroka 40).

Two other synagogues face each other across ulica Miodowa,

three blocks northwest of ulica Szeroka. **Tempel Synagogue** (Synagoga Templu) has the grandest interior—big and dark, with elaborately decorated, gilded ceilings and balconies—and the most lived-in feel of the bunch (5 zł, Sun–Fri 9:00–16:00, closed Sat, corner of ulica Miodowa and ulica Podbrzezie). The smaller **Kupa Synagogue** (Synagoga Kupa) sometimes hosts temporary exhibits (Miodowa 27).

Galicia Jewish Museum (Galicja Muzeum)—This new museum, the brainchild of a visionary English photojournalist named Chris Schwarz, focuses on the present rather than the past. With a series of beautiful photographs displayed around a restored Jewish furniture factory, the exhibit shows today's remnants of yesterday's Judaism in the area around Kraków (a region known as "Galicia"). From forgotten synagogues to old Jewish gravestones flipped over and used as cobblestones, these giant postcards of Jewish artifacts (with good English descriptions) ensure that an important part of this region's heritage won't be forgotten (7 zł, daily April–Oct 9:00–20:00, Nov–March 10:00–20:00, 1 block east of ulica Szeroka at ulica Dajwór 18, tel. 012/421-6842, www.galiciajewishmuseum .org). The museum also serves as a sort of cultural center, with a good bookstore, kosher shop, café, and programming that caters to both locals and visitors (from Jewish dancing lessons to Yiddish classes to Jewish karaoke).

Kazimierz Market Square (Plac Nowy)—The natives shop at plac Nowy's market stalls. This is a gritty, factory-workers-on-lunch-break contrast to Kraków's touristy Main Market Square (stalls open Tue–Sat 6:00–14:00, a few also open later and Sun 7:00–14:00, closed Mon). Consider dropping by here for some shopping (sorry, no souvenirs), people-watching, or a quick, cheap, and local lunch (see "Eating," page 253). Other, much trendier restaurants are popping up all around this square.

▲Polish Folk Museum (Muzeum Etnograficzne)—This clever and refreshingly good museum hides a few blocks west of the Jewish area of Kazimierz, in the former town hall. The square it's on, plac Wolnica, was Kazimierz's primary market square, once almost as big as Kraków's. Inside the museum, you'll find models of traditional rural Polish homes, as well as musty replicas of the interiors (like an open-air folk museum—but inside). On the second floor are traditional Polish folk costumes, Christmas decorations, and even bagpipes. The top floor has some imaginatively carved beehives (6.50 zł, free on Sun; May–Sept Mon and Wed–Fri 10:00–17:00, Sat–Sun 10:00–14:00, closed Tue; Oct–April Mon 10:00–18:00, Wed–Fri 10:00–15:00, Sat–Sun 10:00–14:00, closed Tue; ulica Krakowska 46, tel. 012/430-6023).

Podgórze—This neighborhood, directly across the Vistula from Kazimierz, is where the Nazis forced Kraków's Jews into a ghetto in early 1941. (*Schindler's List* and the films in the Isaac Synagogue depict the sad scene of the Jews loading their belongings onto carts and trudging over the bridge into Podgórze.) The ghetto was surrounded by a wall with a fringe along the top that resembled Jewish gravestones—a chilling premonition of what was to come. A short section of this wall is still standing along Lwowska street.

Ghetto Heroes' Square (plac Bohaterow Getta) is the focal point of the visitor's Podgórze. To get there, continue through Kazimierz on trams #3, #13, or #24 (described under "Getting to Kazimierz," above) to the stop called plac Bohaterow Getta. On the square you'll find the **Pharmacy under the Eagle** (Apteka pod Orłem), with a modest exhibit about the Jewish experience before and after the ghetto.

Most people coming to Podgórze are actually looking for...

Schindler's Factory—Fans of the Holocaust movie and book— and the compassionate Kraków businessman who did his creative best to save the lives of his Jewish workers—can see Oskar Schindler's actual factory. This is where Schindler worked, and where Spielberg filmed much of *Schindler's List*. After the war, the factory became the Telpod electronics manufacturing plant. But it went bust a few years back, and now most of the buildings are abandoned. Starting in the fall of 2005, the city began converting this facility into a new "Museum of the Place." If you're interested in visiting, inquire at the Kraków TI about what kind of progress they're making. Just inside the main building is a long staircase (immortalized in a scene from *Schindler's List*) to Oskar Schindler's office. Gestapo agents and other Nazi troops were also stationed in this building to keep an eye on Schindler and his workers. Just behind that are crumbling factory buildings (also slated for future reconstruction).

Getting There: From Ghetto Heroes' Square (plac Bohaterow Getta, described above), it's about a five-minute walk: Head up Kącik street (to the left of the big, glass skyscraper), go under the railroad underpass marked *Kraków–Zabłocie*, and continue two blocks to the second big building on the left (marked *Fabryka Oskara Schindlera Emalia* (ulica Lipowa 4).

Closer to the center, **Schindler's apartment** is a block from Wawel Castle at ulica Straszewskiego 7 (unmarked and not available for tours).

Wieliczka Salt Mine (Kopalnia Soli Wieliczka)

Wieliczka (vee-LEECH-kah), 10 miles southeast of Kraków, is beloved by Poles. Though it's a bit overrated, most visitors find it's worth ▲▲.

This remarkable mine has been producing salt since at least the 11th century. Under Kazimierz the Great, one-third of Poland's income came from these precious deposits. Wieliczka miners spent much of their lives underground, leaving for work before daybreak and returning after sundown, rarely emerging into daylight. To pass the time, and to immortalize their national pride and religiosity in art, 19th-century miners began to carve figures, chandeliers, and eventually even an elaborate chapel out of the salt.

From the lobby, your guide leads you 210 feet down a winding staircase. From this spot, you begin a 1.5-mile generally downhill stroll past 20 of the mine's 2,000 chambers (with signs saying when they were dug), finishing 443 feet below the surface. When you're done, an elevator beams you back up.

The tour shows how the miners lived and worked, using horses  who spent their whole lives without ever seeing the light of day. It takes you through some impressive underground caverns past subterranean lakes, and introduces you to some of the mine's many sculptures (including an army of salt elves and this region's favorite son, Pope John Paul II). Your jaw will drop as you enter the enormous **Chapel of the Blessed Kinga,** carved over three decades in the early 20th century. Look for the salt-relief carving of the Last Supper.

While advertised as two hours, your tour finishes in a deep-down shopping zone 90 minutes after you started (they hope you'll hang out and shop). Note when the next elevator departs (just 3/hr), and you can be outta there on the next lift. Zip through the shopping zone in two minutes, or step over the rope and be immediately in line for the great escape (you'll be escorted 300 yards to the skinny industrial elevator, into which you'll be packed like mine workers).

Cost and Hours: Visits are by tour only (55 zł for a guided tour, 10 zł extra to use your camera). English tours are generally daily year-round at 10:00, 11:30, 12:30, 13:45, 15:00, and 17:00; June and Sept also at 9:00; July–Aug every half hour between 8:30 and 18:00. If you miss the English-language tour (or decide to just show up and take whatever's going next), buy the informative guidebook, which narrates the exact route the tours do (daily April–Oct 7:30–19:30, Nov–March 8:00–17:00, ulica Daniłowicza 10, tel. 012/278-7302, www.kopalnia.pl). Dress warmly—the mine is a constant 57 degrees Fahrenheit.

Mine Museum: Your ticket includes a dull mine museum at the end of the tour. It adds an hour to the mine tour and is discouraged by local guides ("1.5 miles more walking, colder, more of the same"). Make it clear when you buy your ticket that you're not interested in the museum.

Getting to Wieliczka: The salt mine, 10 miles from Kraków, is best reached by minibus (3 zł, 4/hr or with demand). These minibuses (with *Wieliczka Soli* sign in window) normally leave from the streets around Kraków's bus station. However, during the ongoing construction around the station (see "Arrival in Kraków," page 210), the minibuses depart from the Main Post Office (Poczta Główna, east of Main Market Square, just beyond the Planty, at the start of Starowiślna street). Ask at the TI where these minibuses are currently leaving from. Taking a taxi (about 50 zł) is fastest, and taking the train makes no sense.

Nowa Huta

Nowa Huta (literally, "New Steel Works"), an enormous planned workers' town, offers a glimpse into the stark, grand-scale aesthetics of the communists. While it's five miles east of central Kraków, a little tricky to see on your own, and worth only ▲ for most visitors, architects and communists may want to make a pilgrimage here.

Getting There: Tram #4 goes from Kraków's old center (meet it at one of two handy stops: by the Main Post Office—from Main Market Square, follow Szczepańska to the ring road outside the Planty park; or on the ring road near Kraków's Main Train Station) along Pope John Paul II Avenue (aleja Jana Pawła II) to Nowa Huta's main square, plac Centralny (about 30 min total). From there, tram #4 continues a few minutes farther to the main gate of the Tadeusz Sendzimir Steelworks, and then it returns to Kraków.

Tours: True to its name, Mike Ostrowski's **Crazy Guides** is a very loosely run operation that takes tourists to Nowa Huta in genuine communist-era vehicles (mostly Trabants and Polski Fiats). While the content is excellent, be warned that Mike and his comrades are laid-back, very informal, and sometimes crude. If you're offended by a foul-mouthed guide who reminds you of a scruffy college student, or if you don't like the idea of careening down the streets of Kraków in a car that feels like a cardboard box with a lawnmower engine, skip this tour. For the rest of us, it's a fun and convenient way to experience Nowa Huta (119 zł per person for 2.5-hr Nowa Huta tour; 159 zł per person for 4-hr Communism Deluxe tour that also includes their makeshift "museum"—a communist-era apartment that's decorated to give you a taste of the way things were; 159 zł per person for 4-hr "Real Kraków" tour that covers the basic Nowa Huta trip plus other outlying sights; cash only, reserve ahead and they'll pick you up at your hotel, tel. 0888-686-871, mobile 0500-091-200, www.crazyguides .com, mike@crazyguides.com).

History: Nowa Huta was the communists' idea of paradise— to them, it was perfect. It's one of only three towns outside the Soviet Union that were custom-built to showcase socialist ideals. (The others are Dunaújváros—once called Sztálinváros—south of Budapest, Hungary; and Eisenhüttenstadt—once called Stalinstadt—near Brandenburg, Germany.) Completed in just 10 years (1949–1959), Nowa Huta was primarily built because the Soviets felt that intellectual and potentially dissident Kraków needed a taste of heavy industry. Farmers and villagers were imported to live and work in Nowa Huta. Many of the new residents weren't accustomed to city living, and brought along their livestock (who grazed in the fields around unfinished buildings). For commies, it was downright idyllic: Dad would cheerily ride the tram into the steel factory, mom would dutifully keep house, and the kids could splash around at the manmade beach and learn how to cut perfect red stars out of construction paper. But Krakovians had the last laugh: Nowa Huta, along with Lech Wałęsa's shipyard in Gdańsk, was one of the home bases of the Solidarity strikes that eventually brought down the regime. Now, with the communists long gone, Nowa Huta remains a sooty suburb of Poland's cultural capital, with a whopping 200,000 residents.

Sights: Nowa Huta's focal point used to be known simply as **Central Square** (plac Centralny), but in a fit of poetic justice, it was recently renamed for the anti-communist Ronald Reagan (plac Centralny im. Ronalda Reagana). This square is the heart of the planned town. A map of Nowa Huta looks like a clamshell: a thoughtful, semi-circular design radiating out from Central/ Reagan Square. Numbered streets fan out like spokes on a wheel, and trolleys zip workers directly to the immense factory (described below).

Believe it or not, the inspiration for Nowa Huta was the Renaissance (which, thanks to the textbook Renaissance design of the Cloth Hall and other landmarks, Soviet architects considered typically Polish). Note the elegantly predictable arches and galleries that would make Michelangelo proud. When first built (before it was layered with grime), Nowa Huta was delightfully orderly, primly painted, impeccably maintained, and downright beautiful (if a little boring). It was practical, too: Each of the huge apartment blocks is a self-contained unit, with its own grassy inner courtyard, school, and shops. Driveways (which appear to dead-end at underground garage doors) lead to vast fallout shelters.

Today's Nowa Huta is a far cry from its glory days. Wander around. Poke into the courtyards. Reflect on what it would be like to live here. It may not be as bad as you imagine. Ugly as they seem from the outside, these buildings are packed with happy little apartments filled with color, light, and warmth.

Up the wide, dramatic boulevard running northeast of Central/Reagan Square, Solidarity Avenue (aleja Solidarności, lined with tracks for tram #4), is the **Tadeusz Sendzimir Steelworks**. Originally named for Lenin, this factory was supposedly built using plans stolen from a Pittsburgh plant. It was designed to be a cog in the communist machine—reliant on iron ore from Ukraine, and therefore worthless unless Poland remained in the Soviet Bloc. Down from as many as 40,000 workers at its peak, the steelworks now employs only about 10,000. Today there's little to see other than the big sign, stern administration buildings, and smokestacks in the distance. Examine the twin offices flanking the sign—topped with turrets and a decorative frieze inspired by Italian palazzos, these continue the Renaissance theme of the housing districts.

Another worthwhile sight in Nowa Huta is the **Lord's Ark Church** (Arka Pana, several blocks northwest of Central/Reagan Square on ulica Obrońców Krzyża). Back when he was archbishop of Kraków, Karol Wojtyła fought for years to build a church in this most communist of communist towns. When the regime refused, he insisted on conducting open-air Masses to crowds in fields—until the communists finally capitulated. Consecrated on May 15, 1977, the Lord's Ark Church has a Le Corbusier-esque design that looks like a fat, exhausted Noah's Ark resting on Mount Ararat—encouraging Poles to persevere through the floods of communism. While architecturally interesting, the church is mostly significant as a symbol of an early victory of Catholicism over communism. The year after his monumental triumph, Karol Wojtyła became Pope John Paul II.

SLEEPING

Accommodations can be miserable in some Eastern European cities, but Kraków is the happy exception. Healthy competition—with new, cleverly run places cropping up all the time—keeps prices reasonable and makes choosing a hotel fun rather than frustrating.

I've focused my accommodations on two areas: in and near the Old Town; and in Kazimierz, which is a local-style, more affordable neighborhood that is home to both the old Jewish quarter and Kraków's most happening nightlife.

Rates are soft. Hoteliers don't need much of an excuse to

Sleep Code

(3.40 zł = about $1, €1 = about $1.20, country code: 48, area code: 012)
S = Single, **D** = Double/Twin, **T** = Triple, **Q** = Quad, **b** = bathroom, **s** = shower only. Breakfast is included, credit cards are accepted, and English is spoken (unless otherwise noted). Some hotels quote prices in euros.

To help you sort easily through these listings, I've divided the rooms into three categories, based on the price for a standard double room with bath:

$$$ **Higher Priced**—Most rooms 400 zł (€100) or more.
$$ **Moderately Priced**—Most rooms between
                     300–400 zł (€75–100).
$ **Lower Priced**—Most rooms 300 zł (€75) or less.

offer you 10 to 20 percent off, especially on weekends or in the off-season.

In the Old Town

While you could stay away from the center, accommodations values here are so good that there's little sense in sleeping beyond the Planty. Most of my listings are inside (or within a block or two of) the old city walls.

The Old Town has three basic types of accommodations: small, well-run guest houses (my favorite); big hotels (comfortable but overpriced); and upstart youth hostels. I've listed the best of each type.

Guest Houses

Over the last three years, more than a dozen cheap, new guest houses have sprung up inside Kraków's Old Town. These almost invariably come with lots and lots of stairs, and are run by smart, can-do, entrepreneurial owners. Usually just as nice as a big hotel, these pensions are Kraków's best accommodations values.

$ At **Pensjonat Trecius,** Michał Palarczyk offers surprising class for low prices. Hiding upstairs in a nondescript building, its six rooms are nicely decorated (cheap S with bathroom down the hall-100 zł, Sb-130–200 zł depending on size, cheap D with bathroom down the hall-130 zł, Db-170–250 zł depending on size, extra bed-25 zł, continental breakfast-8 zł, full breakfast-16 zł, non-smoking, 2 blocks from the Main Market Square at ulica Św. Tomasza 18, tel. 012/421-2521, fax 012/426-8730, www.trecius.krakow.pl, hotel@trecius.krakow.pl).

Kraków Hotels and Restaurants

1. Hotel Maltański
2. Hotel Senacki
3. Hotel Saski
4. Hotel Wawel Tourist
5. Hotel Gródek
6. Hotel Classic
7. Pensjonat Trecius
8. Hotel Pugetów
9. Bed & Breakfast
10. Nathan's Villa Hostel
11. La Fontaine B&B
12. "Globtroter" Guest House
13. Mama's Hostel
14. Restauracja Pod Aniołami
15. Chłopskie Jadło Rest. (3 locations)
16. Rest. Samoobsługowa Polakowski
17. Rest. Hawełka & Tetmajerowska
18. Restauracja Jarema
19. Milk Bar (Bar Mleczny) & Kwandras Lunch Bar
20. Cukiarnia Jama Michalika
21. Restauracja Redolfi
22. Chimera Cafeteria
23. Cyklop Pizza
24. Bombaj Tandoori Restaurant
25. Jazz Club U Muniaka
26. Pizzeria Trzy Papryczki
27. Rest. Farina
28. Massolit Books

$ La Fontaine B&B, run by a French woman named Charlotte, is one of Kraków's best deals for the location. The four rooms and two apartments are up several flights of stairs over a cellar restaurant just a few steps off the Main Market Square. Tastefully decorated with French flair, they're cute as a poodle (Sb/Db-€58, extra bed-€10, apartment for up to 4-€98, cheaper off-season, low slanted ceilings, ulica Sławkowska 1, tel. 012/422-6564, fax 012/431-0955, www.bblafontaine.com, biuro@bblafontaine.com).

$ Globtroter Guest House offers 12 rooms with high ceilings and big beams around a serene garden courtyard. Jacek (Jack) conscientiously focuses on value, keeping prices as low as possible by not offering needless extras (June–Aug: Sb-155 zł, Db-240 zł; April–May and Sept–Oct: Sb-135 zł, Db-225 zł; Nov–March: Sb-120 zł, Db-180 zł; 2 people can cram into a single to save money, larger suites for up to 6 also available, cash only, no breakfast at hotel, but you can buy 10-zł breakfast from courtyard restaurant, fun 700-year-old brick cellar lounge down below, plac Szczepańska 7/15, tel. 012/422-4123, fax 012/422-4233, www.cracow-life.com /globtroter, globtroter@cracow-life.com).

$ Bed & Breakfast is a suitable last resort, with 20 cheap, ramshackle rooms, a treehouse floor plan, thin walls, and mix-and-match furniture in a great location (S-85 zł, Sb-100 zł, D-155 zł, Db-180 zł, T-240 zł, Tb-270 zł, extra bed-50 zł, they'll do your laundry for 10 zł, ulica Wiślna 10, tel. & fax 012/421-9871, mobile 0604-199-902, www.noclegi.tk, wislna@wp.pl).

Hotels

$$$ Donimirski Boutique Hotels, with three different locations in or near Kraków's Old Town, offer the city's best splurge experience (Web site for all: www.donimirski.com). All Donimirski hotels offer my readers a 15 percent discount through 2006 (in the off-season, try to negotiate an even better deal—up to 25 percent off). You can expect any of these hotels to have some of the friendliest staff in Kraków, and all the classy little extras that add up to a pleasant experience (like a fluffy white bathrobe for every guest). **Hotel Maltański** has 16 rooms in the beautifully renovated former royal stables, just outside the Planty and only two blocks from Wawel Castle (Sb-510 zł, Db-540 zł, parking-30 zł/day, ulica Straszewskiego 14, tel. 012/431-0010, fax 012/431-0615, maltanski@donimirski.com). **Hotel Pugetów,** with seven plush rooms and a fun breakfast cellar, is on the other side of town. It's actually slightly closer to the Main Market Square—on the way to Kazimierz—but the neighborhood's a tad dingy (Sb-350 zł, Db-480 zł, Db suite-590 zł, ulica Starowiślna 13–15, tel. 012/432-4950, pugetow@donimirski.com). The brand-new **Hotel Gródek**—the fanciest and most central of the bunch—offers 20 rooms a three-minute walk behind St. Mary's Church on a quiet street overlooking the Planty (Sb-590 zł, Db-630 zł, Na Gródku, tel. 012/431-0010, grodek@donimirski.com).

$$$ Hotel Senacki is a professional-feeling, business-class splurge renting 20 elegant rooms between Wawel Castle and the Main Market Square (Sb-€105, Db-€120, deluxe Db-€155, extra bed-€25, €10 cheaper Fri–Sun, 15 percent cheaper Nov–March, parking-80 zł/day, non-smoking rooms, elevator—but doesn't go to top floor, ulica Grodzka 51, tel. 012/421-1161, fax 012/422-7934, www.senacki.krakow.pl, recepcja@senacki.krakow.pl).

$$$ Hotel Classic, a modern home in old Kraków (on a peaceful street just inside the Planty), has 33 rooms, a sleek marble lobby, professional staff, reasonable prices, and little character (Sb-€100, Db-€110, 25 percent cheaper Nov–March, readers of this book get a 20 percent discount on weekdays and 25 percent discount Fri–Sun in 2006, elevator, ulica Św. Tomasza 32, tel. 012/424-0303, fax 012/429-3680, www.hotel-classic.pl, hotel@hotel-classic.pl).

$$ Hotel Wawel Tourist, with a swanky marble lobby and the history of the hotel painted on the walls, was recently renovated. Its 40 rooms are a little musty, but the location is good (Sb-260 zł, Db-380 zł, big "retro" Db-370 zł, Tb-450 zł, prices higher with air-con, elevator—but doesn't go to top floor, ulica Poselska 22, tel. 012/424-1300, fax 012/424-1333, www.wawel-tourist.pl, hotel@wawel-tourist.pl).

$$ Hotel Saski rents 60 high-ceilinged rooms a few steps from the Main Market Square (6 of them with institutional-feeling bathrooms down the hall). My other hotel recommendations are modern, but this is your best old-fashioned-feeling option, with a frou-frou lobby, kitschy gift shops, uniformed bellhop, and antique elevator. The rooms have worn furniture and the hotel somehow lacks soul, but it's a decent value for the location (S-220 zł, Sb-280 zł, D-250 zł, Db-360 zł, fancy "superior" Db-430–450 zł, Tb-400 zł, elevator, ulica Sławkowska 3, tel. 012/421-4222, fax 012/421-4830, www.hotelsaski.com.pl, info@hotelsaski.com.pl).

Hostels

New hostels are born—and go extinct—every other day in Kraków. But these two are the real deal. Accept no substitutes. My first listing is just steps off the Main Market Square; the second one is in a lively, up-and-coming neighborhood between Wawel Hill and Kazimierz.

$ Mama's Hostel is ideally located and more dignified than most hostels—like an old apartment taken over by vagabonds with good manners, but who still know how to have a good time (55 zł per person in a 6-bed room, 50 zł in an 8–10-bed room; includes sheets, breakfast, laundry, and lockers; no curfew, ulica

Bracka 4, tel. & fax 012/429-5940, www.mamashostel.com.pl, hostel@mamashostel.com.pl).

$ **Nathan's Villa Hostel** is run by an energetic young Bostonian and his wife. It's loose, easygoing, and fun, with 18 cleverly painted rooms, a bar, a beer garden, an art gallery, and plenty of backpacker bonding. Their advertising promises advice on how to "get hammered"...if that's not your scene, sleep elsewhere (bunk in 4-bed room-60 zł, in 6-bed room-55 zł, in 8-bed room-50 zł, in 10-bed room-45 zł, 5 zł less Nov-Feb; includes breakfast, sheets, laundry facilities, and lockers; free Internet in lobby, no curfew or lockout time, ulica Św. Agnieszki 1, tel. 012/422-3545, www.nathansvilla.com, krakow@nathansvilla.com).

Kazimierz

Sleep in Kazimierz to be close to Kraków's Jewish heart—or simply to experience a cheaper, less touristy, more local-feeling neighborhood outside the Old Town. With the highest concentration of pubs and nightclubs in town, Kazimierz is emerging as *the* spot for nightlife. The downside: You are a 20-minute walk from the fairytale medieval ambience of Kraków's old center. For locations, see the map on page 236.

The following are the best values in the neighborhood. Some of the klezmer music restaurants listed in "Eating," below, also rent rooms—but they're generally an afterthought to the food and music, and not a good value.

$$ **Hotel Astoria** is your best big-hotel option in Kazimierz, even though it lacks character. This hotel, renting 33 comfy rooms a couple of blocks from the center of Kazimierz, is popular with Israeli tour groups (Sb-280 zł, Db-360 zł, Db suite-400 zł, extra bed-70 zł, less on weekends and with an online reservation, free underground parking, air-con, non-smoking floor, elevator, ulica Józefa 24, tel. 012/432-5010, fax 012/432-5020, www.astoriahotel.pl, biuro@astoriahotel.pl).

$ **Karmel Pensjonat,** on a pleasant side-street near the heart of Kazimierz, feels elegant, but the prices are reasonable (Sb-200 zł, twin Db-280 zł, "komfort plus" Db with 1 big bed-350 zł, extra bed-50 zł, 20 percent less Nov–Feb, ulica Kupa 15, tel. 012/430-6697, fax 012/430-6726, www.karmel.com.pl, hotel@karmel.com.pl).

$ **El-jot Art Center** rents 15 rooms, in addition to running a theater and an art gallery. It's a tasteful mix of old and new, with huge discounts (up to 25 percent) for booking rooms online or via e-mail (Sb-239 zł, Db-299 zł, Tb-379 zł, 2-room apartment-429 zł, prices 15 percent lower on weekends and Nov–March, ulica Miodowa 15, tel. & fax 012/421-3326, www.eljotartcenter.pl, recepcja@eljotartcenter.pl).

$ Tournet Guest House, well-run by friendly Piotr Działowy, offers 10 cheap, colorful rooms near the edge of Kazimierz towards Wawel Hill (Sb-140 zł, basic Db with no breakfast or TV-100 zł, standard Db-180 zł, Tb-220 zł, extra bed-50 zł, 20 zł less Nov–March—except basic Db, ulica Miodowa 7, tel. 012/292-0088, fax 012/292-0089, www.accommodation.krakow.pl, tournet@accommodation.krakow.pl).

EATING

Kraków is one of Eastern Europe's best dining towns, with surprising diversity, high quality, and low prices. For Polish food, you have several inexpensive options (plus some splurges) in the Old Town. For Jewish food, head to Kazimierz.

In the Old Town
Kraków's Old Town is littered with delightful restaurants. Prices are reasonable even on the Main Market Square. And a half block away, they get even better.

Polish Food
Restauracja Pod Aniołami (literally, "Under Angels") offers a dressy, jazz-and-candles atmosphere outside on a covered patio, or inside in a romantic cellar with rough wood and medieval vaults. The cuisine is traditional Polish, with an emphasis on grilled foods and trout (on a wood-fired grill). Don't go here if you're in a hurry—only if you want to really slow down and enjoy your dinner (main dishes 20–40 zł, daily 13:00–24:00, reservations smart, ulica Grodzka 35, tel. 012/421-3999). If you want a fast, cheap, and tasty lunch, drop by their tiny sandwich bar for delightful open-faced sandwiches to take away or enjoy on their sidewalk tables (Mon–Fri 9:00–19:00, Sat 9:00–18:00, Sun 11:00–17:00).

Chłopskie Jadło (literally, "Peasant Food") is part of a successful chain serving inexpensive, authentic Polish food (most main dishes 15–40 zł, fish dishes around 45 zł). The peasant theme begins with rustic bread that comes with farmer cheese and lard *(smalec)*. It's kitschy—touristy and fun, with "bed board" chairs—but the food is good, and it's packed with foreign visitors, Polish tourists, and locals. It's comparable to restaurants in the United States with cheesy down-home decor that promise "good country cookin'"...and deliver. As the chain has become more successful, the food quality has gone a little downhill, but it's still a reliable bet for a typical Polish meal. There are two central locations just off the Main Market Square: a smaller one north (daily 12:00–24:00, ulica Św. Jana 3, tel. 012/429-5157), and one to the south with a farmyard patio and a sprawling, labyrinthine series of cellars (daily 12:00–24:00, ulica Grodzka 9, tel. 012/429-6187). A third, less touristy location is between Wawel Hill and Kazimierz (Sun–Thu 12:00–22:00, Fri–Sat 12:00–24:00, ulica Agnieszki 1, tel. 012/421-8520).

Restauracja Samoobsługowa Polakowski is a homey little self-service cafeteria with a surprisingly elegant interior—sort of a dressed-up milk bar. They serve fast, inexpensive, and tasty traditional meals a block off the Main Market Square, with delicious borscht and *gołąbki* (stuffed cabbage rolls) at a fraction of what you'd pay elsewhere. Curt service...cute hats (main dishes about 6 zł, point to what you want, daily 10:00–22:00, ulica Św. Tomasza 5, tel. 012/422-4822). There's another location in Kazimierz (see below).

Restauracja Farina, with a fish-and-bottles theme, features welcoming atmosphere, friendly service, and Polish and Mediterranean cuisine with an emphasis on fresh fish (most main dishes 25–45 zł, daily 12:00–23:00, 2 blocks north of the Square at ulica Św. Marka 16, at intersection with ulica Św. Jana, tel. 012/422-1680).

Restauracja Jarema offers a tasty reminder that Kraków used to rule a large swath of Ukraine and Lithuania. They serve eastern Polish/Ukrainian cuisine, with savory borscht, amid 19th-century aristocratic elegance. You'll feel like you're dining in an old mansion (main dishes 25–40 zł, daily 12:00–22:00, sometimes live music from 19:00, reservations wise, across the street from barbican at plac Matejki 5, tel. 012/429-3669).

Chimera, just off the Main Market Square, is a cafeteria that serves fast traditional meals to a steady stream of students, either outside on their quiet courtyard, or inside in what seems like a fake Old World stage set (good salad buffet: small plate-8 zł, big plate-12 zł, good for vegetarians, daily 9:00–23:00, near University at ulica Św. Anny 3). I'd skip their attached full-service restaurant (main dishes 20–40 zł, daily 12:00–24:00).

Kwandras Lunch Bar (literally, "Quarter"—as in, you can eat here in a quarter-hour) has fast and cheap milk bar-type bites in a modern, no-frills ambience (pierogi and other mains for 5–7 zł, daily 9:00–22:00, ulica Grodzka 32).

Cukiarnia Jama Michalika—filled with green balloons—is legendary for its great homemade ice cream, *szarlotka* (apple cake), *kawa* (coffee), and early-1900s atmosphere. Though it's a bit over-rated, this café is a Kraków institution (also serves light 20-zł meals, Sun–Thu 9:00–22:00, Fri–Sat until 23:00, a rare smoke-free interior, ulica Floriańska 45, tel. 012/422-1561). Expect a grouchy greeting and a fee for the coat-check and miserable bathrooms.

Non-Polish Options

Pizza: **Cyklop,** with 10 tables wrapped around the cook and his busy oven, has excellent wood-fired pizzas (1-person pizzas for

15–20 zł, daily 11:30–22:00, near St. Mary's Church at Mikołajska 16, tel. 012/421-6603). **Pizzeria Trzy Papryczki** (literally, "Three Peppers")—also dishing out wood-fired pizzas at similar prices— has better ambience, but the pizza's not quite as good as Cyklop's (daily 11:00–24:00, ulica Poselska 17, tel. 012/292-5532).

Indian: If you need a tandoori-and-naan fix, **Bombaj Tandoori** offers decent Indian fare two blocks off the Main Market Square (main dishes 20–30 zł, daily 12:00–23:00, ulica Mikołajska 11).

Splurging on the Main Market Square

You'll find plenty of traditional, relatively expensive, tourist-oriented Polish food on the Square. While tourists go for the ye olde places, natives hang out at pizza joints (like Sphinx, part of a wildly popular Poland-wide chain). Poles generally afford this zone on their meager incomes by just having a drink on the Square after eating at home.

Restauracja Redolfi comes with my favorite Square view, friendly service, great salads, French cuisine, and a wide selection of desserts. This place is fine for just a drink or for a full meal (25-zł salads, main dishes 35–50 zł, daily 9:00–24:00, Rynek Główny 38, tel. 012/423-0579).

Restauracja Hawełka, with good seats overlooking the Square's action, serves traditional Polish cuisine. This was a rowdy pub in the communist days, but now the interior has a genteel painting-gallery ambience. They're especially proud of their mush-room soup in a bread bowl (main dishes 20–50 zł, daily 11:00–23:00, near the corner of Szczepańska at Rynek Główny 34).

Tetmajerowska serves up some of the finest cooking in town—game, Polish, and European—in a plush, elegant modernist (c. 1911) interior upstairs from Restauracja Hawełka. The presentation is classy, the service formal, and the ambience as romantic as the piano is live. It's on the Square, but has no view (main dishes 50–70 zł, daily 13:30–23:00, reservations recommended, near the corner of Szczepańska at Rynek Główny 34, tel. 012/422-0631). You'll reach it by climbing a staircase lined with paintings by Młoda Polska also-rans.

Kazimierz

The entire district is bursting with lively cafés and bars—it's a happening night scene. Jewish food is the specialty here. The non-Jewish places I've listed are fast, cheap, and convenient, but not worth going out of your way for. For locations, see the map on page 247.

Klezmer Concerts and Jewish Food: Kazimierz is a hub of Jewish restaurants, featuring cuisine and music that honors the neighborhood's Jewish heritage (and caters to its Jewish visitors).

On a balmy summer night, the air is filled with the sound of klezmer music—traditional Jewish music from 19th-century Poland, generally with violin, string bass, clarinet, and accordion. Skilled klezmer musicians can make their instruments weep or laugh like human voices. Several places on ulica Szeroka (Kazimierz's main square) offer klezmer concerts nightly in the summer at 20:00 (unless otherwise noted). Each restaurant has a similar menu, with main dishes for 20–40 zł. You'll pay an additional cover charge just for the music (15–22 zł per person). While it'd be nice to pop into each restaurant to compare the performers, it's customary to reserve ahead at a single place to dine. At **Klezmer-Hois,** which fills a venerable former Jewish ritual bathhouse, you'll feel like you're dining in a rich grandparent's home (22-zł cover, daily 8:00–22:00, music nightly year-round, #6, tel. 012/411-1245, www .klezmer.pl). **Restauracja Arka Noego** (literally, "Noah's Ark") has a good reputation for its music (15-zł cover, daily 9:00–2:00 in the morning, music nightly at 20:30 March–Oct, shares building with Jarden Bookshop at #2, tel. 012/429-1528). **Ariel** is a popular restaurant that has gone downhill in recent years, and receives mixed reviews for its food (20-zł cover, daily 10:00–24:00, music in up to 4 different rooms, best upstairs in the larger dining hall, #18, tel. 012/421-7920).

Inexpensive Polish Food: **Restauracja Samoobsługowa Polakowski,** the cheap and tasty milk bar near the Main Market Square in central Kraków (see above), has another handy location in the heart of Kazimierz (similar decor and menu, main dishes about 6 zł, point to what you want, daily 8:00–22:00, 100 yards from Szeroka at ulica Miodowa 39, tel. 012/421-2117). **Pierożki U Vincenta** is a tiny, Vincent van Gogh–inspired eatery serving great pierogi (Polish-style ravioli) with both traditional fillings and creative new-fangled versions (7 zł, Sun–Thu 12:00-20:00, Fri–Sat 12:00–21:00, ulica Józefa 11, tel. 012/430-6834). The **plac Nowy market** offers a fully authentic, blue-collar Polish experience—join the workers on their lunch break at the little food windows on Kazimierz's market square.

Bagels and Burritos: **Bagel Mama**, run by an American named Nava, offers good 14-zł burritos, plus 9-zł bagels with various spreads. Though the menu's limited, it offers a break from Polish fare (Tue–Sun 10:00–21:00, closed Mon, behind Tempel Synagogue at ulica Podbrzezie 2, tel. 012/431-1942).

TRANSPORTATION CONNECTIONS

For getting between Kraków and Auschwitz, see page 268 in the next chapter.

From Kraków by Train to: Warsaw (hrly, 2.75 hrs), **Gdańsk** (2/day direct, 7 hrs; plus 1 direct night train, 10.75 hrs; more with transfer in Warsaw), **Toruń** (1/day direct, 7.75 hrs; better to transfer at Warsaw's Zachodnia station: 4/day, 5.75–6.5 hrs), **Prague** (1 direct night train/day, 8.5 hrs; otherwise transfer in Katowice, Wrocław, or Ostrava-Svinov, 8-11 hrs), **Berlin** (2/day direct, including 1 night train, 9.5–10.5 hrs; otherwise transfer in Warsaw, 9–11 hrs), **Budapest** (1 direct night train/day, 11 hrs; otherwise transfer in Katowice, Poland, or Břeclav, Czech Republic, 9–10 hrs), and **Vienna** (2/day direct, including 1 night train, 6.5–8.25 hrs).

AUSCHWITZ-BIRKENAU

The unassuming regional capital of Oświęcim (ohsh-VEENCH-im) was the site of one of humanity's most unspeakably horrifying tragedies: the systematic murder of at least 1.1 million innocent people. From 1941 until 1945, Oświęcim was the home of Auschwitz, the biggest, most notorious concentration camp in the Nazi system. Today, Auschwitz is the most poignant memorial anywhere to the victims of the Holocaust.

A visit here is obligatory for Polish 14-year-olds; students usually come again during their last year of school, as well. You'll often see Israeli high school groups walking through the grounds waving their Star of David flags. Many visitors, including Germans, leave flowers and messages. One of the messages reads: "Nations who forget their own history are sentenced to live it again."

ORIENTATION

"Auschwitz" actually refers to a series of several camps in Poland—most importantly Auschwitz I, in the village of Oświęcim (50 miles, or a 75-minute drive, west of Kraków), and Auschwitz II (a.k.a. Birkenau, about 2 miles west of Oświęcim). Those visiting Auschwitz generally see both Auschwitz I and Birkenau.

Begin at Auschwitz I. The museum's main building has ticket booths, bookstores (consider the good 3-zł *Guide-Book* and the 5-zł map), exchange offices, WCs, and eateries. You'll also find maps of the camp (posted on the walls), a tour office (tours described below), and a theater that shows a powerful film (see below).

Why Visit Auschwitz?

Why visit a notorious concentration camp on your vacation? Auschwitz-Birkenau is one of the most moving sights in Europe, and certainly the most important of all the Holocaust memorials. Seeing the camp can be difficult: Many visitors are overwhelmed by a combination of sadness and anger over the tragedy, as well as inspiration at the remarkable stories of survival. But Auschwitz survivors and victims' families want tourists to come here and experience the scale and the monstrosity of the place. In their minds, a steady flow of visitors will ensure that the Holocaust is always remembered—so it never happens again.

Auschwitz isn't for everyone. But I've never met anyone who toured Auschwitz and regretted it. For many, it's a profoundly life-altering experience—and at the very least, it will forever affect the way you think about the Holocaust.

Cost, Hours, Information: Entrance to the camp is free, but donations are gladly accepted. The museum opens every day at 8:00, and closes June–Aug at 19:00, May and Sept at 18:00, April and Oct at 17:00, March and Nov–mid-Dec at 16:00, and mid-Dec–Feb at 15:00. Information: tel. 033/844-8107, www .auschwitz.org.pl.

Getting There: For details on getting between Kraków and Auschwitz, see "Transportation Connections" on page 268.

Getting from Auschwitz I to Birkenau: Buses shuttle visitors two miles between the camps nearly hourly (leaving Auschwitz I at the bottom of the hour and Birkenau at the top of the hour, times posted at the bus stop outside the main building of each site, buy the 3-zł ticket on the bus). Taxis are also standing by (about 20 zł). Many visitors, rather than wait for the next bus, decide to walk between the camps—offering a much-needed chance for reflection. Along the way, you'll pass the Judenrampe, a new exhibit featuring an old train car like the ones used to transport prisoners, explained by an informational sign.

Film: The 17-minute movie (too graphic for children) was shot by Ukrainian troops days after the Soviets liberated the camp (3.50 zł, buy ticket on arrival; generally in English at 11:00, 11:30, 13:00, 13:30, 15:00, and 17:00).

Eating: There's a café and decent cafeteria (Bar Smak) at the main Auschwitz building. More options are in the newer commercial complex across the street.

On the Way to Auschwitz: The Polish Countryside

You'll spend about an hour gazing out the window as you drive or ride the bus to Auschwitz. This may be your only real look at the Polish countryside. Ponder these thoughts about what you're passing...

The small houses you see are traditionally inhabited by three generations at the same time. Nineteenth-century houses (the few that survive) often sport blue stripes. Back then, parents announced that their daughters were now eligible by getting out the blue paint. Once they saw these blue lines, local boys were welcome to come a-courtin'.

Big churches mark small villages. Tiny roadside memorials and crosses indicate places where fatal accidents have occurred.

Polish farmers traditionally had small lots that were notorious for not being very productive. These farmers somewhat miraculously survived the communist era without having to merge their farms. For years, they were Poland's sacred cows: producing little, paying almost no tax, and draining government resources. But since Poland joined the European Union in 2004, they're being forced to get up to snuff...and, in many cases, collectivize their farms after all.

Since most people don't own cars, bikes are common and public transit is excellent. There are lots of bus stops and minibuses that you can flag down anywhere for a 2-zł ride. The bad roads are a legacy of communist construction, exacerbated by heavy truck use and brutal winters.

Poland has more than 2,000 counties, or districts, each with its own coat of arms; you'll pass several along the way. The forests are state-owned, and locals enjoy the right to pick berries in the summer and mushrooms in the autumn. The mushrooms are dried and then boiled to make tasty soups in the winter.

TOURS

Round-trip tours from Kraków to Auschwitz take care of transportation for you (see "Tours" in the Kraków chapter, page 213). But with a tour, you pay triple and have to adhere to a strict schedule. The most rewarding way to visit is to go by yourself, take one of the camp's organized tours, and then explore the grounds on your own.

The Auschwitz Museum has a network of excellent guides who are serious and frank, and feel a strong sense of responsibility about sharing the story of the camp. The 3.5-hour **English tour** covers Auschwitz, Birkenau, and the film (26 zł, or 23 zł off-season; tour office on right-hand side in main building, about halfway down the long hallway). There are generally at least three English tours scheduled each day (at 11:00, 13:00, and 15:00, possibly more with demand); try to arrive at least 30 minutes ahead, because if the tour's full, you'll have to wait until the next one.

You can also hire your own **private guide** for the basic 3.5-hour tour of the camp (192 zł), or for a longer six-hour "study tour" (383 zł). This guide service is an exceptional value and worthwhile if you have special interest in the camp (to arrange, call 033/844-8100, or book online at www.auschwitz.org.pl). Remember, you can also hire your own private guide in Kraków with a car (about 400 zł—see "Tours" in the Kraków chapter, page 213).

Visiting without a guide (given the abundance of English descriptions and the self-guided tour of both camps described below) works just fine.

SELF-GUIDED TOUR

Auschwitz I

Before World War II, this camp was a base for the Polish army. When Hitler occupied Poland, he took over these barracks and

turned it into a concentration camp for his Polish political enemies. The location was ideal, with a nearby rail junction and rivers providing natural protective boundaries. In 1942, Auschwitz became a death camp for the extermination of European Jews and others that Hitler considered "undesirable." By the time the camp was liberated in 1945, at least 1.1 million people had been murdered here—approximately 960,000 of them Jewish.

As you exit the entry building's back door and go towards the camp, you see the notorious gate with the cruel message, *Arbeit Macht Frei* (Work Sets You Free). Note that the B was welded on upside down by belligerent inmates. On their arrival, new prisoners were told the truth: The only way out of the camp was through the crematorium chimneys.

Just inside the gate and to the right, the camp orchestra (made up of prisoners) used to play marches; having the prisoners march made them easier to count.

The main road leads past the barracks. An average of 14,000 prisoners were kept at this camp at one time. (Birkenau could hold

Auschwitz I

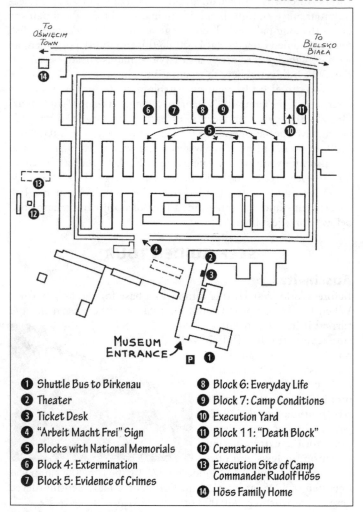

To Oświęcim Town

To Bielsko Biała

MUSEUM ENTRANCE

1. Shuttle Bus to Birkenau
2. Theater
3. Ticket Desk
4. "Arbeit Macht Frei" Sign
5. Blocks with National Memorials
6. Block 4: Extermination
7. Block 5: Evidence of Crimes
8. Block 6: Everyday Life
9. Block 7: Camp Conditions
10. Execution Yard
11. Block 11: "Death Block"
12. Crematorium
13. Execution Site of Camp Commander Rudolf Höss
14. Höss Family Home

up to 100,000.) The first row of barracks contains the **National Memorials,** created by the home countries of the camps' victims. The most worthwhile are the "Suffering, Struggle, and Destruction of the Jews" exhibit (block 27) and the nearby Roma (Gypsy) exhibit. Most of the other national memorials were created during the communist era, so they have a decidedly socialist spin; some have been updated (including Hungary, block 18, and the Czech and Slovak Republics, block 16).

The most interesting part of the camp is the second row of barracks, which holds the museum exhibitions. Blocks 4 and 5 focus on how Auschwitz prisoners were killed. Blocks 6, 7, and 11 explore the conditions for prisoners who survived here a little longer than most.

Block 4 features exhibits on extermination. In the first room is a map showing all of the countries Auschwitz prisoners were brought from—as far away as Norway and Greece. You'll also find an urn filled with ashes, a symbolic memorial to all of the camp's victims. In Room 2, a map shows that victims were transported here from all over Europe. To prevent a riot, the Nazis claimed at first that this was only a transition camp for resettlement in Eastern Europe. Room 3 displays some of the only photos that exist of victims inside the camp—taken by arrogant SS men.

Upstairs in Room 4 is a chilling model of a Birkenau crematorium. People entered on the left, then got undressed in the underground rooms (hanging their belongings on numbered hooks and encouraged to remember their numbers to retrieve their clothes later). They then moved into the "showers" and were killed by Zyklon-B gas. This efficient factory of murder took about 20 minutes to kill 20,000 people in four gas chambers. Elevators brought the bodies up to the crematorium. Members of the *Sonderkommand*—Jewish inmates who were kept isolated and forced by the Nazis to work here—removed the corpses' gold teeth and shaved off their hair (to be sold) before putting the bodies in the ovens. It wasn't unusual for a *Sonderkommand* worker to discover a wife, child, or parent among the dead. A few committed suicide by throwing themselves at electric fences; those who didn't were systematically executed by the Nazis after a two-month shift. Across from the model of the crematorium are canisters of Zyklon-B (hydrogen cyanide), the German-produced cleaning agent that is lethal in high doses. Across the hall in Room 5 is a wall of victims' hair—4,400 pounds of it. Also displayed is cloth made of the hair, used to make Nazi uniforms.

Back downstairs in Room 6 is an exhibit on the plunder of victims' personal belongings. People being transported here were encouraged to bring luggage—and some victims had even paid in advance for houses in their new homeland. After they were killed, everything of value was sorted and stored in warehouses that prisoners named "Canada" (after a country they associated with great wealth). Although the Canada warehouses were destroyed, you can see a few of these items in the next building.

Block 5 focuses on material evidence of the crimes that took place here. It consists mostly of piles of the victims' goods, a tiny fraction of everything the Nazis stole. As you wander through the rooms, you'll see eyeglasses; fine Jewish prayer shawls; crutches and prosthetic limbs (the first people the Nazis ever exterminated were mentally and physically ill German citizens); a seemingly endless

Chilling Statistics: The Holocaust in Poland

The majority of people murdered by the Nazis during the Holocaust were killed right here in Poland. For centuries, Poland was known for its tolerance of Jews, and right up until the beginning of World War II, Poland had Europe's largest concentration of Jews: 3,500,000. Throughout the Holocaust, the Nazis murdered 4,500,000 Jews in Poland (many of them brought in from other countries) at camps, including Auschwitz, and in ghettos such as Warsaw's.

By the end of the war, only 300,000 Polish Jews had survived—less than one in 10 of the original population. Many of these survivors were granted "one-way passports" (read: deported) to Israel by the communist government in 1968 (following a big student demonstration with a strong Jewish presence). Today, only a few thousand Jews live in all of Poland.

mountain of shoes; and suitcases with names of victims—many marked Kind, or "child." Visitors often wonder if the suitcase with the name "Frank" belonged to Anne, one of the Holocaust's most famous victims. After being discovered in Amsterdam by the Nazis, the Frank family was transported here to Auschwitz, where they were split up. Still, it's unlikely this suitcase was theirs. Anne Frank and her sister Margot were sent to the Bergen-Belsen camp in northern Germany, where they died of typhus shortly before the war ended. Their father, Otto Frank, survived Auschwitz and was found barely alive by the Russians, who liberated the camp in January of 1945.

Although the purpose of Auschwitz was to murder its inmates, not all of them were killed immediately. After an initial evaluation, some prisoners were registered and forced to work. (This did not mean they were chosen to live—but rather to die later.) In **Block 6,** you see elements of the everyday life of prisoners. The halls are lined with photographs of victims. Notice the dates of arrival *(przybył)* and death *(zmarł)*—those who were registered survived here an average of two to three months. (Flowers are poignant reminders that these victims are survived by loved ones.) Room 1 displays drawings of the arrival process—sketched by survivors of the camp. After the initial selection, those chosen to work were showered, shaved, and photographed. After a while, photographing each prisoner got to be too expensive, so prisoners were tattooed instead (see photographs): on the chest, on the arm, or—for children—on the leg. A display shows the symbols that prisoners had to wear to show their reason for internment—Jew,

Roma (Gypsy), homosexual, political prisoner, and so on.

Room 4 shows the starvation that took place. The 7,500 survivors that the Red Army found here when the camp was liberated were living skeletons (the healthier ones had been forced to march to Germany). Of those liberated, 20 percent died soon after of disease and starvation. Look for the prisoners' daily ration (in the glass case): a pan of tea or coffee in the morning; thin vegetable soup in the afternoon; and a piece of bread (often made with sawdust or chestnuts) for dinner. This makes it clear that Auschwitz was never intended to be a "work camp," where people were kept alive, healthy, and efficient to do work. Rather, people were meant to die here—if not in the gas chambers, then through malnutrition and overwork.

You can see scenes from the prisoner's workday (sketched by survivors after liberation) in Room 5. Prisoners worked as long as the sun shone—eight hours in winter, up to 12 hours in summer—mostly on farms or in factories. Room 6 is about Auschwitz's child inmates, 20 percent of the camp's victims. Blond, blue-eyed children—like the girl in the bottom row on the right—were either "Germanized" in special schools or, if younger, adopted by German families. Dr. Josef Mengele conducted experiments on children, especially twins and triplets, to try to figure out ways to increase fertility for German mothers.

Block 7 shows living and sanitary conditions at the camp—which you'll see in more detail later at Birkenau. Blocks 8–10 are vacant (medical experiments were carried out in Block 10). Step into the **courtyard** between Blocks 10 and 11. The wall at the far end is where the Nazis shot several thousand political prisoners, leaders of camp resistance, and religious leaders. Notice that the windows are covered, so that nobody could witness the executions. Also take a close look at the memorial—the back of it is made of a material designed by Nazis to catch the bullets without a ricochet. Inmates were shot at short range—about three feet. The pebbles represent prayers from Jewish visitors.

The most feared place among prisoners was the **"Death Block" (#11),** from which nobody ever left alive. In Room 5, you can see how prisoners lived in these barracks—three-level bunks, with three prisoners sleeping in each bed (they had to sleep on their sides so they could fit). Death here required a trial (the room in which sham trials were held—lasting about 2 minutes each—is on display). In Room 6, people undressed before they were executed. In the basement, you'll see several different types of cells. The Starvation Cell (#18) held prisoners selected to starve to death when a fellow prisoner escaped; Maksymilian Kolbe voluntarily spent two weeks here to save a man's life (see sidebar). In the Dark Cell (#20), which held up to 30, people had only a small window

St. Maksymilian Kolbe
(1894–1941)

Among the many inspirational stories of Auschwitz is that of a Polish priest named Maksymilian Kolbe. Before the war, Kolbe traveled as a missionary to Japan, then worked in Poland for a Catholic newspaper. While he was highly regarded for his devotion to the Church, some of his writings had an unsettling anti-Semitic sentiment. But during the Nazi occupation, Kolbe briefly ran an institution that cared for refugees—including Jews.

In 1941, Kolbe was arrested and interned at Auschwitz. When a prisoner from Kolbe's block escaped in July of that year, the Nazis punished the remaining inmates by selecting 10 of them to put in the Starvation Cell until they died—based on the Nazi "doctrine of collective responsibility." After the selection had been made, Kolbe offered to replace a man who expressed concern about who would care for his family. The Nazis agreed. (The man Kolbe saved is said to have survived the Holocaust.)

All 10 of the men—including Kolbe—were put into Starvation Cell 18. Two weeks later, when the door was opened, only Kolbe had survived. The story spread throughout the camp, and Kolbe became an inspiration to the inmates. To squelch the hope he had given the others, Kolbe was executed by lethal injection.

In 1982, Kolbe was canonized by the Catholic Church. Some critics—mindful of his earlier anti-Semitic rhetoric—still consider Kolbe's sainthood controversial. But most Poles feel he redeemed himself for his earlier missteps through this noble act at the end of his life.

for ventilation—and if it became covered with snow, the prisoners suffocated. At the end of the hall in Cell 21, you can see where a prisoner scratched a crucifix (left) and image of Jesus (right) on the wall. In the Standing Cells (#22), four people would be forced to stand together for hours at time (of course, the bricks went all the way to the ceiling then). Upstairs is an exhibit on resistance within the camp.

Before you leave Auschwitz, visit the **crematorium** (from Block 11, exit straight ahead and go past the first row of barracks, then turn right and go straight on the road between the two rows of barracks; pass through the gap in the fence and look for the chimney on your left). People undressed outside, or just inside the door. Up to 700 people at a time could be gassed here. Inside the door, go into the big room on the right. Look for the vents in the ceiling—this is where the SS men dropped the Zyklon-B. Through the door is a replica of the furnace. This facility could burn 340 bodies a day—so it took two days to burn all of the bodies from one round of executions. The Nazis didn't like this inefficiency, so they built four more huge crematoria at Birkenau.

Shortly after the war, camp commander Rudolf Höss was tried, convicted, and sentenced to death. Survivors requested that he be executed at Auschwitz. In 1947, he was hanged. The site is preserved behind the crematorium (about a hundred yards from his home where his wife—who loved her years here—read stories to their children, very likely by the light of a human-skin lampshade).

Take your time with Auschwitz I. When you're ready, continue to the second stage of the camp—Birkenau (see "Getting from Auschwitz I to Birkenau," page 257).

Auschwitz II—Birkenau

In 1941, when the original Auschwitz camp got to be too small for the capacity the Nazis envisioned, they began a second camp in some nearby farm fields. The original plan was for a camp that could hold 200,000 people, but at its peak, Birkenau (Brzezinka) held only about 100,000. They were still adding onto it when the camp was liberated in 1945.

Train tracks lead past the main building and into the camp. The first sight that greeted prisoners was the guard tower (familiar to Americans from the stirring scenes in *Schindler's List*). Climb to the top of the entry building (also houses WCs and bookstore) for an overview of the massive camp. As you look over the camp, you'll see a vast field of chimneys and a few intact wooden and brick barracks. The train tracks lead straight back to the dividing platform, and then dead-end at the ruins of the crematorium and camp monument at the far side.

Some of the barracks were destroyed by Germans. Most were dismantled to be used for fuel and building materials shortly after the war. But the first row has been reconstructed (using components from the original structures). Visit the barracks on the right.

The first of these barrack buildings was the **latrine:** The front half of the building contained washrooms, and the back was a row of toilets. There was no running water; prisoners were in charge of keeping these clean. Because of the unsanitary conditions, the Nazis were afraid to come in here—so it was the heart of the black market and the inmates' resistance movement.

Auschwitz II—Birkenau

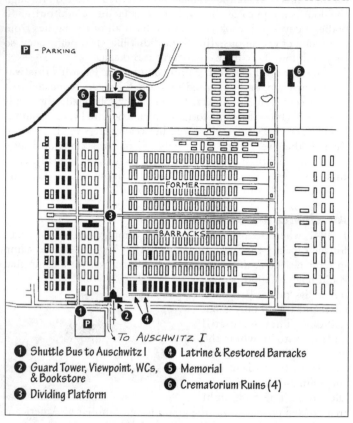

1 Shuttle Bus to Auschwitz I
2 Guard Tower, Viewpoint, WCs, & Bookstore
3 Dividing Platform
4 Latrine & Restored Barracks
5 Memorial
6 Crematorium Ruins (4)

The fourth barrack was a **bunk** building. Each inmate had a personal number, a barrack number, and a bed number. Inside, you can see the beds (angled so that more could fit). An average of 400 prisoners—but up to 1,000—would be housed in each of these buildings. These wooden structures, designed as stables by a German company (look for the horse-tying rings on the wall), came in prefab pieces that made them cheap and convenient. Two chimneys connected by a brick duct provided a little heat. The bricks were smoothed by inmates who sat here to catch a bit of warmth.

Follow the train tracks toward the monument about a half mile away, at the back end of Birkenau. At the intersection of these tracks and the perpendicular gravel road (halfway to the monument) was the gravel **dividing platform.** A Nazi doctor would stand facing the guard tower and evaluate each prisoner. If he pointed to the right, the prisoner was sentenced to death, and trudged—unknowingly—to the gas chamber. If he pointed to the left, the person would be registered and live a little longer. It was here that families from all over Europe were torn apart forever.

On the left-hand side of the tracks are some **brick barracks.** The supervisors lived in the two smaller rooms near the door. Farther in, most barracks still have the wooden bunks that held about 700 people per building. Four or five people slept on each bunk, including the floor—reserved for new arrivals. There were chamber pots at either end of the building. After a Nazi doctor died of typhus, sanitation improved, and these barracks got running water.

As you walk along the camp's only road, which leads along the tracks to the crematorium, imagine the horror of this place—no grass, only mud, and all the barracks packed with people, with smoke blowing in from the busy crematoria. This was an even worse place to die than Auschwitz I.

The train tracks lead to the camp memorial and crematorium. At the end of the tracks, go 50 yards to the left and climb the three concrete steps to view the ruin of the **crematorium**. This one of four crematoria here at Birkenau, with a capacity to cremate more than 4,400 people per day. At the far-right end of the ruins, see the stairs where people entered the rooms to undress. People were given numbered lockers, conning them into thinking they were coming back. (Nazis didn't want a panic.) Then they piled into the "shower room"—the underground passage branching away from the memorial—and were killed. Their bodies were burned in the crematorium (on the left), giving off a scent of sweet almonds (the Zyklon-B). Beyond the remains of the crematorium is a hole—once a gray lake where tons of ashes were dumped. This efficient factory of death was destroyed by the Nazis as the Red Army approached, leaving today's evocative ruins.

The Soviets arrived on January 27, 1945, and the nightmare of Auschwitz was over. The Polish parliament voted to turn these grounds into a museum, so that the world would understand, and never forget, the horror of what happened here. The **monument** at the back of the camp, built in 1967 (by the communist government in its heavy "Social Realist" style), represents gravestones and the chimney of a crematorium. The plaques, written in each of the languages spoken by camp victims (including English, far right), explain that the memorial is "a cry of despair and a warning to humanity."

TRANSPORTATION CONNECTIONS

Remember that Auschwitz Museum is in the town of Oświęcim, about 50 miles west of Kraków.

From Kraków to Auschwitz

Frequent **buses** connect Kraków and Auschwitz, mostly run by PKS Oświęcim (about 10 zł, roughly hourly, 1.5 hrs). Get the most recent schedule (and confirm the departure point) at any Kraków TI. When you board the bus, tell the driver you want "Auschwitz Museum." Once in the town of Oświęcim, buses from Kraków stop first at the train station, then continue on to a low-profile bus stop on the edge of the Auschwitz camp grounds (you'll see a small *Muzeum Auschwitz* sign on the right just before the stop). From this bus stop, follow the sign down the road and into the parking lot; the main building is across the lot on your left. Note that since most buses don't actually go into the museum's parking lot, the Auschwitz stop can be easy to miss.

Several **minibuses** also depart from near Kraków's bus station, and head directly to the Auschwitz Museum (8 zł, 1.5 hrs, get details at TI).

You could ride the **train** to Oświęcim, but it's less convenient than the bus (14/day, 1.25–1.75 hrs).

If you wind up at the Oświęcim **train station**, it's about a 20-minute walk to the camp (turn right out of station, go straight, then turn left at roundabout, camp is several blocks ahead on left). Or, from the Oświęcim station, you can reach the camp by catching a local bus (about 2 zł) or taking a taxi (around 10 zł).

A **taxi** between Kraków and Auschwitz runs about 200 zł one-way. But if you're splurging for a taxi, you might as well pay for a private guide to drive you here, as well as show you around once you arrive (see "Tours" in the Kraków chapter, page 213).

Returning from Auschwitz to Kraków

Buses back to Kraków do not leave from the camp parking lot itself (though some minibuses do). Instead, you'll catch the bus from the stop on the edge of the Auschwitz I grounds (described above). To reach this bus stop, leave the Auschwitz I building through the main entry and walk straight along the parking lot, then turn right on the road near the end of the lot. At the dead end, cross the street to the little bus stop. As this can be confusing and frustrating, figure out your return with the help of the information desk upon arrival in Auschwitz. Note that there's no public transportation back to Kraków from Birkenau, where most people end their tours; you'll have to take the shuttle bus back to Auschwitz I first.

WARSAW

(Warszawa)

Warsaw (Warszawa, vah-SHAH-vah in Polish) is Poland's capital and biggest city. It's huge, famous, and important...but not particularly romantic. If you're looking for Old World quaintness, head for Kraków. If you're tickled by spires and domes, get to Prague. But if you want to experience a truly 21st-century city, Warsaw's your place.

Like Berlin, Warsaw is modernizing—fast. Mindful of its history, yet optimistic about the future, Warsaw has happily emerged from a long hibernation. Varsovians are embracing their role as the capital city of an influential nation in the "New Europe." The European Union has two universities aimed at educating future political leaders (or "Eurocrats"). One is in Bruges, Belgium—just down the road from the EU capital of Brussels. The other one is right here. Warsaw also has gleaming new skyscrapers and street signs, stylishly dressed locals, cutting-edge shopping malls, and a gourmet coffee shop on every corner.

Warsaw has good reason to be a city of the future: The past hasn't been very kind. Since becoming Poland's capital in 1596, the city has seen wave after wave of foreign rulers and invasions—especially during the last hundred years. Warsaw is an open-air display of tragic 20th-century history. But in this horrific crucible, the enduring spirit of the Polish people was forged. As one proud Varsovian told me, "Warsaw is ugly because its history is so beautiful."

The city's darkest days came during the Nazi occupation of World War II. First, its Jewish residents were forced into a tiny ghetto. They rose up...and were slaughtered. Then, its Polish residents rose up...and were slaughtered. Hitler sent word to systematically demolish this troublesome city. At the war's end,

Warsaw was devastated. An estimated 800,000 residents were dead—almost two out of every three Varsovians.

The Poles almost gave up on what was then a pile of rubble to build a brand-new capital city elsewhere. But ultimately they decided to rebuild, creating a city of contrasts: painstakingly restored medieval lanes, crumbling communist apartment blocks (*bloki* in Polish), and sleek, super-modern, glass-and-steel skyscrapers. Between the buildings, you'll find fragments of a complex, sometimes tragic, and often inspiring history.

A product of its complicated past, sprinkled with the big-city style and sophistication of the present, while remaining quintessentially Polish, Warsaw is a place worth grappling with to understand the Poland of today...and the Europe of tomorrow.

Planning Your Time

Though you can get a good taste in a short visit—as a day-trip, or en route elsewhere—Warsaw deserves at least a full day.

With a few hours, gape at Stalin's towering Palace of Culture and Science, then wander through the reconstructed Old Town. With a little more time, relax in Łazienki Park or seek out the sights of whichever topics interest you: art, Holocaust history, the Warsaw Uprising, Polish royalty, or Chopin.

If you're coming from Germany, consider connecting to Warsaw via an overnight train from Berlin. See Warsaw, and then move on to Kraków later that same day (hourly trains, 2.5 hours).

ORIENTATION

(area code: 022)

Warsaw sprawls with 1.6 million residents. Everything is on a big scale—it seems to take forever to walk just a few "short" blocks. Get comfortable with public transportation and plan your sightseeing wisely to avoid backtracking. Virtually everything of interest to travelers is on the west bank of the Vistula River. The city's Central Train Station (Warszawa Centralna) is in the shadow of its biggest landmark: the can't-miss-it, skyscraping Palace of Culture and Science. To the east of the station, parallel to the river, runs the "Royal Way" boulevard, connecting the sights in the north (Old Town and New Town) with the sights in the south (Łazienki Park, and beyond that, Wilanów Palace). Most major sights and recommended hotels and restaurants are along this spine.

Another tip: You'll hear about two distinct uprisings that occurred against the Nazis during World War II. They're easy to confuse, but try to keep them straight: the **Ghetto Uprising** was staged by Warsaw's dwindling Jewish population in the spring of 1943 (see page 293); the **Warsaw Uprising**, a year later, came

Central Warsaw

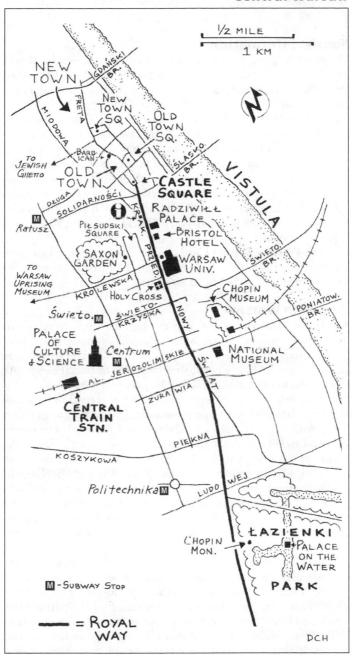

at the hands of the (mostly non-Jewish) Polish Home Army (see page 296).

Tourist Information

Warsaw's helpful, youthful TI has four offices: on the **Royal Way** near Castle Square (daily May–Sept 9:00–20:00, Oct–April 9:00–18:00, Krakowskie Przedmieście 39), the **Central Train Station** (daily May–Sept 8:00–20:00, Oct–April 8:00–18:00), the **western bus station** (same hours as Central Train Station TI, aleja Jerozolimskie 144), and the **airport** (same hours as Central Train Station TI). The general information number for all TIs is 022/9431 (www.warsawtour.pl). All four branches offer several free, useful materials: a city map (with key phone numbers on the back), a well-produced booklet called *Warsaw: In Short*, and a series of brochures on sights (Jewish heritage, Chopin) and neighborhoods (Old Town, Royal Way). The TI also has a free room-booking service.

The **Warsaw Tourist Card**, which covers public transportation and admission to over 20 museums, isn't worth the price for most travelers (35 zł/24 hrs, 65 zł/3 days).

Arrival in Warsaw

By Train: Most trains arrive at the big, dreary Central Train Station (Warszawa Centralna), a *Flying Nun* monstrosity next to the Palace of Culture and Science. You'll emerge from your platform *(peron)* into a confusing labyrinth of passageways. At this underground level, you'll find **lockers** near *peron* 4—look for *przechowalnia bagażu*. Emerge into the **main arrival hall** (follow signs to *Hala Główna*) to get your bearings (and take your first gawk at the nearby Palace of Culture and Science). For **international tickets,** look for the *Kasy Międzynarodowe* office in the corner of the main hall (under the big, orange *Apteka Non Stop* sign). **Bus #175** takes you right to the Royal Way and Old Town in about 10 minutes (see "Getting Around Warsaw," below; catch bus in front of the skyscraper with the LOT airlines office and Hotel Marriott across busy aleja Jerozolimskie from the station; exit to the south—near *peron* 1—and follow signs for *Hotel Marriott*). Train info: tel. 022/9436.

By Car: Warsaw is a stressful city to drive and park in. Arrange parking with your hotel, and get around by foot or public transit. You must pay to park in the city Monday–Friday 8:00–18:00. Park your car (likely on a sidewalk), find the parking pay station, and insert coins until the proper amount of time appears in the left-hand window (about 2 zł/hr). Press the green button, wait for your ticket, and put it on your dashboard. Sometimes public parking areas are monitored by "attendants"—unemployed creeps

Warsaw Essentials

English	Polish	Pronounced
Warsaw	Warszawa	vah-SHAH-vah
Central Train Station	Warszawa Centralna	vah-SHAH-vah tsehn-TRAHL-nah
Palace of Culture and Science	Pałac Kultury i Nauki (or simply "Pałac")	PAH-wahts kool-TOO-ree ee nah-OO-kee
New Town	Nowe Miasto	NOH-vay mee-AH-stoh
Old Town	Stare Miasto	STAH-reh mee-AH-stoh
Old Town	Rynek Starego	REE-nehk stah-RAY-goh
Market Square	Miasta	mee-AH-stah
Royal Way	Szłak Królewski	shwock kroh-LEHV-skee
Royal Castle	Zamek Królewski	ZAH-mehk kroh-LEHV-skee
Castle Square	Plac Zamkowy	plahts zahm-KOH-vee
Piłsudski Square	Plac Marszałka Józefa Piłsudskiego	plahts mar-SHAW-kah yoh-ZEH fah pew-sood-SKYAY-goh
Łazienki Park	Park Łazienkowski	park wah-zhehn-KOV-skee
Vistula River	Wisła	VEES-wah

who kindly help you find a spot, then ask if you want them to "watch your car" for you. Try to avoid parking where you see these crooks, but if you do, 1–2 zł is a small investment to prevent the car from being damaged.

By Plane: Warsaw's **Frederic Chopin International Airport** (Port Lotniczy im. Fryderyk Chopina) is about six miles southwest of the center. The airport is small and user-friendly, with English signs. You'll find a branch of the TI, plus lots of ATMs and exchange offices *(kantor)*. Bus #175 runs into the center (Central Train Station, Royal Way, and Old Town) from the bus stop just in front of the terminal (sold for 2.40 zł at kiosk, or 3 zł from driver, 4–6/hr, fewer Sat–Sun, 30 min). A 20-minute taxi ride to the center shouldn't cost you more than 40 zł (though hucksters who approach you offering a ride may try to charge you astronomical rates—ask for an estimate, and if it's more than 40 zł, ask the next guy). The trip into town can take much longer during rush hour, because only one main thoroughfare connects the airport to the center. Airport info: tel. 022/650-4100.

Getting Around Warsaw

By Public Transit: Warsaw's trams and city buses help make the city more manageable—the Metro is virtually useless to tourists. All three systems use the same tickets. A single ticket costs 2.40 zł (called *bilet jednorazowy,* good for one trip, no transfers); a one-day ticket costs 7.20 zł (*bilet dobowy,* good for 24 hours); and a three-day ticket is 12 zł *(bilet trzydniowy).* Buy your ticket at any kiosk with a *RUCH* sign, and be sure to validate it as you board by inserting it in the little yellow box (24-hour and 3-day tickets need only be validated the first time you ride). You can also buy the basic one-ride tickets from your bus or tram driver for an extra 0.60 zł.

Bus #180 (marked with an eye icon because it's a special sightseeing route) conveniently connects virtually all of the sights and neighborhoods of interest to tourists: the former Jewish Ghetto, Castle Square/Old Town, Royal Way, Łazienki Park, and Wilanów Palace (south of the center). **Bus #175** links the airport, the Central Train Station, Royal Way, and Old Town. Those two buses, as well as buses #116, #122, #175, #195, #503, and #518, go along the most interesting stretch of the Royal Way (between aleja Jerozolimskie and Castle Square in the Old Town). Bus routes beginning with "E" are express, so they go long distances without stopping.

By Taxi: As in most big Eastern European cities, it's wise to use only cabs that are clearly marked with a company logo and telephone number (or call your own: Locals like MPT Radio Taxi, tel. 022/9191). All official taxis have similar rates: 6 zł to start, then 2–3 zł per kilometer (more after 22:00 or in the suburbs). The drop fee may be higher if you catch the cab in front of a big, fancy hotel.

TOURS

Various companies offer bus tours (which include some walking) for 120–130 zł (3–4.5 hrs, get information at TI and most hotels). A tourist train does a 30-minute circuit, leaving from in front of the Royal Castle (16 zł, daily May–Oct, doesn't run Mon Nov–April).

SELF-GUIDED WALK

Warsaw's Royal Way

The Royal Way (Szłak Królewski) is the six-mile route that kings of Poland used to take from their main residence (at Castle Square in the Old Town) to their summer home (Wilanów Palace, south of the center). In the heart of the city, the Royal Way is a busy boulevard with two different names: vibrant **Nowy Świat** (at the south end), which offers a good look at urban Warsaw, and **Krakowskie Przedmieście** (at the north end, ending at the Old Town), lined with historic landmarks and better for sightseeing.

Since this spine connects most hotels, restaurants, and sights, you'll probably use it—on foot or by bus (for example, bus #175 from the Central Train Station)—sometime during your trip. This commentary should make the commute more interesting. I've focused more on the intriguing stretch closest the Old Town, where the street is called Krakowskie Przedmieście. To skip directly to this point ("Part 2," below), take the bus to the Uniwersytet stop and backtrack one block. Figure about 20 minutes to walk along Nowy Świat ("Part 1"), then another 30 minutes along Krakowskie Przedmieście to the Old Town ("Part 2").

Royal Way Walk Part 1: Nowy Świat

Begin at the head of the boulevard called Nowy Świat—literally, "New World"—at the intersection with aleja Jerozolimskie. In the middle of the intersection, notice the giant model of a palm tree. Why a palm tree? Nobody knows. As you face it, look across the street and up the block to the left to see the National Museum—a good place for a Polish art lesson (more interesting than it sounds—see page 289). To the right of that, directly across from Nowy Świat, stands a big, blocky building that used to be the headquarters of the Communist Party. A popular communist-era joke: What do you see when you turn your back on the Communist Party? A new world (Nowy Świat).

Today's Poland is confidently striding into a new world...and so should we. Get marching.

Nowy Świat is a charming, nearly traffic-free shopping boulevard—nicknamed the "Champs-Elysées of Warsaw" by Varsovians...well, maybe not quite. But, lined with shops, cafés, restaurants, and happy locals, it's less dreary-urban and more romantic-elegant than other parts of the city. Rents are higher here than anywhere else in Warsaw. Between Nowy Świat and the Palace of Culture and Science, one of Warsaw's trendiest shopping and dining neighborhoods stretches to your left.

Ulica Chmielna, the first street to the left, is an appealing pedestrian boutique street leading to Emil Wedel's chocolate heaven. After another block on Nowy Świat, on the left, don't miss the A. Blikle pastry shop and café—*the* place in Poland to buy sweets. (For more on these two places, see page 301.)

Eat and shop your way up Nowy Świat. After three long blocks, you'll reach the big Copernicus statue in the middle of the street.

Old Town and Royal Way

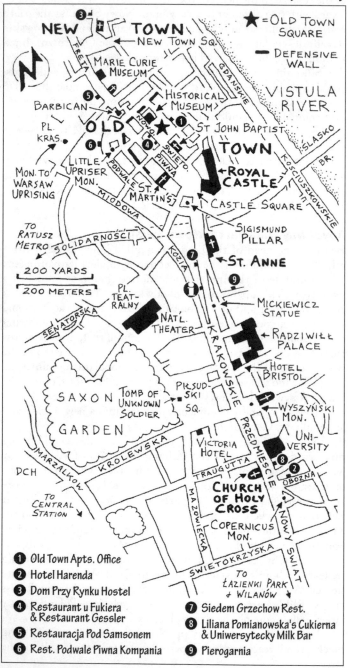

1 Old Town Apts. Office
2 Hotel Harenda
3 Dom Przy Rynku Hostel
4 Restaurant u Fukiera
  & Restaurant Gessler
5 Restauracja Pod Samsonem
6 Rest. Podwale Piwna Kompania

7 Siedem Grzechow Rest.
8 Liliana Pomianowska's Cukierna
  & Uniwersytecky Milk Bar
9 Pierogarnia

Royal Way Walk Part 2: Krakowskie Przedmieście

The street changes its name to Krakowskie Przedmieście at the big statue of **Copernicus**, in front of the Polish Academy of Science. Mikołaj Kopernik was born in Toruń (see page 359) and went to college in Kraków. The Nazis stole this statue and took it to Germany (which, like Poland, claims Copernicus as its own). Now it's back where it belongs.

We'll pass many churches along this route, but the **Church of the Holy Cross** is unique (Kościół Św. Krzyża, across from Copernicus). Composer Fryderyk Chopin's heart is inside one of the pillars of the nave (2nd big pillar on the left, look for the marker). After two decades of exile in France, Chopin's final wish was to have his heart brought back to his native Poland. During World War II, the heart was hidden away in the countryside for safety. Chopin's organs aside, this church feels more alive than most. Locals often drop in. Check out the bright gold chapel, located on the left as you face the altar, at the front of the church. It's dedicated to a saint who Polish Catholics believe helps them with "desperate and hopeless causes." People praying here are likely dealing with some tough issues. The beads draped from the altarpieces help power their prayers, and the many little brass plaques are messages of thanks for prayers answered.

After leaving the church, continue up the street and take the pedestrian underpass to the other side. You're at the gates to the main campus of **Warsaw University**, founded in 1816. This area is a lively student district with plenty of bookstores and cafés. If you're still hungry after all those pastries and chocolate, consider a couple of very cheap and characteristic places nearby: up at the start of the block, a passageway (at Krakowskie Przedmieście 8) leads to Liliana Pomianowska's *cukierna* (pastry shop). For something heartier, duck into the Uniwersytecky Bar (at #20). This is a **milk bar** *(bar mleczny)*—a subsidized government cafeteria filled with students and anyone who wants a bargain (for more about milk bars, see page 202).

The 18th century was a time of great political decline for Poland, as a series of incompetent foreign kings mishandled crises and squandered funds. But ironically, it was also Warsaw's biggest economic boom time. Along this boulevard, aristocratic families of the period built **mansions**—destroyed during World War II and rebuilt since, some with curious flourishes. (Just past the university on the right, look for the doorway supported by four bearded brutes admiring their overly defined abs.) Over time, many of these families donated their mansions to the university.

The yellow church a block up from the university is the Church of the Nuns of the Visitation (Kościół Sióstr Wizytek). The monument in front commemorates **Cardinal Stefan Wyszyński,** who was the Polish primate (the head of the Polish Catholic Church) from 1948 to 1981. He took this post soon after the arrival of the communists, who opposed the Church, but also realized it would be risky for them to shut down the churches in such an ardently religious country. The Communist Party and the Catholic Church coexisted tensely in Poland, and when Wyszyński protested a Stalinist crackdown in 1953, he was arrested and imprisoned. Three years later, in a major victory for the Church, Wyszyński was released. He continued to fight the communists, becoming a great hero of the Polish people in their struggle against the regime.

Farther up, you'll see the elegant **Hotel Bristol,** Warsaw's classiest. Leave the Royal Way briefly to reach Piłsudski Square (a block away on the left, up the street opposite Hotel Bristol).

The vast, empty-feeling **Piłsudski Square** (Plac Marszałka Józefa Piłsudskiego)—a ▲ sight—has been important Warsaw real estate for years, constantly changing with the times. An Orthodox cathedral here was torn down in the 1920s, when anti-Russian passions ran high in newly independent Poland. During the Nazi occupation, it took the name "Adolf-Hitler-Platz." Under the communists, it was Zwycięstwa, meaning "Victory" (of the Soviets over Hitler's fascism). When the regime imposed martial law in 1981, the people of Warsaw silently protested by filling the square with a giant cross made of flowers. The huge plaque in the ground near the busy road commemorates two monumental communist-era Catholic events on this square: John Paul II's first visit as pope to his homeland on June 2, 1979; and the funeral on May 31, 1981, of Cardinal Stefan Wyszyński, whom we met across the street.

Find the sewer lid at the very center of the square, and stand on it for this quick spin-tour orientation: Ahead are the Tomb of the Unknown Soldier and Saxon Garden; to the right is the old National Theater, eclipsed by a modern shopping mall/parking garage; farther to the right is a statue of Piłsudski (which you passed to get here—described below); and to the right of that—past the big gray Polish Ministry of Defense building—is the Victoria Hotel, the ultimate plush, top-of-the-top hotel where all communist-era VIPs stayed.

Walk to the fragment of colonnade by the park that marks the **Tomb of the Unknown Soldier** (Grób Nieznanego Żołnierza). The colonnade was once part of a much larger palace built by the Saxon prince electors (Dresden's Augustus the Strong and his son), who became kings of Poland in the 18th century. After the palace was destroyed in World War II, this fragment was kept to memorialize Polish soldiers. The names of key battles are etched into the columns, urns contain dirt from major Polish battlefields, and the two guards are pretty stiff.

Just behind the Tomb is **Saxon Garden** (Ogród Saski), a pleasant park to stroll in, also built by the Saxon kings of Poland. Like most foreign kings, Augustus the Strong and his son cared little for their Polish territory, building gardens like these for themselves instead of investing in more pressing needs. Poles say that foreign kings such as Augustus did nothing but "eat, drink, and loosen their belts" (it rhymes in Polish). According to Poles, these selfish absentee kings are the culprits for Poland's eventual decline.

Walk back out toward the Royal Way, stopping at the statue you passed earlier. In 1995, the square was again re-named—this time for **Józef Piłsudski,** the guy with the big walrus moustache. Piłsudski (1867–1935) forced out the Russian Bolsheviks from Poland in 1920 in the so-called Miracle on the Vistula. Piłsudski is credited with creating a once-again-independent Poland after over a century of foreign oppression, and he essentially ran Poland after World War I. Of course, under the communists, Piłsudski was swept under the rug, but today he's enjoying a renaissance as Poland's favorite prototype anti-communist hero (his name adorns streets, squares, and bushy-mustachioed monuments all over the country).

Return to Hotel Bristol, turn left, and continue your Royal Way walk. Next door to the hotel, you'll see the huge **Radziwiłł Palace**—the Polish White House, with the offices of Poland's new president, who was elected in October of 2005. The Warsaw Pact was signed here in 1955, officially uniting the Soviet satellite states in a military alliance against NATO. The newest flag in the courtyard is Europe's (celebrating the May 1, 2004, entry of Poland into the EU).

Beyond Radziwiłł Palace, you'll reach a statue (on a pillar) of **Adam Mickiewicz,** Poland's national poet. Polish high school students have a big formal ball (like a prom) 100 days before graduation. After the ball, if students come here and hop around the statue on one leg, it's supposed to bring them good luck on their finals. Mickiewicz, for his part, looks like he's suffering from a heart attack—perhaps in response to the impressively ugly National Theater and Opera a block in front of him.

For a scenic finale to your Royal Way stroll, climb the 150 steps of the view tower by **St. Anne's Church** (3 zł, sporadic hours but generally open daily 10:00–18:00). You'll be rewarded with a great view of the Old Town, river, and Warsaw's skyline.

From St. Anne's Church, it's just another block—past inviting art galleries and restaurants—to the Castle Square, the TI, and the start of the Old Town (to continue your walk all the way to the New Town, see "Warsaw's Old Town," page 280).

Warsaw at a Glance

▲▲**Old Town Market Square** Recreation of Warsaw's glory days, with lots of colorful architecture. **Hours:** Always open.

▲▲**National Museum** Collection of mostly Polish art, with unknown but worth-discovering works by Jan Matejko and the Młoda Polska (Art Nouveau) crew. **Hours:** Tue–Sun 10:00–16:00, Thu until 18:00, closed Mon.

▲**Piłsudski Square** Tomb of the Unknown Soldier, Saxon Garden, National Theater, and historic monuments. **Hours:** Always open.

▲**Castle Square** Colorful spot with whiffs of old Warsaw—Royal Castle (below), monuments, and a chunk of the city wall, with cafés just off the square. **Hours:** Always open.

▲**Royal Castle** Warsaw's best palace, rebuilt after World War II, but stocked with original furnishings (hidden during the war). **Hours:** Various tour routes with different hours. Generally open Tue–Sun 10:00–16:00 or 18:00, summer Mon 11:00–16:00 or 18:00, shorter tours and permanent exhibition closed on Sun, closed Mon in winter.

▲**Chopin Museum** Elegant old mansion with Chopin bric-a-brac and occasional piano concerts. **Hours:** May–Sept Mon, Wed, and Fri 10:00–17:00, Thu 12:00–18:00, Sat–Sun 10:00–14:00, closed Tue;

SIGHTS

Warsaw's Old Town

In 1945, not a building remained standing in Warsaw's "Old" Town (Stare Miasto). Everything you see is rebuilt, mostly finished by 1956. This is the city's only must-see sight. Some find it artificial and phony, in a Disney World kind of way. For others, the painstaking postwar reconstruction just feels right, with Old World squares and lanes charming enough to give Kraków a run for its money. Before 1989, stifled by communist repression and choking on smog, the Old Town was an empty husk of its historic self. But now, the market stalls have returned, and the locals are out strolling.

These sights are listed in order from south to north, beginning at the Castle Square and ending at the entrance to the New Town. For the best route from the Central Train Station to the Old Town, see the "Royal Way" self-guided walk on page 274.

Oct–April Mon–Wed and Fri–Sat 10:00–14:00, Thu 12:00–18:00; closed Sun.

▲**Łazienki Park** Lovely, sprawling green space with Chopin statue, peacocks, and neoclassical buildings. **Hours:** Always open.

▲**Ghetto Walking Tour** Pilgrimage from Ghetto Heroes Square along the Path of Remembrance to the infamous Nazi "transfer spot" where Jews were sent to death camps. **Hours:** Always open.

▲**Warsaw Uprising Museum** High-tech exhibit tracing the history of the Uprising and celebrating its heroes. **Hours:** Wed–Mon 10:00–18:00, Thu until 20:00, closed Tue.

Warsaw Historical Museum Glimpse of the city before and after World War II, with excellent movie in English. **Hours:** Museum—Tue and Thu 11:00–18:00, Wed and Fri 10:00–15:30, Sat–Sun 10:30–16:30, closed Mon; Movie—Tue–Sat at noon.

Palace of Culture and Science Huge "Stalin Gothic" skyscraper with a more impressive exterior than interior, housing theaters, multiplex cinema, observation deck, and more. **Hours:** Observation deck—daily June–Sept 9:00–20:00, Oct–May 9:00–18:00.

▲**Castle Square (Plac Zamkowy)**—This lively square is dominated by the big, pink Royal Castle, the historic heart of Warsaw's political power. After the second great Polish dynasty—the Jagiellonians—died off in 1572, the Republic of Nobles (about 10 percent of the population) elected various foreign kings to their throne.

The guy on the 72-foot-tall **pillar** is Sigismund III, the first Polish king from the Swedish Waza family. In 1596, he relocated the capital from Kraków to Warsaw. This move made sense, since Warsaw was closer to the center of 16th-century Poland (which had expanded to the east), and because the city had been gaining political importance as the meeting point of the Sejm, or parliament of nobles, over the preceding 30 years. Along the right side of the castle, notice the two previous versions of this pillar lying on a lawn. The first one, from 1644, was falling apart and had to be replaced in 1887 by a new one made of granite. In 1944, a Nazi tank broke this second pillar—a symbolic piece of Polish heritage—into the four pieces that you see here today. As Poland rebuilt, its citizens put Sigismund III back on his pillar.

Across the square from the castle, you'll see the partially reconstructed defensive wall. This rampart once enclosed the entire Old Town. Situated at the crossroads of Central Europe, Warsaw—like all of Poland—has seen invasion from all sides.

Explore the café-lined lanes that branch downhill off Castle Square. Street signs (from the early 1950s) indicate the year that each street was originally built.

The first street leading off the square is **ulica Piwna** (literally, Beer Street), where you'll find **St. Martin's Church** (Kościół Św. Martina, on the left). Run by Franciscan nuns, this church has a simple, modern interior. Notice the partly destroyed crucifix—all that survived World War II. Across the street and closer to Castle Square, admire the carefully carved doorway of Restauracja Pod Gołębiami (literally, "Under Doves")—dedicated to the memory of an old woman who fed birds amidst the Old Town rubble after World War II.

Back on the Castle Square, find the white **plaque** with the red stripes in the middle of the second block (by plac Zamkowy 15/19). It explains that 50 Poles were executed by Nazis on this spot on September 2, 1944. You'll see plaques like this all over the Old Town, each one commemorating victims or opponents of the Nazis. Notice the brick planter under the plaque; it's often filled with fresh flowers to honor the victims.

▲Royal Castle (Zamek Królewski)—After Warsaw became the capital in 1596, this massive building was used both as the king's residence and as the meeting place of the parliament (Sejm). There has been a castle here since the Mazovian dukes built a wooden version in the 14th century. It has shifted shape with the tenor of the times, being rebuilt and remodeled by many different kings.

After it was destroyed in World War II, rebuilding began again in the 1950s and was not completed until the 1970s.

Of all of Warsaw's many castles, this one is most interesting to tour—which isn't saying much. While the exterior is entirely reconstructed, many of the furnishings are original (hidden away

when it became clear the city would be demolished). Each room is well-described in English.

The castle makes a great Polish history textbook. In fact, you'll likely see grade-school classes sitting cross-legged on the floors. Watching the teachers drilling eager young history buffs, you can only imagine what it's like to be a young Pole, with such a tumultuous recent history.

Warning: The information below—the castle opening times, tour routes, and castle layout—is maddeningly sporadic. Things frequently change depending on special events, temporary exhibitions, the direction the wind is blowing, and the inexplicable whims of palace administrators.

Touring the Castle: The castle has various parts, each with separate tickets. For a basic visit, you'll choose between two completely different tour routes: **Route I** (10 zł, year-round Tue–Sun 10:00–16:00, mid-April–Sept also open Mon 11:00–16:00); or **Route II**, which is more expensive since it includes a mandatory tour with a Polish-speaking guide (18 zł, mid-April–Sept Tue–Sat 10:00–18:00, Mon 11:00–18:00; Oct–mid-April Tue–Sat 10:00–16:00, closed Mon). On Sundays, a special **Sunday Route** includes the "greatest hits" of both routes (free entry, mid-April–Sept 11:00–18:00, Oct–mid-April 11:00–16:00).

Route I—including the Senators' Chamber and the Matejko rooms (see below)—is better. The last entry for any route is one hour before closing.

There's also a **permanent exhibition** that includes decorative arts (17th–18th centuries), a porcelain gallery, a coin collection, some paintings (including a pair of Rembrandts), and various exhibits of interest only to Polish historians (10 zł, Tue–Sat 10:00–16:00, mid-April–Sept also open Mon 11:00–16:00, always closed Sun). Rounding out the attractions is a series of temporary exhibitions. The palace is at Plac Zamkowy 4 (tel. 022/657-2170, www.zamek-krolewski.art.pl). A public WC is on the courtyard just around the corner of the castle.

Route I Highlights: The grand **Senators' Chamber,** with the king's throne, is surrounded by different coats of arms. Each one represents a region that was part of Poland during its Golden Age, back when it was united with Lithuania and its territory stretched from the Baltic to the Black Sea. In this room, Poland adopted its 1791 constitution. It was the first in Europe, written soon after America's and just months before France's. And, like the Constitution of the United States, it was very progressive, based on the ideals of the Enlightenment. But the final partitions followed in 1793 and 1795, Poland was divided between neighboring powers and disappeared from the map until 1918, and the constitution was never really put into action.

The next room features paintings by **Jan Matejko** that capture the excitement surrounding the adoption of this ill-fated constitution (for more on Matejko, see page 287).

Route II Highlights: Climb the stairs and wander through the ornate rooms. In the **Throne Room,** note the crowned eagle, the symbol of Poland, decorating the banner behind the throne. The Soviets didn't allow anything royal or aristocratic, so postwar restorations came with crown-less eagles. Only after 1989 were the crowns replaced (in the case of this banner, sewn on). A few rooms later is the **Canaletto Room,** filled with canvases of late-18th-century Warsaw painted in exquisite detail by this talented artist. These paintings came in handy when the city needed to be rebuilt. (This Canaletto, also known for his panoramas of Dresden, was the nephew of another artist with the same nickname, famous for painting Venice's canals.) Continue wandering through the sumptuous halls, saying hello to U.S. Constitution co-signer Ben Franklin (by the door in the Green Room) and gaping at the Marble Room (with portraits of Polish kings around the ceiling—find your favorite).

After you finish touring the castle and you're ready to resume exploring the Old Town, turn left at the end of the square onto...

St. John's Street (Świętojańska)—On the plaque under the street name sign, you can guess what the dates mean, even if you don't speak Polish: This building was constructed 1433–1478, destroyed in 1944, and rebuilt 1950–1953.

Partway down the street on the right, you'll come to the big brick...

Cathedral of St. John the Baptist (Katedra Św. Jana Chrzciciela)—This cathedral-basilica is the oldest (1339) and most important church in Warsaw. Poland's constitution was consecrated here on May 3, 1791. This church became the final battleground of the 1944 Warsaw Uprising—when a Nazi tank (appropriately named *Goliath*) drove into the church and intentionally exploded, massacring the rebels. You can still see part of that tank's tread hanging on the outside wall of the church (around the right side).

Despite the church's importance, the its interior is pretty dull (free, open long hours daily, closed 13:00–15:00 and during services). Look for the crucifix ornamented with real human hair (chapel left of high altar). The high altar holds a copy of the Black Madonna—proclaimed "everlasting queen of Poland" after a victory over the Swedes in 17th century. The original Black Madonna is in Częstochowa (125 miles south of Warsaw)—a mecca for Slavic Catholics, who visit in droves in hopes of a miracle.

Continue up the street and enter Warsaw's grand...

▲▲Old Town Market Square (Rynek Starego Miasta)—Seventy years ago, this was one of the most happening spots in Central

Europe. Sixty years ago, it was rubble. And today, like a phoenix rising from the ashes, it reminds residents and tourists alike of the prewar glory of the Polish capital. Enjoy the colorful architecture.

Go to the **mermaid fountain** in the middle of the square.

The mermaid is an important symbol in Warsaw—you'll see her everywhere. Legend has it that a mermaid *(syrenka)* lived in the Vistula River and protected the townspeople. While this siren supposedly serenaded the town, Varsovians like her more for her strength (hence the sword). In fact, the woman who modeled for this sculpture, Krystyna Krahelska, served as a paramedic for the Polish Home Army during the Warsaw Uprising (code name: "Danuta").

On the second day of the fighting, she was shot in the chest and died—becoming a martyr for the Polish people.

Each of the square's four sides is named for an prominent 18th-century Varsovian: Kołłątaj, Dekert, Barss, and Zakrzewski. These men served as "Presidents" of Warsaw (more or less the mayor), and Kołłątaj was also a framer of Poland's 1791 constitution. Take some time to explore the square. Notice that many of the buildings were intentionally built to lean out into the square—to simulate the old-age wear and tear of the original buildings.

On the Dekert (north) side of the square is the...

Warsaw Historical Museum (Muzeum Historyczne Warszawy)—This labyrinthine museum rambles through several reconstructed buildings fronting the Old Town Market Square. With limited descriptions in English (and only a couple of paltry English brochures available for purchase), the museum is difficult to appreciate. You'll twist your way through room after room of historical bric-a-brac. The exhibits near the end—photos of the Old Town before and immediately after its WWII destruction—are the most interesting (6 zł, free entry but no movie on Sun, open Tue and Thu 11:00–18:00, Wed and Fri 10:00–15:30, Sat–Sun 10:30–16:30, closed Mon, last entry 45 min before closing, Rynek Starego Miasta 28/42, tel. 022/635-1625).

The museum's saving grace is its excellent 20-minute **film** in English, worth ▲▲ and the price of admission alone; unfortunately, it runs only Tuesday through Saturday at 12:00. With somber narration and black-and-white scenes from before, during, and after the wartime devastation, this film is best appreciated after you've had a chance to see some of today's Warsaw (especially along the Royal Way). The movie ends with, "They say that there are no miracles. Then what is this city on the Vistula?" Emotionally drained, you can only respond, "Amen."

Leave the square on Nowomiejska (at the mermaid's 2 o'clock, by the 2nd-story niche sculpture of St. Anne). After a block, you'll reach the...

Barbican (Barbakan)—This defensive gate of the Old Town, similar to Kraków's, protected the medieval city from invaders. Just outside the gate, you may be accosted by a pair of **village idiots**, dressed as medieval executioners. These unemployed (but undeniably creative) punks, in a sort of aggressive, costumed pan-handling, will steer you to their "executioner's block" and playfully threaten to liberate your head from your body until you give them some pocket change. Actually, these guys speak English, and if you talk to them, they'll explain that at least two buildings within the Old Town actually were used for executions once upon a time.

Once you've crossed through the barbican and received a stay of execution, you're officially in Warsaw's...

New Town (Nowe Miasto)—This 15th-century neighborhood is new in name only: It was the first part of Warsaw to spring up outside of the city walls (and therefore slightly newer than the Old Town). The New Town is a fun place to wander: Only a little less charming than the Old Town, but with a more real-life feel—like people live and work here. It's also packed with affordable restaurants (see "Eating," page 300). Its centerpiece is the **New Town Square** (Rynek Nowego Miasta), watched over by the distinctive green dome of St. Kazimierz Church.

Scientists will want to pay homage at the museum for Warsaw native **Marie Skłodowska-Curie** (at her birthplace, ulica Freta 16). This Nobel Prize winner was the world's first radiologist—discovering both radium and polonium (named for her native land) with her husband, Pierre Curie. Since she lived at a time when Warsaw was controlled by oppressive Russia, she conducted her studies in France.

From the New Town to Castle Square: You can backtrack the way you came, or, to get a look at Warsaw's back streets, consider this route from the big, round Barbican gate (where the New Town meets the Old): Go back through the Barbican and turn right, walking along the inside of the wall. You'll pass a courtyard on the left—a reminder that people actually live in the tourist zone within the Old Town walls. Just beyond the garden on the right, look for the carpet-beating rack, used to clean rugs (these are common fixtures in people's backyards). Go left into the square called Szeroki Dunaj (Wide Danube) and look for another mermaid (over the Thai restaurant). Continue through the square and turn right at Wąski Dunaj (Narrow Danube). After about 100 yards, you pass the city wall. Just to the right (outside the wall), you'll

Jan Matejko
(1838–1893)

Jan Matejko (yawn mah-TAY-koh) is Poland's most important painter, period. In the late 19th century, the nation of Poland had been dissolved by foreign powers, and Polish artists struggled to make sense of their people's place in the world. Rabble-rousing Romanticism seemed to have failed (inspiring many brutally suppressed uprisings), so Polish artists and writers turned their attention to educating the people about their history, with the goal of keeping the Polish traditions alive.

Matejko was at the forefront of this so-called "positivist" movement. Matejko saw what the tides of history had done to Poland, and was determined to make sure his countrymen learned from it. He painted two types of works: huge, grand-scale epics depicting monumental events in Polish history; and small, intimate portraits of prominent Poles. Polish schoolchildren study history from books with paintings of virtually every single Polish king—all painted by the incredibly prolific Matejko.

Matejko is admired not for his technical mastery (he's an unexceptional painter), but for the emotion behind—and inspired by—his works. Matejko's paintings are utilitarian, straightforward, and dramatic enough to stir the patriot in any Pole...precisely his goal. The intense focus on history by Matejko and other positivists is one big reason why today's Poles are still so in touch with their heritage.

You'll see Matejko's works in Warsaw's National Museum and Royal Castle, as well as in Kraków's Gallery of 19th-Century Polish Art (above the Cloth Hall). You can also visit his former residence in Kraków.

see the monument to the **Little Upriser** of 1944, an imp wearing a grown-up's helmet and too-big boots, and carrying a machine gun. Children—and especially Scouts (Harcerze)—played a key role in the resistance against the Nazis. Their job was mainly carrying messages and propaganda.

Now continue around the wall—admiring more public art—back to Castle Square.

Near the Central Train Station

These sights are within a few blocks of the train station.

Palace of Culture and Science (Pałac Kultury i Nauki, or PKiN)—This massive skyscraper, dating from the early 1950s, is Poland's tallest building (760 feet). It was a "gift" from Stalin that the people of Warsaw couldn't refuse. Varsovians call it

Near Warsaw's Central Station

1 Novotel
2 Hotel Mazowiecki
3 Hotel Gromada
4 Boutique B&B
5 IYHF Szkolne Schronisko Hostel
6 Oki Doki Hostel
7 Hotel Harenda
8 Café Brama
9 Bar Rest. Wegetariańska Zielony Świat ("Greenland")
10 Sandwicz
11 Blikle Bakery
12 E. Wedel Pijalnia Czekolady (Chocolate Shop)
13 Bus #175 to Royal Way
14 Observation Deck Entrance

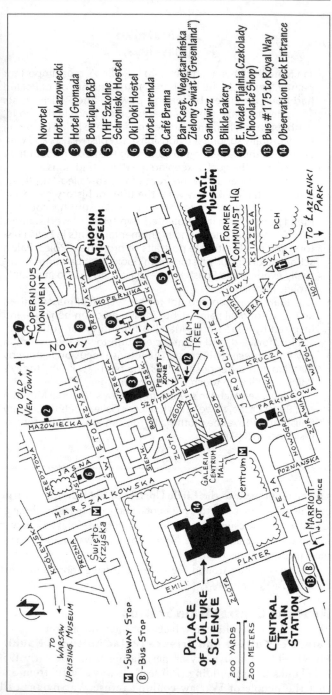

"Stalin's Penis," using even cruder terminology than that. There were seven such "Stalin Gothic" erections in Moscow. Because it was to be "Soviet in substance, Polish in style," Soviet architects toured Poland to absorb local culture before starting the project. Since the end of communism, the younger generation doesn't mind the structure so much—and some even admit to liking it. The clock was added in 1999 as part of the millennium celebrations.

Everything about the Pałac is big. It's designed to show off the strong, grand-scale Soviet aesthetic and architectural skill. The Pałac contains various theaters (the Culture), a museum of evolution (the Science), a congress hall, a multiplex (showing current movies), an observation deck (see below), and lots of office space (including UNICEF's Polish headquarters). With all of this Culture and Science under one Roof, it's a shame that none of it makes for worthwhile sightseeing. While the interior is highly skippable, viewing the building from the outside is a quintessential, ▲▲ Warsaw experience.

If you're killing time between trains, you could zip up to the observation deck (20 zł, more for special exhibitions, daily June–Sept 9:00–20:00, Oct–May 9:00–18:00, enter through main door on east side of Pałac—opposite from train station, tel. 022/656-6000, www.pkin.pl). Better yet, snap a photo from down below and save your money, since the view's a letdown. You can hardly see the Old Town, and Warsaw's most prominent big building—the Pałac itself—is missing.

▲▲**National Museum (Muzeum Narodowe)**—This museum, while short on big-name pieces, interests art-lovers and offers a fine introduction to some talented Polish artists unknown outside their home country (12 zł, more for temporary exhibits, permanent collection free on Sat, open Tue–Sun 10:00–16:00, Thu until 18:00, closed Mon, 1 block east of Nowy Świat at aleja Jerozolimskie 3, tel. 022/629-3093, www.mnw.art.pl).

On the ground floor are exhibits of ancient art (from Egyptian and Greek pieces to works by early Polish tribes), as well as room upon room of medieval altarpieces and crucifixes (including some of the most graphic I've seen). The upper floors have temporary exhibits and collections of Polish and European decorative arts and European paintings. But the reason we're here is the Gallery of Polish Painting, one floor up. Focus on the two most important eras, at opposite ends of the building.

First, find the **Jan Matejko** room. From the lobby, take the left staircase up one level, then go in the door on the left. Matejko is hiding at the back (if you can't find him, ask the guards, "mah-TAY-koh?"). On the way, you'll pass through a whole room of Napoleon portraits. The Poles loved Napoleon, who bravely marched on Russia in an era when this part of Poland was occupied and oppressed by the Russians...sadly, not for the last time.

The Matejko room is dominated by the enormous *Battle of Grunwald*. This epic painting commemorates one of Poland's high-water marks—the dramatic victory of a Polish-Lithuanian army over the Teutonic Knights, who had been terrorizing northern Poland for decades (for more on the Teutonic Knights, see page 348). On July 15, 1410, some 40,000 Poles and Lithuanians (led by the sword-waving Lithuanian in red, Grand Duke Vytautas) faced off against 27,000 Teutonic Knights (under their Grand Master, in white) in one of the medieval world's bloodiest battles. Matejko plops us right in the thick of the battle's chaos, painting life-size figures and framing off a 32-foot-long slice of the actual two-mile battle line.

In the center of the painting, the Teutonic Grand Master is about to become a shish kebab. In red, Duke Vytautas leads the final charge. And waaaay up on a hill (in the upper right-hand corner) is Władysław Jagiełło, the first king of the Jagiellonian dynasty...ensuring his bloodline will survive another 150 years.

Matejko spent three years covering this 450-square-foot canvas in paint. The canvas was specially made in a single seamless piece. At the unveiling, this was such a popular work that there were almost as many fans as there are figures in the painting.

From Poland's high point in the *Battle of Grunwald*, turn to the canvas on the left, *Stańczyk after the Loss of Smolensk*, to see how Poland's fortunes shifted drastically a century later. This smaller, more intimate portrait by Matejko depicts a popular Polish figure: the court jester Stańczyk, who's smarter than the king, but not allowed to say so. This complex character, representing the national conscience, is a favorite symbol of Matejko's. Stańczyk slumps in gloom. He's just read the news (on the table beside him) that the city of Smolensk has fallen to the Russians after a three-year siege (1512–1514). The jester had tried to warn the king to send more troops, but the king was too busy partying (behind the curtain). The painter Matejko—who may have used his own features for Stańczyk's face—also blamed the nobles of his own day for fiddling while Poland was partitioned.

Other Matejko paintings include one depicting the tragic couple of the last Jagiellonian king and his wife, Barbara—whom the king loved deeply, even though she couldn't bear him an heir. (In the next room, see the painful end to their sad tale: Barbara on her deathbed.)

Then take a look at the **Młoda Polska** (Young Poland) collection, featuring paintings from Poland's version of Art Nouveau (see page 221). From the lobby, take the right staircase up, then go in the right-hand door and work your way all the way to the back. In addition to a room of works by movement headliner Stanisław Wyspiański, you'll see the hypnotic *Strange Garden* by Józef Mehoffer, as well as several works by Jacek Malczewski. Malczewski's paintings depict the goateed, close-cropped artist in a variety of different semi-surrealistic, Polish countryside contexts. There's also a room of canvases by the only prominent female Polish painter, Olga Boznańska—with a softer and more impressionistic touch than her male Młoda Polska counterparts.

▲**Chopin Museum (Muzeum Fryderyka Chopina)**—The reconstructed Ostrogski Castle houses this modest museum honoring Poland's most famous composer. Everything of interest is upstairs: manuscripts, letters, and original handwritten compositions. You'll also see Chopin's last piano, which he used for composing during the final two years of his life (1848-1849). Nearby, flip through the guest book. Chopin's music is popular in Japan, and Japanese music-lovers flock here, almost as a pilgrimage. In the next room, find Chopin's bronze death mask and admire his distinctively Polish nose, shaped like an eagle's beak (10 zł; May–Sept Mon, Wed, and Fri 10:00–17:00, Thu 12:00–18:00, Sat–Sun 10:00–14:00, closed Tue; Oct–April Mon–Wed and Fri–Sat 10:00–14:00, Thu 12:00–18:00; closed Sun, 3 blocks east of Nowy Świat at ulica Okólnik 1, tel. 022/826-5935).

The top floor has a **concert hall**, open only for special concerts. If you're in town for one, go. There's nothing like hearing Chopin's music fill this fine mansion, passionately played by a teary-eyed Pole who really feels the music (call museum or check online for concert schedules, www.tifc.chopin.pl).

The **Ostrogski Castle** was destroyed down to the brick cellar in World War II. A plaque by the staircase around back notes that it was "voluntarily reconstructed" by the communists in 1970 "to celebrate the 25th anniversary of the People's Republic of Poland." In the courtyard behind is a statue of a golden duck *(złota kaczka)*, a mythical creature that supposedly lived in the castle's cellar. An often-repeated but strangely anticlimactic parable explains that this duck gave a cobbler's apprentice a huge amount of money, telling him that if he frittered it away by the end of the day, he'd win great rewards. The boy gave some to a beggar, which didn't fit the duck's idea of "frittering"—but the boy found happiness anyway.

Chopin's birth house is in Żelazowa Wola, 34 miles from Warsaw. It's tourable, but not worth the trek for anyone but the most rabid Chopin fan.

South of the Center

▲**Łazienki Park (Park Łazienkowski)**—This huge, idyllic park is where Varsovians go to play. The park is sprinkled with fun neo-classical buildings, strutting peacocks, and young Poles in love. It was built by Poland's very last king (before the final partition), Stanisław August Poniatowski, to serve as his summer residence and provide a place for his citizens to relax.

On the edge of the park (along Belwederska) is a **monument to Fryderyk Chopin**. The monument, in a rose garden, is

flanked by platforms, where free summer piano concerts are given weekly (generally Sun at 12:00 and 16:00). The statue (from 1926) shows Chopin sitting under a wind-blown willow tree. While he spent his last 20 years and wrote most of his best-known music in France, his inspiration came from wind blowing through the willow trees of his native land, Poland. The Nazis melted the statue down for its metal. Today's copy was recast after World War II. Savor this spot; it's great in summer, with roses wildly in bloom, and in autumn, when the trees provide a golden backdrop for the black, romantic statue.

Venture to the center of the park, where (after a 10-min hike) you'll find King Poniatowski's striking **Palace on the Water** (Pałac na Wodzie)—literally built in the middle of a river. Nearby, you'll spot a clever amphitheater with seating on the riverbank and the stage on an island. The king was a real man of the Enlightenment, hosting weekly dinners here for artists and intellectuals.

Getting There: The park is just south of the city center on the Royal Way. Buses #116, #180, #195, and #503 run from Castle Square in the Old Town along the Royal Way directly to the park (get off at stop Bagatela, by Belweder Palace). Maps at park entrances locate the Chopin monument, Palace on the Water, and other park attractions.

Jewish Warsaw

After centuries of living peacefully in Poland, Warsaw's Jews suffered terribly at the hands of the Nazis (see sidebar, page 293). You can visit several sights in Warsaw that commemorate those who were murdered—and those who fought back. Because the Nazis leveled the ghetto, there is literally nothing left except the street plan and the heroic spirit of its former residents.

Warsaw's Jews and the Ghetto Uprising

From the Middle Ages until World War II, Poland was a safe haven for Europe's Jews. When other kings were imprisoning and deporting Jews in the 14th century, the progressive king Kazimierz the Great welcomed Jews into Poland, even granting them special privileges (see page 218).

By the 1930s, there were more than 380,000 Jews in Warsaw—nearly a third of the population (and the largest concentration of Jews in the world). The Nazis arrived in 1939. Within a year, they had pushed all of Warsaw's Jews into one neighborhood and surrounded it with a wall, creating a miserably overcrowded ghetto (crammed full of half a million people, including many from nearby towns). Over the next year, the Nazis brought in more Jews from throughout Poland, and the number grew by a million.

By the summer of 1942, more than a quarter of the Jews in the ghetto had already died of disease, murder, or suicide. The Nazis started moving Warsaw's Jews (at the rate of 5,000 a day) into what they claimed were "resettlement camps." Most of these people were actually murdered at Treblinka or Auschwitz. After hundreds of thousands of Jews had been taken to concentration camps, the waning population—now about 60,000—began to get word from concentration camp escapees about what was actually going on there. Spurred by this knowledge, Warsaw's surviving Jews staged a dramatic uprising.

On April 19, 1943, the Jews attacked Nazi strongholds and had some initial success—but within a month, the Nazis crushed the Ghetto Uprising. The ghetto's residents and structures were "liquidated." About 300 of Warsaw's Jews survived, thanks in part to a sort of "underground railroad" of courageous Varsovians.

Warsaw's Jewish sights are moving, but even more so if you know some of their stories. Many Americans have heard of **Władysław Szpilman,** a Jewish concert pianist who survived the war with the help of Jews, Poles, and even a Nazi officer. Szpilman's life story was turned into the highly acclaimed, Oscar-winning 2002 film *The Pianist,* which powerfully depicts events in Warsaw during World War II.

Less familiar to Americans—but equally affecting—is the story of Henryk Goldszmit, better known by his pen name, **Janusz Korczak.** Korczak wrote imaginative children's books that are still enormously popular among Poles. He worked at an orphanage in the Warsaw ghetto. When his orphans were sent off to concentration camps, the Nazis offered the famous author a chance at freedom. Korczak turned them down, and chose to die at Treblinka with his children.

▲**Ghetto Walking Tour**—For a quick walking tour of the former ghetto site, begin at **Ghetto Heroes Square** (plac Bohaterow Getta). To get here from the Old Town, either hop a taxi (10 zł) or walk (go through Barbican gate 2 blocks into New Town, turn left on Świętojerska, and walk straight 10 min—passing the new green-glass Supreme Court building—until you reach grassy park on Zamenhofa Street). The square is in the heart of what was the Jewish ghetto—now surrounded by bland Soviet-style apartment blocks. After the Uprising, the entire ghetto was reduced to dust by the Nazis—leaving the communists to rebuild to their own specifications. The district is called Muranów (literally, "Rebuilt") today.

The **monument** in the middle of the square commemorates those who fought and died "for the dignity and freedom of the Jewish Nation, for a free Poland, and for the liberation of humankind." The big park across the street is the future site of the Museum for the History of Polish Jews. It's been in the works for years, with its progress slowed by controversy over exactly what form the museum will take (for the latest, see www.jewishmuseum .org.pl).

Facing the monument, head left (with the park on your left) up Zamenhofa—which, like many streets in this neighborhood, is named for a hero of the Ghetto Uprising. From the monument, you'll follow a series of three-foot-tall black stone monuments to Uprising heroes—the **Path of Remembrance.** Like Stations of the Cross, each recounts an event of the uprising. Every April 19th (the day the Uprising began), huge crowds follow this path. In a block, at the corner of Miła, you'll find a **bunker** where organizers of the Uprising hid out (and where they committed suicide when the Nazis discovered them on May 8, 1943).

Continue following the black stone monuments up Zamenhofa, then turn left around the corner and cross busy Stawki street. A long block up Stawki and on the right, you'll see the **Umschlagplatz** monument—shaped like a cattle car. That's German for "transfer place," and it marks the spot where the Nazis brought Jewish families to prepare them to be loaded onto trains bound for Treblinka or Auschwitz (a harrowing scene vividly depicted in *The Pianist*). In the walls of the monument are inscribed the first names of some of the victims.

Jewish Historical Institute of Poland (Żydowski Instytut Historyczny)—For more in-depth information about Warsaw's Jewish community, including the Ghetto Uprising, visit this museum housed in the former Jewish Library building. The main floor displays well-described old photos. The 37-minute movie about life and death in the ghetto—played in English upon request—is graphic and powerful. Upstairs, you'll find more on Jewish art, culture, and temporary exhibits (10 zł, Mon–Wed and

Fri 9:00–16:00, Thu 11:00–18:00, closed Sat–Sun, ulica Tłomackie 3/5, tel. 022/827-9221, www.jewishinstitute.org.pl).

The Peugeot building next door—appropriately and simply dubbed "the blue tower" by locals—was built on the former site of Warsaw's biggest synagogue, destroyed by the Nazis as a victorious final kick.

The Warsaw Uprising

While the 1944 Warsaw Uprising (see page 296) is a recurring theme in virtually all Warsaw sightseeing, two sights in particular are worth a visit for anyone with a special interest. Neither is right on the main tourist trail; the monument is closer to the sightseeing action, while the museum is a tram or taxi ride away.

Warsaw Uprising Monument—The most central sight relating to the Warsaw Uprising is the monument at plac Krasińskich (intersection of ulica Długa and Miodowa, a few blocks northwest of the New Town). Larger-than-life soldiers and civilians race for the sewers in a desperate attempt to flee the Nazis. Just behind the monument is the rusting copper facade of Poland's Supreme Court.

▲Warsaw Uprising Museum (Muzeum Powstania Warszawskiego)—This new museum opened on August 1, 2004—the 60th anniversary of the Warsaw Uprising. Thorough, well-presented, and packed with Polish field-trip groups, the museum celebrates the heroes of the Uprising. The location is inconvenient (a 15-min tram ride west of Central Train Station), and probably not worth the trip for those with a casual interest. But for history buffs, it's Warsaw's single best museum.

The museum has several parts. The beautifully restored 1905 red-brick building, once an electrical plant, houses the permanent exhibition. The more recent gray addition behind it displays temporary exhibitions. And the park stretching around the back of the complex also has some moving sights.

The high-tech **main exhibit** occupies three floors. It chronologically tells the story of the Uprising, with a keen focus on military history. Everything is well-described in English; also look for the printed pages of English information, and collect the clever calendar pages tracing the events of the two-month Uprising day by day. The ground floor focuses on Germany's invasion and occupation of Poland. Then you'll take the elevator up to the top floor, which features exhibits on the Uprising itself. Finally you'll climb through a simulated sewer—just as many Home Army soldiers and civilians did to evade the Germans—and climb stairs down into an exhibit on the Uprising's aftermath. A chilling section at the end describes how Warsaw became a "city of graves," with burial mounds and makeshift crosses scattered everywhere.

The Warsaw Uprising

By the summer of 1944, it was becoming clear that the Nazis' days in Warsaw were numbered. The Red Army drew near, and by late July, Soviet tanks were within 25 miles of downtown Warsaw.

The Varsovians could have simply waited for the Soviets to cross the river and force the Nazis out. But they knew that Soviet "liberation" would also mean an end to Polish independence. The Polish Home Army numbered 400,000—30,000 of them in Warsaw alone—and was the biggest underground army in military history. The uprisers wanted Poland to control its own fate, and they took matters into their own hands. The resistance's symbol was an anchor made up of a P atop a W (which stands for *Polska Walcząca*, or "Poland Fighting"—you'll see this icon all around town). Over time, the Home Army had established an extensive network of underground tunnels and sewers, which allowed them to deliver messages and move around the city without drawing the Nazis' attention. These tunnels gave the Home Army the element of surprise.

On August 1, 30,000 Polish resistance fighters launched an attack on their Nazi oppressors. They poured out of the sewers and caught the Nazis off guard, initially having great success.

But the Nazis regrouped quickly, and within a few days, they had retaken several areas of the city—murdering tens of thousands of innocent civilians as they went. In one notorious incident, some 5,500 Polish soldiers and 6,000 civilians who were surrounded by Nazis in the Old Town were forced to flee through the sewers; many were drowned or shot. (This scene is depicted in the Warsaw Uprising Monument on plac Krasińskich—see page 295.)

Just two months after it had started, the Warsaw Uprising was over. The Home Army called a cease-fire. About 18,000 Polish uprisers were killed, along with nearly 200,000 innocent civilians. An infuriated Hitler ordered that the city be destroyed—which it was, systematically, block by block, until virtually nothing remained.

Through all of this, the Soviets stood still, watched, and waited. When the smoke cleared and the Nazis left, the Red Army marched in and claimed the wasteland that was once called Warsaw. After the war, General Dwight D. Eisenhower said that the scale of destruction here was the worst he'd ever seen.

Depending on whom you talk to, the desperate uprising of Warsaw was incredibly brave, stupid, or both. As for the Poles, they remain fiercely proud of their struggle for freedom. The city of Warsaw has recently commemorated this act of bravery with the new Warsaw Uprising Museum (see page 295).

The **park** features several thought-provoking sights. Around the right side, photographs along the wall show the history of the museum building. Also find the reconstructed German bunker, used by the Nazis during the occupation. Finally, along the back is the Wall of Memory, a Vietnam Wall–type monument to soldiers of the Polish Home Army who were killed in action. You'll see their rank and name, followed by their codename, in quotes. The Home Army observed a strict policy of anonymity, forbidding members from calling each other anything but their codenames. The bell in the middle is dedicated to the commander of the uprising, Antoni Chruściel (codename "Monter").

The museum also has an observation deck (in the temporary exhibits building) and a café with drinks and light snacks, decorated in prewar Warsaw style (museum entry-4 zł, Wed–Mon 10:00–18:00, Thu until 20:00, closed Tue, on the west edge of downtown at ulica Przyokopowa 28, tel. 022/626-9506, www.1944 .pl). Take tram #12 or #24 from the Central Train Station or from across the street from the National Museum (near the start of Nowy Świat). Get off at the stop called Muzeum Powstania Warszawskiego, cross the tracks and the busy street, walk straight one short block up Grzybowska, and take a left on Przyokopowa. The museum is the big, red-brick building on the left.

SLEEPING

The accommodations scene in central Warsaw is difficult. There's an abundance of overpriced business hotels and cheap hostel-type accommodations, with little in between. Desk clerks do their best to reinforce the communist-era stereotype of grouchy, incompetent service. Thankfully, there are a few happy exceptions—such as Boutique B&B (see below), easily the best option in Warsaw. Since this is a convention town, prices can go up during convention times and way down on weekends. For locations, see the maps on pages 276 and 288.

$$$ Novotel, with 740 rooms across the street from the Palace of Culture and Science, overlooks Poland's busiest intersection. Recently renovated inside and out, this is a good option for a big, downtown hotel. Its prices plummet on weekends and in summer (Mon–Fri: Sb or Db-€110; Sat–Sun: Sb or Db-€80; sometimes even better deals in summer, elevator, ulica Nowogrodzka 24/26, tel. 022/621-0271, fax 022/625-0476, www.orbis.pl, nov.warszawa @orbis.pl).

$$ Old Town Apartments offers 40 studio, one-bedroom, and two-bedroom apartments (all with kitchen) inside Warsaw's Old Town. The prices are good and the location is excellent, but you're pretty much on your own (no real reception, no breakfast).

Sleep Code

(3.40 zł = about $1, €1 = about $1.20, country code: 48, area code: 022)
S = Single, **D** = Double/Twin, **T** = Triple, **Q** = Quad, **b** = bathroom, **s** = shower only. Unless otherwise noted, English is spoken, breakfast is included, and credit cards are accepted.

To help you sort easily through these listings, I've divided the rooms into three categories, based on the price for a standard double room with bath:

$$$ **Higher Priced**—Most rooms 400 zł (€100) or more.
 $$ **Moderately Priced**—Most rooms between
                             300–400 zł (€75–100).
  $ **Lower Priced**—Most rooms 300 zł (€75) or less.

View the apartments on their Web site, pick the one that looks best, make arrangements with them, and they'll set up a meeting to give you the keys. This is an especially good value for families and longer stays (studio-€60–80, 1-bedroom-€95, 2-bedroom-€110, some more expensive "featured" apartments also available, slightly cheaper Oct–April and last-minute, tel. 022/887-9800, fax 022/831-4956, www.warsawshotel.com, booking@warsawshotel.com). They have an office right on the Old Town Market Square that acts as a sort of reception desk, though communication can be a little frustrating (Mon–Fri 9:00–20:00, Sat–Sun 9:00–17:00, Rynek Starego Miasta 12/14, same contact information as above).

$$ Hotel Harenda rents out 43 rooms on the third floor of an office building right on the Royal Way, where Nowy Świat becomes Krakowskie Przedmieście. The rooms are nothing special, but the location is good, and the ground-floor pub is a popular hangout spot (March–June and Sept–Oct: Sb-295 zł, Db-315 zł; July and Nov–Feb: Sb-250 zł, Db-270 zł; breakfast-20 zł, second night is free Fri–Sun, some rowdy street noise—especially on weekends—so request a quiet room, Krakowskie Przedmieście 4/6, tel. & fax 022/826-0071, www.hotelharenda.com.pl, hh@hotelharenda.com.pl).

$$ Hotel Gromada, a 320-room conference hotel, has a dreary communist exterior, but the lobby and most rooms have been refurbished. There are three types of rooms: "tourist" (decent, but could be spruced up); "standard" (nicely renovated and modern); and "plus" (almost identical to standard, but in a newer building—not worth the extra expense). Though it has zero personality, the place offers a decent value and a good location, between the Palace of Culture and Science and Nowy Świat ("tourist" rooms: Sb-200 zł, Db-230 zł; "standard" rooms: Sb-320 zł, Db-350 zł; "plus" rooms:

Sb-420 zł, Db-450 zł; standard and plus rooms about 25 percent cheaper Fri–Sat, non-smoking rooms, elevator, plac Powstańców Warszawy 2, tel. 022/582-9900, fax 022/582-9527, www.hotels .gromada.pl, warszawahotele.centrum@gromada.pl).

$ **Boutique B&B** is Warsaw's best value by far. Don't let the low prices fool you: This place offers more comfort and class than a hotel twice its price, in a beautifully renovated and well-located old building. Jarek Chołodecki, who lived near Chicago for many years, returned to Warsaw and converted apartments into this wonderful bed-and-breakfast. It's a friendly, casual, stylish place, creatively decorated and impeccably maintained. Quirky, charismatic Jarek loves to chat with his guests (standard Db-€55, junior suite-€75, big suite-€110, 15 percent cheaper Oct–March, elevator, ulica Smolna 14, tel. 022/829-4801, fax 022/829-4882, www.bedandbreakfast.pl, office@bedandbreakfast.pl). Let Jarek know what time you're arriving. To make things easier, he offers a no-stress ride in from the airport for the same price as a taxi (40 zł, arrange when you reserve your room).

$ **Hotel Mazowiecki** is a local-style place on a drab urban street between the Palace of Culture and Science and Nowy Świat. Its 56 rooms are old and basic, but well-located for the price (S-150 zł, Sb-200 zł, D-200 zł, Db-250 zł, 20 percent cheaper Fri–Sun, elevator, ulica Mazowiecka 10, tel. & fax 022/827-2365, www .mazowiecki.com.pl, recepcja.mazowiecki@hotelewam.pl).

$ **Oki Doki Hostel**, on a pleasant square a few blocks in front of the Palace of Culture and Science, is colorful, creative, and easygoing. Each of its 40 rooms was designed by a different artist with a special theme—such as Van Gogh, Celtic spirals, heads of state, or Lenin. It's well-run by Ernest—a Pole whose parents loved Hemingway—and his wife Łucja, who are energetic and welcoming (S-110 zł, D-140 zł, Db-180 zł, T-180 zł; dorm bed in 4- to 5-bed room-50 zł, in 6-bed room-45 zł, in 8-bed room-42 zł, includes breakfast except for dorm-dwellers—who pay 10 zł, free Internet in lobby, free self-service laundry, kitchen, lots of stairs, plac Dąbrowskiego 3, tel. 022/826-5112, fax 022/826-8357, www .okidoki.pl, okidoki@okidoki.pl).

Hostels: $ The IYHF **Szkolne Schronisko** hostel is well-run, bright, and very clean. The downside: It's on the fifth floor, with no elevator (non-members welcome, all prices per person: dorm beds-36 zł, S-65 zł, twin D-60 zł, T-55 zł, Q-45 zł, plus 5 zł per person for sheets and 2 zł for towels, cash only, no breakfast but members' kitchen, closed 10:00–16:00, curfew at 24:00; e-mail or fax ahead in summer to reserve limited S, D, and T rooms; good location across the street from National Museum at ulica Smolna 30, tel. & fax 022/827-8952, www.ssmsmolna30.pl, ssmsmolna@poczta.onet.pl).

$ Dom Przy Rynku is a small, friendly, charming, 40-bed hostel with two goals: housing kids from dysfunctional families, and raising money for its work by renting out beds to tourists (when it's not housing children). Located in the peaceful New Town, the cozy rooms are decorated for grade-schoolers. Beds are rented in July and August, and on Friday and Saturday nights all year (35 zł per bed in 2- to 5-bed rooms, rooms segregated by gender, bus #175 from station or airport to Franciszkańska stop, corner of Kościelna and Przyrynek streets at Rynek Nowego Miasta 4, tel. & fax 022/831-5033, www.cityhostel.net, info@cityhostel.net).

EATING

In or near the Old Town

Rather than wasting my money dining on the Old Town Market Square, I prefer to venture a few blocks to find a place with good food and much lower prices. Most restaurants say they're open until the "last guest," which usually means about 23:00 (sometimes later in summer). For locations, see the maps on pages 276 and 288.

At **Restauracja Pod Samsonem** (literally, "Under Samson"), dine on affordable Polish-Jewish fare with well-dressed locals. The ambience is pleasant, the service is playfully opinionated, and the low prices make up for the fact that you have to pay to check your coat and use the bathroom (most main dishes 15–25 zł, daily 10:00–23:00, ulica Freta 3/5, tel. 022/831-1788).

Pierogarnia offers several types of pierogi, tasty soups, and a fun variety of drinks (from fruit juices to non-alcoholic dark beer). Order at the counter and take a seat—they'll call you when your food's ready. With mellow country decor, wooden menus, and a loyal local crowd, this is my favorite spot for a quick, cheap meal along the Royal Way (12-zł plates of pierogi, daily 11:00–21:00, hiding on a quiet street behind the statue of Adam Mickiewicz at ulica Bednarska 28/30, tel. 022/424-1387).

Podwale Piwna Kompania, a lively, smoky place filled with Varsovians, feels more like Prague than Warsaw. You'll enjoy the large plates of tasty food and the Czech beer-hall ambience (most main dishes 20–30 zł, daily 11:00–24:00, just outside Old Town walls near the Barbican at ulica Podwale 25, tel. 022/635-6314).

Siedem Grzechów (literally, "Seven Sins") is an old-style Warsaw restaurant serving top-notch Polish and international cuisine in a 1930s lace, velvet, and burgundy ambience. The place fills a dressy cellar with jazz and photos of prewar Warsaw (main dishes 30–60 zł, daily 11:00–23:00, a few blocks before the Old Town on the Royal Way at Krakowskie Przedmieście 45, tel. 022/826-4770).

On the Old Town Market Square: You'll pay triple to eat right on the Old Town Market Square, but some visitors figure it's worth the splurge (plan on 60–100 zł per main dish). If money's no object, these two places are tops. **U Fukiera,** at #27, offers traditional Polish and pan-European meals in a sophisticated setting (daily 12:00–23:00, tel. 022/831-1013). The pricier option is **Gessler,** at #21, with two parts: traditional Polish dishes in an atmospheric cellar with dramatic brick vaults, or very expensive (up to 140 zł) international cuisine in a swanky dining room (daily 10:00–23:00, tel. 022/831-4427). In Gessler's lobby hang photos of famous patrons. It's the only place you'll see Hillary Rodham Clinton, George H. W. Bush, and Henry Kissinger side by side—and smiling. (A sly Fidel Castro watches over the three of them.)

Quick and Tasty on Nowy Świat

These restaurants offer a fast bite close to the National Museum and Central Train Station on Nowy Świat.

Café Brama, part of a trendy chain popular with local students, offers great sandwiches, salads, soups, and pierogi (sandwiches around 18 zł, salads about 20 zł, Mon–Fri 9:00–22:00, Sat–Sun 10:00–22:00, Nowy Świat 60, actually just down Ordynacka street).

Bar Restauracja Wegetariańska Zielony Świat (a.k.a. "Greenland") offers a wide range of Asian-style vegetarian food, making liberal use of vegetarian "ham," "chicken," and even "fish." The decor is nothing special—contemporary Asian kitsch—but the food is good, healthy, and well-priced (most dishes 20–30 zł, daily 10:30–21:30, enter through passageway at Nowy Świat 42 to reach ulica Gałczyńskiego 5/9, tel. 022/826-4677).

Sandwicz, a colorful glorified milk bar with Polish grub, has a self-serve salad bar, and—of course—sandwiches (Mon–Fri 7:30–20:30, Sat–Sun 10:00–20:30, aleja Jerozolimskie 11/19).

Uniquely Polish Treats

These two places are on or close to the busy Nowy Świat boulevard.

A. Blikle, Poland's most famous bakery, serves a wide variety of delicious pastries. This is where locals shop for cakes when they're having someone special over for coffee. The specialty: *pączki* (2 zł)—the quintessential Polish doughnut, filled with rose-flavored jam. You can get your goodies "to go" in the shop (Mon–Fri 9:00–19:00, Sat 9:00–18:00, Sun 10:30–17:00), or enjoy them with coffee in the swanky, classic café (Mon–Sat 9:00–22:00, Sun 10:00–22:00; both at Nowy Świat 35).

E. Wedel Pijalnia Czekolady thrills chocoholics. Emil Wedel made Poland's favorite chocolate, and today, his former residence houses this chocolate shop and café (Mon–Sat 8:00–22:00, Sun 11:00–20:00, between Palace of Culture and Science and Nowy

Świat at ulica Szepitalna 1, tel. 022/827-2916). This is the spot for delicious pastries and a *real* hot chocolate, *czekolada do picia* (9 zł; that means a cup of melted chocolate, not just hot chocolate milk). The menu describes it as "true Wedel ecstasy for your mouth that will take you to a world of dreams and desires." Or, if you fancy pudding, try *pokusa*. Wedel's was *the* Christmas treat for locals under communism. Cadbury bought the company when Poland privatized after communism, but they kept the E. Wedel name, which is close to all Poles' hearts...and taste buds.

TRANSPORTATION CONNECTIONS

Virtually all trains into and out of Warsaw go through the hulking Central Train Station (see "Arrival in Warsaw," page 272.) If you're heading to Gdańsk, note that the red-brick Gothic city of Toruń and the impressive Malbork Castle are on the way (though on separate train lines, so you can't do both en route; see Gdańsk and Pomerania chapters).

From Warsaw by Train to: **Kraków** (hrly, 2.75 hrs), **Gdańsk** (nearly hrly, 4 hrs), **Toruń** (5/day, 3 hrs direct, more with a transfer in Kutno), **Malbork** (nearly hrly, 3.5 hrs direct), **Prague** (2/day direct, including 1 night train, 9–12 hrs; or 1/day, 9 hrs, with transfer in Ostrava-Svinov), **Berlin** (3/day direct, 5.75 hrs; plus 1 direct night train, 7.75 hrs), **Budapest** (2/day direct, including 1 night train, 10.5–11.5 hrs; or 1 each per day with transfer in Győr, Hungary, or Břeclav, Czech Republic, both 10 hrs), **Vienna** (2/day direct, including 1 night train, 7.75 or 10 hrs; or 1/day with transfer in Břeclav, Czech Republic, 7.75 hrs).

GDAŃSK
and the TRI-CITY

Gdańsk (guh-DANSK) is a true find on the Baltic Coast of Poland. You may associate Gdańsk with the images of dreary dock-workers you saw on the nightly news in the 1980s—but there's so much more to this city than shipyards, Solidarity, and smog. It's surprisingly easy to look past the urban sprawl to find one of northern Europe's most historic and picturesque cities.

Gdańsk is second only to Kraków as Poland's most appealing city. The gem of a Main Town boasts block after block of red-brick churches and narrow, colorful, ornately decorated Hanseatic burghers' mansions. It's also fascinating—from its medieval Golden Age to the headlines of our own generation, major events happen here. You might even see old Lech Wałęsa still wandering the streets.

But Gdańsk is just the beginning. From here, the "Tri-City" continues north along the coast, offering several day-trip opportunities. The faded elegance of the seaside resort Sopot beckons to tourists, while the modern burg of Gdynia sets the pace for today's Poland. Beyond the Tri-City, the sandy Hel Peninsula is a popular spot for summer sunbathing.

Planning Your Time

This region merits at least two days to make the trip here worthwhile. Gdańsk has more than enough sightseeing for a full day, but a second day allows you to see everything in town at a more relaxing pace. Gdańsk sightseeing has two major components: the "Royal Way" (historic main drag with small but good museums—described in my self-guided walk) and the modern shipyard where Solidarity was born (with a fascinating museum, fully described

Gdańsk

400 YARDS
400 METERS

SOLIDARITY SHIPYARD

❶ Great Mill
❷ Small Mill
❸ Madison Shopping Mall

GATE
SOLIDARITY MONUMENT
FINISH

••• WALKING TOUR ROUTE TO
SOLIDARITY SHIPYARD

WATOWA
LIBRARY

PODWALE GRODSKIE
OLD
❸
TOWN
❷
ST. BRIDGET'S
ST. CATH.
ST. KATARZYNKI
MKT. HALL
CENTRAL MARITIME MUSEUM
SS SOŁDEK
MOTŁAWA RIVER
TRAM STOP
TRAIN STN.
❶
Tower
PODWALE
STRAGA
NIARSKA
SWIETO-JANSKA
ST. NIC.
THE CRANE
TARG DRZEWNY
SZEROKA
MAIN
ST. MARY'S
TOWN
SW. DUCHA
ARCHAEO-LOGICAL MUS.
Armory
GOLDEN GATE
MARIACKA
GRANARY ISLAND
LOT OFFICE
PIWNA
TOWN HALL
ARTUS COURT
BOATS TO HEL
TRAM STOP
UPLAND GATE
START
UPHAGEN House
DŁUGA
Post
DŁUGI TARG
STAGIEWNA
NEPTUNE STATUE
GREEN GATE
OGARNA
TO NAT'L MUSEUM

DCH

below). With just one day, do one of these activities in the morning, and the other in the afternoon. With two days, do one each day, and round your time out with other attractions: art-lovers enjoy the National Museum (with a stunning painting by Hans Memling), history buffs make the pilgrimage to Westerplatte (where World War II began), and church fans visit Oliwa Cathedral in Gdańsk's northern suburbs (on the way to Sopot).

With more time, consider the wide variety of side-trips. The most popular option is the full-day round-trip to Malbork Castle

(45 min each way by train, plus at least 3 hours to tour the castle—see next chapter). Closer to Gdańsk, it only takes a few hours to get a feel for the resort town of Sopot (30 min each way by train); with more time, laze around longer on Sopot's beaches, or make a quick visit to Gdynia to round out your take on the Tri-City. If you have a full day and great weather, and you don't mind fighting the crowds for a patch of sandy beach, head out to Hel Peninsula.

Gdańsk gets busy in late June, when school holidays begin, and it's downright crowded in July and August—especially during St. Dominic's Fair (Jarmark Św. Dominika, 2 weeks in early Aug), with market stalls, concerts, and other celebrations. The city is dead in the winter.

ORIENTATION

(area code: 058)
Gdańsk, with 460,000 residents, is part of a larger metropolitan area called the Tri-City (Trójmiasto, total population 750,000). But

if you break it into chunks, Gdańsk feels small. The city has several surprisingly good museums and pretty churches, but only two knockout sights: the color-ful showpiece main drag, ulica Długa (also known as the "Royal Way"); and the shipyard at the north end of

the Old Town where the Solidarity movement began (now home to a stirring monument and exceptional museum).

Gdańsk's "Old Town" (Stare Miasto) has a handful of old brick buildings and faded, tall, skinny houses—but the area is mostly drab and residential, and not worth much time. Focus instead on the "Main Town" (Główne Miasto), home to most sights described in this chapter.

The second language in this part of Poland is German, not English—and German tourists (many of them retracing their fam-ily roots) flock here in droves. Scandinavian shoppers come across the Baltic Sea to take advantage of the low prices.

You'll win no Polish friends calling the city by its more famil-iar German name, Danzig.

Tourist Information
Gdańsk's most central TI is in a red, high-gabled building across **ulica Długa** from the Town Hall. Pick up the free map and bro-chure, and browse through the other brochures and guidebooks

Gdańsk History

Visitors to Gdańsk are surprised at how "un-Polish" the city's history is. In this cultural melting pot of German, Dutch, and Flemish merchants (with a smattering of Italians and Scots), Poles were only one part of the picture until the city became exclusively Polish after World War II. And yet, in Gdańsk, cultural backgrounds traditionally took a back seat to the bottom line. Wealthy Gdańsk was always known for its economic pragmatism—no matter who was in charge, Gdańsk merchants made money. Jealous Poles from poorer towns called it *Gdańsk Chłańsk*—"Gdańsk the Greedy One."

Gdańsk is Poland's gateway to the waters of Europe—where its main river (the Vistula) meets the Baltic Sea. The town was first mentioned in the 10th century, and was seized in 1308 by the Teutonic Knights (who called it "Danzig"; for more on the Teutonic Knights, see page 345). The Knights encouraged other Germans to come settle on the Baltic coast, and gradually turned Gdańsk into a wealthy city. In 1361, Gdańsk joined the Hanseatic League, a trade federation of mostly Germanic merchant towns that provided mutual security. By the 15th century, Gdańsk was a leading member of this mighty network, which virtually dominated trade in northern Europe (and also included Toruń, Kraków, Lübeck, Hamburg, Bremen, Bruges, Bergen, Tallinn, Novgorod, and nearly a hundred other cities).

In 1454, the people of Gdańsk rose up against the Teutonic Knights, burning down their castle and forcing them out of the city. Three years later, the Polish king borrowed money from wealthy Gdańsk families to hire Czech mercenaries to take the Teutonic Knights' main castle, Malbork (see page 345). In exchange, Gdańsk merchants were granted special privileges, including exclusive export rights. Gdańsk now acted as a middleman for all trade passing through the city, but paid only a modest annual tribute to the Polish king.

The 16th and 17th centuries were Gdańsk's Golden Age. Now a part of the Polish kingdom, the city had access to an enormous hinterland of natural resources to export—yet it maintained a

(May–Sept daily 9:00–20:00, Oct–April Mon–Fri 9:00–17:00, closed Sat–Sun, ulica Długa 45, tel. 058/301-9151).

There are two other, less central TIs run by a different organization. The one in the modern **Madison shopping mall,** just north of the Main Town, has information about the entire region (Mon–Sat 9:00–21:00, Sun 10:00–21:00; between Main Town and Solidarity shipyard and across from big silver Mercure hotel skyscraper, at corner of Heweliusza and Rajska, go in main entrance of Madison mall and turn right, look for blue *it* sign; ulica Rajska privileged, semi-independent status. Like Amsterdam, Gdańsk became a tolerant, progressive, and booming merchant city. Its mostly Germanic and Dutch burghers imported Dutch, Flemish, and Italian architects to give their homes an appropriately Hanseatic austerity. At a time of religious upheaval in the rest of Europe, Gdańsk became known for its tolerance—a place that opened its doors to all visitors (many Mennonites and Scottish religious refugees emigrated here). It was also a haven for great thinkers, including philosopher Arthur Schopenhauer and scientist Daniel Fahrenheit (who invented the mercury thermometer).

Gdańsk declined, along with the rest of Poland, in the late 18th century, and became a part of Prussia (today's Germany) during the partitions. But the people of Gdańsk—even those of German heritage—had taken pride in their independence, and weren't enthusiastic about being ruled from Berlin. After World War I, Gdańsk once again became an independent city-state, the Free City of Danzig (populated by 400,000 Germans and only 15,000 Poles). The city, along with the so-called Polish Corridor connecting it to Polish lands, effectively cut off Germany from its northeastern territory. On September 1, 1939, Adolf Hitler started World War II when he invaded Gdańsk to bring it back into the German fold. Nearly 80 percent of the city was destroyed in the war.

After World War II, Gdańsk officially became part of Poland, and was painstakingly reconstructed (mostly replicating its 16th- and 17th-century Golden Age). In 1970, and again in 1980, the shipyard of Gdańsk witnessed strikes and demonstrations by the trade union Solidarity that would lead to the fall of European communism. Poland's great anti-communist hero and first post-communist president—Lech Wałęsa—is Gdańsk's most famous resident, and still lives here today.

After a recent history both tragic and uplifting, Gdańsk celebrated its 1,000th birthday in 1997. This came with a wave of renovation and refurbishment, which left the gables of the atmospheric Hanseatic quarter gleaming.

10, tel. 058/766-7466). There's also a small window in the *RUCH* kiosk in front of the **Main Train Station**.

Arrival in Gdańsk

By Train: Gdańsk's Main Train Station (Gdańsk Główny) is a pretty brick palace on the western edge of the old center. Trains to other parts of Poland (marked "PKP") use tracks 1–3; regional trains with connections to the Tri-City (marked "SKM") use the shorter tracks 3–5 (for more on regional SKM trains, see page 340).

In front of the station is a *RUCH* kiosk (where you can buy tram tickets) and a TI window. The pedestrian underpass by the McDonald's takes you beneath the busy road (1st set of exits: tram stop; end of corridor: Old Town). To reach the heart of the Main Town, you can ride the **tram** (buy tickets—*bilety*—at *RUCH* kiosk or at any window marked *Bilety ZKM* in pedestrian underpass; access tram stop via underpass, then board tram #8, #13, or #14 going to the right with your back to the station; go just 1 stop to Brama Wyżynna, in front of the LOT airlines office). But by the time you buy your ticket and wait for the tram, you might as well **walk** the 15 minutes to the same place (go through underpass, exit to the right and follow the busy road until you reach LOT airlines office, then head left towards all the brick towers). Or even easier, take a **taxi** (shouldn't cost more than 15 zł to any of my recommended hotels).

By Plane: Gdańsk's small airport (recently named for Lech Wałęsa) is about five miles west of the city center (tel. 058/348-1163, www.airport.gdansk.pl). Bus #B connects the airport with downtown (2.50 zł, 30 min, buy ticket on board). A taxi into town will cost you about 50 zł.

Helpful Hints

Blue Monday: In the off-season, most of Gdańsk's museums are closed Monday. In the busy summertime, some of these museums are open limited hours on Monday. If museums are closed, Monday is a good day to visit churches or take a side-trip to Sopot (but not Malbork Castle, which is also closed Mon).

Last Entry: The "last entry" time for museums is 30 minutes before closing—and it's strictly enforced. Museum-goers who cut it close discover that ticket-sellers sometimes clock out a few minutes early.

Local Help/Travel Agent: Gdynia-based **Sports-Tourist** (so named because they used to help the Polish Olympic team get visas during the communist days), run by friendly Mirek, is a reliable and helpful contact in the Tri-City area. They can book you a good local guide or driver, set you up with a rental car, book you a room at a big hotel for discounted rates, help with ferry and plane tickets (including the red tape for a day trip to Kaliningrad, Russia, by boat), or anything else you need (tel. 058/621-9164, fax 058/621-9921, www.sports-tourist.com.pl, info@sports-tourist.gdynia.pl).

Private Guides: There are no regularly scheduled bus or walking tours of Gdańsk, but hiring a private local guide for yourself is an exceptional value. I've worked with two young, bright, energetic guides who are equally good (both charge

300 zł for up to 4 hrs, 50 zł/hr after that): **Agnieszka Syroka** is bubbly and personable, and also does tours of Malbork Castle (mobile 0502-554-584, asyroka@interia.pl); **Paweł Grochola** is smart as a whip and brings Gdańsk's history to life with humor (mobile 0505-085-814, www.tourguide.gd.pl, office@tourguide.gd.pl). If these two are busy, contact Sports-Tourist (listed above) for help finding a guide.

Getting Around Gdańsk

If you're staying at one of my recommended hotels, everything is within easy walking distance. Public transportation is useful for residents, but not really for sightseers.

By Public Transportation: Gdańsk has a fine network of trams and buses. Buy tickets (*bilety*) at kiosks marked *RUCH* or *Bilety ZKM*. Prices depend on the time limit on the ticket (about 1.50 zł/10 min, 2.50 zł/30 min, 4 zł/1 hr, 8 zł/24 hrs). Stops worth knowing about: Plac Solidarności (near the shipyards), Gdańsk Główny (in front of the Main Train Station), and Brama Wyżynna (near the heart of the tourist zone, in front of LOT airlines office). Don't confuse *ZKM* (the company that runs Gdańsk city transit) with *SKM* (the company that runs regional trains to outlying destinations).

To get beyond central Gdańsk to visit the Oliwa cathedral, see "Outer Gdańsk," (page 332). For directions to towns of Sopot and Gdynia, and the Hel Peninsula, see "Getting Around the Tri-City" (page 340).

By Taxi: They cost 5 zł to start, then 2 zł per kilometer. Find a taxi stand, or call a cab (try Super Hallo Taxi, tel. 058/9191, or City Plus Hallo Taxi, tel. 058/9686).

SELF-GUIDED WALKS

Gdańsk's Royal Way

In the 16th and 17th centuries, Gdańsk was Poland's wealthiest city, with gorgeous architecture (much of it in the Flemish Mannerist style) rivaling that in the two historic capitals, Kraków and Warsaw. During this Golden Age, Polish kings would visit this city of well-to-do Hanseatic League merchants, and they gawked along the same route trod by tourists today. The following walk, worth ▲▲▲, introduces you to the best of historic Gdańsk. It only takes about 45 minutes, not counting multiple worthwhile sightseeing stops.

Begin at the west end of the Main Town, between the big, white gate and the big brick gate (near the LOT airlines office, the busy road, and the Brama Wyżynna tram stop).

City Gates: Medieval Gdańsk had an elaborate network of

Gdańsk at a Glance

▲▲▲**Ulica Długa** Gdańsk's colorful showpiece main drag, cutting a picturesque swath through the heart of the wealthy burghers' neighborhood. **Hours:** Always open.

▲▲▲**Solidarity Sights and Gdańsk Shipyard** The shipyard that was home to the beginning of the end of European communism, housing a towering monument and an excellent museum. **Hours:** April–Oct Tue–Sun 10:00–17:00, Nov–March Tue–Sun 10:00–16:00, always closed Mon.

▲▲**Uphagen House** Tourable 18th-century interior, typical of the pretty houses that line ulica Długa. **Hours:** June–Sept Tue–Sat 10:00–18:00, Sun 11:00–18:00, Mon 10:00–15:00; Oct–May Tue–Sat 10:00–16:00, Sun 11:00–16:00, closed Mon.

▲▲**Main Town Hall** Ornately decorated meeting rooms, exhibits of town artifacts, and climbable tower with sweeping views. **Hours:** Museum open June–Sept Tue–Sat 10:00–18:00, Sun 11:00–18:00, Mon 10:00–15:00; Oct–May Tue–Sat 10:00–16:00, Sun 11:00–16:00, closed Mon; tower open same hours, but mid-May–mid-Oct only.

▲**Artus Court** Grand meeting hall for guilds of Golden Age Gdańsk, boasting an over-the-top tiled stove. **Hours:** June–Sept Tue–Sat 10:00–18:00, Sun 11:00–18:00, Mon 10:00–15:00; Oct–May

---

protection for the city, including several moats and gates—among them the white **Upland Gate** (Brama Wyżynna); the shorter, red-brick **Torture House** (Wieża Więzienna); and the taller, red-brick **Prison Tower** (Katownia). These three were all connected back then, and visitors had to pass through all of them to enter the city. These buildings, with walls up to 15 feet thick, are being turned into a museum. But they keep discovering hidden passages, rooms, and other archaeological finds (such as spectacularly well-preserved 14th-century toilets)...so the plans keep getting delayed.

Now walk around the left side of the Torture House and Prison Tower. Look to your left to see a long brick building with four gables. This is the 16th-century **Armory** (Zbrojownia), one of the best examples of Dutch Renaissance architecture in Europe. Though this part of the building looks like houses, it's a kind of urban camouflage to hide its real purpose from potential attackers. But there's at least one clue to what it's for: Find the exploding cannonballs at the tops of the turrets. The round, pointy-topped tower next door is the **Straw Tower.** Gunpowder was stored here,

Tue–Sat 10:00–16:00, Sun 11:00–16:00, closed Mon.

▲St. Mary's Church Giant red-brick church crammed full of Gdańsk history. **Hours:** Mon–Sat 9:00–17:30, Sun 13:00–17:30.

▲Central Maritime Museum Sprawling exhibit on all aspects of the nautical life, housed in several venues (including the landmark medieval Crane and a permanently moored steamship) connected by a ferry boat. **Hours:** Mid-June–Aug daily 10:00–18:00, Sept–mid-June Tue–Sun 10:00–16:00, closed Mon.

Archaeological Museum Decent collection of artifacts from this region's past. **Hours:** July–Aug Tue–Sun 10:00–17:00, closed Mon; Sept–June Tue and Thu–Fri 9:00–16:00, Wed 10:00–17:00, Sat–Sun 10:00–16:00, closed Mon.

National Museum in Gdańsk Ho-hum art collection with a single blockbuster highlight: Hans Memling's remarkable *Last Judgment* altarpiece. **Hours:** Tue–Fri 9:00–16:00, Sat–Sun 10:00–16:00, closed Mon.

Oliwa Cathedral Suburban church with long, skinny nave and playful organ. **Hours:** Church open long hours daily; frequent organ concerts in summer.

and the roof was straw—so if it exploded, it would blow its top without destroying the walls.

• *Continue around the brick buildings until you're face-to-face with the...*

Golden Gate (Złota Brama): The other gates were defensive, but this one's purely ornamental. The four women up top represent

virtues that the people of Gdańsk should exhibit towards outsiders: Peace, Freedom, Prosperity, and Fame. The inscription, a psalm in medieval German, compares Gdańsk to Jerusalem: famous and important. In the middle is one of the coats of arms of Gdańsk—two crosses under a crown. You'll see this symbol many times today.

• *Now go through the gate, entering the "Long Street"...*

Ulica Długa: Look back at the gate you just came through. The women on top of this side represent virtues the people of Gdańsk should cultivate in themselves: Wisdom, Piety, Justice, and Concord (if an arrow's broken, let's take it out of the quiver and fix it).

Begin to wander this intoxicating promenade. Gdańsk was cosmopolitan and exceptionally tolerant in the Middle Ages, attracting a wide range of people (including many who were persecuted elsewhere): Jews, Scots, Dutch, Flemish, Italians, Germans, and more. Members of each group brought with them strands of their culture, which they wove into the tapestry of this city. The eclectic homes along this street are one of the ways that cultures from throughout Europe left their mark on Gdańsk.

This lovely street was nothing but rubble at the end of World War II. The city was damaged when the Germans first invaded, sparking the war. But the worst devastation came when the Soviets arrived. This was the first traditionally German city that the Red Army reached on their march towards Berlin—and the soldiers were set loose to level the place in retaliation for all of the pain the Nazis had caused. (Soviets didn't destroy nearby Gdynia—which they considered Polish, not German.) Soviet officers turned a blind eye as their soldiers raped and brutalized residents. An entire order of horrified nuns committed suicide by throwing themselves into the river. And upwards of 80 percent of this area was destroyed. It was only thanks to detailed drawings and photographs that these buildings could be so carefully reconstructed, mostly using the original brick.

Like the homes lining Amsterdam's canals, these houses were taxed based on frontage—so they were built skinny and deep (about 10 times as long as they are wide). The widest houses belonged to the super-elite. Different as they are from the outside, each house has the same general plan inside (with 3 parts, starting with the front and moving back). First was a fancy drawing room, to show off for visitors. Then came a narrow corridor to the back rooms—often along the side of an inner courtyard. Because the houses had only a few windows facing the outer street, this courtyard provided much-needed sunlight to the rest of the house. The residential quarters were in the back, where the people actually lived: bedroom, kitchen, office. To see the interior of one of these homes, pay a visit to the **Uphagen House** (#12, on the right, a block in front of the gate; described on page 317).

Across the street and a little farther down are some of the most striking **facades** along all of ulica Długa. The big blue house with the three giant heads is from the 19th century, when eclecticism was hot—borrowing bits and pieces from various architectural eras. This was one of the few houses on the street that survived World War II.

A bit farther up on the right is the huge, blocky **post office**, which doesn't quite fit with the skinny facades lining the rest of the street. But step inside. With doves fluttering under an airy glass atrium, the interior's a class act. (To mail postcards, take a number—category C—from the machine on the left.)

Across the street and a few doors down from the post office, notice the colorful **scenes** just overhead on the facade of the cocktail bar. These are slices of life from 17th-century Gdańsk: drinking, talking, buying, fighting, playing music. The ship is a *koga*, a typical symbol of Gdańsk.

A couple of doors down from the cocktail bar is **Neptun Cinema** (marked *KINO*). In the 1980s, this was the only movie theater in the city, and locals lined up all the way down the street to get in. Young adults remember coming here with their grandparents to see a full day of cartoons. Now, like in the United States, the rising popularity of multiplexes is threatening to close this place down.

Across the street from the theater are three houses belonging to the very influential medieval **Ferber family**, which produced many burghers, mayors, and even a bishop. On the house with the little dog over the door (#29), look for the heads in the circles. These are Caesars of Rome. At the top of the building is Mr. Ferber's answer to the constant question, "Why build such an elaborate house?"—*PRO INVIDIA*, "For the sake of envy."

Now you're just a few steps from the **Main Town Hall** (Ratusz Głównego Miasta). This building features a climbable observation tower and houses a superb museum with ornately decorated meeting rooms for the city council (see description on page 317).

• *Just beyond the Main Town Hall, ulica Długa widens and becomes...*

Długi Targ: The centerpiece of "Long Square" is one of Gdańsk's most important landmarks, the statue of **Neptune**—god of the sea. He's a fitting symbol for a city that dominates the maritime life of Poland. Behind him is the third good museum on this tour, **Artus Court** (see page 318). This meeting hall for various Gdańsk brotherhoods is home to the most impressive stove you've ever seen.

As you continue down Długi targ, notice the **balconies** extending out into the square, with access to cellars underneath. These were far more common along ulica Długa in Gdańsk's Golden Age, but were removed in the 19th century to make way for a new tram system. You'll find more balconies like these on Mariacka street, which runs parallel to this one (2 blocks to the left).

• *At the end of Długi targ is the...*

Green Gate (Zielona Brama): This huge gate was actually built as a residence for visiting kings...who usually preferred to stay back by Neptune instead (maybe because the river, just on the other side of this gate, stunk). It might not have been good enough for kings and queens, but it's plenty fine for a former president—Lech Wałęsa's office is upstairs (see the plaque, *Biuro Lecha Wałęsy*). Other parts of the building are used for temporary exhibitions.

Notice that these bricks are much smaller than the ones we've seen earlier on this walk. That's because those were locally made, but these are Dutch. Boats would come here empty, load up with goods, and take them back to Holland. For ballast, they brought bricks on the trip from Holland—which they left here to be turned into this gate.

• *Now go through the gate, and turn left along the...*

Riverfront Embankment: This is it—the source of Gdańsk's phenomenal medieval wealth. Actually, this isn't the Vistula, but a side channel called the Motława—still, you get the idea. This place was jam-packed in its heyday, the 14th and 15th centuries. It was so crowded with boats that you could hardly see the water, and boats had to pay a time-based tax for tying up to a post. Instead of an actual embankment (which was built later), there was a series of wooden piers to connect the boats directly to the gates of the city. Now it's a popular place to buy amber.

Across the river is **Granary Island** (Spichrze), where grain was stored until it could be taken away by ships. Before World War II, there were some 400 granaries here; now it's still in ruins. Three granaries have been reconstructed on the next island up, and house exhibits for the Central Maritime Museum (see "Sights," below); another is Hotel Królewski (see "Sleeping," page 333).

Continue along the embankment until you see the five big, round stones on your left. These are the **five little ladies**—mysterious ancient sculptures. If you look closely, you can make out their features, especially the chubby one on the end. If you touch one, you'll come back to Gdańsk...or so the tour guides say.

The next huge red-brick fort houses the **Archaeological Museum** and a tower you can climb for a good view (see "Sights," below). The gate in the middle leads to **Mariacka Street**, a calm, atmospheric drag leading to St. Mary's Church (see page 319) and lined with old balconies, amber shops, and imaginative gargoyles (which locals call "pukers" when it rains).

• *Just up ahead on the embankment is Gdańsk's number one symbol, and our last stop...*

The Crane (Żuraw): This monstrous 15th-century crane was used for loading ships, picking up small crafts for repairs, and uprighting masts... beginning a shipbuilding tradition that continued to the days of Lech Wałęsa. The crane mechanism was operated by several guys scrambling around in giant hamster wheels up top (you can see the wheels if you look up). The Crane houses part of the Central Maritime Museum (described on page 321, below).

• *Our orientation tour is over. Now get out there and enjoy Gdańsk... do it for Lech!*

From the Main Town to the Solidarity Shipyard

This lightly guided walk links Gdańsk's two most important sightseeing areas. Along the way, you'll see some important historic landmarks, tour two of Gdańsk's more interesting red-brick churches, and wander through the city's best shopping district. The stroll takes about 20 minutes, not counting stops for sightseeing and shopping.

Begin at the top of ulica Długa, with your back to the Golden Gate. Head a few steps down the street and take a left on Tkacka. After one long block, you'll see back of the **Armory** building (described in "Self-Guided Walks—Gdańsk's Royal Way," above).

After two more blocks, detour to the right down Świętojańska and use the side door to enter the big, brick **St. Nicholas Church** (Kościół Św. Mikołaja). Near the end of World War II, when the Soviet army reached Gdańsk on its march westward, they were given the order to burn all of the churches. Only this one—dedicated to Russia's patron saint—was spared. Step inside. As the best-preserved church in town, today it has a more interesting interior than the others, with lavish golden Baroque altars.

Backtrack out to the main street and continue north. Immediately after the church (on the right), you'll see Gdańsk's newly renovated **Market Hall**. Look for the coat of arms of Gdańsk over each of its four doors. Inside you'll find mostly local shoppers—browsing through produce, other foods, and clothing—as well as the graves of medieval Dominican monks (discovered here when renovation began, and covered by protective glass).

Across the street from the Market Hall is a round red-brick **tower**, once part of the city's protective wall. This marks the end of the Main Town, and the beginning of the Old Town.

Another long block up the street is the huge **St. Catherine's Church** (Kościół Św. Katarzyny, on the right). While this church has an unexceptional interior, the church hiding behind it—named for Catherine's daughter Bridget—has important ties to Solidarity, and is worth a quick visit. To get there, walk along the side of St. Catherine's Church (passing the monument to Pope John Paul II).

St. Bridget's Church (Kościół Św. Brygidy) was the home church of Lech Wałęsa during the tense days of the 1980s. This church and its priest, Henryk Jankowski, were particularly aggressive in supporting the ideals of Solidarity. Jankowski became a mouthpiece for Solidarity, and Wałęsa named his youngest daughter Brygida in gratitude for the church's support. In the back corner, find the tomb of Jerzy Popiełuszko, a martyr of Solidarity. This famously outspoken Warsaw priest was kidnapped, beaten, and murdered by the communist secret police. At the front of the church, check out the enormous, unfinished altar made entirely of amber—the ongoing megalomaniacal project of Wałęsa's former priest, Father Jankowski. The altar is just one example of Jankowski's recent missteps. Sadly, Jankowski has become a highly controversial figure recently—just in the last two years, he's been accused of anti-Semitism and implicated in pedophilia and corruption charges. Despite his celebrity and noble past, Jankowski has been demoted, and no longer leads this church.

Backtrack out past St. Catherine's Church to the main street. Just across from St. Catherine's is a red-brick building with lots of little windows in the roof. This is the **Great Mill** (Wielki Młyn), which has been converted into a shopping mall. As you continue north and cross the stream, you'll also see the cute **Small Mill** (Mały Młyn) straddling the stream on your right.

After another block, on your right, is the modern **Madison shopping mall** (Centrum Handlowa Madison; TI on ground floor—see "Tourist Information," above). Two blocks to your left (up Heweliusza) are more shopping malls and the Main Train Station. But to get to the shipyard, keep heading straight up Rajska. After another long block, jog right (between the big, green-glass skyscraper and today's Solidarity headquarters) and head for the three tall crosses.

For a self-guided tour of the shipyard and Solidarity museum, see page 324.

SIGHTS

Main Town (Główne Miasto)

The following sights are all in the Main Town, listed roughly in the order you'll see them on the self-guided walk of the Royal Way. The first three sights are all part of the **Gdańsk Historical Museum,** and covered on the same discounted 12-zł combo-ticket (you'll save 6 zł if you visit all 3, and break even if you visit only 2; buy it at any of the included museums).

▲▲**Uphagen House (Dom Uphagena)**—This wonderful place is your chance to get a glimpse into what's behind the colorful facades lining ulica Długa. Check out the model in the ticket office to see the three parts you'll visit: dolled-up visitors' rooms in front, a corridor along the courtyard, and private rooms in the back (6 zł, included in 12-zł combo-ticket with Main Town Hall and Artus Court, June–Sept Tue–Sat 10:00–18:00, Sun 11:00–18:00, Mon 10:00–15:00; Oct–May Tue–Sat 10:00–16:00, Sun 11:00–16:00, closed Mon; ulica Długa 12, tel. 058/301-2371).

You'll begin upstairs, in the salon—used to show off for guests. Most of this furniture is original (saved from WWII bombs by locals who hid it in the countryside). Then you'll pass into the dining room, with knee-high paintings of hunting and celebrations. Along the passage to the back, each room has a theme: butterflies in the smoking room, then flowers, then birds in the music room. In the private rooms at the back, notice how much simpler the decor is (and how low the ceilings are). Back downstairs, you'll pass through the kitchen, the pantry, and a room with photos from the house before the war, which they used to reconstruct what you see today.

▲▲**Main Town Hall (Ratusz Głównego Miasta)**—Inside this landmark building, you'll find some remarkable decorations from Gdańsk's Golden Age (6 zł, included in 12-zł combo-ticket with Uphagen House and Artus Court, June–Sept Tue–Sat 10:00– 18:00, Sun 11:00–18:00, Mon 10:00–15:00; Oct–May Tue–Sat 10:00–16:00, Sun 11:00–16:00, closed Mon; ulica Długa 47, tel. 058/767-9100). You can also climb to the top of the **tower** for commanding views (3 zł extra, mid-May–mid-Oct only).

Buy your ticket down below (good gift shop), then head up the stairs and inside. In the entry room, examine the photo showing this building at the end of World War II (you'll see more upstairs). The ornately carved wooden **door**, which you'll pass through in a minute, also deserves a close look. Above the door are two crosses under a crown. This seal of Gdańsk is being held—as it often is—by a pair of lions. The felines are stubborn and independent, just like Gdańsk. Close the door partway to look at the carvings of crops. Around the frame of the door are mermen, reminding us that these crops, like so many other resources of Poland, are transported on the Vistula and out through Gdańsk.

Go through the door into the **Red Hall,** where the Gdańsk city council met in the summertime. (The lavish fireplace—with another pair of lions holding the coat of arms of Gdańsk—was just for show.) City council members would sit in the seats around the room, debating city policy. The shin-level paintings depict the earth; the exquisitely detailed inlaid wood just over the seats are animals; the paintings on the wall above represent the seven virtues the burghers meeting in this room should have; and the ceiling is all about theology. Examine that ceiling. You'll see 25 paintings total, with both Christian and pagan themes—meant to inspire the decision-makers in this room to make good choices. The smaller ones around the edges are scenes from mythology and the Bible. The one in the middle (from 1607) shows God's relationship to Gdańsk. In the foreground, the citizens of Gdańsk go about their daily lives. Above them, high atop the arch, God's hand reaches down (from within clouds of Hebrew characters) and grasps the city's steeple. The rainbow arching above also symbolizes God's connection to Gdańsk. Mirroring that is the Vistula River, which begins in the mountains of southern Poland (on the right), runs through the country, and exits at the sea in Gdańsk (on the left—where the rainbow ends).

Continue into the not-so-impressive Winter Hall, with another fireplace and coat of arms held by lions. Keep going through the next room, into a room with before-and-after photos of **WWII damage**. At the foot of the destroyed crucifix is a book with a bullet hole in it. The twist of wood is all that's left of the main support for the spiral staircase (today reconstructed in the room where you entered). Ponder the tragedy of war...and the inspiring ability of a city to be reborn.

Upstairs are some temporary exhibits, and several examples of **Gdańsk-style furniture**. These pieces are characterized by three big, round feet along the front, lots of ornamentation, and usually a virtually-impossible-to-find lock (sometimes hidden behind a movable decoration). You'll also see a coin collection, from the days when Gdańsk had the elite privilege of minting its own currency.

▲**Artus Court (Dwór Artusa)**—In the Middle Ages, there were many businessmen's clubs in Gdańsk. For their meetings, the city provided this elaborately decorated hall, named for King Arthur (who was a medieval symbol for prestige and power). Halls like this one were once common in Baltic Europe, but only three survive, and Gdańsk's is by far the best (6 zł, included in 12-zł combo-ticket with Uphagen House and Main Town Hall, June–Sept Tue–Sat 10:00–18:00, Sun 11:00–18:00, Mon 10:00–15:00; Oct–May Tue–Sat 10:00–16:00, Sun 11:00–16:00, closed Mon; in tall, white, 3-arched building behind Neptune statue at ulica Długi Targ 43-44, tel. 058/767-9100).

In the grand hall, you'll see various **cupboards** lining the walls. Each organization that met here had a place to keep its important documents and office supplies.

In the far back corner is the museum's highlight: a towering **stove** decorated with 520 colorful tiles featuring the faces of kings, queens, nobles, mayors, and burghers. Half of these people were Protestant, and half were Catholic, mixed together in no particular order—a reminder of the importance of religious tolerance. About 90 percent of these tiles are original, having survived WWII bombs. Of the missing tiles, three were recently discovered by a bargain-hunter wandering through a flea market in the southern part of the country—and returned to their rightful home.

Notice the huge **paintings** on the walls above, with 3-D animals emerging from flat frames. Hunting is a popular theme in local artwork. Like minting coins, hunting was a privilege usually reserved for royalty, but extended in special circumstances to special towns...like Gdańsk. If you look closely, it's obvious that these "paintings" are digitally generated reproductions of the original ones, which were damaged in World War II.

The next room—actually in the next-door building—is a typical front room of the burghers' homes lining ulica Długa. As you exit to the back, you'll see a miniature reconstruction of the whole grand room, including paintings that have yet to be re-created. As you leave, you're just down the street from St. Mary's Church (below); to get back to the main drag, go back around the block, to the left.

▲**St. Mary's Church (Kościół Mariacki)**—Gdańsk has so many striking red-brick churches, it's hard to keep track of them. But if you visit only one, make it St. Mary's. This is the biggest brick church in the world, accommodating up to 25,000 people (standing room only). Built over 159 years in the 14th and 15th centuries, the church is an important symbol of Gdańsk. If you've got the energy, climb the 408 steps up the church's 270-foot-tall tower. You'll be rewarded with sweeping views of the entire city (church entry-2 zł, tower climb-3 zł, tower climb price includes church entry—so don't pay twice, open for tourists Mon–Sat 9:00–17:30, Sun 13:00–17:30).

As you enter the church, notice all of the white, empty space—unusual in a Catholic country, where frilly Baroque churches are the norm. In the Middle Ages, Gdańsk's tolerance attracted people who were suffering religious persecution (especially Mennonites). As the Protestant population grew, they needed a place to worship. St. Mary's, like most other Gdańsk churches, eventually became Protestant—leaving these churches with the blank walls you see now. Today you'll find only one Baroque church in central Gdańsk (the domed pink-and-green chapel behind St. Mary's).

Most Gothic stone churches are built in the basilica style—with a high nave in the middle, shorter naves on the side, and flying buttresses to support the weight. (Think of Paris' Notre-Dame.) But that design doesn't work with brick. So, like all Gdańsk churches, St. Mary's is a "hall church"—with three naves the same height, and no exterior buttresses.

Also like other Gdańsk churches, St. Mary's gave refuge to the Polish people after the communist government declared martial law in 1981. If a riot broke out and violence seemed imminent, people would flood into churches for protection. The ZOMO riot police wouldn't follow them inside.

Most of the church decorations are original. A few days before World War II broke out in Gdańsk, locals hid precious items in the countryside. Take some time now to see a few of the highlights.

Head up the right nave and find the opulent family marker to the right of the main altar. Look for the falling baby. This is Constantine Ferber. As a precocious child, Constantine leaned out his window on ulica Długa to see the king's processional come through town. He slipped and fell, but landed in a salesman's barrel of fish. Constantine grew up to become the mayor of Gdańsk.

At the next post down, look for the coat of arms with the three pigs' heads. This story relates to another member of the illustrious Ferber clan. An enemy army was laying siege to the town, and tried to starve them out. A clever Ferber decided to load the cannons with pigs' heads to show the enemy that they had plenty of food—it worked, and the enemy left.

Circle around, past the front of the beautifully carved main altar. Behind it is the biggest stained-glass window in Poland, and below the window is a huge, empty glass case. The case was designed to hold Hans Memling's *Final Judgment* painting, which used to be on display here, but is currently being held hostage by the National Museum. The museum claims the church isn't a good environment for such a precious work, but the priest had this display case built to convince the museum to give it back. You can see a smaller replica up by the main door of the church (in the little chapel on the right just before you exit), but true art fans will want to venture to the National Museum to see the much larger original (described below).

Before you head back out to the mini-Memling (and the exit), venture to the far side of the altar and check out the elaborate astronomical clock. Below is the calendar and the saint's day, and above are zodiac signs and the time (only 1 hand).

Archaeological Museum (Muzeum Archeologiczne)—This modest museum is worth a quick peek for those interested in archaeology. The ground floor has exhibits on excavated finds from Sudan, where the museum has a branch program. Upstairs, look for the distinctive urns with cute faces, dating from the Hallstatt Period and discovered in slate graves around Gdańsk. Also upstairs are a small display of amber artifacts (but the exhibit at Malbork Castle is worlds better); some Bronze and Iron Age tools; before-and-after photos of WWII Gdańsk; and a reconstructed 12th-century Viking-like Slavonic longboat (5 zł; July–Aug Tue–Sun 10:00–17:00, closed Mon; Sept–June Tue and Thu–Fri 9:00–16:00, Wed 10:00–17:00, Sat–Sun 10:00–16:00, closed Mon; ulica Mariacka 25–26, tel. 058/301-5031).

▲Central Maritime Museum (Centralne Muzeum Morskie)—Gdańsk's history and livelihood are tied to the sea. This collection,

spread out among several buildings on either side of the river, examines all aspects of this connection. While nautical types may get a thrill out of the creaky, sprawling museum, most visitors find it little more than a convenient way to pass some time and enjoy a cruise across the river.

There are four parts of the exhibit. Two of them are on the Main Town side of the river:

1. The Crane (Żuraw): The medieval Crane—Gdańsk's most important symbol—houses an exhibit on living in the city during its Golden Age (16th–17th centuries). You'll see models of Baltic buildings (including the Crane you're inside), plus traditional tools and costumes. For more on the Crane itself, see page 315.

2. Boats of the World: The building next to the Crane houses different kinds of boats from around the world, mostly from non-European cultures. A Venetian gondola greets you at the entry.

The other two parts of the museum are across the river on Ołowianka Island. You'll reach the island via the little **ferry** (*prom*, 1 zł 1-way, included in 14-zł ticket). The ferry runs about every 15 minutes in peak season (during museum hours only), but frequency declines sharply in the off-season (and it doesn't run if the river freezes). This also gives fine views back on the Crane. Once on the island, you'll visit the other two parts:

3. The Old Granaries (Spichlerze): These three rebuilt granaries make up the heart of the exhibit, tracing the history of Gdańsk—particularly as it relates to the sea—from prehistoric days to the present. Models of the town and region help put things into perspective. You'll see exhibits on underwater exploration, navigational aids, artifacts of the Polish seafaring tradition, peek-a-boo cross-sections of multi-level ships, and models of the modern-day shipyard where Solidarity was born. This place is home to more miniature ships than you ever thought you'd see, and the Nautical Gallery upstairs features endless rooms with paintings of boats. The whole thing would probably be great...if you could speak Polish (paltry English loaner descriptions available in some rooms).

4. The *Sołdek*: Crawl through the holds and scramble across the deck of this decommissioned steamship docked permanently across from the Crane. Below decks, you'll see where they shoveled the coal; wander through a maze of pipes, gears, valves, gauges, and ladders; and visit the rooms where the sailors lived, slept, and ate. You can even play captain in the bridge. The place would be much improved with a smarter exhibit and more English information—both of which are planned for the future (ship sometimes closed in winter).

Cost, Hours, Location: Each part of the museum costs 6 zł, but the 14-zł ticket gets you in everywhere and also covers the ferry across the river. It's open mid-June–Aug daily 10:00–18:00, Sept–mid-June Tue–Sun 10:00–16:00, closed Mon (ulica Ołowianka 9–13, tel. 058/301-8611, www.cmm.pl). Throughout the museum, there's an irritating lack of English information. But a new guidebook is supposedly in the works, and hiring your own guide is cheap.

Tour: If you have a serious fascination with all matters maritime, pay the unbelievably cheap price of 20 zł to get your own private English-speaking guide (reserve ahead: tel. 058/301-8611, if they speak only Polish, they'll figure it out and find an English-speaker). The tour can last two hours or more, so if you have only a passing interest, skip the guide and see the museum at your own pace.

National Museum in Gdańsk (Muzeum Narodowe w Gdańsku)—This art collection, housed in what was a 15th-century Franciscan monastery, is worth ▲▲ to art-lovers for one reason: Hans Memling's glorious *Last Judgment* triptych altarpiece, one of the two most important pieces of art to be seen in Poland (the other is da Vinci's *Lady with an Ermine* in Kraków—see page 232). If you're not a purist, skip the 10-minute walk here from the Main Town and settle for seeing the much smaller replica in St. Mary's Church. But if medieval art is your bag, make the trip here (9 zł, Tue–Fri 9:00–16:00, Sat–Sun 10:00–16:00, last entry at 15:30, closed Mon; walk 10 min due south from ulica Długa's Golden Gate, taking the pedestrian underpass beneath the busy street; ulica Toruńska 1, tel. 058/301-7061, www.muzeum .narodowe.gda.pl).

From the entry, the altarpiece by Hans Memling (c. 1440–1494) is at the top of the stairs. The history of the painting is as interesting as the work itself. It was commissioned in the mid-15th century by the Medicis' banker in Florence, Angelo di Jacopo Tani. The ship delivering the painting from England to Florence was hijacked by a Gdańsk pirate named Paul Bendecke, who brought the altarpiece to his hometown to be displayed in St. Mary's Church. For centuries, it was admired from afar by kings, emperors, and czars, until it was finally seized by Napoleon in the early 19th century and taken to Paris, where it hung in the Louvre. Gdańsk got the painting back, only to have it exiled again—this time into St. Petersburg's Hermitage Museum—after World War II. On its return to Gdańsk in 1956, it was claimed by this museum—though St. Mary's wants it back (see above).

Have a close look at Memling's well-traveled work. It's the end of the world, and Christ rides in on a rainbow to judge humankind. Angels blow reveille, waking the dead, who rise from their graves. The winged archangel Michael—dressed for battle and wielding the cross like a weapon—weighs the grace in each person, sending them either to the fires of hell (right panel) or up the sparkling-crystal stairway to heaven (left).

It takes all 70 square feet of paneling to contain this awesome scene. Jam-packed with dozens of bodies, a Bible's worth of symbolism, and executed with astonishing detail, the painting can keep even a non-art-lover occupied. Notice the serene, happy expressions of the righteous, as they're greeted by St. Peter (with his giant key) and clothed by angels. And pity the condemned, their faces filled with terror and sorrow as they're tortured by grotesque devils more horrifying than anything Hollywood can devise.

Tune into the exquisite details: the angels' robes, the devils' genetic-mutant features, the portrait of the man in the scale (a Medici banker), Michael's peacock wings. Get as close as you can to the globe at Christ's feet and Michael's shining breastplate, and you'll even make out the whole scene in mirror reflection. Then back up and take it all in—three panels connected by a necklace of bodies that curves downward through hell, across the earth, then rising up to the towers of the New Jerusalem. On the back side of the triptych, you'll see reverent portraits of the painting's patron, Angelo Tani, and his new bride, Catarina.

Beyond the Memling, the rest of the collection features local works from the Gothic period, more Flemish and Dutch art, fabrics and gold- and silverware from the city's Golden Age, characteristic Gdańsk-style furniture, and lots more.

Solidarity (Solidarność) and the Gdańsk Shipyard (Stocznia Gdańska)

Gdańsk's single best experience—easily worth ▲▲▲—is exploring the shipyard that witnessed the beginning of the end of communism's stranglehold on Eastern Europe. Here in the industrial wasteland that Lech Wałęsa called the "cradle of freedom," you'll learn the story of the brave Polish shipyard workers who took on and defeated an Evil Empire.

A visit to the Solidarity sights has two main parts: the memorial and gate out in front of the shipyard, and the excellent "Roads to Freedom" exhibit, housed in the meeting hall where the agreement to end the strike was signed. Allow 90 minutes to tour the grounds and learn the entire story.

Cost, Hours, Information: Visiting the memorial and the shipyard gate is free. The "Roads to Freedom" exhibit costs 5 zł (April–Oct Tue–Sun 10:00–17:00, Nov–March Tue–Sun 10:00–16:00, always closed Mon, ulica Doki 1, tel. 058/769-2920, www.fcs.org.pl).

Getting to the Shipyard: The Solidarity monument and shipyard are at the north end of the Old Town, about a 20-minute walk from ulica Długa. For the most interesting approach, see my self-guided walk on page 315.

● **Self-Guided Tour:** After the communists took over Eastern Europe at the end of World War II, the oppressed people

throughout the Soviet Bloc rose up in different ways. The most dramatic uprisings—Hungary's 1956 Uprising (see page 408) and Czechoslovakia's 1968 "Prague Spring" (see page 54)—were both brutally crushed under the treads of Soviet tanks. The formula for freedom that finally succeeded—and was lucky enough to coincide with the *perestroika* and *glasnost* policies of Soviet premier Mikhail Gorbachev—was a patient, decade-long series of strikes spearheaded by Lech Wałęsa and his trade union, called Solidarność— "Solidarity." While some American politicians would like to claim responsibility for defeating communism, Wałęsa and his fellow workers were the ones fighting on the front lines, armed with nothing more than guts. The following tour leads you through the place where the inspirational events of August 1980 took place, while explaining the story as it unfolded. Begin at the towering monument—with three anchor-adorned crosses—near the entrance gate to the shipyard.

Monument of the Fallen Shipyard Workers: The seeds of August 1980 were sown a decade before. Since becoming part of the Soviet Bloc, the Poles staged frequent strikes, protests, and uprisings to secure their rights, all of which were put down by the regime. But the bloodiest of these took place in December 1970—a tragic event memorialized by this monument.

The 1970 strike was prompted by price hikes. The communist government set the prices for all products. As Poland endured drastic food shortages in the 1970s, the regime frequently announced what they called "regulation of prices"—increasing the cost of essential foodstuffs, while at the same time symbolically lowering prices of unimportant items (like elevators and TV sets). The regime was usually smart enough to raise prices on January 1—when the people were fat and happy after Christmas, and too hung over to complain. But on December 12, 1970, bolstered by an ego-stoking visit by West German Chancellor Willy Brandt, Polish premier Władysław Gomułka hiked up prices. The people of Poland—who cared more about the price of Christmas dinner than relations with Germany—struck back.

A wave of strikes and sit-ins spread along the heavily industrialized north coast of Poland, most notably in Gdańsk, Gdynia, and Szczecin. Thousands of angry demonstrators poured through the gate of this shipyard, marched into town, and set fire to the Communist Party Committee building. In an attempt to quell the riots, the government-run radio implored the people to go back to work. On the morning of December 17, workers showed up at shipyard gates across northern Poland—and were greeted by the army and police. Without provocation, the Polish army opened fire on the workers. While the official death toll for the massacre stands at 44, others say the true number is much higher.

This monument, with a trio of 140-foot-tall crosses, honors those lost to the regime that December. Go to the middle of the wall behind the crosses, to the monument of the worker wearing a flimsy plastic work helmet, attempting to shield himself from bullets. Behind him is a list—pockmarked with symbolic bullet holes—of workers murdered on that day. *Lat* means "years"—many teenagers were among the dead. The quote at the top of the wall was from Pope John Paul II, who was elected eight years after this tragedy. The Pope was known for his clever way with words, and this very carefully phrased quote—which served as an inspiration to the Poles during their darkest hours—skewers the regime in a way subtle enough to still be tolerated: "Let thy spirit descend, and renew the face of the earth—*this* earth" (that is, specifically, Poland). Below that is the

Lech Wałęsa

In 1980, the world was turned on its ear by a walrus-mustachioed shipyard electrician. Within three years, this seemingly run-of-the-mill Pole had precipitated the collapse of communism, led a massive 10 million-member trade union with enormous political impact, was named *Time* magazine's Man of the Year, and won a Nobel Peace Prize.

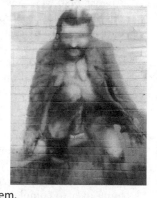

Lech Wałęsa was born in Popowo, Poland, in 1943. After working as a car mechanic and serving two years in the army, he became an electrician at the Gdańsk Shipyard in 1967. Like many Poles, Wałęsa felt stifled by the communist government, and was infuriated that a system that was supposed to be for the workers clearly wasn't serving them.

When the shipyard massacre took place in December 1970, Wałęsa was at the forefront of the protests. He was marked as a dissident, and in 1976, he was fired. He hopped from job to job and was occasionally unemployed—a rock-bottom status reserved for only the most despicable protesters. But Wałęsa soldiered on, fighting for the creation of a trade union and building up quite a file with the secret police.

In August 1980, Wałęsa heard news of the beginnings of the Gdańsk strike, and raced to the shipyard. In an act that has since become the stuff of legends, Wałęsa scaled the shipyard wall to get inside.

Before long, Wałęsa's dynamic personality won him the unofficial role of the workers' leader and spokesman. He negotiated with the regime to hash out the August Agreements, becoming a rock star-type hero during the so-called "16 Months of Hope"...until martial law came crashing down in December of 1981. Wałęsa was arrested and interned for 11 months in a country house. After being released, Wałęsa continued to struggle under-

dedication: "They gave their lives so you can live decently."

Stretching to the left of this center wall are plaques representing labor unions from around Poland—and around the world (look for the Chinese characters)—expressing solidarity with these workers. To the right is an enormous Bible verse: "May the Lord give strength to his people. May the Lord bless his people with the gift of peace" (Psalms 29:11).

More than a decade after the strike, this monument was finally constructed. It marked the first time a communist regime ground, becoming a symbol of anti-communist sentiment.

Finally, the dedication of Wałęsa and Solidarity paid off, and Polish communism dissolved—with Wałęsa rising from the ashes as the country's first post-communist president. But the skills that made Wałęsa a rousing success at leading an uprising did not translate to the president's office. Wałęsa proved to be a stubborn, headstrong politician, frequently clashing with the parliament. He squabbled with his own party, declaring a "war at the top" of Solidarity and rotating higher-ups to prevent corruption and keep the party fresh. He also didn't choose his advisors well, enlisting several staffers who wound up immersed in scandal. His overconfidence was his Achilles' heel, and his governing style verged on authoritarian.

Unrefined and none too interested in scripted speeches, Wałęsa was a simple man, who preferred playing ping-pong with his buddies to attending formal state functions. Though lacking a formal education, Wałęsa had unsurpassed drive and charisma... but that's not enough to lead a country—especially during an impossibly complicated, fast-changing time, when even the savviest politician would certainly have stumbled.

Wałęsa was defeated at the polls (by the Poles) in 1995, and when he ran again in 2000, he received a humiliating 1 percent of the vote. Since leaving office, Wałęsa has kept a lower profile, but still delivers speeches worldwide. Many poor Poles grumble that Lech, who started life simple like them, has forgotten the little people. But his fans point out that he gives much of his income to charity. And he still always wears a pin featuring the Black Madonna of Częstochowa—the symbol of Polish Catholicism—on his lapel.

Poles say there are at least two Lech Wałęsas: the young, working-class idealist Lech, at the forefront of the Solidarity strikes, who will always have a special place in their hearts; and the failed President Wałęsa, who got in over his head and tarnished his legacy.

ever allowed a monument built to honor its own victims. Wałęsa called it a harpoon in the heart of the communists. Inspired by the brave sacrifice of their true comrades, the shipyard workers rose up here in August of 1980, formulating the "21 Points" of a new union called Solidarity. These demands are listed in Polish on the panel at the far end of the right wall, marked *21 X TAK Solidarność* ("21 times yes Solidarity").

• *Now continue to the gate and peer through into the birthplace of Eastern European freedom.*

Gdańsk Shipyard (Stocznia Gdańska) Gate #2: When a Pole named Karol Wojtyła was elected Pope in 1978—and visited his homeland in 1979—he inspired his 40 million countrymen to believe that impossible dreams can come true. Prices continued to go up, and the workers continued to rise up. It began with general strikes in response to an increase in meat prices in the southeastern city of Lublin on July 11, 1980. While quickly resolved, the Lublin strikes were a sign to Poland that the dam was about to break.

A few weeks later in Gdańsk, Anna Walentynowicz—a crane operator and known dissident—was fired unceremoniously just short of her retirement. This sparked a strike in the Gdańsk Shipyard (then called the Lenin Shipyard) on August 14, 1980. An electrician named Lech Wałęsa had been fired as an agitator years before, and wasn't allowed into the shipyard. But on hearing news of the strike, Wałęsa went to the shipyard and climbed over the wall to get inside. The strike had a leader.

Imagine being one of the 16,000 workers who stayed here for 18 days during the strike—hungry, cold, sleeping on sheets of Styrofoam, inspired by the new Polish pope, excited about finally standing up to the regime...and terrified that you might be gunned down at any moment, like your friends who were massacred a decade before. Because you're afraid to leave the shipyard, your only way to communicate with the outside world is through this gate—your wife or brother shows up here and asks for you, and those inside spread the word until you come talk to them. Occasionally, a truck pulls up to the gate, and Lech Wałęsa stands on its cab with a megaphone and faces the thousands of people assembled here—giving them progress reports of the negotiations, and pleading for food. The people of Gdańsk respond, bringing armfuls of bread and other food, keeping the workers going. This truly is Solidarity.

Two items hung on the fence. One of them (which still hangs there today) was a picture of Pope John Paul II—a reminder to believe in your dreams and have faith in God (for more on the pope and his role in Solidarity, see page 224). The other item was a makeshift list of the strikers' 21 Points—demands scrawled in red paint and black pencil on pieces of plywood. The demands included the right to strike and form unions, the freeing of political prisoners, and an increase in wages.

• *Go around the gate (to the right, past the souvenir stand) and enter the shipyard. Keep an eye out for graffiti depicting important symbols and events from Solidarity history—including pudgy Lech leaping over the shipyard wall like a superhero.*

Path Through the Shipyard: As you walk toward the "Pathways to Freedom" exhibit, you'll pass through two huge symbolic gateways. The first resembles the rusted hull of a ship, representing the protest of the shipbuilders. Inside are two electronic strips: on the left, displaying communist slogans; on the right, the wisdom of Lech Wałęsa and Solidarity.

The next gate—a futuristic, colorful tower—is a small-scale version of a 1,000-foot-tall monument planned by the prominent Soviet constructivist architect Vladimir Tatlin. This fanciful but unfulfilled design represents the misguided, failed optimism of the communist "utopia."

After the gateways, on the left, look for the two **wall fragments**. On the right is the shipyard wall that Lech Wałęsa famously scrambled over in August of 1980 to join his comrades in the shipyard strikes. On the left, with the map of Europe, is a piece of another Wall—from Berlin—which fell less than a decade later. The message is simple: What began in this shipyard culminated in the fall of the Berlin Wall. The map showing Europe in 1980 and again in 2004 drives the point home.

At the end of the path, you see an **armored personnel carrier**, just like the ones used by the ZOMO (riot police) to terrorize Polish citizens after martial law was declared in 1981 (described below).

• *Now continue into the red-brick building.*

"Roads to Freedom" Exhibit in BHP Conference Hall: Step inside and buy your ticket, which is designed to look like the communist ration coupons that all Poles had to carry and present before they could buy certain goods. Cashiers would stand with scissors at the ready, prepared to snip off a corner of your coupon after making the sale.

A renovation of the exhibit was planned for late 2005. Things may be in a slightly different order than what's listed below, but everything should be close by.

The first room shows a typical **Polish shop** (marked *spożyw*, a truncated version of *spożywczy*, or "grocery store") from the 1970s, at the worst of the food shortages. Great selection, eh? Often the only things in stock were vinegar and mustard. Milk and bread were generally available, but they were low quality—it wasn't unusual to find a cigarette butt in your loaf. The few blocks of cheese and other items in the case aren't real—they're props (marked *atrapy*—"fake"), so the shop wouldn't look completely empty. Sometimes they'd hang a few pitiful, phony salamis from the hooks—otherwise, people might think it was a tile shop. The only real meat in here was the flies on the flypaper. Shockingly, shoppers (mostly women) would sometimes have to wait in line literally all day long just to pick over these scant choices.

In the corner, the phone booth is marked *Automat Nieczynny*—"Out of Order"—as virtually all phone booths were back then. The sign in the shop window *(22 Lipca)*, draped in the Polish flag, celebrates July 22, the Soviet Liberation Day, honoring the regime. Over the cash register is a picture of Bolek and Lolek, popular cartoon characters of the era. Unlike the Polish people, these two were able to travel around the world. (They seem to be in Turkey.)

Consider picking up a Solidarity book or other souvenir at the excellent gift shop before moving into the next room. If friendly, English-speaking Tomasz is around, he'd be happy to answer any questions.

The first part of the exhibit, called **"They Were the First,"** explains the roots of the 1980 shipyard strikes. Then you move into the heart of the exhibit, **August 1980.** There are the original plywood boards featuring the 21 Points, which hung on the front gate we just saw. As you enter the next room, keep an eye out for a giant, historic pen with the image of Pope John Paul II.

The next room is **the Hall.** After 18 days of protests, it became clear to the communist government that Solidarity would not simply go away. On the afternoon of August 31, 1980, the Governmental Commission and the Inter-Factory Strike Committee (MKS) came together in this very room and signed the August Agreements, which legalized Solidarity—the first time any communist government permitted a workers' union. A video shows the giddy day. Lech Wałęsa--sitting at the big table, with his characteristic walrus moustache—signed the agreement with the big red pope pen. Other union reps, sitting at smaller tables, tape-recorded the proceedings, and played them later at their own factories to prove the unthinkable had happened. While the government didn't take the agreements very seriously, the Poles did...and before long, 10 million of them—one in every four Poles—became members of Solidarity.

So began the **16 Months of Hope**—the theme of the next room. Newly legal, Solidarity continued to stage strikes and made its opposition known. Slick Solidarity posters and children's art convey the childlike enthusiasm with which the Poles seized their hard-won kernels of freedom. The poster with a baby in a Solidarity T-shirt—one year old, just like the union itself—captures the sense of hope. The grasp of the communist authorities on the Polish people began to slip. The rest of the Soviet Bloc looked on nervously, and the Warsaw Pact army assembled at the Polish border and glared at the uprisers. The threat of invasions hung heavy in the air.

In the next room, Solidarity's progress comes crashing down. On Sunday morning, December 13, 1981, the Polish head of state, General Wojciech Jaruzelski, appeared on national TV and announced the introduction of **martial law.** Solidarity was outlawed. Frightened Poles heard the announcement and looked out their windows to see Polish Army tanks rumbling through the snowy streets. Jaruzelski claimed that he imposed martial law to prevent the Soviets from invading. Today, many historians question whether martial law was really necessary—though Jaruzelski remains remorseless. Martial law was a tragic, terrifying, and bleak time for the Polish people. But Solidarity moved underground and continued the fight for freedom. Notice that their martial law era propaganda was produced with far more primitive printing equipment than their earlier posters. As you leave the room, look for the clandestine print shop, and for the shipbuilding equipment surrounding a Styrofoam pad on the floor. Remember, this was where those first strikers, who had no beds in the shipyard, were forced to sleep.

The next room, with sobering displays of **ZOMO riot gear,** shows a film about the ugliness of martial law. Watch the footage of General Jaruzelski—wearing his trademark dark glasses—reading the announcement of martial law. Listen to the music of the Polish Bob Dylan as he laments the evils of the regime. Chilling scenes show riots, demonstrations, and crackdowns by the ZOMO police— including one demonstrator who's run over by a truck. Another old woman is stampeded by a pack of fleeing demonstrators.

But the ZOMO couldn't crush the human spirit. The exhibit ends with two uplifting **films:** a retrospective on the entire communist era in Poland, and a general look at the fall of the Iron Curtain across Eastern Europe.

Here's your happy ending: By the time the Pope visited his homeland again in 1983, martial law was lifted, and Solidarity— still technically illegal—had gained momentum, gradually pecking away at the communists. With the moral support of the Pope and the entire Western world, the brave Poles were the first European country to throw off the shackles of communism when, in the spring of 1989, the "Round Table Talks" led to the opening up of elections. The government arrogantly called for parliamentary elections, reserving 65 percent of seats for themselves. The plan backfired, as virtually every contested seat went to Solidarity. This success inspired people all over Eastern Europe, and by that winter, the Berlin Wall had crumbled and the Czechs and Slovaks had staged their Velvet Revolution. Lech Wałęsa—the shipyard electrician who started it all by jumping over a wall—became the first president of post-communist Poland. And a year later, in Poland's first true elections since World War II, 29 different parties won seats in the *Sejm* (Parliament). This celebration of democracy was brought to the Polish people by a brave electrician and the workers of Gdańsk.

Outer Gdańsk

These two sights—worthwhile only to those with a special interest—are each within the city limits of Gdańsk, but they take several hours to see round-trip.

Oliwa Cathedral (Katedra Oliwska)—The suburb of Oliwa, at the northern edge of Gdańsk, is home to this visually striking church. The quirky, elongated facade hides a surprisingly long and skinny nave. The ornately decorated 18th-century organ over the main entrance features angels and stars that move around when the organ is played. While locals are proud of this place, it's hard to justify the effort it takes to get out here...Skip it unless you just love Polish churches or you're going to a concert.

Concerts: Concerts of the animated organ occur frequently, especially in summer (June–Aug generally at the top of each hour Mon–Fri 10:00–16:00—except at 14:00, Sat 10:00–15:00, Sun 15:00–17:00; May and Sept Mon–Sat at the top of each hour 10:00–13:00, Sun at 15:00 and 16:00; less off-season). Confirm the schedule before making the trip. Note that on Sundays and holidays, there are no concerts before 15:00.

Getting There: Oliwa is about six miles northwest of central Gdańsk, on the way to Sopot and Gdynia. To get to Oliwa, you have two options: Take **tram #6** or **#12** from Gdańsk's Main Train Station. These trams let you off right at the entrance to Oliwski Park. Go straight through to the back of the park; near the end, you'll see the copper roof and two skinny, pointy spires of the cathedral on your right. Exit through the back of the park, bear right, and go one block to find the entrance to the church. Your other option is to take a **commuter SKM train** from Gdańsk's Main Station 15 minutes to the "Gdańsk Oliwa" stop (see "Getting Around the Tri-City," page 340). From the Oliwa train station, it's a 15-minute walk or 10-zł taxi ride to the cathedral. Walk straight ahead out of the station and turn right when you get to the busy road. Cross the road at the light and enter the tree-filled Park Oliwski at the corner, then follow the directions above.

Westerplatte—World War II began on September 1, 1939, when Adolf Hitler sent the warship *Schleswig-Holstein* to attack this Polish munitions depot, which was guarding Gdańsk's harbor. Though it may interest WWII history buffs, there's little to see at this site aside from a modest museum and a towering monument. To get to Westerplatte, take bus #106 to the end (about 40 min). Even better, take a boat (see "Transportation Connections," page 339).

SHOPPING

As a major tourist town, Gdańsk offers plenty of enticing shopping opportunities. The big story here is amber *(bursztyn)*, a fossil resin available in all shades, shapes, and sizes (see "All About Amber," page 353). While you'll see amber sold all over town, the best place to browse and buy is along the atmospheric ulica Mariacka (between the Motława River and St. Mary's Church). This pretty street, with old-fashioned balconies and dozens of display cases, is fun to wander even if you're not a shopper. Other good places to buy amber are along the riverfront embankment and on ulica Długa. To avoid rip-offs—such as amber that's been melted and reshaped—always buy it from a shop, not from someone standing on the street. (But note that most shops also have a display case and salesperson out front, which are perfectly legit.) Prices everywhere are about the same, so rather than seeking out a specific place, just window-shop until you see what you want. Styles range from gaudy necklaces with huge globs of amber, to tasteful smaller pendants in a silver setting, to cheap trinkets. All shades of amber—from near-white to dark brown—cost about the same, but you'll pay more for inclusions (bugs or other objects stuck in the amber). You can get a basic amber pendant on a silver chain or a pair of small earrings for about 30 zł. If you want to pay more for bigger pieces or a more stylish setting, merchants will happily take your money.

Gdańsk also has several modern shopping malls, most of them in the Old Town or near the Main Train Station. The walk between the Main Town and the Solidarity shipyards goes past some of the best malls (see page 315).

SLEEPING

Central Gdańsk has fine splurges and acceptable dives, with little in between. Budget travelers can pay a pretty penny for a plush place, settle for a hostel, or stay farther from the Old Town. Prices virtually everywhere go up in the summer (at least July–Aug, often longer).

Across the River

Just across the Motława from the heart of the Main Town, you'll find Gdańsk's two best values. While they're a few minutes farther by foot from the action, they're both well-priced and in pleasant neighborhoods.

$$ Hotel Królewski is my favorite hotel in Gdańsk: a new, classy hotel in a beautifully renovated red-brick granary with 30 stylish rooms, great rates, and a friendly staff. It's just beyond

Sleep Code

(3.40 zł = about $1, €1 = about $1.20, country code: 48, area code: 012)
S = Single, **D** = Double/Twin, **T** = Triple, **Q** = Quad, **b** = bathroom, **s** = shower only. Unless otherwise noted, breakfast is included, credit cards are accepted, and English is spoken.

To help you sort easily through these listings, I've divided the rooms into three categories, based on the price for a standard double room with bath:

$$$ **Higher Priced**—Most rooms 400 zł (€100) or more.
$$ **Moderately Priced**—Most rooms between
                                300–400 zł (€75–100).
$ **Lower Priced**—Most rooms 300 zł (€75) or less.

the three granaries of the Maritime Museum and across from the Crane (Sb-260–290 zł, Db-310–350 zł, fancier suite-like Db "plus"-350–390 zł, higher prices are for May–Sept, cheaper Fri–Sun, request view room—they cost the same as non-view rooms, elevator, non-smoking rooms, good restaurant, ulica Ołowianka 1, tel. 058/326-1111, fax 058/326-1110, www.hotelkrolewski.pl, office@hotelkrolewski.pl). You can commute to your sightseeing by ferry (take the 1-zł boat trip across the river offered by the Maritime Museum—see page 321). But the ferry runs only during the museum's opening hours, and is sporadic off-season. If the ferry isn't running, it's a scenic 10-minute walk along the river and over the bridge into the Main Town.

$ **Dom Muzyka,** a 10-minute walk from the Main Town, is a great deal, with 87 simple, new-feeling rooms. The catch: It's hiding in the back of the big Academy of Music building (Akademia Muzyczna)—virtually impossible to find in a nondescript residential neighborhood. Still, the prices are worth the hunt (Sb-150 zł, Db-210 zł, deluxe Db-230 zł, apartment-320 zł, extra bed-60 zł, cheaper Oct–April, elevator, ulica Łąkowa 1–2, tel. 058/326-0600, fax 058/326-0601, www.dom-muzyka.pl, biuro@dom-muzyka.pl). From the Green Gate in the Main Town, cross the two bridges, then take the second right (on Łąkowa, across from the big brick church). Walk to the end of the block; just before the busy road, go through the gate of the big, yellow-brick building on the right. Once through the gate, the hotel is around the back of the yellow building, the farthest door down (unmarked). If you get lost, just ask people, "Hotel?"

Gdańsk Hotels and Restaurants

1. Kamienica Goldwasser Hotel/Rest.
2. Hanza Hotel
3. Hotel Mercure Hevelius
4. Pensjonat Dom Aktora
5. Przy Targu Rybnym Hostel
6. To Baltic Hostel
7. Hotel Królewski
8. To Dom Muzyka Hotel
9. Dom Harcerza Hostel
10. Bar Mleczny Neptun Rest.
11. Bar pod Rybą Rest.
12. Pierogarnia u Dzika Rest.
13. Dom pod Łososiem Rest.
14. Tawerna Rest.
15. Pi Kawa Café
16. Cukiernia Kaliszczak (Bakery)

In the Main Town

You'll pay a premium to stay in the Main Town itself, but many find it worth the extra expense.

$$$ Kamienica Goldwasser, renting seven rooms over a good restaurant, is perfectly located, right on the river embankment next door to the Crane. Each room is different, but all are thoughtfully decorated, with windows facing both the river and the back. Three of the rooms are smaller and cheaper—similar to the bigger rooms, but with cramped bathrooms, and an especially good value. The restaurant has a special room that guests are encouraged to use as a lounge for congregating and socializing (small Sb-250 zł, big Sb-340 zł, small Db-340 zł, big Db-430 zł, extra bed-90 zł, lots of stairs and no elevator, Długie Pobrzeże 22, tel. & fax 058/301-8878, www.goldwasser.pl, kamienica@goldwasser.pl).

$$$ Hanza Hotel, also on the riverfront, offers a fun, neo-Hanseatic exterior and 60 modern, uninspired rooms. The location is ideal, but it's a lesser value than my other listings, with little character and a disinterested staff. Prices are sky-high in the summer, but drop to tempting lows off-season (June–Aug: Sb-665 zł, Db-695 zł; Sept–Oct and May: Sb-565 zł, Db-595 zł; Nov–April: Sb-395 zł, Db-465 zł; request riverview room in summer, when it costs the same as non-view room; non-view rooms 100 zł cheaper Nov–April only, elevator, air-con, Tokarska 6, tel. 058/305-3427, fax 058/305-3386, www.hanza-hotel.com.pl, hotel@hanza-hotel.com.pl).

$$$ Hotel Mercure Hevelius, the mighty silver tower dominating the Gdańsk skyline, doesn't look too inviting. But its 281 rooms are pleasant, well-located, and fairly priced—an unusual combination in central Gdańsk. One problem: It can be booked up far in advance with tour groups in the peak season (rack rates: Sb-410 zł, Db-470 zł, but you'll usually pay about 20 zł less, cheaper Fri–Sun and Nov–March; ask for a newer room, which costs the same as older rooms; elevator, air-con, between the Main Town and Solidarity shipyard at ulica Jana Heweliusza 22, reception tel. 058/321-0000, reservation tel. 058/321-0021, www.orbis.pl, mer .hevelius@orbis.pl).

$$ Pensjonat Dom Aktora, on a drab street in the Main Town, comes with no frills and challenging communication. Though it's not a great value, the location is good. Ten of its 12 rooms are actually multi-room apartments with kitchenettes, and the cheaper rooms go fast (1 Sb-200 zł, 1 twin Db-280 zł, small apartment-350 zł, bigger apartment-420 zł, even bigger apartment-500 zł, 20 percent cheaper Oct–April, ulica Straganiarska 55–56, tel. & fax 058/301-5901, www.domaktora.pl, biuro@domaktora.pl).

$ Przy Targu Rybnym is your best hostel option. It's well-located at the north end of the river embankment, just a three-minute walk from the Crane. Waldemar runs this easygoing, low-key place with a spirit of fun that permeates the chummy common room. Since it offers double rooms (bathroom down the hall), it's an attractive budget option even for non-hostelers ("private" room for 2–4 people-60 zł per person, bunk in dorm or crowded basement slumbermill-40 zł, private rooms might be more expensive in peak season, prices include sheets and breakfast, free Internet in lobby, free laundry service, ulica Grodzka 21, tel. 058/301-5627, www.gdanskhostel.com, gdanskhostel@hotmail.com). If they're booked up, Waldemar might send you to his **Baltic Hostel**, which is cheaper (45 zł per person in 2–4-person room, 35 zł for dorm bunk) but in a much less convenient location (away from the center, north of the train station at 3. Maya #25; tel. 058/721-9657, www.baltichostel.com, baltichostel@hotmail.com).

$ Dom Harcerza is a Polish-style budget hotel/hostel with 17 old, musty, but well-maintained rooms on the second floor of a dreary office building. It won't win any prizes for personality, but it's nicely located, in a quiet corner of the Main Town just two blocks south of the Golden Gate (bunk in 5- to 12-bed dorm-25 zł, D-100 zł, Db-200 zł, T-120 zł, Tb-250 zł, Q-140 zł, 25 percent cheaper Oct–April, includes sheets, breakfast-8 zł, cash only, fun ground-floor café, ulica Za Murami 2–10, tel. 058/301-3621, fax 058/301-2472, www.domharcerza.prv.pl, domharcerza@go2.pl).

EATING

In addition to the traditional Polish fare, Gdańsk has some fine Baltic seafood. Herring *(śledź)* is popular here, as is cod *(dorsz)*. Natives also brag that their salmon *(łosoś)* is better than Norway's. For a stiff drink, sample *Goldwasser* (better known in the U. S. as Goldschlager). This strong liqueur, flecked with gold, was supposedly invented here in Gdańsk. The following options are all in the Main Town, within three blocks of ulica Długa.

Budget Restaurants on the Main Drag

These two places are incredibly cheap, tasty, quick, and wonderfully convenient—right on ulica Długa. They're worth considering even if you're not on a tight budget.

Bar pod Rybą ("Under the Fish") is nirvana for fans of baked potatoes *(pieczony ziemniak)*. They offer more than 20 varieties, piled high with a wide variety of toppings and sauces, from Mexican beef to herring to Polish cheeses. They also offer fish dishes with salad and potatoes, making this a cheap place to sample local seafood. The surprisingly tasteful decor—walls lined with old bottles, antique wooden hangers, and paintings by the owner—is squeezed into a single cozy room packed with happy eaters (potatoes and fish dishes are each about 10–15 zł, daily 11:00–19:00, until

22:00 in summer, Długi Targ 35–38, tel. 058/305-1307).

Bar Mleczny Neptun is your best milk-bar option in the Main Town. A good meal, including a drink, runs about 10 zł. This popular place has more charm than your typical institutional milk bar. The items on the counter are for display—rather than take what's there, point to what you want and they'll dish it up fresh (Mon–Fri 7:00–18:00, until 19:00 in summer, Sat 9:00–18:00, open Sun only in summer 9:00–18:00, ulica Długa 33–34, tel. 058/301-4988). For more on milk bars, see page 202.

Moderately Priced Polish Fare

Kamienica Goldwasser, which also rents rooms (see "Sleeping," page 336), offers good Polish and international cuisine at fair prices. This is the best choice for dining along the riverfront embankment. Choose between cozy, romantic, austere indoor seating on several levels, or scenic outdoor seating (most main dishes 30–50 zł, open long hours daily, live piano music Thu–Sat nights, near the Crane at Długie Pobrzeże 22, tel. 058/301-8878).

Pierogarnia u Dzika ("By the Boar") offers 16 varieties of pierogi (Polish ravioli)—plus meat and fish dishes—in a contemporary setting enhanced by all manner of stuffed and skinned boar (pierogi-12–17 zł, main dishes-20–30 zł, daily 10:00–22:00, ulica Piwna 59–60, tel. 058/305-2676).

Splurges

If you don't mind paying top prices for top-quality cuisine, consider going high-class at these restaurants. They're both very expensive by local standards (most main dishes 50–80 zł), with long wine lists, Old World atmosphere, and fine food (with an emphasis on fish).

Dom pod Łososiem ("House under the Salmon"), with over-the-top formality, will make you feel like a rich burgher's family invited you over for dinner. This elegant restaurant has been serving guests for more than 400 years, racking up an impressive guest list—and, somewhere in there, inventing *Goldwasser* (daily 12:00–23:00, ulica Szeroka 52–54, tel. 058/301-7652).

Tawerna, a venerable old place just off the end of Długi Targ, is everyone's recommendation for fish dishes (mostly Polish-style, with some French elements). The *żurek* (sour soup) served in a bread bowl is delicious (main dishes 50–70 zł, seafood splurges to 100 zł, daily 11:00–23:00, reservations smart, ulica Powroźnicza 19–20, tel. 058/301-4114).

Coffee and Sweets

Pi Kawa (pronounced "pee" in Polish) is a trendy, atmospheric café with a wide variety of coffee drinks and herbal teas, best accompanied by the delicious *szarlotka* (Polish apple cake). The decor is cozy Old World, and it's packed with socializing locals (daily 10:00–22:00, ulica Piwna 5–6).

Cukiernia Kaliszczak, a bakery right on ulica Długa, is a no-frills throwback to the communist days, with delicious cakes and ice cream and delightfully grumpy service (daily 9:00–20:30, ulica Długa 74).

TRANSPORTATION CONNECTIONS

Trains

Gdańsk is well-connected to the Tri-City via the commuter SKM trains (see below). It also has frequent connections to Warsaw, and handy night trains to Berlin and Kraków.

From Gdańsk by Train to: Hel (town on Hel Peninsula, 3/day direct, 2.25–3.25 hrs, more with transfer in Gdynia), **Malbork** (about 2/hr, 1hr), **Toruń** (4/day direct, 3 hrs; more with a transfer in Bydgoszcz or Ilawa, at least hrly, 3–4 hrs), **Warsaw** (nearly hrly, 4 hrs), **Kraków** (3/day direct, 7 hrs; plus 1 night train, 10 hrs; more with transfer in Warsaw), **Berlin** (4/day, 8.25–9.25 hrs, transfer in Szczecin, Poznań, or Frankfurt an der Oder; plus 1 direct night train, 10 hrs).

Boats

Zegluga Gdańska offers several boat trips, which leave from the riverfront near the Green Gate, just upriver from the Crane (tel. 058/301-4926, www.zegluga.pl). Boats generally don't run in winter (Dec–March). All boat trips are weather permitting, especially for the faster hydrofoils.

The easiest quick cruise option is the 50-minute hydrofoil trip to **Westerplatte,** where World War II started—see page 332 (40 zł round-trip, 6/day in each direction, less off-season).

Boats from Gdańsk to other parts of the Tri-City (**Sopot, Gdynia**, and the town of **Hel**) run only in the summer (late June–Aug). During this time, two boats per day go in each direction between Gdańsk and Hel (1 of which stops at Sopot). Other boats conect Gdańsk with Sopot and Gdynia. Because the schedule can be very confusing, it's best to check details with the TI, who can help you sort through your options to find the best bet.

From April through late June and from September through mid-November, there are no boats from Gdańsk to Hel. But boats from Sopot and Gdynia still go to Hel—so you can take the SKM commuter train to those cities and continue on to the peninsula (see "Getting Around the Tri-City," below).

Near Gdańsk: The Tri-City
(Trójmiasto)

Gdańsk is the anchor of the three cities that make up the metropolitan region known as the Tri-City (Trójmiasto). The other two parts are as different as night and day: a once-swanky resort town (Sopot) and a practical, nose-to-the-grindstone business center (Gdynia). The Tri-City as a whole is home to bustling industry and a sprawling university, with several campuses and plenty of well-dressed, English-speaking students.

Sopot—boasting sandy beaches, tons of tourists, and a certain elegance—is clearly the more interesting day-trip option, while Gdynia offers a glimpse into workaday Poland. Beyond the Tri-City, the long, skinny Hel Peninsula—a sparsely populated strip of fishing villages and fun-loving beaches—arches dramatically into the Baltic Sea.

Getting Around the Tri-City

Gdańsk, Sopot, and Gdynia are connected both by regional commuter trains (*kolejka*, operated by SKM) and trains of Poland's national railway (operated by PKP). Trains to Hel are always operated by PKP. Tickets for one system can't be used on the other. While the two different trains chug along the same tracks, they use different (but nearby) stations. For example, at Gdańsk's Main Station, national PKP trains use tracks 1–3, while regional SKM trains use tracks 3–5. And in Sopot, the SKM station is a few hundred feet before the PKP station.

Regional SKM trains are much more frequent—they go in each direction about every 10 minutes (less frequently after 19:30). In Gdańsk, buy tickets at any kiosk marked *SKM Bilety*. Figure on 3 zł to Sopot, 4 zł to Gdynia. Before boarding, be sure to validate your ticket by punching it in the very easy-to-miss yellow or blue slots under the boards with SKM price information. Each city has multiple stops. In Gdańsk, use "Gdańsk Główny" (the end of the line); for Sopot, use the stop called simply "Sopot" (only one word); and for Gdynia, it's "Gdynia Główna" (the main station). For a more romantic approach, take the **boat** (see Gdańsk's "Transportation Connections," above).

Sopot

Sopot (SOH-poht), dubbed the "Nice of the North," was a celebrated haunt of beautiful people during the 1920s and 1930s, and remains a popular beach resort to this day.

Sopot was created in the late 19th century by Napoleon's doctor, Jean Georges Haffner, who believed Baltic Sea water to be therapeutic. By the 1890s, it had become a fashionable beach resort. This gambling center boasted enough high-roller casinos to garner comparisons to Monte Carlo.

The casinos are gone, but the health resorts remain, and you'll still see more well-dressed people here per capita than just about anywhere in the country. While it's no Cannes, Sopot features a relative feeling of high class unusual in otherwise unpretentious Poland. But even so, a childlike spirit of summer-vacation fun pervades—making it an all-around enjoyable place.

ORIENTATION

The main pedestrian drag, Monte Cassino Heroes Street (ulica Bohaterów Monte Cassino), leads to the Molo, the longest pleasure pier in Europe. From the Molo, a broad, sandy beach stretches in each direction. Running parallel to the surf is a tree-lined, people-filled path made for strolling.

Tourist Information: Sopot's TI is in front of the train station at ulica Dworcowa 4 (daily June–mid-Sept 9:00–20:00, mid-Sept–May 10:00–18:00, tel. 058/550-3783, www.sopot.pl).

Arrival in Sopot: From the station, exit to the left and walk five minutes. You'll run into the main drag, ulica Bohaterów Monte Cassino (marked by the big red-brick church). Follow it to the right, down to the seaside.

SIGHTS

Monte Cassino Heroes Street (Ulica Bohaterów Monte Cassino)—This in-love-with-life promenade may well be Poland's most manicured street. Especially after all the suburban and industrial dreck you passed through to get here, you'll be charmed by this pretty drag. The street is lined with happy tourists, trendy cafés, movie theaters, and late-19th-century facades (known for their wooden balconies). At the bottom of the boulevard, just before the Molo, pay 2 zł to climb to the top of the Art Nouveau lighthouse for a waterfront panorama.

Molo (Pier)—At more than 1,600 feet long, this is Europe's longest wooden entertainment pier. While you won't find any amusement-park rides, you will be surrounded by vendors, artists, and Poles having the time of their lives. Buy a *gofry* (Belgian waffle topped with whipped cream and fruit) or an oversized cloud of *wata cukrowa* (cotton candy), grab your partner's hand, and stroll with gusto.

For a jarring reality check, look over to Gdańsk. Visible from the Molo are two of the most important sites in 20th-century history: the towering monument at Westerplatte, where World War II started; and the cranes rising up from the Gdańsk Shipyard, where Solidarity was born and European communism began its long goodbye.

In spring and fall, the Molo is a favorite venue for pole vaulting—or is that Pole vaulting?

The Beach—Yes, Poland has beaches. Nice ones. When I heard Sopot compared to places like Nice, I'll admit that I scoffed. But when I saw those stretches of inviting sand as far as the eye can see, I wished I'd packed my Speedos. (You could walk from Gdańsk to Gdynia on beaches like this.) Most of the beach is public, except for a small private stretch in front of the Hotel Grand Sopot. Year-round, it's crammed with locals. At these northern latitudes, the season for bathing is brief and crowded.

SLEEPING AND EATING

Sopot is littered with resort hotels—but if you're staying here, you might as well sleep at one of the kitschiest. These two places, flanking the Molo and right on the beach, are expensive but fun. Both hotels have well-priced, well-regarded, extremely atmospheric seaview restaurants open long hours daily, serving good cuisine (Polish and Chinese, respectively).

$$$ Hotel Grand Sopot, a can't-miss-it landmark Art Nouveau place right next to the Molo, has 113 classic rooms—characteristic and only lightly renovated since the town's Golden Age. Outmoded, but clean and well-maintained, this is the best spot to capture the spirit of old Sopot. The three-story atrium, sumptuous dining room, and private stretch of beach will take you right back (July–Aug: Sb-355 zł, Db-445 zł, seaview Db-550–650 zł; April–June and Sept–Oct: Sb-345 zł, Db-430 zł, seaview Db-550–560 zł; Nov–March Sb-270 zł, Db-340 zł, seaview Db-440–520 zł; elevator, non-smoking rooms, ulica Powstańców Warszawy 12–14, tel. 058/551-0041, fax 058/555-6124, www.orbis .pl, rez.sogrand@orbis.pl). They could charge admission for room #226, a multi-room suite that has hosted the likes of Adolf Hitler, Marlene Dietrich, and Fidel Castro (but not all at the same time). With all the trappings of Sopot's belle époque—dark wood, plush upholstery, antique furniture—this room had me imagining Hitler sitting at the desk, looking out to sea, and plotting the course of World War II (890 zł April–Oct, 700 zł Nov–March).

$$$ Hotel Zhong Hua, co-owned by a Chinese businessman, takes its Asian theme seriously. With 49 rooms, it's smaller and humbler than the Hotel Grand Sopot, but it looks a little out of place—a Chinese pagoda right on the beach (Db-440 zł June–Aug, 330 zł April–May and Sept–Oct, 220 zł Nov–March, cheaper on weekends off-season, view rooms 50–100 zł more in summer, aleja Wojska Polskiego 1, tel. 058/550-2020, fax 058/551-7275, www.zhonghua.com.pl, minhong@gdy.pl).

Gdynia

Compared to its flashier sister cities, straightforward Gdynia (guh-DIN-yah) has retained a more working-class vibe, still in touch with its salty, fishing-village roots. Gdynia feels much younger than Gdańsk or Sopot, as it was mostly built in the 1920s to be Poland's main harbor after Gdańsk became a free city. Although not as attractive as Gdańsk or Sopot, Gdynia has an authentic feel and a fine waterfront promenade (www.gdynia.pl).

Gdynia is a major business center, and—thanks to its youthful, progressive city government—has edged ahead of the rest of Poland in transitioning from communism. It enjoys a certain affluence, with one of the highest income levels in the country. Many of the crumbling downtown buildings have been renovated, and Gdynia is becoming known for its top-tier shopping—all the big designers have boutiques here. If a local woman has been shopping on Świętojańska street in Gdynia, it means that she's got some serious złoty.

Because Gdańsk's port is relatively shallow, the biggest cruise ships must put in at Gdynia...leaving confused tourists to poke around town looking for some medieval quaintness, before coming to their senses and heading for Gdańsk. Gdynia is also home to a major military harbor, and an important NATO base.

To get a taste of Gdynia, take the SKM train to the "Gdynia Główna" station and walk down Starowiejska towards the Southern Pier (Molo Południowe). At the pier, you'll find a smattering of sights—an aquarium and a pair of permanently moored museum boats—but it's most interesting just to soak in this real-world Polish city.

Hel Peninsula
(Mierzeja Helska)

Out on the edge of things, this slender peninsula juts 20 miles into the ocean, providing a sunny retreat from the big cities—even as its shelters them from Baltic winds. Trees line the peninsula, and the northern edge is one long, sandy, ever-shifting beach.

On hot summer days, Hel is a great place to frolic in the sun with Poles. Sunbathing and windsurfing are practically a religion here. Small resort villages line Hel Peninsula: Władysławowo (at the base), Chałupy, Kuźnica, Jastarnia, Jurata, and—at the tip—a town also called Hel. Beaches right near the towns can be crowded in peak season, but you're never more than a short walk away from your own stretch of sand. There are few permanent residents, and the waterfront is shared by budget campgrounds and hotels hosting middle-class families, and mansions of Poland's rich and famous (former president Aleksander Kwaśniewski has a summer home here).

The easiest way to go to Hel—aside from coveting thy neighbor's wife—is by boat (see "Transportation Connections," page 339). Trains from Gdańsk also reach Hel, and from Gdynia, you can take a train, bus, or minibus. Hel is immensely popular in the summer, when it's notorious for its traffic jams.

POMERANIA

Malbork Castle and Toruń

The northwestern part of Poland—known as Pomerania (Pomorze)—has nothing to do with excitable little dogs, but it does offer plenty of attractions. Two in particular are worth singling out, both conveniently located between Gdańsk and Warsaw. Malbork, the biggest Gothic castle in Europe, also happens to be the most interesting castle in Eastern Europe. Farther south, the Gothic town of Toruń—the birthplace of Copernicus, and a favorite spot of every proud Pole—holds hundreds of red-brick buildings (and even more varieties of tasty gingerbread).

Planning Your Time

Malbork works well as a side-trip from Gdańsk (frequent 1-hour trains), and it's also on the main train line from Gdańsk to Warsaw. Toruń doesn't merit a long detour, but it's worth a stroll or an overnight if you want to sample a smaller Polish city. Ideally, if traveling round-trip from Warsaw, see one of these destinations coming to Gdańsk, and visit the other on the way back. Or do Malbork as a side-trip from Gdańsk, then visit Toruń on the way to Warsaw. If choosing one or the other, do Malbork.

Malbork Castle

Malbork Castle is soaked in history. The biggest brick castle in the world, the largest castle of the Gothic period, and one of Europe's most picturesque fortresses, it sits smugly on a marshy plain at the edge of the town of Malbork, 35 miles southeast of Gdańsk. This was the headquarters of the notorious Teutonic Knights, a

Gdańsk Day Trips

Germanic band of ex-Crusaders who dominated northern Poland in the Middle Ages.

When the Teutonic Knights were invited to Polish lands to convert neighboring pagans in the 13th century, they found the perfect site for their new capital here, on the bank of the Nogat River. Construction began in 1274. After the Teutonic Knights conquered Gdańsk in 1308, the order moved its official headquarters from Venice to Malbork. The Teutonic Knights remained here for nearly 150 years. They called the castle Marienburg, the "Castle of Mary," in honor of the order's patron saint.

At its peak in the early 1400s, Malbork was both the imposing home of a seemingly unstoppable army, and the final bastion of the ideals of chivalry in Europe. Surrounded by swamplands, with only one gate in need of defense, it was a tough nut to crack. Malbork Castle was never taken by force in the Middle Ages, though it had to withstand various sieges by the Poles during the Thirteen Years' War (1454–1466)—including a siege that lasted over three years. Finally, in 1457, the Polish king gained control of Malbork by buying off Czech mercenaries guarding the castle. Malbork became a Polish royal residence for 300 years. But when

Poland was partitioned in the late 18th century, this region went back into German (Prussian) hands. The castle became a barracks, windows were sealed up, delicate vaulting was damaged, bricks were quarried for new buildings, and Malbork deteriorated.

In the late 19th century, Romantic German artists and poets rediscovered the place. An architect named Konrad Steinbrecht devoted 40 years of his life to Malbork, painstakingly restoring the palace to its medieval splendor. A half century later, the Nazis used the castle to house POWs, and about half of it was destroyed by the Soviet army, who saw it as a symbol of longstanding German domination. If you look closely, you can still see the original and reconstructed parts.

Today Malbork has been restored once again to its Teutonic glory, and ranks among the most visit-worthy sights in Poland.

Cost, Hours, Information: Malbork has two seasons: high season (mid-April–Sept) and low season (Oct–mid-April). In high season, entry costs 30 zł, and the castle exhibits are open Tue–Sun 9:00–19:00 (grounds open until 20:00, last entry 19:30). In low season, it costs 19 zł, and the exhibits are open Tue–Sun 10:00–15:00 (grounds open until 17:00, last entry 15:30). It's always closed on Mon and holidays. The ticket office (marked *kasa*) generally opens 30 minutes before the castle. You'll pay an extra 16 zł for a sticker allowing you to take photos inside. In summer, they also offer a Family Ticket for a small savings (covers 1 or 2 adults and their children: 80 zł/3 people total, 102.50 zł/4 people, 125 zł/5 people, 147.50 zł/6 people). For details, see www.zamek.malbork.pl.

Tours of Malbork: You are required to enter the castle with a three-hour tour (Polish tour included in your ticket). This sounds like an intimidating commitment—but thoroughly seeing the place actually takes about that long. This policy is very loosely enforced, so you can easily tour the place on your own (using my self-guided tour, below) without being hassled—just enter with any tour, then wander off. Getting an **English tour** can be frustrating. In July and August, there are English tours three times a day (likely at 11:00, 13:30, and 15:30; included in your ticket). But the schedule can be unpredictable, and if there's not enough demand, you

may have to wait until a quorum of English-speakers gather (generally no longer than an hour). September through June, you have to pay 150 zł for an English tour, but this cost can be divided by everyone in your group. Take the initiative, play "tour guide," and get together a group of frustrated English-speakers by the cashier.

The Teutonic Knights

The Order of the Teutonic Knights began in the Holy Land in 1191, during the Third Crusade. Officially called the "Order of the Hospital of the Blessed Virgin Mary of the German House of Jerusalem," these German monks and knights took vows of poverty, chastity, and obedience. They also built hospitals, and cared for injured knights. When the Crusades ended in the 12th century, the order found itself out of a job, and went back to Europe. They set up shop in Venice, and reorganized as a chivalric order of Christian mercenaries—pagan-killers for hire.

The Teutonic Knights were hired for a gig in northern Poland in 1226. Duke Konrad of Mazovia wanted to subdue a tribe of pagans, called the Prussians, who had been attacking his lands. (Confusingly, these were pagan Slavs—*not* the same as the later goose-stepping Prussians who lived in what would become eastern Germany.) The Teutonic Knights—claiming to be missionaries (and wearing white cloaks decorated with black crosses)—spent 60 years "saving" the pagan Prussians by turning them into serfs or brutally massacring them.

Like houseguests who didn't know when to leave, the Teutonic Knights decided they enjoyed northern Poland—and stuck around. The Knights made themselves at home, building one of Europe's biggest and most imposing fortresses: Malbork. Because they were fanatical Christians, they won the support of the pope and the Holy Roman Emperor. When the Teutonic Knights seized large parts of northern Poland in 1308, including Gdańsk—cutting off Polish access to the Baltic Sea—the Polish royals began to realize their mistake. The Teutonic Knights invited more Germans to come join them, building their numbers and tightening their grasp on the region. They grew rich from Hanseatic trade, specializing in amber, grain, and timber. The Knights conquered Estonia and Latvia, and began to threaten the Poles' pagan neighbor to the east, Lithuania. By the late 14th century, the Teutonic Knights were enjoying a Golden Age at the expense of the Prussians, Poles, and Lithuanians.

On my last trip, it only took me a few minutes to gather together 10 strangers (only half of us Americans) eager for some English information—bringing the per-person cost of the tour down to just 15 zł. Ideally, contact the castle a day or two ahead to see if you can join a scheduled English tour, or to reserve a guide for yourself (tel. 055/647-0978, kasa@zamek.malbork.pl); communication can be difficult, so try to get a Polish person (such as your hotelier) to help you. Agnieszka Syroka, an excellent Gdańsk-based local guide, also does tours of Malbork (see page 309).

At about this time, Poland's long-lived Piast dynasty died out. Inspired by a mutual desire to fight back against the Teutonic Knights, the Poles and the Lithuanians decided to join their kingdoms. In 1386, the Polish Princess Jadwiga married Lithuanian Prince Władysław Jagiełło (who converted to Christianity for the occasion), uniting Poland and Lithuania and kick-starting a grand new dynasty, the Jagiellonians.

Just as every American knows the date July 4, 1776, every Pole knows the date July 15, 1410—the Battle of Grunwald. King Władysław Jagiełło and Grand Duke Vytautas the Great led a ragtag army of some 40,000 soldiers—Lithuanians, Poles, other Slavs, and even speedy Tartar horsemen—against 27,000 Teutonic Knights. At the end of the day, some 18,000 Poles and Lithuanians were dead—but so were half of the Teutonic Knights (and the other half had been captured). Poland and Lithuania were victorious. Though the Teutonic Knights remained in Poland—extending their Germanic cultural influence on the region well into the 20th century—their political power waned, they pulled out of Lithuania, and they once again allowed free trade on the Vistula. A generation later, the Thirteen Years' War (1454–1466) finally put an end to the Teutonic Knights' domination of northern Poland. The order officially dissolved in 1575, when they converted to Protestantism...though some conspiracy theorists (and *Da Vinci Code* enthusiasts) claim the Teutonic Knights are still very much active.

The Knights' influence on Poland persists today—even beyond the striking red-brick churches and castles scattered around the northern part of the country. The Polish novelist Henryk Sienkiewicz's *The Teutonic Knights* is a cultural benchmark and a favorite work of many Poles. The 19th-century Romantics who fanned the flames of Polish patriotism turned the Teutonic Knights into a symbol of Germanic oppression. Even today, Poles—and all Slavs—think of the Teutonic Knights as murderous invaders...while the Germans see them as a mere footnote in their history.

Again, if getting an English guide proves too complicated, simply enter with a Polish group and split off to do your own thing.

Best Views: The views of massive Malbork are stunning—especially at sunset, when the red brick glows. Be sure to walk out across the bridge over the Nogat River. The most scenic part of the castle is probably the twin-turreted, riverside Bridge Gate, which used to be connected by a bridge to the opposite bank.

Sound-and-Light Show: Every night from May through mid-September, there's a sound-and-light show in the castle courtyard. Though the commentary is in Polish, the show gives you a different perspective on the mighty fortress (15 zł, begins after dark—which can be as late as 22:00 at these northern latitudes). Don't make a special trip (or stay late) for this show—it really only makes sense if you're spending the night (see "Sleeping," page 358).

Getting There: Malbork is on the train line between Gdańsk and Warsaw. Coming by train from Gdańsk, you'll enjoy striking views of the castle on your right as you cross the Nogat River. The Malbork train station has a handy baggage-check office (*przechowalnia bagażu,* by ticket windows, 4 zł/bag); if it's closed, be insistent, and someone should eventually help you. To get from the station to the castle, consider taking a **taxi** (shouldn't cost more than 10 zł, though many corrupt cabbies charge twice that—keep asking until someone agrees to 10 zł). Or you can **walk** 15 minutes to the castle: Leave the station to the right, walk straight, and go through the pedestrian underpass beneath the busy road (by the red staircase). When you emerge on the other side, follow the busy road (noticing peek-a-boo views on your right of the castle's main tower) and take your first right turn (onto Kościuszki, the main shopping street). When you reach the fork at the end of the street, jog right, and head for the big, red castle (ticket office at far end).

SELF-GUIDED TOUR

The official tour of Malbork lasts about three hours. And, while there's plenty to see, this self-guided tour allows you to see it at your own pace. (Remember, you can split off from your group at any time.) This tour also works if you're tagging along with a Polish group, since it corresponds more or less to the route most Malbork guides take. Still, every guide is a little different, exhibits tend to move around, and entrances can be unexpectedly closed. Use a map to navigate and jump around as needed. The castle complex is a bit of a maze, with various entrances and exits for each room, often behind closed (but unlocked) doors. Don't be shy about grabbing a medieval doorknob and letting yourself in.

Lower Castle and Entrance Gate

Stand in front of the gate to one of Europe's most intimidating fortresses—home to the Grand Master, monks, and knights of the Teutonic Order. Across from the gate is the Lower Castle, which was an infirmary and hospital for injured knights and retirees. The end closest to you is the Chapel of St. Lawrence; farther away, the former farm buildings have been converted into hotel rooms and restaurants (see "Sleeping," page 358).

Malbork Castle

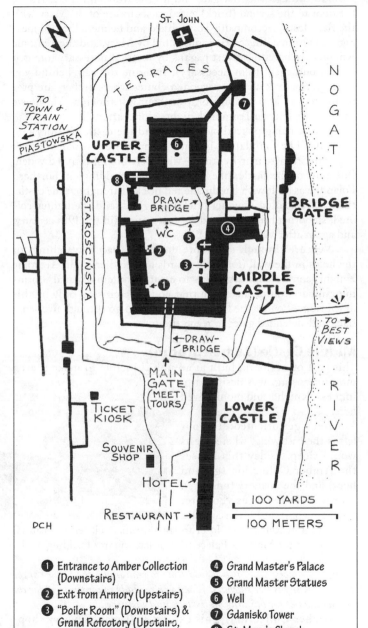

TO TOWN & TRAIN STATION

PIASTOWSKA

STAROŚCIŃSKA

ST. JOHN

TERRACES

N O G A T

UPPER CASTLE

6 Well

8 St. Mary's Church

DRAW-BRIDGE

WC

5

4

BRIDGE GATE

2

3

1

MIDDLE CASTLE

TO BEST VIEWS

DRAW-BRIDGE

MAIN GATE (MEET TOURS)

LOWER CASTLE

R I V E R

TICKET KIOSK

SOUVENIR SHOP

HOTEL →

RESTAURANT →

100 YARDS

100 METERS

DCH

1 Entrance to Amber Collection (Downstairs)

2 Exit from Armory (Upstairs)

3 "Boiler Room" (Downstairs) & Grand Refectory (Upstairs, but usually closed)

4 Grand Master's Palace

5 Grand Master Statues

6 Well

7 Gdanisko Tower

8 St. Mary's Church

Go through the first gate and up the wooden bridge. Above the door to the second (brick) gate is a sculpture of St. Mary with the Baby Jesus...accompanied by a shield and helmet. The two messages to visitors: This castle is protected by Mary, and the Teutonic Knights are here to convert pagans by force, if necessary (or, as it turned out, even if not necessary). Imagine the gate behind you closing. You look up to see wooden chutes where archers are preparing to rain arrows down on you. Your last thought: Maybe we should have left the Teutonic Knights alone, after all.

Before being pierced by arrows, read the castle's history into its walls: The foundation is made of huge stones, which aren't abundant in these marshy lands—they were brought from Sweden. But most of the castle, like so many other buildings in northern Poland, was built with handmade red brick. Throughout the castle, the darker-colored, rougher brick is original, and the lighter-colored, smoother brick was used for restoration (in the 19th century, and again after World War II).

Venture through two more enclosed spaces, watching for the holes in the wall (for more guards and soldiers). The Teutonic Knights connected nearby lakes to create a system of canals, forming a moat around the castle that could be crossed only by this drawbridge. Ponder the fact that you have to go through five separate, well-defended gates to reach the...

Middle Castle (Zamek Średni)

This part of Malbork, built at an uphill incline to make it even more imposing, was designed to impress. Knights and monks lived here.

Let's get oriented: To your left is the east wing, where guests would sleep. Today this houses the Amber Collection (ground floor) and the Armory (upstairs). To the right (west) as you enter the main courtyard is the complex of the Grand Refectory (closer to the entrance, closed to visitors) and the Grand Master's Palace (the taller, squarer building at the far end).

• *Before we move on, this is a good time to read up on the history of the Teutonic Knights (see sidebar). When you're ready to continue, enter the ground floor of the building on the left, and visit the...*

Amber Collection: This exhibit will make jewelry shoppers salivate. (Even as someone with zero interest in amber, I enjoyed it.) View the displays clockwise (and chronologically) from the entrance. Begin at the huge chunks of raw amber, and

All About Amber

Poland's Baltic seaside is known as the Amber Coast. You'll see amber *(bursztyn)* in the exhibit at Malbork, as well as in shop windows in Gdańsk (and throughout the country). This petrified pine-tree sap originated here on the north coast of Poland 40 million years ago. It comes in as many different colors as Eskimos have words for snow: 300 distinct shades, from yellowish-white to yellowish-black, from opaque to transparent. (I didn't believe it either, until I toured Malbork's collection.) Darker-colored amber is generally mixed with ash and sand—making it more fragile, and generally less desirable. Lighter amber is mixed with gasses and air bubbles.

Amber has been popular since long before there were souvenir stands. Archaeologists have found graves of Roman citizens (and their coins) who were buried with crosses made of amber. Almost 75 percent of the world's amber is mined in northern Poland, and it often simply washes up on the beaches after a winter storm. Some of the elaborate amber sculptures displayed at Malbork are created by joining pieces of amber with "amber glue"—made of melted-down amber mixed with an adhesive agent.

In addition to being good for the economy, some Poles believe amber is good for their health. A traditional cure for arthritis pain is to pour strong vodka over amber, let it set, and then rub it on sore joints.

the illuminated display of inclusions (bugs stuck in the amber, à la Jurassic Park). In the next cases are ancient amber artifacts, some of them up to 3,000 years old. These were found in graves, presumably put there by people who thought amber would help the deceased enter a better world. Along the rest of this wall are all manner of amber creations, from boxes and brooches to chess sets and pipes. Many of the finely decorated jewelry boxes and chests have ivory, silver, or shell inlays—better for contrast than gold. The portable religious shrines and altars could be used for travel, allowing people to remain reverent on the road and still pack light. At the end of the hall are two truly exquisite boxes of amber—the museum's prize possessions.

Working your way back up the other side of the room, you'll see more modern uses for amber—necklaces and other jewelry, miniature ships, wine glasses, and belts for skinny-waisted, fashion-conscious women. Look for the amber crucifix. This is a small replica of a six-foot-tall amber and silver cross presented to Pope John Paul II by the people of Gdańsk. In the display case by the door, you can see the full range of amber colors, from opaque white at the top, to transparent yellow in the middle, to virtually black at the bottom.

• *Now head upstairs to the...*

Armory: At the top of the stairs, flags commemorate the Battle of Grunwald, where the united forces of Poland (on the left) and Lithuania (on the right) defeated the Teutonic Knights (in the middle). Browse your way through the staggering array of swords, armor, and other armaments (English descriptions). Look for the 700-year-old "one-and-a-half-hand swords"—too big to be held in one hand. At the end, in the display of cannons, pikes, and spears, look for the giant shield. These shields could be lined up to form a portable "wall" to protect the knights.

Head downstairs to the second room of the armory, displaying suits of armor (including for horses). Here you'll see some seven-foot-long "two-hand swords" even bigger than the ones upstairs. On the left, find the suit of armor from the Hussars—Polish knights on horseback who had wings on their armor, which created a terrifying sound when galloping.

• *Head back outside and across the main courtyard, entering the smaller courtyard through the passage next to the dark-wood-topped tower. Find the steep steps down into the...*

"Boiler Room": The Teutonic Knights had a surprisingly sophisticated method for heating this huge complex. You see a furnace for fire down below, and a sort of a holding area for super-heated rocks up above. This method allowed the rocks to send heat through the vents without also filling them with smoke. This is one of 11 such "boiler rooms" in the castle complex. Later on, keep an eye out for little saucer-sized vents in the floor where the heat came through.

• *Near the boiler room—but generally closed to the public due to ongoing renovation work—is the...*

Grand Refectory: This enormous dining hall, damaged in World War II, is still being rebuilt. With remarkable palm vaulting and grand frescoes, the Grand Refectory hosted feasts for up to 400 people to celebrate a military victory or to impress a visiting king.

• *Now we're moving on into the Grand Master's Palace. There are two entrances to the palace, either of which might be locked: one in the small courtyard near the boiler room steps, and another one a bit farther up in the main courtyard. However you get there, climb the stairs up into the...*

Grand Master's Palace: This was one of the grandest royal residences in medieval Europe, used in later times by Polish kings and German Kaisers. From the top of the stairs, you'll head down the hall to the right. The door on your right leads to the **private rooms of the Grand Master**, with show-off decor (including some 15th-century original frescoes of wine leaves and grapes). The

Grand Master even had his own chapel, dedicated to St. Catherine. Though the Teutonic Order dictated that the monks sleep in dormitories, the Grand Master made an exception for himself—and you'll see his private bedroom (with rough original frescoes of 4 female martyrs).

• *Continue down the hall, noticing the troughs in the ground—anyone wanting an audience with the Grand Master had to wash both his hands and his feet.*

At the end of the hall, on the left, enter the elegant...

Summer Refectory: where the G.M. dined. With big stained-glass windows, and all of the delicate vaulting supported by a single pillar in the middle, this room was clearly not designed with defense in mind. In fact, medieval Polish armies focused their attacks on this room. On one legendary occasion, the attackers—tipped off by a spy—knew that an important meeting was going on here, and fired a cannonball into the room. It just barely missed the pillar. (You can see where the cannonball hit the wall, just above the fireplace.) The ceiling eventually did collapse during World War II.

As you continue into the **Winter Refectory,** notice fewer windows (better insulation) and the little manhole-like openings in the floor where the "central heating" came into the room.

• *Head back outside. At the top of the main courtyard, look for the four...*

Grand Master Statues: These four statues came from a 19th-century Prussian monument that was mostly destroyed when the Soviets took Malbork at the end of World War II. Though this was a religious order, these powerful guys look more like kings than monks. From right to left, shake hands with Hermann von Salza (who was Grand Master when the Teutonic Knights came to Poland); Siegfried von Feuchtwangen (who actually moved the T.K. capital from Venice to Malbork, and who conquered Gdańsk for the Knights—oops, can't shake his hand, which was supposedly chopped off by Soviet troops); Winrich von Kniprode (who oversaw Malbork's Golden Age, and turned it into a castle fit for a king); and Markgraf Albrecht von Hohenzollern (the last Grand Master before the order dissolved and converted to Protestantism).

• *To the right of the statues, continue over the...*

Drawbridge: As you cross, notice the extensive system of fortifications and moats protecting the innermost part of the castle. Check out the cracks in the walls—a increasing threat to the ever-settling castle set on this marshy, unstable terrain. The passage is lined with holes (for guards to view who was entering), with chutes up above (to pour scalding water or pitch on unwanted visitors). It's not quite straight—so a cannon fired here would hit the side wall of the passage, rather than entering the High Castle. Which is what you're about to do now.

High Castle (Zamek Wysoki)

This is the heart of the castle, and its oldest section. As much a monastery as a fortress, the High Castle was off-limits to all but 60 monks of the Teutonic Order and their servants. (The knights stayed in the Middle Castle.) Here you'll find the monks' dormitories, chapels, church, and refectory. As this was the heart and nerve center of the Teutonic Knights—the T.K. H.Q.—it was also their last line of defense. They stored tremendous amounts of food here in case of a siege.

In the middle of the High Castle courtyard is a **well.** At the top is a sculpture of a pelican. Because this noble bird is known to kill itself to feed its young (notice that it's piercing its own chest with its beak), it was often used in the Middle Ages as a symbol for the self-sacrifice of Jesus.

• *Take some time to explore the...*

Ground-Floor Exhibits: Working clockwise around the courtyard from where you entered, you'll find the following: A door leads to the prison and torture chamber (with small "solitary confinement" cells near the entrance), and a long hall behind with a single tiny window. Along the back of the cloister are WWII photos of Malbork. Beyond those, hiding in the far corner, is an exhibit on medieval stained-glass windows.

• *To the right from where you entered, you'll find the most interesting exhibit on this floor, the...*

Kitchen: This exhibit really gives you a feel for medieval monastery life. The monks who lived here ate three meals a day, along with lots of beer (made here) and wine (imported from France, Italy, and Hungary). A cellar under the kitchen was used as a primitive refrigerator—big chunks of ice were cut from the frozen river in winter, stored in the basement, and used to keep food cool in summer. Behind the long table, see the big dumbwaiter (with shelves), which connects this kitchen with the refectory upstairs. Step into the giant stove and look up the biggest chimney in the castle. In the next room is a demonstration of how medieval money was made. The Teutonic Knights minted their own coins—and you can buy your very own freshly minted replica today.

• *Now go back out into the courtyard, and climb up the stairs near where you came in. From the top of the stairs, the first door on the left leads to the most important room of the High Castle, the...*

Chapter Room: Monks gathered here after Mass, and it was also the site for meetings of Teutonic Knights from around the countryside. If a Grand Master was killed in battle, the new one would be elected right here. Each monk had his own seal and a name over his seat (for example, a hospitaler, who cared for the sick). The big chair belonged to the Grand Master. Above his chair, notice the little windows, connecting this room to St. Mary's

Church next door (described below). Church music would come into this room through these windows...Imagine the voices of 60 monks bouncing around these acoustics.

While monks are usually thought to pursue simple lives, the elegant vaulting in this room is anything but plain. The 14th-century frescoes (restored in the 19th century) depict Grand Masters. In the floor are more vents for the central heating.

Leave the Chapter House and walk straight ahead, imagining the monk-filled corridors of Teutonic times. The first door on the right is the...

Treasury: The first room has a small display of coins and amber (which helped make the Teutonic Knights rich). As you explore the rooms of the tax collector and the house administrator, notice the wide variety of safes and other lock boxes. Near the end, look for the small bed—for a small medieval person.

• *Continue around the cloister. At the end of the corridor, look for the little devil at the bottom of the vaulting (on the right, about eye level). He's pulling his beard and crossing his legs—pointing you down the long corridor to the....*

Gdanisko Tower: From the devil's grimace, you might have guessed that this tower houses the toilets. Follow his directions to the medieval WCs, in a tower set apart from the main part of the castle. The toilets dropped straight down into the moat; the bins were for cabbage leaves, used by the T.K. as T.P. This tower could also serve as a final measure of defense—it's easer to defend than the entire castle. Food was stored above, just in case.

• *Head back to the main part of the High Castle and continue around the cloister. The door halfway down on the right leads to the....*

Church Exhibition: These rooms used to be dormitories for the monks, and today they display a wide range of relics from the church (with English descriptions). The first room features an elaborate monstrance (vessel used to carry the Communion host) and a hands-less 15th-century sculpture of Jesus praying in the Garden of Gethsemane. The next room displays pictures of various eras of Malbork Castle, as well as some fragments of statues rescued from the destroyed St. Mary's Church. The huge, mangled crucifix dates from the mid-14th century. At the end of this exhibition is a replica of a Gothic altarpiece, with graphic paintings of the murder and dismemberment of Poland's patron saint, Adalbert.

• *Go back out into the hall and continue down to the end, arriving at the...*

Golden Gate: This elaborate doorway—covered in protective glass—marks the entrance to St. Mary's Church. Ringed with detailed carvings from the Old Testament, and symbolic messages about how monks of the Teutonic Order should live their lives, it's a marvelous example of late-13th-century art. On the left, find the five wise virgins who filled their lamps with oil, conserved it wisely, and are headed to heaven. On the right, the five foolish virgins who overslept and used up all their oil are damned, much to their dismay. The church itself is still pretty glum, though ongoing renovations should eventually restore it to its medieval splendor.

• *If the door's open, go ahead on into...*

St. Mary's Church: This holy site was destroyed in World War II and sat for decades with no roof. After so much neglect, it's finally being renovated...slowly. Pictures of the original church with English descriptions explain some of the fragments.

• *Go through the door on the left (as you exit St. Mary's Church) and take the narrow spiral staircase upstairs to the final set of exhibits.*

Top-Floor Exhibits: Walk through the two long hallways of temporary exhibits. At the end, go down the stairs into the monks' common room. Over the fireplace is a relief depicting the Teutonic Knights fighting the Prussians. To the left of that is the balcony where musicians could perform to entertain the monks after a meal. The next, very long room, with seven pillars, is the refectory, where the monks ate in silence. Along the right-hand wall are confessional-like, lockable storage boxes. At the end of this room, just before the door, notice the grated hole in the wall. This is where the dumbwaiter comes up from the kitchen (which we saw below).

Your Malbork tour ends here. A nearby door (sometimes locked) leads to the stairs up to the top of the tower. When finished, you can head back the way you came. En route, you can walk around terraces lining the inner moat, between the castle walls (stairs lead down off of the drawbridge). It's hardly a must-see, but it's pleasant enough, with the Grand Master's garden, a cemetery for monks, and the remains of the small St. Anne's Chapel (with Grand Master tombs).

SLEEPING

Malbork is so well-connected by rail to Gdańsk and Warsaw that there's little sense in sleeping here. The most compelling reason to stay in Malbork is to be here for the nighttime sound-and-light show in the castle courtyard.

$$ Hotel Zamek is housed in Malbork's Lower Castle, a red-brick building that was once a hospital, just across from the main part of the fortress. The 42 rooms are overpriced, dark, old-feeling, and a little creepy...but, hey—you're next door to Europe's grandest Gothic castle (Sb-210–270 zł, Db-250–320 zł, Tb-330–500 zł, higher prices are for mid-May–Oct, elevator, ulica Starościńska 14, tel. & fax 055/272-3367).

Sleep Code

(3.40 zł = about $1, €1 = about $1.20, country code: 48, area code: 012)
S = Single, **D** = Double/Twin, **T** = Triple, **Q** = Quad, **b** = bathroom, **s** = shower only. Unless otherwise noted, breakfast is included, credit cards are accepted, and English is spoken.

To help you sort easily through these listings, I've divided the rooms into three categories, based on the price for a standard double room with bath:

$$$ **Higher Priced**—Most rooms 400 zł (€100) or more.
  $$ **Moderately Priced**—Most rooms between
                            300–400 zł (€75–100).
    $ **Lower Priced**—Most rooms 300 zł (€75) or less.

TRANSPORTATION CONNECTIONS

From Malbork by Train to: Gdańsk (about 2/hr, 45 min), **Toruń** (about every 2 hrs, 3 hrs, transfer in Tcew or Iława), **Warsaw** (nearly hrly, 3.5 hrs direct).

Toruń

Toruń is a pretty, lazy, Gothic town conveniently located about halfway between Warsaw and Gdańsk. It's worth a couple of hours to stroll the wide pedestrian boulevards, ogle the huge red-brick buildings, and savor the flavor of one of Poland's most enjoyable mid-sized cities. With about 210,000 residents and 30,000 students (at Copernicus University), Toruń is a thriving burg.

Locals brag that Toruń is a "mini-Kraków." The squares are not nearly so grand, and the sights not as plentiful or as impressive. But the street life is arguably better—at once more bustling (with in-love-with-life, promenading locals who greet each other like they're long-lost friends) and more laid-back (fewer tourists and aggressive salesmen).

Toruń has two claims to fame: It's the proud birthplace of the astronomer Copernicus (Mikołaj Kopernik), and home to a dizzying variety of gingerbread treats *(piernikowa nuta)*.

ORIENTATION

(area code: 056)
Everything in Toruń worth seeing is in the Old Town, climbing up a gentle hill from the Vistula River. From the station (Toruń Główny, lockers available), take the underpass beneath track 4 (following signs for *wyjście do miasta*—"exit to the town"), and catch bus #22 or #27 into the center (a little over a mile, get off at first stop after long bridge, called Plac Rapackiego). A taxi into town should cost no more than 10 zł.

Tourist Information

The TI is on the main square, behind the Town Hall. Pick up the free map, and get information about hotels in town and city tours (Tue–Fri 9:00–18:00, Mon and Sat 9:00–16:00, closed Sun except May–Aug, when it's open 9:00–13:00, Rynek Staromiejski 25, tel. 056/621-0931, www.it.torun.pl).

SELF-GUIDED WALK

Welcome to Toruń

From the Plac Rapackiego bus stop, head into the town (through the passageways under the colorful buildings). Within a block, you're at the bustling **Old Town Market Square** (Rynek Staromiejski), surrounded by huge brick buildings and lively locals. The big building in the center is the **Old Town Hall** (Ratusz Staromiejski), with a boring museum and a climbable tower.

The guy playing his violin in front of the Town Hall is a **rafter**—one of the medieval lumberjacks who lashed tree trunks together and floated them down the Vistula to Gdańsk. This particular rafter came to Toruń when the town was infested with frogs. He wooed them with his violin and marched them out of town. (Hmm...sounds like a certain visitor to another medieval Hanseatic city, Bremen....)

The bigger statue, at the other end of the Town Hall, is of favorite son **Mikołaj Kopernik.** There's some dispute about Copernicus' origins; he was born in Toruń, all right, but at a time when it was a predominantly German town. So is he Polish or German? You can visit his birth house, now a museum to the astronomer, in a marvelously decorated brick building a block away (head down Żeglarska, lined with gingerbread shops, and take the first right—on Kopernika, of course—to #15/17).

Pick up some of Toruń's trademark **gingerbread** at one of the shops on the square, or down ulica Żeglarska. You can get it topped with any kind of jam or chocolate—take your pick.

Then join the human stream down the appropriately named **ulica Szeroka** ("Wide Street"), an enjoyable pedestrian promenade through the heart of town. At Przedzamcze, you leave the Old Town and enter the New Town (chartered only about 30 years later—both in the 13th century). While these areas are both collectively known today as the unified "Old Town," they were quite different in the Middle Ages—each with its own market square, and separated by a wall.

For a detour, follow that wall to the right, down Przedzamcze, to reach the **ruins** of the castle built by the Teutonic Knights who were so influential in northern Poland in the Middle Ages (see page 348). The castle was destroyed in the 15th century by the locals—who, aside from a heap of bricks, left only the tower that housed the Teutonic toilets.

Beyond the castle ruins is the **Vistula** riverbank. The road that runs along the river here is called Bulwar Filadelfijski—for Toruń's sister city in Pennsylvania.

SLEEPING

There are plenty of great options; Toruń has a surprising abundance of central, good-value places. The TI has a brochure listing the options, and can help you find a room for no extra charge.

$ Hotel Karczma "Spichrz" is a fresh, atmospheric hotel in a renovated old granary. Its 19 rooms and public spaces are a fun meld of old and new—with huge wooden beams around every corner, and the odor of the restaurant's wood-fired grill wafting through the halls. It's a little kitschy, but it's comfortable, central, and well-priced (Sb-190 zł, Db-250 zł, elevator, a block off the main drag towards the river at ulica Mostowa 1, tel. 056/657-1140, fax 056/657-1144, www.spichrz.pl, hotel@spichrz.pl).

TRANSPORTATION CONNECTIONS

Toruń is a handy stopover on the way between Warsaw and Gdańsk. Unfortunately, it's on a different train line than Malbork—so visiting both Toruń and the mighty Teutonic castle in the same day is surprisingly time-consuming, and not worth the bother.

From Toruń by Train to: Warsaw (5/day direct, 3 hrs; more with a transfer in Kutno), **Gdańsk** (4/day direct, 3 hrs; more with a transfer in Bydgoszcz or Ilawa, at least hrly, 3–4 hrs).

HUNGARY

HUNGARY

(Magyarország)

Hungary is an island of Asian-descended Magyars in a sea of Slavs. Even though the Hungarians have thoroughly integrated with their Slavic and German neighbors in the millennium since they arrived, there's still something about the place that's distinctly Magyar (MUD-jar). Visiting quirky, idiosyncratic Hungary is like looking at the rest of Eastern Europe in a mirror: Everything's a little different—in terms of history, language, culture, customs, and cuisine—but it's hard to put your finger on exactly how.

Just a century ago, Hungary controlled half of one of Europe's grandest empires. Today, perhaps clinging to their former greatness, Hungarians remain old-fashioned and nostalgic. With their dusty museums and bushy moustaches, they love to remember the good old days. Buildings all over the country are marked with plaques boasting *MŰEMLEK* ("historical monument").

Thanks to this focus on tradition, the Hungarians you'll encounter are generally polite, formal, and professional. Hungarians have class. Everything here is done with a proud

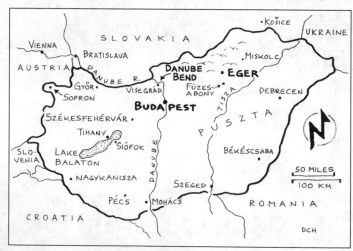

flourish. You get the impression that people in the service industry wear their uniforms as a badge of honor rather than a burden. When a waiter comes to your table in a restaurant, he'll say, *"Tessék parancsolni*—literally, "Please command, sir." The standard greeting, *"Jó napot kívánok,"* means "I wish you a good day." And when your train or bus makes a stop, you won't be alerted by a mindless, blaring beep or hoot—but instead, peppy music. (You'll be humming these contagious little ditties all day.)

Hungarians are just as orderly and tidy as Germans...in their own sometimes unexpected ways. Yes, Hungary has as much litter, graffiti, and crumbling buildings as any other Eastern European country, but you'll find great reason within the chaos. My favorite town name in Hungary: Hatvan. This means "Sixty" in Hungarian...and it's exactly 60 kilometers from Budapest. You can't argue with that kind of logic.

This tradition of left-brained thinking hasn't produced many great Hungarian painters or poets. But it has made tremendous contributions to the field of science, technology, business, and industry. Hungarians of note include Edward Teller (instrumental in creating the A-bomb), John von Neumann (a pioneer of computer science), Andy Grove (who, as András Grof, immigrated to the United States and founded Intel), and George Soros (who fled to the United States under communism, became a billionaire through shrewd investment, and is loved by the Left and loathed by the Right as a major contributor to liberal causes). Perhaps the most famous Hungarian "scientist" created something you probably have in a box in your basement: Ernő Rubik, and his famous cube. Hungary's enjoyment of a good mind-bending puzzle is also evident in their fascination with chess, which you'll see played in cafés, parks, and baths.

Like their Austrian neighbors, Hungarians know how to enjoy the good life. Favorite activities include splashing and soaking in their many thermal baths (see sidebar on page 430). "Taking the waters," Hungarian-style, should be your top priority while you're here. Though public baths can sound intimidating, they're a delight. I've recommended my two favorite baths in Budapest and a fine one in Eger, and given you careful instructions to help you enjoy the warm-water fun like a pro. (To allay your first fear: Yes, you can wear your swimsuit the entire time.)

Hungarians are also reviving an elegant, Vienna-style café culture that was dismantled by the communists. Classical music is revered, perhaps nowhere else outside Austria. Aside from scientists and businessmen, the best-known Hungarians are composers: Béla Bartók, Zoltan Kodály (who developed the famous solfege sight-singing method taught in music schools worldwide), and Franz Liszt (actually German, but of Hungarian ancestry).

Hungary Almanac

Official Name: Magyar Köztársaság, or simply Magyarország.

Snapshot History: Settled by the Central Asian Magyars in A.D. 896, Hungary became Catholic in the year 1000, and went on to become Christian Europe's front line in fighting against the Ottoman Turks in the 16th–17th centuries. After serving as co-capital of the vast Austro-Hungarian Empire and losing World Wars I and II, Hungary became a Soviet satellite until achieving independence in 1989.

Population: Hungary's 10 million people (similar to Michigan) are 90 percent ethnic Hungarians who speak Hungarian. One in 50 is Roma (Gypsy). Half the populace is Catholic, with 20 percent Protestants and 25 percent listed as "other" or unaffiliated. Of the world's approximately 12 million ethnic Hungarians, one in six lives outside Hungary (mostly in areas of Romania, Slovakia, Serbia, and Croatia that were once part of Hungary).

Latitude and Longitude: 47°N and 20°E, similar latitude to Seattle, Paris, and Vienna.

Area: 36,000 square miles, similar to Indiana or Maine.

Geography: Hungary is situated in the Carpathian Basin, bound on the north by the Carpathian Mountains and on the south by the Dinaric Mountains. Though it's surrounded by mountains, Hungary itself is relatively flat, with some gently rolling hills. The Great Hungarian Plain—which begins on the east bank of the Danube in Budapest—stretches all the way to Asia. Hungary's two main rivers—the Danube and Tisza—run north-south through the country, neatly dividing it into three regions.

Biggest Cities: Budapest (the capital on the Danube, 1.8 million), Debrecen (in the east, 210,000), and Miskolc (in the north, 180,000).

Economy: The Gross Domestic Product is $150 billion (a third of Poland's), but the GDP per capita is $15,000 (nearly 20 percent more than Poland's). Thanks to its progressive "Goulash communism," Hungary had a headstart on many other former Soviet Bloc countries and is now thriving, privatized...and largely foreign-owned. Despite high deficits, the country maintains a good credit rating. In the 1990s, many communist-era workers lost their jobs (especially women). Today, the workforce is small (only 57 percent of eligible workers) but highly skilled, producing and earning more than in other Eastern European countries. Grains, metals, and machinery are major products, and nearly a third of trade is with Germany.

Currency: 200 forints (Ft, or HUF) = about $1.

Government: The single-house National Assembly (386 seats) is the only ruling branch directly elected by popular vote. The legislators in turn select the figurehead President (currently the right-of-center László Sólyom) and the ruling Prime Minister (the Socialist Ferenc Gyurcsány). In April of 2006, Hungarians go to the polls to vote for a political party—there are two major parties and many lesser ones—which will in turn determine the next Prime Minister.

Flag: Three horizontal bands, top to bottom: red (representing strength), white (faithfulness), and green (hope). It's identical to the Italian flag—only flipped 90 degrees counterclockwise. It often includes the Hungarian coat of arms: horizontal red-and-white stripes (on the left); the patriarchal, or double-barred, cross (on the right); and the Hungarian crown (on top). In the communist era, a socialistic emblem was placed in the center of the flag. A memorable symbol of dissent in those times (especially during the 1956 Uprising) was a Hungarian flag with a hole cut in the middle.

The Average Hungarian: ...Eats a pound of lard a week (they cook with it). One in five Hungarians uses the Internet. The average family has three members, and they spend almost three-fourths of their income on (costly) housing. According to a recent condom-company survey, the average Hungarian has sex 131 times a year (behind only France and Greece), making them Europe's third-greatest liars.

First Name Last: In Hungary, a person's family name is listed first, and the given name is last—just as in many other Eastern cultures (think of Kim Jong Il). The composer known as "Franz Liszt" in German is "Liszt Ferenc" in his homeland. To help reduce confusion, many Hungarian business cards list the surname in capital letters.

As you can guess from the many grandiose structures built in Budapest in the late 1800s, Hungarians are also romantic. Over-the-top, melodramatic Latin American soap operas are popular here (dubbed into Hungarian, of course). When the European Union expanded on May 1, 2004, the biggest celebrations anywhere were here in Hungary—where people love an excuse to party.

While one in every four Hungarians lives in Budapest, the countryside plays an important role in Hungary's economy—this has always been a highly agricultural region. You'll pass fields of wheat and corn, but the grains are secondary to Hungarians' (and tourists') true love: the wine. After Hungarian winemaking standards plummeted under the communists, many vintner families are now reclaiming their land, returning to their precise traditional methods, and making their wines worth being proud of once more.

Somehow Hungary, at the crossroads of Europe, has managed to become cosmopolitan while remaining perfectly Hungarian. In the countryside, where less mixing has occurred, Magyar culture and occasional Central Asian facial features are more evident. But in the cities, the Hungarians—like Hungary itself—are a cross-section of Central European cultures: Magyars, Germans, Czechs, Slovaks, Poles, Serbs, Jews, Turks, Romanians, Roma (Gypsies), and many others. Still, no matter how many generations removed they are from Magyar stock, there's something different about a Hungarian—and not just the language. Look a Hungarian in the eye, and you'll see a glimmer of the marauding Magyar, stomping in from the Central Asian plains a thousand years ago.

Practicalities

Telephones: Like many things in Hungary, the telephone system is uniquely confusing. You must dial different codes whether you're calling locally, long distance within the country, or internationally to Hungary.

To dial a number in the same city, simply dial direct, with no area code.

To dial long-distance within Hungary, you have to add the prefix 06, followed by the area code (e.g., Budapest's area code is 1, so you dial 06-1, then the rest of the number).

To make an international call to Hungary, start with the international access code (00 if calling from Europe, 011 from the United States or Canada), then Hungary's country code (36), then the area code (but not the 06) and number.

To make an international call from Hungary, dial 00, the country code of the country you're calling (see chart in appendix), the area code if applicable (may need to drop initial zero), and the local number.

Top 10 Dates that Changed Hungary

A.D. **896**—The nomadic Magyars (a tribe from Central Asia) arrive in the Carpathian Basin and begin to terrorize Europe.

1000—The pope crowns King István (Stephen), marking the domestication of the Magyars.

1541—Invading Ottoman Turks take Buda and Pest...and cook with paprika.

1686—The Austrian Hapsburgs drive out the Turks, making Hungary part of their extensive empire (despite occasional rebellions from nationalistic Hungarians).

1848—A Golden Age begins, as Hungary gains semi-autonomy from Austria, rebuilds Budapest, rules surrounding territories, and inspires great artists.

1920—Losers in World War I, Hungary is stripped of two-thirds its territory and half its population in the Treaty of Trianon... and they're still angry about it.

1945—After World War II, the Soviet Union "liberates" the country and establishes a communist state.

1956—Hungarians bravely revolt, bringing a massive invasion of Soviet tanks and soldiers who brutally suppress the rebellion, killing 25,000.

1989—Hungary is the first of the Soviet satellites to open its borders with the West, sparking similar reforms throughout Eastern Europe.

2004—Hungary joins the European Union.

Hungarian phone numbers beginning with 0680 are toll-free; those beginning with 0620, 0630, or 0670 are mobile phones; and 0681 or 0690 are expensive toll lines. To call these numbers from within Hungary, simply dial direct. To dial them from outside Hungary, you need to drop the 06 at the beginning. So to call the Hungarian mobile phone number 0620-926-0557 from the United States, you dial 011 (the U.S. international access code), then 36 (Hungary's country code), then 20 (omitting the 06), then 926-0557.

Telephone cards, which you insert into pay phones, are sold locally at tobacco shops and newsstands. Cheap international telephone cards (which aren't insertable but can be used from virtually any phone—see page 35) are just catching on in Hungary.

Hungarian History

Hungary has a colorful and illustrious history. In terms of political influence in Eastern Europe's past, the Hungarians rank with the Germans and the Russians.

Who Are the Magyars?

The Magyars—the ancestors of today's Hungarians—are a mysterious lot. Of all Asian invaders to Europe, they were arguably the most successful—integrating more or less smoothly with the Europeans, and thriving well into the 21st century. Centuries after the Huns, Tatars, and Turks retreated east, leaving behind only fragments of their culture, the Hungarians remain a fixture in contemporary Europe.

The history of the Magyars before they arrived in Europe in A.D. 896 is hotly contested. Because their language is related only to Finnish and Estonian, it's presumed that these three peoples were once a single group, which likely originated east of the Ural Mountains (in the steppes of present-day Asian Russia).

After the Magyars' ancestors spent some time in Siberia, climatic change pushed them south and west, eventually (likely around the 5th century A.D.) crossing the Ural Mountains and officially entering Europe. They settled near the Don River (in today's southwestern Russia) before local warfare pushed them farther and farther west. The Magyars began running raids into European lands, eventually setting up camp in the Carpathian Basin—today's Hungary—in A.D. 896.

After dominating Europe for many decades, the Hungarians were routed in battle and forced to adopt Christianity—a turning point that ultimately allowed them to flourish in Europe. Over the next several centuries, the Hungarians' Asian features and customs mostly faded away as they intermarried with Germans,

Welcome to Europe

The Magyars, led by the mighty Árpád, thundered into the Carpathian Basin in A.D. 896. They were a rough-and-tumble nomadic people from Central Asia who didn't like to settle down in one place. They'd camp out in today's Hungary in the winters, and in the summers, they'd go on raids throughout Europe—terrorizing the Continent from Constantinople (modern-day Istanbul) to the Spanish Pyrénées. For half a century, they ranked with the Vikings as the most feared people in Europe.

After decades of running roughshod over Europe, the Hungarians were finally defeated by a German and Czech army at the Battle of Augsburg in 955. If they were to survive, the nomadic Magyars had to settle down. King Géza baptized his son, István (who was Árpád's great-great-grandson), and married him to a Bavarian princess at an early age.

Magyars Tamed

On Christmas Day in the year 1000, King István (Stephen) was

Slavs, and other European peoples. In fact, by the 16th century, the Hungarians became Europe's front line in fending off the invasion of another Asian group, the Ottoman Turks. Hungarian integration with the other peoples of Europe continued over the next several centuries, and through to the present day. In fact, a recent genetic study found that Hungarians are the most ethnically diverse nationality on the planet.

But even though certain aspects of their Magyar heritage have been lost, the Hungarians have done a remarkable job of clinging on to their Asian roots. They still do things their own way, making Hungary subtly but unmistakably different from its neighboring countries. And people of German-Hungarian, Slavic-Hungarian, and Jewish-Hungarian descent still speak a language that's not too far removed from the Asian tongue spoken by those original Magyars.

Were the Hungarians (Magyars) descended from the Huns, a similarly violent nomadic tribe that lived in the same area centuries earlier? Until recently, legends and historians speculated a tie between these two groups. In fact, the word "Hungarian" is at least partly derived from "Hun." But, even though it's a popular romantic notion to link these two mysterious tribes, recent historians strongly doubt that the two ever had anything to do with each other. Even so, many Hungarians still take pride in the legendary link to the Huns...and "Attila" remains a popular name even today.

crowned by the pope, and Hungary became a legitimate Christian nation (see page 404). The domestication of the nomadic Magyars was difficult, but Hungary eventually emerged as a major European power. The kingdom reached its peak in the late 15th century, when the enlightened King Mátyás Corvinus fostered the arts and sparked a mini-Renaissance (see page 402).

Turkish Invasion

Soon after the reign of good king Mátyás, the Turks came slicing their way through the Balkan Peninsula towards Central Europe. In 1526, they entered Hungary. By 1541, they took Buda. During the Turkish occupation, the Magyars moved the capital of the little that remained of their land—"rump Hungary"—to Bratislava (which they called "Pozsony"). During this era, the Ottomans built many of the baths that you'll still find throughout Hungary—and spiced up the food with paprika.

Crippled by the Turks and lacking power and options, Hungary came under control of the Austrian Hapsburg Empire, which finally wrested Buda from the Turks in 1686. The Hapsburgs repopulated Buda and Pest with Germans, while Magyars reclaimed the countryside.

The Hapsburgs

The Hungarians resisted Hapsburg rule, and three Magyars in particular are still noted for their rebellion against Vienna: Ferenc Rákóczi, who led Hungarians in the War of Independence (1703–1711); Lajos Kossuth, who was at the forefront of the 1848 Revolution; and Kossuth's contemporary, Count István Széchenyi, who fought the Hapsburgs with money—building structures like Budapest's iconic Chain Bridge. Countless streets, squares, and buildings throughout the country are named for these three Hungarian patriots.

But centuries of alliance with the Hapsburgs eventually paid off. After the 1848 Revolution in Hungary and an important military loss to the Prussians, Austria realized that it couldn't control its rebellious Slavic holdings all by itself. With the Compromise of 1867, Austria granted Budapest the authority over the eastern half of their lands, creating the so-called Dual Monarchy of the Austro-Hungarian Empire.

Hungary enjoyed a Golden Age and Budapest prospered, governing large parts of today's Slovakia, Croatia, and Transylvania (northwest Romania). Composers Franz Liszt (more German than Magyar) and Béla Bartók incorporated the folk and Gypsy songs of the Hungarian and Transylvanian countryside into their music.

The Crisis of Trianon

Hungary, allied with Austria and Germany, came up on the losing end of World War I. As retribution, the 1920 Treaty of Trianon (named for the palace on the grounds of Versailles where it was signed) reassigned two-thirds of Hungary's former territory and half of its population to Romania, Czechoslovakia, Slovenia, Croatia, and Serbia. Not unlike the overnight construction of the Berlin Wall, towns along the new Hungarian borders were suddenly divided down the middle. Many Hungarians found themselves unable to cross over to visit relatives or commute to a job that was in the same country the day before. This sent hundreds of thousands of Hungarian refugees—now "foreigners" in their own towns—into Budapest, sparking an enormous boom in the capital.

To this day, the Treaty of Trianon is regarded as one of the greatest tragedies of Hungarian history. More than two million ethnic Hungarians live outside Hungary (mostly in Romania)—and many Hungarians claim that these lands still belong to the Magyars. The sizeable Magyar minorities in neighboring countries have often been mistreated—particularly in Romania (under

Ceauçescu), Yugoslavia (under Milošević), and Slovakia (under Mečiar). You'll see maps, posters, and bumper stickers with the distinctive shape of a much larger, pre-WWI Hungary...patriotically displayed by Magyars who feel as strongly about Trianon as if it happened yesterday. When the European Union expanded in 2004, some Hungarians saw it as a happy ending in the big-picture sense—they were once again united with Slovakia, part of the territory they had lost.

After World War I, the newly shrunken Kingdom of Hungary had to reinvent itself. The WWI hero Admiral Miklós Horthy had won many battles with the Austro-Hungarian navy. Though the new Hungary had no sea and no navy, Horthy retained his rank and ruled the country as a regent. A popular joke points out that during this time, Hungary was a "kingdom without a king" and a landlocked country ruled by a sea admiral. This sense of compounded deficiency pretty much sums up the morose attitude Hungarians have about those gloomy post-Trianon days.

World War II and the Arrow Cross

As Hitler rose to power, some countries that had felt unfairly treated in the aftermath of World War I—including Hungary and Croatia—saw Nazi Germany as a vehicle to greater independence. Admiral Horthy ceded power to the Nazis with the hope that they might help Hungary regain the crippling territorial losses of Trianon. Being an ally of the Nazis, rather than an occupied state, also allowed Hungary a certain degree of self-determination through the war—including saving its sizeable Jewish population from concentration camps. Winning back chunks of Slovakia, Transylvania, and Croatia in the early days of World War II also bolstered the Nazis' popularity in Hungary.

As Nazism took hold in Germany, the Hungarian fascist movement—spearheaded by the Arrow Cross Party (Nyilaskeresztes Párt)—gained popularity within Hungary. And as Germany increased its demands for Hungarian soldiers and food, Admiral Horthy resisted...until Hitler's patience wore thin. In March of 1944, the Nazis invaded and installed the Arrow Cross in power. The Arrow Cross made up for lost time, immediately beginning a savage campaign of executing Hungary's Jews—not only sending them to concentration camps, but butchering them in the streets. Almost 600,000 Hungarian Jews were murdered. For more on this dark era of Hungarian history, see the "House of Terror" museum listing on page 420 of the Budapest chapter.

The Soviet Army eventually liberated Hungary—but at the expense of Budapest, where a months-long siege reduced the proud city to rubble.

Communism...with a Pinch of Paprika

After World War II, the Soviets installed Mátyás Rákosi as head of state. In 1956, the Hungarians staged an uprising, led by Communist Party reformer Imre Nagy (see page 408). Moscow sent in troops, 25,000 Hungarians were killed, and 250,000 fled to the West. (If you know any Hungarians back home, their families more than likely fled to the U.S. in 1956.) János Kádár was installed to run a harder-line government, and though he cooperated with Moscow, he gradually allowed the people of Hungary more freedom than citizens of neighboring countries had.

Life here was better and more colorful than elsewhere in the Soviet bloc—a system dubbed "goulash communism." With little fanfare, the Hungarian parliament—always skeptical of the Soviets—peacefully voted to end the communist regime in February of 1989. Later that year, Hungary was the first Eastern Bloc nation to open its borders to the West, a major advance in the fall of communist regimes across Eastern Europe.

In 2004, Hungary eagerly joined the EU, excited about its future in a united Europe.

Hungarian Food

Hungary is known in Eastern Europe for its spicy food. Hungarian cuisine is as rich and complex as Polish and Czech food are simple. Everything is heavily seasoned: with paprika, tomatoes, and peppers of every shape, color, size, and flavor.

Hungarians dine at a *vendéglő* or *étterem* (restaurant). They gather with friends at a *kávéház* (café, literally, "coffeehouse"), which sometimes has light food, too. And for dessert, it's a *cukrászda* (pastry shop—*cukr* means "sugar").

Many American visitors to Hungary can't wait to taste goulash in its homeland—only to be disappointed that it isn't quite what they expected. The word "goulash" comes from the Hungarian *gulyás leves,* or "shepherd's soup." Here in its homeland, it's a clear, spicy broth with chunks of meat, potatoes, and other vegetables. Only outside of Hungary is the word used to describe a thick stew.

Aside from the obligatory *gulyás,* make a point of trying another unusual Hungarian specialty: cold fruit soup *(hideg gyümölcs leves).* This cream-based treat—generally eaten, like other soups, before the meal, even though it tastes more like a dessert—is usually made with *meggy* (sour cherries), but you'll also see versions with *alma* (apples) or *körte* (pears). Other Hungarian soups *(levesek)* include *bableves* (bean soup), *zöldségleves* (vegetable soup), *gombaleves* (mushroom soup), and *halászlé* (fish broth with paprika).

Hungarians adore all kinds of meat *(hús).* *Csirke* is chicken, *borjú* is veal, *kacsa* is duck, *liba* is goose, *libamáj* is goose liver (which shows up more often than you'd think), *sertés* is pork, *sonka*

Paprika Primer

The quintessential ingredient in Hungarian cuisine is paprika. In Hungarian, the word *paprika* can mean both peppers (red or green) and the spice that's made with them. Peppers can be stewed, stuffed, sautéed, baked, grilled, or pickled. For seasoning, red shakers of dried paprika join the salt and pepper on tables.

There are more than 40 varieties of paprika spice, with two main types: hot (*csípős* or *erős*) and sweet (*édesnemes* or simply *édes*, often comes in a white can). A can of paprika is a handy and tasty souvenir of your trip (see "Shopping" in the Budapest chapter, page 436). On menus, anything cooked *paprikás* (PAH-pree-kash) will be a little spicy.

In the fall of 2004, Hungary endured a paprika crisis. The spice was banned because some warehouse supplies were contaminated with aflatoxin, a poisonous substance caused by fungus. Because aflatoxin doesn't grow in the Hungarian climate, imported paprika from the tropics was blamed. After this scare, you can rest assured that today's Hungarian paprika is top-quality.

is ham, *kolbász* is sausage, *szelet* is schnitzel (*Bécsi szelet* means Wiener schnitzel)—and the list goes on. Fat is used quite a bit in cooking, making Hungarian cuisine very rich and filling. Meat goes well with *káposzta* (cabbage), which may be *töltött* (stuffed) with the meat.

Vegetarians have a tricky time in Hungary, with many restaurants able to offer only a plate of deep-fried vegetables. They haven't quite figured out how to do a good, healthy, leafy salad; a traditional restaurant will generally offer only marinated cucumbers (listed on menus as "cucumber salad"), a plate of sliced-up pickles ("pickled cucumbers"), marinated spicy peppers, or something with cabbage—using lettuce only as a garnish.

In Hungary, you sometimes pay for *köretek* (starches) separately from the meat course, which can be confusing for foreigners. You'll be asked to choose between *galuska* (noodles, traditional and recommended), *burgonya* (potatoes), *krumpli* (French fries), *krokett* (like Tater Tots), or *rizs* (rice). *Kenyér* (bread) often comes with the meal.

A popular snack, especially in Budapest, is *lángos*—a savory deep-fried doughnut spread with cheese, garlic, and sour cream. In restaurants, a fancier version (often with meat) can be served as an entrée.

Pastries are a big deal here. Hungary's streets are lined with *cukrászda* (pastry shops). You have many options; simply point to what you want, and chow down. Try the *Dobos torta* (a layered chocolate-and-caramel cream cake), *somlói galuska* (a dumpling with vanilla, nuts, and chocolate), anything with *gesztenye* (chestnuts), and *rétes* (strudel with various fillings, including *túrós*, curds). On dessert menus at restaurants, you'll also see *palacsinta* (pancakes), usually served *diós* (with walnuts), *mákos* (with poppy seeds), or *gündel* (with nuts, chocolate, cream, and raisins). And many *cukrászda* also serve *fagylalt* (ice cream, *fagyi* for short), sold by the *gomboc* (ball).

To drink: *Sör* means "beer," and *bor* means "wine" (*vörös* is red and *fehér* is white). For more on Hungarian wines, see page 475 in the Eger chapter. *Kávé* and *tea* (pronounced TEY-ah) are coffee and tea, and *víz* (water) comes as *szódavíz* (soda water, sometimes just carbonated tap water) or *ásványvíz* (spring water, more expensive).

Unicum is a unique and beloved Hungarian liqueur made of 40 different herbs and aged in oak casks. The flavor is powerfully unforgettable—like Jägermeister, but harsher. A swig of Unicum is often gulped before the meal, but it's also used as a cure for an upset stomach (especially if you've eaten too much rich food—not an uncommon problem in Hungary). The liqueur has a history as unique and complicated as its flavor. Invented by a Doctor Zwack in the late 18th century, the drink impressed Hapsburg emperor Josef II, who supposedly declared: *"Das ist ein Unikum!"* ("This is a specialty!"). The Zwack company went on to thrive during Budapest's late-19th-century Golden Age (when Unicum was the subject of many whimsical Guinness-type ads). But when the communists took over after World War II, the Zwacks fled to America—taking their secret recipe for Unicum with them. The communists continued to market the drink with their own formula, which left Hungarians (literally and figuratively) with a bad taste in their mouths. In a landmark case, the Zwacks sued the communists for infringing on their copyright...and won. In 1991, Péter Zwack—who had been living in exile in Italy—triumphantly returned to Hungary and resurrected the original family recipe. To get your own taste of this family saga, look for the round bottle with the red cross on the label (www.zwack.hu).

If you're drinking with some new Magyar friends, impress them with the standard toast: *Egészségedre* (EH-gehs-sheh-geh-dreh; "to your health"). But don't clink your glasses with theirs. They still remember the 1848 Revolution against the Hapsburgs, which ended with the Hapsburg execution of 13 great Hungarian leaders. The Hapsburgs clinked their beer mugs to the victory. To this very day, clinking mugs is, for many Hungarians, just bad style.

When your waiter brings your food, he'll probably say, *"Jó étvágyat!"* (Bon appétit!). When you're ready for the bill, you can simply say, *"Fizetek"* (FEE-zeh-tehk—literally, "I'll pay").

Key Hungarian Phrases

English	Hungarian	Pronounced
Hello. (formal)	*Jó napot kívánok.*	yoh NAH-pot KEE-vah-nohk
Hi. / Bye. (informal)	*Szia.*	SEE-yah
Do you speak English?	*Beszél angolul?*	BEH-sehl AHN-goh-lool
Yes. / No.	*Igen. / Nem.*	EE-gehn / nehm
Please.	*Kérem.*	KAY-rehm
You're welcome.	*Szívesen.*	SEE-veh-shehn
Can I help you?	*Tessék.*	TEHSH-shehk
Thank you.	*Köszönöm.*	KUR-sur-nurm
I'm sorry. / Excuse me.	*Bocsánat.*	BOH-chah-nawt
Good.	*Jól.*	yohl
Goodbye.	*Viszont látásra.*	VEE-sohnt-lah-tahsh-rah
one / two	*egy / kettő*	edj / KEH-tur
three / four	*három / négy*	HAH-rohm / nedj
five / six	*öt / hat*	urt / hawt
seven / eight	*hét / nyolc*	heht / NEE-ohlts
nine / ten	*kilenc / tíz*	KEE-lehnts / teez
hundred	*száz*	sahz
thousand	*ezer*	EH-zehr
How much?	*Mennyi?*	MEHN-yee
local currency	*forint (Ft)*	FOH-reent
Where is...?	*Hol van...?*	hohl vawn
...the toilet	*...a toalet*	aw TOH-ah-leht
men	*férfi*	FEHR-fee
women	*női*	NUR-ee
water / coffee	*víz / kávé*	veez / KAH-veh
beer / wine	*sör / bor*	shewr / bohr
Cheers!	*Egészségedre!*	EH-gehs-sheh-geh-dreh
the bill (literally, "I'll pay")	*fizetek*	FEE-zeh-tehk

Hungarian Language

Hungarians have an endearing habit of using the English word "hello" for both "hi" and "bye," just like the Italians use *"ciao."* You'll often overhear a Hungarian end a telephone conversation with a cheery "Hello!" While the language is overwhelming for tourists, one easy word is *"Szia"* (SEE-yah), which actually does mean hello or goodbye.

Even though Hungary is surrounded by Slavs, Hungarian is not at all related to Slavic languages. In fact, Hungarian isn't related to *any* European language (except for very distant relatives Finnish and Estonian). It isn't even an Indo-European language—which means that English is more closely related to Hindi, Russian, and French than it is to Hungarian.

Hungarian is agglutinative, which means that you start with a simple root word and then start tacking on suffixes to create meaning—sometimes resulting in a pileup of extra sounds at the end of a very long word. The emphasis always goes on the first syllable, and the following syllables are droned downhill in a kind of a monotone—giving the language a distinctive cadence that Hungary's Slavic neighbors love to tease about.

Hungarian pronunciation is straightforward, once you remember a few key rules. The trickiest: *s* alone is pronounced "sh," while *sz* is pronounced simply "s." This explains why you'll hear in-the-know travelers pronouncing Budapest as "BOO-dah-pesht." You might catch the *busz* up to Castle Hill—pronounced just like we say "bus." And "Franz Liszt" is easier to pronounce than it looks: It sounds just like "list."

The letter *c* and the combination *cz* are both pronounced "ts" (as in "cats"). The combination *zs* is pronounced "zh" (like "measure"). The letters *j* and *ly* are interchangeable, and both are pronounced as "y."

Hungarian has a set of unusual palatal sounds that don't quite have a counterpart in English. To make these sounds, gently press the thick part of your tongue to the roof or your mouth (instead of using the tip of your tongue behind your teeth, as we do in English): *gy* sounds more or less like "dg" in "ledger"; *ny* sounds kind of like the "ny" in "canyon"; and *cs* sounds like "ch."

As for vowels: The letter *a* almost sounds like o (aw); but with an accent *(á)*, it brightens up to the more standard "ah." As with Czech, an accent *(á, é, í, ó, ú)* indicates that you linger on that vowel (but not necessarily that you stress that syllable). Like German, Hungarian has umlauts *(ö, ü)*, meaning you purse your lips when you say that vowel. A long umlaut *(ő, ű)* is the same sound, but you hold it a little longer.

Okay, maybe it's not *so* simple. But you'll get the hang of it.

As you're tracking down addresses, these definitions will help: *tér* (square), *utca* (road), *út* (boulevard), *körút* (ring road), *fürdő* (bath), and *híd* (bridge). Words ending in *k* are often plural.

BUDAPEST

Budapest is the capital of Eastern Europe. It's a city of nuance and paradox—cosmopolitan, complicated, and challenging for the first-timer to get a handle on. Novices are sometimes overwhelmed by Budapest—but seasoned travelers enjoy this grand city more with each return visit. Though Prague and Kraków have more romance (and crowds), travelers in the know find Budapest to be Eastern Europe's most fascinating and rewarding destination.

Budapest is hot—literally. The city sits on a thin layer of earth above thermal springs, which power its many baths. Even the word *Pest* comes from a Slavic word for "oven." Two thousand years ago, the Romans had a settlement, Aquincum, on the north edge of today's Budapest. Several centuries later, in A.D. 896, the Magyars arrived from the steppes of Russia and took over the Carpathian Basin (roughly today's Hungary). In the 16th century, the Ottoman Turks invaded—occupying the region for 145 years. When the Turks were forced out, Buda and Pest were in ruins. The Hapsburgs repopulated them, giving the cities a more Austrian style.

The Great Compromise of 1867 granted Hungary an equal stake in the Austro-Hungarian Empire. Six years later, the cities of Buda, Pest, and Óbuda united to form the capital city of Budapest, which governed a huge chunk of Eastern Europe. For the next few decades, Hungarian culture enjoyed a Golden Age, and Budapest was a boomtown. The expansion reached its peak with a flurry of construction surrounding the year 1896—Hungary's 1,000th birthday (see page 389).

During the Soviet era, Hungary's milder "goulash" communism meant that Budapest, though still oppressed, was a place

Budapest Overview

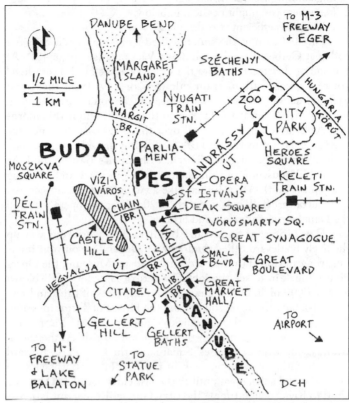

To M-3
FREEWAY
& EGER

DANUBE BEND

MARGARET
ISLAND

SZÉCHENYI
BATHS

HUNGÁRIA KÖRÚT

1/2 MILE
1 KM

MARGIT BR.

NYUGATI
TRAIN
STN.

ZOO

CITY
PARK

BUDA

PARLIA-
MENT

HEROES'
SQUARE

MOSZKVA
SQUARE

VÍZI-
VÁROS

PEST

ANDRÁSSY ÚT

OPERA

KELETI
TRAIN STN.

DÉLI
TRAIN
STN.

CHAIN
BR.

ST. ISTVÁN'S

DEÁK SQUARE

VÖRÖSMARTY SQ.

CASTLE
HILL

ELIS.
BR.

VÁCI UTCA

GREAT SYNAGOGUE

HEGYALJA ÚT

SMALL
BLVD.

GREAT
BOULEVARD

CITADEL

LIB.
BR.

GREAT
MARKET
HALL

DANUBE

TO
AIRPORT

GELLÉRT
HILL

GELLÉRT
BATHS

TO M-1
FREEWAY
& LAKE
BALATON

TO
STATUE
PARK

DCH

where other Eastern Europeans felt they could let loose. Twenty years ago, a stroll down Váci utca was the closest Czechs and Poles could get to a day pass to the West—including a chance to taste a Big Mac at the first McDonald's behind the Iron Curtain.

Budapest was built as the head of a much larger empire than it currently governs. Like Vienna, the city today feels a bit too grandiose for the capital of a relatively small country. But Budapest remains the heart and soul of Eastern Europe. It's a rich cultural stew made up of Hungarians, Germans, Slavs, and Jews, with a dash of Turkish paprika—simmered for centuries in a thermal bath. Each group has left its mark, but through it all, something has remained that is distinctly...Budapest.

Planning Your Time

Budapest demands at least three nights and two full days. Budapest has oodles of good museums, but none of them is strictly must-see; which ones you visit depends entirely on your interests. Skim my

listings and figure out which sights sound good to you. I've suggested where you might fit them in below.

I like this efficient two-day plan:

Day 1: Begin at the square called Vörösmarty tér, consider
coffee at Gerbeaud, and stroll down Váci utca (see page 412). At
the end of the street, explore the Great Market Hall. From here,
you're a quick walk or tram ride (#47 or #49) from the Great
Synagogue and the National Museum. If you're interested in
touring the Parliament—farther to the north—do it this morning. After lunch in Pest, stroll over the Chain Bridge and ride
the funicular up to Castle Hill. Following my self-guided walk
(page 395), visit Matthias Church, Fishermen's Bastion, and the
Castle Hill museums of your choice (the Commerce and Catering
Museum is best). After dinner, take a twilight sightseeing cruise,
go to a concert (folk music nightly at 20:00) or the opera, or stroll
the Danube embankments and bridges.

Day 2: Start at St. István's Basilica, then work your way up
the lively boulevard called Andrássy út. Depending on your interests, you can stop at (in this order): the Postal Museum, the Opera
House (duck in to see the lobby, or return later for a full-blown
tour at 15:00 or 16:00), Franz Liszt Square (lots of cafés and restaurants), busy Oktogon square, and the House of Terror museum.
To skip ahead (or backtrack quickly), hop on the M1 Metro line,
which runs beneath Andrássy út from start to finish. At the end of
Andrássy út, explore Heroes' Square and the City Park. Reward
yourself with a nice, long soak in the Széchenyi Baths (secure
lockers, rental suits, open until 19:00, last entry 18:00, get there by
17:00 to have enough time). The ritzy Gundel Restaurant is across
from the baths, and other, less-fancy dining options are nearby.
For the evening, consider the same options as for Day 1.

To speed things up and fit in Statue Park, start with the statues in the morning of Day 2 (bus departs Deák tér at 11:00), then
do an accelerated ramble down Andrássy boulevard.

You'll have no trouble filling a third day—it gives you more
time to fit in Statue Park, more museums, and outlying areas (such
as Óbuda and Szentendre). After many years, I still discover new
joys each time I return.

Eger is the best day trip (2.25 hrs by train each way, even
better if you spend the night—see Eger chapter). Szentendre, on
the Danube Bend, is closer but very touristy (doable in a half day
or even just in the late afternoon/evening). With a car (or a hired
driver—see "Drivers," page 391), you could spend a day seeing the
entire Danube Bend—Szentendre, Visegrád, and Esztergom—
ideally on the way to Vienna or Bratislava (see Danube Bend
chapter).

Budapest Essentials

English	Hungarian	Pronounced
Square	Tér	tehr (said pulling cheeks back)
Street	Utca	OOT-zah
Boulevard	Út	oot
Bridge	Híd	heed
Ring Road	Körút	KUR-root
Funicular	Sikló	SHEE-kloh
Bath	Fürdő	FEWR-dur
Pest's Main Pedestrian Street	Váci utca	VAH-tsee OOT-zah
Pest's Main Square	Vörösmarty tér	VOO-roosh-mar-tee tehr
Pest's Grand Boulevard	Andrássy út	AHN-drah-shee oot
City Park	Városliget	VAH-rohsh-lee-geht
(Buda) Castle	(Budai) Vár	BOO-die vahr
Castle Hill	Várhegy	VAHR-hayj
Chain Bridge	Széchenyi lánchíd	SAY-chehn-yee LAHNTS-heed
Liberty Bridge (green, a.k.a. Franz Josef Bridge)	Szabadság híd	SAW-bawd-shahg heed
Elisabeth Bridge (white, modern)	Erzsébet híd	EHR-zheh-bayt heed
Margaret Bridge (crosses Margaret Island)	Margit híd	MAWR-geet heed
Danube River	Duna	DOO-naw
Eastern Train Station	Keleti pályaudvar	KEH-leh-tee PAH-yuh-uhd-vahr
Western Train Station	Nyugati pályaudvar	NYOO-gaw-tee PAH-yuh-uhd-vahr
Southern Train Station	Déli pályaudvar	DAY-lee PAH-yuh-uhd-vahr
Suburban Train System	HÉV	hayv

ORIENTATION

(area code: 1)

Budapest is big—with nearly two million people, it's much larger than Prague. The city is split down the center by the Danube River. On the west side of the Danube is hilly **Buda,** dominated by Castle Hill (packed with tourists by day, dead at night). The pleasant Víziváros (literally "Water Town"; VEE-zee-vah-rohsh) neighborhood is between the castle and the river.

On the east is flat **Pest** (pesht), the commercial heart of the city, which bustles day and night. The red-domed, riverside Parliament, visible from any point along the Danube, marks the northern edge of the tourists' Pest. A few blocks to the south, the Váci utca pedestrian drag runs parallel to the Danube, ending at the steps of the Great Market Hall. From Deák Square in the center of Pest, Andrássy út (and the yellow M1 Metro line beneath it) runs out past the Opera House to the Oktogon, House of Terror museum, Heroes' Square, City Park, and Széchenyi Baths.

Buda and Pest are connected by a series of very different **bridges.** From north to south, there's the relatively dull Margaret Bridge (Margit híd, crosses Margaret Island), the famous Chain Bridge (Széchenyi lánchíd), the white and modern Elisabeth Bridge (Erzsébet híd), and the green Liberty Bridge (Szabadság híd). The bridges are fun to cross by foot, but it's faster to go under the river (on the M2 Metro line), or to cross over it by tram (#47 and #49 over the Liberty Bridge) or by bus (#16 over the Chain Bridge and #8 across the Elisabeth Bridge are both handy).

Pest is surrounded by a series of **ring roads** (körút). The innermost ring road—called the Kiskörút, or "Small Boulevard"—surrounds central Pest. The outer ring road—Nagykörút, or "Great Boulevard"—is about halfway between the river and City Park. The ring roads change names every few blocks, but they are always called körút. Arterial **boulevards** called út (such as Andrássy út) stretch from central Pest into the suburbs, like spokes on a wheel. Almost everything a tourist wants to see in Pest is either inside the innermost ring—in the **Belváros** (literally "Inner City")—or along one of these main boulevards (and therefore well-covered by public transit). Buda is also surrounded by a ring road, and the busy Hegyalja út rumbles through the middle of the tourists' Buda (between Castle and Gellért hills).

Budapest uses a **district** system (like Paris and Vienna), and addresses often start with the district number (as a Roman numeral). Districts are called kerület. Castle Hill is district I. Notice that the district number does not necessarily indicate how central a location is: Districts II and III are to the north of Buda, where few tourists go, while the heart of Pest is district V.

Tourist Information

Budapest has five TIs (www.budapestinfo.hu): **Franz Liszt Square,** a block south of the Oktogon on Andrássy út (May–Oct daily 9:00–19:00; Nov–April Mon–Fri 10:00–18:00, Sat 10:00–16:00, closed Sun; Liszt Ferenc tér 11, tel. 1/322-4098); **Deák tér** (daily 8:00–20:00, Sütő utca 2, tel. 1/318-8718); **Castle Hill,** across from Matthias Church (May–Oct daily 9:00–20:00; Nov–March Mon–Fri 10:00–19:00, Sat–Sun 10:00–16:00; April Mon–Sat 10:00–19:00, Sun 10:00–16:00; Szentháromság tér, tel. 1/488-0453); **Nyugati Train Station** (May–Oct daily 9:00–19:00; Nov–April Mon–Fri 9:00–18:00, Sat–Sun 9:00–15:00; tel. 1/302-8580); and at the **airport.**

At all of the TIs, you can collect a pile of free brochures (on sights, bus tours, and more). Most important: the free, good city map; the *Budapest Panorama* events guide; and the information-packed *Budapest Cityguide* booklet. TIs are handy places to buy your Budapest Card.

Budapest Card: Even though this sightseeing card has shot up in price in recent years, it can still be a good value for busy sightseers. You get free travel on public transportation and entry to virtually all of Budapest's museums, plus discounts on other worthwhile attractions (including boat tours and visits to the baths). With the Budapest Card, you have the freedom to hop the Metro for one stop to save 10 minutes of walking, or drop into semi-interesting sights for a peek. This is especially useful since Budapest has lots of "quickie" museums that don't really merit a long visit. The card costs 4,700 Ft for 48 hours, or 5,900 Ft for 72 hours (includes handy 100-page booklet with maps, updated hours, and brief museum descriptions). You can buy the card all over Budapest—at TIs, travel agencies, major Metro stations, sights, and many hotels. Be sure to sign and date your card before you use it.

Note that all state-run museums (including Budapest History Museum, Museum of Military History, Museum of Ethnography, Hungarian National Museum, Museum of Fine Arts, and Museum of Hungarian Agriculture) are free, but charge for special exhibitions. The Budapest Card gets you a 20 percent discount on the entrance fee to these special exhibitions.

Alternative Tourist Information Offices: Ben Frieday, an American in love with Budapest (and one of its women), runs **Discover Hungary.** This alternative to the TIs specializes in answering the questions Americans (especially backpackers) have about Budapest. They have two locations in central Budapest: at Deák tér (Sütő utca 2, in the courtyard between the McDonald's and TI, marked "Yellow Zebra") and near Andrássy út (behind the Opera House at Lázár utca 16). At either branch, you can use

Sightseeing Modules

Budapest is a sprawling city, with sights scattered over a huge area. But if you organize your sightseeing efficiently and dive into the easy-to-master public transportation system, Budapest gets small. Break the city into manageable chunks, and digest them one at a time:

Buda
1. **Castle Hill** (Royal Palace, Matthias Church, and various museums)
2. **Gellért Hill** (Gellért Baths, Citadella, and Cave Church)

Pest
1. **Central Pest, a.k.a. Belváros** (north to south: Parliament, Vörösmarty Square, Váci utca pedestrian drag, Danube embankment and cruises, Great Synagogue, National Museum, and Great Market Hall)
2. **Andrássy út** (from center to outskirts: St. István's Basilica, Opera House, Franz Liszt Square, Oktogon, House of Terror, Heroes' Square, City Park, and Széchenyi Baths)

Outer Budapest
1. **Óbuda** (Vasarely Museum, Imre Varga Collection, and Aquincum Roman ruins)
2. **Statue Park**
3. **Danube Bend** (begins just north of Óbuda: Szentendre, Visegrád, and Esztergom; see Danube Bend chapter)

the Internet (100 Ft/15 min), rent a bike, and find out more about Budapest (both offices open May–Oct daily 9:30–19:30, shorter hours off-season, tel. 1/266-8777, www.discoverhungary.com). The Andrássy út office has a fun exhibit of communist relics in the basement (500 Ft). Ben also runs Yellow Zebra bike tours and Absolute Walking Tours (see "Tours," below).

Arrival in Budapest

Budapest has three major train stations (*pályaudvar*, abbreviated *pu.*): Keleti (Eastern) Station, Nyugati (Western) Station, and Déli (Southern) Station. A century ago, the name of the station indicated which part of Europe it served. But these days, there's no connection: Trains going to the east might leave from the Western Station, and vice-versa. Even more confusingly, the station used by a particular train can change from year to year, so it's essential to carefully confirm which station your train departs from.

The Keleti (Eastern) Station and Nyugati (Western) Station,

both in Pest, are the ones you're most likely to use. Déli (Southern) Station, in Buda, is less useful for most tourists.

The taxi stands in front of each train station are notorious for ripping off tourists—it's better to call for one (see "Getting Around Budapest—By Taxi," page 393).

By Train at the Keleti (Eastern) Station: The Keleti Station (Keleti pu.) is just south of City Park, east of central Pest. On arrival, go to the front of the long tracks 6–9 to reach the exits and services. Near the head of the tracks cluster several travel agencies with "Tourist Information" signs. None is official, but all have a few helpful fliers, and most can sell you a Budapest Card. Along track 6, you'll find a baggage-check desk, an ATM (at K&H Bank), money exchange booths (avoid Interchange, which has bad rates), and international information and ticket windows (hiding down a hallway, look for *nemzetközi pénztár*—lockers nearby).

If you go out the front door, you'll stumble over a cluster of suspicious-looking taxis. Either try to negotiate—the fair rate to downtown is about 1,500 Ft—or telephone for a taxi (phone numbers listed on page 393). The big staircase at the front of the tracks leads down to domestic ticket windows and WCs. To reach the Metro, go straight at the bottom of the stairs, then proceed straight through the open-air courtyard to the big "M" sign (M2 line, see "Getting Around Budapest—by Metro," page 392).

By Train at the Nyugati (Western) Station: The Nyugati Station (Nyugati pu.) is the most central of Budapest's stations, on the northeast edge of downtown Pest. Most international arrivals use tracks 1–9, which are set back from the main entrance. With these tracks at your back, exit straight ahead into a parking lot with taxis and buses, or use the stairs just inside the doors to reach an underpass and the Metro (M3 line, see "Getting Around Budapest—by Metro," page 392). If you're homesick, leave through the door and go immediately to the right to discover the huge, American-style **WestEnd City Center mall** (complete with a T.G.I. Friday's, daily 8:00–23:00).

To reach an official TI and ticket windows, follow tracks 10–13 to the station's main entrance. The TI is by the head of track 10 (May–Oct daily 9:00–19:00; Nov–April Mon–Fri 9:00–18:00, Sat–Sun 9:00–15:00; tel. 1/302-8580). The TI can call you an honest taxi to avoid the crooked cabbies parked out front. Ticket windows are through an easy-to-miss door, across the tracks by platform 13 (marked *cassa* and *információ;* once you enter the ticket hall, international windows are in a second room at the far end—look for *nemzetközi*).

From the front of tracks 10–13, exit straight ahead and you'll be on Teréz körút, the very busy Great Boulevard ring road. (Váci utca, at the center of Pest, is dead ahead, about 20 min away by foot). In front of the building is another taxi stand and access to handy trams #4 and #6 (zipping all the way around Pest's great ring); to the right you'll find stairs leading to an underpass (use it to avoid crossing this busy intersection, or to reach the Metro's M3 line); and to the left you'll see the classiest Art Nouveau McDonald's on the planet. (Seriously. Take a look inside.)

By Car: A car is unnecessary at best and a headache at worst. Unless you're heading to an out-of-town sight (such as Statue Park), park the car at your hotel and take public transportation. Public parking costs 120–400 Ft per hour (pay in advance at machine and put ticket on dashboard—watch locals and imitate; free parking Mon–Fri after 18:00, and all day on weekends—but you'll have to pay all the time in touristy zones). Be careful to park within the lines—otherwise, your car is likely to get booted. A guarded parking lot is safer, but more expensive (figure 3,000–4,000 Ft/day, ask your hotel or look for the blue *P*s on maps).

By Plane: Budapest Ferihegy Airport is 15 miles southeast of the center (tel. 1/296-7000, www.bud.hu). For two or more people, it's best to take a taxi (should be about 5,000 Ft to downtown). An inexpensive alternative is the **minibus** (2,300 Ft/person to any hotel in the city center, 15 percent discount with Budapest Card—buy at airport TI, minibus desk at arrival lobby, call 1/296-8555 to arrange a pickup), but they prefer to take several people at once—so you may have to wait a while. The cheapest option is to take the **public bus** to the Kőbánya-Kispest M3 Metro station, and then take the Metro into town; allow about an hour total for the trip to the center.

Helpful Hints

Rip-Offs: Budapest feels—and is—safe, especially for a city of its size. There's little risk of violent crime here. And, while people routinely try to rip me off in Prague, I've never had a single problem in Budapest. Still, many of my readers report falling victim to scams and con artists in Budapest. As in any big city, it's especially important to beware of pickpockets in crowded and touristy places, particularly on the Metro and in trams. Wear a money belt and watch your valuables closely.

Keep your wits about you and refuse to be bullied or distracted. Any deal that seems too good to be true—such as "discounted taxi vouchers" from the boat dock to your hotel—probably is.

Budapest restaurants—especially on the Váci utca shopping street—are notorious for overcharging tourists. Never eat at a restaurant that doesn't list prices on the menu, and always check your bill carefully. It's best to steer clear of those

Tonight We're Gonna Party Like It's 1896

Visitors to Budapest need only remember one date: 1896. For the millennial celebration of their ancestors' arrival in Europe, Hungarians threw a huge blowout party. In a thousand years, the Magyars had gone from being a nomadic Central Asian tribe that terrorized the Continent to sharing the throne of one of the most successful empires Europe had ever seen.

Much as the year 2000 saw a fit of new construction worldwide, Budapest used their millennial celebration as an excuse to build monuments and buildings appropriate for the capital of a huge empire, including:

- Heroes' Square **Millennium Monument**
- **Vajdahunyad Castle** (in City Park)
- The riverside **Parliament** building (96 meters tall, with 96 steps at the main entry)
- **St. István's Basilica** (also 96 meters tall)
- The M1 (yellow) Metro line, a.k.a. *Földalatti* (literally, "Underground")—the first subway on the Continent
- The **Great Market Hall** (and 4 other market halls)
- **Andrássy út** and most of the fine buildings lining it
- The **Opera House**
- A complete rebuilding of **Matthias Church** (on Castle Hill)
- The **Fishermen's Bastion** decorative terrace (by Matthias Church)
- The green **Liberty Bridge** (then called Franz Josef Bridge, in honor of the ruling Hapsburg emperor)

Ninety-six is the key number in Hungary—even the national anthem (when sung in the proper tempo) takes 96 seconds. But after all this fuss, it's too bad that the date was wrong: A commission—convened to establish the exact year of the Magyars' debut—determined it happened in 895. But city leaders knew they'd never make an 1895 deadline, and requested the finding be changed to 896.

overpriced Váci utca eateries entirely—even if they charge you what's listed, it's still a rip-off.

If you're a male in a touristy area and a gorgeous local girl (*konzumlany*, or "consumption girl") takes a liking to you, avoid her. The only foreplay going on here will climax in your grand rip-off. Another common scam involves a man stopping you on the street to "change money." A policeman arrests him—and you—and needs to see your wallet to find out if he's a con artist. They are a team and you are being robbed. And, as in many big cities, the famous shell games on the streets have everybody winning...until you give it a try.

Budapest's biggest crooks? Unscrupulous cabbies (see "Getting Around Budapest—By Taxi," page 393). I've said it before, I'll say it again: Locals *always* call for a cab, rather than hail one on the street or at a taxi stand. If you're not comfortable making the call yourself, ask your hotel or restaurant to call for you.

Blue Monday: Virtually all of Budapest's museums are closed on Mondays. But never fear—you can still take advantage of these sights and activities: Both major baths, Statue Park, Great Synagogue, Matthias Church and Budapest History Museum on Castle Hill, St. István's Basilica, Parliament tour, Opera House tour, City Park (and Zoo), Great Market Hall, Danube cruises, concerts, and bus and walking/biking tours.

Internet Access: Internet cafés are everywhere—just look for signs or ask your hotel. In Pest, I like **Discover Hungary/Yellow Zebra,** with fast access and good prices (100 Ft/15 min; for locations, hours, and contact information, see "Discover Hungary" listing on page 385). In Buda's Víziváros neighborhood, try the **Soho Coffee Company** (on Fő utca—see page 451).

Post Offices: These are marked with a smart green *posta* logo (usually open Mon–Fri 8:00–18:00, Sat 8:00–12:00, closed Sun).

Laundry: Options are scarce, and there's not yet a coin-op, self-serve launderette in town. The easiest solution is simply to have your hotel do it for you. Or, if it's a weekday, try the cheap and central **Patyolat** (drop off your clothes in the morning with the monolingual laundry ladies, pick it up in the afternoon, allow 2,500 Ft to wash and dry a load, Mon–Fri 7:00–19:00, closed Sat–Sun, just up from Váci utca at the corner of Vármegye utca and Városház utca).

English Newspapers: Newsstands sell two weekly English newspapers: *The Budapest Sun* (359 Ft) and *The Budapest Times* (420 Ft, more business-oriented).

Local Guidebook: András Török's *Budapest: A Critical Guide* is the best book by a local writer (available in English at most souvenir stands).

English Bookstores: Pendragon, the recently expanded bookstore of Central European University, sells guidebooks and popular American magazines and paperbacks, and offers the best selection anywhere of scholarly books about this region (all in English; Mon–Fri 10:00–18:00, closed Sat–Sun, enter Central European University building at Nádor utca 9 and look left, tel. 1/327-3096). This university—offering graduate study for Americans and students from all over Eastern Europe—is predominantly funded by George Soros, a Hungarian who emigrated to the United States and became a billionaire and high-profile donor to left-wing causes. **Red Bus Bookstore**, run by the hostel of the same name, has shelves of used books in English—and they buy books, too (Mon–Fri 11:00–18:00, Sat 10:00–14:00, closed Sun, Semmelweis utca 14, tel. 1/337-7453).

Travel Agencies: Carlson Wagonlit Travel, conveniently located 40 yards north of Pest's Vörösmarty tér, is handy for taking care of your rail and air travel needs (no extra fee for rail tickets or reservations, Mon–Thu 9:00–12:45 & 13:30–17:00, Fri 9:00–12:45 & 13:30–15:30, closed Sat–Sun, Dorottya utca 3, tel. 1/483-3380, www.carlsonwagonlit.hu). **Vista Travel Center,** at the base of Andrássy út, is a sprawling, user-friendly travel service with cheap flights, guidebooks, hotels, tours, and so on. Step in and grab a number (Mon–Fri 9:00–18:30, Sat 10:00–14:30, closed Sun, Andrássy út 1, tel. 1/429-9999). The central **MÁV** (National Hungarian Railways) train office, a block past the Opera House at the corner of Andrássy and Nagymező, is useful for any train ticket business you may have (Mon–Fri 9:00–18:00, until 17:00 Oct–March, closed Sat–Sun, www.mav.hu).

Bike Rental: Rent a bike at **Yellow Zebra,** part of Discover Hungary (500 Ft/hr, 2,000 Ft/half-day, 3,000 Ft/full day; for locations, hours, and contact information, see "Discover Hungary" listing on page 385).

Drivers: Friendly, English-speaking **Gábor Balázs** can drive you around the city or into the surrounding countryside (3,500 Ft/hr, 3-hr minimum in city, 4-hr minimum in countryside—good for a Danube Bend excursion, mobile 0620-936-4317, balazs.gabor@chello.hu). **József Király** runs a 10-car company, Artoli, with good, generally English-speaking drivers (€17/hr, more for larger cars and vans, tel. 20/369-8890, mobile 0630-949-1253, artoli@t-online.hu).

Best Views: Budapest is a city of marvelous vistas. Some of the best are from the Citadella (high on Gellért Hill), the promenade in front of Buda Castle, the embankments or many bridges spanning the Danube (especially the Chain Bridge), and tour boats on the Danube—lovely at night.

Getting Around Budapest

Budapest is huge. Connecting your sightseeing by foot is tedious and unnecessary; use the excellent public transportation system instead. The same tickets work for the Metro, trams, and buses (buy them at kiosks, Metro ticket windows, or machines; the new machines are slick and easy, but the old orange ones are trickier: Put in the appropriate amount of money, then press button).

Your options are:

• Single ticket (*vonaljegy*, for a ride of up to an hour with no transfers)—170 Ft;

• Short single Metro ride (*metroszakaszjegy*, 3 stops or fewer on the Metro)—120 Ft;

• Transfer ticket (*átszállójegy*—allowing up to 90 minutes, including 1 transfer)—290 Ft; or

• Unlimited multi-day tickets (1,350 Ft/1 day, 2,700 Ft/3 days, 3,100 Ft/7 days)—but if you're here more than a day and plan to do lots of sightseeing, consider a Budapest Card instead (see "Tourist Information," page 385).

Always validate your ticket as you enter the bus, tram, or Metro station (stick it in the little elbow-high box). A transfer ticket must be validated a second time when you transfer. The stern-looking guys with red armbands waiting as you exit the Metro want to see your validated ticket or signed and dated Budapest Card. Cheaters get fined 2,000 Ft on the spot, and you'll be surprised how often you're checked (they're widely believed to target tourists, and are most commonly sighted at train stations and along the touristy M1 line). All public transit runs from 4:30 in the morning until 23:10. A useful route-planning Web site is www.bkv.hu.

By Metro: Riding Budapest's Metro, you really feel like you're down in the efficient guts of the city. It's every bit as convenient and slick as Vienna's or Berlin's—but it has more character than those stodgy systems.

There are three lines:

• **M1 (yellow)**—The first Metro line on the Continent, this shallow line runs under Andrássy út from the center to City Park (see "The Millennium Underground of 1896," page 416).

• **M2 (red)**—Built during the communist days, it's 115 feet deep, doubles as a bomb shelter, and comes with a tornado ventilation system—notice the gale. The only line going under the Danube to Buda, M2 connects the Déli train station, Moszkva tér (where you catch the *vár* bus to the top of Castle Hill), Batthyány tér (where you catch the HÉV train to Óbuda or Szentendre), and the Keleti train station.

• **M3 (blue)**—This line makes a broad, boomerang-shaped swoop north to south. Key stops include the Nyugati Train Station and Kálvin tér (near the Great Market Hall and many recommended hotels).

The three lines cross only once: at the **Deák tér** stop (sometimes signed as "Deák Ferenc tér") in the heart of Pest, where Andrássy út begins. Most M2 and M3 Metro stations are at intersections of ring roads and other major arterials. You'll usually exit the Metro into a confusing underpass packed with kiosks, fast-food stands, and makeshift markets.

Orange directional signs help you find the right exit.

The Metro stops themselves are usually very well marked, with a list of upcoming stops on the wall behind the tracks. The red digital clocks tell you how long it's been since the last train left; you'll rarely wait more than five minutes for the next.

You'll ride very long, steep, fast-moving escalators to access the M2 and M3 lines. Hang on tight, enjoy the breeze as trains below shoot through the tunnels...and don't make yourself dizzy by trying to read the Burger King ads.

Note that Budapest is renovating its Metro stations. If a particular stretch of Metro line is closed, buses run the same route instead. Ask at the TI or check www.bkv.hu.

By Tram: Budapest's trams are handy and frequent, taking you virtually anywhere the Metro doesn't. Here are some trams you might use:

Trams #2 and #2A: Run along Pest's Danube embankment parallel to Váci utca, between the Parliament and the Great Market Hall.

Trams #19 and #41: Runs along Buda's Danube embankment, stopping at Gellért Hotel, the bottom of the Castle Hill funicular (Adam Clark tér), several recommended Víziváros hotels, and Batthyány tér (end of the line, M2 Metro station and HÉV trains to Óbuda and Szentendre).

Trams #4 and #6: Zip around Pest's Great Boulevard ring road (Nagykörút), connecting the Nyugati Train Station and Oktogon with Buda's Moszkva tér (M2 Metro station).

Trams #47 and #49: Connect the Gellért Baths in Buda with Pest's Small Boulevard ring road (Kiskörút), with stops at the Great Market Hall, the National Museum, the Great Synagogue (Astoria stop), and Deák tér (end of the line).

By Bus: The tram and Metro network can get you nearly anywhere, so you're less likely to take a bus. One exception is getting to the top of Castle Hill—accessible only by the *várbusz* ("castle bus," from Moszkva tér—see page 399). Bus #16 is handy (Deák tér, Roosevelt tér, crosses Chain Bridge, Adam Clark tér, and up to Dísz tér atop Castle Hill near the Royal Palace).

By Taxi: Budapest's public transportation is good enough that you probably won't need to take many taxis. If you do, you may run into a dishonest driver. Locals always call a cab from a reputable company; try **Taxi 6x6** (tel. 1/266-6666) or **City Taxi** (tel. 1/211-111).

Cabbies are not allowed to charge more than a drop rate of 300 Ft, and then 240 Ft per kilometer (more expensive 22:00–6:00)—though the more reputable companies charge less. Prices are per ride, not per passenger. A 10 percent tip is expected. A typical ride within central Budapest shouldn't run more than 2,000 Ft. Despite what some slimy cabbies may tell you, there's no legitimate extra charge for crossing the river.

Many cabs you'd hail on the streets are there only to prey on rich, green tourists. Avoid hotel taxis, unmarked taxis, and cabs waiting at tourist spots and train stations. If you do wave down a cab on the street, choose one that's marked with a company logo and telephone number. Ask for a rough estimate before you get in—if it doesn't sound reasonable, walk away. If you wind up being dramatically overcharged for a ride, simply pay what you think is fair and go inside. If the driver follows you (unlikely), your hotel receptionist will defend you.

TOURS

Walking Tours—A youthful, backpacker-oriented company, **Absolute Walking Tours,** is run by Oregonian Ben Frieday. You can choose from several different itineraries: the Absolute Walk overview tour (4,000 Ft, mid-May–Sept daily at 9:30 and 13:30, Oct–mid-May daily at 10:30, 3.5 hrs); the Hammer and Sickle Tour, including a visit to Statue Park (5,500 Ft, 4/week, 3 hrs); and the Absolute Night Stroll (4,000 Ft, mid-May–Sept only, 3/week, 2.5 hrs). There's also a cuisine-oriented tour, called Absolute Hungro Gastro, which includes a visit to a market to buy ingredients, traditional Hungarian recipes, and a chance to taste several specialties at a local restaurant (6,500 Ft, 3/week, 1/week in winter, 3 hrs). The Pub Crawl sometimes continues late into the night (5,500 Ft, departs 20:00, 4/week, at least 3 hrs). Consider the day-long excursion to Eger (13,500 Ft, 3/week, 1/week in winter). All tours depart from Deák tér (tel. 1/266-8777, www.absolutetours .com). Travelers with this book get a 500-Ft discount on any tour in 2006, as does anyone under 26.

Private Guides—Budapest has plenty of enthusiastic, hardworking young guides who speak fine English and enjoy showing off their exciting city. Given the reasonable fees and efficient use of your time, hiring your own personal expert is an excellent value. I have two favorites: **Péter Pölczman** charges €70 for a four- or five-hour tour and €100 for a full-day tour (mobile 0620-926-0557, polczman@freestart.hu or peter.polczman@guideclub. net). **Andrea Makkay** leads four-hour tours (23,000 Ft) and seven-hour tours (39,000 Ft; mobile 0620-9629-363, www .privateguidebudapest.com, amakkay@t-online.hu—arrange details by e-mail), can also also tour outside of Budapest by car or minivan—ask. Both Péter and Andrea are good within town and for side-tripping up the Danube Bend.

Danube Boat Tours—Cruising the Danube, while touristy, is fun and convenient. The most established company, **Legenda**, runs boats day and night. By day, the one-hour cruise costs 3,600 Ft

(2,750 Ft with Budapest Card) and includes an optional one-hour walking tour around Margaret Island, Budapest's playground (6/day July–Aug, 4/day May–June and Sept, 2/day mid-March–April, 1/day Oct, 1/day Fri–Sun only Nov–Feb).

By night, the one-hour cruise (with no Margaret Island option) costs 4,200 Ft (3,250 Ft with Budapest Card, 3/day May–Sept, 1/day Oct–April).

Both cruises include two drinks and headphone commentary. TV monitors show the interior of the great buildings as you float by. The Legenda dock is in front of the Marriott on the Pest embankment (find pedestrian access under tram tracks just downriver from Vigadó tér, tel. 1/317-2203, www.legenda.hu).

Bike Tours—A sister company of Absolute Walking Tours, **Yellow Zebra,** wheels by Budapest's major sights on a four-hour tour (5,500 Ft, April–Oct daily at 11:00, also at 16:00 July–Aug, no tours Nov–March, meet at Deák tér, tel. 1/266-8777, www.yellowzebrabikes.com).

Segway Tours—In addition to walking and bike tours, Ben Frieday's **Discover Hungary** also offers tours of Budapest by Segway (stand-up electric scooter). While expensive, it's a unique way to see the city while trying out a Segway (12,500 Ft, daily at 10:00, also daily at 18:30 April–Oct, 3 hrs with 30-min training beforehand, 6 people per group, must reserve and pre-pay at www.citysegwaytours.com or call the office when in Budapest—tel. 1/266-8777).

Bus Tours—Several companies run bus tours that glide past all the big sights. A basic three-hour bus tour will run you 6,000–6,500 Ft per person, and the different companies are essentially the same. Budatours runs a shorter, cheaper two-hour version (4,300 Ft). A new hop-on, hop-off bus tour by City Circle Sightseeing makes five stops as it cruises around town (4,500 Ft for the 2-hour tour, or 7,000 Ft for an all-day ticket). Most companies also offer a wide variety of other tours, including dinner boat cruises and trips to the Danube Bend. Pick up fliers about all these tours at the TI or in your hotel lobby.

SIGHTS
Buda
Castle Hill (Várhegy)
Buda's main sights are all on Castle Hill. While many visitors expect this high-profile district to be time-consuming, for most it's enough to simply stroll through in a couple of hours. The major landmarks are the huge, green-domed Royal Palace at the south end of the hill (housing a pair of ho-hum museums) and the frilly-spired Matthias Church near the north end. In between are

Budapest at a Glance

In Buda

▲▲Matthias Church Landmark neo-Gothic church with gilded history-book interior and revered 16th-century statue of Mary and Jesus. **Hours:** Mon–Sat 9:00–17:00, Sun 13:00–17:00, sometimes closed Sat after 13:00 for weddings.

▲▲Gellért Baths Touristy baths in elegant hotel. **Hours:** May–Sept daily 6:00–20:00; Oct–April Mon–Fri 6:00–19:00, Sat–Sun 6:00–17:00.

▲▲Statue Park Larger-than-life communist big shots all collected in one park, on the outskirts of town. **Hours:** Daily 10:00–sunset.

▲Hungarian Commerce and Catering Museum Intriguing time-tunnel look at 19th-century businesses. **Hours:** Wed–Fri 10:00–17:00, Sat–Sun 10:00–18:00, closed Mon–Tue.

▲Imre Varga Collection Evocative sculpture collection capturing communist times, in Óbuda. **Hours:** Tue–Sun 10:00–18:00, closed Mon, artist visits at 10:00 Sat.

Royal Palace Reconstructed fortress on Castle Hill housing a pair of decent museums (Budapest History Museum and National Gallery). **Hours:** History Museum—mid-May–mid-Sept daily 10:00–18:00; March–mid-May and mid-Sept–Oct Wed–Mon 10:00–18:00, closed Tue; Nov–Feb Wed–Mon 10:00–16:00, closed Tue. National Gallery—Tue–Sun 10:00–18:00, closed Mon.

Cave Church House of worship carved into the cliff face of Gellért Hill. **Hours:** Open long hours daily, but closed to sightseers during frequent services).

In Pest

▲▲▲Széchenyi Baths Budapest's steamy soaking scene in the City Park—the city's single best attraction. **Hours:** Daily 6:00–19:00, may close at 17:00 Sat–Sun in winter.

▲▲Váci utca Hopping pedestrian boulevard and tourist magnet, featuring Eastern Europe's first McDonald's. **Hours:** Always open.

▲▲Great Market Hall Colorful Old World mall with produce, cheap eateries, souvenirs, and great people-watching. **Hours:** Mon 6:00–17:00, Tue–Fri 6:00–18:00, Sat 6:00–14:00, closed Sun.

▲▲**House of Terror** Harrowing remembrance of Nazis and communist secret police in former headquarters/torture site. **Hours:** Tue–Fri 10:00–18:00, Sat–Sun 10:00–19:30, closed Mon.

▲▲**Heroes' Square** Mammoth tribute to Hungary's historic figures, fringed by a couple of art museums and Countryrama 3-D movie. **Hours:** Square always open; Museum of Fine Arts— Tue–Sun 10:00–17:30, closed Mon; Palace of Art—Tue–Wed and Fri–Sun 10:00–18:00, Thu 12:00–20:00, closed Mon; Countryrama 3-D—mid-March–Sept Tue–Sun 10:30–17:30, closed Mon; Oct– mid-March Fri–Sun 10:30–17:00, closed Mon–Thu.

▲▲**City Park** Budapest's backyard, with Art Nouveau zoo, Transylvanian castle replica, amusement park, and Széchenyi Baths. **Hours:** Park always open.

▲**Hungarian Parliament** Vast, riverside neo-Gothic government center. **Hours:** English tours usually daily at 10:00, 12:00, and 14:00.

▲**Postal Museum** Funky tribute to old postal service objects in elegant old Andrássy út mansion. **Hours:** Tue–Sun 10:00–18:00, closed Mon.

▲**Hungarian State Opera House** Neo-Renaissance splendor and affordable opera. **Hours:** Lobby/box office open Mon–Sat 11:00–19:00, Sun 16:00–19:00, until 17:00 on days when there's no performance; English tours nearly daily at 15:00 and 16:00.

▲**Vajdahunyad Castle** Disney World–type complex in the City Park with replicas of historic Hungarian architecture, anchored by a massive Transylvanian castle. **Hours:** Grounds always open.

▲**Great Synagogue** The world's second-largest after New York's, with museum and garden memorial. **Hours:** April–Oct Mon–Thu 10:00–17:00, Fri and Sun 10:00–14:00; Nov–March Mon– Thu 10:00–15:00, Fri and Sun 10:00–14:00; always closed Sat and Jewish holidays.

▲**Holocaust Memorial Center** Excellent memorial and museum honoring Hungarian victims of the Holocaust. **Hours:** Tue–Sun 10:00–18:00, closed Mon.

Hungarian National Museum Extensive collection of fragments from Hungary's history. **Hours:** Tue–Sun 10:00–18:00, closed Mon.

Buda Center Sights

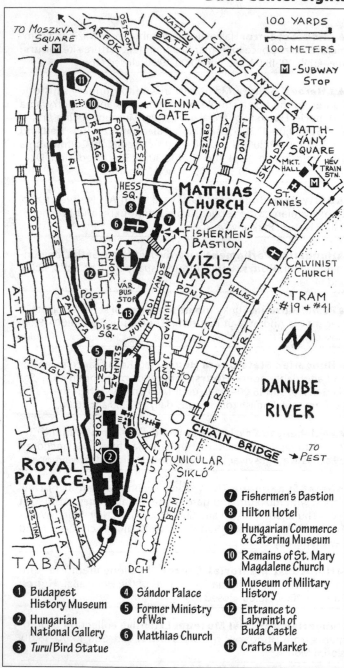

100 YARDS

100 METERS

Ⓜ - SUBWAY STOP

TO MOSZKVA SQUARE & Ⓜ

VIENNA GATE

BATTHYÁNY SQUARE

MKT. HALL

HÉV TRAIN STN.

ST. ANNE'S

MATTHIAS CHURCH

HESS SQ.

FISHERMEN'S BASTION

VÍZI-VÁROS

CALVINIST CHURCH

TRAM #19 & #41

POST

VÁR. BUS STOP

DISZ SQ.

SZÍNHÁZ

SZN.

DANUBE RIVER

CHAIN BRIDGE

TO PEST

FUNICULAR "SIKLÓ"

ROYAL PALACE

TABÁN

DCH

⓻ Fishermen's Bastion
⓼ Hilton Hotel
⓽ Hungarian Commerce & Catering Museum
⓾ Remains of St. Mary Magdalene Church
⑪ Museum of Military History
⑫ Entrance to Labyrinth of Buda Castle
⑬ Crafts Market

❶ Budapest History Museum
❷ Hungarian National Gallery
❸ Turul Bird Statue
❹ Sándor Palace
❺ Former Ministry of War
❻ Matthias Church

tourist-filled pedestrian streets and historic buildings. A few other interesting but non-essential museums are scattered around the hill. I've listed the sights in order from south to north, and linked them together on a self-guided tour.

When to Visit: Castle Hill is packed with tour groups in the morning, but it's much less crowded in the afternoon. Since restaurants up here are expensive and low-quality, Castle Hill is an ideal after-lunch activity.

Getting to Castle Hill: The Metro and trams won't take you to the top of Castle Hill. You can hike, taxi, ride the funicular (see below), or catch **bus #16** from either side of the Chain Bridge (departs from Deák, Roosevelt, and Adam Clark squares). A special **castle bus** *(várbusz)* does a loop from Moszkva tér (Moscow Square) north of the castle (M2: Moszkva tér, bus stops just uphill from Metro station, look for small bus with the words *vár* or *Dísz tér* and a little picture of a castle). Castle Hill buses are specially designed to be light, as the hill is honeycombed with limestone caves. The handiest stop for either of these buses is at Dísz tér, right in the middle of the hill (across from old Ministry of War building). If you arrive at Dísz tér, you can backtrack to the Royal Palace and *turul* bird statue, or skip ahead to the Dísz tér listing in the walking tour (all of this is described below).

The **funicular** *(sikló*, SHEE-kloh), lifting visitors from the Chain Bridge to the top of Castle Hill, is a Budapest landmark. Built in 1870 to provide cheap transportation to Castle Hill workers, today it's a pricey little tourist trip. Read the fun first-person history you'll see in glass cases at the top station (600 Ft up, 500 Ft down, not covered by Budapest Card, daily 7:30–22:00, departs every 5 min, closed for maintenance every other Mon).

• *From the funicular, enjoy the views of the Danube and go a few yards to the big bird at the top of the stairs. You can survey the immense palace and Danube panorama from here, or wander to the equestrian statue and circle through and around the huge building.*

The Turul—This mythical bird of Magyar folk tales watches over the palace. The *turul* supposedly led the Hungarian migrations in the 9th century. He dropped his sword in the Carpathian Basin, indicating that this was to be the permanent home of the Magyar people. During a surge of nationalism in the 1920s, a movement named after this bird helped revive traditional Hungarian culture. *Turul* birds also top the towers of the green Liberty Bridge, just downriver.

Royal Palace (Királyi Palota)—The imposing palace on Castle Hill is a dull contemporary construction, barely hinting at the colorful story of this hill since the day that the legendary *turul* dropped his sword.

Originally, the main city of Hungary wasn't Buda or Pest, but Esztergom (just up the river; see Danube Bend chapter). In the 13th century, Tatars swept through Eastern Europe, destroying much of Hungary. King Béla IV decided to rebuild a walled Buda here, a more protected location in the interior of the country. The city has dominated the region ever since, gradually becoming the Hungarian capital.

The first Hungarian dynasty (the Árpáds) died out in 1301, and a new French line—the Anjous (or Angevins)—took over Buda and the rest of Hungary. They replaced Béla IV's modest castle with a luxurious palace that expanded over the years. It was one of Europe's biggest by the early 15th century, when King Mátyás Corvinus made the palace even more extravagant, putting Buda—and Hungary—on the map.

Just a few decades later, the invading Ottoman Turks occupied Buda and turned the palace into a military garrison. When the Hapsburgs laid siege to the hill for 77 days in 1686, gunpowder stored in the cellar exploded, destroying the palace. The Hapsburgs took the hill, but Buda was deserted and in ruins. The town was resettled by Austrians, who built a new Baroque palace, hoping that the Hapsburg monarch would move in—but none ever did. (They preferred to live up the river in Vienna, and occasionally in Prague.) The useless palace became a garrison, then a university, and later the viceroy's residence. It was damaged again during the 1848 Revolution, but was repaired and continued to grow right along with Budapest's prominence (for more on the 1848 Revolution, see page 408).

As World War II drew to a close, Buda became the front line between the Nazis and the approaching Soviets, who laid siege to the hill for six months. The palace was again destroyed.

Most Budapesters (and historians) don't much care for the current tame, and historically inaccurate, post-WWII reconstruction of the palace. It's a loose rebuilding of previous versions, lacking the style and sense of history that this important site deserves. The most prominent feature of today's palace—the green dome—didn't even exist in earlier versions.

• *The palace houses a pair of mediocre museums. Visit your choice now (listed below), or head to Matthias Church from here (Castle Hill self-guided tour continues below).*

Castle Museums—The palace houses two worthwhile (but not must-see) museums. The history museum is decent, but the art museum ranks low on a European scale. Both of these museums are off of the big enclosed courtyard (make your way into the courtyard on the other side of the dome; once you're there, face the dome: the history museum is behind you, and the National Gallery is at 2 o'clock, using an imaginary clock for directions).

The **Budapest History Museum** (Budapesti Történeti Múzeum), a good but stodgy museum begging for a makeover, celebrates the earlier grandeur of Castle Hill. If Budapest really intrigues you, this is a fine place to explore its history. You'll start at the top floor and work down. Along the way, you'll see artifacts of Budapest's prehistoric residents and a good collection of 14th-century sculptures, many of them with strong Magyar features—notice that they look Central Asian, like Mongolians. The highlight is the "Budapest in the Modern Times" exhibit, tracing the last two rocky centuries of the city, with a focus on the gradual movement towards merging Buda and Pest. The cellar illustrates just how much this hill has changed over the centuries—and how dull today's version is in comparison. You'll wander through a maze of old palace parts, including the remains of an original Gothic chapel, a knights' hall, and marble remnants (reliefs and fountains) of Mátyás Corvinus' lavish Renaissance palace (800 Ft, covered by Budapest Card, good English descriptions posted, other descriptions are borrowable, mid-May–mid-Sept daily 10:00–18:00; March–mid-May and mid-Sept–Oct Wed–Mon 10:00–18:00, closed Tue; Nov–Feb Wed–Mon 10:00–16:00, closed Tue; tel. 1/225-7815).

The huge **Hungarian National Gallery** (Magyar Nemzeti Galéria) has an excellent collection of 15th-century winged altars, plus halls and halls of paintings and sculptures by Hungarian artists you've never heard of—for good reason (free, charge for special exhibitions, Tue–Sun 10:00–18:00, closed Mon, tel. 1/224-3700).

From the Funicular and Royal Palace to Matthias Church: To connect the palace to Matthias Church, the closest major sight, follow this self-guided walk:

From the *turul* bird and the top of the funicular (with your back to the Royal Palace), walk along the non-river side of the big white building **Sándor Palace.** This mansion underwent a very costly renovation under the previous Hungarian prime minister, who hoped to make it his residence. But in 2002, the same year it was finished, he lost his bid for reelection. The spunky new PM refused to move in. By way of compromise, now the president's office is here.

As you continue along the side of Sándor Palace, you'll notice the remains of a medieval monastery and church in the field to your left. Beyond that, past the flagpoles, is the ongoing excavation of the medieval Jewish quarter—more reminders that most of what you see on today's Castle Hill has been destroyed and rebuilt many times over.

After Sándor Palace, you'll pass the yellow National Dance Theater, where Beethoven once performed. Beyond that, you'll come to **Dísz tér** (Parade Square), which has a convenient bus stop

Mátyás Corvinus: The Last Hungarian King

The Árpád dynasty—descendants of the original Magyar tribes—died out in 1301. For more than 600 years, Hungary would be ruled by foreigners...with one exception.

In the middle of the 15th century, Hungary had bad luck hanging on to its foreign kings: Two of them died unexpectedly within seven years. Meanwhile, homegrown military general János Hunyadi was enjoying great success on the battlefield against the Turks. When the five-year-old Ladislas V was elected king, Hunyadi was appointed regent and essentially ruled the country. Hunyadi defeated the Turks in the crucial 1456 Battle of Belgrade, which temporarily prevented them from entering Hungary and made him an even greater hero to the Hungarian people. Tragically, soon after this great victory, Hunyadi died of the plague.

When King Ladislas also died (at the tender age of 16), the nobles looked for a new hero...and found Hunyadi's son, Mátyás (Matthias). He became the first Hungarian-descended king in more than 150 years, taking the nickname Corvinus (Latin for "raven," which appears on his coat of arms).

Progressive and well-educated, Mátyás Corvinus (r. 1458–1490) was the quintessential Renaissance king—a benefactor of the poor and a true humanist. He patronized the arts and built

for connecting to other parts of Budapest (see "Getting to Castle Hill," above).

On the Royal Palace end of Dísz tér—before the street—is the still-damaged building that used to house the **Ministry of War.** Most of the bullet holes are from World War II, while others were left by the Soviets who occupied this hill in response to the 1956 Uprising (see page 408). The building is a political hot potato—prime real estate, but nobody can decide what to do with it. (Note that 50 yards beyond the Ministry of War is a bus stop for bus #16, offering a quick return to the Pest side of the Chain Bridge.)

Across the street from the Ministry of War (on the right) is the entrance to a courtyard with an open-air Hungarian **crafts market.** While it's fun to browse, prices here are high (haggle away). The Great Market Hall has a better selection and generally lower prices (see page 413).

Cross the street and continue uphill through and up **Tárnok utca.** This area often disappoints visitors. After being destroyed by Turks, it was rebuilt in sensible Baroque, lacking the romantic time-capsule charm of a medieval old town (like perfectly preserved Prague or Kraków). But if you poke your head into some palaces legendary for their beauty. He dressed up as a commoner and ventured into the streets to see firsthand how the nobles of his realm treated his people.

Mátyás was a strong, savvy leader. He created Central Europe's first standing army—30,000 mercenaries known as the Black Army. No longer reliant on the nobility for military support, Good King Mátyás was able to drain power from the nobles and make taxation of his subjects more equitable—earning him the nickname the "people's king."

King Mátyás was also a shrewd military tactician. Realizing that squabbling with the Turks would squander his resources, he made peace with the Ottoman sultan to stabilize Hungary's southern border. Then he swept north, invading Moravia, Bohemia, and even Austria. By 1485, Mátyás moved into his new palace in Vienna, and Hungary was enjoying a Golden Age.

Five years later, Mátyás died mysteriously at the age of 47, and his empire disintegrated. It is said that when Mátyás died, justice died with him. To this day, Hungarians consider him the greatest of all kings, and they sing of his siege of Vienna in their national anthem. They're proud that for a few decades in the middle of half a millennium of foreign oppression, they had a truly Hungarian king—and a great one at that.

courtyards, you'll almost always see some original Gothic arches and other medieval features.

• *Continue along the street; after two blocks, past the TI (on your right), you'll see a warty plague column marking the main square of old Buda. Across the square is the...*

Fishermen's Bastion (Halászbástya)—This neo-Romanesque fantasy rampart offers beautiful views over the Danube to Pest. In the Middle Ages, the fish market was just below here (in today's Víziváros, or "Water Town"), so this part of the rampart actually was guarded by fishermen. The current structure, though, is completely artificial—an example of Budapest sprucing itself up for 1896 (see page 389). Its seven towers represent the seven Magyar tribes. The cone-headed arcades are reminiscent of tents the nomadic Magyars called home before they moved west to Europe.

Survey Pest across the Danube from this viewpoint. The two domes are the Parliament and St. István's Basilica—both 96 meters high, built in...you guessed it...1896. The Chain Bridge cuts Pest in two: The left half is administrative, with government ministries, embassies, banks, and so on; the right half (stretching to the modern, white Elisabeth Bridge) is the commercial center of Pest, with the best riverside promenade.

Paying to climb up the bastion makes little sense (330 Ft, not covered by Budapest Card, buy ticket at kiosk near TI in park, daily May–Oct 9:00–23:00, Nov–April 9:00–19:00, gates are generally open and entry is free after closing time). Enjoy virtually the same view through the windows (left of café) for free. The café offers a scenic break if you don't mind the tour groups.

• *Between the bastion and the big church stands a...*

Statue of St. István (Stephen)—Hungary's first Christian king tamed the nomadic, pagan Magyars and established strict laws and the concept of private property. István's father, King Géza, lost a major battle against the forces of Christian Europe—and realized that he must raise his son as a Catholic and convert his people, or they would ultimately be forcefully driven out of Europe. The reliefs on this statue show the Pope crowning St. István (EESHT-vahn) in the year 1000, bringing Hungary into Christendom. This meant the rest of Europe was now inclined to help Hungary against the Turks and to bully Slavs. Without this pivotal event, locals believe that the Magyar nation would have been lost. A passionate evangelist—more for the survival of his Magyar nation than for the salvation of his people—István beheaded those who wouldn't convert. To make his point perfectly clear, he quartered his reluctant uncle and sent him on four separate, simultaneous tours of the country to show Hungarians that Christianity was a smart choice. Gruesome as he was, István was sainted within 30 years of his death.

• *Next to St. István is the can't-miss-it...*

▲▲Matthias Church (Mátyás-Templom)—Budapest's best church has been destroyed and rebuilt several times in the 800 years since it was founded by King Béla IV.  Today's version—renovated at great expense in the late 19th century, and restored after World War II—is an ornately decorated lesson in Hungarian history. While it's officially called the "Church of Our Lady," everyone calls it the Matthias Church, for the popular Renaissance king who got married here...twice (600 Ft, covered by Budapest Card, 12-stop audioguide-300 Ft, Mon–Sat 9:00–17:00, Sun 13:00–17:00, sometimes closed Sat after 13:00 for weddings, Szentháromság tér 2, tel. 1/488-7716, www.matyas-templom.hu).

Examine the **exterior**. While the nucleus of the church is Gothic, most of what you see outside—including the frilly, flamboyant steeple—was added for the 1896 celebrations. At the top of the spire facing the river, notice the raven (*corvinus* in Latin) with a ring in his mouth. This symbol, which you'll see all over Castle Hill, is from the coat of arms of King Mátyás Corvinus. According to legend, Mátyás' father—the military leader János Hunyadi—was imprisoned by the Turks, and his family feared him dead. But a raven appeared in the window of his cell, and Hunyadi gave the bird his ring. The raven flew it to the family to reassure them that he lived on. (For more on Mátyás, see the sidebar on page 402.)

The sumptuous **interior** is wallpapered with gilded pages from a Hungarian history textbook. Different eras are represented by symbolic motifs. For example, the wall immediately to the left of the entry represents the Renaissance, with a giant coat of arms of the beloved King Mátyás Corvinus. (The tough guys in armor on either side are members of his mercenary Black Army, the source of his power.) Notice the raven with a ring. Meanwhile, the wall across from the entry—with Oriental motifs—commemorates the Turkish reign of Buda.

The first chapel to the left, the **Loreto Chapel**, holds the church's prize possession. Peer through the black iron grill to see the 1515 statue of Mary and Jesus. Anticipating Turkish plundering, locals walled over this precious statue. The occupying Turks used the church as their primary mosque—oblivious to the statue plastered over in the niche. Then, a century and a half later, during the siege of Buda in 1686, gunpowder stored in the castle up the street detonated, and the wall crumbled. Mary's triumphant face showed through, terrifying the Turks. According to legend, this was the only part of town taken from the Turks without a fight.

Continue circling around the church. As you look down the **nave**, notice the 500-year-old Hungarian battalion banners, left here after the Mass that celebrated János Hunyadi's victory over the Turks at the Battle of Belgrade in 1456. The stained glass is 160 years old; during World War II, it was removed and hidden to avoid destruction.

At the rear left of the church, towards the altar from the gift shop, is the tomb of St. Imre, the son of the great King (and later Saint) István. This heir to the Hungarian throne was mysteriously killed by a boar while he was hunting when he was only 19 years old. Though he didn't live long enough to do anything important, he rode his father's coattails to sainthood. The next chapel is the tomb of Béla III, utterly insignificant except that this is one of only two tombs of Hungarian kings that still exist in the country. The rest—including all of the biggies—were defiled by the Turks. Up next to the main altar is the chapel of László—St. István's nephew, who stepped in as king of Hungary when the rightful heir, St. Imre, was killed.

The upstairs gallery holds the **Museum of Ecclesiastical Art** (Egyházművészeti Gyűjteménye, same ticket and hours as church). The original Hungarian crown is under the Parliament's dome, and a hassle to visit (see page 414)—but a replica is up here, and worth a peek. The church also hosts concerts (about 2/month, signs posted outside, ticket desk inside).

• *To continue your exploration of Buda, take a self-guided walk along...*

North Castle Hill: The following stroll takes you through Buda north of Matthias Church. As this was the site of a Nazi military headquarters, it was heavily bombed towards the end of World War II. (During a 6-week siege, 30 percent of the city was destroyed.)

Leave the courtyard beside the church and turn right—passing the 1713 Holy Trinity plague column on your left—so that you're walking along the front of the glassy modern **Hilton Hotel.** To minimize the controversy of building upon so much history, architects thoughtfully incorporated the medieval ruins into its modern design. Built in 1976, the Hilton was the first plush Western hotel in town. Before 1989, it was a gleaming center of capitalism, offering a cushy refuge for Western travelers and a stark contrast to what was, at the time, a very gloomy city. Halfway down the hotel's facade, you'll see fragments of a 13th-century wall, with a monument to Mátyás Corvinus.

After the wall, continue along the second half of the Hilton Hotel facade. Turn right into the gift-shop entry, and then go right again inside the second glass door. Stairs on the left lead down to a reconstructed 13th-century Dominican cloister; at the far end of the cloister are more stairs, to the Faust Wine Cellar (daily 16:00–23:00), a friendly place with fine wine by the glass. For an even better look at what was here back then, go back up the stairs and turn left. As you enter the lounge, look out the back windows to see fragments of the 13th-century Dominican church incorporated into the structure of the hotel. If you stood here eight centuries ago, you'd be looking straight down the church's nave. You can even see tomb markers in the ground.

Back out on the street, cross the little park and duck into the entryway of the **Fortuna Passage.** Along the passageway to the courtyard, you can see the original Gothic arches of the house that once stood here. In the Middle Ages, every homeowner had the right to sell wine without paying taxes—but only in the passage of his own home. He'd set up a table here, and his neighbors would come by to taste the latest vintage. These passageways evolved into very social places, like the corner pub.

• *Leaving the Fortuna, turn left down Fortuna utca, where after a block you'll find the excellent little...*

▲**Hungarian Commerce and Catering Museum (Magyar Keres-kedelmi és Vendéglátóipari Múzeum)**—Far more interesting than it sounds, this museum—which fills two ground-floor wings of an old building—takes a nostalgic look at workaday 19th-century Pest commerce. With the help of good English descriptions, you'll enjoy a peek into the fancy hotels, restaurants, and coffeehouses of the day. There's even a section on the 1896 festivities, including kitschy souvenirs. The second half (across the driveway, opposite the main entrance) is the "Made in Hungary 1900–1950" exhibit, with fun ads, toys, and fashions. The attendants are enthusiastic grannies who seem old enough to remember all this history first-hand. If you're lucky, one of them will speak English well enough to take you by the hand and explain it all to you (500 Ft, covered by Budapest Card, audioguide-600 Ft, Wed–Fri 10:00–17:00, Sat–Sun 10:00–18:00, closed Mon–Tue, Fortuna utca 4, Budapest I, tel. 1/375-6249).

• *At the end of Fortuna utca, you'll see the Vienna Gate. If you go through it and walk for about 10 days, you'll get to Vienna. (For now, settle for climbing up to the top for a view of some Buda residential neighborhoods.) Now walk along the hulking National Archive building (with your back to the Danube) until you reach the...*

Remains of St. Mary Magdalene Church–This was once known as the Kapisztrán Templom, named after a hero of the Battle of Belgrade in 1456, an early success in the struggle to keep the Turks out of Europe. (King Mátyás' father, János Hunyadi, led the Hungarians in that battle.) The Pope was so tickled by the victory that he decreed that all church bells should toll at noon in memory of the battle—and, technically, they still do. Californians will recognize the Kapisztrán's Spanish name: San Juan de Capistrano. This church was destroyed by bombs in World War II, though no worse than Matthias Church. But, since this part of town was depopulated after the war, there was no longer a need for a second church. The remains of the church were torn down, the steeple was rebuilt as a memorial, and a carillon was added—so that every day at noon, the bells can still toll.

• *Across the square from the church is a monument to San Juan de Capistrano. Walking around the big building, you come to a viewpoint overlooking modern Buda, and on the green hill beyond that, you find the Beverly Hills of Budapest—where the local rich and famous live. To the right, near the flagpole, is the entry to the...*

Museum of Military History (Hadtörténeti Múzeum)—This fine museum explains in painstaking detail the history of various Hungarian military actions, with a special emphasis on the 1848 Revolution against the Hapsburgs. With enough old uniforms and flags to keep an army-surplus store in stock for a decade, this place will interest military and history buffs (free, charge for special

408 Rick Steves' Best of Eastern Europe

Foreign powers who have oppressed the Hungarians have found them tough to keep under control. Two revolutions in particular stand out. In each case, the Hungarians initially encountered bloodshed and more oppression, but ultimately brought about positive change. The dates these revolutions began remain national holidays.

Lajos Kossuth and the 1848 Revolution

Of the many Hungarian uprisings against Hapsburg rule (1526–1918), the 1848 Revolution was the most dramatic. In 1848, a wave of nationalism spread across Europe. The spirit of change caught on in Hungary, where lawyer and parliamentarian Lajos Kossuth led an uprising sparked on March 15. Though the Austrians were initially overwhelmed by the revolt, they eventually brought in Russian troops to regain control. For a few years, the Hapsburgs cracked down on their Hungarian subjects—but within 20 years, they ceded half the authority of their empire to Budapest, creating the Dual Monarchy.

Imre Nagy and the 1956 Uprising

The Hungarian politician Imre Nagy (EEM-ray nodge, 1896–1958) was a lifelong communist. In the 1930s, he allegedly worked for the Soviet secret police. In the late 1940s, he quickly moved up the hierarchy of Hungary's communist government, becoming prime minister in 1953. But in the Moscow shuffle following Stalin's death, Nagy was quickly demoted.

When violence broke out in Budapest on October 23, 1956, Nagy reemerged as the leader of the reform movement. For a few short days, it seemed as though Hungary's communism would moderate—until Soviet tanks rumbled into Budapest, brutally put down the uprising, and occupied the city. By the time the Red Army left, 25,000 protesters were dead, and 250,000 Hungarians had fled to Austria. Nagy was arrested, given a sham trial, and executed in 1958. He was buried disgracefully, face-down in an unmarked grave, and his name was taboo in Hungary for 30 years.

Though the uprising met a tragic end, within a few years Hungary's harshness did soften, and the milder, so-called "goulash communism" emerged. As the Eastern Bloc thawed in 1989, Nagy became a martyr and a hero. His body was discovered and given a proper reburial in July of that exciting year—heralding the quickly approaching end of the communist era.

exhibitions, April–Sept Tue–Sun 10:00–18:00, closed Mon; Oct–March Tue–Sun 10:00–16:00, closed Mon; closed mid-Dec–mid-Jan, Tóth Árpád sétány 40, Budapest I, tel. 1/356-9522).

• *Our guided stroll is finished. Under your feet lies one more sightseeing attraction:*

Labyrinth of Buda Castle (Budavári Labirintus)—There are miles of caves burrowed under Castle Hill, carved out by water, expanded by the Turks, and used by locals during the siege of Buda at the end of World War II. If you've done everything else in town, you can explore these caverns and see a conceptual exhibit that traces human history (1,200 Ft, 25 percent discount with Budapest Card, daily 9:30–19:30, last entry 19:00, entrance between Royal Palace and Matthias Church at Úri utca 9, Budapest I, tel. 1/212-0207, www.labirintus.com). After 18:00, they turn the lights out and give everyone gas lanterns. The exhibit loses something in the dark, but it's nicely spooky and a fun chance to startle amorous Hungarian teens—or be startled by mischievous ones.

Gellért Hill (Gellérthegy)

The hill rising from the Danube banks just downriver from the castle is Gellért Hill. When King István converted Hungary to Christianity in the year 1000, he brought in Bishop Gellért, a monk from Venice, to tutor his son. But some rebellious Magyars had other ideas. They put the bishop in a barrel, drove long nails in from the outside, and rolled him down this hill...tenderizing him to death. Gellért became the patron saint of Budapest and gave his name to the hill that killed him.

Gellért Hill's only real attraction is the **baths** at Gellért Hotel (see page 433 of "Budapest's Baths"). The hill is a fine place to commune with nature on a hike or jog.

Monument Hike—The north slope of Gellért Hill is good for a low-impact hike. You'll see many interesting monuments, most notably the memorial to Bishop Gellért himself (you can't miss it as you cross the Elisabeth Bridge on Hegyalja út). A bit farther up, seek out a newer monument to the world's great philosophers—Eastern, Western, and in between, from Gandhi to Plato to Jesus. Nearby is a scenic overlook with a king and a queen holding hands on either side of the Danube.

Citadella—This strategic, hill-capping fortress was built by the Hapsburgs after the 1848 Revolution to keep an eye on their Hungarian subjects. There's not much to do up here (no museum or exhibits, just a hotel), but it's a good destination for an uphill hike, and provides excellent views over all of Budapest.

The hill is crowned by the **Liberation Monument,** featuring a woman holding aloft a palm branch. The locals call it "the lady with the big fish" or "the great bottle opener." The heroic Soviet soldier—who once inspired the workers with a huge red star from the base of the monument—is now in Statue Park (see page 428).

Cave Church (Sziklatemplom)—Hidden in the hillside on the south end of the hill (across the street from Gellért Hotel) is Budapest's atmospheric cave church—literally burrowed into the rock face. The communists bricked up this church when they came to power, but now it's open for visitors once again (free entry, but closed to sightseers during frequent services).

Pest

Central Pest (Belváros), Along Váci utca

▲**Vörösmarty tér**—The prominent square called Vörösmarty tér (VOO-roosh-mar-tee tehr), at the north end of the Váci utca pedestrian boulevard, is named for a 19th-century Romantic poet (see his statue in the center) who stirred nationalistic spirit with his writing. It's a good place to get oriented in Pest.

Find the landmark **Gerbeaud** pastry shop at the north end of the square. Between the World Wars, the well-to-do ladies of Budapest would meet here after shopping their way up Váci utca. Today it's still *the* meeting point in Budapest (described under "Cafés and Pastry Shops," page 450).

As you face Gerbeaud, the street to your left leads to the Danube embankment (ideal for a scenic stroll), and the street to your right leads past Erzsébet tér (once Pest's market square) to Andrássy út, lined with sights, restaurants, and hotels (see "Andrássy út and City Park," below). If you were to jog left around the Gerbeaud and then go straight, you'd reach the Parliament in about 10 minutes (see "More Sights in Central Pest," page 414).

The yellow Metro stop in the middle of the square is the entrance to the shallow *Földalatti*, or "underground"—the first subway on the Continent (built for the millennial celebration in 1896). Today, it still carries passengers to Andrássy út sights (it runs under that street all the way to City Park).

Three hundred years ago, Vörösmarty tér was a rough-and-tumble, often flooded quarter just outside the Pest city walls. People came here to enjoy brutal, staged fights between bloodhounds and bears (like cockfights, only bigger and angrier, with more fur and teeth). The Turkish invaders had finally been forced out of Pest, and the city was nearly deserted. After a series of battles for Hungarian independence, the Hapsburgs moved into ruined Pest in the 1710s. They populated the city with Austrians. (While there was a small Hungarian minority, most Magyars lived in the countryside.) The Austrians of Pest began rebuilding the city, virtually from scratch—most of the buildings you'll see are no older than 300 years.

Pest Center Sights

① Attila József Statue
② Imre Nagy Statue
③ Kossuth Lajos Square
④ Szabadság Square
⑤ Roosevelt Square
⑥ Vigadó Square
⑦ Vörösmarty Square
⑧ Erzsébet Square
⑨ Deák Square
⑩ Liszt Ferenc Square
⑪ Pendragon Bookstore
⑫ Carlson Wagonlit Travel
⑬ Vista Travel Center
⑭ Párisi Udvar Shopping Gallery
⑮ Red Bus Bookstore
⑯ Danube Palace (Duna Palota Concert Tickets)

For more of the story, stroll down the street across the square from Gerbeaud: Váci utca.

▲▲**Váci utca**—This pedestrian boulevard—Budapest's shopping and tourism artery—was dreamland for Eastern Europeans back in the 1980s. It was here that they fantasized about what it might be like to be free, while drooling over Nikes, Reeboks, and Big Macs before any of these Western evils were introduced elsewhere in the Warsaw Pact region.

Many tourists are mesmerized by this people-friendly stretch of souvenir stands, Internet cafés, and upscale boutiques—thinking wrongly that this is the "real" Budapest. But a ramble along Váci utca (VAH-tsee OOT-zah) does have stories to tell, and you're sure to stroll here at some point during your visit. The following self-guided walk will help you uncover artifacts of authentic Pest between the postcard racks.

"Váci utca" means "street to Vác"—a town 25 miles to the north. This has long been the street where the elite of Pest would go shopping, then strut their stuff for their neighbors on an evening promenade (*korzó* in Hungarian). Today, the tourists do the strutting here—and the Hungarians go to suburban shopping malls.

As you walk, be sure to look up. Along this street and throughout Pest, spectacular facades begin on the second floor, above a plain entryway (in the 1970s, ground-floor shop windows were made uniformly dull by the communist government). Pan up to see some of Pest's best architecture. These were the townhouses of the aristocracy whose mansions dotted the countryside.

At the end of the first block, next to the Tatuum store on the right, a **plaque** notes that Pest's medieval town wall was torn down in 1789. The no-longer-needed wall had been gradually crumbling for centuries, and as residents rebuilt from the Turkish occupation, it was just getting in the way.

On the next block, find the quirky **Modernist facade** at #8 on the left (over the Clinique shop). Compare this one to the building marked *Douglas* (#11A, across the street a few doors up). The first is more traditional Modernism, but the second is a great example of the **Secession** style. Modernist architecture was rebellious: It rejected what came before—which is why it still looks weird to us today. But the Secession did one better and rejected Modernism.

At the end of the block, the unassuming **McDonald's** (on the right, down Régiposta utca) was a landmark in Eastern Europe—the first McDonald's behind the Iron Curtain. Budapest has always been a little more rebellious, independent, and cosmopolitan than its Eastern European neighbors, who flocked here during the communist era. Long lines for a burger famously went down the street—but it wasn't "fast food," it was "West food."

Continuing your stroll, you'll notice that some of the **facades** are plain (like the one above the tobacco shop on the right, just after the street leading to McDonald's). Many of these used to be more ornate, like the others, but they were destroyed by WWII bombs and rebuilt in a stripped-down style.

At the halfway point on your Váci utca stroll (midway between the square and Great Market Hall), an underpass takes you below busy Szabad street (Szabad sajtó út). While you're down there, enjoy photos of Budapest (with English descriptions) from the turn of the 20th century, when the city was booming.

The last stretch of Váci utca dead-ends at the huge market hall. This used to be a strongly Serbian neighborhood. (Around the next corner to the left, on Szerb utca, there's still a **Serbian Orthodox church**—heavy with incense and packed with icons.) Traditionally, Hungary's territory included most of Slovakia and large parts of Romania, Croatia, and Serbia—and people from all of those places (along with Jews and Gypsies) flocked to Buda and Pest. And yet, most of the residents of this cosmopolitan city still speak Hungarian. Through centuries of foreign invasions and visitors, Budapest remains Magyar. (Remember that after the Turks left, Budapest was mostly Austrian. The Austrians didn't go anywhere...they became Hungarian, assimilated into the local culture.)

At the end of Váci utca, you'll come to the...

▲▲**Great Market Hall (Nagyvásárcsarnok)**—This market hall (along with 4 others) was built—you know it—around the year

1896. The cavernous interior features three levels. The ground floor has produce stands, bakeries, butcher stalls, heaps of paprika, goose liver, and sausages. Upstairs are fun, super-cheap, stand-up, Hungarian-style fast-food joints and six-stool pubs, along with a great selection of souvenirs both traditional (paprika) and not-so-traditional (commie kitsch T-shirts; for all the details, see "Shopping" on page 436). Along the upstairs back wall are historic photos of the market hall (and WCs). The basement is pungent with tanks of still-swimming carp, catfish, and perch, and piles of pickles.

The market was kept open during communism. Margaret Thatcher came to visit in 1989. She expected atrocious conditions compared to English markets, but was pleasantly surprised to find this place up to snuff. This was, after all, "goulash communism" (Hungary's pragmatic mix, which allowed a little private enterprise to keep people going). On the steps of this building, she delivered a historic speech about open society, heralding the impending arrival of the market economy.

The market hall is ideal for lunch, picnic shopping, and people-watching (Mon 6:00–17:00, Tue–Fri 6:00–18:00, Sat 6:00–14:00, closed Sun, Fővám körút 1–3, Budapest IX, M3: Kálvin tér). See "Eating," page 445, for ideas.

From the market, walk to the river. You'll pass (on the left) the University of Economics, which was called Karl Marx University 15 years ago. The bridge leads straight to Gellért Hotel, with its famous hot-springs bath, at the foot of Gellért Hill (see "Budapest's Baths," page 429). Trams #2 and #2A run from here along the Danube directly back to central Pest, the Chain Bridge, and the Parliament.

More Sights in Central Pest

▲**Hungarian Parliament (Országház)**—The Parliament building, like so much of Budapest, was built around the city's millennial celebration in 1896. Its elegant neo-Gothic design and riverside location were inspired by its counterpart in London. This enormous building—with literally miles of stairs—was appropriate for a time when Budapest ruled much of Eastern Europe. But today it's just plain too big—the legislature only occupies an eighth of the building. Architecture snobs shake their heads and wonder why this frilly Gothic monstrosity is topped with a Renaissance dome. (To make matters worse, there used to be a huge red communist star on top of the tallest spire.) But I think it's beautiful.

The best views of the building are from across the Danube—especially in the late afternoon sunlight. Tours of the Parliament's opulent interior include the elegant main entryway, a legislative chamber, and the Hungarian crown, under the ornate dome (2,300 Ft, English tours usually daily at 10:00, 12:00, and 14:00, but can change so confirm in advance; follow signs around to entry X, find the line for individual tickets, join the disorganized queue, and make it clear to the guard that you want an *individual* ticket; eventually you'll be allowed to enter the door marked X, pay cashier, and return to the mob to wait for your tour; Kossuth tér 1–3, Budapest V, M2: Kossuth tér, tel. 1/441-4904, www.mkogy.hu).

Kossuth Tér—The square behind the Parliament building has several interesting monuments. Just behind the Parliament is a grassy park with statues of various important Hungarians. A newer monument features a Hungarian flag with a hole cut out of the middle. This commemorates the 1956 Uprising, when protesters removed the socialist-style seal the Soviets had added to their flag.

Also near the Parliament are two other interesting monuments. By the tram tracks on the end of the Parliament facing the Chain Bridge, look for a statue of the pensive **Attila József**, a popular modern poet who committed suicide at age 32. He's looking over the Danube, a common motif in his works. Straight back from the river, on Vértanúk tere, a statue of the pensive **Imre Nagy**, hero of the 1956 Uprising, stands on a bridge (see page 408).

At the top end of Kossuth tér is the...

Museum of Ethnography (Néprajzi Múzeum)—This museum, housed in one of Budapest's grandest venues, feels deserted. Its fine exhibit on Hungarian folk culture (mostly from the late 19th century) only takes up a small corner of the cavernous building. This permanent exhibit, with surprisingly good English explanations, shows off costumes, tools, wagons, boats, beehives, furniture, and ceramics of the many peoples who lived in pre-WWI Hungary (which also included much of today's Slovakia and Romania). The museum also has a collection of artifacts from other European and world cultures, which it cleverly assembles into good temporary exhibits (free, charge for special exhibitions, Tue–Sun 10:00–18:00, closed Mon, Kossuth tér 12, Budapest V, M2: Kossuth tér, tel. 1/473-2400).

Hungarian National Museum (Magyar Nemzeti Múzeum)—One of Budapest's biggest museums features all manner of Hungarian historic bric-a-brac, from the Paleolithic age to a more recent infestation of dinosaurs (the communists). The first floor focuses on the Carpathian Basin in the pre-Magyar days, with ancient artifacts and Roman remains. The basement features a lapidarium, with medieval tombstones and more Roman ruins. On the second floor, 20 rooms take you on a very fast overview trip from the arrival of the Magyars in 896 up to the 1989 revolution. Unless you've got a pretty good handle on Hungarian history, the exhibits are difficult to appreciate (with only a few big-picture English explanations). The most interesting part comes at the very end, with an exhibit on the communist era, featuring both pro- and anti-Party propaganda. The exhibit ends with video footage of the 1989 end of communism—demonstrations, monumental parliament votes, and a final farewell to the last Soviet troops leaving Hungarian soil. Another uprising—the 1848 Revolution against Hapsburg rule—was declared from the steps of this impressive neoclassical building (free, charge for special exhibitions, Tue–Sun 10:00–18:00, closed Mon, last entry 30 min before closing, near Great Market Hall at Múzeum körút 14–16, Budapest VIII, tel. 1/338-2122, www.hnm.hu).

The Millennium Underground of 1896

Built to get the masses of visitors conveniently out to Heroes' Square, this fun and extremely handy little Metro line follows Andrássy út from Vörösmarty Square (Pest's main square) to City Park. Just 20 steps below street level, it's so shallow that you must follow the signs on the street (listing end points) to gauge the right direction, because there's no underpass for switching platforms. The first underground on the Continent (London's is older), it originally had horse-drawn cars. Trains depart every couple of minutes. Recently renovated, the M1 line retains its 1896 atmosphere, along with fun black-and-white photos of the age.

▲**Courtyards and Galleries**—If you only experience what's on the street in Budapest, you'll miss a big part of the story. Pest is filled with once-grand, now crumbling facades, and behind most of them, you'll find cozy courtyards where residents carry out much of their lives. These courtyards, shared among neighbors and ringed by a common balcony, stay cool through the summer. Poking into some of these courtyards (which are generally open to the public, offering a handy shortcut through city blocks) is an essential Back Door experience for understanding the inner life of the city.

Pest's streets also hide some impressive galleries—once used for elegant shopping, now faded and ignored. The most spectacular—with delicate woodwork and a breathtaking stained-glass dome—is the **Párisi Udvar**. It's dead-center in Pest, along the busy Lajos Kossuth út, a few blocks up from the big, white Elisabeth Bridge (enter at Lajos Kossuth út 11; can also enter the other end, around the corner at Petőfi Sándor utca 2). If you're passing by (it's near the recommended local-style Jégbüfé café and the Leo Panzió hotel—see "Eating" and "Sleeping," below), it's certainly worth a look. While many of the storefronts inside are abandoned, a few are still alive and kicking (including a bookstore with English guidebooks).

Andrássy út and City Park

Connecting central Pest to City Park, Andrássy út is Budapest's main boulevard, lined with shops, theaters, cafés, and locals living well. Budapesters claim it's like the Champs-Elysées and Broadway rolled into one. While that's a stretch, it is a good place to stroll and get a feel for today's urban Pest. The best part to wander is between the boulevard's beginning at Deák tér and the Oktogon.

The following sights are listed in order, from Deák tér (in central Pest) to City Park. The M1 line runs every couple of minutes

Andrássy út

1 K+K Hotel Opera
2 Cotton House
3 Hotel Ambra
4 Hotel Medosz
5 Hotel Délibáb

6 Bohémtanya Pub
7 Bagolyvár Rest.
8 Menza Rest.
9 Articsóka Rest.
10 Rest. Művészinas & Duran Szendvics

11 Gundel Restaurant
12 Müvész Kávéház Café
13 Robinson Restaurant
14 MÁV Office (Train Tickets)
15 Discover Hungary/Yellow Zebra Bike & Internet (2)

Count Andrássy and Sissy

You'll see the names Andrássy and Sissy (or Elisabeth) a lot in Budapest. A key player in the 1848 Revolution, **Count Julius Andrássy** ultimately helped forge the Dual Monarchy of the Austro-Hungarian Empire. He served as the Hungarian prime minister and Austro-Hungarian foreign minister (1871–1879), eventually being forced to step down after his unpopular campaign to appropriate Bosnia and Herzegovina (and consequently boost the Slav population).

Sissy was **Empress Elisabeth,** the Princess Diana of the early 20th-century Hapsburgs (see page 700). Her pet project was advancing the cause of Hungarian autonomy within the empire. While she was married to Emperor Franz Josef, she spent seven years in Budapest—enjoying horseback riding, the local cuisine, and the company of the charming and good-looking Count Andrássy. Her third daughter—believed to be the count's—was known as the Little Hungarian Princess.

just under the street—so if you get tired of walking it's easy to skip several blocks ahead (stops marked by yellow Földalatti signs; see sidebar).

St. István's Basilica (Szent István Bazilika)—Step into Budapest's largest Catholic church and you'll see not Jesus, but St. István

(Stephen), Hungary's first Christian king, glowing above the high altar. (See the "Statue of St. István" listing on page 404 for more on this important Hungarian.) The church is only about 100 years old—like most Budapest landmarks, it was built around 1896. Recently renovated, the interior sparkles proudly. But even though it looks like a major landmark and it's packed with tour groups, the church isn't that compelling (free, Mon–Fri 9:00–17:00, Sat 9:00–13:00, Sun 13:00–17:00, Szent István tér, Budapest V, M1: Bajcsy-Zsilinszky út or M3: Arany János utca).

The church's primary claim to fame is that it's the resting place of the **"holy right hand"** of St. István. The sacred fist—a somewhat grotesque, 1,000-year-old withered stump—is in a jeweled box in the chapel to the left of the main altar (follow signs for *Szent Jobb Kápolna*, chapel often closed). Pop in a coin for two minutes of light.

The church also has a measly treasury (250 Ft) and panoramic

observation deck, with a decent view that gives a sense of the sprawl of Pest (500 Ft, 20 percent discount with Budapest Card, elevator to midlevel, then 137 stairs or smaller elevator, plus a few stairs to top of tower, daily April–May 10:00–16:30, June–Aug 9:30–18:00, Sept–Oct 10:00–17:30, closed Nov–March).

▲**Postal Museum (Postamúzeum)**—This quirky museum, in a fine old apartment from Budapest's Golden Age, features a delightful collection of postal artifacts. You'll see post office coats of arms, 100-year-old postal furniture, antique telephone boxes, historic mailman uniforms, and all manner of postal paraphernalia that was cutting-edge a century ago. It's displayed in an elegant old merchant's mansion with big Murano crystal chandeliers, all the original ornate woodwork, and creaky parquet floors. The apartment—decorated as it was when built in the 1880s—is as interesting as the museum's collection. English-speaking Nora, who's usually around, loves to explain the place and demonstrate the old telephone-operator switchboard (200 Ft, covered by Budapest Card, Tue–Sun 10:00–18:00, closed Mon, loaner English information in each room, or buy the 500-Ft guidebook, just up the street from St. István's Basilica at Andrássy út 3, Budapest VI, M1: Bajcsy-Zsilinszky út, look for easy-to-miss sign and dial 10 to get upstairs, tel. 1/269-6838, www.postamuzeum.hu).

▲**Hungarian State Opera House (Magyar Állami Operaház)**— The neo-Renaissance home of the Hungarian State Opera features performances almost daily. Designed by Miklós Ybl, the building was constructed in the 1890s using almost entirely Hungarian materials. After being damaged in World War II, it was painstakingly restored in the early 1980s. Today, with lavish marble-and-frescoes decor, a gorgeous gilded interior, and high-quality performances at bargain prices, this is one of Europe's finest opera houses. To take in an opera here, see "Budapest Music Scene," page 434.

Even if you don't see an opera, you can slip in the front door and check out the sumptuous entryway when the box office is open (Mon–Sat 11:00–19:00, Sun 16:00–19:00, until 17:00 on days when there's no performance, Andrássy út 22, Budapest VI, M1: Opera). Better yet, take one of the excellent 45-minute **tours** in English (nearly daily at 15:00 and 16:00, reservations not necessary, but it's smart to call ahead and confirm schedule; 2,400 Ft, 200 Ft less with Budapest Card, buy in opera shop—around to the right as you face main entrance, shop open Mon–Fri 10:30–12:45 & 13:30–17:00, Sat–Sun 13:30–17:00, open later during performances, tel. 1/332-8197).

Franz Liszt Square (Liszt Ferenc tér)—This leafy, trendy square on the right (south) side of Andrássy út is surrounded by hip, expensive cafés and restaurants. (The best is the kitschy communist theme restaurant Menza—see page 447.) This is *the* scene for Budapest's yuppies. At the far end of the square is the Music Academy also named for Liszt—a German composer with a Hungarian name, who loved his family's Magyar heritage (though he didn't speak Hungarian) and spent his last five years in Budapest.

Oktogon—During the communist era, this square—at the intersection of Andrássy út and the Great Ring Road (Nagykörút)—was called "November 7 tér" in honor of the Bolshevik Revolution. (Andrássy út was renamed "Sztálin út"; later, after Stalin fell out of fashion, it was simply "People's Republic Boulevard.") Today kids have nicknamed it "American tér" for the fast-food joints littering the square and streets nearby. From this square, Andrássy út gradually becomes the dull diplomatic quarter—less colorful, with tame, embassy-lined streets and stately mansions. From the center of Andrássy út, you can see the column of Heroes' Square at the end of the boulevard.

▲▲House of Terror (Terror Háza)—The former headquarters of the darkest sides of two different regimes—the Arrow Cross (Nazi-occupied Hungary's version of the Gestapo) and the ÁVO/ÁVH (communist Hungary's secret police)—is now, fittingly, an excellent museum of that time of terror.

Hungary initially allied with Hitler to retain a degree of self-determination and self-preservation (for itself and its Jewish population) and to try to regain their huge territorial losses after World War I. But in March 1944, the country was taken over by the Nazi-affiliated Arrow Cross. The Arrow Cross immediately set to work exterminating Budapest's Jews; by May, trains were already heading for Auschwitz. As the end of the war neared, Arrow Cross members resorted to more desperate measures, lining Jews up along the Danube and shooting them into the river. To save bullets, they'd sometimes tie several victims together, shoot one of them, and throw him into the freezing Danube—dragging the others in with him. They executed hundreds in the basement of this building. When the communists moved into Hungary, they took over the same building as headquarters for their secret police (the ÁVO, later renamed ÁVH). To keep dissent to a minimum, the secret police terrorized, tried, deported, or executed anyone suspected of being an enemy of the state.

An overhang casts the shadow of the word "TERROR" onto the building. The museum's atrium features a Soviet tank and a huge wall covered with portraits of the victims of this building.

The modern, stylish, high-tech exhibit (starting on the top floor and spiraling down) is designed for Hungarians, but the English audioguide (1,000 Ft extra) and free handouts help visitors appreciate the experience.

The museum has many memorable exhibits, including rooms featuring gulag life, social realist art and propaganda, a labyrinth of pork-fat bricks reminding old-timers of the harsh conditions of the 1950s (lard on bread for dinner), and religion (joining the Church was a way to express rebellion). This is a powerful experience, particularly for elderly Hungarians who knew many of the victims and perpetrators and have personal memories of the terrors that came with Hungary's "double occupation."

The last section begins with a three-minute video of a guard explaining the execution process, which plays as you descend by elevator into the prison basement. In the early 1950s, this basement was the scene of torture; in 1956, it became a clubhouse of sorts for the local communist youth club. It has now been reconstructed circa 1955. During the 1956 Uprising, 250,000 fled to Austria and the West during the two weeks of chaos before the U.S.S.R. pulled a Tiananmen Square–style crackdown (see page 408). The Hall of Tears remembers 25,000 who died in '56. The last two rooms—with the only color video clips—show the festive and exhilarating days in 1991 when the Soviets departed, making way for freedom. Scenes include the reburial of the Hungarian hero, Imre Nagy; the Pope's visit; and walls of "victimizers"—members and supporters of the Arrow Cross and ÁVO, many of whom are still living, and who were never brought to justice.

Cost, Hours, Location: 1,200 Ft, 20 percent discount with Budapest Card (that's 960 Ft), more for special exhibitions, Tue–Fri 10:00–18:00, Sat–Sun 10:00–19:30, closed Mon, café, bookshop, Andrássy út 60, Budapest VI, M1: Vörösmarty utca, tel. 1/374-2600, www.terrorhaza.hu.

Audioguide: The 1,000-Ft English audioguide is good but almost too thorough, and can be difficult to hear over the din of the Hungarian soundtracks in each room. You can't fast-forward through the very dense and sometimes long-winded commentary. As an alternative, note that each room is stocked with good, free English fliers.

▲▲**Heroes' Square (Hősök tere)**—Like much of Budapest, this *Who's Who* of Hungarian History at the end of Andrássy út was built to celebrate the city's 1,000th birthday in 1896 (M1: Hősök tere). More than just the hottest place in town for skateboarding, this is the site of several museums and the gateway to City Park (filled with diversions for sightseers).

Step right up to the **Millennium Monument** to meet the world's most historic Hungarians (who look to me like their

language sounds). The granddaddy
of all Magyars, Árpád, stands
proudly at the bottom of the pillar,
peering down Andrássy út. The
118-foot-tall pillar supports the
archangel Gabriel as he offers the
crown to St. István (he accepted it
and Christianized the Magyars). In
front of the pillar is the Hungarian
War Memorial (fenced in now to

keep skateboarders from enjoying its perfect slope). Behind the
pillar, colonnades feature Hungarian VIPs. Look for names you
recognize: István, Béla IV, Mátyás Corvinus. But hey...where
are the Hapsburgs? At the time of the monument's construction,
Budapest was part of the Austrian Empire, and Hapsburgs stood
in the right-hand colonnade. When Hungary regained its independence in World War I, the people tore down the sculpture of the
unpopular Franz Josef. (A statue of the less-hated Maria Theresa
was left alone...but was ultimately destroyed by a WWII bomb.)
After World War II, the Hapsburgs were replaced by Hungarians.
In fact, the last two heroes—Ferenc Rákóczi and Lajos Kossuth—
were revolutionaries who fought against Austria. The sculptures on
the top corners of the two colonnades represent, in order from left
to right: Work and Welfare, War, Peace, and the Importance of
Packing Light.

As you face Árpád, the **Museum of Fine Arts** (Szépművészeti
Múzeum), which has an especially good Spanish collection, is to
your left (free, charge for special exhibitions, Tue–Sun 10:00–17:30,
closed Mon, tel. 1/469-7100). The **Palace of Art** (Műcsarnok),
used for temporary contemporary art exhibits, is to your right
(1,600 Ft, covered by Budapest Card, Tue–Wed and Fri–Sun
10:00–18:00, Thu 12:00–20:00, closed Mon, tel. 1/460-7000). In
the basement of the Palace of Art, you'll find a fun but overpriced
20-minute **Countryrama 3-D movie** about Hungary (1,000 Ft,
30 percent discount with Budapest Card, shown every 30 min
on the half hour; mid-March–Sept Tue–Sun 10:30–17:30, closed
Mon; Oct–mid-March Fri–Sun 10:30–17:00, closed Mon–Thu;
tel. 1/460-7014). While the 3-D is fuzzy, this tired video overview
of the countryside is relaxing, and affords a quick swing through
Hungary in a Travel Channel kind of way. Since majority rules for
language, the movie is generally in English (and everyone else gets
headphones).

If you leave Heroes' Square between the two colonnades
behind the main pillar, you'll cross a bridge into...

▲▲**City Park (Városliget)**—This is the city's not-so-cen-
tral Central Park. The park was the site of the overblown 1896

Millennium Exhibition, celebrating Hungary's 1,000th birthday... and it's still packed with huge party decorations: a zoo with quirky Art Nouveau buildings, a replica of a Transylvanian castle, a massive bath/swimming complex, walking paths, and an amusement park. The park is filled with unwinding locals. If the sightseeing grind gets you down, spend the afternoon taking a mini-vacation from your busy vacation the way Budapesters do—stroll in the park and soak in the baths.

Orient yourself from the bridge behind Heroes' Square: The huge Vajdahunyad Castle is on your right (go straight and look for bridge to enter complex). Straight into the park and on the left are the big copper domes of the fun, relaxing Széchenyi Baths (see "Budapest's Baths," below). And the zoo is past the lake on the left. Three recommended restaurants are at the end of the lake near the zoo (see "Eating," page 445).

▲**Vajdahunyad Castle (Vajdahunyad Vára)**—The huge complex is a replica of a famous castle in Transylvania (part of Hungary for centuries), surrounded by other styles of traditionally Hungarian architecture (textbook Romanesque, Gothic, Renaissance, and Baroque). Some find it artificial in a Walt Disney World sort of way; others think it's pretty cool. You can enter the castle complex for free to poke around the grounds. (After crossing the bridge behind Heroes' Square, turn right.)

As you enter the complex through the castle facade, you'll see a replica of a 13th-century **Benedictine chapel** on the left—Budapest's most popular spot for weekend weddings in the summer. Farther ahead on the right, you'll see a big Baroque mansion—which houses, of all things, the **Museum of Hungarian Agriculture** (Magyar Mezőgazdasági Múzeum, free, charge for special exhibitions; mid-Feb–mid-Nov Tue–Sun 10:00–17:00, closed Mon; mid-Nov–mid-Feb Tue–Fri 10:00–16:00, Sat–Sun 10:00–17:00, closed Mon; last entry 30 min before closing, tel. 1/363-2711). The museum brags that it's Europe's biggest agriculture museum...but the lavish interior is more interesting than the exhibits.

Across the street from the museum entry, you'll see a monument to **Anonymous;** specifically, the Anonymous who penned the first Hungarian history in the Middle Ages.

Zoo (Állatkert)—Aside from animals, the zoo also has redeeming sightseeing value: Many of its structures are playful bits of turn-of-the-20th-century Art Nouveau. To reach the beautiful Art Nouveau elephant house, turn right inside the main entry, then right again at the fork, and look for the white-and-turquoise tower. The zoo is a perfect example of a sight that's not really worth the price of entry, but makes for a fun 15-minute walk-through with the Budapest Card (1,300 Ft, covered by Budapest Card, May–Aug Mon–Thu

9:00–18:30, Fri–Sun 9:00–19:00; March–April and Sept–Oct daily 9:00–17:00; Nov–Feb daily 9:00–16:00; Állatkerti körút 6–12, Budapest XIV, tel. 1/364-0109, www.zoobudapest.com).

Jewish Budapest

As the former co-capital of an empire that included millions of Jews, Budapest always had a high concentration of Jewish residents. Before World War II, 5 percent of Hungary's population and 25 percent of Budapest's was Jewish (the city was dubbed "Judapest" by their snide Viennese neighbors up the river). Hungary lost nearly 600,000 Jews to the Holocaust, at the hands of the brutal Nazi puppet government called the Arrow Cross. (For more about the Holocaust in Hungary, see the "House of Terror" listing on page 420.) Today, only half of one percent of Hungarians are Jewish—and most of them are in Budapest. In recent years, since the thawing of communism, Hungarian Jews have been taking a renewed interest in their heritage.

The first sight listed here is very central, close to Pest's Deák tér; the other is just outside central Pest, a Metro ride plus a five-minute walk away.

▲**Great Synagogue (Zsinagóga)**—This impressively restored synagogue is the second biggest in the world, after one in New York City.

While several traditional synagogues are nearby (this is Pest's Jewish quarter), the Great Synagogue is reformed, and—with its nave, pulpit, and pipe organ flanking the high altar—it looks like

a church with the symbols switched. It was built in the 1850s, when Jews wanted to feel more integrated into the community. The balconies were originally for women, but today men and women sit together anywhere. The Moorish-flavored decor is a reminder of how Jewish culture flourished in Iberia. After World War II, the synagogue was refurbished with financial support from Tony Curtis, an American actor of Hungarian-Jewish origin (he and his daughter Jamie Lee continues to support these causes today).

Your synagogue ticket also includes the **Jewish Museum** (Zsidó Múzeum, in the same building; entry for both-1,000 Ft, maybe covered by Budapest Card, April–Oct Mon–Thu 10:00–17:00, Fri and Sun 10:00–14:00; Nov–March Mon–Thu 10:00–15:00, Fri and Sun 10:00–14:00; always closed Sat and Jewish holidays, often closed mid-Dec–mid-Jan, last entry 30 min before closing, Dohány utca 2, Budapest VII; between M2: Astoria and M1, M2, or M3: Deák tér; tel. 01/344-5131).

Behind the synagogue, the *Tree of Life* sculpture was built on the site of mass graves of those killed by the Nazis. The willow makes an upside-down menorah, each individual leaf lists the name of a victim, and pebbles represent prayers. You can visit the *Tree* even if you don't buy a ticket for the synagogue (enter through synagogue security gate and go straight ahead through doors and under arcade to the park behind the synagogue; if synagogue is closed, go around left side to view monument through a fence).

Aviv Travel leads **tours** of the synagogue and the Jewish quarter (basic 1-hr English tour covers synagogue, museum, and *Tree of Life*, 1,900 Ft, includes admission, Mon–Thu hourly on the half hour 10:30–15:30; Fri and Sun 10:30, 11:30, and 12:30 only; kiosk by synagogue entry).

▲**Holocaust Memorial Center (Holokauszt Emlékközpont)**— This brand-new center is making great strides in honoring the nearly 600,000 Hungarian victims of the Nazis. The impressive modern complex (with a beautifully restored 1920s synagogue as its centerpiece) is intended to serve as a museum of the Hungarian Holocaust, a monument to its victims, and a research and documentation center of Nazi atrocities. A black marble wall in the courtyard is etched with the names of victims, and an information center downstairs helps teary-eyed Hungarians locate the names of their relatives.

The center—which opened on April 16, 2004, the 60th anniversary of the ghettoization of Hungary—presents very good temporary exhibitions. A permanent exhibit detailing the history of the Hungarian Holocaust opened in the fall of 2005 (free, Tue–Sun 10:00–18:00, closed Mon, Páva utca 39, Budapest IX, M3: Ferenc körút, tel. 1/216-6557, www.hdke.hu). To reach the complex, take the M3 Metro line to Ferenc körút. Use the exit marked *Üllői út 45–51*, walk straight ahead three blocks, and look right.

The Danube (Duna)

The mighty river coursing through the heart of the city defines Budapest. For many visitors, a highlight is taking a touristy but beautiful boat cruise up and down the Danube—especially at night (see "Tours," above). Here are some other river-related activities to consider.

▲**Danube Embankment (Dunakorzó)**—Pest's breezy riverfront promenade (from Elisabeth Bridge to the Chain Bridge) is a fine place for a stroll. Start on Vigadó tér, two blocks towards the river from Vörösmarty tér, and head southward. Along the way, keep an eye out for the Little Princess statue leaning on the railing—one of Budapest's symbols, even though it's just over a decade old. When

Prince Charles visited Budapest, he liked this statue so much that he had a replica made for himself. You'll pass a few souvenir stalls and big, fancy hotels (including Hyatt and InterContinental), and enjoy sweeping views of Buda, some of the international river-cruise ships, and the city's many bridges. While dining values aren't good here, Spoon—on the boat moored in front of the InterContinental Hotel—is fun (see "Eating," page 445).

▲Chain Bridge (Széchenyi Lánchíd)—One of the world's great bridges connects Pest's Roosevelt tér and Buda's Adam Clark tér. This historic, iconic bridge, guarded by lions (symbolizing power), is Budapest's most enjoyable and convenient bridge to cross on foot. (This is especially handy for commuting to the top of Castle Hill, since both bus #16 and the funicular to the top begin from the Buda end of the bridge.)

Until the mid-19th century, only pontoon barges spanned the Danube between Buda and Pest. In the winter, the pontoons had to be pulled in, leaving locals to rely on ferries (in good weather) or a frozen river. People often walked across the frozen Danube, only to get stuck on the other side during a thaw, with nothing to do but wait for another cold snap.

Count István Széchenyi was stranded for a week trying to get to his father's funeral. After missing it, Széchenyi decided to commission Budapest's first permanent bridge. The Chain Bridge was built by Scotsman Adam Clark between 1842 and 1849, and it immediately became an important symbol of Budapest. Széchenyi—a man of the Enlightenment—charged both commoners and nobles a toll for crossing his bridge, making it a symbol of equality in those tense times. Like all of the city's bridges, the Chain Bridge was destroyed by Nazis at the end of World War II, but was quickly rebuilt.

Margaret Island (Margitsziget)—Budapesters come to play in this huge, leafy park, a wonderful spot for strolling and people-watching (accessible from Margaret Bridge—trams #4 and #6 stop at the gateway to the island). The island is also home to some of Budapest's many baths.

Outer Budapest

The following sights, while technically in Budapest, take a little more time to reach.

Óbuda

Budapest was originally three cities: Buda, Pest, and Óbuda. Óbuda (or "Old Buda") is the oldest of the three—the first known residents of the region (Celts) settled here, and today it's still littered with ruins from the next occupants (Romans). Despite all the history, the district is disappointing, worth a look only for those interested in Roman ruins or 20th-century Hungarian painting and sculpture. To reach the first three sights listed here, go to Batthyány tér in Buda (M2 Metro line) and catch the HÉV suburban train north to the Árpád híd stop. The Vasarely Museum is 50 yards from the station. The town square is 100 yards beyond that, and 200 yards later (turn left at the ladies with the umbrellas), you'll find the Imre Varga Collection. Aquincum is three stops further north on the HÉV line.

Vasarely Museum—This museum features two floors of eye-popping, colorful paintings by the founder of Op Art, Victor Vasarely. The exhibition follows his artistic evolution from his youth as a graphic designer to the playful optical illusions he was most famous for. (If this art gets you pondering Rubik's Cube, it may come as no surprise that Ernő Rubik was a professor of mathematics right here in Budapest.) Vasarely, and the movement he pioneered—which was heavy on optical illusions—helped to inspire the trippy styles of the 1960s (400 Ft, covered by Budapest Card, Tue–Sun 10:00–17:30, closed Mon, Szentlélek tér 6, Budapest III, tel. 1/388-7551). This museum is immediately on the right as you leave the Árpád híd HÉV station.

Óbuda Main Square (Fő Tér)– If you keep going past the Vasarely Museum and turn right, you enter Óbuda's cute Main Square. The big, yellow building was the Óbuda Town Hall when this was its own city. Today it's still the office of the district mayor. To the right of the Town Hall, you'll see a whimsical, much-photographed statue of women with umbrellas. Replicas of this sculpture, by local artist Imre Varga, decorate the gardens of wealthy summer homes on Lake Balaton. Varga created many of Budapest's distinctive monuments. His museum is just down the street (turn left at the umbrella ladies).

▲Imre Varga Collection (Varga Imre Kiállítóház)—Imre Varga worked from the 1950s through the 1990s. His statues, while occasionally religious, mostly commented on life during communist times, when there were three types of artists: banned, tolerated, and supported. Varga was tolerated. His themes included forced marches and mass graves. One headless statue comes with medallions nailed into his chest. (These medallions were Varga's own, from his pre-communist military service. Anyone with such medallions was persecuted by communists in the 1950s...so Varga disposed of his this way.) Varga actually drops by each Saturday

428 Rick Steves' Best of Eastern Europe

morning at 10:00 to chat with visitors. He speaks English, and, while now in his 80s, he enjoys explaining his art. Don't miss the garden, where you'll see three prostitutes illustrating "the passing of time" (500 Ft, covered by Budapest Card, Tue–Sun 10:00–18:00, closed Mon, Laktanya utca 7, Budapest III, tel. 1/250-0274).

Aquincum Museum—Long before Magyars laid eyes on the Danube, Óbuda was the Roman city of Aquincum. Here you can explore the remains of the 2,000-year-old Roman town and amphitheater. The museum is proud of its centerpiece, a water organ (700 Ft, covered by Budapest Card, May–Sept Tue–Sun 9:00–18:00, closed Mon; Oct and latter half of April Tue–Sun 9:00–17:00, closed Mon; closed Nov–mid-April, Szentendrei út 139, Budapest III, HÉV north to Aquincum stop, tel. 1/250-1650). From the HÉV stop, cross the busy road and turn to the right. Go through the railway underpass, and you'll see the ruins ahead and on the left as you emerge.

Statue Park (Szoborpark)

When regimes fall, so do their monuments. Just think of all those statues of Stalin and Lenin—or Saddam Hussein—crashing to the ground. Throughout Eastern Europe, people couldn't wait to get rid of these reminders of their oppressors. But some clever entrepreneur hoarded Budapest's, and now has collected them in a park just southwest of the city—where tourists flock to get a taste of the communist era. Though it can be time-consuming to visit, this collection is worth ▲▲ (or ▲▲▲ for those fascinated by the Red old days).

Under the communists, creativity was discouraged. Art was acceptable only if it furthered the goals of the state. The only sanctioned art in communist Europe was **Social Realism.** Aside from a few important figureheads, individuals didn't matter. Everyone was a cog in the machine—strong, stoic, doing their job well and proudly for the good of the people. Individual characteristics and distinguishing features were unimportant; people are represented as machines serving their nation.

At Statue Park, you'll see the Communist All-Stars (Marx, Engels, and Lenin—in his favorite "hailing a cab" pose). They couldn't save the biggest "star" of all, Stalin—he was destroyed in the 1956 Uprising (but you can see a chunk of him in the Budapest History Museum on Castle Hill). Statue Park also features other socialist symbols (the stoic soldier, the faceless worker, and the tireless and heroic mother). The gift shop is a fun parade of communist kitsch; consider picking up the good English guidebook, the CD of *Communism's Greatest Hits*, and maybe a model of a Trabant.

Cost, Hours, Location: 600 Ft, covered by Budapest Card, daily 10:00–sunset, six miles southwest of center at the corner of Balatoni út and Szabadka út, Budapest XXII, tel. 1/424-7500, www.szoborpark.hu.

Getting There: The park runs a direct bus from Deák tér in downtown Budapest (where all three Metro lines converge, bus stop marked with Statue Park logo, year-round daily at 11:00, July-Aug also at 15:00; round-trip takes 105 min total, including a 40-min visit to the park, 2,450 Ft round-trip, 1,950 Ft with Budapest Card, price includes park entry).

The trip by public transportation is complicated, but doable. The most enjoyable approach is to take tram #47 from Pest's central Deák tér around the Small Boulevard, over the Liberty Bridge, past the Hotel Gellért, and south along the Danube to the community of Budafok (30-min ride, Városház tér stop, end of the line). This area has wine cellars (including Lics Pince), which you can wander through before catching bus #50 (at Budatétény) to Statue Park (10 min, end of the line). Since the park is open until sunset, this approach works best in the long daylight hours of summer, when seeing the surreal statues can be a fun and tipsy after-dinner experience.

An alternate but more confusing route is this: Take the Metro to Ferenciek tere, then the red #7 bus to its end at Etele tér, then the yellow Volán Bus from stall 7–8 in the direction Diosd-Erd (let the driver know your destination when you board); Statue Park is about 15 minutes into the trip—look for the red-brick entry and the statues on your right, and then signal for a stop.

EXPERIENCES

Perhaps more than anything else, Budapest is about enjoying the good life. Two experiences in particular are "must-dos" while in Budapest: soaking in a thermal bath and taking in a fine musical performance.

Budapest's Baths

Splashing and relaxing in Budapest's thermal baths is the city's only ▲▲▲ activity. Though it might sound intimidating, bathing with the Magyars is far more accessible than you'd think. Before you go—or if you need more convincing—read the "Taking the Waters" sidebar. The short version: These baths are not that different from an American water park. The procedure can be confusing, but you can wear your swimsuit the whole time, and you really can't "do it wrong." Overcome your jitters, follow my instructions, and

Taking the Waters

American tourists often feel squeamish at the thought of bathing with Speedo-clad, pot-bellied Hungarians. The worst-case scenario leaps to mind: wandering naked into a room filled with clothed members of the opposite sex. Relax! If you choose the right bath (such as the ones I've recommended), "taking the waters" is no more challenging than a trip to a water park. I was nervous on my first visit, too. But now I feel like a trip to Hungary just isn't complete without a splish-splash in the bath.

All this fun goes way back. Hungary's Carpathian Basin is a thin crust on top of a lot of hot water. The Romans named their settlement at present-day Budapest "Aquincum"—meaning "abundant waters"—and took advantage of those waters by building many baths. Centuries later, the occupying Turks revived the custom. Locals brag that if you poke a hole in the ground anywhere in Hungary, you'll find a hot-water spring. Judging from Budapest, they may be right: The city has 123 natural springs and some two dozen thermal baths *(fürdő)*. While these spas have traditionally served a medicinal purpose for the elderly, today Hungary is trying a new angle on its hot water: entertainment. Adventure water parks are springing up all over the country. (The preventative-health component is a bonus.)

While Hungary has several mostly nude, segregated Turkish baths, the places I list are more like your hometown swimming pool: Men and women are usually together, and you can keep your swimsuit on the entire time (though there generally are a few clothing-optional, gender-segregated areas, where locals are likely to be nude—or wearing a *kötény*, or flimsy, loose-fitting loincloth).

The baths I recommend have various types of pools. Big pools with cooler water are for serious swimming, while the

dive in...or miss out on *the* quintessential Budapest experience.

Budapest's two dozen baths *(fürdő)* were taken over by the communist government, and they're all still owned by the city. The two baths listed here are the best known, most representative, and most convenient for first-timers: Széchenyi Baths are more casual and popular with locals, while the Gellért Baths are more elegant and touristy. To me, Széchenyi is second to none, but some travelers prefer the famous, swankier Gellért experience. For more smaller, hotter thermal baths (*gyógyfürdő*, or simply *göz*) are for relaxing, enjoying the jets and current pools, playing chess, and splashing around. Most pools are marked with the water temperature in Celsius (cooler pools are about 30°C/86°F; warmer pools are closer to 36°C/97°F or 38°C/100°F, about like the hot tub back home; and the hottest are 40°C/104°F...yowtch!). You'll also usually find a steam room, as well as sunbathing areas (which may be segregated and clothing-optional).

The most daunting part of visiting a Hungarian bath is the inevitably complicated entrance procedure (which I've described carefully). Expect monolingual staff, a complex payment and locker-rental scheme, and lengthy menus of massages and other treatments. Hang in there, go where people direct you, and enjoy this unique cultural experience. Remember, they're used to tourists—so don't be afraid to act like one. If you can make it through these first few confusing minutes, you'll have the time of your life.

If you stay less than a designated time (usually 3 hours), you will usually get a refund when you leave—if you get a receipt, take it to the ticket window and see if they'll give you anything back.

Here are some useful phrases:

English	Hungarian	Pronounced
Bath	*Fürdő*	FEWR-dur
Men	*Férfi*	FEHR-fee
Women	*Női*	NUR-ee
Changing Cabin	*Kabin*	KAH-been
Locker	*Szekrénye*	SEHK-rayn
Ticket Office	*Pénztár*	PAYNZ-tar
Thermal Bath	*Gyógyfürdő, Göz*	JODGE-fewr-dur, gorz

Please trust me, and take the plunge. If you go into it with an easygoing attitude and a sense of humor, I promise you'll have a blast.

information, see www.spasbudapest.com.

▲▲▲**Széchenyi Baths (Széchenyi Fürdő)**—To soak with the locals, head for this bath complex—the big, yellow, copper-domed building in the middle of City Park. Széchenyi (SAY-chehn-yee) Baths is the best of Budapest's many bath experiences—and, thanks to an ongoing renovation, it's becoming nearly as classy as the Gellért Baths. Relax and enjoy some Hungarian good living. Magyars of all shapes and sizes stuff themselves into tiny swimsuits and strut their stuff. Housewives float blissfully in the warm water. Intellectuals and Speedo-clad elder statesmen stand in chest-high water around chessboards and ponder their next moves. This is Budapest at its best.

Cost: The sliding entry-fee scale covers thermal baths, the swimming pool, sauna, and a changing cabin (2,300 Ft if you arrive before 15:00, 2,100 Ft if you arrive by 16:00, 1,800 Ft if you arrive by 17:00, 1,500 Ft if you arrive after 17:00; you also get money back later if your stay is short—explained below; 100-Ft discount with Budapest Card). If you want a locker instead of a private changing cabin, you'll save 300 Ft. Couples can share a changing cabin (one person pays the cabin rate, the other pays the locker rate). There's also a wide array of massages and other special treatments—find the English menu in the lobby (make an appointment as you enter). Once inside the complex, you can rent a swimsuit or towel (about 600 Ft each with deposit).

Hours and Location: Daily 6:00–19:00, may stay open until 22:00 in summer and close at 17:00 Sat–Sun in winter, last entry 1 hour before closing, Állatkerti körút 11, Budapest XIV, M1: Széchenyi fürdő. The huge bath complex has three entries. The busiest one is the grand main entry, facing south (roughly towards Vajdahunyad Castle). During peak times, you may have to wait to enter here. But you'll usually be able to walk in without a wait if you use the entry on the other side of the complex (facing the Zoo). The third entry, to the right as you face the Zoo entry (near the Metro stops), is smaller (and therefore comes with longer lines), but has windows with nice views into the complex.

Procedure: Pay the cashier, and you'll be given a receipt (keep this for later) and an electronic chit (yellow for a changing cabin, blue for a locker). Remember, men are *férfi* and women are *női*—but if you've paid for a private cabin, you'll be ushered into the same changing area, where everyone gets their own cabin (couples can share a cabin). If you've paid for a locker, the locker rooms are gender-segregated.

As you enter the changing area, pass your electronic chit over the turnstile, and an attendant will point you to a changing cabin and give you a key or a little metal disc, either of which goes around your wrist. (This is where you can rent a swimsuit or towel if you need one. If using the entrance facing the zoo, you'll have to go downstairs before you head to the cabins—do this before you change, as you'll need money.) After you change, lock your belongings in your cabin and hang on to your key or little metal disc. (An attendant might double-lock the cabin with his or her own key.) While leaving things in these cabins is at your own risk, I've found them to be safe. Still, you have the option of leaving valuables in a locker for 500 Ft (ask at desk). Many locals bring plastic shopping bags with the essentials: towels, leisure reading, and sunscreen.

Follow the crowds to a series of indoor pools. The water here is quite hot—most about 40 degrees Celsius, or 104 Fahrenheit—and some with green water, supposedly caused by the many healthy minerals. Beyond the pools you'll find your way outside, where the action is.

There are three outdoor pools. Orient yourself with your back to the main building: The pool to the right is for fun (cooler water—30 degrees Celsius, or 86 Fahrenheit, warmer in winter, lots of jets and bubbles, lively and often crowded current pool); the pool on the left is for relaxation (warmer water—38 degrees Celsius, or 100 Fahrenheit, mellow atmosphere, chess); and the main pool in the center is all business (the coolest water, doing laps, swimming cap required). Stairs to saunas are below the doors to the inside pools. You get extra credit for joining the gang in a chess match.

On your way out, drop your electronic chit in the slot. A receipt will print out, indicating how much of a refund you get *(Visszatérités: Jár* [amount] *Ft)*. Present this and your original receipt at the cashier on your way out to claim your "time-proportional repayment." Then continue your sightseeing...soggy, but relaxed.

▲▲**Gellért Baths (Gellért Fürdő)**—Budapest's classic bath experience is at Gellért Hotel. You'll pay more, won't have as much fun, and won't run into nearly as many locals—this is definitely a more upscale, touristy, spa-like scene. But if you want a soothing, luxurious bath experience in an elegant setting, this is the place.

Cost: 2,900 Ft includes changing cabin, 2,400 Ft includes locker, cheaper after 15:00, 10 percent discount with Budapest Card. A "visitor ticket" to see—but not use—the baths costs 700 Ft. When you buy your ticket, tell them if you want to buy a massage (described below) or rent a towel (600 Ft with a 4,000-Ft deposit) or a swimsuit (600 Ft, with a 2,500-Ft deposit for men or a 2,800-Ft deposit for women).

Hours and Location: May–Sept daily 6:00–20:00; Oct–April Mon–Fri 6:00–19:00, Sat–Sun 6:00–17:00; last entry 1 hour before closing. It's on the Buda side of the green Liberty Bridge (trams #47 and #49 from Deák tér in Pest, or tram #19 along the Buda embankment from Víziváros below the castle). The entrance to the baths is under the white dome opposite the bridge (Kelenhegyi út 4–6, Budapest XI, tel. 1/466-6166).

Procedure: As you enter, a generally English-speaking information desk is dead ahead, cashiers are on either side, and beyond the cashier on the left is the safe (150 Ft). Buy a basic ticket to simply splash about, or—if you want to get a treatment—choose from the dizzying array of options at the ticket window (from mud baths to foot massages—1,300–3,300 Ft). Pay for everything you want (including massages or towel rentals), enter, and glide through the swanky lobby. Look for the swimming pool on your right about halfway down the main hall, and you'll find the stairs leading down to a maze of corridors that take you to the changing rooms (left for *férfi*—men—and right for *nöi*—women). If you paid to rent a towel or swimsuit, get it from the attendant on your way.

Once you've changed, you have three options: Outside is a big **wave pool** and several smaller pools (closed Oct–April). Inside is a cool-water **swimming pool** (swimming cap required—free loaners available) and a crowded hot-water pool. Off of that pool are doors to the gender-segregated, clothing-optional massage rooms and **thermal baths,** with nude and loinclothed locals stewing in pools at 36 and 38 degrees Celsius (97 and 100 degrees Fahrenheit), as well as cold plunge pools and eucalyptus-scented steam rooms. If you paid for a massage, report to the massage room when you're ready (no appointments—first-come, first-served; you may have to wait up to 30 min).

When you're finished, return your towel and swimsuit to get the slip to reclaim your deposit money (at cashier as you leave). If you were at the bath for less than four hours, you'll also get money back when you leave (if the change isn't automatically dispensed when you go through the exit turnstile, take your plastic card to the cashier).

Budapest Music Scene

Budapest is a great place to catch a good—and inexpensive—concert. In fact, Viennese music lovers often make the three-hour trip here just to take in some fine, cheap opera in a luxurious setting. Options range from a performance at one of the world's great opera houses to light, touristy "Gypsy" folk concerts (with musicians and routines suspiciously similar to tomorrow's "Hungarian folk music" concerts). The tourist concerts are the simplest option—you'll see the fliers everywhere—but you owe it to yourself to do a little homework and find something more authentic. The monthly *Budapest Panorama* brochure makes it easier (free, available at the TI)—listing performances with dates, venues, performers, and contact information for getting tickets. Or check schedules online (try www.wherebudapest.com).

A Night at the Opera—Consider taking in an opera by one of the best companies in Europe, in one of Europe's loveliest opera houses, for bargain prices. The Hungarian State Opera performs almost nightly, both at the main Opera House (Andrássy út 22, Budapest VI, M1: Opera, see page 419) and in the Erkel Színház theater (not nearly as impressive, near the Keleti train station at Köztársaság tér 30, Budapest VIII, tel. 1/333-0540). Be careful to get a performance in the Opera House—not the Erkel Színház. Ticket prices range from 800 to 15,000 Ft, but the best music deal in Europe may be the 400-Ft, obstructed-view tickets (easy to get, as they rarely run out). If you chose to buy one of these opera-tickets-for-two-bucks, you'll have a seat, and won't be able to see the stage—but you'll hear every note along with the big spenders. If a full evening of opera is too much for you, you can leave early or come late (but buy ticket ahead of time, as box office closes when performance starts). Note that there are no performances in July and August, when Budapest's outdoor music season is in full swing. To get tickets, call, fax, or visit the box office at the main Opera House, or order online (box office open and phone answered Mon–Sat 11:00–19:00, Sun 16:00–19:00, until 17:00 on days when there's no performance, box office tel. 1/353-0170 or 1/472-0447, fax 1/311-9017, www.opera.hu). If you reserve by phone, fax, or online, pick up tickets at the Opera House two days before the performance (Andrássy út 22, Budapest VI, M1: Opera). You can pick up tickets 30 minutes before performance by request. There are often a few tickets available at the door.

Tourist Concerts—A company called Duna Palota offers a wide range of made-for-tourist concerts. The most popular options are Hungarian folk music and dancing by various interchangeable troupes (4,600–5,600 Ft, May–Oct almost daily at 20:00) and classical "greatest hits" by the impressively named Danube Symphony Orchestra (the best group, 6,400–8,100 Ft, 12–15 percent discount with Budapest Card for this concert only, May–Oct Sat at 20:00). These concerts take place in one of three historic venues: the Budai Vigadó (literally, "Buda Concert Hall"—on Corvin tér in Víziváros, between Castle Hill and the Danube); the Bábszínház (literally, "Puppet Theater"—near the House of Terror at Andrássy út #69, M1: Vörösmarty utca); or a former casino called the Duna Palota (literally, "Danube Palace"—3 long blocks north of Vörösmarty tér in Pest, at Zrínyi utca 5). You can also take in an organ concert in the Baroque St. Anne's Church (3,600 Ft, June–Sept Fri and Sun at 20:00, May only Fri at 20:00, on Batthyány tér at the north end of Víziváros).

While highbrow classical music buffs will want a more serious concert, these shows are real crowd-pleasers. Your hotel can book for you (and take a commission), or you can book directly with Duna Palota (main office in Danube Palace at Zrínyi utca 5, call or visit for tickets, daily April–Dec 8:00–20:00, Jan–March 8:00–18:00, open later during concerts, tel. 1/317-2754, http://ticket.info.hu).

SHOPPING

Budapest's single best shopping venue is the Great Market Hall (see page 413). Aside from all the colorful produce downstairs, the upstairs gallery is full of fiercely competitive souvenir vendors (bargaining is the norm). There's also a folk-art market on Castle Hill (near the bus stop at Dísz tér), but it's generally more touristy and a little more expensive. And, while Váci utca has been Budapest's main shopping thoroughfare for generations, today it features the city's highest prices and worst values. At any outdoor markets, you're welcome to haggle, but not inside shops.

The most popular souvenir is the quintessential Hungarian spice: **paprika**. Sold in metal cans, linen bags, or porcelain vases—and often accompanied by a tiny wooden scoop—it's a fun way to spice up your cooking with memories of your trip. (But remember that only sealed containers will make it through Customs on your way back home.) For more on paprika, see page 375.

Another popular local item is a hand-embroidered **linen tablecloth**. The colors are often red and green—the national colors of Hungary, of course—but white-on-white designs are also available (and classy). You'll see **crystal** sold in some shops; it's mostly of Czech origin, but cut in Hungary. Other handicrafts to look for include **chess sets** (most from Transylvania) and **nesting dolls**. While these dolls have more to do with Russia than with Hungary, you'll see just about every modern combination available: from *South Park* characters, to Russian heads of state, to infamous terrorists, to American Presidents. Tacky...but fun. Fans of communist kitsch can look for cool **T-shirts** that poke fun at that bygone era (but the very best selection is at the Statue Park gift shop—see page 428).

If you're looking for a modern, American-style shopping mall, look no further than **WestEnd City Center** (daily 8:00–23:00, next door to Nyugati train station at Váci útca 1–3, M3: Nyugati pu., www.westend.hu) or **Mammut** (literally, "Mammoth"; Mon–Sat 10:00–21:00, Sun 10:00–18:00, next to Moszkva Square at Lövőház utca 2–6, M2: Moszkva tér, www.mammut.hu).

SLEEPING

The hotel scene in Budapest is decent, but not ideal. Over the last few years, supply has not kept up with demand—so prices have gone up without a corresponding improvement in quality. Still, I've unearthed a few gems. Book as far ahead as possible to get the best deal. Most rates drop 10–25 percent in the off-season (generally Nov–March). The Formula 1 races (a weekend in early Aug) send rates through the roof. If you're arriving on an international train, you may be approached by room-hawkers on board, offering accommodations in private homes and hotels. These places get mixed reviews; you're better off using my listings.

Pest

Staying in Pest is more convenient, but a little less romantic, than sleeping in Buda. Most sights worth seeing are in Pest, and this half of the city also has a much higher concentration of Metro and tram stops, making it a snap to get around. Pest also feels more lively and local than stodgy, touristy Buda. I've arranged my listings by neighborhood, clustered around the most important sightseeing sectors.

Central Pest (Belváros), near Váci utca

Sleeping on the very central and convenient Váci utca comes with overly inflated prices. But these gems—just a block or two off Váci utca—offer some of the best values in Budapest.

$$$ **Peregrinus Hotel** is a little overpriced despite its good location. The 25 high-ceilinged rooms are outmoded but spacious.

Sleep Code

(€1 = $1.20, 200 Ft = about $1, country code: 36, area code: 1)
S = Single, **D** = Double/Twin, **T** = Triple, **Q** = Quad, **b** = bathroom, **s** = shower only. Unless otherwise noted, breakfast is included and credit cards are accepted. Everyone speaks English, and most prices are quoted in euros.

To help you sort easily through these listings, I've divided the rooms into three categories, based on the price for a standard double room with bath:

$$$ **Higher Priced**—Most rooms €100 (24,000 Ft) or more.

$$ **Moderately Priced**—Most rooms between €70–100 (16,800–24,000 Ft).

$ **Lower Priced**—Most rooms €70 (16,800 Ft) or less.

Pest Hotels and Restaurants

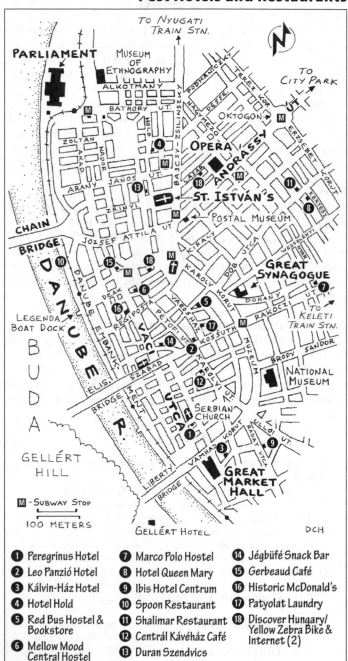

TO NYUGATI TRAIN STN.

PARLIAMENT

MUSEUM OF ETHNOGRAPHY

TO CITY PARK

ALKOTMANY

BATHORY UT.

ZOLTAN

NADOR

ARANY JANOS UT.

ZRINYI

OKTOGON

OPERA

ANDRASSY

ST. ISTVÁN'S

POSTAL MUSEUM

CHAIN BRIDGE

JOZSEF ATTILA UT

DANUBE

KIRALY

DOB UTCA

GREAT SYNAGOGUE

DOHANY

TO KELETI TRAIN STN.

LEGENDA BOAT DOCK

DEAK

KAROLY KORUT

RAKOCZI

BUDA

EMBANKMENT

VACI UTCA

KOSSUTH

MUZEUM KORUT

BRODY SANDOR

NATIONAL MUSEUM

ELIS.

SZABAD

BRIDGE

SERBIAN CHURCH

GELLÉRT HILL

LIBERTY BRIDGE

VAMHAZ KORUT

RADAY UCA

ULLOI UT.

GREAT MARKET HALL

M – SUBWAY STOP

100 METERS

GELLÉRT HOTEL

DCH

1. Peregrinus Hotel
2. Leo Panzió Hotel
3. Kálvin-Ház Hotel
4. Hotel Hold
5. Red Bus Hostel & Bookstore
6. Mellow Mood Central Hostel
7. Marco Polo Hostel
8. Hotel Queen Mary
9. Ibis Hotel Centrum
10. Spoon Restaurant
11. Shalimar Restaurant
12. Centrál Kávéház Café
13. Duran Szendvics
14. Jégbüfé Snack Bar
15. Gerbeaud Café
16. Historic McDonald's
17. Patyolat Laundry
18. Discover Hungary/ Yellow Zebra Bike & Internet (2)

Because it's run by the big ELTE university, many of its guests are visiting professors and lecturers (Sb-18,000 Ft, Db-24,000 Ft, extra bed-7,000 Ft, 20 percent cheaper Nov–March, elevator, just off Váci utca at Szerb utca 3, Budapest V; 5-min walk to M3: Kálvin tér, or tram #47 or #49 to Fövám tér; tel. 1/266-4911, fax 1/266-4913, www.peregrinushotel.hu, peregrinushotel@elte.hu).

$$ Leo Panzió is a peaceful oasis with 14 modern rooms in a hulking building that's seen better days. The location is central, the antique elevator is wonderfully rickety, the staff is polite and professional, and the double-paned windows keep out most of the noise from the busy street below (Sb-€66, Db-€82, extra bed-€26, 15 percent cheaper Nov–March, air-con, Kossuth Lajos utca 2A, Budapest V, M3: Ferenciek tér, tel. 1/266-9041, tel. & fax 1/266-9042, www.leopanzio.hu, leo@leopanzio.hu).

$$ Kálvin-Ház, a long block up from the Great Market Hall, offers 28 big rooms with old-fashioned furnishings and squeaky parquet floors. The location is convenient and the price is good, but the rooms could be cleaner (Sb-€69, Db-€89, apartment-€109, extra bed-€20, 20 percent cheaper Nov–March, non-smoking rooms, elevator, free Internet in lobby, Gönczy Pál utca 6, Budapest IX, M3: Kálvin tér, tel. 1/216-4365, fax 1/216-4161, www .kalvinhouse.hu, info@kalvinhouse.hu).

$$ Ibis Hotel Budapest Centrum, with 126 rooms, is part of the no-frills chain that's sweeping Europe. Like all other Ibis branches, this place has thin, spongy carpets, cookie-cutter predictability, and utterly no charm. But it's cheap, well-equipped for the price, and beautifully located at the start of the happening Ráday utca restaurant scene, just up the street from the Great Market Hall and Váci utca (Sb/Db-€75 April–Oct, Sb/Db-€65 Nov–March, plus 3 percent tax, breakfast-€8/person, air-con, elevator, Ráday utca 6, M3: Kálvin tér, tel. 1/456-4100, fax 1/456-4116, www.ibis-centrum.hu, h2078@accor.com).

$ Mellow Mood Central Hostel is Budapest's biggest, best-run, best-located, and most expensive hostel. With 176 beds in 33 bright, cheery, clean rooms (including 4 twins), it's a winner (prices per person: twin Db-7,500 Ft, T-6,250 Ft, Q-6,000 Ft, bunk in 6-bed dorm-5,500 Ft, in 8-bed dorm-5,000, cash only, prices soft—especially off-season, includes sheets, towel-500 Ft, breakfast-400 ft, pay laundry and Internet, a block north of Váci utca at Bécsi utca 2, tel. 1/411-1310, fax 1/411-1494, www .mellowmoodhostel.com, info@mellowmoodhostel.com). Their sister hostel, **Marco Polo**, has dorm beds and 36 more twin rooms with similar rates in a less convenient location (Nyár utca 6, M2: Blaha Lujza tér, tel. 1/413-2555, fax 1/413-6058, www.marcopolohostel .com, info@marcopolohostel.com).

Near Andrássy út

Andrássy Boulevard is handy, local-feeling, and endlessly enter-taining. It's lined with appealing cafés, restaurants, theaters, and bars—and the living is good. The frequent Metro stations make getting around the city easy from here. None of these hotels is on Andrássy út, but they're all within a two-block walk away. For locations, see the map on page 417.

$$$ K+K Hotel Opera is wonderfully located beside the opera in the fun "Broadway Quarter." True to its name, it's a regal splurge, where wicker seems classy. It has helpful, professional service and 207 rooms. The high rack rates (Sb-€110, Db-€130) are pretty firm in the summer, but drop to wonderful lows in the winter (Sb/Db-€90 Nov–Feb; non-smoking floors, air-con, eleva-tor, free Internet in lobby, parking garage-€14/day, Révay utca 24, Budapest VI, M1: Opera, tel. 1/269-0222, fax 1/269-0230, www.kkhotels.com, kk.hotel.opera@kkhotel.hu).

$$$ Hotel Ambra is centrally located on a somewhat dingy street two blocks in front of the Opera House. It's bright and mod, with 16 spacious, well-decorated apartments and five rooms (rooms: Sb-€85, Db-€105; apartments: Sb-€95, Db-€115, Tb-€125, Qb-€140; 20 percent cheaper Oct–March, air-con, non-smoking rooms, elevator, garage-€10/day, Kisdiófa utca 13, Budapest VII, M1: Opera, tel. 1/321-1533, fax 1/321-1540, www.hotelambra.hu, hotelambra@hotelambra.hu). They plan to open an annex next door with cheaper rooms—four singles, six doubles—in early 2006.

$ Hotel Medosz is cheap and dumpy, overlooking a seedy square. But the prices are low and the location is wonderfully cen-tral, around the corner from the Oktogon and the trendy Franz Liszt Square. Beyond the chilling concrete communist facade and gloomy lobby are 67 rooms—old and uninspired but perfectly ade-quate, comrade (Sb-€47, Db-€57, 15 percent cheaper Nov–March, elevator, Jókai tér 9, Budapest VI, M1: Oktogon, tel. 1/374-3000, fax 1/332-4316, www.medoszhotel.hu, info@medoszhotel.hu). When I asked if prices had gone up since last year, the tired, com-munist-era receptionist chuckled and said, "Nothing ever changes around here."

Elsewhere in Pest

These fine values are scattered around central Pest.

$$$ Cotton House is a fun, blast-from-the-past theme hotel. Its 18 retro rooms are fresh and comfy, with 1930s themes; each room is devoted to a different mobster (Al Capone) or old-time performer (Ella Fitzgerald, Elvis Presley, Frank Sinatra). The styl-ish furnishings are a clever mix of actual old and neo-old (Sb or Db-€100 with shower, €110 with bath, €120 with whirlpool tub, 20 percent less Jan–March, air-con, close to the Nyugati Station and a few blocks from the Oktogon at Jókai utca 26, Budapest V, M3: Nyugati pu., tel. 1/354-2600, fax 1/354-1341, www.cottonhouse .hu, info@cottonhouse.hu). In the basement is an elaborate jazz club, with a restaurant, "cigar room" (with a wall of rentable humidor lockers), and oodles of atmosphere. Live ragtime music fills the lower floors almost nightly until 23:00—request a quieter upstairs room if you turn in early.

$$ Hotel Hold is in a peaceful business district between the Parliament and Váci utca, across from the interesting, old, beehive-lined facade of the National Bank building. The 28 rooms—with old furniture, but adequate for the price—cluster around a quiet courtyard (Sb-€70, Db-€80, €10 less Oct–April, mostly air-con, cleverly decorated breakfast cellar, Hold utca 5, Budapest V, M3: Arany János utca, tel. 1/472-0480, fax 1/472-0484, www.hotelhold .hu, info@hotelhold.hu).

$$ Hotel Queen Mary (named not for the British monarch, but for the owner's wife) is simple and affordable, with 26 tight, unimaginative, but new-feeling rooms. The neighborhood—a block south of the Great Boulevard ring road and two blocks beyond the end of Franz Liszt Square—is central and safe, but not very pretty (Sb-€69, Db-€75, Tb-€94, 30 percent cheaper Nov–March, air-con, elevator, Kertész utca 34, between M1: Oktogon and M2: Blaha Lujza tér, tel. 1/413-3510, fax 1/413-3511, www.hotelqueenmary .hu, info@hotelqueenmary.hu).

$$ Hotel Délibáb is spartan but a great value, located across the street from Heroes' Square. The 34 rooms are a little old and worn, but clean and comfy enough. Most face a busy street and come with some noise (Sb-€68, Db-€79, 15 percent cheaper Nov–March, free Internet in lobby, parking-€10/day, Délibáb utca 35, Budapest VII, M1: Hősök tere, tel. 1/342-9301, fax 1/342-8153, www.hoteldelibab.hu, info@hoteldelibab.hu).

$ Mária and István, your chatty Hungarian aunt and uncle, are saving a room for you in their Old World apartment. For warmth and hospitality at youth-hostel prices, consider bunking in one of their two rooms, which share a bathroom (S-€18–22, D-€28–34, T-€36–42, price depends on size of room and length of stay—longer is cheaper, no breakfast but guests' kitchen, cash only, elevator, Ferenc körút 39, Budapest IX, M3: Ferenc körút, tel. & fax 1/216-0768, www.mariaistvan.hu, mariaistvan@mariaistvan .hu). Mária and István also rent two apartments farther from the center (Db-€44–54, Tb-€54–64, Qb-€60–72, family apartment, both near M3: Nagyvarad tér).

$ Red Bus Hostel is in an old apartment with cheap flooring and nine nicely renovated rooms. This loosely run place is popular, so it's smart to book ahead (S/D-8,000 Ft, T-11,000 Ft, dorm bed-3,000 Ft, Internet in lobby, laundry service-1,200 Ft, no curfew, Semmelweis utca 14, Budapest V, M2: Astoria, tel. & fax 1/266-0136, www.redbusbudapest.hu, redbusbudapest@hotmail .com). They also have a second, less central location (Szövetség utca 35, tel. & fax 1/321-7100).

Buda

Víziváros

The Víziváros neighborhood—literally, "Water Town"—is the lively part of Buda, squeezed between Castle Hill and the Danube, where fishermen and tanners used to live. Across the river from the Parliament building, it comes with fine views. Today, it's the most pleasant central area to stay on the Buda side of the Danube. It's expensive and a little less convenient than Pest, but also more charming.

The following hotels (except the last one) are between the Chain Bridge and Buda's busy Margit körút ring road. Trams #19 and #41 zip along the embankment in either direction. Batthyány tér, a few minutes' walk away, is a handy center with a Metro stop (M2 line). For a good hangout with Internet access near these hotels, try Soho Coffee Company (see page 451). Each of these places comes with professional, helpful staff.

$$$ art'otel impresses New York City sophisticates. Every detail of the 165-room art'otel—from the breakfast dishes to the carpets to the good-luck blackbird perched in each room—was designed by American artist Donald Sultan. This big, stylish hotel is a fun, classy splurge (rack rates: Sb-€198, Db-€218, Danube view-€20 more, bigger "executive" rooms-€30 more, deluxe "art suites"-€100 more, rates drop as low as Sb-€148/Db-€168 during slow times, even lower rates—often Db-€150—if you book online, non-smoking rooms, elevator, free Internet in business lounge, free sauna and mini-exercise room, Bem rakpart 16–19, Budapest I, tel. 1/487-9487, fax 1/487-9488, www.artotel.hu, budapest@artotel.hu).

$$$ Hotel Victoria, with 27 business-class rooms—each with a grand river view—is a fine value. This tall, narrow place (9 floors, 3 rooms on each) is run with pride (Sb-€102, Db-€107, extra bed-€41, 30 percent less Nov–March, elevator, free sauna, Internet in lobby, parking garage-€10/day or park free on street, Bem rakpart 11, Budapest I, tel. 1/457-8080, fax 1/457-8088, www.victoria.hu, victoria@victoria.hu).

$$$ Hotel Astra is quiet, old-fashioned, and well-maintained. Its 12 rooms—surrounding a peaceful courtyard—are woody, elegant, and spacious (Sb-€90, Db-€105, sumptuous Sb or Db suite-€135, extra bed-€20, 10 percent less Nov–March, cash only, Vám utca 6, Budapest I, tel. 1/214-1906, fax 1/214-1907, www .hotelastra.hu, hotelastra@euroweb.hu).

Buda Hotels and Restaurants

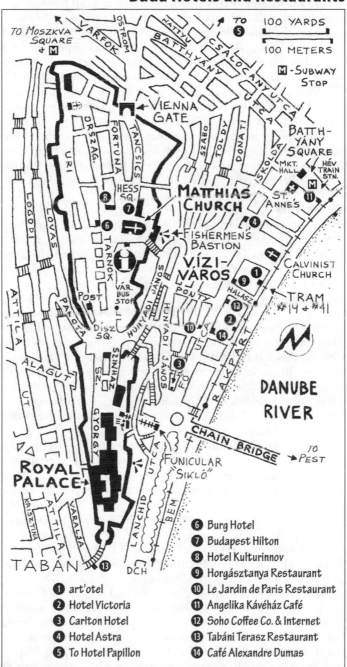

TO MOSZKVA SQUARE & M

VARFOK
OSTROM
HATTYU
BATTHYANY
CSALOCANYUTCA

TO 5

100 YARDS
100 METERS

M - SUBWAY STOP

VIENNA GATE

ORSZAG.
FORTUNA
TANCSICS
URI
SZABO
TOLDY
DONATI
ISKOLA
MKT. HALL

BATTHYÁNY SQUARE

HÉV TRAIN STN. **M**

HESS SQ.

MATTHIAS CHURCH

St. ANNE'S **11**

8
7
6
TARNOK

4

FISHERMEN'S BASTION

VÍZI-VÁROS

PONTY
HALASZ

1
9

CALVINIST CHURCH

TRAM #14 & #41

LOGODI
LOVAS
Post
VÁR. BUS STOP
DISZ SQ.

SONS
HUNYADI JANOS

13
10
2
14

ATTILA
PALOTA
SZINHAZ
SN.

FŐ UTCA
RAKPART

3

ALAGUT CT.
GYORGY

DANUBE RIVER

M

ROYAL PALACE

KRISZTINA
ATTILA
VARALJA
LANCHID UTCA
BEM

FUNICULAR "SIKLÓ"

CHAIN BRIDGE

TO **PEST**

TABÁN

13
DCH

1 art'otel
2 Hotel Victoria
3 Carlton Hotel
4 Hotel Astra
5 To Hotel Papillon

6 Burg Hotel
7 Budapest Hilton
8 Hotel Kulturinnov
9 Horgásztanya Restaurant
10 Le Jardin de Paris Restaurant
11 Angelika Kávéház Café
12 Soho Coffee Co. & Internet
13 Tabáni Terasz Restaurant
14 Café Alexandre Dumas

\$\$\$ Carlton Hotel, with 95 small rooms, is all business and no personality. But the location—where the Castle Hill funicular meets the Chain Bridge—is handy for getting to both Buda and Pest (Sb-€90, Db-€105, extra bed-€21, prices 15 percent lower Nov–March, non-smoking rooms, elevator, Internet in lobby, parking garage-€12/day, Apor Péter utca 3, Budapest I, tel. 1/224-0999, fax 1/224-0990, www.carltonhotel.hu, carltonhotel@t-online.hu).

\$ Hotel Papillon is farther north, in a forgettable residential area a 10-minute walk past Moszkva tér. It's a cheery little place with 20 homey, pastel rooms, a garden with a tiny pool, and great prices (Sb-€39, Db-€49, 25 percent less Nov—March, tram #4 or #6 from Moszkva tér to Mechwart stop, Rózsahegy utca 3B, tel. 1/212-4750, www.hotelpapillon.hu, rozsahegy@t-online.hu).

Castle Hill

Romantics often like calling Castle Hill home. The next three hotels share Holy Trinity Square (Szentháromság tér) with Matthias Church. They couldn't be closer to the Castle Hill sights, but they're in a tourist zone—dead at night—and less convenient to Pest than other listings.

\$\$\$ Burg Hotel, with 26 rooms, is simply efficient: concrete, spacious, and comfy, with a professional staff. You'll find more conveniently located hotels for less money elsewhere, but if you simply *must* stay in a modern hotel across the street from Matthias Church, this is it (Sb-€105, Db-€115, Db apartment-€134, extra bed-€39, 30 percent cheaper for 3-night stays, prices 15 percent cheaper Nov–March, no elevator, entirely non-smoking, top-floor rooms are incredibly long, Szentháromság tér 7–8, Budapest I, tel. 1/212-0269, fax 1/212-3970, www.burghotelbudapest.com, hotel .burg@mail.datanet.hu).

\$\$\$ Budapest Hilton is a 322-room landmark—the first big Western hotel in town, back in the gloomy days of communism. Today it remains the top of the top, offering a complete escape from Hungary and a chance to be surrounded by rich tourists mostly from Japan, Germany, and the United States (rack rates: Sb/Db-€220, you'll usually pay closer to Db-€120 in slower times, check for deals online, €30 more for Danube-view rooms, breakfast-€20, elevator, Hess András tér 1 on Castle Hill next to Matthias Church, tel. 1/889-6000, fax 1/889-6644, www.budapest.hilton .com, reservations.budapest@hilton.com).

\$\$ Hotel Kulturinnov, run by the Hungarian Culture Foundation, is in a big building that feels more like a museum than a hotel. The 16 rooms are basic, with old, frumpy furnishings. But it's still a great value for the location—or for anywhere in central Budapest (Sb-€64, Db-€80, Tb-€100, extra bed-€20, 25 percent less Nov–March, elevator, through the lobby and upstairs at

Szentháromság tér 6, Budapest I, tel. 1/224-8102, fax 1/375-1886, www.mka.hu, hotel@mka.hu).

EATING

Dining in Budapest is surprisingly expensive (by Eastern European standards). Don't even bother trying to find a "local" restaurant in central Budapest. With the recent influx of tourists, and the resulting increase in prices, most Budapesters can't afford to eat out in the areas where you'll be spending your time. If you really want to eat local-style, head for the big shopping malls (like the WestEnd City Center near Nyugati Station, or Mammut near Moszkva tér). There, you can truly dine with the Budapesters...at T.G.I. Friday's and McDonald's, just like back home.

In lieu of actual "local" restaurants, I've unearthed a few good options with an at least partly local clientele—along with a few memorable, decidedly touristy places that are just plain fun. I've focused on eateries serving traditional Hungarian fare (see page 374), but also included a few international and ethnic alternatives.

Pest

I've listed these options by neighborhood, for easy reference with your sightseeing.

Central Pest (Belváros), near Váci utca

When you ask natives about good places to eat on Váci utca, they just roll their eyes. Budapesters know that only rich tourists who don't know better would throw their money away on the relatively bad food and service along this high-profile pedestrian drag. But wander a few blocks off the tourist route, and you'll discover alternatives with fair prices and better food.

Centrál Kávéház, while famous as a grand, old-fashioned café, is also one of Budapest's best spots for a central, characteristic meal. Since it's across the street from the university library, it's popular with students and professors. Choose between the lively, vast downstairs, or the more refined upstairs dining room—both featuring elegant, early-1900s ambience. The enticing menu offers traditional specials (small but filling 1,100-Ft "Solo" plates and larger 1,000–2,500-Ft main dishes), sandwiches (750–1,200 Ft), elaborate salads (1,600–1,900 Ft), serious vegetarian offerings, tempting desserts, and some fun history you should read. The "Solo" plates includes some very traditional, home-style Hungarian dishes that you usually won't find in restaurants, including *lecsó* (chopped-up onion, tomato, peppers, and paprika with sausage) and creamed spinach with fried egg (daily 8:00–24:00, Károlyi Mihály utca 9, Budapest V, tel. 1/266-2110).

Great Market Hall: At the far south end of Váci utca, you can eat a quick lunch on the upper floor of the Great Market Hall (Nagyvásárcsarnok). The **Fakanál Étterem** (literally, "Wooden Spoon Cafeteria")—a glassed-in, sit-down cafeteria above the entrance—is good, with real tables and English on the blackboard. It's frequented mostly by tourists, but it's a convenient spot for heavy, traditional Hungarian food (main dishes 1,400–2,400 Ft, Mon–Fri 10:00–17:00, Sat 10:00–14:00, closed Sun, Fővám körút 1–3, Budapest IX, M3: Kálvin tér). The stalls along the side of the building offer better prices with more choice and adventure. Grab a bar stool or you'll stand while you munch. Produce and butcher stands line the main floor, but it's easy to miss the big, modern grocery store in the basement (the end nearest Váci utca).

Ráday Utca: Ráday utca is Budapest's "restaurant row." While tourists foolishly blow their budgets a few blocks away on Váci utca, Budapesters dine on good food at decent prices in trendy, inventive eateries and pubs. This is one of the hottest bits of central Budapest, and while the similar scene at Franz Liszt Square (described below) is becoming more touristy, locals still outnumber visitors on Ráday utca. It's worth going out of your way to come here and simply wander, choosing the place that looks best. Just take the M3 Metro line to Kálvin tér Metro stop—a three-minute walk from the Great Market Hall—and stroll south.

Danube Promenade: The riverbank facing the castle is lined with hotel restaurants and permanently moored restaurant boats. You'll find bad service, mediocre food, mostly tourists, and sky-high prices...but the atmosphere and people-watching are marvelous. **Spoon**, a boat in front of the InterContinental Hotel next to the Chain Bridge, is your best Danube dining option. This hip, upscale place offers expensive, elaborately prepared European and Asian cuisine (2,500–5,000 Ft). Choose between a dressy candlelit dining room or outdoor tables above decks. The bathrooms—Budapest's most scenic—are a must, even if you don't have to go. If you're going to pay too much to eat along the river, you might as well do it here (daily 12:00–24:00, reservations smart, Vigadó tér 3, tel. 1/411-0933, www.spooncafe.hu).

On or near Andrássy Út

Articsóka is hip, classy, romantic, and mellow. This is where young Budapesters go to celebrate special occasions. In a well-decorated interior or on the rooftop terrace, you'll enjoy delicious Mediterranean cuisine, including vegetarian and pasta options... with a few Hungarian standbys on the menu, just in case (2,500–4,500 Ft, daily 12:00–24:00, reservations smart, a few blocks behind the Opera at Zichy Jenő utca 17, Budapest VI, tel. 1/302-7757).

Franz Liszt Square (Liszt Ferenc Tér): Franz Liszt Square, on the most interesting stretch of Andrássy út, has sprouted a stylish cluster of yuppie restaurants, many with outdoor seating (lively on a balmy summer evening). This is the place for Budapesters to see and be seen...but only for the ones who can afford it (most main dishes hover around 2,500 Ft). Take the Metro to Oktogon and follow your nose. My favorite, **Menza** (the old communist word for "School Cafeteria"), wins the "Best Design" award. Recycling 1970s furniture and an orange-and-brown color scheme, it's an ingenious postmodern parody of an old communist café. Half kitschy-retro, half brand-new-feeling, it's got more personality than all the other Franz Liszt Square eateries combined. When locals come in here, they can only chuckle and say, "Yep. This is how it was." With tasty and well-priced updated Hungarian cuisine, embroidered leather-bound menus, and indoor or outdoor seating, it's a winner (main dishes 1,400–2,800 Ft, daily 10:00–24:00, halfway up Andrássy út at Liszt Ferenc tér 2, tel. 1/413-1482, www.menza.co.hu).

Cheap Sandwiches: **Duran Szendvics,** a cheery little eatery, is reminiscent of Scandinavian open-faced sandwich shops, where a dozen or so tempting little treats are displayed. Two sandwiches and a drink make a quick and healthy meal for about $3 (they'll also box things to go for a classy picnic). Look at the window outside before ordering. This is your chance to try caviar cheaply (120–150 Ft per sandwich, Mon–Fri 8:00–18:00, Sat 9:00–13:00, Sun 8:00–12:00; near Basilica, Postal Museum, and Deák tér Metro stop at the start of Andrássy út; Bajcsy-Zsilinszky utca 7, tel. 1/267-9624). There's a second location a few blocks in front of St. István's Basilica on Oktober 6 utca (Mon–Fri 8:00–17:00, Sat 9:00–13:00, closed Sun), and similar places are popping up all over the city.

Indian: **Shalimar** hides in a cellar two blocks beyond the end of Franz Liszt Square. Everything about this place is unexceptional...except the food. Serving the most delicious Indian food I've had in continental Europe, the restaurant is packed with young locals who know they're on to something good (1,700–2,500 Ft, daily 12:00–16:00 & 18:00–24:00, reservations smart, Dob utca 50, tel. 1/352-0297).

Restaurant Művészinas is expensive, fancy, and central, serving traditional Hungarian and international cuisine. Its 1920s and 1930s atmosphere is plush yet homey—like the candlelit living room of an artist who happens to be playing his favorite jazz on the phonograph (2,000–4,000 Ft, always several good vegetarian options, daily 12:00–24:00, reservations wise, 100 yards from Deák tér Metro stop, Bajcsy-Zsilinszky út 9, Budapest VI, tel. 1/268-1439).

Bohémtanya (literally, "Bohemian Pub") serves inexpensive, hearty Hungarian food in a humble restaurant actually frequented by some locals, huddled around their beers in a smoke-filled room (and neatly segregated from the tourists in the non-smoking room). The service can be stand-offish, the chef seems to have a thing for pigs' brains, and the food's pretty basic...but that's the point (most main dishes 1,300–2,000 Ft, daily 12:00–23:00, Paulai Ede utca 6, Budapest VI, tel. 1/267-3504). It's around the corner from Duran Szendvics (above), a block off Andrássy út and just up from Deák tér.

Near City Park

These three touristy eateries cluster around the end of the lake behind the Millennium Monument in City Park. All are open for both lunch and dinner. The first one is Budapest's best-known, fanciest splurge; the other two are more reasonable and casual, but still pretty pricey.

Gundel Restaurant has been *the* dining spot for VIPs and celebrities since 1894. The place is an institution—President Bill Clinton ate here. Pope John Paul II didn't, but when his people called out for dinner, they called Gundel. The elegant main room is decorated with fine 19th-century Hungarian paintings and an Art Deco flair, while the more casual outdoor garden terrace is leafy and delightful. The Hungarian cuisine flirts with sophisticated international influences (4,200–10,000-Ft main courses, 17,000–20,000-Ft *menus*). At lunch, choose from the same pricey à la carte items, or opt for a more affordable lunch *menu* (3,300–4,300 Ft). Sunday brunch is popular here (5,000 Ft, served 11:30–14:30). Reserve ahead for dinner, and request near or far from the live "Gypsy" music (open daily 12:00–15:00 & 18:30–23:00, music nightly, open daily 12:00–15:00 & 18:30–23:00, live music nightly, Állatkerti út 2, tel. 1/468-4040, www.gundel.hu). The dress code is formal: Jackets are required for dinner in the dining room, but not for lunch, for Sunday brunch, or if you sit outside. (You can borrow a free jacket at the door if you travel like me. Ties and dresses are not required.)

Bagolyvár (literally, "Owl's Castle") is managed and staffed entirely by women. Owned by the Gundel people, it has lower prices and a strict focus on traditional Hungarian cuisine (1,300–3,600-Ft main dishes, 3,500-Ft *menu*, daily 12:00–22:30, reservations smart, around the corner from Gundel at Állatkerti út 2, tel. 1/468-3110, www.bagolyvar.com).

Robinson, stranded on an island in City Park's lake, is a hip, playful, mellow theme restaurant. With island-castaway ambience and more outdoor seating than indoor, it's made to order for lazing away a sunny afternoon at the park. The upstairs terrace café has a long menu of ice-cream treats, coffee drinks, and light 2,000-Ft salads (daily in summer 12:00–24:00). The downstairs terrace and elegant, glassed-in dining room feature pricey Mediterranean and Hungarian cuisine (2,500–5,000 Ft, daily 12:00–16:00 & 18:00–24:00, reserve ahead, Városligeti tó, tel. 1/422-0222, www .robinsonrestaurant.hu).

Buda

Eateries on Castle Hill are generally overpriced and touristy—as with Váci utca, locals never eat here. Instead, they head down the hill into the Víziváros (Water Town) neighborhood.

Víziváros

My first listing is just beyond the southern tip of Castle Hill, near the Elisabeth Bridge. The other three are in the heart of Víziváros, right between Castle Hill and the river. For specific locations, see the map on page 443.

Tabáni Terasz offers delicious, well-priced food (1,600–2,800 Ft) between the castle and the big, white Elisabeth Bridge. The historic 250-year-old building has several seating options: in a cozy, classy drawing-room interior; on a terrace out front; or in the inner courtyard (daily 12:00–24:00, by the single-spired yellow church at Arpód utca 10, tel. 1/201-1086).

Horgásztanya (literally, "Fishermen's Pub") is a local spot for reliable, traditional Hungarian food—and a confused fisherman suspended from the ceiling. The staff can be quirky, but the restaurant is tasty and popular, with lots of fish on the menu (1,000–2,000 Ft, daily 12:00–23:00, a block up from Danube at corner of Halász utca and Fő utca, Fő utca 27, Budapest I).

Le Jardin de Paris is small and peaceful, with an upscale clientele and live jazz nightly from 19:00 to 23:00. Depending on the weather, the music is either in the leafy garden (May–Sept) or in the charming dining room (Oct–April). While the menu is mostly French fare, there are some Hungarian options, too (2,500–4,000 Ft, daily 12:00–23:00, reservations smart, Fő utca 20, Budapest I, tel. 1/201-0047).

Café Alexandre Dumas—an airy, modern, glassy eatery on the ground floor of the French Institute—is a good option for Internet access and 1,000-Ft salads and sandwiches. Ideal for a quick and inexpensive meal in Víziváros, this place is filled with students...and their cigarette smoke (Mon–Fri 8:00–20:30, Sat 9:00–13:00, closed Sun, a block up from the Danube promenade and across the street from Jardin de Paris at Fő utca 17).

Cafés and Pastry Shops
(Kávéház and Cukrászda)

Budapest once had a thriving café culture, like Vienna's. But realizing that these neighborhood living rooms were breeding grounds for dissidents, the communists closed the cafés or converted them into *esszpresszó*s (with uncomfortable stools instead of easy chairs) or *bisztro*s (stand-up fast-food joints with no chairs at all). Today Budapest's café scene is slowly coming back to life. Unless otherwise noted, these places serve only coffee and cakes—not light meals.

In Pest

On Vörösmarty Square: **Gerbeaud** (zher-BOW) isn't just a café—it's a landmark, the most famous restaurant in Budapest. Aside from coffee and pastries, you can also get a sandwich, salad, or other light meals. It's touristy, but central, historic, and great for people-watching (650-Ft coffee drinks, 500–650-Ft cakes, 1,300–2,500-Ft salads and sandwiches, daily 9:00–21:00, on Vörösmarty tér, tel. 1/429-9020).

Two Blocks up from Váci utca: **Centrál Kávéház** is the Budapest café that best recaptures the early-1900s ambience, with elegant cakes and coffees, loaner newspapers, and a management that encourages loitering (daily 8:00–24:00, Károlyi Mihály utca 9, Budapest V, tel. 1/266-2110). This is also a great spot for a meal (see page 445).

Near Ferenciek tere: **Jégbüfé** is where Pest urbanites get their quick, cheap, stand-at-a-counter fix of coffee and cakes. And for those feeling nostalgic for the communist days, little has changed here. First, choose what you want at the counter. Then try to explain it to the cashier across the aisle. Finally, take your receipt back to the appropriate part of the counter (look up at the 4 signs: coffee, soft drinks, ice cream, cakes), trade your receipt for your goodie, go to the bar, and enjoy it standing up (Mon–Sat 7:00–21:30, Sun 8:00–21:30, Ferenciek tere 10). Now...back to work.

Across from the Opera House: **Müvész Kávéház** is a classic coffeehouse with 19th-century elegance, indoor or outdoor seating, a wide variety of tasty cakes, and a convenient location (daily 9:00–23:45, Andrássy út 29, tel. 1/352-1337).

In Buda's Víziváros Neighborhood

Angelika Kávéház, in the heart of Víziváros, has coffee, pastries, and light food inside—or outside, with a riverside Parliament view. While the terrace is simply riverfront, the charmingly stale 1960s interior was a famous spot during communist days. Today it's retro-chic, still filled with locals (main dishes 1,500–2,500 Ft, daily 9:00–24:00, Batthyány tér 7, tel. 1/212-3784).

Soho Coffee Company is a taste of Seattle with a Hungarian accent, combining good American-style lattes, cozy stay-awhile atmosphere, Internet access, and a jazz soundtrack (Mon–Fri 8:00–21:00, Sat–Sun 9:00–21:00, Fő utca 25).

TRANSPORTATION CONNECTIONS

Budapest has three main stations (pályaudvar, or pu. for short): Keleti (Eastern), Nyugati (Western), and Déli (Southern). There's no telling which station each train will use, especially since it can change from year to year—always confirm carefully which station your train leaves from. For general rail information in Hungary, call 1/461-5400; for information about international trains, call 1/461-5500.

From Budapest by Train to: Vienna (that's *Bécs* in Hungarian, 6/day direct, 3 hrs), **Bratislava** (that's *Pozsony* in Hungarian, hrly, direct, 2.5–3 hrs), **Prague** (4/day direct, including 1 night train, 7–9.5 hrs), **Kraków** (1 direct night train/day with early arrival in Kraków, 11 hrs; otherwise transfer in Katowice, Poland, or Břeclav, Czech Republic; 9–10 hrs), **Ljubljana** (2/day direct, 9 hrs, no convenient night train), **Munich** (1/day direct, 7.5 hrs; plus 1 direct night train/day, 10 hrs; otherwise transfer in Regensburg, Germany, or Vienna), **Berlin** (2/day direct, 12 hrs; plus 1 direct night train/day, 14 hrs), **Zagreb** (2/day direct, 5 or 7 hrs), **Eger** (5/day direct, 2 hrs, more with transfer in Füzesabony), **Szentendre** (4–7/hr, 40 min on suburban HÉV train, leaves from Batthyány tér), **Visegrád** (trains arrive at Nagymaros-Visegrád station, across the river—take shuttle boat to Visegrád; hrly, 1 hr), and **Esztergom** (hrly, 1.5 hrs). Note that Nagymaros (the Visegrád station) and Esztergom are on opposite sides of the river—and on different train lines.

By Boat: In the summer, Mahart runs daily high-speed hydrofoils up the Danube to Vienna. While this is not particularly scenic, and slower than the train, it's a fun alternative for nautical types. The boat leaves Budapest in April and mid-September–October at 9:00 and arrives in Vienna at 15:20 (Vienna to Budapest: 9:00–14:30); May through mid-September, the boat leaves Budapest at 8:00 and arrives in Vienna at 14:20 (Vienna to Budapest: 8:00–13:30). The trip costs €79 one-way. On any of these boats, you can also stop in the Slovak capital, Bratislava. To confirm times and prices, and to buy tickets, contact Mahart (Budapest tel. 1/484-4010, www.mahartpassnave.hu).

THE DANUBE BEND

(Dunakanyar)

The Danube, which begins as a trickle in Germany's Black Forest, becomes the Mississippi River of Central Europe as it flows east through Vienna, then makes a sweeping right turn—called the Danube Bend—south towards Budapest, Belgrade, and the Black Sea. Three river towns, north of Budapest on the Danube Bend, offer a convenient day-trip getaway for urbanites who want to commune with nature.

Hungarians sunbathe and swim along the banks of the Danube, or hike in the rugged hills that rise up from the river. This is also one of Hungary's most historic stretches—for centuries, Hungarian kings ruled not from Buda or Pest, but from Visegrád and Esztergom.

Closest to Budapest is Szentendre, whose colorful, storybook-cute Baroque center is packed with tourists. The ruins of a mighty castle high on a hill watch over the town of Visegrád. Esztergom, birthplace of Hungary's first Christian king, has the country's biggest and most important church. All of this is within a one-hour drive of the capital, and also reachable (up to a point) by public transportation.

Planning Your Time

Szentendre is the easiest Danube Bend destination—just a quick suburban-train (HÉV) ride away, it can be done in a half day. Visegrád and Esztergom are more difficult to reach by public transportation; both require a substantial walk from the train or bus stop to the town's major sight.

Don't try to see all three towns in one day by public transportation—focus on one or two. Take a tour, rent a car, or hire a driver

The Danube Bend

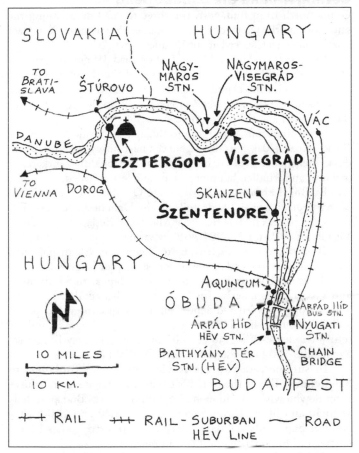

SLOVAKIA   HUNGARY

TO BRATI-SLAVA   ŠTÚROVO   NAGY-MAROS STN.   NAGYMAROS-VISEGRÁD STN.   VÁC

DANUBE   **ESZTERGOM**   **VISEGRÁD**

TO VIENNA   DOROG   SKANZEN ■   **SZENTENDRE**

HUNGARY

10 MILES

10 KM.

AQUINCUM   ÓBUDA   ÁRPÁD HÍD BUS STN.   NYUGATI STN.

ÁRPÁD HÍD HÉV STN.

BATTHYÁNY TÉR STN. (HÉV)   CHAIN BRIDGE

BUDA-PEST

┼┼┼ RAIL   ┼┼┼ RAIL-SUBURBAN HÉV LINE   〜 ROAD

to see all three (for recommended drivers, see "Helpful Hints" on page 388 of the Budapest chapter). With a car, do the Danube Bend this way: 9:00-Leave Budapest; 9:30-Arrive at Szentendre and see the town; 12:00–Leave Szentendre; 12:30–Lunch in Visegrád; 13:30–Tour Visegrád Royal Palace and Citadel; 15:30–Leave Visegrád, 16:00–Visit Esztergom Basilica, 17:00–Head back to Budapest. With extra time, or if you enjoy folk architecture, add a visit to the Hungarian Open-Air Folk Museum ("Skanzen") near Szentendre.

If you're driving between Budapest and Vienna (or Bratislava), the Danube Bend towns are a fine way to break up the journey, but seeing all three en route makes for a very long day. Again, choose one or two.

Getting Around the Danube Bend

Going north from Budapest, the three towns line up along the same road on the west side of the Danube—Szentendre, Visegrád, Esztergom—each spaced about 15 miles apart.

By Car: It couldn't be easier. Get on road #11 going north out of Buda, and it'll take you through each of the three towns—the road bends with the Danube. As you approach Szentendre, watch for signs for *Centrum Szentendre* to branch off to the right, towards the old center and the river promenade.

Returning from Esztergom to Budapest, consider cutting the "bend." Road #10 is most direct, but can have heavy traffic on weekdays. The smaller road farther north (by way of Pilisszentkereszt) is slower and windier, but more scenic and less crowded.

By Boat: From early April to late October, Budapest-based Mahart runs boats and hydrofoils up the Danube Bend. Confirm times and prices and buy tickets at Mahart in Budapest (dock near Vigadó tér in Pest, tel. 1/484-4010, www.mahartpassnave.hu). For details on this company's trips up to Vienna, see "Transportation Connections" at the end of the Budapest chapter (page 451).

Slower **"pleasure boats"** connect **Budapest to Szentendre and Visegrád** from early April to late October (daily May–Aug, Sat–Sun only in April and Sept–Oct). Departure from Budapest is at 9:00 (about 1.5 hrs to Szentendre, 2.5 hrs to Visegrád), and the return trip leaves Visegrád at 16:00 or 16:30 (one-way Budapest–Szentendre-990 Ft, Budapest–Visegrád-1,090 Ft).

In summer, an express service runs from **Budapest to Szentendre.** This is the only boat that uses Szentendre's convenient downtown dock (June–mid-Sept: boat leaves Budapest daily at 10:30 and 14:00, leaves Szentendre at 12:20 and 17:00; May and late Sept: only the daily 10:30 boat goes; trip takes 1.5 hrs upstream, 1 hr downstream, 1,400 Ft one-way).

Another boat goes from **Budapest via Visegrád to Esztergom** (daily May–Aug, Sat–Sun only in April and Sept; leaves Budapest 7:30, arrives Visegrád 10:50 and Esztergom 13:00; leaves Esztergom 16:00, arrives Visegrád 17:30 and Budapest 19:55). From early June to early September, yet another boat runs just between **Esztergom and Visegrád** (leaves Esztergom 9:00, arrives Visegrád 10:25; returns from Visegrád 16:00, arrives Esztergom 18:00). One-way prices: Budapest–Visegrád-1,090 Ft, Budapest–Esztergom-1,490 Ft, Esztergom–Visegrád-790 Ft.

Finally, on summer weekends only, a high-speed **Budapest–Visegrád–Esztergom hydrofoil** leaves Budapest at 9:30, arriving in Visegrád at 10:30 and Esztergom at 11:00; the return trip leaves Esztergom at 16:30 and Visegrád at 17:15, arriving back in Budapest at 18:15 (runs Sat–Sun late May–mid-Sept, one-way to Visegrád-2,000 Ft, to Esztergom-2,500 Ft; round-trip to Visegrád-3,500 Ft, to Esztergom-4,000 Ft; doesn't stop in Szentendre).

By Train: The three towns are on three separate train lines. Szentendre is truly handy by train, while Esztergom and Visegrád are less convenient.

Getting to **Szentendre** is a breeze by train—the HÉV, Budapest's suburban rail, zips you right there (catch train at Batthyány tér Metro station, 4–7/hr, 40 min each way, 430 Ft, 280 Ft with Budapest Card, last train returns from Szentendre around 23:00).

The nearest train station to **Visegrád** is actually across the river in Nagymaros (this station is called "Nagymaros-Visegrád"; don't get off at the station called simply "Nagymaros"). From the station, you'll walk five minutes to the river and take a ferry across to Visegrád (see "Arrival in Visegrád," page 459). Trains between Nagymaros-Visegrád and Budapest take an hour (hrly, 500 Ft).

To **Esztergom**, trains run hourly from Budapest's Nyugati Station (1.5 hrs, 500 Ft), but the Esztergom train station is 45 minutes' walk from the basilica.

By Bus: Buses are the best way to hop between the three towns. They're as quick as the train if you're coming from Budapest, but can be standing-room only. All buses to the Danube Bend leave from Budapest's Árpád híd bus station (by the M3 Metro station of the same name). There are two main routes. The river route (roughly hourly, more frequent during weekday rush hours) runs from Budapest along the Danube through Szentendre (30 min) and Visegrád (80 min), then past Esztergom Basilica to the Esztergom bus station (2 hrs). The inland route goes over the hills and through the town of Piliscsaba on the way to the Esztergom bus station (every 15–30 min, 80 min, last bus back leaves Esztergom 22:00). Buses make many stops en route, so you'll need to pay attention. One-way prices: Budapest–Szentendre-about 250 Ft, Szentendre–Visegrád-about 300 Ft, Visegrád–Esztergom Basilica-about 300 Ft.

By Tour from Budapest: If you want to see all three towns in one day, don't have a car, and don't want to shell out for a private driver, a bus tour is the most convenient way to go. All of the companies are about the same (all three towns in 9–10 hrs, including Renaissance lunch feast in Visegrád and shopping stops, plus return on boat, for around 18,000 Ft); look for fliers at the TI or in your hotel's lobby.

Szentendre

The old town of Szentendre (SEHN-tehn-dreh, "St. Andrew" in English, pop. 23,000) rises gently from the Danube, a postcard-pretty village with a twisty Mediterranean street plan filled with Austrian Baroque houses. Szentendre's old center rivals Budapest's Castle Hill as the most touristy spot in Hungary. It promises a taste of Hungarian village life without having to stray far from Budapest...but it sometimes feels like too many people had this same idea. In addition to tourists, Szentendre is also where Budapesters bring their wives or girlfriends for that special weekend lunch. The town has a long tradition as an artists' colony, and it still has more than its share of museums and galleries. The downside: crowded streets, ice-cream stands, and tacky shops. But venture off the tourist-clogged main streets and you'll soon have quiet back lanes under colorful Baroque steeples all to yourself.

Tourist Information

The TI is along the tourist-clogged route between the station and the main square (Mon–Fri 9:30–13:00 & 13:30–16:30, closed Sat–Sun, Dumtsa Jenő utca 22, just by the stream, tel. 26/317-965, www.szentendre.hu, tourinform@szentendre.hu).

Arrival in Szentendre

The combined **train/HÉV and bus station** is at the southern edge of town. To reach the center from the station, go through the pedestrian underpass at the head of the train tracks. This funnels you onto the small Kossuth Lajos utca, which leads in 10 minutes to the main square. (A handy map of town is posted by the head of the tracks.) Some **boats** arrive right near the main square, but most come to a pier about a 15-minute walk north of the center. After you get off the boat, take the first path to your left; stay on this, and it'll lead you straight ahead into town.

SIGHTS

▲**Main Square (Fő Tér)**—Szentendre's top sight is the town itself. Start at the main square, Fő tér. Take a close look at that cross, erected in 1763 to give thanks for surviving the plague. Notice the Cyrillic lettering. After the Turks were forced out of Hungary, this town was rebuilt primarily by Serbs who had fled those same Turks down south. Look at the very narrow alleyways around the square. Mediterranean towns often have walls close together to create shade in the hot sun. Even though Hungary has a milder climate, old habits die hard: The Serbs built the town in that style anyway. Various minor sights and museums line the lanes that branch off this square.

Just up Alkotmány utca from the square, the tallest of Szentendre's church spires belongs to the red-painted **Serbian Orthodox cathedral,** with a fine iconostasis (partition with icons) inside, and an icon collection in the attached museum (400 Ft, Tue–Sun 10:00–18:00, closed Mon).

Leave the square on Görög utca and take your first right to find the **Margaret Kovács Museum** (Kovács Margit Múzeum), dedicated to a local artist (1902–1977) famous for whimsical, wide-eyed pottery sculptures based on Hungarian folktales and biblical themes (600 Ft, daily 9:00–17:00, somtimes until 19:00 in summer, Vastagh György utca 1).

Between the square and the TI, you'll find the **Marzipan Museum**—a candy and ice cream store whose upper floor displays marzipan models of the Hungarian Parliament, the *turul* bird, the Muppets, Michael Jackson, and much more. It's fun for kids, but skippable for adults (shop free, upper floor 350 Ft, daily May–Sept 9:00–19:00, Oct–April 10:00–18:00, Dumtsa Jenő utca 12, tel. 26/311-931).

Enjoy a stroll through town. Head off to the back streets (try the hill behind the square) and you'll be surprised at how quickly you find yourself alone with Szentendre.

▲Hungarian Open-Air Folk Museum (Szabadtéri Néprajzi Múzeum, a.k.a. Skanzen)—Three miles northwest of Szentendre is an open-air museum featuring examples of traditional Hungarian architecture from all over the country. As with similar museums all over Europe, these aren't replicas—each building was taken apart at its original location, transported piece by piece, and reassembled here. The museum is huge and spread out, so a thorough visit could take several hours. The admission price includes a map in English, and the museum shop sells a more comprehensive English guidebook (600–800 Ft depending on special exhibits, April–Oct Tue–Sun 9:00–17:00, closed Mon and Nov–March, last entry 30 min before closing, Sztaravodai út, tel. 26/502-500, www.skanzen.hu).

Buses leave from the Szentendre station for Skanzen every 60–90 minutes (100 Ft, departs from platform 7, 12-min trip, no buses 12:00–14:00 on weekends). A **taxi** to the museum should cost no more than 2,000 Ft; the TI can call one for you.

SLEEPING

(200 Ft = about $1, country code: 36, area code: 26)
In recent years, the delightful little burg of Szentendre has become a bedroom community for nearby Budapest. I don't advise staying here if Budapest is your main interest—it takes too long to get into the city. But if you must stay here, these two places rent acceptable second-story rooms along the Danube embankment just north of the center.

Corner Panzió has five cozy, woody rooms. Prices rise in the summer, when they turn on the air-conditioning (Sb/Db: June–Sept 10,000 Ft, breakfast-1,000 Ft; Oct–May 8,000 Ft, breakfast-500 Ft; cash only, Duna korzó 4, tel. & fax 26/301-524, www.radoczy.hu).

Centrum Panzió has six pleasant enough rooms with a dark red color scheme (Sb-8,000 Ft, Db-10,000–12,000 Ft, includes breakfast, cash only, Bogdányi utca 15, at corner of Duna korzó, tel. & fax 26/302-500, hotel.centrum@t-online.hu).

Visegrád

Visegrád (VEE-sheh-grahd, Slavic for "High Castle," pop. 1,400) is a small village next to the remains of two major-league castles: a hilltop citadel and a royal riverside palace.

At this strategic site overlooking the river, there has been—since Roman times—a citadel atop the steep hill. When Károly Róbert (Charles Robert), from the French Anjou dynasty, became Hungary's first non-Magyar king in 1323, he was so unpopular with the nobles in Buda that he had to set up court in Visegrád, where he built a new residential palace down closer to the Danube. Later, King Mátyás Corvinus—notorious for his penchant for Renaissance excess—ruled from Buda but made Visegrád his summer home, and turned the riverside palace into what some called a "paradise on earth." Mátyás knew how to party; during his time here, red marble fountains flowed with wine.

In memory of these grand times, **Hotel Visegrád** today runs a Renaissance-themed restaurant, with period cookware, food, costumed waitstaff, and live lute music—just the spot for Danube Bend tour groups (can't miss it, by the palace).

Today, both citadel and palace are but a shadow of their former splendor. The citadel was left to crumble after the Hapsburg reoccupation of Hungary in 1686, while the palace was covered by a mudslide during the Turkish occupation, and is still being excavated. The citadel is more interesting, but difficult to reach by public transport. Non-drivers who don't want to make the steep hike to the citadel, and are in too much of a hurry to sort through the taxi and bus options up, should skip this town.

ORIENTATION

The town of Visegrád is basically a wide spot in the riverside road, squeezed between the hills and the riverbank. At the main intersection of Visegrád (coming from Szentendre/Budapest), the cross road leads to the left through the heart of the village, then hairpins up the hills to the citadel. To the right is the dock for the ferry to Nagymaros (home to the closest train station, called Nagymaros-Visegrád—see "Arrival in Visegrád," below).

The Visegrád Connection

The Royal Palace at Visegrád has been the site of two important meetings of Central European leaders. In 1335, as Hapsburg Austria was rising to the west, the kings of Hungary, Poland, and Bohemia converged on the Visegrád Palace to strategize against this new threat. But the meeting wasn't successful; all of the countries involved ultimately lost territory to the Hapsburgs.

In February of 1991, the Iron Curtain had fallen, and the East was looking to the future. The heads of state of these same countries—Hungary, Poland, and Czechoslovakia—once again came together in the Visegrád Palace, this time to compare notes about Westernization. To this day, these countries are still sometimes referred to as the "Visegrád countries."

The town has two sights. The less interesting riverside Royal Palace is a 15-minute walk downriver (towards Szentendre/Budapest) from the village center. The hilltop citadel, high above the village, is the focal point of a larger recreation area best explored by car.

Tourist Information: The **Visegrád Tours** travel agency at the village crossroads is not an official TI, but does have transport schedules posted in the window, sells maps, and hands out a few free leaflets (daily April–Oct 8:00–17:30, Nov–March 10:00–16:00, Rév utca 15, tel. 26/398-160).

Arrival in Visegrád

Train travelers arrive across the river at the Nagymaros-Visegrád station (don't get off at the station called simply "Nagymaros"). Walk five minutes to the river and catch the ferry to Visegrád, which lands near the village's main crossroads (250 Ft, hrly, usually in sync with the train, last ferry 20:45). Visegrád's most convenient **bus stop** is at the main crossroads, but there's also a stop a little downstream, by the river boat dock. This **dock**, near the Royal Palace and Hotel Visegrád, is where boats from Budapest stop. To reach the village center from the dock, follow the paved riverside footpath 15 minutes upriver (towards Esztergom).

SIGHTS

▲**Visegrád Citadel (Fellegvár)**—The remains of Visegrád's hilltop citadel are fun to explore. Scramble across the ramparts, try your hand with a bow and arrow, or pose with a bird of prey

perched on your arm. See fun
wax sculptures enjoying a medieval feast—and demonstrating
the collection of torture devices.
Only a few exhibits have English
labels, but borrow the free English
audioguide. You can also sometimes find a small English book
about the citadel. At the top, you
have commanding views over the

Danube Bend—which, of course, is exactly why they built it here
(750 Ft, mid-March–mid-Oct daily 10:00–18:00; mid-Oct–mid-
March Sat–Sun 10:00–16:00 in good weather only, usually closed
Mon–Fri; last entry 30 min before closing, tel. 26/398-101, www
.visegrad.hu).

Around the citadel is a **recreational area** that includes three
restaurants, a picnic area, a luge and toboggan run, a network of
hiking paths, a Waldorf school, and a children's nature education
center and campground. By the luge run and walkable from the
citadel, the **Nagy-Villám restaurant** is elegant, with breathtaking
views from the best tables (April–Oct daily 12:00–22:00, closed
Nov–March, tel. 26/398-070). A bit farther away, the simpler
Mogyoróhegy restaurant is in an early building by Organic architecture pioneer Imre Makovecz, who also designed the striking
school gymnasium in Visegrád village—white and brown, with a
row of 12 spikes on the roof (restaurant open mid-April–Sept daily
9:00–20:00, closed Oct–mid-April, tel. 26/398-237). For more on
Makovecz, see page 475. Only drivers can reach the **picnic area**
(called Telgárthy-rét), in a shady valley with paths and waterfalls.

Getting to Visegrád Citadel: To **drive** to the citadel, simply
follow signs for *Fellegvár* down the village's main street and up
into the hills. To get to the citadel from the town center without a
car, you have three options:

1. **Hike.** Buy a map at the Visegrád Tours office and figure on
40 steep minutes from the village center.

2. Take the **taxi service** called "City Bus." The minivan trip
up and back costs 2,000 Ft total, no matter how many people ride
along (ask at Visegrád Tours or call 26/397-372).

3. Take the **public bus** (200 Ft, April–Sept only, 2/day, catch
from bus stop on Danube side of main road at the crossroads at
12:28 and 15:28 or 1 min earlier at Royal Palace, reconfirm schedules in advance; this bus comes from Szentendre, where it departs
at 11:45 and 14:45).

Royal Palace (Király Palota)—Under King Mátyás Corvinus,
this riverside ruin was one of Europe's most elaborate Renaissance
palaces. During the Turkish occupation, it was deserted and

eventually buried by a mudslide. For generations, the existence of the palace faded into legend, so its rediscovery in 1934 was a surprise. Today, the partially excavated remains are tourable; unfortunately, there's no English-language guidebook. Keep your eye out for the red marble fountain, which spouted wine for parties (500 Ft, Tue–Sun 9:00–16:30, closed Mon, tel. 26/398-026, www .visegrad.hu/muzeum).

Esztergom

Esztergom (EHS-tehr-gohm, pop. 29,000) is an unassuming town with a big Suzuki factory. You'd never guess it was the first capital of Hungary—until you see the towering 19th-century Esztergom Basilica, built on the site where István (Stephen) I, Hungary's first Christian king, was crowned in A.D. 1000.

Arrival in Esztergom

Esztergom's **boat dock** is more convenient to the basilica than the bus or train stations are (can't miss the basilica as you disembark—hike on up). If arriving by **bus** from Visegrád, get off by the basilica, not at the bus station. (Buses taking the inland route from Budapest via Piliscsaba do not pass the basilica.) To reach the basilica on foot from the **train station**, allow at least 45 minutes. Continue in the same direction as the train tracks, and when the street forks go straight along the residential Ady Endre utca. After a few minutes, you'll pass the bus station, from which it's 30 minutes farther to the basilica. Local buses run between the train station and the basilica roughly hourly. On Wednesdays and Fridays, an open-air market livens up the street between the bus station and the center.

If you happen to be on your way to Bratislava, there is also a handy train station across the river in **Štúrovo, Slovakia** (cross the border on foot as you cross the bridge).

SIGHTS

Esztergom Basilica

The basilica commemorates Hungary's entry into the fold of Western Christendom. It tops a hill a steep hike up from the center of town and the boat dock. The hill was once strongly fortified, and some ruins of its castle survive (housing a mediocre museum). The neoclassical basilica, completed in 1869, was built on top of these remains. With a 330-foot-tall dome, this is the biggest church in Hungary. St. István was born in Esztergom, and on Christmas Day in the year 1000—shortly after marrying the daughter of the

Cardinal József Mindszenty
(1892–1975)

Mindszenty was a Catholic Church leader who spoke out aggressively against the communist government. In 1948, the communists arrested him and tortured him for 39 days. He was imprisoned in Budapest until the 1956 Uprising, when he was freed and took refuge in the U.S. Embassy. There he stayed for 15 years, unable to leave for fear of being captured. (Many Catholic Americans remember praying for Cardinal Mindszenty every day when they were kids.) In 1971, he agreed to step down from his position, then fled to Austria.

On his deathbed in 1975, Mindszenty said that he did not want his body returned to Hungary as long as there was a single Russian soldier still stationed there. As the Iron Curtain was falling in 1989, Mindszenty emerged as an important hero to post-communist Hungarians, who wanted to bring his remains back to his homeland. But Mindszenty's secretary, in accordance with the Cardinal's final wishes, literally locked himself to the coffin—refusing to let the body be transported as long as any Soviet soldier remained in Hungary. In May 1991, when only a few Russians were still in Hungary, Mindszenty's remains were finally brought to the crypt in the Esztergom Basilica.

king of Bavaria and accepting Christianity—he was crowned here by the Pope (for more on St. István, see page 404).

Enter through the side door, which is on the left as you face the front of the basilica (free, daily 6:00–18:00). In the foyer, the stairway leading down to the right takes you to the crypt housing the remains of Cardinal József Mindszenty, revered for standing up to the communist government (100 Ft, daily 9:00–16:30, last entry 15 min before closing). The stairway leading up goes to the church tower (200 Ft).

Enter the cavernous **nave**. There are plenty of fancy tour-guide stats about this church—for example, the altarpiece supposedly has the biggest single-canvas painting in the world. But mostly, the sheer size of the church is what impresses visitors.

As you face the altar, find the chapel on the left before the transept. This Renaissance **Bakócz Chapel** actually predates the basilica by 350 years. When the basilica was built, they dissasembled the chapel into 1,600 pieces and rebuilt it inside the new structure. The heads around the chapel's altar had been defaced by Turks, who believed that only God—not sculptors—can create man.

The **treasury** is to the right of the main altar (400 Ft, daily 9:00–16:30). Though the collection is standard ecclesiastical stuff, there are some interesting models inside the entry: a big one showing off the even more ambitious original plans for the basilica complex; smaller ones of the frames of the basilica's wooden nave and metal dome; and yet another showing what Esztergom looked like in the early 16th century (notice the more modest church that stood where this basilica is today).

When you're finished in the basilica, head around to the back for a thrilling **Danube overview**. That's Štúrovo, Slovakia, across the river. The bridge connecting them was destroyed in World War II and rebuilt only recently. Before its reconstruction, no bridges spanned the Danube between Budapest and Bratislava.

A huge restaurant catering to tour groups is built into the fortifications underneath the basilica (enter from bus parking lot). On Batthyány Lajos utca, a block into the residential neighborhood across the street, are two smaller restaurants with garden seating: the Szent Tamás-hegyi Kisvendeglő and the more expensive Csülök Csárda.

EGER

You've probably never heard of the enchanting Back Door town of Eger (EH-gehr). It's a mid-sized city (pop. 70,000) in northern Hungary, the seat of a bishop and home to a small teacher-training college. Hungarians think proudly of Eger as the town that, against all odds, successfully held off the Turkish advance into Europe in 1552. This stirring history makes Eger the mecca of Hungarian school field trips. If the town is known internationally for anything, it's for the surrounding wine region (its best-known red wine is Bull's Blood, or Egri Bikavér).

But don't let its lack of fame keep you away—in fact, that's part of Eger's charm. Rather than growing jaded from floods of American tourists, Egerites go about their daily routines amidst lovely Baroque buildings, watched over by one of Hungary's most important castles. Everything in Eger is painted with vibrant colors, and even the communist apartment blocks seem quaint. The city also has its share of cultural life, with plans to be a European City of Culture in 2010 (www.eger2010.hu). It all comes together to make Eger an ideal introduction to small-town Hungary.

Planning Your Time

Mellow Eger is just the spot to catch your breath in the middle of an intense itinerary. The town is worth a relaxing day on a trip between Kraków and Budapest, or as a side-trip from Budapest (possible in a day, but better as an overnight). The sights are few but fun, the ambience is great, and strolling is a must.

A perfect day in Eger begins with a browse through the colorful market and a low-key ramble on the castle ramparts. Then head to the college building called the Lyceum to visit the library

Eger

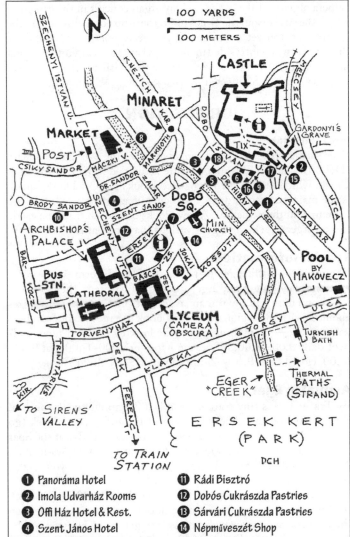

100 YARDS

100 METERS

1. Panoráma Hotel
2. Imola Udvarház Rooms
3. Offi Ház Hotel & Rest.
4. Szent János Hotel
5. Senator Ház Hotel & Rest.
6. Dobó Vendégház Rooms
7. HBH Bajor Sörház Rest.
8. Elefanto Pizza
9. Palacsintavár Rest.
10. Szantofer Vendéglő Restaurant

11. Rádi Bisztró
12. Dobós Cukrászda Pastries
13. Sárvári Cukrászda Pastries
14. Népművészét Shop
15. Castle Entrance
16. Hist. Exhibition of Weapons
17. Palóc Folklore Museum
18. Menny és Pokol (Internet)

and astronomy museum, and climb up to the thrillingly low-tech camera obscura. Take in the midday organ concert in the cathedral across the street from the Lyceum. In the afternoon, unwind on the square or, better yet, at the spa. If you need more to do, consider a drive into the countryside (including visits to local vintners—get details at TI). Round out your day with a visit to Eger's touristy wine caves in the Sirens' Valley.

ORIENTATION

(area code: 36)
Eger Castle sits at the top of the town, hovering over Dobó Square (Dobó István tér). This main square is divided in half by the Eger Creek, which bisects the town. Two blocks west of Dobó Square is the main pedestrian drag, Széchenyi utca, where you'll find the Lyceum and the cathedral. A few blocks due south from the castle (follow Eger Creek) are Eger's various spas and baths.

Tourist Information
Eger's on-the-ball, eager-to-please TI (TourInform) is the most efficient place to get any Eger question answered. They give out a free brochure and town map, as well as piles of other brochures about the city and region. They can't book rooms, but they can help you find one—or anything else you're looking for (mid-June–mid-Sept daily 9:00–18:00; off-season Mon–Fri 9:00–17:00, Sat 9:00–13:00, closed Sun; Bajcsy-Zsilinszky utca 9, tel. 36/517-715).

Arrival in Eger
By Train: Eger's tiny train station is a 20-minute walk south of the center. You can check your bag at the information desk (go through door marked *Information*). The closest ATM is at the Spar grocery store just up the street (turn left out of station, walk about 2 blocks, and look for red-and-white supermarket on your right; ATM is around front).

A **taxi** into the center will cost you about 1,000 Ft. To catch the **bus** toward the center, go straight out of the station, and when the road you're on veers right, cross it to get to the bus stop on the busier road above it. Bus #11, #12, or #14 cut about 10 minutes off the walk into town (160 Ft, buy ticket from driver; or 110 Ft if you buy it inside train station—ask for *helyijárat buszjegy*). Get off the bus when you see the big, yellow cathedral. To **walk** all the way, leave the station straight ahead, turn right with the road, and then continue straight ahead (on Deák Ferenc utca) until you run into the cathedral. With your back to the cathedral entry, the main square is two blocks in front of you and to the left.

```
┌─────────────────────────────────────────────────────────┐
│                  Eger Essentials                          │
│  English            Hungarian          Pronounced         │
│  Main Square        Dobó István tér     DOH-boh           │
│  ("Dobó Square")                          EESHT-vahn tehr │
│  (Eger) Castle      (Egri) Vár          (EHG-ree) vahr    │
│  Market Hall        Csarnok             CHAWR-nohk        │
│  Bull's Blood (local Egri Bikavér       EH-gree           │
│   blend of red wines)                     BEE-kah-vehr    │
└─────────────────────────────────────────────────────────┘
```

By Car: In this small town, most hotels will provide parking or help you find a lot. For a short visit, the most central lot is behind the department store on Dobó Square.

Getting Around Eger
Everything of interest in Eger is within walking distance, except maybe the Sirens' Valley wine caves—for these, catch a cab (starts at 220 Ft, then around 250 Ft/km; try City Taxi, tel. 36/555-555).

Helpful Hints
Language Barrier: Having fewer American visitors means that Egerites are not as likely to speak English as in more mainstream Eastern European destinations. (Consider it part of the adventure.) Eger does get lots of German tourists, so if you speak any German, it may come in handy. The TI is happy to act as a go-between with a Hungarian-only sight or business.

Tours: A couple of hokey little **tourist trains** do circuits around Eger, leaving the main square every hour on the hour. The bigger one includes a trip to Sirens' Valley wine caves (50 Ft, 50 min); the smaller one, which runs only in peak season, is slightly cheaper and runs a shorter route. There are no organized town walking tours, but the TI can put you in touch with a **local guide** (figure 3,000 Ft/hr).

Internet Access: Many small cafés in Eger have one or two Internet terminals. Ask at your hotel about the nearest access. The British-run Menny és Pokol (literally, "Heaven and Hell"), just off Dobó Square, has a dessert-bar paradise upstairs and a demonic, smoky lair with Internet access downstairs (daily 10:00–22:00, Dobó utca 23).

Shopping: For folk art, try the **Népművészét** shop (Mon–Fri 9:00–17:00, Sat 9:00–13:00, closed Sun, Bajcsy-Zsilinszky utca 8, at intersection with Jókai utca).

Organ Concert: Daily from mid-May to mid-October, Hungary's second biggest organ booms out a glorious 30-minute concert in the cathedral (500 Ft, Mon–Sat at 11:30, Sun at 12:45).

SIGHTS

▲▲Dobó Square (Dobó István tér)—Dobó Square is the heart of Eger. In most towns this striking, the main square is packed with postcard stalls and other tourist traps. Refreshingly, Eger's square seems mostly packed with Egerites. Ringed by breathtaking Baroque buildings, decorated with vivid sculptures depicting the city's noble past, and watched over by Eger's historic castle, this square is one of the most pleasant spots in Hungary.

The statue in the middle is **István Dobó,** the square's namesake and Eger's greatest hero, who defended the city—and all of Hungary—from a Turkish invasion in 1552 (see his story in the sidebar). Next to Dobó is his co-commander, István Mekcsey. And right at their side is one of the brave women of Eger—depicted here throwing a pot down onto the attackers.

Use the square to orient yourself to the town. Behind the statue of Dobó is a bridge over the stream that bisects the city, and on the other side of the bridge is the charming **Little Dobó Square,** home to the town's best hotels (see "Sleeping," page 477). As you cross the bridge toward Little Dobó Square, look to the left and you'll see the northernmost minaret in Europe—once part of a Turkish mosque (see page 473). Hovering above Little Dobó Square is Eger Castle (see below).

Now face in the opposite direction, with Dobó's statue at your back. On your right is a handy department store. On your left, dominating the square, is the picturesque pink Minorite Church; next to that is the town hall. The **monument** in front of you and on the left also commemorates the 1552 defense of Eger: one Egerite against two Turkish soldiers, reminding us of the townspeople's bravery despite the odds. Straight ahead, two blocks beyond the end of the square, runs Széchenyi utca, Eger's main pedestrian drag. At the left end

István Dobó and the Siege of Eger

In the 16th century, Turkish invaders swept into Hungary. They easily defeated a Hungarian army—in just two hours—at the notorious Battle of Mohács in 1526. After the victory, the Turks gradually worked their way up the Balkan Peninsula, threatening to overrun the entire Continent. When Buda and Pest fell to the Turks in 1541, all of Europe looked to Eger as the last line of defense. István Dobó and his second-in-command, István Mekcsey, were put in charge of Eger's forces. They prepared the castle (which still overlooks the square) for a siege and waited.

On September 11, 1552—after a summer spent conquering more than 30 other Hungarian fortresses on their march northward—40,000 Turks arrived in Eger. Only about 2,000 Egerites (soldiers, their wives, and their children) remained to protect their town. The Turks expected an easy victory, but the siege dragged on for 39 days. Eger's soldiers fought valiantly, and the women of Eger also joined the fray, pouring hot tar down on the Turks...everyone pitched in. A Hungarian officer named Gergely Bornemissza, sent to reinforce the people of Eger, startled the Turks with all manner of clever and deadly explosives. Finally, the Turks left in shame, Eger was saved, and Dobó was a national hero.

The unfortunate epilogue: The Turks came back in 1596 and, this time, succeeded in conquering an Eger Castle guarded by unmotivated mercenaries. The Turks sacked the town and controlled the region for close to a century.

In 1897, a castle archaeologist named Géza Gárdonyi moved from Budapest to Eger, and tales of the siege captured his imagination. Gárdonyi wrote a book about István Dobó and the 1552 Siege of Eger called *Egri Csillagok* (literally, "Stars of Eger," translated into English as *Eclipse of the Crescent Moon*, available at local bookstores and souvenir stands). The book—a favorite of many Hungarians—is taught in schools, keeping the legend of Eger's heroes alive today.

of Széchenyi utca are the cathedral and Lyceum. To reach the TI, jog left at the end of this square, then right onto Bajcsy-Zsilinszky utca (TI one block ahead on right). To visit the Market Hall, leave Dobó Square to the right (on Zalár József utca, with department store on your right-hand side; you'll see Market Hall on left).

▲Eger Castle (Egri Vár)—This castle is Hungary's Alamo, where István Dobó defended Eger from the Turks in 1552. These days, it's usually crawling with school-age kids on field trips from all over the country.

The great St. István—Hungary's first Christian king—built a church on this hill a thousand years ago. The church was destroyed by Tatars in the 13th century, and this fortress was built to repel another attack.

The castle grounds feature several small museums, including a history museum, picture gallery, dungeon, underground casements (tunnels through the castle walls), Heroes' Hall (with the grave of István Dobó), and temporary exhibits. For those of us who didn't grow up hearing the legend of István Dobó, the whole complex is hard to appreciate. Most visitors find that the most rewarding plan is to stroll up, wander around the grounds, enjoy the view overlooking the town (find the minaret and other landmarks), maybe pay a visit to the waxworks (see below), and then head back down past a gaggle of colorful shops.

Cost and Hours: 400 Ft for grounds only; 900-Ft ticket gets you into all of the museums (except the "Other Castle Sights," described below). The underground casements and Heroes' Hall are only accessible by one-hour tour (600 Ft extra, call ahead to ask if English tour is scheduled, tel. 36/312-744, ext. 111; tours likely July–Aug, otherwise depends on guides' schedules). The castle grounds are open April–Aug daily 8:00–20:00, Sept until 19:00, March and Oct until 18:00, Nov–Feb until 17:00. The castle museums are open March–Oct Tue–Sun 9:00–17:00, Nov–Feb Tue–Sun 10:00–16:00 (last entry 40 min before closing). On Monday, everything's closed except the casements, which—as usual—you can only visit with a guided tour (700 Ft, plus 600 Ft extra if you go with English tour). General castle info: tel. 36/312-744, www.div.iif.hu.

Other Castle Sights: In addition to the castle museums, there are three privately run exhibits, each with its own sporadic hours and prices: the **archery** exhibit (100–200 Ft per arrow to use old-fashioned bows and crossbows); the **mint** (200 Ft); and the **waxworks,** or "Panoptikum" (350 Ft, daily 9:00–18:00, less in winter). Of these, the waxworks is by far the best—in fact, it's the most enjoyable part of the whole castle complex. You'll see a handful of eerily realistic heroes and villains from the siege of Eger (including István Dobó himself and the leader of the Turks sitting in his colorful tent). Notice the exaggerated Central Asian features of the Egerites—a reminder that the Magyars were more Asian than European. Sound effects add to the fun...think of it as a very low-tech, walk-through *Ottomans of the Caribbean*. You'll also have the chance to scramble through a segment of the casements that run inside the castle walls.

Getting to Eger Castle: To reach the castle from Dobó Square, cross the bridge toward Senator Ház Hotel, then jog right around the hotel, turning right on Dobó István utca. Take this street a few blocks until it swings down to the right; the ramp up to the castle is to your left.

▲▲**Lyceum (Líceum)**—In the mid-18th century, Bishop Károly Eszterházy wanted a university in Eger, but Hapsburg Emperor Josef II refused to allow it. So instead, Eszterházy built the most impressive teacher-training college on the planet, and stocked it with the best books and astronomical equipment money could buy. The Lyceum still trains local teachers (enrollment: about 2,000). Since Eger is expensive by Hungarian standards, many families live in the surrounding countryside. The kids all come into Eger for school—and lots of teachers are needed. But the halls of the Lyceum are also roamed by tourists who have come to visit its classic old library (500 Ft), and its astronomical museum, with a fascinating camera obscura (another 500 Ft; both parts open April–Sept Tue–Sun 9:30–15:30, closed Mon; Oct–March Sat–Sun only 9:30–13:30, closed Mon–Fri; last entry 30 min before closing, Eszterházy tér 1, at south end of Széchenyi utca at intersection with Kossuth utca, enter through main door across from cathedral and buy tickets just inside and to the left).

First, visit the old-fashioned **library** (from main entry hall, go around the right wing of the courtyard, then climb the stairs partway down the hall on your right-hand side; at top of first flight of stairs, turn right into the hall and look for the library halfway down on the right; watch for easy-to-miss signs). The library houses 50,000 books (here and in the 2 adjoining rooms, with several stacked 2 deep; plus another 100,000 elsewhere in the building). Dr. Imre Surányi and his staff have spent the last decade cataloging these books. This is no easy task, since they're in over 100 languages—from Thai to Tagalog—and are shelved according to size, rather than topic. You'll likely meet Dr. Surányi's assistant, Dénes Szabó (if he's not away for a choral contest), or the resident tour guide, Katalin Bódi. Either of them will happily show you a copy of the library's pride and joy: a letter from Mozart. The shelves are adorned with golden seals depicting great minds of science, philosophy, and religion. Take some time to marvel at the gorgeous ceiling fresco, dating from 1778. If you want to thank the patron of this museum, say *köszönöm* to the guy in the second row up, to the right of the podium (2nd from left, not wearing a hat)—that's Bishop Károly Eszterházy. While the Lyceum now belongs to Eger, his library is still the property of the archbishop.

A few flights above (leave library to the right, go to end of hall to reach stairs) is the **Astronomical Tower,** with some dusty old stargazing instruments, as well as a meridian line in the floor (the dot of sunlight hits the line every day exactly at noon).

Yet a few more flights up is the Lyceum's treasured **camera obscura.** You'll enter a dark room around a big, bowl-like canvas, and the guide will fly you around the streets of Eger. Fun as it is today, this camera must have seemed like a miracle when it was built in 1776—well before anyone had seen "moving pictures." It's a bit of a huff to get up here (9 flights of stairs, 302 steps all together)—but the camera obscura and the view of Eger from the outdoor terrace are worth it. If a Hungarian school group is waiting to see the camera obscura, let them go first, then try to get a viewing session all to yourself.

▲▲**Eger Cathedral**—Eger's 19th-century bishops peppered the city with beautiful buildings—including the second biggest church in Hungary (after Esztergom's—see Danube Bend chapter). With a quirky, sumptuous, Baroque-feeling interior, Eger's cathedral is well worth a visit (free entry, cathedral is the big, can't-miss-it yellow building at Pyrker János tér 1, just off Széchenyi utca).

Eger Cathedral was built in the 1830s by an Austrian archbishop who had previously served in Venice and thought Eger could use a little more class. The colonnaded neoclassical facade, painted a pretty Hapsburg yellow, boasts some fine Italian sculpture. As you walk up the main stairs, you'll pass saints István and László—Hungary's first two Christian kings—and then the apostles Peter and Paul.

Enter the cathedral and walk to the first collection box, partway down the nave. Then, facing the door, look up at the ornate **ceiling fresco:** On the left, it shows Hungarians in traditional dress, and on the right, the country's most important historical figures. At the bottom, you see this cathedral, celestially connected with St. Peter's in Rome (at the top). This symbol of devotion to the Vatican was a brave statement when it was painted in 1950. The communists were closing churches in other small Hungarian towns, but the Eger archbishop had enough clout to keep this one open.

Continue to the **transept.** A few years ago, the windows at either end were donated to the cathedral by a rich Austrian couple to commemorate the 1,000th anniversary of Hungary's conversion to Christianity—notice the dates 1000 (when King István was crowned by the Pope) and 2000.

As you leave, notice the enormous **organ**—Hungary's second largest—above the door. In the summer, try to catch one of the cathedral's daily half-hour organ concerts (500 Ft, mid-May–mid-Oct Mon–Sat at 11:30, Sun at 12:45, no concerts off-season).

If you walk up Széchenyi utca from here, you'll see the fancy Archbishop's Palace on your left—still home to Eger's archbishop.

▲**Market Hall (Csarnok)**—Wandering Eger's big indoor market will give you a taste of local life—and maybe some local food, too. It's packed with Egerites choosing the very best of the fresh produce. Tomatoes plus peppers of all colors and sizes are abundant—magic ingredients that give Hungarian food its kick (and that won't grow in colder Poland or the Czech Republic, with tamer cuisine). To reach the market, leave Dobó Square with the castle to your back; turn right on Zalár József utca, and you'll see the market on your left in two blocks, at the intersection with Dr. Sándor utca (mid-April–mid-Oct Mon–Fri 6:00–18:00, Sat–Sun 6:00–10:00; mid-Oct–mid-April Mon–Fri 6:00–17:00, Sat 6:00–13:00, closed Sun).

Minaret—Once part of a mosque, this slender, 130-foot-tall minaret represents the century of Turkish rule that left its mark on Eger and all of Hungary. The little cross at the top symbolizes the eventual Christian victory over Hungary's Turkish invaders. You can climb the minaret's 97 steps for fine views of Eger, but it's not for those scared of heights or tight spaces (200 Ft, April–Oct daily 10:00–18:00, closed Nov–March; if it's locked, ask for the key at nearby Hotel Minaret).

Minorite Church—The church that stands over Dobó Square is often said to be the most beautiful Baroque church in Hungary—even if it could use some touch-up work. It's exquisitely photogenic outside, but the shabby interior is less interesting, aside from the hand-carved pews, each of which is a little different.

Other Museums—Two small museums lie between Little Dobó Square and the entrance to the castle; neither is worth a visit, unless you have a special interest in the subject matter. The **Palóc Folklore Museum** is a measly little place with a handful of traditional tools, textiles, ceramics, costumes, and pieces of furniture (140 Ft, no English whatsoever, April–Oct Tue–Sun 9:00–17:00, closed Mon and Nov–March, Dobó utca 12). The **Historical Exhibition of Weapons** (Történeti Tárház) is just that, featuring centuries of Eger armaments: clubs, rifles, and everything in between (300 Ft, Tue–Sun 9:00–17:00, closed Mon, 450-Ft booklet labels weapons in English, 1,600-Ft English book gives more info, Dobó utca 9, actually just down Fazola Henrik utca).

EXPERIENCES

Aqua Eger

Swimming and water sports are as important to Egerites as good wine. They're proud that many of Hungary's Olympic medalists in aquatic events have come from this county.

To test the waters of this part of Eger, you can join the locals lounging and laughing around in the city bath (see "Taking the Waters" on page 430). Or you can take a more serious approach—doing laps (and appreciating the unique architecture) at the city swimming pool.

▲Thermal Bath Complex (Eger Thermálfürdő)—For a refreshing break from the sightseeing grind, consider a splash in the spa. This is a fine opportunity to try a Hungarian bath: modern enough to feel accessible (men and women are clothed and together most of the time), but frequented mostly by locals. While Budapest has many great baths (see page 429), you may want to take a dip in low-key Eger and save your Budapest time for big-city sights.

You'll enter and be given a little barcode to swipe across the turnstile scanner. Trade this in for a key to a locker (1,000-Ft deposit per key, which will be refunded when you return the key). Change (private changing cabins available in the locker room for no extra charge), stow your stuff in a locker, put the key around your wrist, then join the fun. The heart of the complex is the new, green-domed, indoor-outdoor "adventure bath." Its cascades, jets, bubbles, geysers, and powerful current pool will make you feel like a kid again. For some warmer water, follow your nose to the old-fashioned sulfur pool—where Egerites sit peacefully, ignore the slight stink, and (supposedly) feel their arthritis ebb away. There's also a big outdoor lap pool (closed off-season).

Note that you can't rent a swimsuit or a towel; bring both with you, along with shower sandals for the locker room (if you've got them).

Cost, Hours, Location: 900 Ft, adventure bath included Oct–April but 500 Ft extra May–Sept; kids get their own adventure bath (650 Ft). Open May–Sept Mon–Fri 6:00–19:30, Sat–Sun 8:00–19:00; Oct–April daily 9:00–19:00. It's at Petőfi tér 2 (tel. 36/314-142, www.egertermal.hu). From Dobó Square, follow the stream four blocks south (signs for *Strand*), past the big, unusual Bitskey Aladár swimming pool building (described below). Continue following the stream into the park; you'll see the main entrance to the bath on your left over a bridge.

Turkish Bath (Török Fürdő)—This very traditional place is open to the public only on weekends (700 Ft, Sat 14:00–18:00, Sun 8:00–18:00, Fürdő utca 1–3, tel. 36/413-356).

Bitskey Aladár Pool—This striking new swimming pool was designed by Imre Makovecz, the father of Hungary's trendy Organic style of architecture. Some Eger taxpayers resented the pool's big price tag, but it left the city with a truly distinctive building. You don't need to be an architecture student to know that the pool is special. It's worth the five-minute walk from Dobó Square just to take a look. Oh, and you can swim in it, too (700 Ft,

Hungary's Organic Architecture

In recent years, a uniquely Hungarian style of architecture has caught on: organic, developed and championed by Imre Makovecz. After being blackballed by the communists for his nationalistic politics, Makovecz was denied access to building materials, so he taught himself to make impressive structures with nothing more than sticks and rocks.

Now that the regime is dead and Makovecz is Hungary's premier architect, he still keeps things simple. He believes that a building should be a product of its environment, rather than a cookie cutter copy. Organic buildings use indigenous materials (especially wood) and take on untraditional forms—often inspired by animals or plants—that blend in with the landscape. Organic buildings look like they're rising up out of the ground, rather than plopped down on top of it. You generally won't find this back-to-nature style in big cities like Budapest; Makovecz prefers to work in small communities such as Eger (see photo on page 474), instead of working for corporations.

Organic architecture has caught on throughout Hungary, becoming *the* post-communist style. Even big supermarket chains are now imitating Makovecz. If you see a building with white walls and a big, overhanging roof (resembling a big mushroom)...that's Organic.

Mon–Sat 6:00–21:30, Sun 7:30–18:00, follow Eger Creek south from Dobó Square to Frank Tivadar utca, tel. 36/511-810). Like the thermal bath complex, this place does not rent out swimsuits—B.Y.O.S.S.

Eger Wine

Eger is at the heart of one of Hungary's best-known wine regions, internationally famous for its **Bull's Blood** (Egri Bikavér). You'll likely hear various stories as to how Bull's Blood got its name during the Turkish siege of Eger. My favorite version: The Turks were amazed at the ferocity displayed by the Egerites, and wondered what they were drinking that boiled their blood and stained their beards so red...it must be potent stuff. Local merchants, knowing that the Turks were Muslim and couldn't drink alcohol, told them it was bull's blood. The merchants made a buck, and the name stuck.

Creative as these stories are, they're all bunk—the term dates only from 1851. Egri Bikavér is a blend—everyone has their own recipe—so you generally won't find it at small producers. Cabernet Sauvignon, Merlot, Kékfrankos, and Kékoportó are the most commonly used grapes.

476 Rick Steves' Best of Eastern Europe

Try Egri Bikavér, but then move quickly on to the more special and characteristic Hungarian wines, such as Leányka ("Little Girl"), Kékfránkos ("Blue Frankish"), Furmint, Hárslevélű, and Kéknyelű. You also might have heard of Tokaji Aszú wine (a sweet white made from a grape of Hungarian origin, also grown in the Alsace region of France—where it's known as *tokay*). Tokaj is a town (not too far from Eger), and Aszú is a "noble rot" grape. These grapes are harvested immediately after the first frost, when they burst and wither on the vine like raisins.

Sirens' Valley (Szépasszony-völgy)—When the Turkish invaders first occupied Eger, residents moved into the valley next door, living in caves dug into the hillside. Eventually the Turks were driven out, the Egerites moved back to town, and the caves became wine cellars. (Most Eger families who can afford it have at least a modest vineyard in the countryside.) There are more than 300 such caves in the valley to the southwest of Eger, several of which are open for visitors.

The best selection of these caves (about 50) is in the Sirens' Valley (sometimes also translated as "Valley of the Beautiful Women," or, on local directional signs, the less poetic "Nice Woman Valley"). It's a fun scene—locals showing off their latest vintage, with picnic tables and tipsy tourists spilling out into the street. Most caves offer something to eat with the wine, and you'll also see lots of non-cave, full-service restaurants. Some of the caves are fancy and finished, staffed by multilingual waiters in period costume. Others feel like a dank basement, with grandpa leaning on his moped out front. (The really local places—where the decor is cement, bottles don't have labels, and food consists of potato chips and buttered Wonder Bread—can be the most fun.) Hopping from cave to musky cave can make for an enjoyable evening, but be sure to wander around a bit to see the options before you dive in (cellars generally open 10:00–22:00 in summer, best June–Aug after 19:00; it's much quieter off-season, when only a handful of cellars remain open, with shorter hours).

Getting to the Sirens' Valley: The valley is a 25-minute walk southwest of Eger. Figure about 1,000 Ft for a **taxi** between your hotel and the caves. To **walk,** leave the pedestrian zone on the street next to the cathedral (Törvényház utca), with the cathedral on your right-hand side. Take the first left just after the back end of the cathedral (onto Trinitárius utca), go one long block, then take the first right (onto Király utca). At the fork, bear to the left. You'll stay straight on this road—crossing busy Koháry István utca—for several blocks, through some nondescript residential areas (on Szépasszony-völgy utca). When you crest the hill and emerge from the houses, you'll see the caves (and tour buses) below you on the left—go left (downhill) at the fork to get there. First you'll come to a stretch of touristy non-cave restaurants; keep going past these, and eventually you'll see a big loop of caves on your left.

SLEEPING

Eger is a good overnight stop, and a couple of quaint, well-located hotels in particular—Senator Ház and Offi Ház—are well worth booking in advance. The TI can help you find a room; if you're stumped, the area behind the castle has a sprinkling of guesthouses *(vendégház)*. A tax of 300 Ft per person will be added to your bill (not included in the prices listed here).

$$$ Panoráma Hotel is a good big-hotel option, still close to Dobó Square. You'll miss the quaintness of some of the other listings—its 38 rooms are all business—but you get free access to its "Unicornis Thermarium" spa facility (Sb-16,500 Ft, Db-19,500 Ft, Tb-23,500 Ft, 10 percent cheaper Nov–March, apartments also available, non-smoking rooms, elevator, free parking, Dr. Hibay K. utca 2, tel. 36/412-886, fax 36/410-136, www.panoramahotels .hu, hoteleger@panoramahotels.hu).

$$$ Imola Udvarház rents six spacious apartments—with kitchen, living room, bedroom, and bathroom—all decorated in modern Scandinavian style (read: Ikea). They're pricey, but roomy and well-maintained, with a great location near the castle entrance (July–Aug: Sb-18,000 Ft, Db-21,000 Ft, Tb-23,000 Ft, Qb-25,000 Ft; each room 2,000 Ft less April–June and Sept–Oct and 4,000 Ft less Nov–March; enter through restaurant courtyard at Dózsa György tér 4, tel. & fax 36/516-180, udvarhaz@imolanet.hu).

Sleep Code

(€1 = about $1.20, 200 Ft = about $1, country code: 36, area code: 36)

S = Single, D = Double/Twin, T = Triple, Q = Quad, b = bathroom, s = shower only, NSE = does not speak English. Unless otherwise noted, English is spoken, breakfast is included, and credit cards are accepted.

To help you sort easily through these listings, I've divided the rooms into three categories, based on the price for a standard double room with bath:

$$$ **Higher Priced**—Most rooms 18,000 Ft (€75) or more.

$$ **Moderately Priced**—Most rooms between 10,000–18,000 Ft (€42–75).

$ **Lower Priced**—Most rooms 10,000 Ft (€42) or less.

$$ **Senator Ház Hotel** is my favorite spot in Eger, and one of the best small, family-run hotels in all of Eastern Europe. Though the 11 rooms are a bit worn, this place is cozy and well-run by András Cseh, with oodles of character and a picture-perfect location just under the castle on Little Dobó Square (Sb-13,000 Ft, Db-17,800 Ft, extra bed-4,600 Ft, 15–30 percent cheaper Nov–April, Dobó István tér 11, tel. & fax 36/411-711, www.senatorhaz .hu, senator@enternet.hu). The Cseh family also runs **Pátria Vendégház**—two doubles (17,800 Ft) and four apartments (19,500 Ft) with new, luxurious decor and a little less character, around a courtyard in a nearby building (same contact info as Senator Ház Hotel).

$$ **Offi Ház Hotel** shares Little Dobó Square with Senator Ház. Its five rooms are classy and romantic (Sb-15,500 Ft, Db-17,500 Ft, Db suite-20,500 Ft, Tb suite-23,500 Ft, extra bed-4,000 Ft, 10 percent cheaper Jan–April, 25 percent cheaper Oct–Dec, non-smoking, Dobó István tér 5, tel. & fax 36/311-005, www .offihaz.hu, offihaz@t-online.hu).

$$ **Szent János Hotel,** less charming and more businesslike than the Senator Ház and Offi Ház, offers a good but less atmospheric location, 11 straitlaced rooms, and a slightly better value (Sb-€50 Db-€68, extra bed-€22, 25 percent cheaper Nov–April, non-smoking rooms, air-con, McDonald's walk-up window across the street can be noisy at night—especially weekends—so request a quiet back room, a long block off Dobó Square at Szent János utca 3, tel. 36/510-350, fax 36/517-101, www.hotelszentjanos.hu, hotelszentjanos@hotelszentjanos.hu).

$ **Dobó Vendégház,** run by friendly Mariann Kleszo, has seven basic but colorful rooms just off Dobó Square. Mariann speaks nothing but Hungarian, but gets simple reservation e-mails and faxes translated by a friend (Sb-€30, Db-€40, Tb-€50, Qb-€60, cash only, Dobó utca 19, tel. 36/421-407, fax 36/516-612, www.hotels.hu/dobo_vendeghaz, csillagd@t-online.hu).

EATING

Bajor Sörház (a.k.a. HBH for the brand of beer on tap) is favored by tourists and locals alike for its excellent Hungarian cuisine. Everything's good here; I especially like their spicy gulyás leves soup (that's real Hungarian goulash—see page 374). They also feature some Bavarian specialties...but with a Hungarian accent (most main dishes 1,000–2,000 Ft, daily 11:30–22:00, right at the bottom of Dobó Square at Bajcsy-Zsilinszky utca 19, tel. 36/515-516). If you're lucky, you may get to meet animated István "Call Me Steve Miller" Molnár, one of my favorite Hungarians.

The recommended hotels **Senator Ház** and **Offi Ház** both have restaurants at the top end of Dobó Square (both open long hours daily). These places have fine food (most main dishes 1,500–2,000 Ft) and postcard-perfect outdoor seating that shares Little Dobó Square with a gazebo featuring cheesy live music in summer. This is *the* place to see and be seen in Eger (see "Sleeping," above).

Elefanto, above the Market Hall, offers good, inexpensive pizzas (600–1,000 Ft), traditional Hungarian dishes (1,000–1,500 Ft), and a pleasant ambience. In warm weather, enjoy the covered terrace seating (daily 12:00–24:00, Katona István tér 2, tel. 36/412-452).

Palacsintavár ("Pancake Castle"), near the castle entrance, isn't your hometown IHOP. This place serves up inventive crêpe-wrapped main courses, popular with local students (most main dishes 1,100–1,400 Ft, daily 12:00–22:30, Dobó utca 9).

Szantofer Vendéglő serves mostly traditional Hungarian food at local prices to both Egerites and tourists. The decent, fill-the-tank food is presented with an artistic flourish—some plates fly miniature Hungarian flags. Steer clear of the few ethnic offerings (like chicken tikka), and you'll do fine (most main dishes 900–1,400 Ft, daily 11:30–22:00, Bródy Sándor utca 3, tel. 36/517-298). The creatively translated menu is good for a laugh while you're choosing your food.

Rádi Bisztró is a popular student hangout and a convenient spot for pastries and inexpensive, pre-made sandwiches (less than 300 Ft, Mon–Fri 7:00–18:00, Sat 7:00–16:00, closed Sun, just down the street from the Lyceum at Széchenyi utca 2).

Dessert: Cukrászda (pastry shops) line the streets of Eger. For deluxe, super-decadent pastries of every kind imaginable—most for less than 400 Ft—drop by **Dobós Cukrászda** (daily 9:30–21:00, point to what you want inside and they'll bring it out to your table, Széchenyi utca 6, tel. 36/413-335). For a more local scene, find the tiny **Sárvári Cukrászda,** behind the Lyceum. Their pastries are good, but Egerites line up here after a big Sunday lunch for their homemade gelato (110 Ft/scoop, Mon–Fri 7:00–18:00, Sat–Sun 10:00–18:00, Kossuth utca 1, between Jókai utca and Fellner utca).

TRANSPORTATION CONNECTIONS

From Eger by Train: The only major destination you'll get to directly from Eger's train station is **Budapest** (5/day direct to Budapest's Keleti Station, 2 hrs; more with a transfer in Füzesabony—see below). For most other destinations, you'll connect through Budapest.

For destinations to the north—such as **Kraków**—you'll save time by transferring in Füzesabony (13/day, 50 min), a nearby smaller village that happens to be on the Budapest–Kraków line. The very rustic Füzesabony station does not have lockers, but—oddly enough—does have a modest museum of local artifacts. There is no ATM at the station—exit straight from the station and walk about two blocks, and you'll find ATMs on either side of the street.

If taking the **night train from Kraków to Eger**, note that your train actually continues on to Budapest—so you'll have to be on your toes to get off at Füzesabony (at 7:39 in 2005; confirm specific time before you travel). When you board the night train, make sure the conductor knows when you're getting off; he should wake you up 20 minutes before reaching Füzesabony, and he'll have to unlock the door to let you off the train. Once in Füzesabony, you'll have about 35 minutes before the next Eger-bound train leaves. That's plenty of time to get some local cash, buy your ticket to Eger (170 Ft), and hop on the train.

SLOVENIA

SLOVENIA

(Slovenija)

Tiny, overlooked Slovenia is one of Europe's most unexpectedly charming destinations. At the intersection of the Slavic, German, and Italian worlds, Slovenia is an exciting mix of the best of each culture. Though it's just a quick trip away from the tourist throngs in Venice, Munich, Salzburg, and Vienna, Slovenia has stayed off the tourist track—a handy detour for in-the-know Back Door travelers.

Today, it seems strange to think that Slovenia was ever part of Yugoslavia. Both in the personality of its people and in its landscape, Slovenia feels more like Austria. Slovenes are more industrious, organized, and punctual than their fellow former Yugoslavs... yet still friendly, relaxed, and Mediterranean. Locals like the balance. Visitors expecting minefields and rusting Yugo factories are pleasantly surprised to find Slovenia's rolling countryside dotted instead with quaint alpine villages and the spires of miniature Baroque churches, with breathtaking, snow-capped peaks in the distance.

Only half as big as Switzerland, but remarkably diverse for its size, Slovenia can be easily appreciated on a brief visit. Travelers can hike on alpine trails in the morning and explore some of the world's best caves in the afternoon, before relaxing with a seafood dinner on the Adriatic.

Slovenia enjoys a powerhouse economy—the healthiest in Eastern Europe. Of the 10 new nations that joined the European Union in 2004, Slovenia was the only one rich enough to be a net donor (with a higher per-capita income than the average), and the only one already qualified to join the euro currency zone (it begins using the euro in 2007). Thanks to its long-standing ties to the West and can-do spirit, Slovenia already feels more Western than any other destination in this book.

The country has a funny way of making people fall in love with it. Slovenes are laid-back, easygoing, and fun. They won't win any world wars (they're too well-adjusted to even try)...but they're exactly the type of people you'd love to chat with over a cup of coffee. Many of today's American visitors are soldiers who participated in the conflict in nearby Bosnia and have good memories of their vacations here. Now they're bringing their families back with them. They're not the only ones. One of your co-authors has decided that Slovenia is his hands-down favorite European country.

The Slovene language is as mellow as the people. While Slovenes use Serb and German curses in abundance, the worst they can say in their native tongue is, "May you be kicked by a horse." For "Darn it!" they say, "Three hundred hairy bears!"

Coming from such a small country, locals are proud of the few things that are distinctly Slovenian, such as the roofed hayrack. Foreigners think that Slovenes' fascination with these hayracks is strange... until they visit, and see them absolutely everywhere (especially in the northwest). Because of the frequent rainfall, the hayracks are covered by a roof that allows

the hay to dry thoroughly. The most traditional kind is the *toplar*, consisting of two hayracks connected by one big roof. It looks like a skinny barn with open, fenced sides. Hay hangs on the sides to dry; firewood, carts, tractors, and other farm implements sit on the ground inside; and dried hay is stored in the loft up above. But these wooden *toplarji* are firetraps, and a stray bolt of lighting can burn one down in a flash. So in recent years, more farmers are moving to single hayracks *(enojni)*; these are still roofed, but have posts made of concrete, rather than wood. You'll find postcards

Slovenia Almanac

Official Name: Republika Slovenija, or simply Slovenija.

Snapshot History: After being dominated by Germans for centuries, Slovenian culture proudly emerged in the 19th century. After World War I, Slovenia merged with its neighbors to become Yugoslavia, then broke away peacefully and achieved independence for the first time ever in 1991.

Population: Slovenia's 2 million people (similar to Nevada) are 83 percent ethnic Slovenes who speak Slovene, plus a smattering of Serbs, Croats, and Bosnians who speak dialects of Serbo-Croatian. The majority of the country is Catholic, but one in 50 is Orthodox and one in 50 faces east to Mecca to pray.

Latitude and Longitude: 46° N and 14° E (latitude similar to Lyon, France; Quebec, Canada; or Bismarck, North Dakota).

Area: At 7,800 square miles, it's about the size of New Jersey, but with a fourth the population.

Geography: Tiny Slovenia has three extremely different terrains and climates: the warm Mediterranean coastline (just 29 miles—about one inch per inhabitant); the snow-capped, forested alpine mountains in the northwest (including 9,400-foot Mt. Triglav); and the moderate, central limestone plateau that includes Ljubljana and the cave-filled Karst region. If you look at a map of Slovenia and kind of squint, it really begins to look like a chicken running towards the east.

Biggest Cities: Nearly one in five Slovenes lives in the two biggest cities: Ljubljana (the capital, pop. 265,000) and Maribor (in the east, pop. 110,000). Half the country lives in rural villages.

Economy: With a Gross Domestic Product of $40 billion and a GDP per capita of nearly $20,000, Slovenia's economy is much stronger than the average Eastern European country. This is thanks to its historical links with the West. Slovenia is on track to adopt the euro currency in January of 2007, if it can rein in inflation, debt, and the corruption of too-close ties between corporations and government. Slovenia's wealth comes largely from manufactured metal products (trucks, machinery) traded with a diverse group of partners.

Currency: 200 tolars (SIT) = about $1.

Government: The country is headed by Prime Minister Janez Janša, who assumes power as the head of the leading vote-getting party in legislative elections. He governs along with the more figurehead president, Janez Drnovšek. (Drnovšek's predecessor,

Milan Kučan, took a brave stand for independence as Yugoslavia was disintegrating. Slovenia's relatively peaceful succession is credited largely to Kučan, who remains a popular figure.) The National Assembly of about 90 elected legislators (along with a second house of parliament, which has much less power) is not currently dominated by any single party. Despite the country's small size, it is divided into some 200 municipalities.

Flag: Three horizontal bands of white (top), blue, and red. A shield in the upper left shows Mount Triglav, with a wavy-line sea below and three stars above.

The Average Slovene: The average Slovene skis, in this largely alpine country, and is an avid fan of the oddly popular sport of team handball. He or she lives in a 250-square-foot apartment, earns $1,400 a month, watches 16 hours of TV a week (much of it in English with Slovene subtitles), and enjoys a drink-and-a-half of alcohol every day.

Notable Slovenes: A pair of prominent Ohio politicians—presidential candidate Dennis Kucinich and Senator George Voinovich, both from the Cleveland area—are each half-Slovene. Classical musicians might know composers Giuseppe Tartini and Hugo Wolf. Even if you haven't heard of architect Jože Plečnik yet, you'll hear his name a hundred times while you're in Slovenia—especially in Ljubljana (see page 485). Most famous of all is the illustrious Melania Knauss—a GQ cover girl who's also Mrs. Donald Trump.

Sporty Slovenes: If you follow alpine sports or team handball, you'll surely know some world-class athletes from Slovenia. NBA fans might recognize basketball players Primož Brezec and Bostjan Nachbar, as well as some lesser players. The athletic Slovenes—perhaps trying to compensate for the miniscule size of their country—have accomplished astonishing feats: Davo Karnicar has skied down from the summits of some of the world's tallest mountains (including Everest, Kilimanjaro, and McKinley); Benka Pulko became the first person ever to drive a motorcycle around the world (that is, all 7 continents, including Antarctica; total trip: 118,000 miles in 2,000 days—also the longest solo motorcycle journey by a woman); Dusan Mravlje ran across all the continents; and ultra-marathon swimmer Martin Strel has swam the entire length of several major rivers, including the Danube (1,775 miles), the Mississippi (2,415 miles), and the Yangtze (3,915 miles).

and miniature wooden models of both kinds of hayracks (a fun souvenir).

Another good (and uniquely Slovenian) memento is a creatively decorated front panel from a beehive *(panjske končnice)*. Slovenia has a strong beekeeping tradition, and beekeepers once believed that painting the fronts of the hives made it easier for bees to find their way home. Replicas of these panels are available at gift shops all over the country. (For more on the panels and Slovenia's beekeeping heritage, see page 548.)

To really stretch your tolar, try one of Slovenia's more than 200 farmhouse B&Bs, called "tourist farms" *(turistične kmetije)*. Use the B&B as a home base to explore the entire country—remember, the farthest reaches of Slovenia are only a day trip away. You can get a comfortable, hotelesque double with private bathroom—plus a traditional Slovenian dinner and a hearty breakfast—for as little as $40. Request a listing from the Slovenian Tourist Board (see page 9), or visit www.slovenia-tourism.si/touristfarms.

Slovenia is poised to become one of Eastern Europe's top destinations in the next few years. Now is the time to visit, while the locals are still friendly, the prices are still reasonable, and the lanes and trails are yours alone.

Practicalities

Telephones: Insertable phone cards, sold at newsstands and kiosks everywhere, get you access to the modern public phones.

When calling locally, dial the seven-digit number. To make a long-distance call within the country, start with the area code (which begins with 0). To call a Slovenian number from abroad, dial the international access number (00 if calling from Europe, 011 from the United States or Canada) followed by 386 (Slovenia's country code), then the area code (without the initial 0) and the seven-digit number. To call out of Slovenia, dial 00, the country code of the country you're calling (see chart in appendix), the area code if applicable (may need to drop initial zero), and the local number.

Slovenian phone numbers beginning with 080 are toll-free; 090 and 089 denote expensive toll lines. Mobile phone numbers usually begin with 031, 041, 051, 040, or 070.

Slovenian History

Slovenia has a long and not very interesting history as part of various larger empires. Charlemagne's Franks conquered the tiny land in the eighth century, and, ever since, Slovenia has been a backwater of the German world—as a holding of the Germanic Holy Roman Empire and, later, the Hapsburg Empire. Slovenia often seems as much German as Slavic. But even as the capital,

Slo-what?-ia

"The only thing I know about Slovakia is what I learned firsthand from your foreign minister, who came to Texas."

—George W. Bush, to a Slovak journalist (Bush had actually met with Dr. Janez Drnovšek, then Slovenia's prime minister)

Maybe it's understandable that many Americans confuse Slovenia with Slovakia. Both are small, mountainous countries that not too long ago were parts of bigger, better known, now defunct nations. But anyone who has visited Slovenia and Slovakia will set you straight—they feel worlds apart.

Slovenia, wedged between the Alps and the Adriatic, is a tidy, prosperous country with a strong economy. Until 1991, Slovenia was one of the six republics that made up Yugoslavia. Historically, Slovenia has had very strong ties with Germanic culture—so it feels German.

Slovakia—two countries away, to the northeast—is slightly bigger. Much of its territory is covered by the Carpathian Mountains, most notably the dramatic jagged peaks of the High Tatras. In 1993, the Czechs and Slovaks peacefully chose to go their separate ways, so the nation of Czechoslovakia dissolved into the Czech Republic and the Slovak Republic (a.k.a. Slovakia). Slovakia was hit hard by the communists, and still suffers from a weak economy and high poverty levels. Slovakia was part of Hungary until the end of World War I, and feels Hungarian (especially the southern half of the country, where many Hungarians still live).

To make things even more confusing, there's also **Slavonia.** This is the thick, inland "panhandle" that makes up the northeast half of Croatia, along Slovenia's southeast border. Much of the warfare in Croatia's 1991–1995 war took place in Slavonia (including Vukovar; see Understanding Yugoslavia chapter).

I won't tell on you if you mix them up. But if you want to feel smarter than the president, do a little homework and get it right.

Ljubljana, was populated by Austrians (called Laibach by its German-speaking residents), the Slovenian language and cultural traditions survived in the countryside.

Ljubljana rose to international prominence for half a decade (1809–1813) when Napoleon named it the capital of his "Illyrian Provinces," stretching from Austria's Tirol to Croatia's Dalmatian Coast. During this time, the long-suppressed Slovene language was used for the first time in schools and the government. Inspired by the patriotic poetry of France Prešeren, national pride surged.

The most interesting chapter in Slovenian history happened in the last century. Some of World War I's fiercest fighting occurred at the Soča (Isonzo) Front in northwest Slovenia—witnessed by young Ernest Hemingway, who drove an ambulance. After the war, from 1918 to 1991, Slovenia was Yugoslavia's smallest, northernmost, and most affluent republic. Concerned about Serbian strongman Slobodan Milošević's politics, Slovenia seceded in 1991. Because more than 90 percent of the people here were ethnic Slovenes, the break with Yugoslavia was simple and virtually uncontested. Its war for independence lasted just 10 days and claimed only a few dozen lives. (For more details, see the Understanding Yugoslavia chapter, page 750.)

After centuries of looking to the West, Slovenia became the first of the former Yugoslav republics to join the European Union in May 2004. The Slovenes are practical about this move, realizing it's essential for their survival as a tiny nation in a modern world. But there are trade-offs, and "Euro-skeptics" are down on EU bureaucracy. As borders disappear, Slovenes are experiencing more crime. Local farming is threatened by EU standards. There are no more cheap bananas (because the brown ones must be trashed), and "you can't sell a cucumber with more than a three-degree curve." Slovenian businesses are having difficulty competing with big German and Western firms. Before EU membership, only Slovenes could own Slovenian land. Now foreigners are buying property, driving up real estate prices.

Still, the Slovenes have kept their sense of humor about the change. The port city of Trieste, which used to be a Yugoslav/Slovenian city, was claimed by Italy after World War II—a move that still strikes many Slovenes as unfair. The day after Slovenia joined the EU, graffiti in the streets of Ljubljana bragged, "We got Trieste back!"

Slovenian Food

Slovenian cuisine has enjoyed influence from a wide variety of sources. Like Croatian food, it features some pan-Balkan elements. The red-bell-pepper condiment *ajvar* is popular here. For fast food, you'll find *burek*, *čevapčiči*, and *ražnjiči* (see "Balkan Flavors," page 580). Italian influence is also notable in Slovenia, with a pizza or pasta restaurant on seemingly every corner. Hungarian food simmers in the northeast corner of the country (where many Magyars reside). But most of all, Slovenian food has a distinctly German vibe—sausages, schnitzels, strudels, and sauerkraut are common here, as well as *repa* (turnip prepared like sauerkraut). Slovenes brag that their cuisine melds the best of Italian and German cooking.

Traditional Slovenian dishes are prepared with groats—kind of a grainy mush made with buckwheat, barley, or corn. Buckwheat, which thrives in this climate, often appears on Slovenian menus. You'll also see plenty of *štruklji* (dumplings), which can be stuffed with cheese, meat, or vegetables. Among the hearty soups in Slovenia is *jota*—a staple for Karst peasants, made from *repa*, beans, and vegetables.

The cuisine of Slovenia's Karst (the arid limestone plain south of Ljubljana) is notable. The small farms and wineries of this region have been inspired by Italy's "Slow Food" movement, and believe that cuisine is meant to be gradually appreciated, not rushed—making the Karst a destination for gourmet tours. Karstic cuisine is similar to France's nouvelle cuisine—several courses in small portions, with a focus on unusual combinations and preparations—but with an Italian flair. The Karst's tasty air-dried ham *(pršut),* available throughout the country, is worth seeking out. Istria (the peninsula just to the south of the Karst, in southern Slovenia and Croatia) produces truffles that, locals boast, are as good as Piedmont's, but much cheaper.

Slovenian food, with all of its influences— Italian, Austrian, Balkan, Hungarian, and Karstic—comes together in Ljubljana. The capital city also has a cosmopolitan diversity of options, from French to Mexican to Chinese to Moroccan.

Voda is water, and *kava* is coffee. Radenska, in the bottle with the three little hearts, is Slovenia's best-known brand of mineral water—good enough that the word *Radenska* is synonymous with bottled water all over Slovenia and throughout the former Yugoslavia.

Adventurous teetotalers should forego the Coke and sample Cockta, a Slovenian cola with a slight cherry, smoky aftertaste. Cockta became popular during the communist period, when Coke was hard to come by. This local variation developed a loyal following...until the Iron Curtain fell, and the real Coke became easy to get. Cockta sales plummeted. But in recent years—prodded by the slogan "The Taste of Your Youth"—nostalgic Slovenes are drinking Cockta once more. Aside from having happy childhood memories of sipping Cockta, Slovenes figure they can be proud that their little country produced a soft drink that rivals Coca-Cola.

To toast, say, *"Na ZDRAHV-yeh!"*—if you can't remember it, think of "Nice driving!" The premier Slovenian brand of *pivo* (beer) is Union (OO-nee-ohn), but you'll also see a lot of Laško, whose mascot is the Zlatorog (or "Golden Horn," a mythical goat-like animal).

Slovenia produces some fine *vino* (wine). The Celts first grew wine in Slovenia; the Romans improved the process and spread it throughout the country. Slovenia has three primary wine regions.

Key Slovene Phrases

English	Slovene	Pronounced
Hello. (formal)	*Dober dan.*	DOH-behr dahn
Hi. / Bye. (informal)	*Živjo.*	ZHEEV-yoh
Do you speak English?	*Ali govorite angleško?*	AH-lee goh-VOH-ree-teh ahng-LEHSH-koh
yes / no	*ja / ne*	yah / neh
Please. / You're welcome.	*Prosim.*	PROH-seem
Can I help you?	*Izvolite?*	eez-VOH-lee-teh
Thank you.	*Hvala.*	HVAH-lah
I'm sorry. / Excuse me.	*Oprostite.*	oh-proh-STEE-teh
Good.	*Dobro.*	DOH-broh
Goodbye.	*Nasvidenje.*	nahs-VEE-dehn-yeh
one / two	*ena / dve*	EH-nah / dveh
three / four	*tri / štiri*	tree / SHTEE-ree
five / six	*pet / šest*	peht / shehst
seven / eight	*sedem / osem*	SEH-dehm / OH-sehm
nine / ten	*devet / deset*	deh-VEHT / deh-SEHT
hundred	*sto*	stoh
thousand	*tisoč*	TEE-sohch
How much?	*Koliko?*	KOH-lee-koh
local currency	*tolar (SIT)*	TOH-lar
Where is...?	*Kje je...?*	kyeh yeh
...the toilet	*...vece*	VEHT-seh
men	*moški*	MOHSH-kee
women	*ženski*	ZHEHN-skee
water / coffee	*voda / kava*	VOH-dah / KAH-vah
beer / wine	*pivo / vino*	PEE-voh / VEE-noh
Cheers!	*Na zdravje!*	nah ZDRAHV-yeh
the bill	*račun*	rah-CHOON

Podravje, in the northeast, is dominated by Laški and Renski Riesling and other top-quality wines. Posavje, in the southeast, produces both white and red wines, but is famous for the light, russet-colored Cviček wine. Primorska, in the southwest, has a Mediterranean climate and produces mostly reds, including Teran, made from *refošk* grapes.

Slovenia's most popular desserts are *potica* (filled nut roll) and *prekmurska gibanica* (pastry filled with poppy seeds, walnuts, apple, and cheese). Bled is known for its *kremna rezina,* a vanilla custard and cream cake. Locals claim that Ljubljana has the finest gelato outside of Italy—which, after all, is just an hour down the road.

Slovenian Language

Slovene is surprisingly different from languages spoken in the other former Yugoslav republics. While Serbian and Croatian are virtually identical, Slovene is another story. Of all Slavic languages, Slovene has changed the least over the centuries—it's still closest to the proto-Slavonic spoken more than a millennium ago in the plains of present-day Ukraine.

Most Slovenes know Serbo-Croatian because, a generation ago, everybody in Yugoslavia had to learn it (along with the Cyrillic alphabet used in Serbia). The tiny country of Slovenia borders Italy and Austria, with important historical and linguistic ties to both. For self-preservation, the Slovene population has always been forced to function in many different languages. All of these factors make Slovenes excellent linguists. Most young Slovenes speak effortless, flawless English—then admit that they've never set foot in the United States or Britain, but love watching American movies and TV shows (which are always subtitled, never dubbed).

Slovene is perhaps the easiest Eastern European language to pronounce. As with most Slavic languages, *c* is pronounced "ts" (like "cats"). The letter *j* is pronounced as "y"—making "Ljubljana" easier to say than it looks (lyoob-lyee-AH-nah). In contrast to other Eastern European languages—which tend to have a wide array of confusing little doohickeys over the letters—Slovene only has one diacritical mark: the *strešica,* or "little roof." This makes *č* sound like "ch," *š* sound like "sh," and *ž* sound like "zh" (as in "measure").

The only trick: As in English, which syllable gets the emphasis is unpredictable. Slovenes use many of the same words as Croatians, but put the stress on an entirely different place.

As you're tracking down addresses, these definitions will help: *trg* (square), *ulica* (street), *cesta* (avenue), and *most* (bridge).

LJUBLJANA

Slovenia's capital, Ljubljana (lyoob-lyee-AH-nah), with a lazy old town clustered around a castle-topped mountain, is often likened to Salzburg. It's an apt comparison—but only if you inject a healthy dose of breezy Adriatic culture, add a Slavic accent, and replace Mozart with local architect Jože Plečnik.

Ljubljana feels much smaller than its population of 265,000. While big-league museums are in short supply, the town itself is an idyllic place that sometimes feels too good to be true. Festivals fill the summer, and people enjoy a Sunday stroll any day of the week. Fashion boutiques and cafés jockey for control of the old town, while the leafy riverside promenade crawls with stylishly dressed students sipping *kava* and polishing their near-perfect English. Laid-back Ljubljana is the kind of place where crumbling buildings seem elegantly atmospheric instead of shoddy.

Batted around by history, Ljubljana has seen cultural influences from all sides—most notably Prague, Vienna, and Venice. This has left the city a happy hodgepodge of cultures. Being the midpoint between the Slavic, Germanic, and Italian worlds gives Ljubljana a special spice.

People often ask me: What's the "next Prague"? I have to answer Kraków. But Ljubljana is the *next* "next Prague."

Planning Your Time

Ljubljana deserves a full day. While there are few must-see sights, the city's biggest attraction is its ambience. You'll spend much of your time strolling the pleasant town center, exploring the many interesting squares and architectural gems, shopping the boutiques, and sipping coffee at sidewalk cafés along the river.

Ljubljana

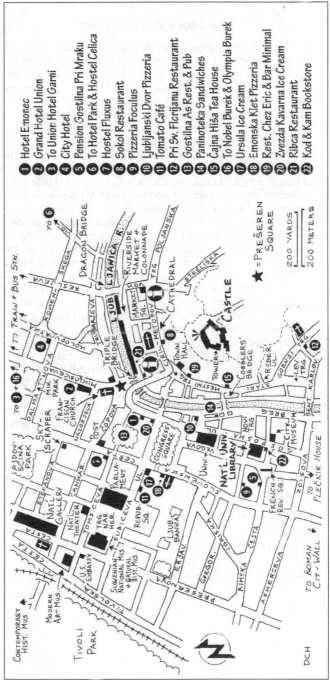

1. Hotel Emonec
2. Grand Hotel Union
3. To Union Hotel Garni
4. City Hotel
5. Pension Gostilna Pri Mraku
6. To Hotel Park & Hostel Celica
7. Hostel Fluxus
8. Sokol Restaurant
9. Pizzeria Foculus
10. Ljubljanski Dvor Pizzeria
11. Tomato Café
12. Pri Sv. Florijanu Restaurant
13. Gostilna As Rest. & Pub
14. Paninoteka Sandwiches
15. Čajna Hiša Tea House
16. To Nobel Burek & Olympia Burek
17. Ursula Ice Cream
18. Emonska Klet Pizzeria
19. Rest. Chez Eric & Bar Minimal
20. Zvezda Kavarna Ice Cream
21. Ribca Restaurant
22. Kod & Kam Bookstore

The Story of Ljubljana

In ancient times, Ljubljana was on the trade route connecting the Mediterranean (just 60 miles away) to the Black Sea (toss a bottle off the bridge here, and it can float to the Danube and, eventually, all the way to Russia). Legend has it that Jason and his Argonauts founded Ljubljana when they stopped here for the winter on their way home with the Golden Fleece. The town was Romanized (and called Emona) before being over-run by Huns—only to be resettled later by Slavs.

In 1335, Ljubljana fell under the jurisdiction of the Hapsburg Emperors (who called it Laibach). After six centuries of Hapsburg rule, Ljubljana still feels Austrian—especially the abundant Austrian Baroque and Viennese Art Nouveau archi-tecture—but with a Mediterranean flair.

Napoleon put Ljubljana on the map when he made it the capital of his Illyrian Provinces, a huge territory stretch-ing from Austria to Albania (1809–1813). For the first time, the Slovene language was taught in schools, awakening a new-found pride in Slovenian cultural heritage. People still look back fondly on this very brief era, which was the first (and probably only) time when Ljubljana rose to prominence on the world stage. After more than 600 years of being part of the Hapsburg Empire, Ljubljana has no "Hapsburg Square"... but they do have "French Revolution Square."

In the mid-19th century, the railway connecting Vienna to the Adriatic (Trieste) was built through town—and Ljubljana boomed. But much of the city was destroyed by an earthquake in 1895. It was rebuilt in the Art Nouveau style so popular in Vienna, its capital at the time. A generation later, architect Jože Plečnik bathed the city in his distinctive, artsy-but-sensible, classical-meets-modern style.

In 1991, Ljubljana became the capital of one of Europe's youngest nations. Today the city is filled with college stu-dents, making it a very youthful-feeling town. Ljubljana has always felt free to be creative, and recent years—with unprec-edented freedoms—have been no exception. This city is on the cutting edge when it comes to architecture, public art, and trendy pubs. But the scintillating avant-garde culture has soft edges—hip, but also user-friendly and fully accessible.

Here's the best plan for a low-impact sightseeing day: Begin on Prešeren Square, the heart of the city. Cross the Triple Bridge and wander through the riverside produce market before joining the town walking tour at 10:00 (daily May–Sept; less frequent off-season). After the tour, enjoy a lunch and some leisurely people-watching in the center before hiking or riding the tourist train up to the castle. After descending, wander along the river to Jože Plečnik's National and University Library, French Revolution Square, and on to my favorite Ljubljana museum, the Jože Plečnik House (note this excellent sight's limited hours, and plan accordingly: Tue–Thu 10:00–14:00 & 16:00–18:00, Sat 10:00–14:00, closed Fri and Sun–Mon). With more time, or if the Plečnik House is closed, stroll from Prešeren Square up Čopova street to Tivoli Park, where you can visit the Contemporary History Museum (Tue–Sun until 18:00, closed Mon).

There are plenty of good day trips close to Ljubljana. With a second day, visit one of the two impressive caves (Škocjan or Postojna) and nearby sights in the Karst region south of the city (see The Karst chapter, page 523).

Ljubljana is dead and disappointing on Sundays (most shops are closed and the produce market is quiet, but museums are generally open, a modest flea market stretches along the riverfront, and the TI's walking tour still runs). The city is also relatively quiet in August, when the students are on break and many locals head to beach resorts. They that say in August, even homeless people go to the coast.

ORIENTATION

Ljubljana—with narrow lanes, architecture that mingles the Old World and contemporary Europe, and cobbles upon cobbles of wonderful distractions—can be disorienting for a first-timer. But the charming central zone is compact, and with a little wandering, you'll quickly get the hang of it.

The Ljubljanica River—lined with cafés, restaurants, and a buzzing outdoor market—bisects the city, running around the base of a castle-topped mountain. Most sights are either on or just a short walk from the river. Visitors enjoy the distinctive bridges that span the Ljubljanica, including the landmark Triple Bridge (Tromostovje) and pillared Cobblers' Bridge (Čevljarski Most)—both by Jože Plečnik. Between them is a very plain wooden bridge dubbed "the Ugly Duckling." The center of Ljubljana is Prešeren Square, watched over by a big statue of Slovenia's national poet, France Prešeren.

I've organized the sights based on which side of the river they're on: the east (castle) side of the river, where Ljubljana began,

---

Ljubljana's Two Big Ps

Jože Plečnik (YOH-zheh PLAYCH-neek, 1872–1957) is the architect who shaped Ljubljana, designing virtually all of the city's most important landmarks. For more information, see page 512.

France Prešeren (FRAHN-tseh preh-SHAY-rehn, 1800–1849) is Slovenia's greatest poet and the namesake of Ljubljana's main square. Some civic-minded candy shops—trying to imitate the success of Austria's "Mozart Ball" chocolates—have started marketing "Prešeren Balls."

Mind your Ps, and your visit to Ljubljana becomes more meaningful.

---

with more medieval charm; and the west (Prešeren Square) side of the river, which has a more Baroque/Art Nouveau feel and most of the urban sprawl. At the northern edge of the tourist's Ljubljana is the train station; at the southern edge is the city's best sight, the Jože Plečnik House.

Tourist Information

Ljubljana's helpful TI has an office at the **Triple Bridge** (across from Prešeren Square; daily June–Sept 8:00–21:00, Oct–May 8:00–19:00, Stritarjeva ulica, tel. 01/306-1215, www.ljubljana -tourism.si). Another TI is at the **train station** (daily June–Sept 8:00–22:00, Oct–May 10:00–19:00, Trg O.F. 6, tel. 01/433-9475). A third TI, at the upper, far end of the **market** at Krekov trg 10, also offers information about the rest of Slovenia and has several Internet terminals (daily June–Sept 8:00–21:00, Oct–May 8:00– 19:00, tel. 01/306-4575).

At any TI, pick up a pile of free resources: the big city map, the Tourist Guide, the *Ljubljana A to Z* directory, the monthly *Where to?* events guide, and *Ljubljana Life* magazine (with restaurant reviews). Skip the **Ljubljana City Card,** which includes access to public transportation and free entry or discounts at several city museums (3,000 SIT/3 days).

Arrival in Ljubljana

By Train: Ljubljana's modern, user-friendly train station (Železniška Postaja) is on the north edge of the city center. Emerging from the passage up to track 1a, turn right to find the Tir Bar (**bike rental**—see "Getting Around Ljubljana," below) and the Cybercity **Internet** joint (Mon–Sat 8:00–23:00, Sun 12:00–23:00). The yellow arrivals hall has a **TI** (see above), an **ATM**, and helpful English signs (station open daily 5:00–22:00).

Ljubljana Essentials

English	Slovene	Pronounced
Ljubljana Castle	Ljubljanski Grad	lyoob-lyee-AHN-skee grahd
Prešeren Square	Prešernov trg	preh-SHEHR-nohv turg
Congress Square	Kongresni Trg	kohn-GREHS-nee turg
French Revolution Square	Trg Francoske Revolucije	turg frant-SOH-skeh reh-voh-LOOT-see-yeh
Square of the Republic	Trg Republike	turg reh-POOB-lee-keh
Triple Bridge	Tromostovje	troh-moh-STOHV-yeh
Cobblers' Bridge	Čevljarski Most	chehv-LAR-skee mohst
Dragon Bridge	Zmajski Most	ZMAY-skee mohst
Jože Plečnik, the architect	Jože Plečnik	YOH-zheh PLAYCH-neek
France Prešeren, the poet	France Prešeren	FRAHN-tseh preh-SHAY-rehn

Arrivals are *prihodi*, departures are *odhodi*, and track is *tir*.

The main square—and all of my recommended hotels—are within easy **walking** distance. It's a 10-minute stroll to get to the city center: Leave the arrivals hall to the right and walk a long block along the busy Trg Osvobodilne Fronte (or "Trg O.F." for short). At the post office (yellow *pošta* sign), cross Trg O.F., head straight down Miklošičeva, and you'll reach Prešeren Square.

Taxis, usually with unscrupulous cabbies, wait for you in front of the station. These mafia-type thugs are accustomed to charging you whatever they want without using the meter. The most likely scenario is that you'll pay a little too much (200–400 SIT extra) for the convenience of taking a taxi to your hotel—but *never* pay more than 1,000 SIT total to any of my recommended hotels. For more on taxis—and how to avoid rip-off cabbies—see "Getting Around Ljubljana—By Taxi," below.

By Bus: Ljubljana's bus station (Autobusna Postaja) is a low-profile building (with ticket windows, Internet access, a bakery, and newsstands) in the middle of Trg O.F., right in front of the train station. To get into the center, see "By Train," above.

By Car: Follow signs for *Center*. For longer visits, park in one of the many well-marked garages (about 400 SIT/hr) or lots (about 250 SIT/hr).

By Plane: See "Transportation Connections," page 521.

Helpful Hints

Important Days: Most Ljubljana museums (except the castle) are closed on Mondays. On Tuesdays and Thursdays, make it a priority to visit the Jože Plečnik House (open only these 2 days 10:00–14:00).

Flea Market: Every Sunday from 8:00 to 13:00, a colorful flea market sprawls along the castle side of the Ljubljanica River (south of the TI)—ideal for bargain-hunting and people-watching.

Banking: Most banks are open Mon–Fri 9:00–12:00 & 14:00–17:00, Sat 9:00–12:00, closed Sun.

Internet Access: Most hotel lobbies have Internet access for guests. The TI at the upper end of the market has several terminals (see "Tourist Information," above). **Cyber Café Xplorer** is more expensive but has longer hours (Mon–Fri 10:00–22:00, Sat–Sun 14:00–22:00, across the river from the market at Petkovškovo nabrežje 23). The other TIs have free terminals allowing you to check your e-mail (but only Hotmail and Yahoo). The train station has its own Internet café (see "Arrival in Ljubljana–By Train," above).

Post Office: The main post office *(pošta)* is a block up Čopova from Prešeren Square, at the intersection with the busy Slovenska cesta (Mon–Fri 7:00–20:00, Sat 7:00–13:00, closed Sun).

Laundry: Most hotels can do your laundry, but it's expensive. Hostel Celica generally lets non-guests use their self-service laundry facilities (1,200 SIT/load, not very central at Metelkova 9; see page 517). Other self-service places, used mainly by students, are even farther from the center (get details at TI).

English Bookstore: Kod & Kam has a huge selection of maps, English guidebooks, and other books about Slovenia (Mon–Fri 9:00–19:00, Sat 8:00–13:00, closed Sun, hiding at the bottom of French Revolution Square by the City Museum at Trg Francoske Revolucije 7, tel. 01/200-2732).

Architecture Guidebook: Ljubljana turns on architecture buffs. If you want to learn more about this city's quirky buildings, consider the excellent but expensive 8,000-SIT *Architectural Guide to Ljubljana* (sold at TIs and many bookstores).

Car Rental: Avis is friendly and central (about €50/day includes tax and insurance, no extra charge for drop-off elsewhere in

Slovenia, Mon–Fri 7:00–19:00, Sat 7:00–13:00, Sun 8:00–12:00, Čufarjeva 2, tel. 01/430-8010).

Best Views: The best view in Ljubljana is from atop The Skyscraper (Nebotičnik, often closed), followed by the castle tower. On sunny, blue-sky days, the colorful architecture on Prešeren Square springs to life, and you'll burn through film quickly along the river promenade.

Getting Around Ljubljana

By Bus: Virtually all of Ljubljana's sights are easily accessible by foot, so public transportation probably isn't necessary. But just in case: A token, or žeton, for a bus trip costs 190 SIT (buy at kiosk, bus station, or TI). If you pay on board, it's 300 SIT and you need exact change. An all-day ticket costs 900 SIT (sold only at bus station, LPP office, or TI).

By Taxi: There are several companies with different rates, but taxis usually start at about 200 SIT, and then charge 200 SIT per kilometer. Additional "surcharges" (such as for luggage) are bogus—and are often tacked on as a surprise after you reach your destination. Crooked cabbies are a huge problem in Ljubljana (especially those hanging out at the train station and tourist attractions). A ride within the city center (such as from the station to a hotel) shouldn't cost more than 1,000 SIT. Your best strategy is to ask for an estimate up front. The cabbie will probably want to just take you for a flat price without using the meter. This is the easiest solution, but realize you'll probably wind up paying 10–20 percent more than you would if he used the meter. (If you're feeling stingy and feisty, try insisting on the meter.) Another common trick is to charge you the "Sunday and holidays" (*nedelja in počitnice*) rate even on weekdays. If you're suspicious, ask your cabbie to explain why he's chosen the tariff. You'll likely (but not definitely) avoid crooked cabbies if you call for a taxi. While this might sound intimidating, dispatchers generally speak a little English. Your hotel, restaurant, or maybe the TI (if they're not too busy) can call a cab for you. **Yellow Taxi** is more reputable than the norm (mobile 041-731-831); **Metro Taxi** is known for being inexpensive (mobile 041-240-200).

By Bike: Ljubljana is a biker's delight, with lots of well-marked bike lanes. Tir Bar rents bikes at the train station (200 SIT/2 hrs, 700 SIT/day, low prices subsidized by mobile phone company Debitel—which puts ads on bikes, Mon–Sat 8:00–23:00, Sun 12:00–23:00, by passageway to tracks). In an attempt to lessen car traffic in the center, the city provides bikes nearly free at various downtown depots—ask the TI for details.

Ljubljana at a Glance

▲▲▲**Jože Plečnik House** Final digs of the famed hometown architect who shaped so much of Ljubljana. **Hours:** Tue–Thu 10:00–14:00 & 16:00–18:00, Sat 10:00–14:00, closed Fri and Sun–Mon.

▲▲**Riverside Market** Lively market area in the old town with produce, clothing, souvenirs—even wild boar salami. **Hours:** Best in the morning, especially Sat; market hall open Mon–Sat 7:00–14:00, Thu–Fri until 16:00, closed Sun.

▲▲**Ljubljana Castle** Tower with stunning views and decent 3-D film. **Hours:** Grounds open daily May–Sept 9:00–22:00, Oct–April 10:00–21:00; film plays on the half hour all day, daily May–Sept 9:00–21:00, Oct–April 10:00–18:00.

▲▲**National and University Library** Plečnik's pièce de résistance, with an intriguing facade, piles of books, and a bright reading room. **Hours:** July–Aug Mon–Sat 8:00–14:00, Wed until 16:00, closed Sun; Sept–June Mon–Fri 8:00–20:00, Sat 8:00–14:00, closed Sun.

▲**Dragon Bridge** Distinctive Art Nouveau bridge adorned with the city's mascot. **Hours:** Always roaring.

▲**Contemporary History Museum** Baroque mansion in Tivoli Park, with exhibit highlighting Slovenia's last 100 years. **Hours:** Tue–Sun 10:00–18:00, closed Mon.

▲**Architectural Museum of Ljubljana** Castle with Plečnik exhibit on the edge of town. **Hours:** Mon–Fri 10:00–14:00, closed Sat–Sun.

TOURS

Most of Ljubljana's museums are disappointing, but the town's ambience, architecture, and public art are its best attraction. To help you appreciate it all, taking a walking tour—either through the TI or by hiring your own local guide—is worth ▲▲.

Walking Tour—The TI organizes excellent two-hour guided town walks of Ljubljana in English, led by knowledgeable guides. From May through September, there are two tours daily: at 10:00 (a walking tour of the Old Town) and at 18:00 (a quick walking tour of the Old Town, followed by a trip by tourist train up to the castle). From October through April, the walking tour (no castle) goes only on Fridays, Saturdays, and Sundays at 11:00 (1,500 SIT for any of these tours, meet at Town Hall around corner from Triple Bridge TI).

Local Guide—Having an expert show you around his hometown for two hours for $45 has to be the best value in town. Ljubljana's hardworking guides lead tours on a wide variety of topics and can tailor their tour to your interests (figure 8,500 SIT/2 hrs, 25 percent more on Sun or for same-day booking, contact TI for details). **Marijan Krišković,** who leads tours for me throughout Eastern Europe, is an outstanding guide (8,500 SIT/2 hrs, mobile 040-222-739, kriskovic@yahoo.com).

Boat Tour—Consider seeing the town from the Ljubljanica River. Guided one-hour cruises leave a block from the Triple Bridge TI (away from the market; 1,500 SIT). From June through September, tours leave daily at 18:30 and 20:30, plus Saturdays and Sundays at 10:30. In April, May, and October, tours leave daily at 17:30 and 19:00, plus Saturdays and Sundays at 10:30 (no tours Nov–March; all trips weather permitting).

Bike Tour—In 2006, the TI plans to offer a new bike tour of the city (3,000 SIT, 2 hrs, get details at TI).

SELF-GUIDED SPIN-TOUR

Prešeren Square

The heart of Ljubljana is lively Prešeren Square (Prešernov trg).

The city's meeting point is the large **statue of France Prešeren,** Slovenia's greatest poet, whose work includes the Slovenian national anthem. Prešeren, an important catalyst of 19th-century Slovenian nationalism, is being inspired from overhead by the Muse. This statue provoked a scandal and outraged the bishop when it went up a hundred years ago—a naked woman sharing the square with a church! To ensure that nobody could be confused about the woman's intentions, she's conspicuously depicted with typical muse accessories: a laurel branch and a cloak.

Stand at the base of the statue to get oriented. Notice the bridge crossing the Ljubljanica River. This is one of Ljubljana's most important landmarks, Jože Plečnik's **Triple Bridge** (Tromostovje). The middle (widest) part of this bridge already existed, but Plečnik added the two side spans to more efficiently funnel the six streets of traffic on this side of the bridge to the one street on the other side. The bridge's Venetian vibe is intentional: Plečnik recognized that Ljubljana, located midway between Venice and then-capital Vienna, is itself a bridge between the Italian and Germanic worlds. Across the bridge is the TI, WCs, the market and cathedral (to the left), and the Town Hall (straight ahead).

Now turn 90 degrees to the right, and look down the first street after the riverbank. Find the pale woman in the picture frame on the second floor of the yellow house. This is **Julija,** the love of Prešeren's life. Tour guides spin romantic tales about how the couple met. But the truth is far less exciting: He was a teacher in her father's house when he was in his 30s and she was four. Later in life, she inspired him from afar—as she does now, from across the square—but they never got together. She may have been his muse, but when it came to marriage, she opted for wealth and status.

Ljubljana—especially the streets around this square—is an architecture-lover's paradise, starting with **Hauptmann House,** to the right of Julija. This was the only building in town that survived the devastating 1895 earthquake. A few years later, the owner renovated it anyway in the then-trendy Viennese Art Nouveau style you see today. All that remains of the original is the Baroque balcony above the entrance.

Just to the right of the Hauptmann House is a car-sized **model** of the city center—helpful for orientation. The street next to it (with the McDonald's) is **Čopova,** once the route of Ljubljana's Sunday promenade. A century ago, locals would put on their Sunday best and stroll from here to Tivoli Park, listening to musicians and dropping into cafés along the way. Plečnik called it the "lifeline of the city," connecting the green lungs of the park to this urban center. Today, busy Slovenska cesta and railroad tracks cross the route, making the promenade less inviting. But in the last decade, Ljubljana has been trying to recapture its golden age, and some downtown streets are pedestrian-only on weekends once again. The new evening *paseo* thrives along the river between the Triple Bridge and Cobblers' Bridge.

Continue looking to the right, past the big, pink landmark Franciscan Church of St. Mary. To the right of the church, the street called **Miklošičeva cesta** connects Prešeren Square to the train station. When Ljubljana was rebuilding after the 1895 earthquake, town architects and designers envisioned this street as a showcase of its new, Vienna-inspired Art Nouveau image. Down the street and on the left is the prominent **Grand Hotel Union,** with a stately domed spire on the corner. When these buildings were designed, Prague was the cultural capital of the Slavic world. The new look of Ljubljana paid homage to "the golden city of a hundred spires" (and copied Prague's romantic image). There was actually a law for several years that corner buildings had to have these spires. Even the trees you'll see around town were part of the vision. When the architect Plečnik designed the Ljubljanica River embankments a generation later, he planted tall, pointy poplar trees and squat, rounded willows—imitating the spires and domes of Prague.

Across from the Grand Hotel Union (not visible from here, but worth a wander up the street) is a Secessionist building with classic red, blue, and white colors (for the Slovenian flag) next to the noisy, pink, zigzagged **Cooperative Bank.** The bank was designed by Ivan Vurnik, an ambitious Slovenian architect who wanted to invent a distinctive national style after World War I, when the Hapsburg Empire broke up and Eastern Europe's nations were proudly emerging for the first time.

On the near corner of Miklošičeva cesta, look for the characteristic glass awning of **Centromerkur**—the first big post-quake department store, today government-protected. At the top of the building is Mercury, god of commerce, watching over the square that has been Ljubljana's commercial heart since the city began. Since this was across the river from medieval Ljubljana (beyond the town's limits...and the long arm of its tax collector), this area was the best place to sell and buy goods. Today it's the heart of Ljubljana's boutique culture. Step into the Centromerkur store to admire the interior, which is exactly the same as when it was built. The old-fashioned layout isn't convenient for modern shoppers—no elevator, tight aisles—but no matter how much anyone complains, the management isn't allowed to change anything.

Prešeren Square is the perfect springboard to explore the rest of Ljubljana. Now that you're oriented, visit some of the areas listed below.

SIGHTS

East of the River, under the Castle

The castle side of the river is the city's most colorful and historic quarter, packed with Old World ambience.

▲▲**Riverside Market**—In Ljubljana's thriving old town market, big-city Slovenes enjoy buying directly from the producer. The market, worth an amble anytime, is best on Saturday mornings, when the townspeople take their time wandering the stalls. In this tiny capital of a tiny country, you may even see the president searching for the perfect melon.

Begin your walk through the market at the Triple Bridge (and TI). The riverside **colonnade** was designed by (who else?) Jože Plečnik. This first stretch—nearest the Triple Bridge—is good for souvenirs: woodcarvings, miniature painted frontboards from beehives, and lots of colorful candles (bubbly Marta will gladly paint a special message on your candle for no extra charge).

Farther in, the market is almost all local, and the colonnade is populated by butchers, bakers, fishermen, and lazy cafés. Peek down at the actual river and see how the architect wanted the town and river to connect. The lower arcade is a people zone, with easy access from the bridge, public WCs, inviting cafés, and a stinky fish market offering a wide variety. The restaurant just below, **Ribca,** serves fun fishy plates, beer, and coffee with great riverside seating (open Mon–Sat only until 16:00; see "Eating," page 517).

Walk along the colonnade with the river on your left. When you come to the first small market square on your right, notice the 10-foot-tall concrete **cone.** Plečnik wanted to make Ljubljana the "Athens of the North," and imagined a huge hilltop cone as the center of a national acropolis—a complex for government, museums, and culture. This ambitious plan never panned out, but part of Plečnik's Greek idea did: the marketplace, based on an ancient Greek *agora.*

At the top of this square, you'll find the 18th-century **cathedral** *(stolnica)* standing on the site of a 13th-century Romanesque church. The cathedral is dedicated to St. Nicholas, patron saint of the fishermen and boatmen who have long come to sell their catch at the market. Take a close look at the intricately decorated side door under the passageway. This remarkable door was created for Pope John Paul II's visit here in 1996. Buried deeply in the fecund soil of their ancient and pagan history, the nation's linden tree of life sprouts with the story of the Slovenes. Crusaders and Turks battle at the bottom. At the top is Pope John Paul II, the Pole who oversaw the fall of communism, and—below him—the man who will become Slovenia's first saint. Around back is a similar door, carved with images of the six 20th-century bishops of Ljubljana. The interior is stunning Italian Baroque.

The building at the end of this first market square is the seminary palace. In the basement is a **market hall,** with vendors selling cheeses, meats, dried fruits, and other goodies (Mon–Sat 7:00–14:00, Thu–Fri until 16:00, closed Sun). This place is worth a graze. Most merchants are happy to give you a free sample (point to what you want, and say *probat, prosim*—"a taste, please").

When you leave the market hall, continue downstream into the big **main market square,** packed with produce and clothing stands. (The colorful flower market hides behind the seminary palace/market hall.) These producers go out of their way to be old-fashioned—many of them still follow the tradition of pushing their veggies on wooden carts (called *cizas*) to the market from their garden patches in the suburbs. Once at their stalls, they handle their produce wearing special gloves—it's considered rude for customers to touch the fruits and vegetables before they're bought. Over time, shoppers develop friendships with their favorite producers. On busy days, you'll see a long line at one stand, while the other merchants stand bored. Your choice is simple: Get in line, or eat sub-par produce.

Look for the little **scales** in the wooden kiosks marked *Kontrola Tehtnica*—allowing buyers to immediately check whether the producer cheated them (not a common problem, but just in case). The Hapsburg days left locals with the old German saying, "Trust is good; control is better."

Near the middle of the market, you'll notice a big gap along the riverfront colonnade. This was to be the site of a huge, roofed **Butchers' Bridge** designed by Jože Plečnik, but the plans never materialized. Aware of Plečnik's newfound touristic currency, some town politicians have recently dusted off the old plans and proposed building the bridge after all these years. (If you look across the river, you'll see that the cornerstone was already put in place by an overzealous politician.) It's a controversial project, and anytime a new mayor is elected, the decision is reversed.

If you want a unique taste as you finish exploring the market, enter the colonnade near the very end and find the **Divjačna Hubert** stand at #22, specializing in game. Ask charming Minka (it's her shop) for a *probat* (taste) of *div. prašič salama*—wild boar salami.

Just beyond the end of the market colonnade is the

▲Dragon Bridge (Zmajski Most)—The dragon has been the

symbol of Ljubljana for centuries, ever since Jason (of Argonauts and Golden Fleece fame) supposedly slew one in a nearby swamp. While the dragon is the star of this very photogenic Art Nouveau bridge, it was officially dedicated to Hapsburg Emperor Franz Josef. (Tapping into the emp's vanity got new projects funded—vital as the city rebuilt after its devastating earthquake of 1895.) But the Franz Josef name never stuck; those dragons are just too darn memorable.

▲▲Town Square (Mestni Trg)—This square is home to the **Town Hall** (Rotovž), highlighted by its clock tower and pillared loggia. Step inside the Renaissance courtyard to see artifacts and a map of late-17th-century Ljubljana. Studying this map, notice how the river, hill, and wall worked together to fortify the town. Courtyards like this (but humbler) are hidden through the city. As rent in these old places is cheap, many such courtyards host funky and characteristic little businesses. Be sure to get off the main drag and poke into Ljubljana's nooks and Back Door crannies.

In the square is the **Fountain of Three Carolinian Rivers,** inspired in style and theme by Rome's many fountains. The figures with vases represent this region's three main rivers: Ljubljanica, Sava, and Krka. Over the centuries, the wild fluctuations in temperature that come with Ljubljana winters took its toll on this fountain—so now you'll have to view it under glass.

In the early 19th century, Ljubljana consisted mainly of this single street, running along the base of Castle Hill (plus a small "New Town" across the river). Stretching south from here are two other "squares"—Stari trg (Old Square) and Gornji trg (Upper Square)—that have long since grown together into one big, atmospheric promenade lined with quaint shops and cafés (perfect for a stroll). Virtually every house along this drag has a story to tell, of residents famous or infamous. As you walk, keep your eyes open for Ljubljana's mascot dragon—it's everywhere. At the end of the pedestrian zone (at Gornji trg), look uphill and notice the village charms of the oldest buildings in town (4 medieval houses with rooflines slanted at the ends, different from the others on this street).

▲▲**Ljubljana Castle (Ljubljanski Grad)**—The castle above town offers marvelous views of Ljubljana and the surrounding countryside. There has probably been a settlement on this site since prehis-

toric times, though the first castle here was Roman. The 12th-century version was gradually added on to over the centuries, until it fell into disrepair in the 17th century. Today's castle was rebuilt in the 1940s, renovated in the 1970s, and is still technically unfinished (subject to ongoing additions). The castle houses a restaurant, a gift shop, temporary exhibition halls, and a Gothic chapel with Baroque paintings of the coat of arms of St. George (Ljubljana's patron saint, the dragon-slayer). Above the restaurant are two wedding halls—Ljubljana's most popular places to get married.

It's free to enter the castle grounds (daily May–Sept 9:00–22:00, Oct–April 10:00–21:00, tel. 01/232-9994). Inside are two optional activities you have to pay for (800 SIT covers both): the **castle tower**, with 92 steps leading to one of the best views in town; and a 20-minute **3-D film** about the history of Ljubljana (touted as a "virtual museum," but barely worth your time; plays on the half hour all day, daily May–Sept 9:00–21:00, Oct–April 10:00–18:00).

Tours of the castle in Slovene and English leave from the entry bridge daily June–September at 10:00 and 16:00 (1,100 SIT, tour lasts 60–90 min). The castle is also home to the Ljubljana Summer Festival, with **concerts** throughout the summer (tel. 01/426-4340, www.festival-lj.si).

Getting to the Castle: A sweat-free route to the top is via the **tourist train** that leaves at the top of each hour from Prešeren Square (600 SIT, daily in summer 9:00–21:00, shorter hours off-season, doesn't run in snow or other bad weather). There are also two handy **trails** to the castle. The steeper-but-faster route begins near the Dragon Bridge (find Studentovska lane, just past the statue of Vodnik in the market). Slower but easier is Reber, just off Stari trg (Old Square), a few blocks south of the Town Hall (once on the trail, always bear left, then go right when you're just under the castle—follow signs). For years, Ljubljana politicians have been debating the construction of a funicular that would connect the market to the castle. Given the project's on-again, off-again history, it may be years more before work begins.

West of the River, beyond Prešeren Square

The Prešeren Square (west) side of the river is the heart of modern Ljubljana, and home to several prominent squares and fine museums. These sights are listed roughly in order from Prešeren Square, and can be linked to make an interesting walk.

• *If you leave Prešeren Square in the direction the poet is looking and bear to your left (up Wolfova, by the picture of Julija), you'll walk a block to...*

Congress Square (Kongresni Trg)—This grassy, tree-lined square is ringed by some of Ljubljana's most important buildings: the University headquarters, the Baroque Ursuline Church of the Holy Trinity, a classical mansion called the Kažina, and the Philharmonic Hall. At the top end of the square, by the entry to a pedestrian underpass, a Roman sarcophagus sits under a gilded statue of a **Roman citizen**, a replica of an artifact from 1,700 years ago, when this town was called Emona. The busy street above you has been the main trading route through town since ancient Roman times. This square hosts the big town events. Locals remember how, when President Clinton visited, tens of thousands packed the square. (When President Bush came, almost nobody showed up.)

• *Take the underpass beneath busy Slovenska street (the town's main traffic thoroughfare) to the...*

▲**Square of the Republic (Trg Republike)**—This unusual square is essentially a parking lot ringed by an odd collection of buildings. While hardly quaint, the Square of the Republic gives you a good taste of a modern corner of Ljubljana. And it's historic—this is where Slovenia declared its independence in 1991.

The **twin office towers** (with the world's biggest digital watch, flashing the date, time, and temperature) were designed by Plečnik's protégé, Edvard Ravnikar. As harrowing as these seem, imagine if they had followed the original plans—twice as tall as they are now, and connected by a bridge, representing the gateway to Ljubljana. These buildings were originally designed as the Slovenian parliament—but the ambitious plans were scaled back when Tito didn't approve (since it would have made Slovenia's parliament bigger than the Yugoslav parliament in Belgrade). Instead, the **Slovenian Parliament** is across the square, in the strangely low-profile office building with the sculpted entryway. The carvings are in the Social Realist style, celebrating the noble Slovenian people conforming to communist ideals for the good of the entire society. Completing the square are a huge conference center (Cankarjev Dom, the white building behind the skyscrapers), a shopping mall, and some intriguing public art.

• *Just a block north (on Trg Narodni Herojev), you'll find the...*

Slovenian National Museum (Narodni Muzej Slovenije) and Slovenian Museum of Natural History (Prirodoslovni Muzej Slovenije)—These two museums share a single historic building facing a park behind the Parliament. While neither collection is particularly good, they're both worth considering if you have a special interest or a rainy day (700 SIT for each museum, or 1,100 SIT for both, some English descriptions, daily 10:00–18:00, Thu until 20:00, Muzejska 1, tel. 01/241-0940, www2.pms-lj.si).

The **National Museum** occupies the ground floor, featuring a lapidarium with carved-stone Roman monuments and exhibits on Egyptian mummies. (Also on this level are temporary exhibits.) Upstairs and to the right are more exhibits of the National Museum, loosely tracing Slovenian history with artifacts ranging from old armor and pottery to the museum's pride and joy, a fragment of a 45,000-year-old Neanderthal flute.

Upstairs and to the left is the **Natural History** exhibit, featuring the flora and fauna of Slovenia. You'll see partial skeletons of a mammoth and a cave bear, plenty of stuffed reptiles, fish, and birds, and an exhibit on "human fish" (*Proteus anguinus*—long, skinny, flesh-colored salamanders).

Behind the museum is a pretty yellow chalet housing the **U.S. Embassy**—my vote for quaintest embassy building in the world.

• *Just up the street are two decent but skippable art museums:*

National Gallery (Narodna Galerija)—This museum has three parts: European artists, Slovenian artists, and temporary exhibits. Find the work of Ivana Kobilca, a late-19th-century Slovenian Impressionist. Art-lovers enjoy her self-portrait in *Summer*. If you're going to Bled, you can get a sneak preview with Marko Pernhart's huge panorama of the Julian Alps (800 SIT, free on

Sat after 14:00, open Tue–Sun 10:00–18:00, closed Mon, enter through big glass box between 2 older buildings at Prešernova 24, tel. 01/241-5435, www.ng-slo.si).

Museum of Modern Art (Moderna Galerija Ljubljana)—This has a ho-hum permanent collection of modern and contemporary Slovenian artists, as well as temporary exhibits by both Slovenes and international artists (1,000 SIT, Sept–June Tue–Sat 10:00–18:00, closed Mon; July–Aug Tue–Sat 12:00–20:00, closed Mon; Tomšičeva 14, tel. 01/241-6800).

• *Near the art museums, look for the...*

Serbian Orthodox Church—The church was built in 1936, soon after the Slovenes joined a political union with the Serbs. Wealthy Slovenia attracted its poorer neighbors from the south—so it built this church for that community. Since 1991, the Serb population continues to rise—people from the poorer parts of the former Yugoslavia, such as Serbia, are flocking to prosperous Slovenia. The church is decorated without a hint of the 20th century, mirroring a very conservative religion. You'll see Cyrillic script in this building, which feels closer to Moscow than to Rome.

• *On the other side of the busy street is...*

Tivoli Park (Park Tivoli)   This huge park, just west of the center, is where Slovenes relax on summer weekends. The easiest access is by underpass from Cankarjeva cesta (between the National Gallery and the Museum of Modern Art). As you emerge, the neoclassical pillars leading down the promenade clue you in that this part of the park was designed by Jože Plečnik.

• *Aside from taking a leisurely stroll, the best thing to do in the park is visit the...*

▲Contemporary History Museum (Muzej Novejše Zgodovine)—In a Baroque mansion (Cekinov Grad) in Tivoli Park, a well-done exhibit called "Slovenians in the 20th Century" traces the last hundred years of Slovenian history. Downstairs are temporary exhibits, and upstairs are several rooms using models, dioramas, and light-and-sound effects to creatively tell the story of one of Europe's youngest nations. It's a little difficult to fully appreciate, even with the English descriptions. But the creativity and the spunky spirit of the place are truly enjoyable. The most moving room has artifacts from the Slovenes' brave declaration of independence from a hostile Yugoslavia in 1991. The well-organized Slovenes had only to weather a 10-day skirmish to gain their autonomy. (It's chilling to think that bombers were en route to leveling this gorgeous city during Slovenia's 10-day war with Yugoslavia. The planes were called back at the last minute, because diplomatic negotiations were improving.) The free English brochure explains everything, but consider the thought-provoking 2,000-SIT essay collection *Over the Hill Is Just Like Here*, which all

Slovenian schoolchildren study (entry-800 SIT, permanent exhibit free first Sun of the month, open Tue–Sun 10:00–18:00, closed Mon, in Tivoli Park at Celovška cesta 23, tel. 01/300-9610).

Getting There: The museum is a 20-minute walk from the center, best combined with a wander through Tivoli Park. The fastest approach: As you emerge from Cankarjeva cesta underpass into park, turn right and go straight ahead for five minutes, continue straight up ramp, then turn left after tennis courts and look for the big pink mansion.

• *On your way back to the center, consider stopping by the...*

The Skyscraper (Nebotičnik)—This 1933 Art Deco building was the first skyscraper in Slovenia, for a time the tallest building in Central Europe, and one of the earliest European buildings that was clearly influenced by American architecture (especially the interior).

The Skyscraper has weathered an often-unlucky history. When it was built, Jože Plečnik was calling the shots when it came to Ljubljana architecture. This building's designer had to get Plečnik's approval before he could build. Plečnik agreed, but didn't like the plan for 12 stories—so he asked to make it nine instead. After agreeing, the building's architect built the last three stories anyway.

Ever since, say the locals, The Skyscraper has been cursed. The 12th-story observation deck—with Ljubljana's best view—had to close a few years back because it had become the most popular spot in the country for suicide attempts. Now it has been (ineffectively) retrofitted to try to prevent people from diving off. Two different restaurants on the top floor have come and gone over the last five years, and plans for a new one are constantly on-again, off-again. If you're in the neighborhood, it's worth poking your head in the door to see if you can take the elevator up top (2 blocks from Prešeren Square at Štefanova ulica 1).

• *A few blocks south, near several Jože Plečnik sights (see below) at the river end of French Revolution Square, you'll find the...*

City History Museum (Mestni Muzej Ljubljana)—This brand-new museum, in the recently restored Auersperg Palace, offers a high-tech, in-depth look at the history of Ljubljana. The cellar features Roman ruins and medieval artifacts; upstairs are exhibits tracing the story of Ljubljana through to modern times. Rounding out the museum's collection is a wide range of special exhibitions (free but may begin charging entry fee in 2006, well-described in English, Tue–Sun 10:00–18:00, closed Mon, Gosposka 15, tel. 01/241-2500, www.mm-lj.si).

Jože Plečnik's Architecture

Jože Plečnik is to Ljubljana what Antoni Gaudí is to Barcelona: a home-grown and amazingly prolific genius who shaped his town with a uniquely beautiful vision. And, as in Barcelona, Ljubljana has a way of turning people who couldn't care less about architecture into huge Plečnik fans. There's plenty to see. In addition to the top sights listed below, Plečnik designed the embankments along the Ljubljanica and Gradaščica Rivers in the Trnovo neighborhood; the rebuilt Roman wall along Mirje street, south of the center; the Church of St. Francis, with its classicist bell-tower; St. Michael's Church on the Marsh; Orel Stadium; Žale Cemetery; and many more buildings throughout Slovenia.

▲▲▲**Jože Plečnik House (Plečnikova Zbirka)**—Ljubljana's favorite son lived here from 1921 until his death in 1957. He added on to an existing house, building a circular bedroom for himself and filling the place with clever furniture and other gizmos he designed, as well as artifacts, photos, and gifts from around the world that inspired him as he shaped Ljubljana.

Today the house is decorated exactly as it was the day Plečnik died, containing much of his equipment, models, and plans. There are very few barriers, so you are in direct contact with the world of the architect. Perhaps no other museum in Europe gives such an intimate portrait of an artist; you'll feel like Plečnik invited you over for dinner. It's still furnished with unique, Plečnik-designed furniture and ingenious, one-of-a-kind inventions. Whether or not you care about Plečnik, architecture, or design, you can't help but be tickled by this man's sheer creativity, and by the world he forged for himself to live in.

The house can be toured only with a guide, whose enthusiasm brings the place to life (1,000 SIT, 500-SIT guidebook, Tue–Thu 10:00–14:00 & 16:00–18:00, Sat 10:00–14:00, closed Fri and Sun–Mon; 30-min tours in English leave at 10:00, 11:00, 12:00, 13:00, 16:00, and 17:00; Karunova ulica 4, tel. 01/280-1600, www .arhmuz.com, pz@aml.si).

Getting There: The 15-minute stroll from the center is nearly as enjoyable as the house itself. First find your way to French Revolution Square, surrounded by other Plečnik works (described below). From the square's obelisk, walk down Emonska for about 10 minutes toward the twin-spired church. You'll pass (on the left) the delightful Krakovo district—a patch of green countryside in downtown Ljubljana. Many of the veggies you see in the riverside market come from these carefully tended gardens. When you reach the Gradaščica stream, head over the bridge (also designed by Plečnik) and go around the left side of the church to find the house.

Jože Plečnik
(1872–1957)

There is probably no single architect who has shaped one city as Jože Plečnik (YOH-zheh PLAYCH-neek) shaped Ljubljana. Everywhere you go, you can see where he left his mark. While he may not yet register very high on the international Richter scale of important architects, the Slovenes' pride in this man's work is understandable.

Plečnik was born in Ljubljana and studied in Vienna under the Secessionist architect Otto Wagner (see page 722). His first commissions, done around the turn of the 20th century in Vienna, were pretty standard Art Nouveau stuff. Then Tomáš Masaryk, president of the new nation of Czechoslovakia, decided that the dull Hapsburg design of Prague Castle could use a new look to go with its new independence. But he didn't want an Austrian architect; it had to be a Slav. In 1921, Masaryk chose Jože Plečnik, who sprinkled the castle grounds with his distinctive touches. By now, Plečnik had perfected his simple, eye-pleasing style, which

▲▲**National and University Library (Narodna in Univerzitetna Knjižnica, or NUK)**—Just a block up from the river at Novi trg is Plečnik's masterpiece. The theme of the building is overcoming obstacles to attain knowledge.

The facade has blocks of odd sizes and shapes, representing a complex numerological pattern that suggests barriers on the path to enlightenment. The sculpture on the river side is Moses—known for leading his people through 40 years of hardship to the Promised Land. On the right side of the building, find the horse-head doorknobs—representing the winged horse Pegasus (grab hold, and he'll whisk you away to new levels of enlightenment). Step inside. The main staircase is dark and gloomy—modeled after an Egyptian tomb. But at the top, through the door marked *Velika Čitalnica*, is the bright, airy main reading room: the ultimate goal, a place of learning.

mixes modern and classical influences, with lots of columns and pyramids—simultaneously serious and playful.

By the time Plečnik finished in Prague, he had made a name for himself. His prime years were spent creating for the Kingdom of Yugoslavia (before the ideology-driven era of Tito). Plečnik returned home to Ljubljana and set to work redesigning the city, both as an architect and as an urban planner. He lived in a simple house behind the Trnovo Church (now a tourable museum—see page 511), and on his walk to work every day, he pondered ways to make the city even more livable. Wandering through town, notice how thoughtfully he incorporated people, nature, the Slovenian heritage, town vistas, and symbolism into his works—it's feng shui on a grand urban scale. Many of his ideas became reality; even more did not. (It's fun to imagine what this city would look like if Plečnik had always gotten his way.)

After his death in 1957, Plečnik was virtually forgotten by Slovenes and scholars alike. His many works in Ljubljana were taken for granted. But in 1986, an exposition about Plečnik at Paris' Pompidou Center jump started interest in the architect. Within a few years Plečnik was back in vogue. Today, scholars hail him as a genius who was ahead of his time, while locals and tourists simply enjoy the beauty of his brilliant works.

You can duck into the main stairwell without a problem, but you'll need a visitor's badge to get into the reading room. (Ask at the reception desk inside and to the right; depending on who's on duty, you'll either get a badge or be told it's impossible. In that case, if you're determined, just stick close to a student going inside (free, July–Aug Mon–Sat 8:00–14:00, Wed until 16:00, closed Sun; Sept–June Mon–Fri 8:00–20:00, Sat 8:00–14:00, closed Sun; corner of Turjaška and Gosposka ulica). To get out, try to stick with another student—or push gently on the door (it usually opens easily). To get here from Prešeren Square, simply follow the river south and turn right up Novi trg (the parking-lot square just after Cobblers' Bridge). Aside from being a great work of architecture, the building also houses the most important library in Slovenia, with more than two million books (about one per Slovene). The library is supposed to receive a copy of each new book printed in the country. In a freaky bit of bad luck, this was the only building in town damaged in World War II, when a plane crashed into it. But the people didn't want to see their books go up in flames—so hundreds of locals formed a human chain, risking life and limb to get the books out of the burning building.

▲French Revolution Square (Trg Francoske Revolucije)—
Many of Plečnik's finest works are on or near this square, just
around the corner from the National and University Library
(described above).

Plečnik designed the **obelisk** in the middle of the square to
commemorate Napoleon's short-lived decision to make Ljubljana
the capital of his Illyrian Provinces. It's rare to find anything honoring Napoleon outside of Paris, but he was good to Ljubljana.
Under his rule, Slovenian culture flourished, schools were established, and roads and infrastructure were improved. Slovene was
made the official language, and Ljubljana became the capital of
a realm that stretched from the Danube to Dubrovnik (for only 4
years, 1809–1813). The monument contains ashes of the unknown
French soldiers who died in 1813, when the region went from
French to Austrian control.

The Teutonic Knights of the Cross established the nearby **monastery** (Križanke, ivy-capped wall and gate, free entry) in 1230. The
adaptation of these monastery buildings into the Ljubljana Summer
Theatre was Plečnik's last major work (1950–1956).

**▲Architectural Museum of Ljubljana (Arhitekturni Muzej
Ljubljana)**—Plečnik fans can make a trek out to this interesting
museum, located in Fužine Castle on the outskirts of Ljubljana.
The permanent exhibit features parts of the 1986 Paris exhibition
that made Plečnik famous all over again. Downstairs is a display
of plans and photos from Plečnik's earlier works in Vienna and
Prague, and upstairs, you'll find an exhibit on his works in Slovenia,
including some detailed plans and models for ambitious projects
he never completed (like the huge, cone-shaped parliament atop
Castle Hill). It's worthwhile, but a bit of a hassle to reach—only
true enthusiasts should pay a visit (500 SIT, Mon–Fri 10:00–14:00,
closed Sat–Sun, Pot na Fužine 2, tel. 01/540-9798, www.arhmuz
.com). Take bus #20 from Congress Square (direction: Fužine) to
the end of the line (about 20 min).

SHOPPING

Ljubljana, with its easygoing ambience and countless boutiques, is
made to order for whiling away an afternoon shopping. It's also a
fun place to stock up on souvenirs and gifts for the folks back home.
Popular items include wood carvings (especially of the characteristic hayracks that dot the countryside), different flavors of schnapps
(the kind with a whole pear inside—cultivated to actually grow
right into the bottle—is the classiest), and those adorable painted
frontboard panels from beehives (see page 548).

The most atmospheric trinket-shopping is in the first stretch of
market colonnade, along the riverfront next to the Triple Bridge

(see page 503). The best souvenir shop in town is **Dom Trgovina**, just a block across the Triple Bridge from Prešeren Square and facing the Town Hall (Mon–Fri 9:00–19:00, Sat 9:00–13:00, closed Sun, Mestni trg 24, tel. 01/241-8300).

Another item you'll see sold all over the country are **Peko shoes**. Made in a town north of Ljubljana called Tržič, Pekos are similar to high-fashion Italian models, but much cheaper. The name is an abbreviation of its founder's name: Peter Kozina (www .peko.si).

SLEEPING

Ljubljana's accommodations scene, once abysmal, is steadily improving. Still, it's challenging. Only a handful of places are within convenient walking distance of the center, and most are overpriced. The higher-priced places listed below are boring business-class hotels that charge way too much and are a rotten value; stick with my moderately priced (**$$**) options and you'll do better. The most expensive hotels raise their prices even more during conventions (often Sept–Oct, and sometimes also June). To locate hotels and restaurants, see map on page 493. The TI can give you a list of cheap private rooms *(sobe)*.

$$$ Grand Hotel Union is as much an Art Nouveau landmark as a hotel. You'll pay dearly for its Old World elegance, professional staff, big pool, and perfect location, right on Prešeren Square. The 193 plush "Executive" rooms are in the main building

---

Sleep Code

(€1 = about $1.20, 200 SIT = about $1, country code: 386, area code: 01)

S = Single, **D** = Double/Twin, **T** = Triple, **Q** = Quad, **b** = bathroom, **s** = shower only. Unless otherwise noted, credit cards are accepted, breakfast is included, and the modest tourist tax (242 SIT per person, per night) is not. Hotels generally quote prices in euros, rather than tolars. Everyone speaks English.

To help you easily sort through these listings, I've divided the rooms into three categories based on the price for a standard double room with bath:

$$$ Higher Priced—Most rooms €100 (24,000 SIT) or more.

$$ Moderately Priced—Most rooms between €50–100 (12,000–24,000 SIT).

$ Lower Priced—Most rooms €50 (12,000 SIT) or less.

(Sb-€136–145, Db-€177, prices 20 percent higher during conventions, can be 20 percent cheaper during slow times—including most weekends and mid-July–mid-Aug, non-smoking floors, elevator, Internet in lobby, parking-€12/day, Miklošičeva cesta 1, tel. 01/308-1270, fax 01/308-1015, www.gh-union.si, hotel.union@gh -union.si). Its 133 "Business" rooms next door are a lesser value: more modern, less fresh, and almost as expensive (Sb-€129–140, Db-€164, same price increases and deals as "Executive" prices, non-smoking floors, elevator, parking and Internet access at main hotel, Miklošičeva cesta 3, tel. 01/308-1170, fax 01/308-1914, www .gh-union.si, hotel.business@gh-union.si).

$$$ Union Hotel Garni was recently bought out by the Grand Hotel Union up the street (above), and will likely change its name in the near future. It has 74 modern, business-class rooms, well-situated between Prešeren Square and the train station (Sb-€107, Db-€140, 20 percent less mid-July–mid-Aug, extra bed-€27, non-smoking rooms, elevator, parking garage-€11/day, Miklošičeva cesta 9, tel. 01/308-4300, fax 01/230-1181, www.gh -union.si, hotel.garni@gh-union.si).

$$$ City Hotel has 123 tight, musty, cookie-cutter rooms in a handy but urban-feeling neighborhood just a few blocks off Prešeren Square (Sb-€90, Db-€109–139, prices depend on room size and demand, non-smoking rooms, elevator, Internet in lobby, bike rental, Dalmatinova 15, tel. 01/234-9130, fax 01/234-9140, www.cityhotel.si, info@cityhotel.si).

$$ Hotel Emonec, an inexpensive new place with some of the best-located rooms in Ljubljana, hides in a courtyard between Prešeren and Congress Squares. Its 26 rooms—in two buildings across a quiet courtyard from each other—are simple and institutional, but the price is right, and you can't be more central (Sb-11,900 SIT, small Db-14,200 SIT, bigger "standard" Db-16,600 SIT, Tb-19,900 SIT, Qb-23,000 SIT, Internet in lobby, Wolfova 12, tel. 01/200-1520, fax 01/200-1521, www.hotel-emonec.com, hotelemonec@siol.net).

$$ Gostilna Pri Mraku has 30 cozy, slightly worn rooms in a pleasant neighborhood near French Revolution Square. Despite its quirks (a so-so breakfast, lots of stairs with no elevator, sometimes-frustrating staff), I find it a very comfortable home-away-from-home in Ljubljana (Sb-14,500 SIT, Db-23,000 SIT, Tb-28,000 SIT, top-floor rooms have air-con and cost about 3,000 SIT more, prices about 20 percent cheaper July–Aug, non-smoking floor, Rimska 4, tel. 01/421-9600, fax 01/421-9655, www.daj-dam.si, mrak@daj-dam.si).

$$ Hotel Park has 145 rooms at good prices. They have two types of rooms: "two-star" rooms, recently renovated and modern-feeling; and "one-star" rooms, with no TV, old linoleum, and worn furniture, but reasonably well-maintained (the cheapest one-star rooms have a toilet in the room, but showers down the hall). The simple but fresh two-star rooms are about the best deal in Ljubljana, nearly as nice as the fancy hotels that charge twice as much. The catch: The hotel is housed in a soulless 12-story communist apartment block in a dull neighborhood a 10-minute walk from Prešeren Square (one-star rooms with toilet but no shower: S-€37, D-€46, 10 percent discount for hostel members for these rooms only; one-star rooms with full bathrooms: Sb-€49, Db-€63; two-star rooms: Sb-€53, Db-€70; elevator, Tabor 9, tel. 01/300-2500, fax 01/433-0546, www.hotelpark.si, hotel.park@siol.net).

Hostels: **$ Hostel Celica** rents the cheapest beds in town in an unforgettable setting. This innovative hostel is funded by the city and run by a nonprofit student arts organization (which can make management a little uneven...but they're learning). Once an old military prison, this remarkable place has 20 cells *(celica)* converted into hostel rooms—each one unique, decorated by a different designer (tours of the hostel daily at 14:00, usually led by the architect on Tue and Wed). On the top floor are several more typical hostel rooms (each with its own bathroom, for 3–14 people). The building also houses an art gallery, tourist information point, Internet in lobby, self-serve laundry, restaurant, and shoes-off Oriental café. The neighborhood is a bit run-down and remote (a dull 15-min walk to Prešeren Square), but safe (all prices listed are per person—cell rooms: S-9,500 SIT, D-5,250 SIT, T-4,250 SIT; top-floor rooms with bathrooms: 3–5-bed room-4,950 SIT, 6–7-bed dorm-4,250 SIT, 14-bed dorm-3,750 SIT; all prices 1,000 SIT more if you're over 35, includes breakfast and sheets, no curfew, non-smoking, a 10-min walk from Prešeren Square or the train station, Metelkova 9, tel. 01/230-9700, fax 01/230-9712, www.souhostel.si, info@souhostel.si).

$ Fluxus, Ljubljana's *other* hostel, is loosely run by brothers Miran and Igor. With two colorful dorm rooms (one for 6 people, the other for 8) and one double (with its own shower) sharing a single toilet, the quarters are tight. I'd consider this a last resort, only if Hostel Celica is full (dorm bed-€21, D with shower-€54, includes sheets, no breakfast but guests' kitchen, Tomšičeva ulica 4, Miran's mobile 031-852-921, Igor's mobile 0410-738-638, www.fluxus-hostel.com, info@hostel-fluxus.com).

EATING

Though heavy, meat-and-starch Slovenian food is available, Ljubljana also offers an abundance of pizza and other Italian fare (you're just 150 miles from Venice)—not to mention plenty of other international options (French, Moroccan, Chinese, even Mexican).

The main drag through the Old Town is lined with inviting restaurants, their tables spilling into the cobbled pedestrian street. Prešeren Square thrives in the evenings, often with live bands leading a celebration of life and youth. To locate restaurants, see map on page 493.

Mid-Range, Local-Style Cuisine

Very few places serve strictly Slovenian food; at this crossroads of cultures (and cuisines), Italian and French flavors are just as "local" as anything else. But the following eateries are as close to "real Slovenian cuisine" as you'll get.

Sokol, with brisk, traditionally clad waiters serving truly typical Slovenian food, is a reliable option (soup in a bread bowl is a favorite starter). The sprawling Slovenian-village interior is fun and woody, jaunty polka plays on the soundtrack, and the location is very central. All of this means it's deluged by tourists, so don't expect top quality or a good value (main dishes 1,000–2,500 SIT, salads, veggie options, daily 12:00–23:00, on castle side of Triple Bridge at Ciril-Metodov trg 18, tel. 01/439-6855).

Gostilna As Pub, a cheaper side-restaurant of the fancy As (described under "Upscale International," below), features drinks, salads (1,000–1,700 SIT), pastas (1,400–2,000 SIT), sandwiches (1,000 SIT), and main dishes (1,700–2,600 SIT) in a cellar or outside, under a canopy and in the lively courtyard (daily 12:00–24:00, Čopova ulica 5A, or enter courtyard with *As* sign near image of Julija, tel. 01/425-8822). This is a great leafy-courtyard scene, with live music (in summer) and several other happening places nearby. They also have a much-loved gelato stand.

Ribca, under the first stretch of market colonnade near the Triple Bridge, is your best bet for a relatively quick and cheap riverside lunch. There's a long menu of straightforward fish dishes (700–1,200 SIT, fish and chips for 1,400 SIT), and with the smelly fish market right next door, you know it's fresh. If you just want to enjoy sitting along the river below the bustling market, this is also a fine spot for a coffee or beer (open Mon–Sat 7:00–16:00, closed Sun).

Emonska Klet, a student favorite, is in a monastery cellar. With energetic music, Ljubljana's longest bar, and good food under a cavernous medieval vault, it's a fun dining experience (main dishes 1,000–2,000, good pizza, so-so salad bar, Mon–Sat 8:00–3:00 in the morning, Sun 12:00–24:00, go through underpass at the top of Congress Square—it's on your left as you emerge on the other side, Plečnikov trg 1, tel. 01/421-9300).

Pizzerias

Ljubljana has lots of great sit-down pizza places. Expect to pay 1,000–1,500 SIT for an average-sized pie (wide variety of toppings).

The Student Curse

In most European cities, it's a smart idea to seek out places where locals eat—and students are a sure sign of cheap, good grub. But in this university town, a student crowd is not necessarily a good omen. Ljubljana's university students can buy government coupons that subsidize 80 percent of their restaurant bill. When a restaurant starts accepting these coupons, locals take it as a sure sign that the place is going downhill. Even if the food is decent, the service is sure to get grouchier.

Pizzeria Foculus, tucked in a boring alleyway a few blocks up from the river, has a loyal local following, an innovative, leafy interior, Ljubljana's best pizza (over 50 types), and a good salad bar (Mon–Fri 10:00–24:00, Sat–Sun 12:00–24:00, just off French Revolution Square and across the street from Plečnik's National and University Library at Gregorčičeva 3, tel. 01/251-5643).

Ljubljanski Dvor enjoys the most convenient location and most scenic setting...even if the pizza isn't quite as good. On a sunny summer day, the outdoor riverside terrace is unbeatable. Inside is a simple pizza parlor downstairs, with a more refined dining room upstairs (selling the same pizzas, plus 2,000–3,000-SIT Italian main dishes; daily 12:00–23:00, upstairs restaurant closed Sun, just 50 yards from Cobblers' Bridge at Dvorni trg 1, tel. 01/251-6555). For cheap take-away, go around back to the walk-up window on Congress Square (400-SIT slices to go, along with other light food, picnic in the park or down on the river—plenty of welcoming benches, Mon–Sat 9:00–24:00, closed Sun).

Fast and Cheap

Tomato offers colorful, inexpensive, and tasty meals in an old-fashioned Slovenian diner (good sandwiches and salads, most items 800–1,500 SIT, Mon–Fri 7:00–22:00, Sat 7:00–16:00, closed Sun, near the top of Congress Square at Šubičeva ulica 1, tel. 01/252-7555).

Paninoteka serves 500–700-SIT grilled sandwiches, just over the Cobblers' Bridge from the castle (order at the display case, Mon–Sat 8:00–23:00, Sun 9:00–23:00, fine outdoor seating, Jurčičev trg 3, tel. 01/425-0055).

Burek, the typical Balkan snack (see "Balkan Flavors" sidebar on page 580), can be picked up at street stands around town. Most are open 24 hours and charge 400 SIT for a hearty portion. Try **Nobel Burek,** next to Miklošičeva cesta 30, or **Olympia Burek,** around the corner on Pražakova ulica.

Upscale International

These fine restaurants—mostly serving French cuisine, with Slovenian and other influences—are good for a splurge. It's important to make a dinner reservation at any of these places.

Gostilna As ("Ace"), tucked into a courtyard just off Prešeren Square, offers fish-lovers the best splurge in town. It's a dressy, pricey, and pretentious place (waiters recommend what's fresh, rather than what's on the menu). Everything is specially prepared each day and beautifully presented (mostly fish and Italian, main dishes 2,000–4,000 SIT, daily 12:00–24:00, enter courtyard with *As* sign near image of Julija at Čopova ulica 5A, tel. 01/425-8822). For cheaper food from the same kitchen, eat at their attached Gostilna As Pub (see above).

Around Levstikov Trg: Several fine restaurants cluster away from the crowds just underneath the castle, near St. Florijan's Church (around Levstikov trg and Gornji trg in the old town). **Pri Sv. Florijanu,** with seating on rustic wood floors under medieval brick vaults (or outside, on a quiet square), is sophisticated but still relaxing. They have two types of food: carefully selected, wide-ranging international (French, Italian, Slovenian, and more); and Moroccan (main dishes 2,500–4,000 SIT, daily 12:00–23:00, Gornji trg 20, tel. 01/251-2214). Their 2,000-SIT lunch *menu,* including a starter, main dish, and dessert, is an excellent value (served daily 12:00–16:00).

Restaurant Chez Eric is *the* place for French cuisine in town, with white-tablecloth-and-shiny-crystal formality. The dining rooms—some under medieval brick vaults, all under fancy chandeliers—are simply elegant, and the outdoor seating is on Ljubljana's most historic square (main dishes 4,000 SIT, dinner *menus* 8,000–10,000, summer Mon–Sat 12:00–22:30, winter Mon–Sat 12:00–16:00 & 19:00–22:30, always closed Sun, a few doors down from Town Hall at Mestni trg 3, tel. 01/251-2839). Their three-course business lunch *menu* is also a good deal (2,000 SIT, served Mon–Fri).

Coffee, Tea, and Treats

Riverfront Cafés: Enjoying a coffee, beer, or ice-cream cone along the Ljubljanica River embankment (between the Triple and Cobblers' Bridges) is Ljubljana's single best experience. Tables spill out into the street, and some of the best-dressed, best-looking students on the planet happily fill them day and night. (A common question from first-time visitors to Ljubljana: "Doesn't anybody here have a job?") This is simply some of the top people-watching in Europe. Rather than recommend a particular place (they're all about the same), I'll leave you to explore and find the spot with the breezy ambience you like best. When ordering, the easiest choice is a *bela kava*—"white coffee," basically a latte.

Tea House: If coffee's not your cup of tea, go a block inland to the teahouse **Čajna Hiša**. They have a shop (called "Cha") with over 100 varieties of tea, plus porcelain teapots and cups from all over (Mon–Fri 9:00–20:00, Sat 9:00–13:30, closed Sun). The café serves about 50 different types of tea, plus light food and desserts (300–600-SIT sandwiches, 900–1,400-SIT salads, Mon–Fri 9:00–23:00, Sat 9:00–15:00 & 18:00–23:00, closed Sun, on castle side of the river a few steps from Cobblers' Bridge at Stari trg 3, tel. 01/421-2444).

Treats: **Zvezda Kavarna**, a trendy, central place at the bottom of Congress Square, is a local favorite for cakes, pastries, and ice cream (Mon–Sat 7:00–23:00, Sun 10:00–20:00, a block up from Prešeren Square at Wolfova 14, tel. 01/421-9090).

Trendy Pub: **Bar Minimal** is my favorite of Ljubljana's many theme cafés and pubs. Stripped down to bare basics, this totally black-and-white place is as simple as it gets. While the cubical chairs aren't the most comfortable, the clever design here turns on architecture students (coffee and cocktails, light food, 600-SIT salads, daily 8:00–1:00 in the morning, next to Town Hall at Mestni trg 4, tel. 01/426-0138).

Ice Cream: Ljubljana is known for its Italian gelato-style ice cream. You'll see fine options all along the Ljubljanica River embankment. Favorites include the courtyard garden at **Gostilna As** (see above), **Ursula** (next to Tomato diner, at the corner of Slovenska cesta just above Congress Square), and **Zvezda Kavarna** (see above).

TRANSPORTATION CONNECTIONS

Note that in Slovene, Vienna is "Dunaj."

Getting to the Dalmatian Coast: If connecting directly to Croatia's Dalmatian Coast, you have three options: Train to Zagreb (2.5 hrs), where you'll catch a cheap Croatia Air flight or a bus; take the long, once-daily train connection from Ljubljana to Split (8 hrs, requires a change in Zagreb); or, much slower, take the train to Rijeka, then cruise on a boat down the coast from there. (For specifics on flights, buses, and boats, see "Getting to the Dalmatian Coast," page 583.)

From Ljubljana by Train to: Lesce-Bled (roughly hrly, 1 hr), **Divača** (close to Škocjan caves and Lipica, hrly, 1.75 hrs), **Postojna** (roughly hrly, 1 hr), **Zagreb** (8/day, 2.5 hrs), **Rijeka** (2–3/day direct, 2.5 hrs), **Split** (1/day, 8 hrs, transfer in Zagreb), **Vienna** (that's *Dunaj* in Slovene, 1/day direct, 6 hrs; otherwise 6/day, 7 hrs with transfer in Villach, Maribor, or Graz), **Venice** (2/day direct, 4 hrs), **Munich** (3/day direct, 7 hrs, including 1 night train; otherwise transfer in

Salzburg), **Salzburg** (5/day direct, 5 hrs), **Budapest** (2/day direct, 9 hrs). Train info: tel. 01/291-3332, www.slo-zeleznice.si.

By Bus to: Bled (Mon–Fri 11/day, Sat–Sun 8/day, 1.25 hrs, 1,470 SIT), **Divača** (close to Škocjan caves and Lipica, every 2 hrs, 1.5 hrs, 1,740 SIT), **Postojna** (at least hrly, 1 hr, 1,320 SIT), **Piran** (6/day, 2.5 hrs, 2,670 SIT). Bus info: tel. 090/4230 (toll number—about 160 SIT/min), www.ap-ljubljana.si. If you pick up the blue phone in the bus station, you'll be connected to a free information line.

Ljubljana's Airports

Slovenia's only airport, **Aerodrom Ljubljana** (airport code: LJU), is at Brnik, 14 miles north of the city—conveniently located about halfway between Ljubljana and Bled. Almost every flight is operated by Adria Airways (www.adria-airways.com), but recently, easyJet (www.easyjet.com) and Czech Airlines (www.csa.cz) have also entered the fray. Since Slovenia joined the EU, it's recommended you arrive two hours before your flight (tel. 04/206-1000, www.lju-airport.si). An airport bus connects Brnik with Ljubljana's bus station (850 SIT for 45-min ride, 1,000 SIT for express 30-min bus, buses run at least hourly, some gaps in the schedule Sat–Sun—confirm in advance). There's also a private shuttle that does the same trip (1,000 SIT, every 2 hrs). Figure about 6,000 SIT for a taxi to the airport.

Since Ljubljana's airport is the only one in the country and thus charges extremely high taxes and airport fees, many Slovenes prefer to fly out of Austria. The airport in **Klagenfurt** (airport code: KLU), just over the Austrian border, is subsidized by the local government to keep prices low and compete with Ljubljana's airport. It's even marketed as the "Alpe-Adria Airport" and the "Carinthian Airport" (after a region in Austria that used to be part of Slovenia) to encourage Slovenes to think of it as regional, not Austrian. Especially if you're leaving from Bled, it's handy to reach (train to Villach, then to Klagenfurt's Annabichl station, which is a 5-min walk from the airport; total trip 3 hrs from Ljubljana, or 2 hrs from Bled; www.klagenfurt-airport.com). Austrian Airlines (www.aua.com) flies from Klagenfurt, as do low-cost carriers such as Ryanair (www.ryanair.com) and Hapag-Lloyd Express (www.hlx.com).

All this competition is keeping Slovenia's national airline, Adria, on its toes. While it's generally pretty pricey to fly Adria, the airline often posts a few heavily discounted fares for each flight on its Web site (such as €49 one-way from Ljubljana to London or Paris; first come, first served, www.adria-airways.com).

THE KARST

Caves, Castles, and Horses

In Slovenia's Karst region, about an hour by expressway south of Ljubljana, you'll find some of the most impressive cave systems on the planet, a chance to see the famous Lipizzaner stallions for a fraction of what you'd pay in Vienna, and one of Europe's most dramatically situated castles—built into the face of a mountain.

The term "karst" is used worldwide to refer to an arid limestone plateau, but Slovenia's is the original. It comes from the Slovenian word "Kras"—a specific region near the Italian border. Since limestone is easily dissolved by water, karstic regions are punctuated by remarkable networks of caves and underground rivers.

Your top Karst priority is a cave visit. Choose between Slovenia's two best caves, Škocjan or Postojna—each with a handy side-trip nearby (to help you pick, see the sidebar on page 525).

In the neighborhood of Škocjan is Lipica, where the Lipizzaner stallions strut their stuff. Just up the road from Postojna is Predjama Castle, picturesquely burrowed into the side of a cliff.

To sleep in the heart of the Karst—a short drive from all these sights—consider Tourist Farm Hudičevec, halfway between Škocjan and Postojna. It's as comfortable and private as a hotel. A roomy, spick-and-span double with a private bathroom—including a delicious Slovenian feast for dinner and farm-fresh eggs for breakfast—costs only €56 for two people (Db without dinner-€40, Razdrto 1, tel. 05/703-0300, fax 05/703-0320, www.hudicevec .com, hudicevec@siol.net, Simčič family).

The Karst Region

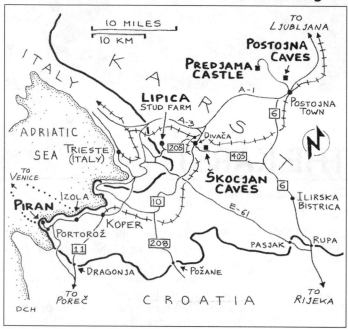

Škocjan Caves and the Lipica Stud Farm

Škocjan Caves (Škocjanske Jame)

Škocjan (SHKOHTS-yahn) offers good formations and a vast canyon with a raging underground river. You'll end up walking around two miles, going up and down more than 400 steps. While anyone in good shape can enjoy Škocjan, those who have trouble walking or tire easily are better off touring Postojna (see below).

Upon arrival, get a ticket for the next tour (they rarely fill up). You'll pass waiting time at a covered terrace with a tiny gift kiosk and a bar serving light meals and drinks. At tour time, your guide (toting an industrial-strength flashlight) calls everyone together, and you march silently for 10 minutes to the cave entrance. There you split into language groups and enter the cave.

The first half of the experience is the "dry caves," with wondrous formations and what seem like large caverns. Then you get to the truly colossal "finale" cavern, with a mighty river crashing through the bottom. You feel like a bit player in a sci-fi thriller. It's a world where a thousand evil *Wizard of Oz* monkeys could

Postojna vs. Škocjan: Which Caves to Visit?

To Postojna or to Škocjan?—that is the question. Each system is massive, cut into the limestone by rivers for more than two million years. Stalagmites and stalactites—in a slow-motion love story—silently work their way towards each other until that last drip never drops. Colors are mixed in by whatever minerals the water seeps through (iron makes red, limestone makes white, and so on). Both caves were excavated and explored in the mid-19th century.

Slovenes debate long and hard about which cave system is better. The formations at Postojna are slightly more abundant, varied, and colorful, with stalagmites and stalactites as tall as 100 feet. Postojna is easier to reach by public transportation, and far less strenuous to visit than Škocjan—of the three-mile route, you'll walk only about a mile (the rest of the time, you're on a Disney World–type people-mover). But Postojna is also more expensive and much more touristy—you'll wade through tour buses and tacky souvenir stands on your way to the entrance. Most importantly, Postojna lacks Škocjan's spectacular, massive-cavern finale. Škocjan also comes with a fairly strenuous hike, leaving you feeling like you really did something adventurous. Finally, the choice of likely side-trip might help you decide: Near Postojna is the cliff-hanging Predjama Castle, while Škocjan is closer to the Lipica Stud Farm.

No matter which cave you visit, you'll find it chilly, but not really cold (a light sweater is fine). Both caves forbid photography (a laughable rule that nobody takes seriously).

comfortably fly their formations. You hike high above the river for about a mile, crossing a breathtaking (but stable-feeling) footbridge 150 feet above the torrent. Far below, the scant remains of century-old trails from the early days of tourism are evocative. The cave finally widens, sunlight pours in, and you emerge—like lost creatures seeking daylight—into a lush canyon. A steep, somewhat strenuous hike leads to a small funicular, which lifts you back to the ticket booth/café/shop.

Cost and Hours: The guided tour is mandatory and takes about two hours (2,500 SIT, June–Sept tours daily at the top of each hour 10:00–17:00, Oct–May tours daily at 10:00 and 13:00 and sometimes also at 15:00 or 15:30, call or pick up current brochure—which you'll find everywhere in Slovenia—to confirm schedule before making the trip, tel. 05/763-2840, www .park-skocjanske-jame.si).

Getting to Škocjan: By car, take the expressway south from Ljubljana about 90 minutes and get off at the Divača exit (also marked with brown signs for *Lipica* and *Škocjanske jame*) and follow signs for *Škocjanske jame*. (Before or after Škocjan, drivers can easily visit the Lipica Stud Farm, described below.) The caves have free and easy parking.

By public transportation, it's trickier. Take the train or bus to Divača (see Ljubljana's "Transportation Connections," page 521), which is about three miles from the caves. Either hike in or take a taxi from the Divača station (tel. 05/734-5428). A better but less predictable option is to take one of the buses from Ljubljana to Piran that goes along the older road (not all of them do; ask for details at bus station). This bus can drop you off closer to the caves (1 mile away—ask for "Škocjanske jame," SHKOHTS-yahn-skeh YAH-meh).

Lipica Stud Farm (Kobilarna Lipica)

The Lipica (LEE-peet-suh) Stud Farm, a 10-minute drive from the Škocjan Caves, was founded in 1580 to provide horses for the Hapsburg court in Vienna. Horse-loving Hapsburg Archduke Charles wanted to create the perfect animal: He imported Andalusian horses from his homeland of Spain, then mixed them with a local line to come up with an extremely intelligent and easily trainable breed. Charles' creation, the Lipizzaner stallions—known for their noble gait and Baroque shape—were made famous by Vienna's Spanish Riding School. Italian and Arabian bloodlines were later added to tweak various characteristics. These regal horses have changed shape with the tenor of the times: They were bred strong and stout during wars, frilly and slender in more cultured eras. But they're always born black, fade to gray, and turn a distinctive white in adulthood.

Until World War I, Lipica bred horses for Austria's needs. Now Austria breeds its own line, and these horses prance for Slovenia—a treasured part of its cultural heritage. Tour the stables to visit the magnificent animals (labeled with purebred bloodlines). Unlike in Vienna, tickets to see the horses perform here are cheap and easy to get. Visitors thrill to the Lipizzaners' clever routine—stutter-stepping sideways to the classical beat.

This excursion—offering an up-close horse encounter—is less polished (and cheaper) than the Lipizzaner experience in Vienna (see page 707). It's worth a visit only if you're a horse enthusiast, or if you have a car and it fits your schedule (for example, drivers visiting the Škocjan Caves are only a few minutes away).

By the way, the hills less than a mile away are in Italy. Aside from the horses, Lipica's big draw is its casino. Italians across the border are legally forbidden from gambling in their own town's casinos—for fear of addiction—so they flock here to Slovenia to try their luck. Farther north, the Slovenian border town of Nova

Gorica has Europe's biggest casino, packed with gamblers from the Italian side of town.

Visiting the Stud Farm: There are three activities at Lipica: **Touring** the farm for a look at the horses; watching a **performance** of the prancing stallions; and, on days when there's no performance, watching a **training session.** If you're coming all the way to Lipica, you might as well time it so that you can do both the tour and a performance (or a training session). Call ahead to confirm performance and tour times before you make the trip.

Cost: Stud farm tour only-€6, tour plus performance-€12, tour plus training session-€8. Tel. 05/739-1580, www.lipica.org.

Tours: April–June and Sept–Oct daily on the hour 10:00–17:00 except 12:00 (also at 9:00 and 18:00 Sat–Sun); July–Aug daily on the hour 9:00–18:00 except 12:00; off-season daily at 11:00, 13:00, 14:00, and 15:00 (plus 10:00 and 15:00 Sat–Sun in March).

Performances: April–Oct Tue, Wed, Fri, and Sun at 15:00, none Nov–March.

Training Sessions: April–Oct Thu at 12:00. Note that on days when there's a performance, you can tour the farm before (14:00) or after (15:40) the show; for a training session, the tour is before (11:00).

Getting to Lipica: Lipica Stud Farm is in Slovenia's southwest corner (a stone's throw from Trieste, Italy). By car, exit the freeway at Divača and follow brown *Lipica* signs. (As you drive into the farm, you'll go through pastures where the stallions often roam.) It's a major hassle by public transportation. You can take the train or bus from Ljubljana to Divača (see "Getting to Škocjan," above)—but that's still about five miles from Lipica, with no bus connections. You could take a taxi (about 3,000 SIT one-way from Divača station, tel. 05/734-5428) or try hitching a ride on a friendly tour bus. Note that there's also no bus connection between Škocjan and Lipica.

Postojna Caves and Predjama Castle

Postojna Caves (Postojnska Jama)

Postojna (poh-STOY-nah) is the most accessible—and touristy—cave experience in the region. It's the biggest cave system in Slovenia (and, before borders shifted a few generations ago, it was the biggest in Italy...a fact that envious Italians still haven't forgotten).

Whether you arrive by car, tour bus, or on foot, you'll walk past a paved outdoor mall of shops, eateries, and handicraft vendors to the gaping hole in the mountain. Buy your ticket and board a train, which slings you deep into the mountain, whizzing past wonderful formations. (The ride alone is exhilarating.) Then you get out, assemble into language groups, and follow a guide on a well-lit, circular, paved path through more formations. You'll see 100-foot-tall stalagmites and stalactites, as well as translucent "curtains" of rock and ceilings dripping with skinny "spaghetti stalactites." You'll wind up peering at the strange "human fish" (a.k.a. olm or *Proteus anguinus*)—sort of a long, skinny, flesh-colored salamander with fingers and toes. The world's biggest cave-dwelling animal, the human fish can survive up to seven years without eating (the live specimens you see here are never fed during the 4 months they're on display). Then you'll load back onto the train and return to the bright daylight.

Cost and Hours: Your visit, which is by tour only, costs 3,700 SIT and lasts 90 minutes. Tours leave May–Sept daily at the top of each hour 9:00–18:00 (off-season daily at 10:00, 12:00, and 14:00; April and Oct also at 16:00; call to confirm schedule or pick up brochure at any TI). From mid-May through August, try to show up 30 minutes early for the morning tours (popular with tour buses); otherwise, aim for 15 minutes ahead. Information: tel. 05/700-0100, www.postojna-cave.com.

"Proteus Vivarium": This new exhibit gives you the chance to learn more about karstic caves and about speleobiology—the study of cave-dwelling animal life. While troglodytes, science nuts, and those who just can't get enough of those human fish may get a charge out of this exhibit, it's basically just an attempt to wring a little more cash out of gullible tourists (1,100 SIT, daily May–Sept 9:30–18:30, April and Oct 10:30–16:30, Nov–March 10:30–14:30).

Getting to Postojna: The caves are just outside the town of Postojna, about an hour by expressway south of Ljubljana (Jamska cesta 30). By car, take the expressway south from Ljubljana and get off at the Postojna exit. Turn right after the tollbooth and follow the *jama/grotte/cave* signs through town until you see the tour buses. Drivers will pay 500 SIT to park 200 yards from the cave entry. The train from Ljubljana to Postojna arrives at a station 20 minutes by foot from the caves. The bus drops you just five minutes from the caves. (For details, see Ljubljana's "Transportation Connections," page 521.)

Predjama Castle (Predjamski Grad)

Burrowed into the side of a mountain close to Postojna is dramatic Predjama Castle (prehd-YAH-mah), one of Europe's most scenic castles. Predjama is a hit with tourists for its striking set-

ting, exciting exterior, and romantic
legend (even if the inside is almost
worthless).

What a wonderful site for a castle. Notice as you approach that you
don't even see Predjama—crouching
magnificently in its cave—until the
last moment. The first castle here was
actually a tiny ninth-century fortress
embedded deep in the cave behind
the present castle (you'll see its front
wall as you explore the place). Over
the centuries, different castles were

built here, and they gradually moved out to the mouth of the cave.
While the original was called "the castle in the cave," the current
one is *pred jama*—"in front of the cave."

While enjoying the view, ponder this legend: In the 15th
century, a nobleman named Erasmus killed the emperor's cousin
in a duel. He was imprisoned under Ljubljana Castle, and spent
years nursing a grudge. When he was finally released, he used his
castle—buried deep inside the cave above this current version—as
a home base for a series of Robin Hood–style raids on the local
nobility and merchants. (Actually, Erasmus stole from the rich and
kept for himself—but that was good enough to make him a hero to
the peasants, who hated the nobles.)

Soldiers from Trieste were brought in to put an end to Erasmus'
raids, laying siege to the castle for over a year. Back then, the only
way into the castle was through the cave in the valley below—then
up, through an extensive labyrinth of caves, to the top. While the
soldiers down below froze and starved, Erasmus' men sneaked out
through the caves to bring in supplies. (They liked to drop their
leftovers on the soldiers below to taunt them, letting them know
that the siege wasn't working.)

Eventually, the soldiers came up with a plan. They waited for
Erasmus to visit the latrine—which, by design, had to be on the
thin-walled outer edge of the castle—and then, on seeing a signal
by a secret agent, blew Erasmus off his throne with a cannonball.
Today, Erasmus is supposedly buried under the huge linden tree in
the parking lot.

As the legend of Erasmus faded, the function of the castle
changed. By the 16th century, Predjama had become a castle for
hunting more than for defense. After driving all the way here, it
seems a shame not to visit the interior—but it's truly skippable. The
management (which also runs the nearby Postojna Caves) is very
strict about keeping the interior 16th-century in style, so there's
virtually nothing inside except 20th-century fakes of 16th-century

furniture, plus a few forgettable paintings and cheesy folk displays. English descriptions are sparse, and the free English history flier is not much help. But for most, the views of the place alone are worth the drive.

Cost and Hours: 1,100 SIT, daily May–Sept 9:00–19:00, April and Oct 10:00–18:00, Nov–March 10:00–16:00. Information: tel. 05/751-6015.

Cave Tours: If you're already visiting the caves at Postojna or Škocjan, a visit to the caves under this castle is unnecessary (1,100 SIT, 45 min, May–Sept daily at 11:00, 13:00, 15:00, and 17:00).

Getting to Predjama: Predjama Castle is on a twisty rural road 5.5 miles beyond Postojna Caves. By car, just continue on the winding road past Postojna, following signs for *Predjama* and *Predjamski Grad* (coming back, follow signs to *Postojna*). By public transportation, it's difficult. There is one bus per day from Postojna to Predjama, and another to Bukovje (about a half mile from Predjama)—but you'll be stranded at Predjama, with no return bus. Consider hitching a ride at Postojna on a friendly Predjama-bound tour bus or tourist's car, as most visitors do both sights.

PIRAN

Along this stretch of the Adriatic, Croatia's Istria Peninsula—just a few hours from Ljubljana—gets all the press. Seedy, touristy, but fun Croatian resort towns such as Rovinj or Poreč deserve a visit. But don't overlook Slovenia's own 29 miles of Adriatic coastline. As with other attractions in Slovenia, it's friendlier, quainter, and tidier than the alternatives in other countries.

The Slovenian coast has only a handful of towns: big, industrial Koper; lived-in and crumbling Izola; and the swanky but soulless resort of Portorož. But the Back Door gem of the Slovenian Adriatic is Piran. Most Adriatic towns are all tourists and concrete, but Piran has kept itself charming and in remarkably good repair while holding the tourist sprawl at bay. In peak season, it's overrun with Italian vacationers and can feel a bit greedy at first. But as you get to know it, Piran becomes one of the most pleasant seaside towns from here to Dubrovnik.

Planning Your Time

You can see everything in Piran (including a pop into the Maritime Museum and a hike up the bell tower) in a quick hour-long walk—then just bask in the town's ambience. Enjoy a gelato or a *kava* (coffee) on the sleek, marbled Tartini Square, surrounded by neoclassical buildings and watched over by the bell tower. Wander its piers and catch the glow of Piran at sunset. Piran also works as a base for visiting the caves, horses, and castles of the nearby Karst region (see previous chapter).

Piran

1 Hotel Tartini
2 Hotel Piran
3 Val Youth Hostel
4 Restaurant Delfin
5 Restaurant Neptun
6 Restaurant Riviera Adriatic
7 Teater Café

ORIENTATION

(area code: 05)

Piran (pee-RAHN) is small; everything is within a few minutes' walk. Crowded onto the tip of its peninsula, the town can't grow. Its population—7,500 a century ago—has dropped to about 4,200 today, as many young people find more opportunity in bigger cities.

Piran clusters around its boat-speckled harbor and main show-piece square, Tartini Square (Tartinijev trg). Up the hill behind

Piran History

Piran (or "Pirano" in *Italiano*) is home to a long-standing Italian community (about 1,500 today)—so it's legally bilingual, with signs in two languages. As with most towns on the Adriatic, it has a Venetian flavor. Piran wisely signed on with Venice as part of its trading empire in 933. Because of its valuable salt industry and strong trade, Piran managed some autonomy in later centuries. In the 15th century, after plagues killed most of Piran's population, local Italians let Slavs fleeing the Turks repopulate the town. As the Turkish threat grew, the town's impressive walls were built. Too much rain ruined its salt basins, but in the 19th century, the Austrian Hapsburg rulers rebuilt the salt industry. With that came a new economic boom, and Piran grew in importance once again. After World War I, this part of the Hapsburg Empire was assigned to Italy, but fascism never sat well with the locals. After World War II, the region was made neutral, then became part of Yugoslavia in 1956. And in 1991, with the creation of Slovenia, the Slovenes of Piran were finally independent.

Tartini Square is the landmark bell tower of the Cathedral of St. George. A few blocks towards the end of the peninsula from Tartini Square is the heart of the old town, May 1 Square (Trg 1 Maja).

From Tartini Square and the nearby marina, a concrete promenade—lined with rocks to break the storm waves, and with expensive tourist restaurants—stretches along the town's waterfront, inviting you to stroll.

Tourist Information: The TI is on Tartini Square facing the marina (daily June–Aug 9:00–13:30 & 15:00–21:00, Sept–May 10:00–17:00, at #2, tel. 05/673-4440, www.portoroz.si). For **Internet access,** get online at the Val Youth Hostel (see "Sleeping," below).

Arrival in Piran: During peak times, parking is a headache. While you can drive inside the town to drop things at your hotel, most visitors end up parking at the harborside lot, a 10-minute walk up the coast (€8/day). Buses drop visitors right on Tartini Square.

SIGHTS AND ACTIVITIES

▲**Tartini Square (Tartinijev trg)**—Tartini Square, with its polished marble, was once part of a protected harbor. In 1894, the harbor smelled so bad that they decided to fill it in. Today, rather than fishing boats, it's filled with kids on skateboards.

The statue honors Giuseppe Tartini (1692–1770), a composer and violinist once known throughout Europe. While the Church of St. Peter has overlooked this spot since 1272, its current facade is neoclassical, from the early 1800s. The neo-Renaissance Town Hall dates from the 1870s.

The fine, little, red palace in the corner (at #4) evokes Venice. This **"Venetian House"** (c. 1450) is the oldest preserved house on the square. Classic Venetian Gothic, it was built by a wealthy Venetian merchant and comes with a legend: The merchant fell in love with a simple local girl when visiting on business, became her "sugar daddy," and eventually built her this flat. When the townsfolk began to gossip about the relationship, he answered them with the relief you see today (with the Venetian lion): *Lassa pur dir* ("Let them talk").

May 1 Square (Trg 1 Maja)—This square marks the center of medieval Piran, where its main streets converged. Once the administrative center of town, today it's the domain of local kids and ringed by a few humble eateries. The stone rainwater cistern dominating the center of the square was built in 1775 after a severe drought. Rainwater was captured here with the help of drains from roofs, and channeled by hardworking statues into the system. The water was filtered through sand and stored in the well, clean and ready for townspeople to draw—or, later, pump—for drinking.

Cathedral and Bell Tower of St. George (Stolna Cerkev Sv. Jurija)—Piran is proud of its many churches, numbering more than 20. While none is of any real historic or artistic importance, the Cathedral of St. George—dating from the 14th century, and decorated Baroque by Venetian artists in the 17th century—is worth a look. It dominates the old town with its bell tower (campanile), a miniature version of the more famous one in Venice. The tower (with bells dating from the 15th century) welcomes tourists willing to pay 100 SIT to climb 146 rickety steps for the best view in town and a chance for some bell fun. Stand inside the biggest bell. Chant, find the resonant frequency, and ring the clapper ever so softly. Snap a portrait of you, your partner, and the rusty clapper. Brace yourself for *fortissimo* clangs on the quarter hour.

Sergej Mašera Maritime Museum (Pomorski Muzej Sergej Mašera)—The humble museum faces the harbor and the square, filling an elegant old building with meager but faintly endearing exhibits about the "Slovenian sailors" and this town's history (600 SIT, 100-SIT English booklet, poorly described in English, July–Aug Tue–Sun 9:00–12:00 & 18:00–21:00, closed Mon; Sept–June 9:00–12:00 & 15:00–18:00, closed Mon; Cankarjevo nabrežje 3, www.pommuz-pi.si).

Harborfront Stroll—Wandering along the harborfront is a delight: almost no pesky mopeds or cars, and virtually no American or Japanese tourists—just Slovenes and Italians. Children sell shells on cardboard boxes. Husky sunbathers lay like large limpets on the rocks. Walk around the lighthouse at the tip of the town and around the corner, checking out the cafés and fishy restaurants along the way.

Swimming—While there is no sandy beach, the water is warm and clean, and swimming is a major activity in Piran. There are two pebbly beaches (one just outside of town before the car park, and the other at the end of the harbor promenade past the lighthouse). From the town promenade, there are two designated swimming areas—both very slippery concrete embankments, with ladders and showers (one in front of Hotel Piran, the other around the corner from the lighthouse).

SLEEPING

$$$ *Big, Top-End Hotels:* Piran has two comparable hotels, each very central, big, unsmiling, and expensive (Db-€80–120, price depends on view, size, air-con, and season—mid-July–Aug is priciest): **Hotel Tartini** faces the main square 50 yards from the waterfront (42 rooms, Tartinijev trg 15, tel. 05/671-1000, fax 05/671-1665, www.hotel-tartini-piran.com, booking@hotel-tartini-piran.com). **Hotel Piran** is right on the water, with swimming and a concrete "beach" directly in front of it (80 rooms, Kidričevo nabrežje 4, tel. 05/676-2502, fax 05/676-2520, www.hoteli-piran.si, marketing@hoteli-piran.si).

Sleep Code

(€1 = about $1.20, 200 SIT = about $1, country code: 386, area code: 05)

S = Single, **D** = Double/Twin, **T** = Triple, **Q** = Quad, **b** = bathroom, **s** = shower only. Unless otherwise noted, credit cards are accepted and breakfast is included. Everyone speaks English and quotes prices in euros.

To help you sort easily through these listings, I've divided the rooms into three categories based on the price for a standard double room with bath:

$$$ **Higher Priced**—Most rooms €85 or more.
$$ **Moderately Priced**—Most rooms between €50–85.
$ **Lower Priced**—Most rooms €50 or less.

$ Val Youth Hostel rents the cheapest beds in this otherwise expensive town. It's a friendly place, a half block off the waterfront (56 beds in 22 2-, 3-, or 4-bed rooms, €24 per person mid-May–mid-Sept, €20 per person off-season, €2 more for 1-night stays in peak season, includes breakfast and sheets, prices are the same regardless of room size, laundry, kitchen, Internet in lobby, 20 yards in from waterfront near tip of peninsula, Gregorčičeva 38A, tel. 05/673-2555, fax 05/673-2556, www.hostel-val.com, yhostel .val@siol.net).

EATING

Pricey tourist bars and restaurants face the sea (figure about €20 per person), while the laid-back, funky, and colorful local joints seem to seek an escape from both the tourists and the sun in the back lanes. Get off the beaten track to find one of my recommended restaurants, and you'll enjoy a seafood-and-pasta feast for a third what you'd pay in Venice (just across the sea). If you can't resist dining at the touristy harborfront places, watch your bill and be deliberate with prices (e.g., notice that fish is priced by the 100-gram unit, rather than by the portion).

Restaurant Delfin serves good fish at a good price, as it's family-run and off the waterfront on the old town's May 1 Square (daily 8:00–24:00, good indoor and outdoor seating, Kosovelova ulica 4, tel. 05/673-2448).

Restaurant Neptun is another fine place, offering tasty food just inland from the waterfront (daily 12:00–24:00, Župančičeva ulica 7, tel. 05/673-4111).

Restaurant Riviera Adriatic, overlooking a pebbly beach at the parking-lot end of town (a 10-min walk from the old center), serves good-value seafood with a wonderfully fishy ambience (daily 10:00–24:00, Dantejeva ulica 8, mobile 041-673-846).

Drinks: **Teater Café** is the place for drinks with Adriatic views and a characteristic old interior. Catching the sunset here is a fine way to kick off your Piran evening (open long hours daily, Stjenkova ulica 1).

TRANSPORTATION CONNECTIONS

The best way to connect Piran with Ljubljana is by bus (6/day, 2.5 hrs, 2,670 SIT). By train, the trip takes 90 minutes longer (train to Koper, then catch bus). By car, Piran is a straight shot—about 90 minutes—on the expressway from Ljubljana.

From Piran by Boat to Venice: Piran is a fun and handy gateway for connecting Eastern Europe to Venice. A boat called the *Prince of Venice*—designed for day-trippers, but also convenient for one-way transport—sails from the nearby town of Izola four times each week in peak season (generally on weekends, fewer departures off-season, 2.5-hr trip; €32–46 1-way, depending on season; departs Izola at 8:00, or 7:30 on Mon; shuttle bus picks up at Piran's Tartini Square 1 hr before departure; boat returns from Venice on the same day at 17:00, arriving Izola at 19:30, or 20:30 on Mon; book through Kompas Travel Agency in nearby Portorož: tel. 05/617-8000, portoroz@kompas.si). Once a week from May through September, Italian-run **Venezia Lines** does a similar trip, departing directly from Piran (€45 1-way, departs Piran at 8:45 or 9:00, arrives Venice at 11:00 or 11:15, boat returns same day 17:00–19:15; from the U.S., dial Italian tel. 011-39-041-242-4000; from within Europe, dial 00-39-041-242-4000; www.venezialines.com).

BLED
and the JULIAN ALPS

The Alps begin in France, tumble across Central Europe, and come to an end here, along Slovenia's northern border. These are the Julian Alps—named for Julius Caesar—where mountain culture has a Slavic flavor. The Slovenian mountainsides are laced with hiking paths, blanketed in a deep forest, and speckled with ski resorts and vacation chalets. Around every ridge is a peaceful alpine village sprawled around a quaint Baroque steeple. In the center of it all is Mount Triglav—ol' "Three Heads"—Slovenia's symbol and tallest mountain (see page 558).

Spend a day or two exploring the Julian Alps and Triglav National Park, and relaxing in the region's tourism capital, the resort town of Bled. Hike up to Bled Castle for beautiful views, make a wish and ring the bell at the island church, and wander the dreamy path around the lake. To get up into the mountains, drive the 50 hairpin turns of the breathtaking Vršič Pass, then explore the Hemingway-haunted WWI sights of the Soča River Valley.

Planning Your Time in the Julian Alps

On a three-week trip through Eastern Europe, the Julian Alps deserve two days. With one day, spend it in and around Bled (or, to rush things, spend the morning in Bled and the afternoon day-tripping). With a second day and a car, drive the circular route up and over the stunning Vršič Pass, down the scenic and historic Soča River Valley, and back to Bled (or on to Ljubljana). Without a car, skip the second day, or spend it doing nearby day trips: Bus to Radovljica to see the bee museum, hike to Vintgar Gorge, or visit the more rustic Lake Bohinj.

Getting Around the Julian Alps

By public transportation, you can easily get a good taste of the Julian Alps by visiting Bled and doing nearby side-trips. But to really tackle the high-mountain scenery—the Vršič Pass and Soča Valley—you'll need a car.

By Bus: Bled is a good home base, with easy and frequent bus connections to day-trip destinations (Radovljica, the Vintgar Gorge, and Bohinj; specific bus connections explained under each destination, below).

By Car: The region is ideal by car. The good *Autokarta Slovenija* map is all you need for the country (the black version, without the cardboard cover, is just as good and costs less—cheapest at the TI). Smaller-scale maps focusing on the Bled region and the whole of Triglav National Park are also available. Even if you're doing the rest of your trip by train, consider renting a car here in tiny, easy-to-navigate Slovenia to take advantage of its many enjoyable day trips. Hiring a local guide with a car can be a great value, making your time not only fun, but also informative. (See car rental tips and local guide information under "Helpful Hints," below.)

By Tour: To hit several far-flung day-trip destinations in one go, you could take a tour from Bled (sold by various agencies, including Kompas Bled—see "Helpful Hints," page 543). Destinations range from Ljubljana (see Ljubljana chapter) and the Karst region (see The Karst chapter) to the Austrian or Italian Alps to Venice (yes, Venice—it's doable as a long day trip from here). An all-day Julian Alps trip to the Vršič Pass and Soča Valley runs about 7,500 SIT. This tour is handy, but two people can rent a car for the day for less and do it at their own pace using the information in this chapter.

By "Old-Timer Train": This old-fashioned steam engine chugs from Bled past Lake Bohinj and on to Most na Soči (at the southern end of the Soča River Valley). It's essentially an expensive package tour by train instead of by bus, with a stop at a gorge and a riverboat ride on the Soča (15,000 SIT, 1/week July–Sept, get details at Kompas Bled—see "Tourist Information," below).

Bled

Lake Bled—Slovenia's leading mountain resort—comes complete with a sweeping alpine panorama, a fairytale island, a cliff-hanging medieval castle, a lakeside promenade, and the country's most sought-after desserts. While Bled has all the modern resort-town amenities, its most endearing qualities are its stunning setting, its natural romanticism, and its fun-loving wedding parties.

The first official mention of Bled was in the year 1004, when

Bled Town

1 Grand Hotel Toplice
2 To Vila Bled
3 Mayer Penzion & Penzion Berc
4 Hotel Jadran
5 Hotel Trst
6 Vila Prešeren Hotel/Rest.
7 Penzion Bledec
8 To Alp Penzion
9 Hotel Lovec & Okarina Etno Rest.
10 Pizzeria Rustica
11 Gostilna Pri Planincu Rest.
12 Café à Propos, Mercator Grocery & Kompas Bled Travel Agency
13 Šmon Slaščičarna Pastry Shop
14 Irish Pub
15 Bled Pub

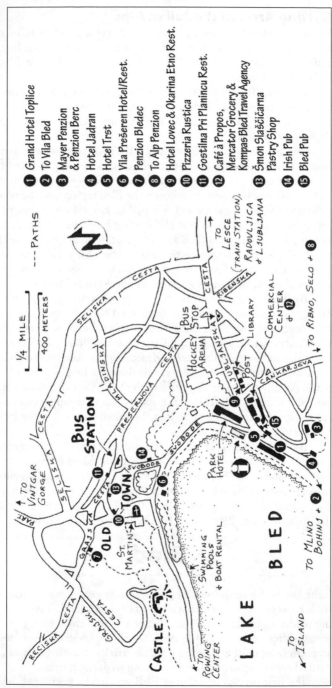

Holy Roman Emperor Henry II turned it over to the Bishops of Brixen. Bled proudly celebrated its millennium in 2004. You'll see the town's symbol everywhere: a peacock, or "bird of paradise," based on an artifact found under the castle.

Since the Hapsburg days, Lake Bled has been the place where Slovenes have wowed visiting diplomats. Tito had one of his vacation homes here (today's Hotel Vila Bled), and more recent visitors have included Prince Charles and Madeleine Albright.

The lake's main town, also called Bled, has plenty of ways to enjoy a lazy afternoon. While the town itself is more functional than quaint, it offers handy access to the region and breathtaking views of the lake. Bled quiets down at night—no nightlife beyond a handful of pubs—giving hikers and other vacationers a chance to recharge.

ORIENTATION

(area code: 04)
The town of Bled is on the east end of 1.5-mile-long Lake Bled. The lakefront is lined with cafés and resort hotels. A 3.5-mile path meanders around the lake.

The tourists' "center" of Bled is a cluster of big resort hotels, dominated by the giant, red Hotel Park (dubbed the "red can"). The busy street **Ljubljanska cesta** leads out of Bled town towards Ljubljana and most other destinations. Just up from the lakefront, across Ljubljanska cesta from Hotel Park, is the modern **commercial center** (Trgovski Center Bled), with a travel agency, Internet café, grocery store, ATM, and (on Thursday evenings) a traditional polka dance. Nicknamed "Gadhafi" by the people of Bled, the commercial center was designed for a Libyan city, but the deal fell through—so the frugal Slovenes built it here instead. Just up the road from the commercial center, you'll find the **post office** and **library** (with more Internet access).

Bled's less-touristy old town is under the castle, surrounding the pointy spire of St. Martin's Church. There you'll find the bus station, several good restaurants, a few hotels, and more locals than tourists.

The mountains poking above the ridge at the far end of the lake (in good weather) are the Julian Alps, crowned by Mount Triglav. The big mountain behind the town of Bled is Stol (literally, "Chair"), part of the Karavanke range that defines the Austrian border.

Tourist Information

Bled's helpful TI is in the long, lakefront building across from the big, red Hotel Park (as you face the lake, the TI is hiding around

Bled and the Julian Alps Essentials

English	Slovene	Pronounced
Slovenia's Biggest Mountain	Triglav	TREE-glahv
Lake Bled	Blejsko Jezero	BLAY-skoh YAY-zay-roh
The Island	Otok	OH-tohk
Bled Castle	Blejski Grad	BLAY-skee grahd
Town near Bled with Train Station	Lesce	lest-SEH
Town with Bee Museum	Radovljica	rah-DOH-vleet-suh
Gorge near Bled	Vintgar	VEENT-gar
Rustic Lake near Bled	Bohinj	BOH-heen
Scenic High-Mountain Pass	Vršič	vur-SHEECH
Historic River Valley	Soča	SOH-chah

front at the far left end, by the casino). Pick up the map with updated prices and schedules, and the free Bled guide booklet (if they have it in stock). Get advice on hikes and day trips. If you're doing any hiking, spring for a good regional map. The TI can't find you a room, but can give you a list of accommodations (open unpredictable hours, but usually July–Aug Mon–Sat 8:00–21:00, Sun 8:00–18:00; May–June and Sept Mon–Sat 8:00–19:00, Sun 11:00–17:00; Oct–April Mon–Sat 9:00–18:00, Sun 12:00–16:00; Cesta Svobode 10, tel. 04/574-1122, www.bled.si).

Arrival in Bled

By Train: Two train stations have the name "Bled." You want the station called "Lesce-Bled." The "Bled Jezero" (literally, "Bled Lake") station isn't on the main line and only sees a few slow regional trains a day. So, if you're buying a train ticket to Bled, specify that you want to go to **Lesce** (lest-SEH)—not just "Bled."

The small Lesce-Bled station is in the village of Lesce, about 2.5 miles from Bled. The nearest ATM is upstairs in the shopping center across the street. A taxi to Bled should run about 2,000 SIT, or you can take the bus (at least hourly, 10 min, 300 SIT). If taking the train out of Lesce-Bled, you can buy tickets at the station or from the conductor on the train.

By Bus: Bled's bus station is just up from the lake in the old town. To reach the lake, walk downhill on Cesta Svobode. To get to the commercial center, jog uphill and turn right on Prešernova cesta, which runs into Ljubljanska cesta just above the commercial center.

By Car: Traffic from the freeway comes into Bled on Ljubljanska cesta, which rumbles through the middle of town before swinging left at the lake. Ask your hotel about parking.

Helpful Hints

Money: The handiest ATMs are **SKB Banka** (upstairs in round building at commercial center) and **Gorenjska Banka** (at far end of Hotel Park).

Internet Access: Most of the bigger hotels have access for guests in the lobby. The public library has fast access (free up to 1 hour per day, Mon 9:00–19:00, Tue–Fri 14:00–19:00, Sat 8:00–12:00, closed Sun, just beyond the post office on Ljubljanska cesta). Several other spots in town—such as **Café à Propos** in the commercial center—also have terminals.

Post Office: Coming up from the lake, it's just beyond the commercial center on Ljubljanska cesta (Mon–Fri 7.00–19.00, Sat until 12:00, closed Sun; July–Aug Mon–Fri until 20.00, Sat until 13:00, closed Sun; tel. 04/575-0200).

Laundry: Most hotels can do laundry for you, but it's expensive. The only self-service option is at the campground at the far end of the lake (1,050 SIT/load, April–Oct only, tel. 04/575-2000). The more convenient Pension Bledec youth hostel does laundry for guests (2,000 SIT/load), and may also do it off-season for non-guests who ask nicely (call first, tel. 04/574-5250).

Car Rental: The Julian Alps are ideal by car. Several big chains rent cars in Bled; **Avis** is in the commercial center (starting at €45/day, no extra charge for drop-off elsewhere in Slovenia, Mon–Sat 9:00–17:00, Sun 8:00–12:00, tel. 04/576-8700).

Travel Agency: Kompas Bled Travel Agency, in the commercial center, exchanges money, rents bikes, offers a room-booking service (including many cheap rooms in private homes—though most are away from the lake), and sells various tours around the region (Mon–Sat 8:00–19:00, Sun 8:00–12:00 & 16:00–19:00, June–Sept until 20:00, Ljubljanska cesta 4, tel. 04/572-7500, www.kompas-bled.si, info@kompas-bled.si).

Local Guides: Tina Hiti and **Sašo Golub** are fine guides who enjoy sharing the town and region they love with American visitors. Hiring one of them can add immeasurably to your enjoyment and understanding of Bled (€30/2 hrs; Tina: mobile 041-375-435, tinahiti@hotmail.com; Sašo: mobile 031-557-331, sasogolub@gmail.com). Either one can drive you in their car on a long day tour into the Julian Alps—or anywhere in Slovenia–for €100, not much more than the cost of renting your own car. (This price is for 2 people; it's more expensive for 3 or more people, since they have to rent a van.) I spent a great day with Tina and was thankful she was behind the wheel.

Getting Around Lake Bled (Literally)

By Bike: You can rent a mountain bike at the Kompas Bled Travel Agency, great for biking around the lake (700 SIT/hr, 1,500 SIT/half-day, 2,200 SIT/day, see "Helpful Hints," above).

By Horse and Buggy: Buggies called *fijakers* are easily the most expensive—and romantic—way to get around the lake. You'll see them along the lakefront between Hotel Park and the castle (5,000 SIT; also 5,000 SIT up to the castle, or 6,000 SIT includes waiting time and trip back down; mobile 041-710-970).

By Tourist Train: A touristy little train makes a circuit around the lake every 40 minutes in summer (600 SIT, daily 9:00–18:00, shorter hours off-season, weather-dependent, tel. 041-608-689).

By Tourist Bus: A handy shuttle bus passes through Bled once daily in summer. It leaves the bus station at 10:00, stops at a few hotels (including Grand Hotel Toplice), then goes up to the castle and on to the Vintgar Gorge entrance (500 SIT, mid-June–Sept only, confirm schedule at TI or bus station).

By Taxi: Bled Tours, run by Sandi Demsar, can take you to various destinations near Bled (2,200 SIT to Lesce-Bled train station, 2,600 SIT to Radovljica, 10,500 SIT to airport, mobile 031-205-611, info@bledtours.si). You'll pay more than these rates if you let your hotel or a travel agency call a taxi for you.

By Boat: For information on boat rental, see "Boating," page 547. For details on the characteristic *pletna* boats, see "Getting to the Island," page 545.

SIGHTS AND ACTIVITIES

Lake Bled

Bled doesn't have many "sights" (except the dull castle museum, described below). But there are plenty of rewarding and pleasant activities.

▲▲**The Island (Otok)**—Bled's little island—topped with a super-cute church—nudges the lake's quaintness level over the top. Locals call it simply "The Island" *(Otok)*. While it's pretty to look at from afar, it's also fun to visit.

The island has long been a sacred site with a romantic twist. On summer Saturdays, a steady procession of brides and grooms cheered on by their entourages head for the island. Leading up

from the island's dock to the Church of the Assumption on top are 98 steps. It's tradition for the groom to carry—or try to carry—his bride up these steps. About four out of five are successful (proving themselves "fit for marriage"). During the communist era, the church was closed, and weddings were outlawed here. But the tradition reemerged—illegally—even before the regime ended, with a clandestine ceremony in 1989.

An eighth-century Slavic pagan temple dedicated to the goddess of love and fertility once stood here; the current Baroque version (with Venetian flair—the bell tower separate from the main church) is the fifth to occupy this spot. As you enter the church, look straight ahead to the fresco of Mary on the wall. She doesn't quite look like other Madonnas, because she has the face of Maria Theresa—the Hapsburg empress who controlled Slovenia when this fresco was done (see page 710). This heavy-handed propaganda was typical in those times.

When the church was being renovated in the 1970s, workers dug up several medieval graves (you can see one through the glass under the bell rope). They also discovered Gothic frescoes on either side of the altar, including, above the door on the right, an unusual ecclesiastical theme: the bris (Jewish circumcision ritual) of Christ. Superstitious natives claim that if you ring the church bell, your dreams will come true. Grab that rope and tug away.

A café and tourist stands are near the church at the top of the steps.

Getting to the Island: The most romantic route to the island is to cruise on one of the distinctive *pletna* boats (€10 per person round-trip, includes 30-min wait time at the island; catch one at several spots around the lake—most convenient from in front of Grand Hotel Toplice or just below Hotel Park; generally run from dawn until around 20:00 in summer, stop earlier off-season, none in winter, mobile 031-316-575). For more on these characteristic little vessels, see the sidebar on page 546. You can also **rent your own boat** to get to the island (see "Boating," below). It's even possible to **swim** to the island, especially from the far end of the lake (see "Swimming," below). But note that you're not allowed into the church in your swimsuit.

▲▲**Walk Around the Lake**—Strolling the 3.5 miles around the lake is enjoyable, peaceful, and scenic. It takes about 1.5 hours—not counting stops to snap photos of the ever-changing view. On the way, you'll pass some great villas, mostly from the beginning of

Pletna Boats

The *pletna* is an important symbol of Lake Bled. These boats provide a pleasant way to reach the island and carry on an  important tradition dating back for generations. In the 17th century, the Hapsburg empress Maria Theresa granted the villagers from Mlino—the little town just along the lakefront beyond Bled—special permission to ferry visitors to the island. (Since Mlino had very limited access to farmland, they needed another source of income.) Mlino residents built their *pletnas* by hand, using a special design passed down from father to son for centuries—like the equally iconic gondolas of Venice. Eventually, this imperial decree and family tradition evolved into a modern union of *pletna* oarsmen, which continues to this day.

Today there are 22 official *pletnas* on Lake Bled, all belonging to the same union. The gondoliers dump all of their earnings into one fund, give a cut to the tourist board, and divide the rest evenly among themselves. Occasionally a new family tries to break into the cartel, underselling his competitors with a "black market" boat that looks the same as the official ones. While some see this as a violation of a centuries-old tradition, others view it as good old capitalism. Either way, competition is fierce.

the 19th century. The most significant one was a former residence of Marshal Tito—today, the Hotel Vila Bled (big, white villa with long staircase at southern end of lake, near village of Mlino—see "Tito's Vila Bled," below). For the more adventurous, there are also hiking paths up into the hills surrounding the lake (ask TI for details and maps; or hike to Vintgar Gorge, described under "Near Bled," below).

▲**Bled Castle (Blejski Grad)**—Bled's cliff-hanging castle, dating in one form or another from a thousand years ago, was the seat of the Austrian Bishops of Brixen. The castle offers a range of sightseeing opportunities: a modest castle museum (with a couple of interesting videos and good English descriptions); a small theater continuously showing a fun 20-minute movie about Bled; a tiny frescoed chapel; a working replica of a printing press from Gutenberg's time (in the castle's oldest tower—from the 11th century, daily April–Sept 10:00–13:00, closed Oct–March); a wine cellar (*klet*, daily April–Sept 10:00–13:00 & 16:00–19:00, closed

Oct–March); a rampart walk with an "herbal gallery" (gift shop of traditional-meets-modern herbal brandies, cosmetics, and perfumes); and a fancy restaurant. None of these attractions is worth the hike up...but the spectacular views are (castle and museum entry-1,200 SIT, daily May–Oct 8:00–20:00, Nov–April 9:00–17:00, tel. 04/578-0525). There's a scenic little picnic spot in the castle courtyard, with fine tables and views.

Getting to the Castle: Most people hike up the steep hill (20 min). The handiest trails are behind big St. Martin's Church: Walk past the church with the lake at your back, and look left after the first set of houses for the *Grad* signs; or, for a longer but less steep route, continue on the street, bear uphill at the fork, and find the *Grad* sign just after the Pension Bledec hostel on the left. Once you're on this second trail, don't take the sharp-left uphill turn at the fork (instead, continue straight up). Instead of hiking, you can take the 10:00 **bus** (see "Getting Around Lake Bled," page 544), your **rental car**, a **taxi** (around 1,500 SIT), or, if you're wealthy and romantic, a **buggy** (5,000 SIT—see "Getting Around Lake Bled," above).

Tito's Vila Bled—Before World War II, this villa on Lake Bled was the summer residence for the Yugoslav royal family. When Tito ran Yugoslavia, he entertained international guests here (big shots from the communist and non-aligned world, from Indira Gandhi to Khrushchev to Kim Il Sung). Since 1984, it's been a classy hotel and restaurant, offering guests grand Lake Bled views and James Bond ambience. For some, this is a nostalgic opportunity to send e-mail from Tito's desk, sip tea in his lounge, and gawk at his Social Realist wall murals.

The villa is a 20-minute lakeside walk from the town of Bled at Cesta Svobode 26 (southern end of lake, near village of Mlino). You can also ask your *pletna* gondolier to drop you off here after visiting the island. Those hiking around the lake will pass the gate leading through Tito's garden to the restaurant, where they are welcome to drop in for a meal, the salad bar, or just a cup of coffee. Tito fans might want to splurge for an overnight here (basic Db-€190, tel. 04/579-1500, www.vila-bled.com).

Boating—Bled is the rowing center of Slovenia. Town officials even lengthened the lake a bit so it would perfectly fit the standard two-kilometer laps, with 100 meters more for the turn. Three world championships have been held here. The town has produced many Olympic medalists, winning gold in Sydney and silver in Athens. You'll notice that local crew guys are characters—with a tradition of wild and colorful haircuts. You'll likely see them running or rowing. This dedication to rowing adds to Bled's tranquility, since no motorized boats are allowed on the lake.

If you want to get into the action, you'll find **rental rowboats** at the swimming pool under the castle (small 3-person boat: 2,300

SIT/hr, bigger 5-person boat: 2,700 SIT/hr) or at the campground on the far side of the lake (4-person boat-2,000 SIT/hr, closed in bad weather and off-season).

Swimming—Lake Bled has several suitable spots for a swim. The swimming pools under the castle are filled with lake water and routinely earn the "blue flag," meaning the water is top-quality (1,200 SIT for all day, less for afternoon only, June–Sept daily 8:00–19:00, closed Oct–May, tel. 04/578-0528). Bled's two beaches are at the far end of the lake. Both are free; the one at the campground (southwest corner) has lots of tourists, while locals prefer the one at the rowing center (northwest corner). If you swim to the island, remember that you can't get into the church in your swimsuit.

Near Bled

The countryside around Bled offers several day trips that can be done easily without a car. The three listed here are the best (one village/museum experience, two hiking/back-to-nature options). They're more convenient than can't-miss, but each one is worth-while on a longer visit, and all give a good taste of the Julian Alps.

▲Radovljica—The village of Radovljica (rah-DOH-vleet-suh) is larger than Bled, perched on a plateau above the Sava River. The town itself is so-so, though its old center pedestrian zone, Linhartov trg, makes for a pleasant stroll. But the town is home to a fascinating and offbeat beekeeping museum—which, with only a few rooms, still ranks as one of Europe's biggest on the topic.

Radovljica's **Apicultural Museum** (Cebelarski Muzej) celebrates Slovenia's long beekeeping heritage. Since the days before Europeans had sugar, Slovenia has been a big honey-producer. The Slovenian farmer Anton Janša is considered the father of modern beekeeping; he was Europe's first official teacher of beekeeping (in Hapsburg Vienna).

The first two rooms of the museum trace the history of bee-keeping, from the time when bees were kept in hollowed-out trees to the present day. Notice the old-fashioned tools in the first room. When a new queen bee is born, the old queen takes half the hive's bees to a new location. Experienced beekeepers used the long, skinny instrument (a beehive stethoscope) to figure out when the swarm would fly the coop. Then, once the bees had moved to a nearby tree, the beekeeper used the big spoons to retrieve the queen—surrounded by an angry ball of her subjects—from her new home before she could get settled in. The beekeeper trans-ported that furious gang into a manmade hive designed for easier, more sanitary collection of the honey. You can also see the tools beekeepers used to create smoke, which makes bees less aggressive. But even today, some of Slovenia's old-fashioned beekeepers simply light up a cigarette and blow smoke on any bees that get ornery.

The third room features the museum's highlight: whimsically painted beehive frontboards (called *panjske končnice*). Nineteenth-century farmers, believing these paintings would actually help the bees find their way home, developed a tradition of decorating their hives with religious, historical, and satirical folk themes (look for the devil sharpening a woman's tongue). The depiction of a hunter's funeral shows all the animals happy...except his dog. There's everything from portraits of Hapsburg emperors, to a "true crime" sequence of a man murdering his family as they sleep, to proto-"Lockhorns" cartoons of marital strife, to 18th-century erotica (one with a woman showing some leg, and another with a flip-up, peek-a-boo panel).

The life-size wooden statues were used to "guard" the beehives—and designed to look like the Slovenes' most feared enemies (Turkish and French soldiers).

You'll also find an interactive multimedia exhibit, a good video in English, temporary exhibitions, and—in the summer only—an actual, functioning beehive (try to find the queen). The gift shop is a good place for souvenirs, with hand-painted replicas of frontboards, honey brandy, candles, ornaments, and other bee products (museum entry-500 SIT, fine English descriptions, free sheet of English info, 400-SIT English-language guidebook is a nice souvenir, May–Oct Tue–Sun 10:00–13:00 & 15:00–18:00, closed Mon; March–April and Nov–Dec Wed and Sat–Sun 10:00–12:00 & 15:00–17:00, closed Mon–Tue and Thu–Fri; closed Jan–Feb; Linhartov trg 1, tel. 04/532-0520, www.muzeji-radovljica.si).

Eating in Radovljica: Several Radovljica restaurants near the bee museum have view terraces overlooking the surrounding mountains and valleys. **Lectar** offers hearty Slovenian fare in a rural-feeling setting with a user-friendly, super-traditional menu (3,000-SIT plates, Wed–Mon 12:00–23:00, closed Tue, family friendly, Linhartov trg 2, tel. 04/537-4800, www.lectar.com). The restaurant is also known for its heart-shaped cookies, decorated with messages of love. **Grajska Gostilnica** dishes up good, basic pub grub closer to the bus station (salads, pizza, pastas, open long hours daily, inside Hotel Grajski Dvor at Kranjska 2, tel. 04/531-5585).

Getting to Radovljica: When planning your day, note that the Bee Museum closes for two hours after lunch. Buses to Radovljica generally leave Bled every half hour (fewer on weekends, check schedules at hotel or station, 400 SIT, buy ticket from driver, trip takes about 15 min). To reach the old town square and the bee museum, leave the station going straight ahead, cross the bus parking lot and the next street, then turn left down the far street (following brown sign for *Staro Mesto*). In five minutes, you'll get to the pedestrianized Linhartov trg (TI on right just before you enter pedestrian zone). At the end of this square, just before the church, you'll see the bee museum, which shares an old Baroque mansion with a music school (bee museum upstairs). Coming back to Bled, there are fewer buses; check the schedule when you arrive (usually at least 2/hr, but fewer Sat–Sun). **Drivers** leave Bled on Ljubljanska cesta, then turn right at the sign for Radovljica and go through the village of Lesce; the road dead-ends at Radovljica's pedestrian zone. A new **bike** path, scenically and peacefully connecting Bled with Radovljica (about 4 miles), is planned to open in 2006.

▲**Vintgar Gorge**—Just north of Bled, the river Radovna has carved this mile-long, picturesque gorge into the mountainside. Boardwalks and bridges put you right in the middle of the action of this "poor man's Plitvice." You'll cross over several waterfalls and marvel at the clarity of the water. The easy hike is on a board-walk trail with handrails (sometimes narrow and a bit slippery). At the end of the gorge, you'll find a restaurant, WCs, and a bridge with a gorgeous view. Go back the way you came, or take a pret-tier return to Bled (see "Scenic Hike Back to Bled," below). The gorge is easily reachable from Bled by bus or foot, and is the best option for those who are itching for a hike but don't have a car (600 SIT, daily May–late Oct 8:00–19:00 or until dusk, June–Aug until 20:00, closed late Oct–April).

Getting to Vintgar Gorge: The gorge is 2.5 miles north of Bled. You can walk (1 hour) or bus (10-min ride plus 15-min walk, or 30-min ride on summer Tourist Bus) to the gorge entrance. **Walkers** leave Bled on the road between the castle and St. Martin's Church and take the uphill (left) road at the fork. Soon after you pass the Pension Bledec hostel, turn right at the stop sign, then turn left at the bend in the road (following signs for *Podhom* and *Vintgar;* ignore the other *Vintgar* sign pointing back toward the way you came). At the fork just after the little bridge, go left for Podhom, then simply follow signs for *Vintgar.* In summer, the easy **Tourist Bus** takes you right to the gorge entrance in 30 minutes (see "Getting Around Lake Bled," above). Otherwise, take a **local bus** to one of two stops: Podhom (10 min, almost hourly, but only on school days) or Spodnje Gorje (take bus in direction of Krnica, hourly). From either the Podhom or the Spodnje Gorje bus stop, it's a 15-minute walk to the gorge (follow signs for *Vintgar*). **Drivers** follow signs to *Podhom,* then *Vintgar* (see walking instructions, above).

Scenic Hike Back to Bled: If you still have energy once you reach the end of the gorge, consider this longer hike back with pan-oramic views. Behind the restaurant, find the trail marked *Katarina Bled.* You'll go uphill for 25 fairly strenuous minutes (following the red-and-white circles and arrows) before cresting the hill and enjoying beautiful views over Bled town and the region. Continue straight down the road 15 minutes to the typical, narrow, old village of Zasip, then walk (about 30 min) or take the bus back to Bled.

Lake Bohinj—The pristine alpine Lake Bohinj (BOH-heen), 16 miles southwest of Bled, enjoys a quieter scene and (some argue) even better vistas of Triglav and the surrounding mountains. This

is a real back-to-nature experience, with just a few campgrounds and lodges. A visit to Bohinj has three parts: a village, a cable car, and a waterfall hike.

Coming from Bled, your first views of Bohinj will be from a little village at the southeast corner of the lake called **Ribčev Laz** (loosely translated as "Good Fishin' Hole"). Here you'll find a TI, a smattering of hotels and ice-cream stands, a bus stop ("Bohinj Jezero"), and boat docks (with boats to other parts of the lake—for example, 45 min to "Bohinj Zlatorog" to catch the cable car to Vogel Mountain, described below). Across from the docks is a fun concrete 3-D model of Triglav (compare to the real thing, hovering—in clear weather—across the lake). The town's church, St. John the Baptist, is one of the area's oldest, with a beautiful rustic exterior and a fresco-packed interior (if it's locked, borrow key from TI).

If you like mountain perches without the sweat, take the cable car up to **Vogel Mountain,** offering panoramic views of the Julian Alps (2,000 SIT round-trip, runs daily every 30 min, 8:00–19:00 in summer, 8:00–18:00 in winter, 8:00–16:00 in shoulder season, www.vogel.si). While you're up there, visit the alpine hut Merjasec ("Wild Boar"), offering tasty strudel and brandy. You can catch the lift from near the Zlatorog Hotel, at the southwest corner of Lake Bohinj (take bus or boat to Bohinj Zlatorog stop).

Hikers follow the moderate-to-strenuous uphill trail to see the **Savica Slap** (sah-VEET-seh) waterfall cascading into a remarkably pure pool of snowmelt. Hardy hikers find it worth the 553 stairs (400 SIT, daily in summer from 8:00 until dusk, round-trip about 2 hours, trailhead at far end of lake). Getting to the trailhead is a hassle without a car off-season. The public bus from Bled (and boats on the lake) get you only as far as the Bohinj Zlatorog stop, which is still a 45-minute walk from the trailhead. (In summer, a shuttle bus takes you right to the trailhead.)

Getting to Lake Bohinj: From Bled, seven **buses** a day head for Bohinj, stopping at two different destinations: "Bohinj Jezero" (at the village of Ribčev Laz, 30 min, 790 SIT), then "Bohinj Zlatorog" (at base of cable car, 45-min walk from waterfall hike, 40 min, 910 SIT). **Boats** connect various points on the lake, including

Ribčev Laz and Zlatorog. **Drivers** leave Bled going south along the lakefront; once you reach the village of Mlino, you'll peel off from the lake and follow signs to *Bohinjska Bistrica* (a midsize town near Lake Bohinj). From there, you'll cruise through Ribčev Laz and along the south side of the lake.

Sleeping near Lake Bohinj: Like most people who live in these parts, **Bojan and Ksenija Kočar** (BOH-yawn and kuh-SAYN-yah KOH-char) have spent years building their alpine home. In addition to housing the Kočars and their two teenagers, this delightful chalet also has several affordable rooms for tourists, as well as a beautifully hand-carved lounge/breakfast room. If you have a car and want to really get away from it all, consider sleeping here, in the countryside less than a mile from Lake Bohinj (about a 30-min drive from Lake Bled). Friendly, English-speaking Bojan—who's a bus driver—is often out of town, but Ksenija (who speaks less English) will take good care of you (Db-€34, or €44 for 1-night stays, includes breakfast, closed Jan–March, tel. 04/574-6660—best to call after 21:00, mobile 041-478-490, kocar .bojan@siol.net). Driving from Lake Bled, you'll go through the town of Bohinjska Bistrica, then the village of Polje; they're just beyond Polje, but just before Lake Bohinj itself (the first farmhouse on the left after Polje, #49, look for *rooms* sign).

NIGHTLIFE

Bled is quiet after hours. If you're not a drinker or a dancer, you're down to mini golf...open late across from the commercial center.

Pubs—Bled is home to three fun bars, all within a few blocks of each other. Gostilna Pri Planincu, near the bus station in the old town, attracts a fun-loving local crowd (see "Eating," below). The Irish pub (a.k.a. simply "The Pub") is rollicking, with Guinness and both indoor and outdoor seating (below Hotel Jelovica, by the path leading from the lake to the bus station). And Bled Pub (a.k.a. "The Cocktail Bar"), between the commercial center and the lake, is a trendy late-night spot. Try a "Smile," a Slovenian, Corona-type lager. *Slivovka* is the local firewater—honey and blueberry are popular flavors.

Polka—Slovenia is the land of polka. Slovenes claim it was invented here, and singer/accordionist Slavko Avsenik—from the nearby village of Begunje—cranks out popular oompah songs that make him bigger than the Beatles (and therefore, presumably, Jesus) in Germany. The easiest way to hear accordion music and yodeling in Bled is by attending a free polka evening with a local band at the commercial center (every Thu from around 20:00, outside on the lower terrace). While the audience is mostly local, tourists are more than welcome. (You can spot the tourists—they're the ones who can't polka.) There's also a Slovenian folk evening once a week at a Bled hotel (ask at TI).

SLEEPING

Bled is packed with gradually decaying, communist-era convention hotels. A few have been halfheartedly renovated, but most are stale, outmoded, and overpriced. It's a strange, incestuous little circle—the vast majority of the town's big hotels and restaurants are owned by the Sava Group (which is in turn part of Goodyear Tire). Only a handful of Bled accommodations are modern and a good value, and I've listed them here—along with a few older places that work in a pinch. Quaint little family-run pensions are rare, and they book up fast with Germans and Brits; reserve these places as far ahead as possible. I've listed the high-season prices (May–Oct). Off-season, the big hotels lower prices 10–15 percent. For cheaper beds, consider one of the many sobe (rooms in private homes) scattered around the lake (about €15–25 per person in peak season, often with a hefty 30 percent surcharge for stays shorter than 3 nights). Several agencies in town can help you find a soba (including Kompas Bled—see page 543). But be sure the location is convenient before you accept.

$$$ **Grand Hotel Toplice** is Bled's best splurge, with 87 rooms, an elegant view lounge, posh service, all the amenities, and a long list of high-profile guests—from Madeleine Albright to Jordan's King Hussein. Rooms in the back are cheaper, but have

---

Sleep Code

(€1 = about $1.20, 200 SIT = about $1, country code: 386, area code: 04)
S = Single, **D** = Double/Twin, **T** = Triple, **Q** = Quad, **b** = bathroom. Unless otherwise noted, breakfast is included and credit cards are accepted. Everyone speaks English, and prices are quoted in euros. Bled levies a €1 tourist tax per person, per night (not included in below prices unless noted).

To help you sort easily through these listings, I've divided the rooms into three categories based on the price for a standard double room with bath:

$$$ **Higher Priced**—Most rooms €100 (24,000 SIT) or more.

$$ **Moderately Priced**—Most rooms between €50–100 (12,000–24,000 SIT).

$ **Lower Priced**—Most rooms €50 (12,000 SIT) or less.

no lake views and overlook a noisy street—try to get one as high up as possible (non-view: Sb-€120, Db-€150; lake view: Sb-€170, Db-€200; suites mostly with lake views-€250, 15–20 percent less Nov–April, elevator, Cesta Svobode 12, tel. 04/579-1000, fax 04/574-1841, www.hotel-toplice.com, info@hotel-toplice.com). The hotel's name—*toplice*—means "spa"; guests are free to use the hotel's natural-spring-fed indoor swimming pool (a chilly 22 degrees Celsius, or 72 degrees Fahrenheit).

$$$ Hotel Lovec, a brand-new Best Western, sits in a convenient (but non-lakefront and less-charming) location just above the commercial center. It's a welcome, very new-feeling alternative to Bled's many old, dreary communist hotels, and its 60 rooms have all the comforts (Sb-€108, Db-€129, €10 more for balcony, €35 more for "deluxe" room with balcony and Jacuzzi, family and "executive" suites available, Ljubljanska Cesta 6, tel. 04/576-8615, fax 04/576-8625, www.lovechotel.com, sales@lovechotel.com).

$$ Mayer Penzion, perched on a bluff above Grand Hotel Toplice, is a steep five-minute uphill walk from lake. Wonderfully run by the Trseglav family, this place comes with 13 great-value rooms, a friendly and professional staff, an excellent restaurant, and an atmospheric wine-tasting cellar. They book up fast in summer with return clients, so reserve early (Sb-€40, Db-€60–75 depending on size and balcony, extra bed-€20, elevator, Želeška cesta 7, tel. 04/576-5740, fax 04/576-5741, www.mayer-sp.si, penzion@mayer -sp.si). They also rent a cute little two-story Slovenian farm cottage next door (Db-€65, Tb-€80, Qb-€85).

$$ Penzion Berc, next door to Mayer Penzion and run by a cousin, offers a brand-new hotel building with pleasantly woody decor and 15 rooms, plus an older, adjacent *penzion* with 11 cheaper, almost-as-nice rooms. Very quiet, with a cozy lounge and breakfast room, it's worth reserving ahead (older *penzion* rooms: Sb-€30–35, Db-€50–60; newer hotel rooms: Sb-€35, Db-€60–65; prices depend on size and balcony, 10 percent more for 1-night stays, 10 percent less off-season, includes tax, cash only, free loaner bikes, free Internet in lobby, free self-serve laundry with hang-dry, Želeška cesta 15, tel. & fax 04/574-1838, www.berc-sp.si, penzion@berc-sp.si, Berc family).

$$ Vila Prešeren, named for Slovenia's national poet, is literally a few steps from the lake. Its eight rooms are small but well-maintained, furnished with classy Biedermeier decor, and beautifully located. This is clearly your best bet for affordable lakeside elegance. Enjoy their buffet breakfast on the waterfront terrace (non-view: Sb-€55, Db-€72; lake view: Sb-€64, Db-€88; cheaper Jan–April, lake-view apartment-€140–155 depending on size, Kidričeva 1, tel. 04/578-0800, fax 04/578-0810, www.vila .preseren.s5.net, vila.preseren@siol.net).

$$ Alp Penzion, sitting in cornfields a 15-minute walk from the lake and just out of town, is the most tranquil and only farm-feeling option. Its 11 rooms are small and faded, but comfortable. The place is enthusiastically run by the Sršen family, who offer lots of fun activities: tennis court, summer barbecue grill, wine-tasting, and a sauna (Sb-€40, Db-€55–60, Tb-€80, 10 percent more for 1-night stays, cheaper Nov–March, family rooms, free Internet in lobby, free loaner bikes, Cankarjeva cesta 20A, tel. 04/574-1614, fax 04/574-4590, www.alp-penzion.com, bled@alp-penzion.com).

Grand Hotel Toplice (listed above) runs two nearby annexes with much lower prices: **$$ Hotel Jadran,** on a hill behind the Toplice, has 45 tired, old rooms (reception tel. 04/579-1365). **$$ Hotel Trst** is less charming, but its 31 rooms are a little bigger and were lightly renovated last year (reception and breakfast at the Toplice, often closed in winter). Both have the same prices and can be reserved through Grand Hotel Toplice (non-view: Sb-€55, Db-€70; lake view: Sb-€75, Db-€90; extra bed-€20, all rooms €10 less Nov–April, Cesta Svobode 12, tel. 04/579-1000, fax 04/574-1841, www.hotel-toplice.com, info@hotel-toplice.com). At either place, ask for a room on the higher floors to avoid road noise (both have elevators).

$ Penzion Bledec is just below the castle at the top of the old town. While it's technically an IYHF hostel, each of the 13 rooms has its own bathroom, and some can be rented as doubles (though "doubles" are actually underutilized triples and quads, with separate beds pushed together—so they're not reservable July–Aug). The friendly staff is justifiably proud of the bargain they offer (bed in 3- to 7-bed dorm-€19, Db-€46, Tb-€60, cheaper Nov–April, members pay 10 percent less, includes sheets and breakfast, non-smoking rooms, great family rooms, Internet in lobby, full-service laundry-2,000 SIT/load, Grajska 17, tel. 04/574-5250, fax 04/574-5251, www.mlino.si, bledec@mlino.si).

EATING

Okarina Etno, run by charming, well-traveled Leo Ličof, serves excellent Slovenian cuisine with an Indian twist. He has a respect for salads and vegetables and a passion for fish. The location and name might change in the future, but Leo's creative cooking, fine presentation, and atmosphere are worth seeking out (daily 11:00–24:00, next to Hotel Lovec at Ljubljanska cesta 8, tel. 04/574-1458). Skim the guest-book to find the page with Paul McCartney's visit from May 2005.

Mayer Penzion, just up the hill from the lakefront, has a dressy restaurant with good traditional cooking that's worth the short hike (2,000–3,000-SIT plates, indoor or outdoor seating,

---

Bled Desserts

While you're in Bled, be sure to enjoy the town's specialty, a vanilla-custard-and-cream cake called *kremna rezina* (KRAYM-nah ray-ZEE-nah). It's often referred to by its German name, *kremšnita* (KRAYM-shnee-tah). This dish was first created right here in Bled, at the big, red Hotel Park. Slovenes travel from all over the country to sample this famous dessert.

Slightly less renowned—but just as tasty—is *grmada* (gur-MAH-dah, literally "bonfire"). This dessert was developed by Hotel Jelovica as a way to get rid of their day-old leftovers. They take yesterday's cake, add rum, milk, custard, and raisins, and top it off with whipped cream and chocolate syrup.

These desserts are typically enjoyed with a lake-and-mountains view—the best spots are the Panorama restaurant by Grand Hotel Toplice, the recommended Vila Prešeren restaurant, and the terrace across from the Hotel Park (figure around 800 SIT for cake and coffee at any of these places). For a more local (but non-lake view) setting, consider Šmon Slaščičarna (only slightly cheaper; see "Dessert," page 557).

Tue–Fri 17:00–24:00, Sat–Sun 12:00–24:00, closed Mon, above Hotel Jadran at Želeška cesta 7, tel. 04/576-5740).

Gostilna Pri Planincu (literally, "By the Mountaineers") is a homey, informal bar packed with fun-loving and sometimes rowdy natives. Behind the small, local-feeling pub sprawls a large dining area. The big menu features good-enough Slovenian pub grub and Balkan grilled-meat specialties (1,200–2,200-SIT plates, huge portions, traditional daily specials, daily 9:00–23:00, Grajska cesta 8, tel. & fax 04/574-1613).

Vila Prešeren serves expensive food in a swanky dining room or on a romantic, scenic terrace right on the water (modern international cuisine with a focus on fish, 2,000–3,000-SIT main dishes, smart to reserve a lakeside table, daily 12:00–23:00, Kidričeva 1, tel. 04/578-0800).

Pizzeria Rustica is convenient and offers good wood-fired pizzas, pastas, and salads (Tue–Sun 12:00–23:00, Mon 15:00–23:00, marked only with low-profile *pizzeria* sign at Riklijeva cesta 13, tel. 04/576-8900). Its upstairs roof terrace is relaxing on a balmy evening.

Café à Propos, in the commercial center, features 400–500-SIT toasted sandwiches, fancy drinks and sweets, slow Internet access, and 800-SIT cocktails in the evening (daily 8:00–24:00, Ljubljanska cesta 4, tel. 04/574-4044).

The **Mercator** grocery store, also in the commercial center, has the makings for a bang-up picnic. They sell 400–500-SIT pre-made sandwiches, or will make you one to order (point to what you want). This is a great option for hikers and budget travelers (Mon–Sat 7:00–19:00, Sun 8:00–12:00).

Dessert: While tourists generally gulp down their cream cakes on a hotel restaurant's lakefront terrace, local residents know the best desserts are at **Šmon Slaščičarna** (a.k.a. the "Brown Bear," for the bear on the sign). It's nicely non-touristy, but lacks the atmosphere of the lakeside spots (daily 7:30–22:00, near bus station at Grajska cesta 3, tel. 04/574-1616).

TRANSPORTATION CONNECTIONS

The most convenient train connections to Bled leave from the Lesce-Bled station, about 2.5 miles away. Remember, when buying a train ticket to Lake Bled, make it clear that you want to go to the "Lesce-Bled" station. The "Bled Jezero" station is closer to the town of Bled, but it takes much longer to reach because it's served by only a handful of regional trains. No one in the town of Bled sells train tickets; buy them at the station or on the train.

From Bled by Train to: Ljubljana (11/day, 1 hr—but bus is better, since it departs conveniently from Bled town, not from train station outside of town), **Salzburg** (5/day, 4 hrs), **Munich** (3/day, 6 hrs), **Vienna** (that's *Dunaj* in Slovene, 5/day, 6 hrs, transfer in Villach, Austria), **Venice** (3/day with transfer in Ljubljana or Villach, 6 hrs), **Zagreb** (5/day, 3.5 hrs).

By Bus to: Ljubljana (Mon–Fri 11/day, Sat–Sun 8/day, 80 min, 1,470 SIT), **Radovljica** (Mon–Fri at least 2/hr, Sat hrly, Sun almost hrly, 15 min, 400 SIT), **Lesce-Bled train station** (at least hrly, 10 min, 300 SIT), **Lake Bohinj** (7/day, 30 min to "Bohinj Jezero" stop, 40 min to "Bohinj Zlatorog" stop), **Podhom** (20-min hike away from Vintgar Gorge, Mon–Fri 9/day, none Sat, 1/day Sun, 15 min, 290 SIT), **Spodnje Gorje** (also near Vintgar Gorge, take bus in direction of Krnica, hrly, 15 min). Confirm times at the Bled bus station.

By Plane: The Ljubljana-Brnik Airport is between Bled and Ljubljana. A taxi costs about 10,500 SIT (set price up front—since it's outside of town, they don't use the meter). The bus connection from Bled to the airport is cheap (total cost: 1,200 SIT), but complicated: First, go to Kranj (Mon–Fri 12/day, Sat–Sun 8/day, 35 min), then transfer to a Brnik-bound bus (at least hrly, 20 min). Many Bled residents prefer to fly from Klagenfurt, Austria. For details on both the Ljubljana and the Klagenfurt airports, see page 522.

Triglav National Park
(Triglavski Narodni Park)

The countryside around Lake Bled has its own distinctive beauty: alpine rivers with superb fishing, rural rest stops, and charming mountain hamlets. But the best day in the Julian Alps is spent driving up and over the Vršič Pass (vur-SHEECH, generally closed in winter, open May–Oct), and back down via the Soča River Valley (SOH-chah). This daylong circular drive features some stunning high-altitude scenery (on challenging, twisty roads), as well as some offbeat WWI sights.

This drive is divided into two parts: the Vršič Pass and the Soča River Valley. You can start and finish in Bled, or start in Bled and end in Ljubljana. Give it a whole day. Not counting stops, figure an hour from Bled to the top of the pass, a half hour back down to the start of the Soča Valley, and an hour on to the town of Kobarid. From Kobarid, figure another two hours back to the expressway via Idrija, then an hour to Ljubljana or 90 minutes back to Bled. Returning via Nova Gorica (explained below) takes slightly longer.

Vršič Pass

This self-guided driving tour takes you up and over the highest mountain pass in Slovenia—with stunning scenery and a few quirky sights along the way. While it's not for stick-shift novices, all but the most timid drivers will agree the scenery is worth the many hairpin turns. The frequent turn-outs offer plenty of opportunity to relax, stretch your legs, and enjoy the vistas.

Begin in Bled. Take the freeway north towards Jesenice (follow green signs), enjoying views of **Mount Triglav** on the left as you drive. You'll drive towards the industrial city of **Jesenice**, whose iron- and steelworks are now all closed. The nearby village of **Kurja Vas** (literally, "Chicken Village") is famous for producing hockey players (18 of the 20 players on the 1971 Yugoslav hockey team—which went to the World Championships—were from this tiny hamlet).

As you approach Jesenice, within yodeling distance of Austria, keep your eye out for the Hrušica exit (also marked for Jesenice, Kranjska Gora, and the Italian

Northwest Slovenia

A U S T R I A

TO VILLACH
TO VILLACH
TO KLAGENFURT

TARVISIO
RATECE
KRANJSKA GORA
202
TO VENICE
PLANICA SKI JUMP
ŠPIK
HRUŠICA EXIT
JESENICE
101
PREDEL
VRŠIČ PASS
TRIGLAV
BLED
LESCE
BEGUNJE
RADOVLJICA
KLUŽE FORT
206
TRENTA NAT'L. PARK INFO CENTER
BOVEC
SOČA
209
UČEJA
LAKE BOHINJ
VOGEL
POLJE
BOHINJSKA BISTRICA
A-2
BRNIK AIRPORT
ROBIC
KOBARID
KRANJ
RIVER
SOČA
TOLMIN
403
ŠKOFJA LOKA
I T A L Y
103
102
210
GORENJA VAS
LJUBLJANA
TO UDINE
KANAL
IDRIJICA RIVER
407
SOČA RIVER
IDRIJA
408
A-1 FREEWAY
102
NOVA GORICA
LOGATEC
TO TRIESTE
10 MILES
20 KM
TO POSTOJNA, ŠKOCJAN, KOPER + PIRAN
DCH

border; it's after the gas station, just before the tunnel to Austria). When you exit, turn left towards Kranjska Gora (yellow sign) and the Italian border.

Slovenes brag that their country—"with 56 percent of the land covered in forest"—is one of Europe's greenest. As you drive towards Kranjska Gora, take in all this greenery...and the characteristic Slovenian hayracks (recognized as part of the national heritage and now preserved; see page 483). The Vrata Valley (on the left) is the starting point for climbing Mount Triglav. On the right, keep an eye out for the statue of Jakob Aljaž, who actually bought Triglav back when such a thing was possible (he's pointing at his purchase). Ten minutes later, you'll cross a bridge and enjoy a great head-on view of Spik Mountain.

Entering Kranjska Gora, you'll see a turnoff to the left marked for *Vršič*. But winter sports fanatics may want to take a 15-minute detour to see the biggest ski jump in the world, a few miles ahead (stay straight through Kranjska Gora, then turn left at signs for **Planica**, the last stop before the Italian border). Every year, tens of thousands of sports fans flock here to watch the ski-jumping world

Mount Triglav

Mount Triglav (literally "Three Heads") stands watch over the Julian Alps and all of Slovenia. Slovenes say that its three peaks are the guardians of the water, air, and earth. This mountain defines Slovenes, even adorning the nation's flag: Look for the national seal, with three peaks. The two squiggly lines under it represent the Adriatic.

From the town of Bled, you'll see Triglav peeking up over the ridge on a clear day. (You'll get an even better view from nearby Lake Bohinj.)

It's said that you're not a true Slovene until you've climbed Triglav. One native took these words very seriously, and climbed the mountain 853 times...in one year. Climbing to the summit—at 9,396 feet—is an attainable goal for any hiker in decent shape. If you're here for a while and want to become an honorary Slovene, befriend a Slovene and ask if he or she will take you to the top.

If mountain climbing isn't your style, relax at an outdoor café with a piece of cream cake and a view of Triglav. It won't make you a Slovene...but it's close enough on a quick visit.

championships. This is where a local boy was the first human to fly more than 100 meters (328 feet) on skis. Today's competitors routinely set new world records (currently 820 feet—that's 17 seconds in the air). From the ski jump, you're a few minutes' walk from Italy or Austria. This region--spanning three nations—lobbied unsuccessfully to host the 2006 Winter Olympics. (Things *"senza confini"*—Italian for "without borders"—are in tune with the European Union's vision for a Europe of regions, rather than nations.)

Back in Kranjska Gora, follow the signs for *Vršič*. Before long, you'll officially enter **Triglav National Park** and come to the first of this road's 50 hairpin turns—each one numbered and labeled with the altitude in meters. In addition to the ever-changing alpine panorama, there are several worthwhile stops along the way, as well as frequent pullouts for photo stops. If the drive seems daunting, remember that 50-seat tour buses routinely conquer this pass...if they can do it, so can you.

After switchback #8, park on the right and hike 100 yards up the stairs to the little **Russian chapel.** This road was built during World War I by 10,000 Russian POWs of the Austro-Hungarian Empire to supply the front lines of the Soča Front. The POWs lived and worked in terrible conditions, and several hundred died of illness and exposure. On March 8, 1916, an avalanche thundered down the mountains, killing hundreds of workers. This chapel was

built where the final casualty was
found. (Notice the group photo of
those comrades on the wall inside the
church.) Sign the little guest book
and pay your respects to the men who
built the road you're enjoying today.

After #22, at the pullout for
Erjavčeva Koča restaurant, you may
see tour buses making a fuss about
the mountain vista. They're looking
for a ghostly face in the cliff wall,
supposedly belonging to the mythical figure **Ajda**. This village girl was
cursed by the townspeople after correctly predicting the death of
the Golden Horn (Zlatorog), a magical, goat-like animal. Her tiny
image (with a Picasso nose) is just above the tree line, a little to the
right—try to get someone to point her out to you (you can see her
best if you stand at the signpost near the road).

After #24, you reach the **summit** (5,285 feet). On the right, a
long gravel chute gives hikers a thrilling glissade down. (From the
pullout just beyond #26, it's easy to view hikers "skiing" down.)
On the 26 hairpin turns on the way down, keep an eye out for old
WWI debris. Just after the pass, the tunnel marked *1916* on the
left used to be the original path of this road. After #28, you'll see
abandoned checkpoints from when this was the border between
Italy and the Austro-Hungarian Empire. At #48 is a statue of
Julius Kugy, an Italian botanist who wrote books about alpine
flora.

At #49, the road to the right leads to the **source of the Soča
River** (20-min uphill hike from the parking lot) and a brand-new,
well-explained hiking path that leads all the way to the town of
Bovec. This is an excellent place for a hike, if you have the time.

Nearing the end of the switchbacks, follow signs for *Bovec.*
Crossing the Soča River, you begin the second half of this trip.

Soča River Valley

During World War I, the terrain between here and the Adriatic
made up the Soča (Isonzo) Front. As you follow the Soča River
south, down what's nicknamed the "Valley of the Cemeteries," the
scenic mountainsides around you tell the tale of this terrible warfare. Imagine a young Ernest Hemingway driving his ambulance
through these same hills.

The last Vršič switchback (#50) sends you into the village of Trenta. On the left, look for the **Triglav National Park**

Information Center (May–Oct daily 10:00–18:00, closed Nov–April, tel. 05/388-9330, www.tnp.si). The humble 900-SIT museum here provides a look (with English explanations) at the park's flora, fauna, traditional culture, and mountaineering history. A poetic 15-minute slideshow explains the wonders and fragility of the park (ask for English version as you enter).

About five miles after Trenta, in the town of Soča, visit the **Church of St. Joseph** (with red onion dome, hiding behind the big tree on the right, damaged in earthquakes of 1998 and 2004). During World War II, an artist hiding out in the mountains filled this church with patriotic symbolism. The interior is bathed in Yugoslav red, white, and blue–a brave statement made when such nationalistic sentiments were dangerous. On the ceiling is St. Michael (clad in Yugoslav colors) with Yugoslavia's three WWII enemies at his feet: the eagle (Germany), the wolf (Italy), and the serpent (Japan). The tops of the walls along the nave are lined with saints–but these are Slavic, not Catholic. Finally, look carefully at the Stations of the Cross and find the faces of hated Yugoslav enemies: Hitler (4th from altar on left) and Mussolini (1st from altar on right). Behind the church is a typical cemetery–with civilian and (on the hillside) military sections.

For a good example of how the Soča River cuts like God's bandsaw into the land, stop about two minutes past the church at Velika Korita Soča, where you can venture out onto a bouncy suspension bridge over a gorge.

Roughly five miles after the town of Soča, you exit the National Park and come to a fork. The main route leads to the left, through Bovec. But first, take a two-mile detour to the right, where the WWI **Kluže Fort** keeps a close watch over the narrowest part of a valley leading to Italy (350 SIT, daily 10:00–19:00). In the 15th century, the Italians had a fort here to defend against the Turks. Half a millennium later, during World War I, it was used by Austrians to keep Italians out of their territory. Notice the ladder rungs fixed to the cliff face across the road from the fort—allowing soldiers to quickly get up to the mountaintop. Today, the fort hosts a peace festival every summer, where costumed Italian and Austro-Hungarian soldiers stop traffic for stern military checks, then perform a show and embrace each other.

Continue back through **Bovec.** This town, which saw some of the most vicious fighting of the Soča Front, was hit hard by a 2004

The Soča (Isonzo) Front

The northwest corner of Slovenia–called Soča in Slovene, and Isonzo in Italian–saw some of World War I's fiercest fighting. While the Western Front gets more press, this eastern border between the Central Powers and the Allies was just as significant. In a series of 13 battles involving 16 different nationalities, 300,000 soldiers died, 700,000 were wounded, and 100,000 were declared MIA. In addition, tens of thousands of civilians died. Among the injured soldiers was a young Ernest Hemingway, who drove an ambulance for the Italian army. (Later in life, he would write the novel *A Farewell to Arms* about his experiences here.)

On April 26, 1915, Italy joined the Allies. A month later, they declared war on the Austro-Hungarian Empire (which included Slovenia). Italy invaded the Soča Valley, quickly taking the tiny town of Kobarid, which they planned to use as a home base for attacks deeper into Austrian territory. For the next 29 months, Italy launched 10 more offensives, all of them unsuccessful. This was difficult warfare–Italy had to attack uphill, waging war high in the mountains, in the harshest of conditions.

In October 1917, the Central Powers of Austria-Hungary and Germany retook Kobarid, launching a downhill attack of 600,000 soldiers. For the first time ever, the Austrian-German army used a new surprise-attack technique called *Blitzkrieg*, which was carried out by a German general named Erwin Rommel–against orders from a superior. (He was demoted for his insolence despite its success, but climbed the ranks again to become famous as Hitler's "Desert Fox" in North Africa.) The Central Powers caught the Italian forces off-guard, quickly breaking through three lines of defense. Within three days, the Italians were forced to retreat. The Austrians called it the "Miracle at Kobarid," but Italy felt differently–to this day, when an Italian finds himself in a mess, he says he had a *Caporetto* (the Italian name for Kobarid).

A year later, Italy came back–this time with the aid of British, French, and U.S. forces. The Allies were successful, and on November 4, 1918, Austria-Hungary conceded defeat. After more than a million casualties, the fighting at Soča was finally over.

earthquake. Today, it's being rebuilt and remains the adventure-sports capital of the Soča River Valley, famous for its whitewater activities. For a good lunch stop in Bovec, try the busiest place in town, Letni Vrt Pizzeria, with pizzas, pastas, salads, and more (closed Tue, on the main square at Trg Golobarskih Žrtev 12, tel. 05/388-6335). Martinov Hram is also good, featuring homemade bread (closed Thu, Trg Golobarskih Žrtev 27, tel. 05/388-6214).

Heading south along the river (with water somehow both perfectly clear and spectacularly turquoise), watch for happy kayakers. When you pass the intersection at Žaga, you're just more than four miles from Italy.

Signs lead to the town of **Kobarid,** home to the world-class **Kobarid Museum** (Kobariški Muzej)—offering a haunting look at the tragedy of the Soča Front (800 SIT, good 600-SIT museum guide, 1,900-SIT *Soča Front* book, April–Sept Mon–Fri 9:00–18:00, Sat–Sun 9:00–19:00; Oct–March Mon–Fri 10:00–17:00, Sat–Sun 9:00–18:00; Gregorčičeva 10, tel. 05/389-0000, www.kobariski-muzej.si). This proud little place, with fine English descriptions, was voted Europe's best museum in 1993. The entry is lined with hastily made cement and barbed-wire gravestones, pictures of soldiers, and flags of all of the nationalities involved in the fighting. Maps show how Europe changed from 1914 to 1918. The rotating ground-floor exhibit features a different country each year. Upstairs are exhibits on the way these soldiers lived, the tragedies they encountered (with some horrific images of war injuries), the devastating effects of the war on civilians, the strategies involved in the various battles (including a huge model of the successful Austrian-German *Blitzkrieg* attack), and the history of this region before and after World War I. Upon arrival, request to watch the English version of the 22-minute video about the history of the Front (plays on top floor). At the museum, WWI buffs can pick up free brochures on self-guided "walks of peace" through town; call ahead if you want a private guide (3,000 SIT/hr, tel. 05/389-0000).

The 55 miles between here and the Adriatic are dotted with more than a hundred cemeteries, reminders of the countless casualties of the Soča Front. One of the most dramatic is the **Italian Mausoleum** (Kostnica) overlooking Kobarid. The access road (across Kobarid's main square from the church, with a gate featuring a cross on one side and a star on the other) leads up Gradič Hill—passing Stations of the Cross—to the mausoleum.

Built in 1938 around the existing Church of St. Anthony, this fascist-style octagonal pyramid holds the remains of 7,014 Italian soldiers. Names are listed alphabetically, along with the names of mass graves for more than 1,700 unknown soldiers *(militi ignoti)*. Walk behind the church and find the WWI battlements high on the mountain's rock face (with your back to church, they're at 10 o'clock). Incredibly, the fighting was done on these treacherous ridges; civilians in the valleys only heard the distant battles. Inside the church, look above the door to see a brave soldier standing over the body of a fallen comrade, fending off enemies with nothing but rocks. When Mussolini came to dedicate the mausoleum, local revolutionaries plotted an assassination attempt that couldn't fail. But at the last minute, the triggerman had a change of heart, Mussolini had an uneventful trip, and fascism continued to thrive in Italy.

Continue south along the Soča to Tolmin. Before you reach Tolmin, decide on your route back to Bled. The fastest option is to load your car onto a train that cuts directly through the mountains. The train departs at 18:05 from Most na Soči (just south of Tolmin) and arrives at Bohinjska Bistrica, near Lake Bohinj, at 18:50 (confirm these times at the TI in Bled before making the trip). From Bohinjska Bistrica, it's a just half-hour drive back to Bled.

But if you'd rather spend more time in your car, you have two possible driving routes back to Bled from Tolmin: Hook south along smoother roads via Nova Gorica, or take windier mountain roads via Idrija. Either option brings you back to the expressway south of Ljubljana.

The option you'll encounter first (turnoff to the right before Tolmin) is the smoother, longer route southwest through Tuscan-esque landscapes towards Nova Gorica (literally divided in half by the Italian border) and eventually to the bustling Italian port of Trieste, which was Slovenian before World War II. From Nova Gorica or from Trieste, freeways lead back to Ljubljana and Bled.

I prefer the more rural second option: Continue through Tolmin, then head southeast through the hills back towards Ljubljana. Keep an eye out for more hay-drying racks—but notice that here, unlike in the northern part of the country, they don't have roofs (less rain). Along the way, you could stop for a bite and some sightseeing at the town of **Idrija** (EE-dree-yah), known to all Slovenes for three things: its tourable mercury mine, fine delicate lace, and tasty *žlikrofi* (like ravioli). Back at the freeway (at Logatec), head north to Ljubljana or on to Bled. If you prefer a more direct, non-expressway route back up to Bled—and don't mind skipping Idrija—you can turn north in Želin (before Idrija) towards Skofja Loka and Kranj.

CROATIA

CROATIA

(Hrvatska)

Croatia is known for two very different reasons: as a top fun-in-the-sun tourist destination, and as the site, just more than a decade ago, of one of the most violent European wars in generations. Thankfully, today the bloodshed is in the past. Be aware of the war, but focus on Croatia's natural wonders: the dramatic Dalmatian coastline and the striking waterfalls of Plitvice Lakes National Park.

Croatia feels more Mediterranean than "Eastern European." Especially on the coast, it's sometimes difficult to distinguish this lively, chaotic place from Italy. Along with this carefree way of life comes a more easygoing attitude. Be prepared to fall victim to the Croatian Shrug—a simple gesture that conveys the message,

"Don't know, don't care." But most visitors happily put up with Croatia's minor frustrations to take advantage of its low prices and postcard beauty. After all, you're on vacation.

If you want to blow through a lot of money here, you can. Croatian hotels, especially on the coast, are a terrible value, and there are plenty of touristy restaurants happy to overcharge you. But there are also wonderful budget alternatives—foremost among them *sobe* (rooms in private homes). While we Americans like our privacy, and may be intimidated by the idea of sleeping in a stranger's house, these *sobe* are a comfortable compromise: new-feeling, fresh, hotelesque doubles with a private bathroom and TV, for half the cost of a moldy room in a crumbling resort hotel just down the beach (for details, see "Dalmatian Accommodation" on page 610). Between sleeping in *sobe* and eating at non-touristy restaurants (which I've also recommended), you'll be amazed how far your money goes here.

In the Yugoslav era, Croatia was flooded with tourists—both European and American—who fell in love with its dramatic beauty and fun-loving ambience. For several years after the war, Croatia floundered, desperately trying to bring its standards back up to snuff. And in the last few years, the country has succeeded—placing itself decisively back on the tourist map.

While timid Americans generally have yet to rediscover Croatia's charms, the country is enjoying an enormous surge in popularity among Europeans looking for a cheap and nearby warm-weather getaway—not unlike Mexico for Americans. Lonely Planet named Croatia the world's "Top Destination" for 2005. For some reason, the country holds a special appeal to French people. On my last visit, I heard more French spoken than Croatian.

Europeans are reverent sun-worshippers, and on sunny days, virtually every square inch of coastal Croatia is occupied by a sunbather on a beach towel. Nude beaches are a big deal, especially for vacationing Germans and Austrians. If you want to work on an all-around tan, seek out one of the beaches marked *FKK* (from the German *Freikörper Kultur*, or "free body culture"). First-timers get comfortable in a hurry, finding they're not the only pink novices on the rocks. But don't get too excited—these beaches are most beloved by people you'd rather see with their clothes on.

Like any seaside resort, Croatia's gift shops are filled with tacky T-shirts, ceramics, and shell sculptures—a wide range of souvenirs with varying degrees of tastelessness. Americans touring Europe are generally more interested in Old World culture than made-in-Taiwan trinkets. But it's surprisingly easy to ignore the tourist sprawl and poke your way into twisty old medieval lanes, draped with drying laundry and populated by gossiping housewives and soccer-playing kids.

After the War

Some Americans shy away from Croatia, clinging to decade-old memories of wartime images on the nightly news. But those who venture here are, without exception, amazed by how peaceful and stable today's Croatia feels. Croatia's primary tourist region—the coast—was barely touched by the war (except Dubrovnik, which has been painstakingly restored). The interior is sprinkled with destroyed homes and churches—some standing gutted, skeletons of their original structures—but these villages are gradually being refurbished.

The only actual danger is that much of the Croatian interior was once full of landmines. However, virtually all of these mines have been removed, and fields that may be dangerous are usually clearly marked. As a precaution, stay on roads and paths, and don't go wandering through overgrown fields and deserted villages.

The biggest impact from the war has been on the people. Throughout the country, but especially in the war-torn interior, sadness and resentment hang heavy in the air. Though the country is repairing itself admirably, the Croatians' souls will take the longest to heal.

For more on Croatia during and after the war, see the Understanding Yugoslavia chapter, page 750.

Croatian music, the mariachi music of Europe, is the ever-present soundtrack of a Dalmatian vacation. Oliver Dragojević—singing soulful Mediterranean ballads with his gravelly, passionate voice—is the Croatian Tom Jones. Known simply as "Oliver," this immensely popular crooner gets airplay across Europe, and has spawned many imitators.

Croatia is known for its idyllic coastline, but there are also worthwhile stops in the interior. The underrated capital, Zagreb—with good museums, colorful street life, and a thriving café culture—is worth exploring. Just to the south is the waterfall wonderland of the Plitvice Lakes, one of Europe's best back-to-nature experiences.

Practicalities

Stow Your Euros: Tourists are notorious for confusing euro bills with Croatian kuna bills (both modeled after the old German *Deutschmark*, and therefore similar). Make a point of deep-storing all euros while outside the euro zone, or you'll be paying about seven times more than you should to enjoy Croatia.

Telephones: Croatia's phone system uses area codes. To make a long-distance call within the country, start with the area code. To call Croatia from another country, first dial the international access code (00 if calling from Europe, 011 from U.S. or Canada), 385 (Croatia's country code), the area code (without the initial zero), and the local number. To call out of Croatia, dial 00, the country code of the country you're calling (see chart in appendix), the area code if applicable (may need to drop initial zero), and the local number.

Croatia's payphones work on insertable phone cards (buy at newsstands or kiosks). Cheap, prepaid international calling cards are appearing here with decent rates (about 1 kn/min). But beware: Some cards (such as one I used, by Dencall) work only with a local Split or Zagreb number—a toll call from a payphone (no toll-free access number).

Free Tourist Help by Phone: The "Croatian Angels" service gives free information over a toll-free line in English (tel. 062/999-999, mid-June–Sept daily 8:00–24:00).

Addresses: Addresses listed with a street name, followed by "b.b.," have no street number.

Anatomy of the Croatian Coast

Croatia's 3,600 miles of coastline is rocky, arid, and dramatic. There are basically three parts to the coast (north to south): Istria, the wedge-shaped peninsula just south of Slovenia; the Kvarner Gulf, with the big, industrial port city of Rijeka and lots of islands; and the Dalmatian Coast (easily the best stretch, and covered in detail in this book). Along the length of the Croatian coast are a few big cities (like Pula, Rijeka, Zadar, Split, and Dubrovnik) and about two dozen more-or-less-interchangeable resort villages, many of them on islands. These include (from north to south) Poreč, Rovinj, Opatija, Krk (on Krk Island), Rab (on Rab Island), Pag (on Pag Island), Šibenik, Trogir, Hvar (on Hvar Island), Korčula (on Korčula Island), Orebić, Neum (in Bosnia-Herzegovina), and Cavtat. People ask me which is best. While each of these towns has its own character, I find them all pretty similar. If I had to pick a favorite, Korčula has an advantage.

Here's an anatomy lesson of the Croatian coast, from north to south.

Istria

The Istrian Peninsula is the northernmost part of the coast. It's got several beach towns; the three most notable are (north to south) **Poreč** (concrete beach resort, not very charming), **Rovinj** (quaint old town on a dramatic peninsula surrounded by concrete resort sprawl), and **Pula** (dull big city with Roman amphitheater). Many people have heard of Istria and are seduced by the fact that it's

Croatia Almanac

Official Name: Republika Hrvatska, or just Hrvatska for short.

Snapshot History: After losing its independence to Hungary in A.D. 1102, Croatia watched as most of its coastline became Venetian and its interior was conquered by Turks. Croatia was "rescued" by the Hapsburgs, but after World War I it became part of Yugoslavia—a decision most Croats regretted until they finally gained independence in 1991 through a bitter war with their Serbian neighbors.

Population: Of the country's 4.5 million people (similar to Louisiana), 90 percent are ethnic Croats (Catholic) and 4 percent are Serbs (Orthodox). (The Serb population was more than double that before the ethnic cleansing of the 1991–1995 war.) About 1 percent of Croatians are Muslim (Bosniak). "Croatians" are citizens of Croatia; "Croats" are a distinct ethnic group made up of Catholic South Slavs. So Orthodox Serbs living in Croatia can be Croatians, but they can't be Croats (since they're not Catholic).

Latitude and Longitude: 45°N and 15°E (similar latitude to Venice, Italy; Ottawa, Canada; or Portland, Oregon).

Area: 22,000 square miles, similar to West Virginia.

Geography: This boomerang-shaped country has two terrains: Stretching north to south is the long, hilly Mediterranean coastline (3,600 miles of beach, including many offshore islands), which is warm and dry. The coast is roughly divided into three areas: the wedge-shaped Istria Peninsula in the north; the island-dappled Kvarner Gulf in the center; and the Dalmatian Coast in the south. Rising up from the sea are the rugged Dinaric Mountains (which also cover virtually all of neighboring Bosnia-Herzegovina). To the northeast, beginning at about Zagreb, Croatia's flat, inland "panhandle" (called Slavonia) has hot summers and cold winters.

Biggest Cities: The capital, Zagreb (in the northern interior), has 765,000; Split (along the southern Dalmatian Coast) has 173,000; and Rijeka (on the northern coast) has 150,000.

Economy: Much of the country's wealth ($50 billion GDP, $11,000 GDP per capita) comes from tourism, banking, and trade with Italy. The country is still recovering from the turmoil of the 1990s: Unemployment is a stiff 14 percent, corruption is deeply rooted, and—unlike the other countries in this book—Croatia is still a European Union outsider.

Currency: 1 kuna (kn, or HRK) = about 17 cents, and 6 kuna = about $1. *Kuna* is Croatian for "marten" (a fox-like animal), recalling the long-ago era when fur pelts were used as currency.

Government: The country's prime minister (currently Ivo Sanader, head of the majority party in parliament) is conservative, while the directly elected (but more figurehead) president, Stipe Mesić, is left-of-center. The single-house assembly (Sabor) of 151 legislators is elected by popular vote. A hot-button issue in today's Croatia is its alleged harboring of war criminals from the wars of the 1990s. This human-rights violation is a potential obstacle to Croatia's EU membership.

Flag: The flag has three horizontal bands (red on top, white, and blue) with a traditional red-checked shield in the center.

The Average Croat: The average Croat will live to age 74 and have 1.39 children. One in four uses the Internet. The average Croat absolutely adores the soccer team Dinamo Zagreb and absolutely despises Hajduk Split...or vice versa.

Notable Croatians: A pair of big-league historical figures were born in Croatia: Roman Emperor Diocletian (A.D. 245–313) and explorer Marco Polo (1254?–1324). More recently, many Americans whose name ends in "-ich" have Croatian roots, including actor John Malkovich and Ohio politicians Dennis Kucinich and John Kasich, not to mention baseball legend Roger Marich...I mean, Maris. More Croatian athletes abound: NBA fans might recognize Toni Kukoč or Gordan Giricek, and at the 2002 Winter Olympic Games, the women's skiing events were virtually swept by Janica Kostelić. Actor Goran Višnjić (from TV's *ER*) was born and raised in Croatia, serving in the army as a paratrooper. Inventor Nikola Tesla (1856–1943) would be world-famous today if America had opted for his alternating current (AC) instead of Thomas Edison's direct current (DC). And a band of well-dressed 17th-century Croatian soldiers stationed in France gave the Western world a new fashion accessory—the *cravate*, or necktie (for the full story, see page 632).

so far north, and therefore more convenient on a multi-country itinerary. But if you want to stay up north and still get some beach time in, I actually prefer **Piran** in Slovenia (see Piran chapter).

Kvarner Gulf

This large gulf has a cluster of islands, each with decent villages frequented mostly by vacationing Europeans: **Rab**, **Pag**, **Krk**, and **Cres**. The big city of **Rijeka** is ugly and industrial, and should be avoided except as a transportation hub. Nearby is the old Hapsburg resort of **Opatija**, with lots of faded-elegant villas.

Dalmatian Coast

As you head south and pass **Zadar** (a relatively dull mid-sized city), you reach the most thrilling part of the Croatian coast. The Dalmatian Coast boasts Croatia's two best cities (Split and Dubrovnik) and some of its most enjoyable small towns (including Korčula). South of Zadar is **Šibenik**, a so-so resort town with some nice old churches, and **Trogir**, a charming little village on an island. On the other side of the bay from Trogir is **Split**—a Mediterranean metropolis featuring Roman ruins inhabited by in-love-with-life locals. Split is the main transport hub for the Dalmatian Coast (lots of boat, bus, and train connections), but it's also a worthwhile destination in its own right.

Dalmatian Islands: Between Split and Dubrovnik are several popular islands, each with its share of resort towns. These include **Brač Island**, **Hvar Island** (with two main towns: Hvar town and Stari Grad), and **Korčula Island**. The main town on Korčula Island, also called **Korčula**, has an extremely charming, historic old town and an especially scenic setting. While some connoisseurs lobby hard for Hvar, Korčula's the one that keeps me coming back.

Pelješac Peninsula: Across the channel from Korčula Island is the town of **Orebić**, which is at the tip of the **Pelješac Peninsula**. This rugged, mountainous peninsula is famous for its wine (Plavec grapes—see page 582). At the base of the peninsula is **Ston**, a humble little town that's unexceptional aside from the dramatic Great Wall of China–type fortifications climbing the hill around it.

Bosnia-Herzegovina: Just north of where the Pelješac Peninsula joins the mainland, the main road along the coast goes through a little segment of Bosnia-Herzegovina, including the town of **Neum** (borders are easy and quick, just flash your passport). Note that about 90 minutes inland (northeast of here) is the Bosnian city of **Mostar**—famous for its still-thriving Muslim culture (tensely sharing the town with Catholic Croats) and its famous old Turkish bridge—destroyed in the recent war, but now rebuilt. While this city still feels a bit too war-scarred for skittish tourists to enjoy, hardy travelers find it to be a safe, illuminating look at Bosnia (you can visit Mostar with a package tour from Split or Dubrovnik, or go on your own—just drive inland, through the border town of Metković and along the Neretva River).

Dubrovnik and Nearby: Dubrovnik is the final stop on the Dalmatian Coast, and easily the single best destination in Croatia. Just before Dubrovnik are the **Elaphite Islands**—an archipelago including **Lopud** (the most developed island), **Koločep**, and **Šipan.** These islands are popular with tourists, but relatively rustic. Beyond Dubrovnik, near the airport and the border, is **Cavtat.** But it's not out of the question to continue over the border, into the country now officially called "Serbia and Montenegro."

The Montenegrin Coast: Just across the border (in Montenegro) is the **Bay of Kotor**, with dramatic fjord-like inlets. You'll pass through little towns as you travel along the twisty road. (Note that you can save time by taking the ferry across the bay.) While this drive is quite time-consuming, it's a popular day trip from Dubrovnik.

Croatian History

For nearly a millennium, bits and pieces of what we today call "Croatia" were batted back and forth between foreign powers: Hungarians, Venetians, Turks, Hapsburgs, and—of course—Yugoslavs. Only in 1991 did Croatia (violently) regain its independence.

Early History

Croatia's first inhabitants were the Illyrians (ancestors of today's Albanians). Romans began to settle the Dalmatian Coast as early as 229 B.C., and Emperor Diocletian had his retirement palace in the coastal town of Split. The Slavic Croats—ancestors of today's Croatians—arrived in the seventh century, and in A.D. 925, the Dalmatian duke Tomislav united most of present-day Croatia.

Loss of Independence

By the early 12th century, the Croatian kings had died out, and neighboring powers (Hungary, Venice, and Byzantium) threatened the Croats. For the sake of self-preservation, Croatia entered into an alliance with the Hungarians in 1102—and for the next 900 years, Croatia was ruled by foreign states. The Hungarians gradually took more and more power from the Croats, exerting control over the majority of inland Croatia. Meanwhile, the Venetian Republic conquered most of the coast and peppered the Croatian Adriatic with bell towers and statues of St. Mark. Through it all, the tiny Republic of Dubrovnik flourished—paying off whomever

Franjo Tuđman
(1922–1999)

Independent Croatia's first president was the complicated, controversial Franjo Tuđman (FRAHN-yoh TOOJ-mahn). Tuđman began his career fighting for Tito on the left, but later had a dramatic ideological swing to the far right. His anti-communist, highly nationalistic HDZ party was the driving force for Croatian statehood, making him the young nation's first hero. But even as he fought for independence from Yugoslavia, his own ruling style grew more and more authoritarian. Just a few years after his death, Tuđman remains a polemical figure.

Before entering politics, Tuđman was a historian. He revered the Ustaše—Croatia's Nazi-affiliated government during World War II, who murdered hundreds of thousands of Serbs and Jews in concentration camps. (Tuđman figured that since that was the first time since the 12th century that Croatia was an independent state, these quasi-Nazis were the original Croatian "freedom fighters.") When Croatia voted for independence and Tuđman was elected president, he immediately reintroduced many Ustaše symbols, including the red-checkerboard flag and the currency (the kuna)—both still fixtures of Croatian life today. These acts raised eyebrows worldwide, and raised alarms in Croatia's Serb communities.

Tuđman espoused many of the same single-minded attitudes about ethnic divisions as the ruthless Serbian leader Slobodan Milošević. In fact, Tuđman and Milošević had secret, Hitler-and-Stalin-esque negotiations for divvying up Bosnia-Herzegovina. When Tuđman's successor moved into the president's office, he

necessary to maintain its independence, and becoming one of Europe's most important shipbuilding and maritime powers.

The Ottoman Turks conquered most of inland Croatia in the 15th century, and challenged the Venetians—unsuccessfully—for control of the coastline. In the 17th century, the Turks were forced out and the Hapsburgs arrived, taking over inland Croatia. After Venice and Dubrovnik fell to Napoleon, the coast went to the Hapsburgs—beginning a long tradition of Austrians basking on Croatian beaches.

The Yugoslav Era, World War II, and the Ustaše

When the Austro-Hungarian Empire broke up at the end of World War I, Croats banded together with the Serbs, Bosnians, and Slovenes in the union that would become Yugoslavia. But virtually as soon as Yugoslavia was formed, many Croats already had regrets. The Croats worried that the Serbs would steer Yugoslavia discovered a top-secret hotline to Milošević's desk. And even today, Croatian newspapers routinely turn up decade-old photos of clandestine summits between the two leaders in Vienna.

To ensure that he stayed in power, Tuđman played fast and loose with his new nation's laws. He was notorious for changing the constitution as it suited him. By the late 1990s, when his popularity was slipping, Tuđman extended Croatian citizenship to anyone in the world who had Croatian heritage—a ploy aimed at getting votes from Croats living in Bosnia, who were sure to line up with him on the far right.

Through it all, Tuđman kept a tight grip on the media, making it illegal to report anything that would disturb the public—even if true. When Croatians turned on their TV sets and saw the flag flapping in the breeze to the strains of the national anthem, they knew something was up...and switched to CNN to get the real story. In this oppressive environment, many bright, young Croatians fled the country, causing a "brain drain" that hampered the country's recovery after the war.

Tuđman died of cancer at the end of 1999. While history will probably judge him harshly, the opinion in today's Croatia is qualified. Most agree that Tuđman was an important and even admirable figure in the struggle for Croatian statehood, but he ultimately went too far and got too greedy. Tuđman's political party is still active, frequently naming streets, squares, and bridges for this "hero" of Croatian nationalism. But if he were still alive, Tuđman would be standing trial in The Hague next to Milošević.

to their own purposes. So when the Nazis invaded and installed a puppet government—called the Ustaše—many Croats supported them, believing that fascism could provide them with greater independence from Serbia. Ustaše concentration camps were used to murder not only Jews and Roma (Gypsies), but also Serbs. Hot-tempered debate rages even today about how many Serbs died at the hands of the Ustaše—estimates vary wildly, from 25,000 to over a million, but most legitimate historians put the number in the hundreds of thousands.

Cardinal Alojzije Stepinac was one Croat who made the mistake of backing the Ustaše. By most accounts, Stepinac was a mild-mannered, extremely devout man who didn't agree with the extremism of the Ustaše...but also did little to fight it. When Tito came to power, he arrested, tried, and imprisoned Stepinac, who died under house arrest in 1960. In the years since, Stepinac has become a martyr for Catholics generally and Croat nationalists specifically. But even though he's the single most revered figure of Croatian Catholicism, Stepinac remains highly controversial and unpopular among Serbs.

At the end of World War II, the Ustaše were forced out by Tito's Partisan army, and Croatia once again became part of a united Yugoslavia. The union would hold together for more than 40 years...until it broke apart under Serbian President Slobodan Milošević and Croatian President Franjo Tuđman.

For all the details on Yugoslavia and its break-up, see the Understanding Yugoslavia chapter, page 750.

Independence Regained

Croatia became its own nation in 1991 after nine centuries of foreign domination. The Croatians seized their hard-earned freedom with a nationalist fervor that bordered on fascism. This was a heady and absurd time, which today's Croatians recall with disbelief, sadness...and maybe a tinge of nostalgia.

In the Croatia of the early 1990s, even the most bizarre notions seemed possible. Croatia's first post-Yugoslav president, the extreme nationalist Franjo Tuđman, proposed implausible directives for the new nation—such as privatizing all of the nation's resources and handing them over to 200 super-elite families (which, thankfully for everyone else, never happened). The government began calling the language "Croatian" rather than "Serbo-Croatian," creating new words from specifically Croat roots (see "Croatian Language," below). The Croats even briefly considered replacing the Roman alphabet with the ninth-century Glagolitic script to invoke Croat culture and further differentiate Croatian from Serbia's Cyrillic alphabet. Fortunately for tourists, this plan didn't take off.

After Tuđman's death in 1999, Croatia began the new millennium with a more truly democratic leader, Stipe Mesić. The popular Mesić, who was once aligned with Tuđman, split when Tuđman's politics grew too extreme. Tuđman spent years tampering with the constitution to give himself more and more power, but when Mesić took over, he reversed those changes and handed more authority back to the parliament.

In 2003, Croatia applied for membership in the European Union. While they're officially an EU candidate country, progress towards membership has occasionally been stalled by Croatia's hesitation to arrest and extradite war criminals to The Hague. But pro-EU President Stipe Mesić's re-election in 2005 is a clear signal that most Croatians are optimistic about becoming a part of a united Europe. After a fitful adjustment to independence, today's Croatia is on the right track.

Croatian Food

Like its people, the food in Croatia's different regions has been shaped by various influences—predominantly Italian, Turkish, and Hungarian. No single cuisine is distinctly Croatian. Choosing between strudel and baklava on the same menu, you're constantly reminded that this is a land where East meets West.

Balkan flavors are everywhere—especially in the inland part of the country (such as near the Plitvice Lakes), where Ottoman influences were strongest (see "Balkan Flavors" on page 580). To the north (Zagreb) and east (Slavonia), the food has more of a Hungarian flavor—heavy on meat, and served with cabbage, noodles, or potatoes (see "Hungarian Food," page 374).

On the Dalmatian Coast, seafood is a specialty, and the Italian influence is obvious. Dalmatians say that a fish should swim three times: first in the sea, then in olive oil, and finally in wine—when you eat it. You can get all kinds of seafood along the coast: fish, scampi, mussels, calamari, you name it. On menus, prices for seafood dishes are listed by the kilogram (figure about a half kilo, or one pound, for a large portion). Consider *riblja juha*—fish soup.

If you're not a seafood eater, there's plenty of pizza and pasta to choose from. Another Dalmatian specialty is *pašticada*—braised beef in a wine-and-herb sauce, usually served with gnocchi (not unlike beef Stroganoff). Dalmatia is also known for its mutton. Since the lambs graze on salty seaside herbs, the meat—often served on a spit—has a distinctive flavor.

Throughout Croatia, salad is served with the main dish unless you request it be served beforehand.

There are many good local varieties of cheese made with sheep's or goat's milk. Pag, an island in the Kvarner Gulf near Rijeka, produces a famous, very salty, fairly dry sheep's-milk cheese *(paški sir)*, which is said to carry the flavor of the sparse herbs that the sheep graze on.

For dessert, you'll find lots of good, homemade ice cream *(sladoled)*. Dalmatia's typical dessert is flan (crème caramel), which they call *rozata*.

As in most Slavic countries, *voda* is water, *kava* gets you coffee, *pivo* is beer, and *vino* gets you wine. Mineral water is *mineralna voda*. Jamnica is the main Croatian brand of bottled water, but I find it strangely salty—I prefer the harder-to-find Bistra or Studenac. The most popular Croatian beers are Ožujsko and Karlovačko, but you'll also see quite a bit of Slovene-produced

Balkan Flavors

All of the countries of the Balkan Peninsula—basically from Slovenia to Greece—have several foods in common. The Ottoman Turks, who controlled much of this territory for centuries, imported some goodies that remained standard fare here long after they left town. Whether you're in Slovenia, Croatia, Bosnia-Herzegovina, Serbia, or Albania, here are some local tastes worth seeking out.

A popular fast food you'll see everywhere is **burek** (BOO-rehk)—phyllo dough filled with meat, cheese, spinach, or apples. The more familiar **baklava** is phyllo dough layered with honey and nuts.

Grilled meats are a staple of Balkan cuisine. You'll most often see **ražnjići** (RAZH-nyee-chee—small pieces of steak on a skewer, like a shish kebab) and **čevapčići** (cheh-VAHP-chee-chee—meat that's chopped up and grilled, sometimes served in a pita wrap), and sometimes you'll come across **pljeskavica** (plehs-kah-VEET-suh—similar to *čevapčići,* except the meat is in the form of a hamburger-like patty).

While Balkan cuisine favors meat, a nice veggie complement is **đuveđ** (JOO-vedge)—a spicy mix of stewed vegetables, flavored with tomatoes and peppers.

And you just can't eat any of this stuff without the ever-present condiment **ajvar** (EYE-var). Made from red bell pepper and eggplant, *ajvar* is like ketchup with a kick. Many Americans pack a bottle of this distinctive, flavorful sauce to remember the flavors of the Balkans when they get back home.

Laško. When toasting with some new Croatian friends, raise your glass with a hearty *"Živjeli!"* (ZHEE-vyeh-lee).

Croatia has good wine, but it's comparatively expensive. The north of the country primarily produces whites *(bijelo vino)*, usually dry *(suho)* but sometimes semi-dry *(polusuho)*. The sunny mountains north of Zagreb are covered with vineyards producing whites. From Slavonia (Croatia's inland panhandle), you'll find *graševina*—crisp, dry, and acidic (like Welsh Riesling); Krauthaker and Enjingi are well-respected brands. The Istrian peninsula corks up some good whites, including *malvazija*, a very popular, light, mid-range wine (Muscat is also popular). Each Adriatic island produces its own wine. For example, on Korčula, look for *pošip* and *grk*; on Vis, it's *vugava*. As you move south, into the Dalmatian Coast, the wines turn red—which Croatians actually call "black wine" *(crno vino)*. The most common grape here is called *plavac* (more specifically *plavac mali*, or "little blue")—a distant cousin of Californian Zinfandel grapes. Generally speaking, the best coastal reds are

Key Croatian Phrases

English	Croatian	Pronounced
Hello. (formal)	*Dobar dan.*	DOH-bahr dahn
Ciao. (both "Hi" and "Bye"—informal)	*Bog.*	bohg
Do you speak English?	*Govorite li engleski?*	GOH-voh-ree-teh lee eng-LEHS-kee
yes / no	*da / ne*	dah / neh
Please. / You're welcome.	*Molim.*	MOH-leem
Can I help you?	*Izvolite?*	EEZ-voh-lee-teh
Thank you.	*Hvala.*	HVAH-lah
I'm sorry. / Excuse me.	*Oprostite.*	oh-PROH-stee-teh
Good.	*Dobro.*	DOH-broh
Goodbye.	*Do viđenija.*	doh-veed-JAY-neeah
one / two	*jedan / dva*	YEH-dahn / dvah
three / four	*tri / četiri*	tree / cheh TEE-ree
five / six	*pet / šest*	peht / shehst
seven / eight	*sedam / osam*	SEH-dahm / OH-sahm
nine / ten	*devet / deset*	DEH-veht / DEH-seht
hundred	*sto*	stoh
thousand	*tisuća*	TEE-soo-chah
How much?	*Koliko?*	KOH-lee-koh
local currency	*kuna*	KOO-nah
Where is...?	*Gdje je...?*	guh-DYEH yeh
...the toilet	*...vece*	VEHT-seh
men	*muški*	MOOSH-kee
women	*ženski*	ZHEHN-skee
water / coffee	*voda / kava*	VOH-dah / KAH-vah
beer / wine	*pivo / vino*	PEE-voh / VEE-noh
Cheers!	*Živjeli!*	ZHEE-vyeh-lee
the bill	*račun*	RAH-choon

produced on the long Pelješac Peninsula, across from Korčula. On the Pelješac Peninsula are specific regions with especially good reputations: Dingač is known as having the best possible climate for growing *plavac* grapes (Grgić, a brand produced by a Croatian-American vintner, is tops), but wines from Postup are also good. Aside from the Pelješac Peninsula, the island of Hvar produces good wines (also using *plavac* grapes).

Along the coast, it's very common to drink wine mixed with mineral water.

To request a menu, say, *"Meni, molim"* (MEH-nee, MOH-leem; "Menu, please"). To get the attention of your waiter, say *"Konobar"* (KOH-noh-bahr; "Waiter"). When he brings your food, he'll likely say, *"Dobar tek!" ("Bon appétit!").* When you're ready for the bill, ask for the *račun* (RAH-choon).

Croatian Language

Croatian was once known as "Serbo-Croatian," the official language of Yugoslavia. Most Yugoslav Republics—including Croatia, Serbia, and Bosnia-Herzegovina—spoke this same language (though Slovene is quite different). And while each of these countries has tried to distance its language from that of its neighbors since the war, the languages spoken in all of these places are still pretty much identical. The biggest difference is in the writing: Croatians and Bosnians use our Roman alphabet, while Serbs use Cyrillic letters.

In recent years, a fit of hyper-nationalism has led Croatia to artificially make its vocabulary different from Serbian. A decade ago, you'd catch a plane at the *Aerodrom.* Today, you'll catch that same flight at the *Zračna Luka*—a new coinage that combines the old Croatian words for "air" and "port." These new words, once created, are artificially injected into the lexicon. Croatians watching their favorite TV show will suddenly hear a character use a word they've never heard before...and think, "Oh, we have another new word."

Croatian is relatively easy to pronounce. The accent is usually on the first syllable (and never on the last). As with other Slavic tongues, c is pronounced "ts" (as in "bats"). The letter *j* is pronounced as "y." The letters *č* and *ć* are slightly different, but they both sound more or less like "ch"; *š* sounds like "sh" and *ž* sounds like "zh" (as in "leisure"). One Croatian letter that you won't see in other languages is *đ,* which sounds like the "dj" sound in "jeans." In fact, this letter is often replaced with "dj" in English.

As you're tracking down addresses, these definitions will help: *trg* (square), *ulica* (road), and *most* (bridge).

THE DALMATIAN COAST

Sunny beaches, succulent seafood, and a taste of *la dolce vita*...in Eastern Europe?

Croatia's Dalmatian Coast—the southern third of the country's coastline, stretching from Zadar to Dubrovnik—is Eastern Europe's Riviera. Many tourists were scared off after the recent war with Serbia (which damaged only Dubrovnik—completely repaired since). But now Croatia's resorts are aggressively advertising their once-again-discovered charms...and the tourists are back in droves. Despite the tourists, this place remains distinctly and stubbornly Croatian. You'll have to search pretty hard to find a McDonald's.

Dalmatia feels like Italy. Historically, it has more in common with Venice and Rome than Vienna or Budapest. People here speak Croatian with a lively Italian rhythm...and live the easygoing lifestyle that comes with it.

Dubrovnik is Croatia's single best destination. With an atmospheric Old Town and an epic history, it's like Venice without the canals. Big, bustling Split is the capital of the coast, boasting an in-love-with-life seaside promenade and a lived-in warren of twisting lanes sprouting out of a massive Roman palace. Right between them, the island town of Korčula is my favorite village on the Croatian coast.

It takes some doing to get down here, but it's worth it. The Dalmatian Coast is the cherry on top of a grand Eastern European adventure.

Getting to the Dalmatian Coast

The biggest problem with the Dalmatian Coast is getting here—it's a long haul from most other worthwhile destinations. But

The Dalmatian Coast

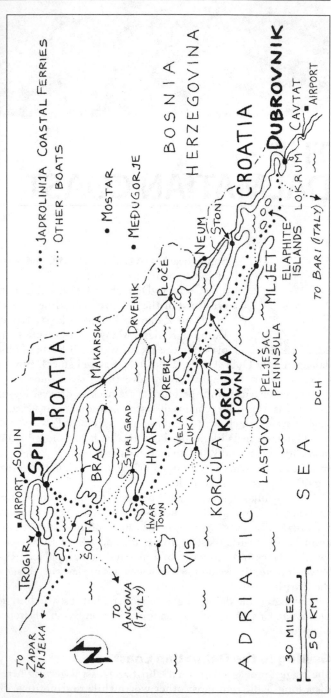

three new developments help make the trip nearly painless: an expressway, a high-speed train line, and budget flights.

By Car or Bus: The road trip from Zagreb to Split—which used to take seven hours—now takes less than five. That's because Croatia's new super-expressway is finally open. Travelers who used to opt for an all-day journey or a bleary-eyed night bus now leave Zagreb after an early dinner, and arrive in Split before bedtime. In the coming years, the expressway will be extended south to Dubrovnik, making that trip even quicker. For the latest, see www.hac.hr.

By Train: In May of 2005, Croatian Railways opened a brand-new "tilting train" line connecting Zagreb to Split. Because the trains can tilt slightly, and the tracks are banked, the new line is able to shave significant time off the trip—making it just less than six hours from the capital to the coast.

By Plane: Several low-cost airlines connect Dalmatia to the rest of Europe (for example, SkyEurope flies Budapest–Dubrovnik for less than $50; www.skyeurope.com). Croatia Airlines flies from Zagreb to Zadar, Split, and Dubrovnik. Ten seats on every Croatia Airlines flight are sold at very cheap promotional discount rates (for example, just €30 from Zagreb to Split or Dubrovnik) These cheap seats sell fast, so try to book at least three weeks ahead. You can find these deals online (www.croatiaairlines.hr), or contact a Croatia Airlines office (Croatian tel. 062-777-777, from outside Croatia call +385-1-487-2727). If the budget seats are already sold out for the flight you need, American-based Europe by Air sells one-way tickets on Croatia Airlines flights for $99, though taxes and other fees bring the price closer to $160 (tickets can be purchased only in the U.S., U.S. tel. 888-321-4737, www.europebyair.com).

By Boat: Overnight boats sail in each direction between Rijeka (on the northern Croatian coast, Rijeka is 3.5 hours by train from Zagreb and 2.5 hours by train from Ljubljana) and Split. While it's still much slower than the first three options, this can be a romantic way for nautical types to get to Dalmatia. (See below, for more about boat connections.)

Getting Around the Dalmatian Coast

There are no trains along the Dalmatian Coast (the southernmost station is in Split, with only a few daily connections to Zagreb). Once here, you'll rely on ferries, buses, or a rental car.

By Boat: Ferries and speedy hydrofoils inexpensively shuttle tourists between major cities and quiet island towns. Most of the ferries are run by Jadrolinija, which conveniently connects the three destinations in this chapter plus a lot more. Advance reservations are not necessary for deck passengers; you can almost always

Sailing between Croatia and Italy

Four different companies cross the Adriatic Sea to connect Croatia to Italy, running boats at least once daily in summer. Split is the primary hub, but you can also go from other cities (usually Dubrovnik or Zadar; some international ferries also stop at smaller Dalmatian towns). Almost all boats go to Ancona, Italy. Most trips are overnight and last 8–10 hours, but there is one super-fast catamaran (by Aliscafi SNAV) that takes only 4.5 hours. All four companies have offices in Split's main ferry terminal.

Slow Night Boats: Figure about €40 per person for one-way deck passage (about 10–20 percent more in peak season, roughly July–Aug; sometimes even more on weekends). On-board accommodation costs extra (about €10 per person for a couchette in a 4-berth compartment, €45 per person in 2-bed compartment with private shower and WC). Three different companies operate night boats to Italy: **Jadrolinija** goes from Split to Ancona, from Zadar to Ancona, and from Dubrovnik to Bari (Croatian tel. 051/211-444, www.jadrolinija.hr); **Blue Line** sails from Split to Ancona, stopping en route at either Stari Grad (on island of Hvar) or Vis (can book at SEM Marina travel agency in Split, tel. 021/352-553, www.bli-ferry.com); and **Tirrenia Navigazione** (Divisione Adriatica) sails from Split to Ancona (can book at Jadroagent in Split, tel. 021/338-335, Italian tel. 081-317-2999, www.tirrenia.it).

Fast Daytime Boat: Aliscafi SNAV is the speedy catamaran that connects Split and Ancona in just 4.5 hours (€64 1-way, or €82 in peak season—late July–early Sept). They also zip from Zadar to Ancona (3 hours, same price), and from Split to Stari Grad (on Hvar island), then on to the Italian town of Pescara (4.75 hours total, €70 1-way or €90 in peak season). Because these boats are faster and smaller, they're also weather-dependent—so they don't run off-season (all boats sail daily mid-June–mid-Sept, Croatian tel. 021/322-252, Italian tel. 081-428-5555, www.snav.it).

Note that in Italian, Split is "Spalato" (which is also the sound you hear if seasickness gets the best of you).

find a seat on the deck or in the on-board café. To reserve a cabin or take a car, it's smart to make the arrangements several weeks in advance (main office in Rijeka: tel. 051/211-444, fax 051/211-485, www.jadrolinija.hr, passdept_e@jadrolinija.hr). I've listed the most useful boat schedules in the "Transportation Connections" section for each destination.

By Bus: Getting to Split by bus is quick and easy—now that the expressway from Zagreb is finished, express buses can make it to Split in just five hours. But once in Dalmatia, things are still fairly slow. While the expressway will eventually be extended to Dubrovnik, for now, busing between Split and Dubrovnik takes five hours (departures nearly hourly). From Dubrovnik, only one direct bus per day goes along the main line to the island town of Korčula (but it's no faster than the boat—about 4 hours). Don't attempt the lengthy bus connection between Split and Korčula; take the boat instead.

If you're headed south along the coast, sitting on the right side while facing forward comes with substantially better scenery (sit on the left for northbound buses).

By Car: Considering the long distances, cheap and frequent buses, fun boat options, and worthlessness of a car in Dubrovnik or Split, those simply lacing together the major sights are better off without a car. Drivers should be prepared for twisty seaside roads, wonderful views, and plenty of tempting stopovers. As you approach any town, follow the signs to *Centar* (usually also signed with a bull's-eye symbol). Get parking advice from your hotel, or look for the blue-and-white *P* signs. Notice that between Split and Dubrovnik, you'll actually pass through Bosnia-Herzegovina for a few miles (the borders are a breezy formality, but you may need to flash your passport). This tiny strip of land, once squeezed between the Republics of Venice and Dubrovnik, was ceded to the Turks in the 18th century...and, in a way, it still belongs to them. The Bosnian resort town of **Neum** has several relatively inexpensive resort hotels (catering to Bosnians, as well as budget-conscious tourists from everywhere). Neum is popular with both Bosnians and Croatians for its cheap shopping. So that future Dalmatian Coast traffic can avoid the borders, the Croatian government is hoping to build a bridge that bypasses Neum (connecting Croatian territory just north of Neum to the Pelješac Peninsula, across the harbor).

Helpful Hints

Slick Pavement: Dalmatian old towns, with their well-polished pavement stones and many slick stairs, can be quite treacherous, especially after a rainstorm. Tread with care.

Siesta: Dalmatians eat their big meal at lunch, then take a traditional Mediterranean siesta. This means that many stores, museums, and churches close in the mid-afternoon. It can make for frustrating sightseeing...but you're on vacation. If you can't beat 'em, join 'em.

Seasonal Changes: Dalmatia's crowds fluctuate wildly by season. Some museums literally double their opening hours overnight when peak season hits. But here on the Adriatic, schedules are made to be broken, and opening times can change suddenly based on demand. The hours I've listed *should* be right...but if you have your heart set on a certain sight, confirm times with the TI on your arrival.

Dubrovnik

Dubrovnik is a living fairytale that shouldn't be missed. It feels like a small town today, but 500 years ago, Dubrovnik was a major maritime power, with the third biggest navy in the Mediterranean. Still jutting confidently into the sea and ringed by thick medieval walls, Dubrovnik deserves its nickname: the Pearl of the Adriatic. Within the ramparts, the traffic-free Old Town is a fun jumble of quiet, cobbled back lanes; tasty seafood restaurants; narrow, steep alleys; and kid-friendly squares. After all these centuries, the buildings still hint at old-time wealth, and the central promenade remains the place to see and be seen.

Dubrovnik, which feels Italian, actually began as a Roman colony. Although Croatian eventually became the official language, even today, people from Dubrovnik are teased by their Zagreb cousins for their Italian-influenced accent and vocabulary.

The city's charm is the sleepy result of its no-nonsense past. Busy merchants, the salt trade, and shipbuilding made Dubrovnik rich. But the city's most valued commodity was always its freedom—even today, you'll see the proud motto *Libertas* displayed all over town (see *"Libertas"* sidebar).

Dubrovnik flourished in the 15th and 16th centuries, but an earthquake destroyed nearly everything in 1667. Most of today's buildings in the Old Town are post-quake Baroque, although a few palaces, monasteries, and convents survive from Dubrovnik's earlier Golden Age.

Dubrovnik remained a big tourist draw through the Tito years, bringing in much-needed hard currency from Western visitors. Consequently, the city was never given the hard socialist patina of other Yugoslav cities (such as the nearby Montenegrin capital Podgorica, then known as "Titograd").

As Yugoslavia fell apart, the Croats fought for their independence. The 1991 war took its toll, and Dubrovnik was devastated (see "The Siege of Dubrovnik" sidebar, page 596). Imagine having your youthful memories of good times spent romping in the surrounding hills replaced by visions of heavily armed soldiers shooting down on your city. The only physical reminders of the war in today's Dubrovnik are lots of new, orange roof tiles...but locals who lived through the war will be forever hardened.

While the war killed tourism in the 1990s, today the crowds are back. The city's popularity is steadily approaching pre-war highs,

Libertas

Libertas—liberty—has always been close to the heart of every Dubrovnik citizen. Dubrovnik was a proudly independent republic for centuries, even as most of Croatia became Venetian and Hungarian. Dubrovnik believed so strongly in *libertas* that it was the first foreign state in 1776 to officially recognize an upstart, experimental republic called the United States of America.

In the Middle Ages, the city-state of Dubrovnik (then called Ragusa) had to buy its independence from whomever was strongest—Byzantium, Venice, Hungary, the Turks—sometimes paying off more than one at a time. Dubrovnik's ships flew whichever flags were necessary to stay free, earning the nickname "Town of Seven Flags." As time went on, Europe's big-league nations were glad to have a second major seafaring power in the Adriatic to balance the Venetian threat. A free Dubrovnik was more valuable than a pillaged, plundered Dubrovnik.

In 1808, Napoleon conquered the Adriatic and abolished the Republic of Dubrovnik. After Napoleon was defeated, the fate of the continent was decided at the Congress of Vienna. But Dubrovnik's delegate was denied a seat at the table. The more powerful nations, no longer concerned about Venice and fed up after years of being sweet-talked by Dubrovnik, were afraid that the delegate would play old alliances off of each other to reestablish an independent Republic of Dubrovnik. Instead, the city became a part of the Hapsburg Empire, and entered a long period of decline.

Libertas still hasn't died in Dubrovnik. In the surreal days of the early 1990s, when Yugoslavia was reshuffling itself, a movement for the creation of a new Republic of Dubrovnik gained some momentum (led by a judge who, in earlier times, had convicted others for the same ideas). But today's locals are content to be part of an independent Republic of Croatia.

the economy is booming, and Dubrovnik is thriving once again.

Planning Your Time

Dubrovnik has several pleasant, one-star sights: a pair of convents turned-museums, a few mildly interesting museums, and Europe's oldest pharmacy. The real attraction here is the city itself. While Dubrovnik could easily be seen in a day, a second day to unwind makes the long trip here more worthwhile.

Start your day at the Pile Gate, just outside the Old Town. Walk around the city's walls to get your bearings, then work your way down the main drag, dropping in at any museums or churches

Greater Dubrovnik

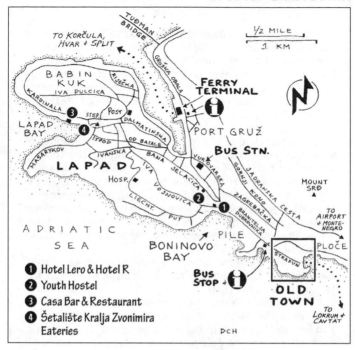

1 Hotel Lero & Hotel R
2 Youth Hostel
3 Casa Bar & Restaurant
4 Šetalište Kralja Zvonimira
   Eateries

that appeal to you. To squeeze in the most into a single day (or with a 2nd day), consider a boat excursion from the Old Port (boating to Lokrum Island, just offshore, requires the least brainpower—see page 606).

ORIENTATION

(area code: 020)
All of the sights worth seeing are in Dubrovnik's traffic-free, walled **Old Town** (Stari Grad) peninsula. The main pedestrian promenade through the middle of town is called Stradun (nobody uses its official name, "Placa"); from this artery, the Old Town climbs uphill in both directions to the walls. The Old Town connects to the mainland through three gates (Pile Gate, to the west; Ploče Gate, to the east; and a small, nameless gate at the top of Boškovićeva). The Old Port (Gradska Luka), with leisure boats to nearby destinations, is at the east end of town. While greater Dubrovnik has about 30,000 people, the local population within the Old Town is just 5,000 in the winter—and even less in summer, when many residents move out to rent their apartments to tourists (see "Sleeping," below).

The **Pile** (PEE-leh) neighborhood, a pincushion of tourist services, is just outside the western end of the Old Town (through Pile Gate). Right in front of the gate, you'll find a TI (with Internet access, see below), ATMs, a post office, the Croatia Airlines office, taxis, buses (heading to hotels on Boninovo Bay and Lapad Peninsula), a cheap Konzum grocery store, and the Atlas travel agency (which books private rooms—see "Helpful Hints," below). Just off this strip are some of Dubrovnik's best *sobe* (rooms in private homes—see "Sleeping," page 607). This is also the starting point for my self-guided "Welcome to Dubrovnik" walk (see page 594).

A mile or two away from the Old Town are beaches peppered with old, expensive resort hotels. My favorites are around **Boninovo Bay** (not too far from the Old Town—see "Sleeping—Hotels," page 613), but most cluster on the lush **Lapad Peninsula** to the west (buses run frequently from just outside Pile Gate and take about 15 min). North of Lapad Peninsula is **Port Gruž**, where ferries connect Dubrovnik to other Adriatic destinations.

In 2005, Dubrovnik re-named two of its busiest streets to commemorate the recent war. The road once called Dr. Ante Starčevića, which stretches from the Pile Gate towards Boninovo Bay and the Lapad Peninsula, became Branitelja Dubrovnika (literally, "Street of the Dubrovnik Defenders"). The road once called Put Republike, in front of the bus station, became Vukovarska (named for the northern Croatian city devastated by a Serb siege—see the Understanding Yugoslavia chapter, page 750). I've used the current names in this chapter, but don't be confused by out-of-date maps and publications.

Tourist Information

Dubrovnik's TI has three branches (hours can fluctuate with demand, www.tzdubrovnik.hr): right on the main drag in the **Old Town**, a few blocks in from the Pile Gate (daily May–Oct 8:00–24:00, Nov–April 8:00–20:00, tel. 020/321-561); in the **Pile** neighborhood just outside the Old Town, 100 yards up the street from the Pile Gate (May–Oct daily 8:00–20:00; Nov–April Mon–Fri 9:00–16:00, Sat 9:00–13:00, closed Sun; Branitelja Dubrovnika 7, tel. 020/427-591; Internet access in the same office—see "Helpful Hints," below); and across the street from the Jadrolinija ferry dock at **Port Gruž** (same hours as Pile TI, Gruška obala, tel. 020/417-983). All are government-run and legally can't sell you anything—but they can answer questions and give you a copy of the free monthly information booklet *Dubrovnik Riviera*, which contains helpful maps, hotel and restaurant listings, bus and ferry schedules, current museum prices and hours, and more. The TIs also give out a free monthly events brochure and a town map. If

Dubrovnik Essentials

English	Croatian	Pronounced
Old Town	Stari Grad	STAH-ree grahd
Old Port	Stara Luka	STAH-rah LOO-kah
Pile Gate	Gradska Vrata Pile	GRAHD-skah VRAH-tah PEE-leh
Ploče Gate	Gradska Vrata Ploče	GRAHD-skah VRAH-tah PLOH-cheh
Main Promenade	Stradun, Placa	STRAH-doon, PLAHT-sah
Adriatic Sea	Jadran	YAH-drahn

you need a room and the TI isn't busy, a staff person might be willing to call around to find a place for you.

Arrival in Dubrovnik

By Boat: The big boats arrive at Port Gruž, two miles northwest of the Old Town. On the road in front of the ferry terminal, you'll find a bus stop (#1a, #1b, and #3 go to Old Town's Pile Gate; wait on side of street facing the water) and a taxi stand (figure 70 kn to the Old Town and most hotels). Across the street is the Jadrolinija office (with an ATM out front) and a TI. You can book a private room *(soba)* at Atlas Travel Agency (room-booking desk in boat terminal building) or at Gulliver Travel Agency (behind TI); you'll likely also be ambushed by locals wanting you to stay at their place (for more on the *sobe* option, see page 607).

By Bus: Dubrovnik's bus station (Autobusni Kolodvor) is 1.5 miles northwest of the Old Town, where Lapad Peninsula connects to the mainland (Vukovarska 19). Out front, you'll find city bus stops (#1a, #1b, #3, #6, and #9 to Old Town's Pile Gate) and a taxi stand (about 50 kn to the Old Town and most hotels). Bus info: tel. 060-305-070.

By Plane: Dubrovnik's small airport (Zračna Luka) is in a place called Ćilipi, 13 miles south of the city. A Croatia Airlines bus leaves from Dubrovnik's bus station 90 minutes before most flights, and meets most arriving flights at the airport (30 kn, 40 min). If you're staying in or near the Old Town, you'll find it more convenient to catch the airport bus at a stop that's just up the stairs from the top of town (follow Boškovićeva up and out of the Old Town, go up the stairs, and swing right at the busy Krešimira street; bus reaches this stop five minutes after leaving station, wave it down or it might pass you by). Airport info: tel. 020/773-333, www.airport-dubrovnik.hr. Figure 220 kn for a taxi or hotel shuttle between the airport and the center.

Helpful Hints

Dubrovnik Summer Festival: Dubrovnik is most crowded during its Summer Festival, a month and a half of theater and musical performances held annually from July 10 to August 25 (www.dubrovnik-festival.hr).

Internet Access: The best access is at the **Dubrovnik Internet Centar,** inside the TI just outside the Pile Gate (5 kn/15 min; May–Oct daily 8:00–23:30; Nov–April Mon–Sat 8:00–21:00, closed Sun; Branitelja Dubrovnika 7). Internet signs advertise handy but more expensive terminals along the Old Town's main drag.

Best Views: Walking the wall at sunset is a treat; film disappears fast. A stroll east of the city walls offers nice views back on the Old Town (the best light is early in the day).

Getting Around Dubrovnik

If you're staying in or near the Old Town, everything is easily walkable. But those sleeping on Boninovo Bay or the Lapad Peninsula will want to get comfortable with the buses—they work great, and the system is easy.

By Bus: Libertas runs Dubrovnik's public buses. Tickets, which are good for an hour, are cheaper if you buy them in advance from a kiosk or your hotel (8 kn, ask for *autobusna karta*) than if you buy them from the bus driver (10 kn, no change given). When you enter the bus, validate your ticket in the machine. All buses stop near the Old Town, just in front of the Pile Gate. From here, they fan out to just about anywhere you'd want to go (hotels on Boninovo Bay and Lapad Peninsula, long-distance bus station, ferry terminal). You'll find bus schedules and a map in the TI booklet.

By Taxi: Taxis start at 25 kn, then cost 8 kn per kilometer. You call for a taxi based on the neighborhood you're in. Old Town's Pile Gate: tel. 020/424-343; Lapad Peninsula: tel. 020/435-715; bus station: tel. 020/357-044; ferry dock: tel. 020/418-112; Ploče (just east of Old Town): tel. 020/423-164.

TOURS

Two big companies (Elite and Atlas) offer tours of Dubrovnik (about 175 kn for a 2.5-hour bus-plus-walking tour of the city), but I wouldn't waste my time with them. Instead, do it on your own using this book, or hire a local guide. I enjoyed working with Štefica Čurić (480 kn for a 2-hour private tour, tel. 020/450-133, mobile 091-345-0133, dugacarapa@yahoo.com).

Elite and Atlas also offer €35–55 **excursions** to nearby destinations. Popular day-trips include the Elaphite Islands, Cavtat (a town just south of Dubrovnik), Montenegro's Bay of Kotor, the national park on Mljet Island, Korčula, and Mostar, in Bosnia-Herzegovina. I went on Elite's day-trip to Mostar. It efficiently packed several interesting destinations into a single day, but it was crowded (49 tourists on a 50-seat bus) and the guide's commentary was uninspired at best ("The bridge is 300 meters long and 90 meters tall"). These trips can be a convenient way to tackle a complicated day trip if you don't want to hassle with public transportation. If you're an independent type, you can slip away from the group as soon as you know the rendezvous time and place. Elite and Atlas are basically interchangeable, and you can buy tickets at most travel agencies and hotel lobbies. If one company isn't running a tour to your preferred destination when you're in town, check with the other one.

SELF-GUIDED WALK

Welcome to Dubrovnik: Strolling the Stradun

Running through the heart of Dubrovnik's Old Town is the Stradun promenade—packed with people and lined with sights. This walk, worth ▲▲▲, offers an ideal introduction to Dubrovnik's charms. It takes about a half hour, not counting sightseeing stops.

• *Begin at the busy square in front of the west entrance to the Old Town, the Pile (PEE-leh) Gate.*

Pile Neighborhood: This bustling area is the nerve center of Dubrovnik's tourist industry—it's where the real world meets the fantasy of Dubrovnik (see "Orientation," page 590). Across from the big Atlas Travel Agency building is a leafy café terrace. Wander over to the edge of the terrace and ponder the imposing walls of the Pearl of the Adriatic. The huge, fortified peninsula just outside the city walls is the **Fort of St. Lawrence** (Tvrđava Lovrijenac), Dubrovnik's oldest fortress and one of the top venues for the Dubrovnik Summer Festival. Shakespearean plays are often performed here, occasionally starring Goran Višnjić, the Croatian actor who has become an American star on the TV show *ER*.

• *Now go through the...*

Pile Gate (Gradska Vrata Pile): Inside the Pile Gate and to the left, a white sign shows where each bomb dropped on the Old Town in the recent war.

Passing the rest of the way through the gate, you'll find a lively little square surrounded by landmarks. To the left, a steep stairway leads up to the imposing **Minčeta Tower.** This is a good starting point for Dubrovnik's best activity, walking around the top of the wall (for details, see page 599).

Next to the stairway is the small **Church of St. Savior** (Crkva Svetog Spasa). This votive church was built as a thanks to God after Dubrovnik made it through a 1520 earthquake. When the massive 1667 quake destroyed the city, this church was one of the only buildings left intact. And during the recent war, the church survived another close call when a shell exploded on the ground right in front of it (you can still see pockmarks from the shrapnel).

The big, round structure in the middle of the square is **Onofrio's Big Fountain** (Velika Onofrijea Fontana). In the Middle Ages, Dubrovnik had a complicated aqueduct system that brought water from the mountains seven miles away. The water ended up here, at the town's biggest fountain, before continuing through the city. This plentiful supply of water, large reserves of salt (a key source of Dubrovnik's wealth), and a massive granary (see Rupe Museum listing, page 605) made little, independent Dubrovnik very siege-resistant.

The big building on the left just beyond the small Church of St. Savior is the **Franciscan Monastery Museum.** This building, with a delightful cloister and one of Europe's oldest pharmacies, is well worth touring (see page 601).

• *When you're finished taking in the sights on this square, continue* ...

Strolling the Stradun: Dubrovnik's main promenade—officially called Placa, but better known as Stradun—is alive with locals and tourists alike. This is the heartbeat of the city: an Old World shopping mall by day and sprawling cocktail party after dark, when everybody seems to be doing the traditional *korzo,* or evening stroll—flirting, ice-cream-licking, flaunting, and gawking. A coffee and some of Europe's best people-watching in a prime Stradun café is one of travel's great $3 bargains.

When Dubrovnik was just getting its start in the seventh century, this street was a canal. Romans fleeing from the invading Slavs lived on the island of Ragusa, and the Slavs settled on the shore. In the 11th century, the canal separating Ragusa from the mainland was filled in, the towns merged, and a unique Slavic-Roman culture and language blossomed. While originally much more higgledy-piggledy, this street was rebuilt in the current, more uniform style after the 1667 earthquake.

• *At the end of the Stradun is the Ploče Gate. Just inside the gate is the lively Luža Square. Its centerpiece is...*

The Siege of Dubrovnik

In June 1991, Croatia declared independence from Yugoslavia. Within weeks, the nations were at war (for more on the war, see the Understanding Yugoslavia chapter, page 750). Though warfare raged in the Croatian interior, nobody expected that the bloodshed would reach Dubrovnik.

At 6:00 in the morning on October 1, 1991, Dubrovnik residents were stunned to see Yugoslav warships on the horizon. The ships shelled the hillsides above Dubrovnik to disable a strategic communications tower (which you can see today) and clear the way for land troops, who quickly surrounded the city. Within a month, the Serb-dominated Yugoslav National Army began bombing the Pearl of the Adriatic. Defenseless townspeople took shelter in their cellars, and sometimes even huddled together in the city wall's 15th-century forts. For the first time in centuries, Dubrovnik's city walls were used to protect its people from an invading army.

Dubrovnik resisted the siege better than anyone expected. The Serbs were hoping that residents would flee the town, allowing the Yugoslav National Army to move in. But the people of Dubrovnik stayed. Many brave young locals lost their lives when they slung old hunting rifles over their shoulders and, under the cover of darkness, climbed the hills above Dubrovnik to meet the Serbs face-to-face.

After eight months of bombing, Dubrovnik was liberated by the Croatian army, which attacked Serb positions from the north. By the end of the war, 100 civilians were dead, along with more than 200 Dubrovnik citizens who lost their lives fighting for their

Orlando's Column (Orlandov Stup): Columns like this were typical of towns in northern Germany. Dubrovnik erected the column in 1417, soon after it had shifted allegiances from the oppressive Venetians to the Hungarians. By putting a northern European

symbol in the middle of its most prominent square, Dubrovnik decisively distanced itself from Venice. Anytime a decision was made by the Republic, the town crier came to Orlando's Column and announced the news. The step he stood on indicated the importance of his message—the higher up, the more important the news. It was also used as the pillory, where people were publicly punished. The thin line on the top step in front of Orlando is exactly as long as the hometown (much revered today as "Dubrovnik Defenders"). More than two-thirds of Dubrovnik's buildings had been damaged, and more than 30,000 people had to flee their homes—but the failed siege was finally over.

Why was Dubrovnik—so far from the rest of the fighting—dragged into the conflict? The Serbs wanted to catch the city and the region off-guard, gaining a toehold on the southern Dalmatian Coast so they could push north to Split, Croatia's second city. They also hoped to ignite pro-Serb passions in the nearby Serb-dominated areas of Bosnia and Montenegro. But perhaps most of all, Yugoslavia wanted to hit Croatia where it hurt—its proudest, most historic, and most beautiful city, the tourist capital of a nation dependent on tourism.

The war initially devastated the tourist industry. Now, to the casual observer, Dubrovnik seems virtually back to normal. Aside from a few pockmarks and bright, new roof tiles, there are few reminders of what happened here just over a decade ago. If you're curious, drop by a souvenir shop and page through the book *Dubrovnik in War*, filled with photos showing the city desolate and in flames.

Though the city itself has been repaired, the people of Dubrovnik are forever changed. Imagine living in an idyllic paradise, a place that attracted and awed visitors from around the world...and then watching it gradually blown to bits. It's understandable that Dubrovnik citizens are a little less in love with life than they once were.

statue's forearm. This mark was Dubrovnik's standard measurement—not for a foot, but for an "elbow" (no kidding).

• Now stand in front of Orlando's Column and orient yourself with a...

Luža Square Spin-Tour: Orlando is looking toward the **Sponza Palace** (Sponza-Povijesni Arhiv). This building, from 1522, is the finest surviving example of Dubrovnik's Golden Age in the 15th to 16th centuries; it's a combination of Renaissance (ground-floor arches) and Venetian Gothic (upstairs windows). Houses up and down the main promenade used to look like this, but after the 1667 earthquake, they were replaced with boring uniformity. This used to be the customs office *(dogana)*, but now it's an exhaustive archive of the city's history, with temporary art exhibits and a war memorial. The poignant **Memorial Room of Dubrovnik Defenders** (on the left as you enter) has photos of dozens of people from Dubrovnik who were killed fighting the Serbs in 1991. A TV screen and images near the ceiling show the devastation of the city. Though the English descriptions are (perhaps unavoidably) slanted to the Croat perspective, it's compelling to look in the eyes of the brave young men who didn't start this war...but were willing to finish it (free, daily 8:00–14:00, often later).

To the right of Sponza Palace is the town's Bell Tower (Gradski Zvonik). The original dated from 1444, but it was rebuilt when it started to slide in the 1920s. The big clock may be an octopus—but it has only one hand. Below that, the circle shows the phase of the moon (the greener, the fuller the moon). At the bottom, the old-fashioned digital readout tells the hour (in Roman numerals) and the minutes (in 5-min increments). At the top of each hour (and again 3 minutes later), the time is clanged out on the bell up top by two bronze bell ringers, Maro and Baro. (If this all seems like a copy of the very similar clock on St. Mark's Square in Venice, locals are quick to point out that this clock predates that one by several decades.) The clock still has to be wound every two days. Notice the little black hole between the moon phase and the "digital" readout: The clock-winder opens this window to get some light. During the recent war, the clock-winder's house was destroyed—with the keys inside. For days, the clock bell didn't run. But then, miraculously, the keys were discovered lying in the street. The excited Dubrovnik citizens came together in this square and cheered as the clock was wound and the bell chimed, signaling to the Serbs surrounding the city that they hadn't won yet.

The big building to the right of the Bell Tower is the **City Hall** (Vijećnica). Next to it is **Onofrio's Little Fountain** (Mala Onofrijea Fontana)—the little brother of the one at the other end of the Stradun—and the **Town Café** (Gradska Kavana), historically Dubrovnik's favorite spot for gossiping and people-watching. Recently renovated, this café is a great place for a scenic coffee break. They have prime seating here, overlooking the pedestrian square, or opposite, with views over the Old Port. Just down the street from the Town Café is the Rector's Palace, and then the cathedral (for more on each, see below).

Behind Orlando is **St. Blaise's Church** (Crkva Sv. Vlaha), dedicated to the patron saint of Dubrovnik. You'll see statues and paintings of St. Blaise all over town, always holding a model of the city in his left hand. According to legend, a millennium ago St. Blaise came to a local priest in a dream and warned him that the up-and-coming Venetians would soon attack the city. The priest alerted the authorities, who prepared for war. Of course, the prediction came true. St. Blaise has been a Dubrovnik symbol—and locals have resented Venice—ever since.

• *Your tour is finished. From here, you've got plenty of sightseeing options (all described below). As you face the Bell Tower, you can go up the street to the right to reach the Rector's Palace and Cathedral; you can walk through the gate straight ahead to reach the Old Port; or you*

can head through the gate and jog left to find the Dominican Monastery
Museum. Even more sights—including an old synagogue, an exhibit of
war photography, and the medieval granary—are in the steep streets
between the Stradun and the walls.

SIGHTS

All of Dubrovnik's sights are inside—or on top of—the Old
Town's walls.

Town Walls (Gradske Zidine)

Dubrovnik's single best attraction—easily worth ▲▲▲—is strolling the scenic mile around the city walls. As you meander along
this lofty perch—with a sea of red roofs on one side, and the actual
sea on the other—you'll get your bearings and snap pictures like
mad of the ever-changing views. Bring extra film and your map,
which you can use to pick out landmarks as you go to get the lay
of the land.

Walking the walls also offers
the best illustration of the damage Dubrovnik sustained during
the recent war. It's easy to see that
more than 70 percent of Dubrovnik's
roofs were replaced after the bomb-
ings (notice the new, bright-orange
tiles—and how some buildings sal-
vaged the old tiles, but have bright
20th-century ones underneath).

There have been walls here
almost as long as there's been a
Dubrovnik. The fortifications were
beefed up in the 15th century, when the Turks became a threat.
Around the perimeter are several substantial forts, which protected
residents both during the Republic of Dubrovnik's Golden Age
and during the recent war with Serbia.

You can enter the walls at three points: just inside the Pile
Gate, near the Dominican Monastery north of the Ploče Gate,
and by the Maritime Museum south of the Old Port. The highest
point is the Minčeta Tower, above the Pile Gate at the west end
of town. The tower, while empty, rewards those who climb it with
a fine view. If you climb here first from the Pile Gate and then
proceed clockwise, it's mostly downhill all the way around. Speed
demons with no cameras can walk the walls in less than an hour;
strollers and shutterbugs should plan on longer (30 kn to enter
walls, July–Aug daily 9:00–20:30, progressively shorter hours off-
season until 10:00–15:00 in mid-Nov–mid-March).

Dubrovnik's Old Town

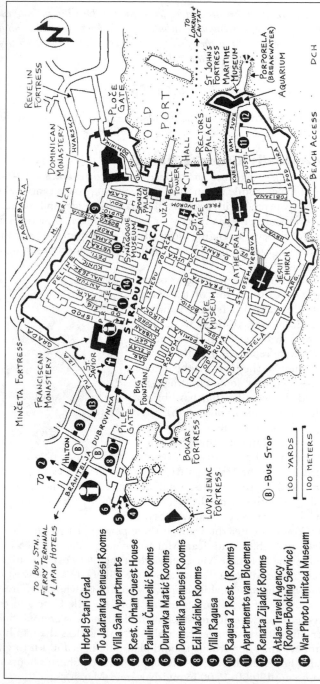

REVELIN FORTRESS

DOMINICAN MONASTERY

PLOČE GATE

OLD PORT

TO LOKRUM & CAVTAT

ST. JOHN'S FORTRESS

MARITIME MUSEUM

PORPORELA (BREAKWATER)

AQUARIUM

DCH

RECTOR'S PALACE

CITY HALL

BELL TOWER

SPONZA PALACE

SYNAGOGUE MUSEUM

PLACA

ST. BLAISE

CATHEDRAL

JESUIT CHURCH

RUPE MUSEUM

BEACH ACCESS

STRADUN

ZAGREBAČKA

MINČETA FORTRESS

FRANCISCAN MONASTERY

ST. SAVIOR

FRANCISCAN MONASTERY

BIG FOUNTAIN

PILE GATE

DUBROVNIKA

HILTON

BOKAR FORTRESS

LOVRIJENAC FORTRESS

TO BUS STN., FERRY TERMINAL & LAPAD HOTELS

B = Bus Stop

100 YARDS
100 METERS

1 Hotel Stari Grad
2 To Jadranka Benussi Rooms
3 Villa San Apartments
4 Rest. Orhan Guest House
5 Paulina Čumbelić Rooms
6 Dubravka Matić Rooms
7 Domenika Benussi Rooms
8 Edi Maćinko Rooms
9 Villa Ragusa
10 Ragusa 2 Rest. (Rooms)
11 Apartments van Bloemen
12 Renata Zijadić Rooms
13 Atlas Travel Agency (Room-Booking Service)
14 War Photo Limited Museum

You can rent a 30-kn audioguide, separate from the admission fee, for a narrated, one-hour circular tour of the walls (look for sales-men near the entry points).

Near the Pile Gate

This museum is just inside the Pile Gate.

▲**Franciscan Monastery Museum (Franjevački Samostan-Muzej)**—In the Middle Ages, Dubrovnik's monasteries flourished. While all you'll see here are a fine cloister and a one-room museum in the old pharmacy, it's a delightful space. Enter through the gap between the small church and the big monastery (15 kn, daily 9:00–18:00, maybe less off-season, Placa 2). Just inside the door, a century-old pharmacy still serves residents. (You'll see the monastery's original medieval pharmacy at the far end of the cloister.)

Explore the peaceful, sun-dappled **cloister.** Examine the capitals at the tops of the 60 Romanesque-Gothic double pillars. Each one is different. Notice that some of the portals inside the courtyard are made with a lighter-colored stone—these had to be repaired after being damaged in the recent war.

In the far corner stands the medieval **pharmacy.** Part of the Franciscans' mission was to contribute to the good health of the citizens, so they opened this pharmacy in 1317. The monastery has had a pharmacy in continual operation ever since. On display are jars, pots, and other medieval pharmacists' tools. The sick would come to get their medicine at the little window (on left side), which limited contact with the pharmacist and reduced the risk of passing on disease. Around the room, you'll also find some relics, old manuscripts, and a detailed painting of 16th-century Dubrovnik.

Near Luža Square

These sights are at the far end of the Stradun (nearest the Old Port, just inside the Ploče Gate). As you stand on Luža Square facing the Bell Tower, the Rector's Palace and Cathedral are up the street to the right (Pred Dvorom), and the Dominican Monastery Museum is through the gate and to the left.

▲**Rector's Palace (Knežev Dvor)**—In the Middle Ages, the Republic of Dubrovnik was ruled by a rector (similar to a Venetian doge), who was elected by the nobility. To prevent any one person from becoming too powerful, the rector's term was limited to one month. Most rectors were in their 50s—near the end of the average lifespan, and less likely to shake things up. During his term, a rector lived upstairs in this palace (20 kn, daily mid-April–Sept 9:00–18:00, Oct–mid-April 9:00–14:00, some posted English information, skip the 30-kn audioguide, 6-kn English booklet is helpful, Pred Dvorom 3).

The exterior is decorated in the Gothic-Renaissance mix (with particularly finely carved capitals) that was so common in Dubrovnik before the 1667 earthquake. The courtyard is a venue for the Summer Festival, hosting music groups ranging from the local symphony to the Vienna Boys' Choir. In the courtyard is the only secular statue created during the centuries-long Republic. Dubrovnik republicans, mindful of the dangers of hero-worship, didn't believe that any one citizen should be singled out. They made only one exception—for Miho Pracat (a.k.a. Michaeli Prazatto), a rich citizen who willed a fleet of ships to the city. But notice that Pracat's statue is displayed in here, behind closed doors, not out in public. Also on the ground floor are old prison cells.

On the mezzanine level (stairs on right as you enter), you'll find an impressive collection of antique pharmacy jars, a wimpy gun exhibit, and a ho-hum coin collection. On the upper floor (stairs on left as you enter) are old apartments that serve as a painting gallery. The only vaguely authentic room is the red room in the corner, decorated more or less as it was in 1500, when it was the rector's office. Mihajlo Hamzić's exquisite *Baptism of Christ* painting, inspired by Italian painter Andrea Mantegna, is an early Renaissance work from the "Dubrovnik School" (see "Dominican Monastery Museum," below).

▲Cathedral (Katedrala)—Dubrovnik's original 12th-century cathedral was funded largely by the English king Richard the Lionhearted. On his way back from the Third Crusade, Richard was shipwrecked nearby. He promised God that if he survived, he'd build a church on the spot where he landed—which happened to be on Lokrum Island, just offshore. At Dubrovnik's request, Richard agreed to build his token of thanks inside the city instead. It was the finest Romanesque church on the Adriatic... before it was destroyed by the 1667 earthquake. This version is 18th-century Roman Baroque.

Inside, you'll find an original Titian *(Assumption of the Virgin)*, a stark contemporary altar, and a quirky **treasury** *(riznica)* packed with 138 relics (church entry free, treasury entry-7 kn, Mon–Sat 9:00–20:00, Sun 11:00–17:30). Notice that there are three locks on the treasury door—the stuff in here was so valuable, three different VIPs (the rector, the bishop, and a local aristocrat) had to agree before it could be opened. On the table near the door are several of St. Blaise's body parts (pieces of his arm, skull, and leg—all encased in fancy silver).

In the middle of the wall above the altar, look for the crucifix with a piece of the "true cross." On a dig in Jerusalem, St. Helen (Emperor Constantine's mother) discovered what she believed to be the cross that Jesus was crucified on. It was brought to Constantinople, and the Byzantine czars doled out pieces of it to Balkan kings. Note the folding three-paneled altar painting (underneath the cross). Dubrovnik ambassadors packed this on road trips (such as their annual trip to pay off the Turks) so they could worship wherever they traveled. On the right side of the room, the silver casket supposedly holds the actual swaddling clothes of the Baby Jesus. Dubrovnik bishops secretly passed these clothes down from generation to generation...until a nun got wind of it, and told the whole town. Pieces of the cloth were cut off to miraculously heal the sick, especially new mothers recovering from a difficult birth. No matter how often it was cut, the cloth always went back to its original form. Then someone tried to use it on the wife of a Bosnian king. Since she was Muslim, it couldn't help her, and it never worked again. Whether or not it's true, this legend hints at the prickly relationships between faiths here in the Balkans.

▲**Dominican Monastery Museum (Dominikanski Samostan-Muzej)**—You'll find many of Dubrovnik's art treasures—paintings, altarpieces, and manuscripts—gathered around the peaceful Dominican Monastery cloister just north of Ploče Gate (10 kn, art buffs enjoy the 70-kn English book, daily May–Sept 9:00–18:00, off-season until 17:00).

One room contains paintings from the **"Dubrovnik School,"** the Republic's circa-1500 answer to the art boom in Florence and Venice. While the 1667 earthquake destroyed most of these paintings, about a dozen survive, and five of those are in this room. Don't miss the triptych by Nikola Božidarović, with St. Blaise holding a detailed model of 16th-century Dubrovnik. You'll see this image all over town.

The striking **church** is decorated with modern stained glass, a fine 13th-century pulpit that survived the earthquake (reminding visitors of the intellectual approach to scripture that characterized the Dominicans), and a precious 14th-century Paolo Veneziano crucifix hanging above the high altar. The most memorable piece of art in the church is the *Miracle of St. Dominic,* showing the founder of the order bringing a child back to life (over the altar to the right, as you enter). It was painted in the Realist style (late 19th century) by Vlaho Bukovac.

Near the Old Port (Stara Luka)

The picturesque Old Port, carefully nestled behind St. John's
Fort, faces away from what was
Dubrovnik's biggest threat, the
Venetians. The long seaside building across the bay on the left was
the medieval quarantine house. In
those days, all visitors were locked
in here for 40 days before entering
town. A bench-lined harborside
walk leads around the fort to a
breakwater, providing a peaceful

perch. At the port, you can haggle with captains selling excursions
(see "Activities," page 605).

Maritime Museum (Pomorski Muzej)—By the 15th century,
when Venice's nautical dominance was on the wane, Dubrovnik
emerged as a maritime power and the Mediterranean's leading
shipbuilding center. The Dubrovnik-built "argosy" boat (from the
word "Ragusa," an early name for the city) was the Cadillac of
ships, frequently mentioned by Shakespeare. This small museum
traces the history of Dubrovnik's most important industry with
contracts, maps, paintings, and models—all well-described in
English. Don't miss the poorly marked upstairs section, with the
best exhibits. Boaters will find the museum particularly interesting (15 kn, English booklet-5 kn, hours depend on demand, usually daily June–Aug 9:00–18:00, Sept–Oct 9:00–17:00, Nov–May
9:00–14:00, upstairs in St. John's Fort, at far—or south—end of
Old Port, tel. 020/323-904).

Aquarium (Akvarij)—Dubrovnik's aquarium, housed in the
cavernous St. John's Fort, is an old-school place, with 27 tanks on
one floor. A visit here allows you a close look at the local marine
life, and provides a cool refuge from the midday heat. The English
descriptions give your visit meaning (20 kn, kids-10 kn, daily
mid-June–Aug 9:00–21:00, mid-April–mid-June and Sept–Oct
9:00–19:00, Nov–mid-April 9:00–13:00, ground floor of St. John's
Fort, enter from Old Port).

Between the Stradun and the Mainland

These two museums are a few steps off the main promenade
towards the mainland.

Synagogue Museum (Sinagoga-Muzej)—When Jews were
forced out of Spain in 1492, many of them passed through here en
route to Turkey. Finding Dubrovnik to be a flourishing and relatively tolerant city, many stayed. Žudioska ulica (literally "Jewish
Street"), just inside Ploče Gate, became the ghetto in 1546. Today,
the same street is home to the second-oldest synagogue in Europe

(after Prague's). The top floor houses the synagogue itself (with the lattice windows through which Orthodox Jewish women would peer). Below that, a small museum with good English descriptions gives meaning to the various Torahs (including a 13th-century one from Spain) and other items—such as the written orders *(naredba)* that Jews in Nazi-era Yugoslavia had to identify their shops as Jewish-owned and wear armbands. (The Ustaše—the Nazi puppet government in Croatia—interned and executed not only Jews, but also Serbs and other people they considered undesirable; see page 576.) Of Croatia's 24,000 Jews, only 3,000 survived the Holocaust. Today, 45 Jews call Dubrovnik home, and a rabbi visits this synagogue five times a year from Zagreb (10 kn, May–Oct daily 10:00–20:00; Nov–April Mon–Fri 10:00–13:00, closed Sat–Sun; Žudioska ulica 5).

War Photo Limited—If the tragic story of wartime Dubrovnik has you in a pensive mood, drop by this new gallery with images of warfare from around the world. The brainchild of photojournalist Wade Goddard, this thought-provoking museum attempts to show the ugly reality of war through raw, often disturbing photographs taken in the field (25 kn; May–Sept daily 9:00–21:00; March–April and Oct Tue–Sat 10:00–16:00, Sun 10:00–14:00, closed Mon; closed Nov–Feb; Antuninska 6, tel. 020/322-166, www.warphotoltd.com).

Between the Stradun and the Sea

This museum hides several blocks uphill from the main promenade towards the sea (climb up Široka, which becomes Od Domina on its way to the museum).

▲**Rupe Granary and Ethnographic Museum (Etnografski Muzej Rupe)**—This huge, 16th-century building was Dubrovnik's biggest granary. *Rupe* means "holes"—and it's worth the price of entry just to look down into these cavernous underground grain stores, designed to maintain the perfect temperature to preserve the seeds (63 degrees Fahrenheit). When the grain had to be dried, it was moved upstairs—which today houses a surprisingly well-presented Ethnographic Museum, with tools, jewelry, clothing, and other artifacts from Dubrovnik's colorful history (5 kn, borrow English-language info sheet; June–Oct daily 9:00–18:00; Nov–May Mon–Sat 9:00–14:00, closed Sun).

ACTIVITIES

Swimming—If the weather's good and you've had enough of museums, spend a sunny afternoon at the beach. There are no sandy beaches on the mainland near Dubrovnik, but there are lots of suitable pebbly options, plus several concrete perches. If your hotel doesn't have a beach of its own, it can direct you to the nearest one. The best public beaches are Banje (just outside Ploče Gate, east of Old Town), the beach in the middle of Lapad Bay (near Hotel Kompas), and the nude beach on Lokrum Island (see below).

Lokrum Island—This island, just offshore from the Old Town, provides a handy escape from the city. Lokrum features a monastery-turned-Hapsburg-palace, a small botanical garden, an old military fort, hiking trails, a café, some rocky beaches, and a little lake called the "Dead Sea" (Mrtvo More) that's suitable for swimming. Since the 1970s, when Lokrum became the "Island of Love," it's been known for its nude sunbathing. If you'd like to subject skin that's never seen the sun to those burning rays (carefully), follow the *FKK* sign from the boat dock for about five minutes to the slabs of waterfront rock, where naturalists feel right at home. Boats run regularly from Dubrovnik's Old Port (35 kn round-trip, 5 kn for map, in summer hourly 9:00–17:00, in peak season until 19:00, none Oct–March).

Other Excursions by Boat from the Old Port—The Old Port is where tenders drop their cruisers, and where local captains set up tiny booths to hawk touristy boat trips. It's fun to chat with them, page through their sun-faded photo albums, and see if they can sell you on a short cruise.

In addition to Lokrum Island (above), boats go regularly to **Cavtat,** a small, forgettable port town 12 miles away...but a fun excuse to take a boat somewhere. You'll sail for 45 minutes, and return when you like (about 60 kn round-trip).

The best day trip from Dubrovnik is to join an excursion to the three **Elaphite Islands,** including a "fish picnic" cooked up by the captain as you cruise. The trip visits all three islands, with short stops at each (about 220 kn with lunch, 160 kn without, prices often soft—feel free to bargain, several boats depart daily at around 11:00, return around 18:00). Each island has sleepy escape mansions of old Dubrovnik aristocracy, fishing ports, shady forests, and sandy beaches. You generally stay 45 minutes each on Koločep and Šipan, and three hours on the most interesting island, Lopud. To get to the Elaphite Islands without a tour (on a cheap ferry), you'll sail from Dubrovnik's less convenient Port Gruž (see "Arrival in Dubrovnik—By Boat," page 592).

NIGHTLIFE

Dubrovnik's Old Town is one big, romantic parade of relaxed and happy people out strolling. The main drag is brightly lit and packed with shops, cafés, and bars, all open late. This is a fun scene. And if you walk away from the crowds, out on the port, or even up on the city walls, you'll be alone with the magic of the Pearl of the

Adriatic. Everything feels—and is—very safe after dark.

Bars—**Cold Drinks "Buža,"** clinging scenically to Dubrovnik's outer wall, is a fine place for a drink day or night (see listing on page 618). **Hard Jazz Caffè Troubadour** is cool, owned by a former member of the Dubrovnik Troubadours—Croatia's answer to the Beatles (or, perhaps more accurately, the Turtles). On balmy evenings, 50 comfy wicker chairs with tiny tables are set up theater-style in the dreamy courtyard facing the musicians. Step inside to see old 1970s photos of the band (30- to 40-kn drinks and light sandwiches, daily 9:00–24:00, live jazz nightly from about 22:00 or whenever the boss shows up, next to cathedral at Bunićeva Poljana 2, tel. 020/323-476). **Hemingway's Cocktail Bar,** a few steps from the cathedral on Pred Dvorom, is an outdoor lounge with big, overstuffed chairs at a fine vantage point for people-watching (open long hours daily, 50-kn cocktails).

Folk Music—Spirited folk-music concerts are performed for tourists twice weekly in the Lazareti (old quarantine building) just outside the Old Town's Ploče Gate (80 kn, usually at 21:30, details at TI).

SLEEPING

You basically have two options in Dubrovnik: a centrally located room in a private home *(soba)*; or a big resort hotel on a distant beach, a bus ride away from the Old Town. Since Dubrovnik hotels are generally a poor value, I highly recommend giving the *sobe* a careful look. For locations, see the map on page 600.

No matter where you stay, prices are much higher mid-June through mid-September. Reserve ahead in these peak times, especially during the Summer Festival (July 10–Aug 25 every year).

Sobe (Private Rooms): A Dubrovnik Specialty

In Dubrovnik, you'll almost always do better with a *soba* than with a hotel. All of my favorite *sobe* are run by friendly English-speaking Croatians, and are inside or within easy walking distance of the Old Town. There's a range of places, from simple and cheap rooms where you'll share your host's bathroom, to downright fancy places with private facilities and satellite TV, where you can be as anonymous as you like.

You'll find the highest concentration of good *sobe* just outside the Old Town's Pile Gate. This Pile (PEE-leh) neighborhood offers all the conveniences of the modern world (grocery store, bus stop, post office, travel agency, etc.), just steps from Dubrovnik's magical Old Town.

Before you choose, carefully read "Dalmatian Accommodation" on page 610. It's easy and smart to book one of these places direct,

Sleep Code

(€1 = about $1.20, 6 kn = about $1, country code: 385, area code: 020)

S = Single, **D** = Double/Twin, **T** = Triple, **Q** = Quad, **b** = bathroom. Unless otherwise noted, English is spoken, credit cards are accepted, and breakfast is included. The modest tourist tax (7 kn or €1 per person, per night, lower off-season) is not included in these rates. Hotels generally accept credit cards and include breakfast in their rates, while most *sobe* accept only cash and don't offer breakfast. All Dubrovnik hotels provide free guest parking.

To help you sort easily through these listings, I've divided the rooms into three categories based on the price for a standard double room with bath in peak season:

$$$ **Higher Priced**—Most rooms 700 kn (€97) or more.
$$ **Moderately Priced**—Most rooms between 400–700 kn (€55–97).
$ **Lower Priced**—Most rooms 400 kn (€55) or less.

but you can also go through an agency (for an additional charge) or make a deal with a *sobe* hustler on arrival. While the town is pretty tight in July and August, you can generally find a €40 double (with a bathroom down the hall) if you're nervy enough to just show up.

In the Pile Neighborhood, behind the Bus Stop

These two places feel plenty private, and each room gets its own bathroom. They're uphill (away from the water) from the Pile Gate's bus stop.

$$ **Jadranka and Milan Benussi,** a middle-aged professional couple, rent four rooms in a quiet, traffic-free neighborhood. Their stony-chic home, complete with a leafy terrace, is a 10-minute hike above the Old Town. Jadranka speaks good English and gives her place modern Croatian class (July–Aug: small Db-€55, big Db-€65, small apartment-€90, big apartment with balcony-€100; June and Sept: small Db-€50, big Db-€55, small apartment-€80, big apartment-€90; Oct–May: small Db-€45, big Db-€50, small apartment-€70, big apartment-€80; 20 percent more for 1-night stays, no breakfast, cash only, all rooms have air-con and kitchenettes; go 2 blocks up busy Branitelja Dubrovnika street from the TI and climb up tiny Miha Klaića lane—across from Chinese restaurant, go up past the small church, then turn right to find Miha Klaića 10; tel. 020/429-339, mobile 098-928-1300, mbenussi@inet.hr).

$$ **Villa San,** run by the Ahmić family, offers four apartments overlooking the busy (and often noisy) bus stop directly in

front of the Pile Gate (July–Sept: Db-€60; May–June: Db-€50; Oct–April: Db-€40; singles discouraged, no extra charge for short stays, no breakfast, cash only; above the bank behind the bus stop, go around left side to find entrance at Tiha 2; tel. 020/411-884, mobile 098-178-5620, www.villa-san.com, info@villa-san.com).

In the Pile Neighborhood, near the Cove by Restaurant Orhan

These places cluster around a quiet, no-name cove a five-minute walk from the Old Town. This waterfront neighborhood's landmark—and best breakfast spot—is Restaurant Orhan, which also rents its own rooms. Dubravka Matić, whose *sobe* are listed here, will do your laundry even if you're not staying with her (50 kn/load). To reach this cove, leave the Pile Gate TI to the right, then go down the first flight of stairs on your right; wind down the lanes to the little bay and the lane called Od Tabakarije.

$ Restaurant Orhan Guest House allows hotel anonymity at *sobe* prices. Its 11 simple rooms—in a couple of different buildings around the corner from the restaurant—are new, air-conditioned, well-located, and quiet, with modern bathrooms (Sb-200 kn, Db-400 kn, Tb-600 kn, Sb is 100 kn more July–Aug, Db and Tb are same prices year-round, no extra charge for 1-night stays, no breakfast, cash only, consider the restaurant your reception desk, Od Tabakarije 1, tel. & fax 020/414-183).

$ Paulina Čumbelić is a kind, gentle woman renting four old-fashioned rooms in her homey, clean, and peaceful house. Staying here is like visiting your Croatian grandma (July–Aug: S-190 kn, D-280 kn, T-400 kn; other times: S-160 kn, D-240 kn, T-300 kn; 20 percent more for 1- or 2-night stays, no breakfast, cash only, closed in winter, Od Tabakarije 2, tel. 020/421-327, mobile 091-530-7985).

$ Dubravka Matić is a charming young mom renting out three classy, tidy, and simple rooms in her cozy home. You'll truly feel you're sharing her house (including her bathroom), but thanks to friendly Dubravka, that's not a problem (July–Aug: S-150 kn, D-300 kn; other times: S-125 kn, D-260 kn; 2-night minimum, no breakfast, cash only, she'll do your laundry for 50 kn/load, Frana Antice 2, tel. 020/311-904, mobile 098-938-8281, m_dubby@yahoo.com).

$ Domenika Benussi, Jadranka Benussi's sister-in-law (see above), rents three modern, new-feeling rooms sharing two bathrooms and a pretty view (July–Aug: D-360 kn, T-400 kn; Sept–May: D-240 kn, T-300 kn; 20 percent more for 1-night stays, no breakfast, cash only, slightly closer to the Old Town than the others and near the small Atlas Travel Agency office at Sv. Đurđa 4, tel. 020/423-062, mobile 098-175-699).

Dalmatian Accommodation

Even under communism, Yugoslavs were savvy businessmen. To maximize beach-tourism occupancy in the 1960s and 1970s, they razed charming Old World buildings to make way for new, big resort hotels. Most of these coastal hotels housed refugees from inland Croatia during the war, and many have been only lightly renovated since. Today, the hotels usually have the same old communist-era dark-wood furnishings, unremarkable rooms with a moldy-college-dorm ambience, "beach" access (often on a concrete pad), a travel-agency desk selling tours in the lobby, and a seaview apéritif bar. They're ridiculously expensive (you'd pay less for the same room in a big city), and those that have been renovated use the new amenities as an excuse to hike prices even higher. These big, ugly hotels are just fine with the busloads of European tourists who head south for a week-long summer holiday. But Americans are appalled at how much you have to spend for such low quality.

Smart travelers forget about the hotels, and opt instead for what locals call "private accommodations": a rented apartment *(apartman)* or a room in a private home *(soba,* pronounced SOH-bah; plural *sobe,* SOH-bay). Private accommodations offer travelers a characteristic and money-saving alternative for a fraction of the price of a hotel. Often run by empty-nesters, these places are similar to British bed-and-breakfasts...minus the breakfast (ask your host about the best nearby breakfast spot). Generally the more you pay, the more privacy and amenities (private bathroom, TV, air-conditioning, kitchenette) you get. The simplest *sobe* allow you to experience Croatia on the cheap, at nearly youth-hostel prices, while giving you a great opportunity to connect with a local family (who could use your money more than the big hotel chains anyway). The fanciest *sobe* are downright swanky, allowing for near-hotel anonymity. Apartments are bigger and cost more than *sobe,* but they're still far cheaper than hotels.

Registered *sobe* have been rated by the government using a system that assigns stars based on amenities. Three stars means that you'll have your own bathroom, two stars means that the bathroom's down the hall, and one star is rock-bottom basic. If you don't like the idea of sharing a toilet with strangers, look for three stars and you'll do fine. (Apartments always have private bathrooms, plus some modest kitchen facilities.) Many, but not all, three-star *sobe* also have TV and air-conditioning (but usually no telephone). The prices for private accommodations generally fluctuate with the seasons, and stays of fewer than three nights almost always come with a 20–30 percent surcharge.

At most *sobe*, you can reserve in advance (usually by e-mail). This represents a major financial risk for your host, who loses money if you don't show up. For this reason, some hosts may ask you to send cash or a check as a deposit. If this happens, ask if you can give them your credit-card number for good faith instead (though you'll still have to pay in cash when you're there). *Sobe* hucksters who accost you on the street can be very aggressive about luring travelers away from their reserved rooms. But if you've booked a room at a particular place, you owe it to them to show up.

If you like to travel spontaneously, you'll have no problem finding *sobe* as you go. It seems natives you encounter on the street don't say "Hello"—they say, "Room?" At any boat dock or bus station in Dalmatia, you'll encounter pushy locals trying to get you to stay in their *soba*. Many of these *sobe* have not been classified by the government, but they can sometimes turn out to be a good deal. If you trust the sales pitch, and the location is convenient, give it a look. Or just keep an eye out as you walk or drive through town—you'll see blue *sobe* and *apartman* signs everywhere. It's actually fun to visit a few homes and make a deal.

As a last resort, you can enlist the help of a travel agency to find you a room—but you'll pay 10–30 percent extra (various agencies listed in this chapter; to search from home, try www .adriatica.net).

I'm accustomed to staying in hotels. But on my last trip to Dubrovnik, I found all of the hotels booked up. With some trepidation, I stayed in a *soba*...and I'll never go back to a Croatian resort hotel again. I've made it my mission to convince you to sleep in *sobe*, too.

$ Edi Maćinko, a can-do, gregarious Robert De Niro look-alike who has lived in Miami, offers three simple, tight rooms in his house. Two of the rooms share a bathroom and feature dramatic views of the harbor; the other has no view, but its own bathroom. The prices are a bit too high, but Edi is a fun character who runs the place with humor (July–Aug D/Db-€50, June and Sept D/Db-€45, Oct–May D/Db-€40, no minimum stay, no breakfast, cash only, U Pilama 7, tel. 020/411-050, mobile 098-905-1844, edi .macinko@inet.hr).

In the Old Town, Off the Stradun Promenade

These two places are more private and hotelesque than my other recommended Dubrovnik *sobe*. However, neither has a reception desk to speak of—so you're basically on your own after you check in.

$$ Villa Ragusa offers the nicest rooms for the price in the Old Town. The Carević family has renovated a 600-year-old house at the top of town that was damaged during the war. The five comfortable, modern rooms come with atmospheric old wooden beams and antique furniture. There are three doubles with bathrooms (including a top-floor room with breathtaking Old Town views for no extra charge—request when you reserve), and two singles that share a bathroom. The Carevićs live off-site, a few miles outside of town, so be sure to let them know when you'll arrive (July–Aug: S-€40, Db-€80; May–June and Sept–Oct: S-€30, Db-€60; Nov–April: S-€25, Db-€50; 30 percent more for 1- or 2-night stays, breakfast-€8, cash only, air-con, lots of stairs with no elevator, Žudioska ulica 15, tel. 020/453-834, mobile 098-765-634, http://villaragusa.netfirms.com, villa.ragusa@hi.htnet.hr).

$$ The similarly named **Ragusa 2 Restaurant** (see page 617) rents out 14 air-conditioned rooms in two buildings (9 over the restaurant, 5 others nearby) a block off the Old Town's main promenade. The rooms are a little musty, with old-fashioned furnishings, and this popular restaurant-and-café neighborhood can get noisy at night. Lora Rudenjak, whose family owns the restaurant, is your main contact, but anyone at Ragusa 2 can help you (June–Sept: Sb-€30, Db-€50–60 depending on size, apartment-€80; Oct–May: Sb-€20, Db-€40, apartment-€60; breakfast in restaurant included in winter but €5 extra in summer, restaurant is your reception desk, cash only, corner of Prijeko and Zamanjina at Zamanjina 12, tel. 020/321-203, Lora's mobile 091-561-2027, loredanada@hotmail.com).

In the Old Town, near St. John's Fort

These two places are near St. John's Fort, at the end of the Old Port. To find them from the cathedral, walk towards the big fort tower along the inside of the wall.

$$$ Apartments van Bloemen, well-run by a Brit named Marc and his Croatian wife Silva, offers four apartments just inside the big fort. The prices are too high, and it's in all the guidebooks, but the apartments are big, well-equipped, and homey-feeling, each with its own bathroom and kitchen (June–Sept-€100, April–May and Oct-Nov-€75, less Dec–March, smaller apartment-30 percent less, 20 percent more for 1- or 2-night stays, no breakfast, cash only, near the aquarium at Bandureva 1, tel. 020/323-433, www.karmendu.tk, apartments@karmendu.tk).

$ Renata Zijadić, a mom who speaks good English, offers four well-located rooms with slanting floors, funky colors, and over-the-top antique furniture. A single and a double (both with great views) share one bathroom; another double features an ornate old cabinet and its own bathroom; and the top-floor apartment comes with low ceilings and fine vistas (July–Aug: S-220 kn, D-300 kn, Db-360 kn, apartment-600 kn, 20 percent more for 1- or 2-night stays; Sept–June: S-180 kn, D-260 kn, Db-300 kn, apartment-400 kn; no breakfast, cash only, follow signs for wall access and walk up the steps marked *ulica Stajeva* going over the street to find Stajeva 1; tel. 020/323-623, renata.zijadic@du.htnet.hr).

Sobe-Booking Agency

If you arrive without a reservation and the TI isn't too busy, they might be able to call around and find you a *soba* for no charge. Otherwise, just about any travel agency in town can help you, on the spot or in advance...for a fee. **Atlas** is the biggest operation, though communication can be difficult. Their newest and most convenient office—scheduled to open in March of 2006—is in the big, can't-miss-it building just outside the Pile Gate; if that's not open yet, try their smaller branch just down the nearby alley at Sv. Đurđa 4 (June–Sept daily 8:00—20:00; Oct—May Mon—Fri 8:00—19:00, Sun 9:00—14:00, closed Sat; tel. 020/442-574, www.atlas-croatia.com). They also have an office at the ferry-terminal building at Port Gruž.

Hotels

If you must stay in a hotel, you have only a few good options. There are just two hotels inside the Old Town walls—and one of them charges $500 a night (Pucić Palace, www.thepucicpalace.com). Any big, resort-style hotel within walking distance of the Old Town will run you at least €130. These inflated prices drive most visitors to the Lapad Peninsula, a 15-minute bus ride west of the Old Town. But values on Lapad aren't much better, so I prefer the closer neighborhood near Boninovo Bay.

In general, Dubrovnik hotels are stuck in one of two ruts: refusing to renovate, and wringing the maximum income out of pathetic old rooms; or aggressively renovating so they can earn that extra star and begin charging lots more.

In the mass-tourism tradition, most European visitors choose to take the half-board option at their hotel (i.e., dinner in the hotel restaurant). This can be convenient and a good value, but I'd rather not be tied down to eating at my hotel—the Old Town is full of well-priced little eateries worth going out of your way for (see "Eating," below).

In the Old Town

$$$ **Hotel Stari Grad** is an ideal splurge: eight modern yet nicely old-fashioned rooms a half-block off the Old Town's main drag. While gloomy, overpriced old hotels sit on desolate beaches two miles away, this smartly appointed, well-run place charges fair rates for true class and an excellent location...for those smart enough to book ahead. The rooftop breakfast terrace (summer only) enjoys a spectacular view over orange tiles (Sb-€95, Db-€136, extra bed-€39, plus silly "insurance" charge of about €1 per person per night, same prices year-round, air-con, Od Sigurate 4, tel. 020/322-244, fax 020/321-256, www.hotelstarigrad.com, info@hotelstarigrad .com). The place is almost too good to be true—and, in fact, they're hoping to earn an extra star so they can raise their rates.

Near Boninovo Bay

If you want a big hotel, Boninovo Bay is your best bet. Around the bay cluster a handful of relatively low-key, well-priced hotels (and the city's only youth hostel). These places offer slightly better prices and closer proximity to the Old Town than the farther-out Lapad Bay resorts. Boninovo Bay is an uphill 20-minute walk from the Old Town (straight up Branitelja Dubrovnika). Once you're comfortable with the buses, the location is great (from Pile Gate, take #1a, #3, #4, #5, #6, #8, or #9). To reach the hotels from the Boninovo bus stop, go down Pera Čingrije (the road running parallel to the cliff overlooking the sea). There's a super little 24-hour bakery, Pekarnica Klas, on the right (across the street from the being-renovated Hotel Bellevue).

$$$ **Hotel Lero**, 250 yards up the street from the bus stop, is modern and fresh, but without the exotic cliffside setting. Its 160 reasonably priced, new-feeling rooms come with small sea views (no extra charge) and access to Hotel Bellevue's beach just down the street (mid-July–mid-Sept: Sb-€90, Db-€120; May–mid-July and mid-Sept–mid-Oct: Sb-€70, Db-€90; even less in winter, air-con, elevator, Internet in lobby, €5 each for lunch or dinner, Iva Vojnovića 14, tel. 020/341-333, fax 020/332-123, www.hotel-lero .hr, hotel-lero@du.htnet.hr).

$$$ Hotel R, next door and similar to Hotel Lero, is a good choice if you prefer a smaller hotel—just 10 rooms (July–mid-Sept: Sb-€75, Db-€116; June and late Sept: Sb-€62, Db-€96; May and Oct: Sb-€50, Db-€76; Nov–April: Sb-€43, Db-€66; 20 percent more for 1- or 2-night stays, 10 percent more for balcony, half-board-€9, Iva Vojnovića 32, tel. 020/333-200, fax 020/333-208, www.hotel-r.hr, helpdesk@hotel-r.hr).

$ Dubrovnik's fine Youth Hostel is a quiet, modern, and well-run by proud manager Laura. It's fairly institutional, with fresh, woody dorms (82 beds in 19 rooms; bed in 4- to 6-bed dorm: 110 kn July–Aug, 95 kn June and Sept, 85 kn May and Oct, 75 kn Nov–April; 10 kn more for non-members, includes sheets and breakfast, 5 kn less without breakfast, open daily 7:00–2:00 in the morning, ulica bana Jelačića 15–17, tel. 020/423-241, fax 020/412-592, www.hfhs.hr, dubrovnik@hfhs.hr). From the Boninovo bus stop, go down Pera Čingrije towards Hotel Bellevue, but take the first right uphill onto ulica bana Jelačića and look for signs up to the hostel on your left.

EATING

In the Old Town

While the Old Town is packed with busy restaurants, my first three recommendations distinguish themselves by providing quality as if there were no easy tourist buck. This makes them very popular with natives and in-the-know visitors—expect lines throughout normal dining hours (no reservations possible). Anywhere you eat, breezy outdoor seating is a no-brainer, and scrawny, adorable kittens beg for table scraps.

Konoba Kamenice, a no-frills fish restaurant, is the locals' unanimous choice for Dubrovnik's best eatery. This place offers inexpensive, fresh, and delicious seafood dishes on a charming market square, as central as can be in the Old Town. Some of the waitstaff is notorious for their playfully brusque service—but loyal patrons put up with it to enjoy the huge, splittable plates. Arrive early, or you'll have to wait (most main dishes 30–50 kn, daily 7:00–2:00 in the morning, until 22:00 off-season, Gundulićeva poljana 8, tel. 020/323-682—no reservations).

Gavun Sandwich Bar is the best sandwich restaurant in town—and also serves some of Dubrovnik's most delicious seafood. This unassuming little hole-in-the-wall has a wide range of exquisitely prepared, homemade specialties, from marinated sardines, octopus, and anchovies to air-dried prosciutto *(pršut)*. If you don't think you like anchovies, try the marinated ones here. Can-do owner Alan is wonderfully flexible, tailoring the perfect combination for each patron's tastes—name your price, and he'll

Dubrovnik's Old Town Restaurants

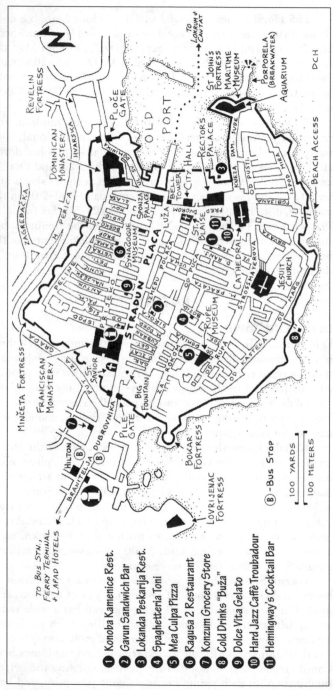

1 Konoba Kamenice Rest.
2 Gavun Sandwich Bar
3 Lokanda Peskarija Rest.
4 Spaghetteria Toni
5 Mea Culpa Pizza
6 Ragusa 2 Restaurant
7 Konzum Grocery Store
8 Cold Drinks "Buža"
9 Dolce Vita Gelato
10 Hard Jazz Caffè Troubadour
11 Hemingway's Cocktail Bar

B – Bus Stop

100 YARDS
100 METERS

whip up an appetizer plate of your favorites, which you can eat at a wooden streetside table with a generous pile of homemade cornbread. Or, for a bite on the go, Alan can wrap it all up in a toasted sandwich. The photo menu and Alan's helpful advice make ordering easy (20–30-kn sandwiches; April–Oct daily 10:00–15:00 & 18:00–24:00; Nov–March Mon–Sat 10:00–14:00 & 18:00–21:00, closed Sun; 50 yards off main drag at Široka 3—the widest side street, midway up the Stradun; tel. 020/323-206).

Lokanda Peskarija, facing the Old Port, is popular for its fine seafood and pretty harborside setting—close to all the tourism, yet still peaceful. Servings are hearty and come in a pot, "home-style." The 40-kn seafood risotto easily feeds two, and sharing is no problem. The menu's tiny—with only seafood options, and not much in the way of vegetables—but the value is appreciated (most main dishes 30–40 kn, daily 12:00–24:00, very limited indoor seating fills up fast, lots of wonderful outdoor tables, tel. 020/324-750, no reservations). This is a good place to try the typical Dubrovnik desert, *rozata* (crème caramel).

Pasta: **Spaghetteria Toni** is a cozy seven-table place popular with natives and tourists for its reliably good pasta and reasonable prices (25–50-kn pastas, Mon–Sat 11:00–15:00 & 18:00–23:00, closed Sun, Nikole Božidarevića 14, tel. 020/323-134).

Pizza: **Mea Culpa** is a popular spot for its cheap and tasty pizzas and salad bar; take-out is also available (30–45-kn pizzas, daily 8:00–24:00, from 11:30 in winter, just off the main drag at Za Rokom 3, tel. 020/323-430).

The Old Town's "Restaurant Row": **Prijeko street,** a block towards the mainland from the Stradun promenade, is lined with outdoor, tourist-oriented eateries—each one with a huckster out front trying to lure in diners. This is hardly a local scene, but a stroll along here is fun, the atmosphere is lively, the sales pitches are entertainingly desperate, and the food is generally acceptable (if overpriced). If any place along here has an edge, it's **Ragusa 2**, which is open year-round and has the longest tradition (the Rudenjak family has been in the restaurant business since 1929). With white tablecloths and fancy presentation, it's a classy place to splurge (most main dishes 50–80 kn, open long hours daily, corner of Prijeko and Zamanjina at Zamanjina 12, tel. 020/321-203). In case you're curious, Ragusa #1—also run by the Rudenjak family—is in New York City.

Picnic in the Old Town: Pick up picnic grub at Konzum (the cheapest grocery store in town, just outside Pile Gate), at the open-air produce market (each morning near the cathedral), or at the Gavun Sandwich Bar (see above). Good picnic spots include the shady benches overlooking the Old Port, the Porporela breakwater (beyond the Old Port and fort—comes with a swimming area, sunny no-shade benches, and views of Lokrum Island), and the green, welcoming park in what was the moat just under the Pile Gate entry to the Old Town.

Drinks with a View: **Cold Drinks "Buža"** offers, without a doubt, the most scenic spot for a drink. Perched on a cliff above the sea, clinging like a barnacle to the outside of the city walls, this is a peaceful, shaded getaway from the bustle of the Old Town... the perfect place to watch cruise ships sail into the horizon. *Buža* means "hole in the wall"—and that's exactly what you'll have to go through to reach this place. Filled with mellow tourists and bartenders pouring wine from tiny screw-top bottles into plastic cups, it comes with castaway views and Frank Sinatra ambience. This is supposedly where Bill Gates hangs out when he visits Dubrovnik (drinks only, 16–30 kn, summer daily 9:00–into the wee hours, closed mid-Nov–Jan, find doorway in city wall marked *Cold Drinks* just up from cathedral, up the stairs and behind Jesuit St. Ignatius' Church). It can be tough to get a table in peak season, but you might be able to reserve by calling owner Danko on his mobile phone (091-589-4936).

Ice Cream: There's lots of great gelato in Dubrovnik; one of the best places is **Dolce Vita** (daily 9:00–24:00, a half block off Stradun at Nalješkovićeva 1A, tel. 020/321-666).

On Lapad Bay

If you want a break from the fantasyland of Dubrovnik, consider venturing to Lapad Bay. Many visitors to Dubrovnik actually sleep here, in overpriced resort hotels. While the accommodations are a bad value, the ambience is pleasant and Lapad is worth an evening stroll (easy bus ride or a 60-kn taxi trip from the Old Town).

The Šetalište Kralja Zvonimira is an amazingly laid-back pedestrian lane where bars have hammocks, Internet terminals are scattered through a forested park, and a folksy Croatian family ambience holds its own against the better-funded force of international tourism. Stroll from near Hotel Zagreb to the bay, where you'll find my favorite splurge restaurant (described below) and schmaltzy music nightly on the harborside terrace of Hotel Kompas. From Hotel Kompas, a romantic walk—softly lit at night—leads along the bay through the woods, with plenty of private little stone coves for lingering.

Casa Bar and Restaurant provides the best harborside, candlelit, romantic dining in the area, with a straightforward, user-friendly menu offering traditional cooking with fresh ingredients. Tables overlook Lapad Bay, and English-speaking owner Gonzales enjoys exploring the menu with his diners (80 kn per fish plate, open long hours daily, on the bay just beyond Hotel Kompas' restaurant, Pučića 1, tel. 020/438-710).

TRANSPORTATION CONNECTIONS

From Dubrovnik by Jadrolinija Ferry: The big boat leaves Dubrovnik in the morning and goes to **Korčula** (3.5–4.5 hrs), **Split** (9–11 hrs), and other coastal destinations (which can include Stari Grad on Hvar Island and the big northern port city of Rijeka). The boat generally cruises four times each week June–Sept, twice weekly off-season. For specific schedules, ask at a local TI or see www.jadrolinija.hr.

By Bus to: Split (almost hrly, 5 hrs), **Korčula** (1/day, 4 hrs), **Zagreb** (4/day, 10 hrs).

By Plane: To quickly connect this remote destination with the rest of your trip, consider a cheap flight (see "Getting to the Dalmatian Coast," page 583.) For information on Dubrovnik's airport, see page 592.

Split

Dubrovnik is the darling of the Dalmatian Coast, but Split is Croatia's second city (after Zagreb), bustling with 173,000 people. If you've been hopping along the coast, landing in urban Split feels like a return to civilization. While most Dalmatian coastal towns seem made for tourists, Split is real and vibrant—a shipbuilding city with ugly sprawl surrounding an atmospheric Old Town. It teems with Croatians living life to the fullest. Though Split throbs to a modern, young beat, its history goes way back—all the way to the Roman Empire. Along with all the trappings of a modern city, Split has some of the best Roman ruins this side of Italy.

In the fourth century A.D., the Roman Emperor Diocletian (245–313) wanted to retire in his native Dalmatia, so he built a huge palace here. Eventually, the palace was abandoned. Then locals, fleeing seventh-century Slavic invaders, moved in and made themselves at home, and a medieval town sprouted from the rubble of the old palace. In the 15th century, the Venetians took over the Dalmatian Coast, adding on to the city and building several small palaces. But even as Split grew, the nucleus remained the ruins of Diocletian's Palace. To this day, 2,000 people live or work inside the former palace walls. A maze of narrow alleys is home to fashionable boutiques and galleries, wonderfully atmospheric cafés, and Roman artifacts around every corner.

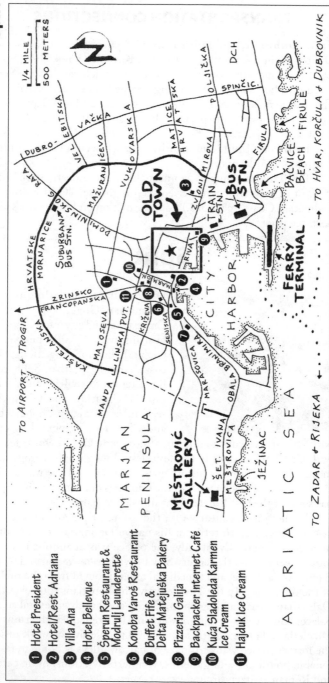

Split

1/4 MILE
500 METERS

1 Hotel President
2 Hotel/Rest. Adriana
3 Villa Ana
4 Hotel Bellevue
5 Šperun Restaurant &
   Modrulj Launderette
6 Konoba Varoš Restaurant
7 Buffet Fife &
   Delta Matejuška Bakery
8 Pizzeria Galija
9 Backpacker Internet Café
10 Kuća Sladoleda Karmen
    Ice Cream
11 Hajduk Ice Cream

Planning Your Time

Split is southern Croatia's transit point—a hub for bus, boat, train, and flight connections to other destinations in the country and abroad. This means that many visitors to Dalmatia only change boats in Split. But the city is the perfect real-life contrast to the tackiness of Dalmatian beach resorts. It deserves a full day. Begin by strolling the remains of Diocletian's Palace, then have lunch or a coffee break along the Riva promenade. After lunch, browse the shops or visit a couple of Split's museums (the Meštrović Gallery is tops). Promenading along the Riva with the natives is *the* evening activity.

With a second day (or en route to or from northern destinations), you could spend some time in nearby Trogir—a charming and enjoyable Dalmatian village.

ORIENTATION

(area code: 021)

Split sprawls, but almost everything of interest to travelers is around the City Harbor (Gradska Luka). At the top of this port is the Old Town (Stari Grad). Between the Old Town and the sea is the Riva, a waterfront pedestrian promenade lined with cafés and shaded by palm trees. The main ferry terminal (Trajektni Terminal) juts out into the harbor from the east side of the port. Along the port between the ferry terminal and the Old Town are the long-distance bus station (Autobusni Kolodvor) and the forlorn little train station (Željeznička Stanica). West of the Old Town, poking into the Adriatic, is the lush and hilly Marjan peninsula.

Split's domino-shaped Old Town is made up of two square sections. The east half was once Diocletian's Palace, and the west half is the medieval town that sprang up next door. The shell of Diocletian's ruined palace provides a checkerboard street plan, with a gate at each end. At the center of the former palace is the Peristyle square (Peristil), where you'll find the TI, cathedral, and highest concentration of Roman ruins.

Tourist Information

Split's TI is on the Peristyle square, in the very center of Diocletian's Palace (Mon–Fri 8:00–20:00, Sat–Sun 8:00–13:00, tel. 021/345-606, www.visitsplit.com). Pick up the free town map, monthly events guide, and other materials. The TI also sells books, maps, and the Splitcard (museum discount card—not worth considering for most visits).

Arrival in Split

By Boat, Bus, or Train: Split's ferry terminal (Trajektni Terminal), bus station (Autobusni Kolodvor), and train station (Željeznička

Split Essentials

English	Croatian	Pronounced
Old Town	Stari Grad	STAH-ree grahd
City Harbor	Gradska Luka	GRAHD-skah LOO-kah
Harborfront Promenade	Riva	REE-vah
Peristyle (old Roman square)	Peristil	PEH-ree-steel
Soccer Team	Hajduk	HIGH-dook
Local Sculptor	Ivan Meštrović	EE-vahn MESH-troh-veech
Adriatic Sea	Jadran	YAH-drahn

Stanica) all share a busy and very practical strip of land called Obala Kneza Domagoja, on the east side of the City Harbor. From any of them, you can see the Old Town and Riva; just walk around the port towards the big bell tower (about a 10-min walk). Along the way, you'll pass travel agencies, baggage-check offices, locals trying to rent rooms, a post office, and Internet cafés. Arriving or leaving from this central location, you never need to deal with the concrete, exhaust-stained sprawl of Split.

Many people arrive in Split **by boat**. After leaving the ferry, wade through the *sobe* hucksters to the main terminal building, where you'll find ATMs, WCs, a grocery store, and offices for all of the main ferry companies, including Jadrolinija (open long hours daily).

By Plane: Split's airport (Zračna Luka Split-Kaštela) is across the big bay (Kaštelanski Zaljev), 15 miles northwest of the center, near the town of Trogir. A bus leaves Split 90 minutes before each Croatia Airlines flight from the small Air Terminal near the southeast corner of Diocletian's Palace, and meets each arriving flight at the airport (30 kn, 40 min). Figure on paying about 300 kn for a taxi to the center. Airport info: tel. 021/203-506, www .split-airport.hr.

By Car: Split is split by its Old Town, which is welded to the harbor by the pedestrian-only Riva promenade. This means drivers needing to get 300 yards from one side of the Old Town to the other must drive about 15 minutes entirely around the center, which can be miserably clogged with traffic. A semicircular ring road makes this better than it might be. To get to the west end, you'll go through a tunnel under the Marjan peninsula. To reach the ferry terminal (east side), follow signs to *Trajektni* (look for the tiny ferry).

Helpful Hints

Internet Access: Internet cafés are plentiful in the Old Town; look for signs, especially around the Peristyle square. Closer to the stations and ferry terminal is **Backpacker C@fé,** run by Australian Steve Potter. This place has Internet access, coffee and drinks with outdoor eating, and used guidebooks and paperbacks for sale (daily in summer 6:00–24:00, off-season daily 8:00–21:00, near the beginning of Obala Kneza Domagoja, tel. 021/338-548).

Post Office: A modern little post office is next to the bus station (daily 7:00–21:00, on Obala Kneza Domagoja).

Laundry: Modrulj Laundrette, Croatia's "only automatic launderette," is run by an Australian couple, Shane and Julie (50 kn/load self-service, 65 kn/load full-service, air-con; Easter–Oct daily 8:00–20:00; Nov–Easter Mon–Sat 10:00–16:00, closed Sun; Šperun 1, tel. 021/315-888). It's conveniently located just off the harbor, near the recommended Šperun and Konoba Varoš restaurants and a couple of Internet cafés—handy if multitasking is your style.

Travel Agency: Turistički Biro, between the two halves of the Old Town on the Riva, books *sobe* and hotels, sells guidebooks and maps, rents scooters and cars, and sells tickets for excursions (mid-July–mid-Aug Mon–Fri 8:00–21:00, Sat 8:00–20:00, Sun 8:00–13:00; off-season Mon–Fri 8:00–20:00, Sat 8:00–13:00, closed Sun, Riva 12, tel. & fax 021/347-100, turist-biro-split@st.htnet.hr).

Baggage Check: Both the train and the bus stations have safe and efficient baggage-check services *(garderoba)*. If one is very crowded, the other may be empty—check both before waiting in a long line.

Folk Performances: Croatian folk-singing groups perform daily May through October at 11:00 in Peristyle square. Each Saturday morning in the summer, there's also a folk-dancing show in Diocletian's Palace (generally 11:00–13:00 in the cellars, details at TI).

Wine Shop: At **Vinoteka Bouquet,** at the west end of the Riva (near the restaurants and launderette on Šperun street), knowledgeable Denis can help you pick out a bottle of Croatian wine to suit your tastes (Mon–Fri 9:00–12:00 & 17:00–20:00, Sat 8:00–12:30, closed Sun, Obala Hrvatskog Narodnog Preporoda 3, tel. 021/348-031). For a wine primer before you visit, see page 580.

Getting Around Split

Most of what you'll want to see is within walking distance, but some hotels and sights (such as the Meštrović Gallery) are a bit farther out than the others.

By Bus: Local buses, run by Promet, cost 9 kn per ride (or 8 kn if you buy ticket from a kiosk; ask for a *putna karta*; zone 1 is fine for any ride within Split, but you need the 19-kn zone 4 ticket for the ride to Trogir). Validate your ticket as you board the bus. Suburban buses to towns near Split (like Salona or Trogir) generally use the Suburban Bus Station (Prigradski Autobusni Kolodvor), a 15-minute walk due north of the Old Town on Domovinskog rata. Bus information: www.promet-split.hr.

By Taxi: Taxis start at 18 kn, then cost around 8 kn per kilometer. Figure 50–60 kn for most rides within the city (for example, from the ferry terminal to most hotels). To call for a taxi, try Radio Taxi (tel. 021/970).

TOURS

Of Split

Unfortunately, there aren't any regularly scheduled walking tours of Split. Your only option is to hire a **local guide.** The guide association, with an office on the Old Town's Peristyle square, has a list of local English-speaking guides who'd love to give you a two-hour tour for 330 kn (this price for 2 tourists, about 50 kn per person after that; May–Sept Mon–Fri 9:00–17:00, Sat 9:00–15:00, closed Sun; shorter hours Oct–April, tel. & fax 021/346-267, mobile 098-361-936).

From Split

Elite Travel and **Atlas Travel** offer a variety of excursions from Split (mostly full-day, about €45–65). Itineraries include: a tour of Split and Trogir, whitewater rafting on the nearby Cetina River, the island of Brač, the island of Hvar, Brač and Hvar together, the island of Korčula, Dubrovnik, and Plitvice Lakes National Park. This can be a quick, convenient way to get to places that are time-consuming to reach by public transportation. Get information and tickets at any travel agency, such as the Turistički Biro on the Riva (see "Tourist Information," above).

Lifejacket Adventures, run by an Australian couple, Shane and Julie, is a new operation with a focus on getting backpackers back to nature. They offer various full-day and multi-day excursions to nearby islands. They also arrange custom excursions, with a focus on kayaking, hiking, wine, history, archaeological sites, and rock climbing. For details, check out www.lifejacketadventures.com or stop by Split's launderette—which Shane and Julie also run (see "Helpful Hints," above).

SELF-GUIDED WALK

Diocletian's Palace (Dioklecijanova Palača)

Split's only ▲▲▲ sight is the remains of Roman Emperor Diocletian's enormous retirement palace, sitting on the harbor in the heart of the city. Since the ruins themselves are now integrated into the city's street plan, exploring them is free (though you'll pay to enter a few parts—such as the cellars and the cathedral/mausoleum). As fragments of the palace are poorly marked, and there are not yet any good guidebooks or audioguides for tracking down the remains, Split is a good place to hire a local guide (330 kn/2 hrs; see "Helpful Hints," above). This self-guided tour explains the basics. To begin the tour, stand in front of the palace (at the east end of the Riva, at the corner with the yellow information pillar) to get oriented.

Background: Diocletian grew up just inland from Split, in the town of Salona (*Solin* in Croatian)—which was then the capital of Dalmatia. He worked his way up the Roman hierarchy and became emperor (A.D. 284–305). Despite all of his achievements, Diocletian is best remembered for two questionable legacies: dividing the huge empire among four emperors (arguably leading to its decline); and torturing and executing Christians, including thousands right here on the Dalmatian Coast.

As Diocletian grew older, he decided to return to his homeland for retirement (since he was in poor health, the medicinal sulfur spring here was another plus). His massive palace took only 11 years to build—and this fast pace required a big push (more than 2,000 slaves died during construction). Huge sections of his palace still exist, modified by medieval and modern developers alike. To get a sense of the original palace, check out the big image on the back of the big map of Split just to your right.

Palace Facade: The "front" of today's Split—facing the harbor—was actually the back door of Diocletian's Palace. The water level was much higher back then, and this part of the palace could be reached only by boat—sort of an emergency exit.

Visually trace the outline of the gigantic palace, which was more than 600 feet long on each side. On the corner to the right stands a big, rectangular guard tower (one of the original 16). To the left, the tower is gone and the corner is harder to pick out (look for the beginning of the newer-looking buildings). Erase in your mind the ramshackle two-story buildings added 200 years ago, which obscure the grandness of the palace wall.

Halfway up the facade, notice the row of 42 arched window frames (mostly filled in today). Diocletian and his family lived in the seaside half of the palace. Imagine him strolling back and forth along this fine arcade, enjoying the views of his Adriatic homeland.

Diocletian's Palace

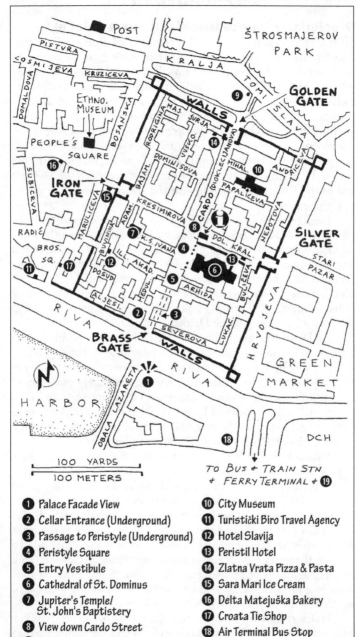

1. Palace Facade View
2. Cellar Entrance (Underground)
3. Passage to Peristyle (Underground)
4. Peristyle Square
5. Entry Vestibule
6. Cathedral of St. Dominus
7. Jupiter's Temple/ St. John's Baptistery
8. View down Cardo Street
9. Bishop Gregory of Nin Statue
10. City Museum
11. Turistički Biro Travel Agency
12. Hotel Slavija
13. Peristil Hotel
14. Zlatna Vrata Pizza & Pasta
15. Sara Mari Ice Cream
16. Delta Matejuška Bakery
17. Croata Tie Shop
18. Air Terminal Bus Stop
19. To Backpacker Internet Café

The inland, non-view half of the palace was home to 700 servants, bodyguards, and soldiers.

• *Now go through the poorly marked, low-profile door in the middle of the palace (known as the "Brass Gate"; look for the "i" sign pointing to the TI). Just inside the door is the entrance to...*

Diocletian's Cellars (Podromi): Since the palace was built on land that sloped down to the sea, these chambers were built to level out the main floor (like a modern "daylight basement"). The cellars weren't used for storage; they were filled with water from three different sources: a freshwater spring, a sulfur spring, and the sea. Later, medieval residents used them as a dump. Rediscovered only in the last century, the cellars enabled archaeologists to derive the floor plan of the long-gone palace. Today, these underground chambers are used for art exhibits and a little strip of souvenir stands. But before you go shopping, explore the cellars at this end (8 kn, skimpy 5-kn guidebook; hours sporadic, but roughly June–Aug daily 9:00–21:00, May daily 10:00–17:00, Sept–mid-Oct daily 10:00–18:00, April and late Oct daily 10:00–14:00; Nov–March Mon–Sat 10:00–14:00, closed Sun).

Wander through the labyrinthine area beyond the ticket desk (on the left, or west, side of the palace). When those first villagers took refuge in the abandoned palace from the rampaging Slavs in 641, the elite lived upstairs, grabbing what was once the emperor's wing. They carved the rough holes you see in the ceiling to dump their garbage and sewage. Over the generations, the basement (where you're standing) actually filled up with waste and solidified, ultimately becoming a once-stinky, then-precious bonanza for 20th-century archaeologists. Notice the unexcavated wings—a compost pile of ancient lifestyles, awaiting the tiny shovels and toothbrushes of future archaeologists. Today, this huge, vaulted hall is used for everything from flower and book shows to fashion catwalks. The headless black granite sphinx is one of 13 that Diocletian brought home from Egypt. The two beams on display once supported floorboards overhead (see the holes on either side of the vaults).

You can also explore the cellars on the east side (same ticket). Among other things, you'll see a semicircular marble table used by the Romans, who—as shown in Hollywood movies—ate lying down (3 would lounge and feast, while servants dished things up from the straight side).

• *When you're finished, head back to the main gallery, where you can shop your way down the passage and up the stairs into the...*

Peristyle (Peristil): This square was the centerpiece of Diocletian's Palace. As you walk up the stairs, the entry vestibule into the residence is above your head, Diocletian's mausoleum (today's Cathedral of St. Dominus) is to your right, and the street

to Jupiter's Temple is on your left. The little chapel straight ahead houses the TI, and beyond that is the narrow street to the former main entrance to the palace, the Golden Gate.

Go to the middle of the square and take it all in. The red granite pillars—which you'll see all over Diocletian's Palace—are from Egypt, where Diocletian spent many of his pre-retirement years. Imagine the pillars defining fine arcades—now obscured by medieval houses. The black sphinx is the only one of Diocletian's collection of 13 that's still intact.

• *Climb the stairs (above where you came in) into the domed, open-ceilinged...*

Entry Vestibule: Impressed? That's the idea. This was the grand entry to Diocletian's living quarters, meant to wow visitors. Emperors were believed to be gods. Diocletian called himself "Jovius"—the son of Jupiter, the most powerful of all gods. Four times a year (at the change of the seasons), Diocletian would stand here and overlook the Peristyle. His subjects would lie on the ground in worship, praising his name. Notice the four big niches at floor level, which once held statues of the four tetrarchs who ruled the unwieldy empire after Diocletian retired. The ceiling was covered with frescoes and mosaics. Wander out back to the harbor side through medieval buildings (some with 7th-century foundations), which evoke the way local villagers came in and took over the once-spacious and elegant palace.

• *Now go back into the Peristyle square and turn right, climbing the steps to the...*

Cathedral of St. Dominus (Katedrala Sv. Duje): The original octagonal structure was Diocletian's elaborate mausoleum,

built in the 4th century. But after the fall of Rome, it was converted into the town's cathedral. Construction on the bell tower began in the 13th century and took 300 years to complete. Before you go inside, notice the sarcophagi ringing the cathedral. In the late Middle Ages, this was prime post-mortem real estate, since being buried closer to a cathedral improved your chances of getting to heaven.

Step inside the oldest building used as a cathedral anywhere in

Christendom (5 kn, get the 10-kn combo-ticket includes Jupiter's Temple—see below, daily 7:00–19:00, may be closed for midday siesta, Kraj Sv. Duje 5, tel. 021/344-121). Imagine the place in pre-Christian times, with Diocletian's tomb in the center. The only surviving decor from those days are the granite columns and the relief circling the base of the dome (about 50 feet up)—a ring of carvings heralding the greatness of the emperor. The small, multi-colored marble pillars around the top of the pulpit (near the entry) were scavenged from Diocletian's sarcophagus. These are all that remains of Diocletian's remains...he was an unpopular guy. What happened to the rest of him is anyone's guess, but it's certainly not a pretty picture.

Diocletian brutally persecuted his Christian subjects, some-times in the crypt of this very building. To kick off his retirement upon his arrival on the Dalmatian Coast, he had Bishop Dominus of Salona killed, along with several thousand Christians. When Diocletian died, there were riots of happiness. In the seventh cen-tury, his mausoleum became a cathedral dedicated to the martyred bishop. The extension behind the altar was added in the ninth century, and the doors are 12th-century walnut originals. The sarcophagus of St. Dominus (to the right of the altar, with early Christian carvings) was once the cathedral's high altar. To the left of today's main altar is the altar of St. Anastasius—lying on a millstone, which is tied to his neck. On Diocletian's orders, this Christian martyr was drowned in Adriatic. Posthumous poetic justice: Now Christian saints are entombed in Diocletian's mauso-leum...and Diocletian is nowhere to be found.

For another 5 kn, you can climb steep steps to the top of the **bell tower**. You'll be rewarded with sweeping views of Split, but it's not for claustrophobes or those scared of heights.

Jupiter's Temple/St. John's Baptistery: Diocletian believed himself to be Jovius (that's Jupiter, Jr.). On exiting the mausoleum of Jovius, worshippers would look straight ahead to the temple of Jupiter. (Back then, of course, all of these medieval buildings weren't cluttering up the view.) Make your way through the nar-row alley, past another headless, pawless sphinx, to explore the small temple (using the 10-kn combo-ticket you bought at the cathedral, same hours as cathedral; if it's locked, go ask the guy at the cathedral to let you in).

The temple has long since been converted into a baptistery—with a big 12th-century baptismal font and a statue of St. John by the great Croatian sculptor Ivan Meštrović (EE-vahn MESH-troh-veech, see page 632). The half-barrel vaulted ceiling is consid-ered the best preserved of its kind anywhere. Every face and each patterned box is different.

• *Back at the Peristyle square, stand in front of the TI with your back to the entry vestibule (and harbor). The little street just beyond the TI (going left to right) connects the east and west gates. If you've had enough Roman history, head right (east) to go through the "Silver Gate" and find Split's busy, open-air Green Market. Or, to the left (west), you'll wind up at the "Iron Gate" and People's Square (see below), and, beyond that, the fresh-and-smelly fish market. But if you want to see one last bit of Roman history, continue straight ahead up the...*

Cardo: This street—literally, "Hot Street"—was the most important in Diocletian's Palace, connecting the main entry with the heart of the complex. As you walk, you'll pass a bank with modern computer gear all around its exposed Roman ruins (1st building on the right, look through window), a Venetian merchant's palace (a reminder that Split was dominated by Venice from the 15th century on—step into his courtyard, 1st gate on left), an alley to the City Museum (on the right—see below), and a fan shop for Hajduk Split, the city's extremely popular soccer team (on left, with Umbro sign).

• *Before long, you'll pass through the...*

Golden Gate (Zlatna Vrata): This great gate was the main entry of Diocletian's Palace. Its name came from the golden statues of Diocletian and other Roman VIPs that once adorned it. Straight ahead from here is Salona (Solin), which was a major city of 60,000 (and Diocletian's hometown) before there was a Split. The big statue by Ivan Meštrović is **Bishop Gregory of Nin,** a 10th-century Croatian priest who convinced the Vatican to allow sermons during Mass to be said in Croatian, rather than Latin. People rub his toe for good luck (though only non-material wishes are given serious consideration).

SIGHTS AND ACTIVITIES

In or near the Old Town

▲▲**Strolling the Riva (Obala Hrvatskog Narodnog Preporoda)**—The official name for this seaside pedestrian drag is the "Croatian National Revival Embankment," but locals just call it "Riva" (Italian for "harbor"). This is the town's promenade, an integral part of Mediterranean culture. After dinner, Split residents collect their families and friends for a stroll on the Riva. It offers some of the best people-watching in Eastern Europe; make it a point to be here for an hour or two after dinner. At the west end of the Riva, the people-parade of Croatian culture turns right and heads away from the water, up Marmontova. The stinky smell that sometimes accompanies the stroll isn't a sewer. It's sulfur—a reminder that the town's medicinal sulfur spas have attracted people here since the days of Diocletian.

▲**People's Square (Narodni Trg)**—The lively square at the center of the Old Town is called by locals simply *Pjaca*, pronounced the same as the Italian *piazza*. Stand in the center and enjoy the bustle. Look around for a quick lesson in Dalmatian history. When Diocletian lived in his palace, a Roman village sprouted here just outside the wall. Face the former wall of Diocletian's Palace (behind and to the right of the clock tower). This was the western gate, or so-called Iron Gate. By the 14th century, the medieval town had developed, making this the main square of Split. The city's grand old café, Gradska Kavana, has been the Old Town's venerable meeting point for generations (drinks and cakes but no meals, daily 7:00–24:00). A few doors down is a cheaper, good take-away bakery called Delta Matejuška (see page 639). To the left, the white building jutting out into the square is the Ethnographic Museum (see below), once the city hall. The loggia is all that remains of the original Gothic building. Directly to your left as you face the museum is the Nakić House, built in Viennese Secession style—a reminder that Dalmatia was part of the Hapsburg Empire, ruled by Vienna, from Napoleon's downfall through World War I. The lane on the right side of this building leads to Split's fish market (Ribarnica).

Ethnographic Museum (Etnografski Muzej)—The museum shows off the colorful art and dress of Dalmatian villages (10 kn; in summer Tue–Fri 10:00–16:00, Sat–Sun 10:00–13:00, closed Mon; in winter Tue–Sun 10:00–13:00, closed Mon; Iza Lože 1, tel. 021/344-164, www.et-mu-st.com).

Split City Museum (Muzej Grada Splita)—Housed in the 15th-century Papalić Palace, this museum traces how the city grew over the centuries. It's a bit dull, but it can help you appreciate a little better the layers of history you're seeing in the streets. The ground floor displays Roman fragments (including coins from the days of Diocletian) and temporary exhibits. The upstairs focuses on the Middle Ages (find the terrace, displaying carved stone monuments), and the top floor goes from the 16th century to the present (10 kn, some English descriptions, 75-kn guidebook is overkill, mid-May–mid-Sept Tue–Fri 9:00–21:00, Sat–Sun 10:00–13:00, closed Mon; off-season Tue–Fri 9:00–16:00, Sat–Sun 10:00–13:00, closed Mon; Papalićeva 1, tel. 021/344-917, www.mgst.net).

Radić Brothers Square (Trg Braće Radića)—A Venetian citadel watches over this square, just off the Riva between the two halves of the Old Town. After Split became part of the Venetian Republic, there was a serious danger of attack by the Turks, so octagonal towers like this were built all along the coast. But this imposing tower had a second purpose—to encourage citizens of Split to forget about any plans of rebellion. In the middle of the square is a sculpture by Ivan Meštrović of the poet Marko Marulić, considered to be the father of the Croatian language.

On the downhill (harbor) side of the square is **Croata,** a necktie boutique that loves to tell how Croatian soldiers who fought with the French in the Thirty Years' War (1618–1648) had a distinctive way of tying their scarves. The French found it stylish, adopted it, and called it *à la Croate*—or eventually, *cravate*—thus creating the modern tie that many people wear to work every day throughout the world. Croata's selection includes ties with traditional Croatian motifs, such as the checkerboard pattern from the flag or writing in the ninth-century Glagolitic alphabet. Though pricey, these ties are good souvenirs (cheaper ties-149 kn, top-quality ties-369 kn, Mon–Fri 8:00–20:00, Sat 8:00–14:00, closed Sun).

Green Market—This lively open-air market bustles at the east end of Diocletian's Palace. Locals shop for produce and clothes here, and there's plenty of tourist souvenirs as well. Browse the wide selection of T-shirts, and ignore the creepy black-market tobacco salesmen who mutter at you: *"Cigaretta?"*

Split's Outskirts

▲▲**Meštrović Gallery (Galerija Meštrović)**—Split's best art museum is dedicated to the sculptor Ivan Meštrović (1883–1962), the most important and famous of all Croatian artists. Many of Meštrović's finest works are housed in this palace, designed by the

sculptor himself. If you have time, it's worth the 20-minute walk or short bus or taxi ride from the Old Town.

Meštrović grew up in a family of poor, nomadic farm workers just inland from Split. At an early age, his drawings and wooden carvings showed promise, and a rich family took him in and made sure he was properly trained. He eventually went off to school in Vienna, where he fell in with the Secession movement and found fame and fortune. Later in life—like Diocletian before him—Meštrović returned to Split and built a huge seaside mansion (today's

Meštrović Gallery). During World War II, Meštrović moved abroad to escape the Nazi puppet government and lectured at Notre Dame (in Indiana, not France) and Syracuse (in New York, not Italy).

You'll see Meštrović's works all over Split and throughout Croatia. Most are cast bronze, depicting biblical, mythological, political, and everyday themes. Whether whimsical or emotional, Meštrović's expressive, elongated faces connect with the viewer. In this collection, don't miss *Job*, howling with an agony verging on insanity—carved by the artist in exile, as his country was turned upside-down by World War II. A moving contrast is the quietly poignant *Roman Pietà*, with mournful faces at painful angles pondering the death of Christ (20 kn, in summer Tue–Sat 9:00–21:00, Sun 12:00–21:00, closed Mon, shorter hours off-season—call to confirm it's open before making the trip, Šetalište Ivana Meštrovića 46, tel. 021/340-800).

If you enjoy the gallery, continue walking five more minutes down Šetalište Ivana Meštrovića to **Kaštelet Chapel** (literally, "Chapel of the Holy Cross"), a 16th-century fortified palace Meštrović bought to display his wooden carvings of Jesus' life. The centerpiece is a powerful wooden crucifix (included in ticket for gallery, but open shorter hours: in summer Tue–Sat 9:30–16:00, Sun 12:00–17:00, closed Mon; even shorter hours off-season).

Marjan Peninsula—This long, hilly peninsula extends west from the center of Split. This is where Split goes to relax, with out-of-the-way beaches and lots of hiking trails (great views and a zoo on top).

Hit the Beach—Since it's more of a big city than a resort, Split's beaches aren't as scenic (and the water not as clean) as towns farther south. The beach that's most popular—and crowded—is Bačvice, in a sandy cove just east of the main ferry terminal. You'll find less crowded beaches just to the east of Bačvice. Locals like to hike around Marjan, the peninsular city park (see above), ringed with several sunbathing beaches.

Near Split: Trogir

Just 12 miles northwest of Split is Trogir, a tiny, medieval-architecture-packed town surrounded by water. This made-for-tourists village lacks the real-world heart and soul of Split, and it's more or less identical to a dozen other Croatian coastal resort towns (Korčula is better—see page 640). But even though it's nothing to jump ship for, Trogir is an easy day trip for those looking to get away from urban Split.

Trogir is a small island, wedged between the mainland and the much bigger Čiovo island. Busy bridges connect it to the rest of the world at the east end, and a big soccer field squeezed between imposing watchtowers anchors the west end. In the middle is a tight medieval street plan of twisty marbled-stone lanes.

Getting There: You have two options for reaching Trogir from Split, both roughly the same price (15–20 kn). The faster, easier option is to take a bus from Split's **main**

bus station, next to the City Harbor. Any bus going north (for example, to Šibenik, Zadar, or even Rijeka) will usually stop at Trogir (2/hr, about 30 min, simply go to ticket window and ask for next bus to Trogir). Note that in the busiest summer months, some long-distance buses may not want to take you (preferring to give your seat instead to someone paying for a longer trip). The other option is to take **local bus #37**, which leaves from the inconveniently located Suburban Bus Station (Prigradski Autobusni Kolodvor, a 15-min walk north of Old Town on Domovinskog rata). Because this bus makes several stops along the way, it can take 45–60 min, depending on traffic (leaves every 20 min)—avoid it if you can. You'll need a ticket for zone 4 (19 kn, buy at ticket window or on bus).

Arrival in Trogir: Both buses drop you off at the mainland market, just across the canal from the island. Cross the bridge into town and wander straight ahead for two blocks (bearing left); you'll run into the main square.

Tourist Information: At the main square, named for Pope John Paul II (Trg Ivana Pavla II), you'll find the TI (June–Sept daily 8:00–21:00, off-season closed afternoons and Sat–Sun, tel. 021/885-628, www.dalmacija.net/trogir.htm).

Sights: On the main square is the town's centerpiece, the **Cathedral of St. Lawrence** (Katedrala Sv. Lovre). Built in the 13th through 17th centuries, the cathedral drips with history. The bell tower alone took 200 years to build, leaving it a textbook lesson in Dalmatian architecture styles: straightforward Gothic at the bottom, Venetian Gothic in the middle, and Renaissance at the top. The cathedral's front entryway—the ornately decorated, recently restored Radovan's Portal—is worth a gander. Inside, it's dark, very old-feeling, and packed with altars. The treasury (5 kn) features some beautiful 15th-century carved-wood cabinets filled with ecclesiastical art and gear.

The town's other sights—both dull—are the **Town Museum** (Muzej Grada), a few blocks north (towards the mainland) from the main square, and the **Monastery of St. Nikola** (Samostan Sv. Nikole), a few blocks south (towards Čiovo island).

But Trogir isn't for museum-going; it's for aimless strolling. And the best place for that is along the wide, beautifully manicured **harborfront promenade** along the southern edge of town (Obala bana Berislavića). Lined with expensive restaurants, and clogged with giddy, ice-cream-licking tourists, this promenade is the highlight of a visit to Trogir. Often the enormous yachts of the rich and famous put in here, giving wanderers something to yak about. At the far end of the promenade, the **Kamerlengo Fortress** has a lookout tower with fine views over the town and region (10 kn).

Sleeping in Trogir: I see no reason to sleep in this little burg.

But if you do, consider **$$ Hotel Concordia,** with 14 fine rooms at the end of the embankment (view Sb-350 kn, non-view Db-500 kn, small Db with view-550 kn, big Db with view-600 kn, 50 kn cheaper in winter, air-con, Obala bana Berislavića 22, tel. 021/885-400, fax 021/885-401, www.concordia-hotel.htnet.hr, concordia -hotel@st.htnet.hr).

NIGHTLIFE

The Riva—Every night in Split, the sea of Croatian humanity laps at the walls of Diocletian's palace along the Riva. Choose a bench and watch life go by, or enjoy a drink at one of the many outdoor cafés lining the promenade.

Old Town Pubs—Wander the labyrinthine lanes of the Old Town to find the pub of your choice. Several cluster along Dioklecijanova (just inside Golden Gate and to the left about a block) and near Radić Brothers Square (Trg Braće Radića; from the square's statue of Marulić, enter the Old Town and bear right, follow sign for *Puls*).

Bačvice Beach—A family-friendly beach by day, it's a throbbing party zone for young locals late at night. All Old Town bars have to close by 1:00 in the morning. This is when night owls hike on over to the Bačvice crescent of clubs. The three-floor club complex is a cacophony of music, with the beat of each club melting into the next—all with breezy terraces overlooking the harbor.

SLEEPING

(6 kn = about $1, country code: 385, area code: 021)
Split's accommodations situation isn't quite as dismal as in other Dalmatian destinations—hotels are a better value here than in Dubrovnik or Korčula. Note that the prices I've listed don't include the tourist tax (6 kn per person, per night July–Sept, less off-season).

Hotels

Villa Ana and Hotel Slavija are clearly the best values. To locate the first and fifth (Hotel Slavija) listings, see the map on page 626. For the rest of these hotels, see the map on page 620.

$$$ Peristil Hotel has 12 new, classy rooms over a restaurant just steps from the couldn't-be-more-central square of the same name. This is your most elegant home inside the Old Town (July–Aug: Sb-700 kn, Db-900 kn; May–June and Sept–Oct: Sb-620 kn, Db-800 kn; Nov–April: Sb-590 kn, Db-750 kn; stairs with no elevator, just behind TI and inside Silver Gate at Poljana Kraljice Jelene 5, tel. 021/329-070, fax 021/329-088, www.hotelperistil.com, hotel.peristil@email.t-com.hr).

$$$ Hotel Adriana has seven nice, new-feeling rooms perched right above the people-packed Riva. Choose between harborview front rooms or quieter back rooms. Unfortunately, the place suffers from absentee management and bad service, and the rooms are an afterthought to the busy restaurant (Sb-650 kn, Db-850 kn, 100 kn less off-season, air-con, elevator, Riva 8, tel. 021/340-000, fax 021/340-008, www.hotel-adriana.hr, info@hotel-adriana.hr).

$$$ Hotel President offers 43 plush, business-class rooms with all the comforts. The downsides: It can be understaffed, and it overlooks a dreary parking lot a 10-minute walk north of the Old Town (Sb-750 kn, Db-975 kn; larger "superior" rooms with Jacuzzi tubs: Sb-985 kn, Db-1,125 kn; plus ridiculous "insurance" fee of 10 kn per person per day, non-smoking rooms, air-con, elevator, parking garage-50 kn/day or park in lot, Starčevićeva 1, tel. 021/305-222, fax 021/305-225, www.hotelpresident.hr, hotel.president@st.htnet.hr).

$$ Villa Ana may just be the best small hotel on the Dalmatian Coast, with five modern, comfortable rooms in a smart little house a five-minute walk from the Old Town. This delightful, free-standing stone home is well-run by Danijel Bilobrk and his family. Though it's in a boring urban neighborhood, it's pristine and welcoming inside (Sb-550 kn, Db-690 kn, Tb-790 kn, air-con, reception open 7:00–24:00, street parking or a tight little parking spot, 2 long blocks east of Old Town up busy Kralja Zvonimira, follow the driveway-like lane opposite Koteks skyscraper 30 yards to Vrh Lučac 16, tel. 021/482-715, fax 021/482-721, www.villaana-split.hr, info@villaana-split.hr).

$$ Hotel Slavija is newly renovated, comfortable, and wonderfully located in the Old Town. It shares a tiny square with some very popular late-night discos and cafés, so it can be noisy—especially on weekends (new windows attempt, with only some success, to keep out the throbbing dance beat; try requesting a quieter back room). Each of its 25 rooms is a little different, some with balconies for no extra charge. Ongoing improvements are planned—including adding an elevator and a rooftop breakfast terrace—so rates may go up in the near future (Sb-500 kn, Db-650 kn, Tb-780, maybe cheaper Nov—May, suites, huge family rooms, air-con, a block from the Riva at Buvinina 2, tel. 021/323-840, fax 021/323-868, www.hotelslavija.com, info@hotelslavija.com).

$$ Hotel Bellevue used to be the grande dame of Split; now it's a communist-era time warp. It's central, at the west end of the Riva, but its 50 rooms are outmoded, grungy, and extremely tired... as is the staff (mid-June—mid-Sept: Sb-490 kn, Db-690 kn, Tb-940 kn; off-season: Sb-425, Db-590, Tb-790; rooms overlooking the square have no traffic noise; 3rd-floor rooms are quietest, but come with tiny portholes for windows; no air-con but fans, elevator, a few handy parking spots, bana Josipa Jelačića 2, tel. 021/347-499, fax 021/362-383, www.hotel-bellevue-split.hr).

Lower-Priced *Sobe* (Private Rooms)

Booking *Sobe* through an Agency: Though there are very few *sobe* inside Split's Old Town, there are plenty within a 10-minute walk. **Turistički Biro,** a booking agency for locals with rooms to rent, helps you find the best fit. Make your reservation in advance; then, on arrival, drop by their office (which serves as a reception desk for the scattered rooms), pick up your welcome packet, pay, and head off to your awaiting landlady (mid-July–mid Aug: S-230 kn, Sb-255 kn, D-340 kn, Db-380 kn; June–mid-July and mid-Aug–Sept: S-190 kn, Sb-210 kn, D-275 kn, Db-315 kn; Oct–May: S-160 kn, Sb-180 kn, D-235 kn, Db-275 kn; plus 6 kn per person, per night for tourist tax, no breakfast, 30 percent less for stays of 4 nights or more; office open mid-July–mid-Aug Mon–Fri 8:00–21:00, Sat 8:00–20:00, Sun 8:00–13:00; off-season Mon–Fri 8:00–20:00, Sat 8:00–13:00, closed Sun; Riva 12, tel. & fax 021/347-100, turist-biro-split@st.htnet.hr).

Going Direct: In addition to the government-regulated *sobe* administered by room-finding agencies, there is also an abundance of unregulated, cash-only rooms within a 10-minute walk of the Old Town (about 250 kn for a double). Locals hawking rooms meet each arrival at the boat, bus, and train terminals. The person generally shows photos of her place, you haggle for a price, then she escorts you to your new home in Split. While it takes nerve to just show up without a room, this is standard operating procedure for backpackers (who spend a third of what others do for similar comfort and a more memorable experience).

EATING

Split's Old Town has oodles of atmosphere, but places to eat are limited mostly to cafés, fast-food joints, and a handful of over-priced, touristy restaurants (Zlatna Vrata is a happy exception—described under "Pizza and Pasta," below). But if you venture just a couple of blocks west of the Old Town, you'll discover my three favorite places (Šperun, Konoba Varoš, and Buffet Fife). To locate most of these eateries, see the map on page 620; for Zlatna Vrata, see the map on page 626.

Šperun Restaurant has a classy, cozy Old World ambience and a passion for good Dalmatian food. Zdravko Banović and his son Damir serve a mix of Croatian and "eclectic Mediterranean," specializing in seafood. This place distinguishes itself by offering a warm welcome and high-quality food for reasonable prices (25–45-kn pastas, 25–60-kn meat and seafood, air-con interior, a few sidewalk tables, reservations wise June–Aug, daily 9:00–23:00, Šperun 3, tel. 021/346-999).

Konoba Varoš, though pricier than Šperun and a bit impersonal, is beloved by natives and tourists alike for its great food. Serious, vest-wearing waiters serve a wide range of Croatian cooking (including pastas, seafood, and meat dishes) under droopy fishnets. Their 50-kn *carpaccio* starter—thinly sliced strips of raw meat or fish sprinkled with lemon and olive oil and served with lettuce and cheese—will get you in an Adriatic-seaside mood (50–85-kn main dishes, lots of groups, reservations smart—busiest after 21:00, daily 9:00–24:00, Ban Mladenova 7, tel. 021/396-138).

Buffet Fife is your cheap, dream-come-true fish joint, where a colorful local crowd shares rough wood tables, and the waitstaff seem brusque until you crack them up. Zvonko (the charming-as-a-cartoon waiter) ignores the menu, declaring, *"Ja sum meni!"* (*"I am the menu!"*) to the chuckles of his regulars. The front room comes with a TV and a little bar action; it's quieter in the back (40-kn grilled fish plate, daily 7:00–24:00, walk 200 yards along the waterfront west of Old Town to Trumbičeva obala 11, poorly marked—look for *Ožujsko Pivo* sign and salty locals standing out front, tel. 021/345-223). When you ask for dessert, they say, "Go to the pastry shop next door" (good suggestion—that's Delta Matejuška, below).

Pizza and Pasta: **Zlatna Vrata** ("Golden Gate"), right in the Old Town, offers wood-fired pizzas and pasta dishes. The food and interior are ho-hum, but there's wonderful outdoor seating in a tingle-worthy Gothic courtyard with pointy arches and lots of pillars (25–45 kn, Mon–Sat 11:00–24:00, closed Sun—except maybe in summer, just inside the Golden Gate and up the skinny alley to the left at Dioklecijanova 7, tel. 021/345-015). **Ristorante Pizzeria Galija,** at the west end of the Old Town, has good wood-fired pizza, pasta, and salads (25–50-kn pizzas and pasta dishes, air-con, Mon–Sat 9:00–24:00, Sun 12:00–24:00, just a block off of the pedestrian drag Marmontova at Tončićeva 12, tel. 021/347-932).

On the Riva: **Restaurant Adriana** is your only choice for dining (not just drinks and desserts) on the harborfront promenade. It's packed with tourists, so you'll get crank-'em-out food and service for top prices. But with entertaining people-watching, it's not a bad place for a slow meal or scenic drink (50–80-kn main dishes, 15–20-kn salads, 35–45-kn pizzas, daily 7:00–24:00, Riva 8, tel. 021/340-000).

Gelato: Split has several spots for delicious Italian gelato-style ice cream *(sladoled).* Convenient and tasty is **Sara Mari,** just inside the west gate of Diocletian's Palace (steps from People's Square, closed off-season). But locals swarm to a pair of ice-cream parlors near Trg Gaje Bulata (the modern shopping square—with a

McDonald's, big Prima mall, and modern-looking church—at the end of the Marmontova pedestrian drag just beyond the northwest corner of the Old Town): **Kuća Sladoleda Karmen** (daily 8:00–24:00, hides behind the building in the middle of the square, facing the modern church on Kačićeva) and **Hajduk** (daily 8:00–24:00, a block west from the top of Marmontova and around the corner from Galija pizzeria at Matošićeva 4).

Other Treats: **Delta Matejuška,** a handy little bakery, sells great pies and cakes by the slice, plus 10-kn sandwiches and pizza to go. They have various locations, including one right on People's Square in the heart of the Old Town (Mon–Sat 7:00–22:00, Sun 7:00–13:00), and next door to the recommended Buffet Fife at Trumbičeva obala 13 (daily 7:00–24:00). After dining at Buffet Fife (described above), drop by here for a special treat, and enjoy it on a bench overlooking the harbor.

TRANSPORTATION CONNECTIONS

Split's Jadrolinija office is in the main ferry terminal (see "Arrival in Split," page 621), with several smaller branch offices between there and the Old Town (tel. 021/338-333).

From Split by Jadrolinija Ferry: The boat generally leaves Split early in the morning and heads south, stopping at **Korčula** (3.5–6 hrs, 5/week in summer, less off-season), **Dubrovnik** (9–11 hrs, 3–4/week in summer, less off-season), and sometimes other coastal destinations.

Other Boat Connections to Korčula: Krilo runs a fast catamaran to Korčula town four times each week (55 kn, about 3 hrs, usually leaves Split mid-afternoon, stops at Hvar en route to Korčula town, also stops at Prigradica on Korčula island in summer). Less convenient are the regional Jadrolinija ferries that connect Split to the town of Vela Luka on Korčula island. From Vela Luka, it's a long bus trip to Korčula town (see page 651). Avoid this roundabout route if you can (inquire locally for schedules; if taking a car, there are no reservations—just show up an hour early and you should be fine).

By Boat to Italy: See "Sailing" sidebar on page 586.

By Bus to: Zagreb (at least hrly, 5–8 hrs, depending on route, about 140 kn), **Dubrovnik** (nearly hrly, 5 hrs, about 100 kn), **Korčula** (1 night bus leaves 24:45 and arrives 6:00, about 100 kn), **Trogir** (at least hrly, 30 min, about 15–20 kn), **Zadar** (at least hrly, 3 hrs, about 70 kn). Zagreb-bound buses sometimes also stop at **Plitvice** (confirm with driver and ask him to stop; 4–6 hrs, 70–80 kn). Each of these routes is served by various companies, which charge slightly different rates, so the prices listed here are rough estimates. Reservations for buses are generally not necessary, but always ask about the fastest option—which can save hours of bus time. Bus info: www.ak-split.hr, tel. 021/338-483 or toll tel. 060-327-327.

   By Train to: Zagreb (3/day, 5.75 hrs, plus 2 direct night trains, 8–8.5 hrs). Train info: tel. 021/338-525 or toll tel. 060-333-444.

Korčula

To get a break from the Dalmatian Coast's two cities, consider the sleepy island getaway of Korčula (KOHR-choo-lah). The Croatian coast has dozens of interchangeable resort towns. But with an extremely atmospheric Old Town, some surprisingly engaging

museums, and a dramatic, fjord-like mountain backdrop, Korčula stands proud above the rest.

   Korčula was founded by ancient Greeks. It became part of the Roman Empire, and was eventually a key southern outpost of the Venetian Republic. Four centuries of Venetian rule left Korčula with a quirky Gothic-Renaissance mix and a strong siesta tradition. Korčulans insist that the great explorer Marco Polo was born here in 1254—even though Venetians also consider him one of their own. Korčula's other claims to fame include shipbuilding and the traditional *Moreška* sword dance.

   Today there are two Korčulas: the tacky seaside resort and the historic Old Town. Like so many other Croatian coastal towns, Korčula comes with crumbling communist-era hotels crammed full of boisterous European holiday-makers, gift shops hawking the tackiest trinkets you've ever seen, and a peak season that hits suddenly and floods the town like a tidal wave, only to recede a couple months later—leaving only empty streets and dazed locals.

   Savvy visitors, on the other hand, ignore the tourist sprawl and focus instead on Korčula's medieval quarter, which pokes out into the sea on a picture-perfect peninsula. Tiny lanes branch off the humble main drag like ribs on a fishbone. This street plan is designed to catch both the breeze and the shade. All in all, this laid-back island village is an ideal place to take a vacation from your busy vacation.

Planning Your Time

Korčula offers little to do besides taking it easy. Wander the medi-eval Old Town, explore the handful of tiny museums, kick back at a café or restaurant, or bask on the beach. If you're here on a Thursday, be sure to catch the performance of the *Moreška* dance (also Mon July–Aug). One day is more than enough for Korčula— but because of sometimes-sparse ferry schedules, you may end up stranded here for longer. With the extra time, consider a one-day package excursion to Mljet Island and its National Park.

Korčula has a couple of fun annual festivals. The "Return to the Age of Marco Polo" festival is the last week of May, with lots of exhibitions, concerts, dances, and a parade with a costumed Marco Polo returning to his native Korčula after his long visit to China. For 10 days at the beginning of September, Korčula remembers the great 1298 naval battle that took place just offshore, when the Genoese captured Marco Polo. The festivities culminate in a 14-ship reenactment, complete with smoke and sound effects.

ORIENTATION

(area code: 020)

The long, skinny island of Korčula runs alongside the even longer, skinnier Pelješac Peninsula (famous for its wine—see page 580). The main town and best destination on the island—just across a narrow strait from Pelješac—is also called Korčula.

Korčula town's compact, highly fortified Old Town (Stari Grad) is on a little peninsula jutting into the Adriatic. Most tourist facilities—ATMs, travel agencies, Jadrolinija ferry office, Internet cafés, Konzum supermarket—are where the Old Town peninsula meets the mainland. Stretching to the south and east of the Old Town is "Shell Bay," surrounded by a strip of tacky tourist shops and resort hotels. This seamier side of Korčula—best avoided— caters mostly to Europeans here to worship the sun for a week or two. To the west of Old Town is the serene waterfront street Put Sv. Nikola, where you'll find my favorite *soba* (Rezi Depolo's—see "Sleeping," page 648) and more locals than tourists.

Warning: Every year, I try to pin down hours for Korčula's TI, travel agencies, and museums. And every year, they change. Be aware that schedules in Korčula revolve entirely around tourist demand. In the busiest peak season (June–Aug), everything is open very long hours daily (occasionally closed for a mid-day siesta). May, September, and October are shoulder season, when opening times can be more limited (especially during siesta times and on weekends). And November through the end of April are dead as a doornail—many of the town's restaurants, museums, and *sobe* close down completely for several months, and everything else has extremely limited hours (basically weekday mornings only). If you're here anytime outside of mid-summer, don't rely on my hours—call a day or two ahead to double-check that the place you

Korčula

100 YARDS
100 METERS

OREBIĆ PASSENGER FERRY DOCK

OLD TOWN WALLS

MARCO POLO'S HOUSE

TUDMANA
SPANICEVA
LUKE
V. FORETICA
TOWN MUSEUM
MIROSEVICA
ISMAELLI
GIUNIO
TEATRA
ZITNICA
OBALA DR. FRANJO

ROZAN
ROKA
KORC. BRAT.
DOM
SET. PETRA
B
LUKE TOLENT.
DEPOLO
DON PAVLA
KANA

ST. MARK'S CATHEDRAL
BISK.
MARK AND
BANIC
CHURCH MUSEUM
KORC. STAT. 1214
IVE MATIJACE
KAPOROVA
VELIKA
ICON MUSEUM
ALL SAINTS' CHURCH

TOWN HALL
FOSA
POST
ST. MICHAEL
DOBRO.
RAMPADA
GREAT LAND GATE

PUT SV. NIK.
TO
PLOKATA 19 TRAVNJA 1921

TO BUS STN.
KORC. BROD.
JADROLINIJA FERRY DOCK

★ = ST. MARK'S SQUARE
DCH

1 Hotel Korčula
2 To Hotels Liburna, Park, Marko Polo, & Bon Repos
3 To Depolo Rooms
4 Modrinić Rooms
5 Konoba Morski Konjic Restaurant
6 Adio Mare Rest.
7 Riblji Rest. Kanavelić
8 Konoba Marinero Rest.
9 Konzum Supermarket
10 Buffet Massimo
11 Marko Polo Travel
12 Atlas Travel
13 *Moreška* Dance Exhibit & Theater
14 Jadrolinija Office

need (like a room-booking agency) will actually be open when you get here.

Tourist Information

Korčula's we-try-harder TI, well-run by Stanka Kraljević, is next to Hotel Korčula on the west side of the Old Town waterfront (mid-June–Sept Mon–Sat 8:00–15:00 & 16:00–22:00, Sun 9:00–14:00; Oct–mid-June Mon–Fri 8:00–15:00, closed Sat–Sun, may be open Sat in shoulder season; tel. 020/715-701, www.korcula .net). Pick up the free cartoon map (marked with "rambling paths") and *Korčula* magazine (with maps, pictures, hotel information, and other town information).

The **Jadrolinija office**—essential for confirming boat schedules and figuring out your options—is located where the Old Town meets the mainland (mid-June–Sept Mon–Fri 8:00–20:00, Sat–Sun 8:00–14:00; Oct–mid-June Mon–Fri 8:00–14:00, Sat–Sun 8:00–13:00, tel. 020/715-410, www.jadrolinija.hr). For a run-down of the confusing boat options to and from Korčula, see page 651.

Arrival in Korčula

By Boat: Jadrolinija ferries usually arrive on the east side of town. As you exit the boat, the fortified Old Town is on your right. To reach the hotels on the far side of Shell Bay (Liburna, Park, Marko Polo), exit left and walk around the bay (about a 10-min walk). To get to the Old Town, Hotel Korčula, and my recommended *sobe*, go straight ahead from the boat landing. In two minutes, you'll come to a big staircase leading to the Great Land Gate (the Old Town's main entrance gate). On the square in front of these steps, you'll find an ATM, the Atlas travel agency (room booking), a colorful outdoor produce market, and the Jadrolinija office.

Sometimes the Jadrolinija ferry arrives on the west side of town, by Hotel Korčula (also used by Orebić passenger ferry). To reach the center, walk with the Old Town on your left-hand side and turn left around the big round tower. In two minutes, you'll reach the staircase described above.

A few boats (car ferries from Orebić and Drvenik) come to the Dominče dock two peninsulas east of Korčula (near Hotel Bon Repos). Hourly buses connect this dock with Korčula.

By Bus: The bus station is at the southeast corner of Korčula's Shell Bay. If you leave the station with the bay on your left, you'll get to hotels Liburna, Park, and Marko Polo. If you leave with the bay on your right, you'll get to the Old Town, Hotel Korčula, and the main ferry terminal (see "By Boat," above).

By Car: See "Transportation Connections," below.

SIGHTS

Korčula's few sights cluster within a few yards of each other in the Old Town. Aside from the Moreška dance, I've listed them roughly in order from the Great Land Gate (the Old Town's main entry) to the tip of the Old Town peninsula. All museums are closed November through April, but most will usually open by request (ask the TI to call for you...or just try knocking on the door).

▲▲**Moreška Dance**—Lazy Korčula snaps to life when locals perform a medieval folk dance called the *Moreška* (moh-REHSH-kah). The plot helps Korčulans remember their hard-fought past: A bad king takes the good king's bride, the dancing forces of good and evil battle, and there's always a happy ending (80 kn, June–mid-Oct every Thu at 21:00, July–Aug also Mon at 21:00, in Gradska Vijećnica theater next to Great Land Gate, or in movie theater if bad weather; buy tickets from travel agency, at your hotel, or at the door).

▲**Great Land Gate (Veliki Revelin)**—An impressive staircase leads up to the main entrance to the Old Town. Like all of the town's

towers, it's adorned with the Venetian winged lion and the coats-of-arms of the doge of Venice (left) and the rector of Korčula (right; the offset coat of arms below was the rector who renovated the gate later). You can climb up the tower to visit a small exhibit on the *Moreška* dance and enjoy panoramic town views (10 kn, May–Oct daily 9:30–21:30, likely closed Nov–April, English descriptions).

Just inside the gate is **Franjo Tuđman Square,** recently (in 2001) renamed for the controversial first president of an independent Croatia (see page 576). During the war, Tuđman was considered a hero. In later years, he grew power-hungry and held secret negotiations with the merciless Serbian leader Slobodan Milošević. But members of his party are still in power and hold local offices throughout the country, sometimes adorning a square or street with his name. (Many Croatians think—or hope—these names will be changed again before too long.)

On the left inside the gate is the 16th-century **Town Hall and Rector's Palace.** The seal of Korčula symbolizes the town's importance as the southernmost bastion of the Venetian Republic: St. Mark standing below three defensive towers. The little church on the other side of the square is dedicated to **St. Michael** (Crkva Sv. Mihovila). Throughout Croatia, you'll often find churches to St.

Michael just inside the town gates, as he is believed to offer saintly protection from enemies. Notice that a passageway connects the church to the building across the street—home to the Brotherhood of St. Michael, one of Korčula's many religious fraternal organizations (see "Icon Museum," page 647).

• *Now continue up the...*

▲**Street of the Korčulan Statute of 1214 (Ulica Korčulanskog Statuta 1214)**—This street is Korčula's backbone—in more ways than one (the street plan is designed as a fish skeleton). While most medieval towns slowly evolved with twisty, mazelike lanes, Korčula was carefully planned. The streets to the west (left) of this one are straight, to allow the refreshing west winds *(maestral)* into town. To the east (right), they're curved (notice you can't see the sea)—to keep out the bad-vibe southeast winds.

The street's complicated name honors a 1214 statute, the oldest known written law in Central Europe, with regulations about everyday life and instructions on maintaining the walls, protecting nature, keeping animals, building a house, and so on.

• *If you continue a few steps up the street, you'll reach St. Mark's Square (Trg Sv. Marka). From here, you're a few steps from the next four sights.*

▲**St. Mark's Cathedral (Katedrala Sv. Marka)**—Korčula became a bishopric in the 14th century. In the 19th century—36 bishops

later—the Hapsburgs decided to centralize ecclesiastical power in their empire, and removed Korčula's bishop. The town still has this beautiful "cathedral"—but no bishop. On the facade, you'll see another Venetian statue of St. Mark (flanked by Adam and Eve). Inside, above the main altar, is an original Tintoretto painting (recently restored in Zagreb). As you leave, notice the weapons on the back wall, used in some of the pivotal battles that have taken place near strategically situated Korčula (10 kn, included in 20-kn combo-ticket with Church Museum—see below, May–Oct daily 9:00–14:00 & 17:00–20:00, maybe open all day long in peak season, closed during church services, generally closed Nov–April but maybe open Mon–Fri 9:00–12:00 after Easter).

▲**Church Museum (Opatska Riznica)**—This small museum has an unusual and fascinating collection. Try to find the following: a ceremonial necklace from Mother Teresa (who came from Macedonia, not too far from here—she gave this necklace to a friend from Korčula), some old 12th-century hymnals, two tiny drawings by Leonardo da Vinci, a coin collection (including a 2,400-year-old Greek coin minted here in Korčula), some Croatian modern paintings (including two in the distinctive "naive art" style—see page 658), and two framed reliquaries with dozens of miniscule relics (15 kn, included in 20-kn combo-ticket with cathedral, May–Oct daily 9:00–14:00 & 17:00–20:00, maybe open all day long in peak season, generally closed Nov–April but maybe open Mon–Fri 9:00–12:00 after Easter).

▲**Town Museum (Gradski Muzej)**—Housed in an old mansion, this museum does a fine job of bringing together Korčula's eclectic claims to fame. It's arranged like a traditional Dalmatian home: shop on the ground floor, living quarters in the middle floors, kitchen on top. Notice that some of the walls near the entry have holes in them. Archaeologists are continually doing actual "digs" into these walls to learn how medieval houses here were built.

On the ground floor is a lapidarium, featuring fragments of Korčula's stone past (see the 1st-century Roman jugs). Upstairs is a display on Korčula's long-standing shipbuilding industry, including models of two modern steel ships built here (the town still builds ship parts today). There's also a furnished living room and, in the attic, a kitchen. This was a smart place for the kitchen—if it caught fire, it was less likely to destroy the whole building. Notice the little WC in the corner. A network of pipes took kitchen and other waste through town and out to sea (10 kn, limited posted English information—pick up the free English guide brochure at entry, mid-June–Aug Mon–Sat 9:30–21:00, closed Sun; Sept–mid-June Mon–Fri 8:00–15:00—if it's locked, try knocking, closed Sat–Sun).

▲**Marco Polo's House (Kuća Marka Pola)**—Korčula's favorite son is the great 13th-century explorer Marco Polo. Though Polo sailed under the auspices of the Venetian Republic, and technically was a Venetian (since the Republic controlled this region), Korčulans proudly claim him as their own. Marco Polo was the first Westerner to sail to China, bringing back amazing stories and goods (like silk) that Europeans had never seen before. After his trip, Marco Polo fought in an important naval battle against the Genoese near Korčula. He was captured, taken to Genoa, and imprisoned. He told his story to a cellmate, who wrote it down, published it, and made the explorer a world-class and much-in-demand celebrity. To this day, kids in swimming pools around the world try to find him with their eyes closed.

Today, Korčula is the proud home to "Marco Polo's House"—actually a more recent building on the site of what may or may not have been his family's property. The house is in poor repair, but most of the property has been purchased by the city to open to visitors. In 2006, you'll probably only be able to climb the tower and wander the gardens, but it's a start (likely open May–Oct only;

just north of cathedral on—where else?—ulica Depolo).

▲**Icon Museum (Zbirka Ikona)**—Korčula is known for its many brotherhoods—centuries-old fraternal organizations that have sprung up around churches. The Brotherhood of All Saints has been meeting every Sunday after Mass since the 14th century, and they run a small but interesting museum of icons. These golden religious images were brought back from Greece in the 17th century by Korčulans who had been fighting the Turks on a Venetian warship (10 kn, May–Oct Mon–Sat 10:00–13:00 & 17:00–20:00, maybe open all day long in peak season, closed Sun and Nov–April—but try knocking, on Kaprova ulica at the Old Town's southeast tip).

Brotherhoods' meeting halls are often connected to their church by a second-story walkway. Use this one to step in to the Venetian-style **All Saints' Church** (Crkva Svih Svetih). Under the loft in the back of the church, notice the models of boats and tools—donated by Korčula's shipbuilders. Look closely at the painting to the right of the altar. See the guys in the white robes kneeling under Jesus? That's the Brotherhood, who commissioned this painting.

▲**Old Town Walls**—For several centuries, Korčula held a crucial strategic position: This was one of the most important southern outposts of the Venetian Republic (the Republic of Dubrovnik started at the Pelješac Peninsula, just across the sea). The original town walls around Korčula date from at least the 13th century, but the fortifications were extended (and new towers built) over several centuries to defend against various foes of Venice—mostly Turks and pirates.

The most recent tower dates from the 16th century, when the Turks attacked Korčula. The rector and other VIPs fled to the mainland, but a brave priest remained on the island and came up with a plan. All of the women of Korčula dressed up as men, and then everybody in town peeked over the wall—making the Turks think they were up against a huge army. The priest prayed for help, and a strong north wind *(bora)* blew. Not wanting to take their chances with the many defenders and the weather, the Turks sailed away, and Korčula was saved.

By the late 19th century, Korčula was an unimportant Hapsburg beach town, and the walls had no strategic value. The town decided to quarry the top half of its old walls to build new homes (and to improve air circulation inside the city). While today's walls are half as high as they used to be, the town has restored many of the towers, giving Korčula its fortified feel today. Each one has a winged lion—a symbol of Venice—and the seal of the rector of Korčula when the tower was built.

ACTIVITIES

Excursions—Various companies offer day-long excursions to nearby destinations (generally available June–Oct). The most popular options are Dubrovnik (about 350 kn, 3/week) and the National Park on Mljet Island (about 200 kn, 2/week). You can buy tickets at any local travel agency (try Marko Polo or Atlas, both listed under "Booking Sobe Through an Agency," below).

Swimming—The water around Korčula is clean and popular for swimming. You'll find pebbly beaches strewn with holiday-goers all along Put Sv. Nikola, the street that runs west from the Old Town. Another popular swimming spot is at the very end of the Old Town peninsula.

SLEEPING

(€1 = about $1.20, 6 kn = about $1, country code: 385, area code: 020)

Korčula's accommodations options are extremely limited. There are five hotels in town—all decaying, overpriced, resort-style hotels, and all owned by the same company (which is, in turn, government-run). The lack of competition keeps quality low and prices ridiculously high—which makes *sobe* a particularly good alternative. No matter where you stay, you'll be charged a tourist tax of about €1 per person, per night (less off-season; not included in these rates).

Sobe

My two favorite *sobe* in Korčula offer similar comfort to the hotels at far lower prices—with TVs and air-conditioning, to boot.

$ Rezi and Andro Depolo, probably distant relatives of Marco, rent four comfy rooms on the bay west of the Old Town. Three of the rooms offer beautiful views to the Old Town, and the five-minute stroll into town is pleasant and scenic. English-speaking Rezi is very friendly and works to make her guests feel welcome (Db-€28, or €33 July–Aug, room with kitchen-€6 more, 30 percent more for 1- or 2-night stays, continental breakfast-25 kn, big breakfast-35 kn, cash only, Put Sv. Nikola 43; walk along waterfront from Old Town with bay on your right, look for *sobe* sign at the yellow house set back from the street, just before the 2 monasteries; tel. 020/711-621, viladepolo@hotmail.com). If Rezi's place is booked up, she's well-connected with neighbors also renting private rooms.

$ Lenni and Periša Modrinić, both of whom speak good English, rent three modern, almost hotelesque rooms and an apartment in the heart of the Old Town (Db-€35, or €40

July–Aug; apartment-€45, or €50 July–Aug; €5 less off-season, 10 percent more for 1-nighters, no breakfast, cash only, near the popular Konoba Marko Polo restaurant at Jakova Baničevića 13, tel. 020/711-400, www.ikorcula.net/lenni, perisa.modrinic@du .htnet.hr).

$ Booking *Sobe* through an Agency: While you can walk along Put Sv. Nikola and generally find a fine deal on a private room, you can also book one through one of Korčula's travel agencies (for an additional 20 percent). **Marko Polo Tours** books private rooms from their selection of 20 places. You'll use their office as a kind of reception desk (Db-€50 in high season, €35 in shoulder season; daily in summer 8:00–22:00; until 20:00 and maybe closed for mid-afternoon break in shoulder season; Jan–March Mon–Sat 8:00–12:00, closed Sun; located just outside the Old Town gate at Biline 5, tel. 020/715-400, fax 020/715-800, marko-polo-tours@du.htnet.hr). **Atlas Travel** is another option (similar hours to Marko Polo, Trg 19. Travnja, tel. 020/711-231, fax 020/715-580).

Hotels

All five of Korčula's hotels are owned by HTP Korčula. If you don't want to stay in a *soba,* these are the only game in town. You can reserve rooms at any of them through the main office (tel. 020/726-336, fax 020/711-746, www.korcula-hotels.com, marketing@htp-korcula.hr; at all hotels, credit cards are accepted, there is no air-con, and there are no non-smoking rooms). I've listed high-season prices with breakfast only; rates are progressively lower the farther off-season you get. You can pay 10 percent more per person for half-board (dinner at the hotel). It's much cheaper to stay a week or longer.

$$$ Hotel Korčula has by far the best location, right on the waterfront alongside the Old Town. It has a fine seaside terrace restaurant and friendly staff, even if the 20 rooms are outmoded and overpriced. The rooms are on two floors: "first-floor" rooms (actually on the 3rd floor) have big windows; "second-floor" rooms (actually on the 4th) have tiny windows (July–Aug: Sb-€90–100, Db-€125–145; June and Sept: Sb-€70–80, Db-€110–125; 10 percent more for seaview, reception tel. 020/711-078).

$$$ *Other Hotels:* Three more hotels cluster a 15-minute walk away, around the far side of Shell Bay. All are poorly maintained, overpriced, and inconvenient to the Old Town, but they share a nice beach. **Hotel Liburna** has 83 rooms—some of them accessible by elevator—and the same prices as Hotel Korčula. Half the rooms face the sea and cost an additional 10 percent (reception tel. 020/726-006). **Hotel Park** has 153 rooms (same rates as Hotel Korčula, reception tel. 020/726-100). **Hotel Marko Polo** has

109 rooms and an elevator (about 15 percent cheaper than Hotel Korčula, reception tel. 020/726-004). The fifth hotel, **Hotel Bon Repos**—another 15 minutes by foot from the Old Town—is, in every sense, the last resort.

EATING

Korčula has plenty of tasty seafood restaurants. Try these suggestions, or follow your nose through the Old Town. The price ranges I've listed don't include seafood splurges, which can be much higher (often listed on the menu by the kilogram; half a kilogram is about right for a large portion).

Konoba Morski Konjic (literally, "Moorish Seahorse") has tables spilling along the seawall, offering atmospheric dining with salty views and jaded service. If you want romantic harborside dining, this is your best option (50- to 60-kn plates, daily 8:00–24:00).

Adio Mare offers fine seafood and pleasant, cave-like, Old World atmosphere near Marco Polo's House (daily 18:00–23:00, sometimes also 12:00–14:00 in peak season, tel. 020/711-253).

Riblji Restoran Kanavelić, near the far end of the Old Town peninsula, serves good seafood in a fancier setting (20–45-kn non-seafood dishes, plus seafood splurges, daily 18:00–23:00, tel. 020/711-800).

Konoba Marinero has nautical decor and a simple menu of Dalmatian specialties on a peaceful alley just two blocks from the main street in the Old Town (most main dishes 50–90 kn, May–mid-Oct daily 11:00–15:00 & 18:00–24:00, dinner only mid-Oct–April, Marka Andrijića 13, tel. 020/711-170).

Picnics: Just outside the main gate, you'll find a lively produce market and a big, modern, air-conditioned Konzum supermarket (next to Marko Polo Tours). A short stroll from there, down Put Sv. Nikola, takes you to beach perches with the best Korčula views. Otherwise, there are plenty of picnic spots along the Old Town embankment.

A Scenic Drink: The best setting for drinks is at **Buffet "Massimo,"** in a city-wall tower at the tip of the Old Town peninsula. The main dining room is just inside the top of the tower, but if you're just having drinks, climb the ladder and sit up top with wonderful views (30–50-kn pizzas, otherwise just drinks, daily 18:00–2:00 in the morning, tel. 020/715-073).

TRANSPORTATION CONNECTIONS

Korčula is reasonably well-connected to the rest of the Dalmatian Coast by boat, but service becomes sparse in the off-season. No matter when you travel, it's smart to carefully study current boat schedules when planning your itinerary.

From Korčula by Boat: Most travelers get to Korčula by Jadrolinija ferry (docks right at Old Town). You can take it to **Split** (5/week in summer, less off-season, stops at Stari Grad on Hvar Island en route, trip takes 3.5–6 hrs) or **Dubrovnik** (3–4/week in summer, less off-season, trip takes 3.5–4.5 hrs).

Krilo runs a speedy catamaran to **Split** four mornings each week (55 kn, about 3 hrs, leaves early in the morning, stops at Hvar, also stops at Prigradica on Korčula island in summer).

There's yet another way to **Split,** but it usually requires a very early bus from Korčula to the port at Vela Luka, an hour away at the other end of the island. Every day, a local Jadrolinija ferry and a faster hydrofoil leave from the Vela Luka dock and go to Hvar, then on to Split (ferry: Mon–Sat at 6:30, Sun at 9:30, 1.5 hrs to Hvar, 3 hrs to Split; hydrofoil: Mon–Sat at 5:30, Sun at 8:00, 30 min to Hvar, 1.5 hrs to Split). There's sometimes a second crossing of the slower boat in summer (late-June–early Sept), leaving Vela Luka in the afternoon. Each ferry arriving at Vela Luka is met by a bus waiting to whisk arriving travelers to Korčula town.

In sum, carefully confirm boat schedules and understand all your options (at the Korčula TI or Jadrolinija office) before you get up early to make the trip.

By Bus to: Dubrovnik (peak season: 2/day, 3–4 hrs; off-season: Mon–Sat 1/day with an early departure, Sun 2/day), **Zagreb** (1/day, 9–12 hrs depending on route), **Split** (1/day, 5 hrs, same bus goes to Zagreb), **Vela Luka** (at far end of island, Mon–Fri 7/day, Sat 6/day, Sun 4/day, 1st bus at 4:10 gets you to the early-morning ferries—see above).

By Car: The island of Korčula is connected to the mainland by a small ferry between Orebić and Dominče (1 mile from Korčula town, 50 kn/car, 12 kn/passenger, 15-min ride, departs Dominče at the top of most but not all hours—check carefully in Korčula, departs Orebić at :30 past most hours).

Rather than take this shorter ferry and then drive the rest of the way between Korčula and Split, I prefer to take the longer ferry the whole way. In summer, there are two each day between Split and Vela Luka (at the far end of Korčula Island—see above; 1/day in winter; 315 kn/car, 35 kn/passenger). The scenic and relaxing four-hour boat ride saves you about that much driving time. Once in Korčula town, there's plenty of free parking at the bus station along the marina.

ZAGREB

While Zagreb doesn't have the world-class sights of Budapest or the stay-awhile charm of Ljubljana, the Croatian capital offers historic neighborhoods, offbeat museums, and an illuminating contrast to the beaches. As a tourist destination, Zagreb pales in comparison to the sparkling coastal towns. But you can't get a complete picture of modern Croatia without a visit here—away from the touristy resorts—in the lively and livable city that is home to one out of every six Croatians (pop. 765,000).

Zagreb began as two walled medieval towns, Gradec and Kaptol, separated by a river. As Croatia fell under the control of various foreign powers—Budapest, Vienna, Berlin, and Belgrade—the two hill towns that would become Zagreb gradually took on more religious and civic importance. Kaptol became a bishopric in 1094, and it's still home to Croatia's most important church. In the 16th century, the *Ban* (Croatia's governor) and the *Sabor* (parliament) called Gradec home. The two towns officially merged in 1850, and soon after, the railroad connecting Budapest with the Adriatic port city of Rijeka was built through the city. Zagreb prospered.

After centuries of being the de facto religious, cultural, and political center of Croatia, Zagreb officially became a European capital when the country declared its independence in 1991. In the ensuing war with Serbia, Zagreb was hardly damaged—Serbian bombs hit only a few strategic targets (the bloodiest fighting was to the east and south of here).

Today, just over a decade later, Zagreb has long since repaired the minimal damage, and the capital feels safe, modern, and accessible.

Zagreb

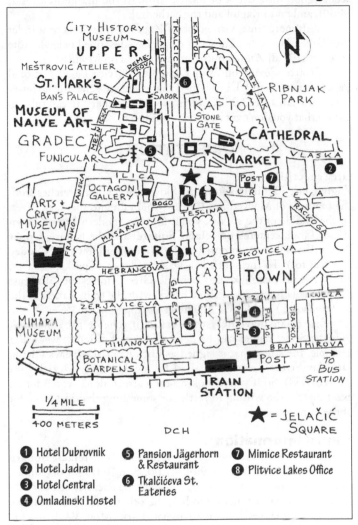

- **1** Hotel Dubrovnik
- **2** Hotel Jadran
- **3** Hotel Central
- **4** Omladinski Hostel
- **5** Pansion Jägerhorn & Restaurant
- **6** Tkalčićeva St. Eateries
- **7** Mimice Restaurant
- **8** Plitvice Lakes Office

★ = JELAČIĆ SQUARE

Planning Your Time

Most American visitors just pass through Zagreb, but the city is worth a look. Check your bag at the station and zip into the center for a quick visit—or consider spending the night.

You can get a decent sense of Zagreb in just a few hours. With whatever time you have, make a beeline for Jelačić Square to visit the TI and get oriented. Take the funicular up to Gradec, visit the excellent Museum of Naive Art, and stroll St. Mark's Square. Then wander down through the Stone Chapel to the lively Tkalčićeva

654 Rick Steves' Best of Eastern Europe

scene (good for a drink or meal), through the market (closes at 14:00), and on to Kaptol and the cathedral.

With more time, visit some of Zagreb's museums or wander the "Green Horseshoe" (a series of parks—described below). Note that virtually all Zagreb museums are closed on Monday.

If you're moving on from Zagreb to Plitvice Lakes National Park (see next chapter), be warned that there are generally no buses between 17:30 and 22:00. Confirm your bus departure carefully to ensure that you don't get stranded in Zagreb.

ORIENTATION

(area code: 01)
Zagreb, just 30 minutes from the Slovenian border, stretches from the foothills of Medvednica ("Bear Mountain") to the Sava River. In the middle of the sprawl, you'll find the modern **Lower Town** (Donji Grad, centered on **Jelačić Square**) and the historic **Upper Town** (Gornji Grad, comprising the original hill towns of **Gradec** and **Kaptol**). To the south is a U-shaped belt of parks, squares, and museums that make up "Lenuci's Green Horseshoe." The east side of the U is a series of three parks, with the train station at the bottom (south) and Jelačić Square at the top (north).

Zagrebians have devised a brilliant scheme for confusing tourists: Street names can be depicted several different ways. For example, the street that is signed as ulica Kralja Držislava ("King Držislav Street") is often called by locals simply Držislavova ("Držislav's"). So if you're looking for a street, don't search for an exact match—be willing to settle for something that just has a lot of the same letters.

Tourist Information

Zagreb has two TIs. The bigger, better one is at **Jelačić Square** (Mon–Fri 8:30–20:00, Sat 9:00–17:00, Sun 10:00–14:00, sometimes longer hours in summer, Trg bana Jelačića 11, tel. 01/481-4051, www.zagreb-touristinfo.hr); the other is just a few blocks south, along the west side of **Zrinjevac Park** (Mon, Wed, and Fri 9:00–17:00, Tue and Thu 9:00–18:00, closed Sat–Sun, Trg Nikole Šubića Zrinskoga 14, tel. 01/492-1645). Zagreb's TIs offer piles of free, well-produced tourist brochures that desperately try to convince visitors to do more than just pass through. Pick up the one-page city map (with handy transit map and regional map on back), the *Zagreb Info A–Z* booklet (including accommodations and restaurant listings), the monthly events guide, the great *City Walks* brochure (with a couple of easy, self-guided walking tours), the museum guide, and more.

The **Zagreb Card** gives you free transportation and discounts

Zagreb Essentials

English	Croatian	Pronounced
Jelačić Square	Trg bana Jelačića	turg BAH-nah YEH-lah-chee-chah
Gradec (original civic hill town)	Gradec	GRAH-dehts
Kaptol (original religious hill town)	Kaptol	KAHP-tohl
Café street between Gradec and Kaptol	Tkalčićeva	tuh-kahl-chee-CHAY-vah
Main Train Station	Glavni Kolodvor	GLAHV-nee KOH-loh-dvor
Bus Station	Autobusni Kolodvor	OW-toh-boos-nee KOH-loh-dvor

on Zagreb sights for 72 hours (90 kn, sold at TI). This usually doesn't make sense for folks who are day-tripping here, but it's a good deal for longer stays, or if you're taking a city tour.

To get oriented, consider the fun daily **city tours**, led by local guides dressed up as important historical Zagrebians (2-hour walking tour: 95 kn, usually Mon–Thu; 3-hr bus-plus-walking tour: 150 kn, usually Fri–Sun; 50 percent discount on either tour with Zagreb Card—a great deal). Call the TI the day before by 14:00 to confirm the schedule, reserve a space, and request an English guide (tel. 01/481-4051, www.event.hr).

Arrival in Zagreb

By Train: Zagreb's Main Train Station (Glavni Kolodvor) is conveniently located a few blocks south of Jelačić Square on the "Green Horseshoe." The straightforward arrivals hall has a train information desk, ticket windows, ATMs, WCs, and newsstands. The left-luggage office is at the left end of the station, with your back to the tracks (look for low-profile *garderoba* sign, open daily 24 hours). To reach the city center, go straight out the front door. You'll run into a taxi stand, and then the tracks for tram #6 (buy 6.50-kn ticket from kiosk, then hop on: direction Črnomerec zips you to Jelačić Square; direction Sopot takes you to the bus station—the 3rd stop, just after you turn right and go under the big overpass). If you walk straight ahead through the long, lush park, you'll wind up at the bottom of Jelačić Square in 10 minutes.

By Bus: The user-friendly bus station (Autobusni Kolodvor) is a few long blocks southeast of the Main Train Station. The station has all the essentials—ATMs, post office, mini-grocery store, left-luggage counter...everything from a smut store to a chapel. Upstairs, you'll find ticket windows and access to the buses (follow signs to *perone;* wave ticket in front of turnstile to open gate). Tram #6 (in direction Črnomerec) takes you to the Main Train Station, then on to Jelačić Square.

By Plane: Zagreb's airport is 10 miles south of the center (tel. 01/626-5222, www.zagreb-airport.hr). The Croatia Air bus connects the airport to Zagreb's bus station (25 kn, every 30 min, 25-min trip). Figure around 200 kn for a taxi from the airport to the center.

Getting Around Zagreb

The main mode of public transportation is the **tram,** operated by ZET (Zagreb Electrical Transport, www.zet.hr). A single ticket (good for 90 min in one direction, including transfers) costs 8 kn if you buy it from the driver (6.50 kn at kiosk, ask for *ZET karta*). A day ticket *(dnevna karta)* costs 18 kn. The most useful tram for tourists is #6, connecting Jelačić Square with the train and bus stations.

Taxis start at 25 kn, then run 7 kn per kilometer (20 percent more Sun and at night, 5 kn extra for each piece of baggage; as always, there are corrupt cabbies—ask for an estimate up front, or call Radio Taxi, tel. 01/970 or 01/668-2505).

Helpful Hints

Ferry Tickets: If you're heading for the Dalmatian Coast, note that there isn't a Jadrolinija ferry office in the center. But you can reserve and buy tickets at the **Marko Polo** travel agency (Masarykova 24, tel. 01/481-5216).

Plitvice Lakes Office: If you're going to Plitvice Lakes National Park, you can get a preview and ask any questions at their helpful information office in Zagreb (Mon–Fri 8:00–16:00, closed Sat–Sun, a block in front of Main Train Station at Trg Kralja Tomislava 19, tel. 01/461-3586).

SIGHTS

The following sights are listed in the order of a handy one-way circular orientation walk, starting at Jelačić Square. The entire route will take you about an hour at a leisurely pace (not counting museum stops).

▲**Jelačić Square (Trg bana Jelačića)**—Zagreb's main square bustles with life. It's lined with cafés, shops, trams, Baroque buildings, and the TI. When Zagreb consisted of the two hill towns of Gradec and Kaptol, this Donji Grad ("lower town") held the townspeople's farm fields. Today, it features a prominent

equestrian statue of national hero **Josip Jelačić** (YOH-seep YEH-lah-cheech, 1801–1859), a 19th-century governor who extended citizens' rights and did much to unite the Croats within the Hapsburg Empire. In Jelačić's time, the Hungarians were exerting extensive control over Croatia, even trying to make Hungarian the official language. Meanwhile, Budapesters revolted against Hapsburg rule in 1848. Jelačić, ever mindful of the need to protect Croatian cultural autonomy, knew that he'd have a better shot at getting his way from Austria than from Hungary. Jelačić chose the lesser of two evils, and fought alongside the Hapsburgs to put down the Hungarian uprising. In the Yugoslav era, Jelačić was considered dangerously nationalistic, and this statue was taken down. But when Croatia broke away in 1991, Croatian patriotism was in the air, and Jelačić returned. Though Jelačić originally faced his Hungarian foes to the north, today he's staring down the Serbs to the south.

Get oriented. If you face Jelačić's statue, a long block to your left is a funicular that takes you up to one of Zagreb's original villages, Gradec. To the right, look for the TI. If you leave the square ahead and to the right, you'll reach the other original village, Kaptol, and the cathedral (you can't miss its huge, pointy, neo-Gothic spires—visible from virtually everywhere in Zagreb). If you leave the square ahead and to the left, you'll come to the market (Dolac) and the lively café street, Tkalčićeva.

▲▲**Gradec**—Eventually absorbed by Zagreb, the city of Gradec (GRAH-dehts) was granted status as a free royal state by the 1242 Golden Bull—meaning that the town answered only and directly to the Holy Roman Emperor (avoiding the pesky bureaucracy of the nobility). In later years, Gradec became the seat of Croatia's government—including its *Sabor*, or parliament, and *Ban*, or governor.

To reach Gradec from Jelačić Square, go a long block down the busy Ilica. On the way, duck inside the big shopping gallery on the left (at #5). If you go down the first passage, you'll come to a beautiful stained-glass ceiling and a tie store called **Croata.** This is a reminder that the French may have "invented" the tie, but they were inspired by Croatian soldiers, who wore jaunty scarves into battle when they went to fight in the Thirty Years' War. The French even named the new accessory *cravate*—after "Croat."

Continue up Ilica and turn right on Tomičeva, where you'll see a small **funicular** (ZET Uspinjača) crawling up the hill. Dating from the late 19th century, this funicular is looked upon fondly by Zagrebians—both as a bit of nostalgia and as a way to avoid some steps. You can walk up if you want, but the ride is more fun and takes only 55 seconds (3 kn, leaves every 10 min daily 6:30–21:00).

From the top of the funicular, you'll enjoy a fine panorama over Zagreb. The tall tower you face as you exit is one of Gradec's original watchtowers, the **Burglars' Tower** (Kula Lotršćak). After the Tatars ransacked Central Europe in the early 13th century, King Béla IV decreed that towns be fortified—so Gradec built a wall and guard towers (just like Kraków and Buda did). Look for the little cannon in the top-floor window. Every day at noon, this cannon fires a shot, supposedly to commemorate a 15th-century victory over the besieging Turks. Zagrebians hold on to other traditions, too—the lamps on this hill are still gas-powered, lit by a city employee every evening.

Head up the street next to the tower. Little remains of medieval Gradec. When the Turks overran Europe, they never managed to take Zagreb—but the threat was enough to scare the nobility into the countryside. When the Turks left, the nobles came back, and replaced the medieval buildings here with Baroque mansions. At the first square, to the right, you'll see the Jesuit **Church of Saint Catherine.** It's not much to look at from the outside, but the interior is intricately decorated. The same applies to several mansions on Gradec. This simple-outside, ornate-inside style is known as "Zagreb Baroque."

As you continue up the street, you'll see the **Croatian Museum of Naive Art** (Hrvatski Muzej Naivne Umjetnosti) on the left. This remarkable museum, rated ▲▲, collects paintings by untrained peasant artists. These stirring images—fantasy worlds rich with detail—are well worth a look. Keep an eye out for works by the movement's star, Ivan Generalić (10 kn, Tue–Fri 10:00–18:00, Sat–Sun 10:00–13:00, closed Mon, ulica Sv. Ćirila i Metoda 3, tel. 01/485-1911, www.hmnu.org).

At the end of the block, you'll come to the low-key **St. Mark's Square** (Markov trg), centered on the **Church of St. Mark.** The original church here was from the 12th century, but only a few fragments remain. The colorful tile roof, from 1880, depicts two coats of arms. On the left, the red-and-white checkerboard symbolizes north-central Croatia, the three lions' heads stand for the Dalmatian Coast, and the marten (*kuna*, like the money) running between the two rivers (Sava and Drava) represent

Slavonia—Croatia's northern, inland panhandle. On the right is the seal of Zagreb: a walled city with wide-open doors (strong, but still welcoming to visitors...like you).

As you face the church, to the right is the *Sabor,* or parliament. From the 12th century, Croatian noblemen would gather to make important decisions regarding their territories. This gradually evolved into today's modern parliament. (If you walk along the front of the *Sabor* and continue straight ahead 2 blocks, you'll run into the Zagreb City Museum, described below.)

Across the square from the *Sabor* (to your left as you face the church) is the **Ban's Palace** (Banski Dvori), today the offices for the president and prime minister. This was one of the few buildings in central Zagreb destroyed in the recent war. In October of 1991, the Serbs shelled it from afar, knowing that Croatian President Franjo Tuđman was inside...but Tuđman survived.

Walk from Gradec to Kaptol: For an interesting stroll from St. Mark's Square to the cathedral, head down the street (Kamenita ulica) to the right of the parliament building. Near the end of the street, you'll see the oldest pharmacy in town (c. 1355, on the right) before coming to Gradec's oldest surviving gate, the **Stone Gate** (Kamenita Vrata). Inside is an evocative chapel. The focal point is a painting of Mary that miraculously survived a major fire in 1731. When this medieval gate was reconstructed in the Baroque style, they decided to turn it into a makeshift chapel. The candles represent Zagrebians' prayers, and the stone plaques on the wall give thanks *(Hvala)* for prayers that were answered. Mary was made the official patron saint of Zagreb in 1990.

As you leave the Stone Gate and come to Radićeva, turn right. Take the next left, onto the street called **Krvavi Most**—literally, "Blood Bridge." At the end of Krvavi Most, you'll come to **Tkalčićeva.** This lively café-and-restaurant street used to be a river—the natural boundary between Gradec and Kaptol. The two towns did not always get along, and sometimes fought against each other. Blood was spilled, and the bridge that once stood here between them became known as Blood Bridge. By the late 19th century, the towns had united, and the river began to stink—so they covered it over with this street.

As you cross Tkalčićeva, you enter the old town of Kaptol. You'll come to the **market** (Dolac), packed with colorful stalls selling produce of all kinds (Mon–Sat 7:00–14:00, Sun 7:00–12:00). Under your feet is an indoor part of the market, where farmers sell farm-fresh eggs and dairy products (same hours as outdoor market, entrance down below in the direction of Jelačić Square).

On the other side of the market, visit the...

▲**Cathedral (Katedrala)**—By definition, Croats are Catholics. Before the recent war, relatively few people practiced their faith.

But as the Croats fought with their Orthodox and Muslim neighbors, Catholicism took on a greater importance. Today, more and more Croats are attending Mass. This is Croatia's single most important church.

In 1094, when a diocese was established at Kaptol, this church quickly became a major center of high-ranking church officials. In the mid-13th century, the original cathedral was destroyed by invading Tatars, who actually used it as a stable. It was rebuilt, only to be destroyed again by an earthquake in 1880. The current version is neo-Gothic. Surrounding the church are walls with pointy-topped towers (part of a larger archbishop's palace) that were built for protection against the Turks. The full name is the Cathedral of the Assumption of the Blessed Virgin Mary and the Saintly Kings Stephen and Ladislav (whew!)—but most locals just call it "the cathedral."

Step inside (free, Mon–Sat 10:00–17:00, Sun 13:00–17:00). Look closely at the silver relief on the first **altar**: a scene of the Holy Family doing chores around the house (Mary sewing, Joseph and Jesus building a fence...and angels helping out).

In the front left corner, find the tombstone of **Alojzije Stepinac**. He was the Archbishop of Zagreb in World War II, when he shortsightedly supported the Nazis—thinking, like many Croatians, that this was the ticket to greater independence from Serbia. When Tito came to power, he put Stepinac on trial and sent him to jail for five years. But Stepinac never lost his faith, and remains to many the most important inspirational figure of Croatian Catholicism.

As you leave the church, look to the back of the left apse. This strange script is the **Glagolitic alphabet** *(glagoljca)*, invented by Byzantine missionaries Cyril and Methodius in the ninth century to translate the Bible into Slavic languages. Though these missionaries worked mostly in Moravia (today's eastern Czech Republic), their alphabet caught on only here, in Croatia. (Glagolitic was later adapted in Bulgaria to become the Cyrillic alphabet—still used in Serbia, Russia, and other parts east.) In 1991, when Croatia became its own country and nationalism surged, the country flirted with the idea of making this the official alphabet (to differentiate Croatian from the very similar Serbian, and to revive old Croat tradition).

Other Zagreb Museums—Zagreb has lots of forgettable museums, but a few others are worth checking out.

The **Mimara Museum** (Muzej Mimara) houses the eclectic collection of a wealthy Dalmatian, ranging from ancient artifacts to paintings by Rubens, Rembrandt, Renoir, and Manet (25 kn, Tue–Sat 10:00–17:00, Thu until 19:00, Sun 10:00–14:00, closed Mon, Rooseveltov trg 5, tel. 01/482-8100).

The **Ivan Meštrović Atelier** features works by the 20th-century Croatian sculptor. Split has the definitive museum of Meštrović's works, but if you're not going there, this gallery is a convenient place to gain an appreciation for the prolific, thoughtful artist (10 kn, Tue–Fri 10:00–18:00, Sat–Sun 10:00–14:00, closed Mon, behind St. Mark's Square at Mletačka 8, tel. 01/485-1123). For more on Meštrović, see page 632.

The **Zagreb City Museum** (Muzej Grada Zagreba), with a modern, engaging exhibit that sprawls over two floors of an old convent, traces the history of the city through paintings, furniture, clothing, and other artifacts. Not surprisingly, the most interesting section is the most recent chapter: the early days of independence from Yugoslavia (including an exhibit on damage sustained during the warfare) and a hall of illuminating propaganda posters (20 kn, English descriptions, Tue–Fri 10:00–18:00, Sat–Sun 10:00–13:00, closed Mon, at north end of Gradec at Opatička 20, tel. 01/485-1361, www.mdc.hr/mgz).

And the **Arts and Crafts Museum** (Muzej za Umjetnost i Obrt) has a good decorative arts collection—mostly furniture, ceramics, and clothes—from the Gothic age to the present (20 kn, Tue–Sat 10:00–19:00, Sun 10:00–14:00, closed Mon, Trg Maršala Tita 10, tel. 01/488-2111, www.muo.hr).

SLEEPING

Hotels in central Zagreb are very expensive—you won't get much for your money. I prefer sleeping in Ljubljana or at Plitvice Lakes National Park, both of which offer better values. But if you must stay in Zagreb, these are the best deals right in the main tourist zone.

$$$ Hotel Dubrovnik has an ideal location (at the bottom of Jelačić Square) and 268 plush, business-class rooms (small Sb-780 kn, bigger Sb-880–950 kn, Db with 1 big bed-1,050 kn, twin Db-1,200 kn, suite-1,400–1,600 kn, extra bed-250 kn, rooms overlooking the square don't cost extra—try to request one, prices soft, non-smoking floors, elevator, Gajeva 1, tel. 01/487-3555, fax 01/481-8447, www.hotel-dubrovnik.hr, reservations@hotel-dubrovnik.hr).

$$ Hotel Jadran has 48 fine rooms near the cathedral, a few blocks east of Jelačić Square (Sb-520 kn, Db-730 kn, Tb-905 kn, some street noise—request quiet room, elevator, Vlaška 50, tel. 01/455-3777, fax 01/461-2151, www.hup-zagreb.hr, jadran@hup-zagreb.hr).

$$ Pansion Jägerhorn, above a restaurant, has 13 small rooms at decent prices (Sb-500 kn, Db-750 kn, suite-900 kn, hiding at the end of a long courtyard a block from Jelačić Square at Ilica 14,

---

Sleep Code

(€1 = about $1.20, 6 kuna = about $1, country code: 385, area code: 01)
S = Single, **D** = Double/Twin, **T** = Triple, **Q** = Quad, **b** = bathroom, **s** = shower only. English is spoken at each place. Unless otherwise noted, credit cards are accepted, breakfast is included, and the modest tourist tax (7 kn per person, per night) is not.

To help you sort easily through these listings, I've divided the rooms into three categories based on the price for a standard double room with bath:

$$$ **Higher Priced**—Most rooms 800 kn or more.
  $$ **Moderately Priced**—Most rooms between
                        500–800 kn.
   $ **Lower Priced**—Most rooms 500 kn or less.

---

tel. 01/483-3877, fax 01/483-3573, www.hotel-pansion-jaegerhorn.hr, info@hotel-pansion-jaegerhorn.hr).

$$ Hotel Central's 79 overly perfumed rooms are comfortable and modern—except the bathrooms, which still feel communist-era (as does the staff). But its prices are acceptable in this difficult accommodations climate, and the location, right across from the Main Train Station, is convenient for rail travelers (Sb-550–600 kn, Db with 1 big bed-720 kn, twin Db-780 kn, bigger Db-830, extra bed-160 kn, Branimirova 3, tel. 01/484-1122, fax 01/484-1304, www.hotel-central.hr, info@hotel-central.hr).

$ Omladinski Hostel Zagreb, with the cheapest beds in the center, is grim, ramshackle, and desperate for a long-promised but never-occurring renovation (bed in 6-person dorm-75 kn, bed in 3-person room-85 kn, S-160 kn, Sb-220 kn, D-220 kn, Db-290 kn, more for non-members, cash only, elevator, handy to the Main Train Station at Petrinjska ulica 77, tel. 01/484-1261, fax 01/484-1269, www.hfhs.hr, zagreb@hfhs.hr).

EATING

For the perfect place to sip a lazy cup of coffee, look no further than Jelačić Square—Zagreb's heart and soul. To venture a little farther, try these places. The last two eateries are both along the main street (called Ilica to the west, Jurišićeva to the east) that runs along the bottom of Jelačić Square.

On Tkalčićeva: This is Zagreb's main café street, "restaurant row," and urban promenade rolled into one. It's a parade of fashionable locals, and *the* place to see and be seen. Wander here and choose your favorite spot (starts a block behind Jelačić Square, next to the market).

At the Market (Dolac): There are plenty of options at Zagreb's lively market (Mon–Sat 7:00–14:00, Sun 7:00–12:00). Buy a fresh picnic direct from the producers. Or, for something already prepared, duck into one of the many cheap restaurants and cafés on the streets around the market. The middle level of the market, facing Jelačić Square, is home to a line of places with cheap food and indoor or outdoor seating.

Jägerhorn offers game (60–90 kn) or simpler grilled dishes (35–50 kn; daily 10:00–23:00, at the end of a courtyard a block from Jelačić Square at Ilica 14, tel. 01/483-3877). They also rent rooms (see "Sleeping," above).

Mimice, frequented by locals, is great for simple fish dishes (20–30 kn, order starches and sauces separately). Choose what you want from the limited menu, pay, and take your receipt to the next counter to claim your food. Then eat it standing or sitting on high stools (closed Sun, Jurišićeva 21).

TRANSPORTATION CONNECTIONS

From Zagreb by Train to: Rijeka (3/day, 4 hrs), **Split** (3/day, 5.75 hrs, plus 2 direct night trains, 8–8.5 hrs), **Ljubljana** (8/day, 2.5 hrs), **Vienna** (2/day, 6.5 hrs), **Budapest** (2/day, 5–7 hrs).

By Bus to: Plitvice Lakes National Park (about hrly until 17:30, 2–2.5 hrs; then none until about 22:00), **Split** (about 2/hr, 5–9 hrs), **Dubrovnik** (2 in the early morning, sometimes 1–2 midday, then 4–6 overnight, 11–12.5 hrs), **Korčula** (1/night, 13.5 hrs). Bus schedules can be sporadic (e.g., several departures clustered around the same time, then nothing for hours)—confirm carefully. Unfortunately, it's impossible to buy bus tickets anywhere in the center —you have to actually go to the bus station. Good bus schedules are at www.akz.hr.

PLITVICE LAKES NATIONAL PARK

(Nacionalni Park Plitvička Jezera)

Plitvice (PLEET-veet-seh) is one of Europe's most spectacular natural wonders. Imagine Niagara Falls diced and sprinkled over a heavily forested Grand Canyon. There's nothing like this lush valley of 16 terraced lakes, laced together by waterfalls and miles of pleasant plank walks. Countless cascades and water that's both strangely clear and full of vibrant colors make this park a misty natural wonderland. Years ago, after eight or nine visits, I thought I really knew Europe. Then I discovered Plitvice, and realized you can never exhaust Europe's surprises.

Planning Your Time

Plitvice deserves at least a few good hours. Since it takes some time to get here (2 hours by car or bus from Zagreb), the most sensible plan is to spend the night in one of the park's hotels (no character, but comfortable and convenient) or a nearby private home (cheaper, but practical only if you're driving). If you're coming from the north (e.g., Ljubljana), head to Zagreb in the morning, spend a few hours seeing the Croatian capital, then take the bus (no buses 17:30–22:00) or drive to Plitvice in the late afternoon to spend the night at the

park. Get up early and hit the trails; by early afternoon, you'll be ready to move on (perhaps by bus to the coast, or back to Zagreb). Two nights and a full day at Plitvice is probably overkill for all but the most avid hikers.

Getting to Plitvice

Plitvice Lakes National Park, a few miles from the Bosnian border, is two hours by car south of Zagreb on National Road #1 (a.k.a. D1).

By **car** from Zagreb, you'll take the expressway south for about an hour, exiting at Karlovac (marked for 1 and *Plitvice*). From here, D1 takes you directly south about another hour to the park.

Buses leave from Zagreb's main bus station in the direction of Plitvice. Various bus companies handle the route; just go to the ticket window and ask for the next departure (about 60 kn, trip takes 2–2.5 hours). Buses run from Zagreb about hourly until 17:30, and then there are generally no departures until 22:00. With the opening of the new freeway connecting Zagreb and Split, some buses now bypass the park altogether. Confirm that your bus actually will stop at Plitvice (the driver may stop at your specific hotel, or, for the worst-case scenario, he'll drop you at the official Plitvice bus stop, which is a 10-min walk beyond the hotels). Confirm the schedule online (www.akz.hr) or at the Plitvice office in Zagreb (Mon–Fri 8:00–16:00, closed Sat–Sun, Trg Kralja Tomislava 19, tel. 01/461-3586).

By car or bus, you'll see some thought-provoking terrain between Zagreb and Plitvice. As you leave Karlovac, you'll pass through the village of **Turanj,** part of the war zone just a decade ago. The destroyed, derelict houses belonged to Serbs who have not come back to reclaim and repair them. Farther along, about 25 miles before Plitvice, you'll pass through the striking village of **Slunj,** picturesquely perched on travertine formations (like Plitvice's) and surrounded by sparkling streams and waterfalls. If you're in a car, this is worth a photo stop. This town, too, looks very different than it did before the war—when it was 30 percent Serb. As in countless other villages in the Croatian interior, the Orthodox church has been destroyed...and locals still seethe when they describe how occupying Serbs "defiled" the town's delicate beauty.

ORIENTATION

(area code: 053)

Plitvice's 16 lakes are divided into the Upper Lakes (Gornja Jezera) and the Lower Lakes (Donja Jezera). The park officially has two entrances *(ulaz),* each with ticket windows and snack and gift shops. Entrance 1 is at the bottom of the Lower Lakes, across the busy D1 road from the park's best restaurant, Lička Kuća (see "Eating," page 672). Entrance 2 is about 1.5 miles south, at the cluster of Plitvice's three hotels (Jezero, Plitvice, and Bellevue; see "Sleeping," page 671). There is no town at Plitvice. The nearest

Plitvice Lakes National Park

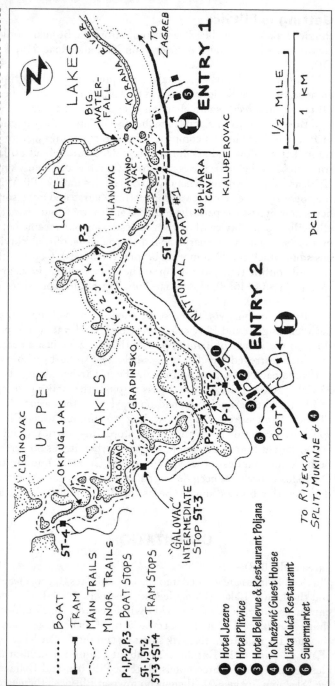

- **BOAT**
- **TRAM**
- **MAIN TRAILS**
- **MINOR TRAILS**

P-1, P-2, P-3 — BOAT STOPS

ST-1, ST-2,
ST-3 + ST-4 — TRAM STOPS

1 Hotel Jezero
2 Hotel Plitvice
3 Hotel Bellevue & Restaurant Poljana
4 To Kneževič Guest House
5 Lička Kuča Restaurant
6 Supermarket

½ MILE

1 KM

DCH

village, Mukinje, is a residential community mostly for park workers (boring for tourists, but has some good private room options).

Cost and Hours: The price to enter the park varies by season (July–Aug 95 kn, May–June and Sept–Oct 80 kn, Nov–April 50 kn; ticket good for entire stay, including park entry, boat, shuttle bus, and parking). Park hours are also changeable (generally from 7:00 in summer, 8:00 in spring and fall, and 9:00 in winter; closes at dusk). Night owls should note that the park never "closes"; these hours are for the ticket booths and the boat and shuttle bus system. You can just stroll right into the park at any time, provided that you aren't using the boat or bus. For fewer tour-group crowds, visit early or late in the day.

Tourist Information

A handy map of the trails is on the back of your ticket, and big maps are posted all over the park. The big 20-kn map is a good investment; the various English-language guidebooks are generally poorly translated and not very helpful (both sold at entrances, hotels, and shops throughout the park). The park has a good Web site: www.np-plitvice.com.

Getting Around Plitvice

Of course, Plitvice is designed for hikers. But the park has a few ways (included in the cost of entry) to help you connect the best parts.

By Shuttle Bus: Buses connect the hotels at Entrance 2 (stop ST2, below Hotel Jezero) with the top of the Upper Lakes (stop ST4) and roughly the bottom of the Lower Lakes (stop ST1, a 10-min walk from Entrance 1). Between Entrance 2 and the top of the Upper Lakes is an intermediate stop (ST3, at Galovac lake)—designed for tour groups, available to anyone, and offering a convenient way to skip the less interesting top half of the Upper Lakes. Buses start running early and continue until late afternoon (frequency depends on demand—generally 3–4/hr; buses run from March until the first snow—often Dec). Note that the park refers to its buses as "trains," which confuses some visitors. Also note that no local buses take you along the major road (D1) that connects the entrances. The only way to get between them without a car is by shuttle bus (within the park) or by foot (about a 40-min walk).

By Boat: Low-impact electric boats ply the waters of the biggest lake, Kozjak, with three stops: below Hotel Jezero (stop P1), the bottom of the Upper Lakes (P2), and at the far end of Kozjak, at the top of the Lower Lakes (P3). From Hotel Jezero to the Upper Lakes is a quick five-minute ride; the boat goes back and forth continuously. From the Upper Lakes to the Lower Lakes takes closer to 20 minutes, and the boat goes about twice

The Science of Plitvice

Nearly everyone is impressed by Plitvice, and eventually asks the same question: How did it happen?

Plitvice's magic ingredient is calcium carbonate ($CaCO_3$), a mineral deposit (from the limestone) that interacts with the plants, algae, and moss in a unique way to create the park's beauty. Remarkably clear water flows into the park from nearby mountains. Minerals coat the vegetation on the bottom of the lakes, reflecting the sunlight to create a striking blue-green coloration. Eventually, this coating becomes thicker, travertine limestone barriers are formed, and waterfalls gradually emerge. The ongoing process means that Plitvice's landscape is always changing.

Wildlife found in the park includes deer, wolves, wildcats, lynx, wild boar, voles, otters, and more than 160 species of birds (including eagles, herons, owls, grouse, and storks). The lakes (and local menus) are full of trout. Perhaps most importantly, Plitvice is home to about 50 brown bears—a species now extremely endangered in Europe. You'll see bears, the park's mascot, plastered all over tourist literature (and in the form of a scary representative in the lobby of Hotel Jezero).

per hour—often at the top and bottom of every hour. (With up to 10,000 people a day visiting the park, you might have to wait for a seat on this boat.) Unless the lake freezes (about every 5 years), the boat runs in the off-season too—though frequency drops to hourly, and it stops running earlier. At P1, you can also rent rowboats (50 kn/hr).

SIGHTS AND ACTIVITIES

Plitvice is a refreshing playground of 16 terraced lakes, separated by natural limestone dams and connected by countless waterfalls. Over time, the water has simultaneously carved out, and, with the help of mineral deposits, built up this fluid landscape.

Plitvice became Croatia's first national park in 1949. On Easter Sunday in 1991, the first shots of Croatia's war with Yugoslavia were fired right here—in fact, the war's first casualty was a park police-man, Josip Jović. The Serbs occupied Plitvice until 1995, and many of the Croatians you'll meet here were evacuated and lived near the coastline as refugees. Today, the war is a fading memory, and the park is again a popular tourist destination, with 750,000 visitors each year (relatively few from the U.S.).

Hiking the Lakes

Plitvice's system of trails and boardwalks makes it possible for visitors to get up close to the park's beauty. (In some places, the paths literally lead right up the middle of a waterfall.) The official park map and signage recommend a variety of hikes, but there's no need to adhere strictly to these suggestions; invest in the big 20-kn map and make your own route.

I like hiking uphill, from Lower Lakes to Upper Lakes, which offers slightly better head-on views of the best scenery. (Even though this route has a gradual uphill slope, remember that if you go the other way—downhill—there's a steep climb back up at the end.) Below, I've described a one-way hiking route (going uphill), divided between Upper and Lower. Walking briskly and with a few photo stops, figure on an hour for the Lower Lakes, an hour for the Upper Lakes, and a half hour to connect them by boat.

Start at the...

Lower Lakes (Donja Jezera)—The lower half of Plitvice's lakes are accessible from Entrance 1. If you start here, the route marked G2 (intended for groups, but doable for anyone) leads you along the boardwalks to Kozjak, the big lake that connects the Lower and the Upper Lakes (see below).

From the entrance, you'll descend down a steep path with lots of switchbacks, as well as thrilling views over the canyon of the Lower Lakes. As you reach water level and begin to follow the boardwalks, you'll have great up-close views of the travertine formations that make up Plitvice's many waterfalls. See any trout? If you're tempted to throw in a line, don't. Fishing is strictly forbidden. (Besides, they're happy.)

Near the beginning of the Lower Lakes trails, an optional 10-minute detour takes you down to the **Big Waterfall** (Veliki Slap). It's the biggest of Plitvice's waterfalls, where the Plitvica River plunges 250 feet over a cliff into the valley below. Depending on recent rainfall, the force of the Big Waterfall varies from a light mist to a thundering deluge.

After seeing the Big Waterfall, continue on the boardwalks. On the left, a smaller trail branches off towards **Šupljara Cave.** You can actually climb through this slippery cave all the way up to the trail overlooking the Lower Lakes (not recommended). This unassuming cavern is a surprisingly big draw. In the 1960s, several German and Italian "Spaghetti Westerns" were filmed at Plitvice and in other parts of Croatia (which, to European eyes, has terrain similar to the American West). The most famous, *Der Schatz im*

Silbersee (The Treasure in Silver Lake), was filmed here at Plitvice, and the treasure was hidden in this cave. The movie—complete with *Deutsch*-speaking "Native Americans"—is still a favorite in Germany, and popular theme tours bring German tourists to movie locations here in Croatia.

After the cave, you'll stick to the east side of the lakes, then cross over one more time to the west, where you'll cut though a comparatively dull forest. You'll emerge at a pit-stop-perfect clearing with squat-and-aim WCs, picnic tables, a souvenir shop, and a self-service restaurant. This is where you can catch the shuttle boat across Lake Kozjak to the bottom of the Upper Lakes (see "Getting Around Plitvice," above). While you're waiting for the next boat (usually every 30 min), visit the friendly old ladies in the kiosks selling wheels of cheese and a variety of strudel (10 kn per piece).

Lake Kozjak (Jezero Kozjak)—The park's biggest lake, Kozjak, connects the Lower and Upper Lakes. The 20-minute boat ride between Plitvice's two halves offers a great chance for a breather. You can hike between the lakes along the west side of Kozjak, but the scenery's not nearly as good as the rest of the park.

Upper Lakes (Gornja Jezera)—Focus on the lower half of the Upper Lakes. That's where nearly all the exotic beauty is. From the boat dock, signs for *C* and *G2* direct you up to Gradinsko Lake through the most striking scenery in the whole park. Enjoy the stroll, take your time, and be thankful you remembered to bring extra film.

At the top of Galovac Lake, you'll have three options: Make your hike a loop by continuing around the lake (following *H* and *G1* signs back to the P2 boat dock); hike a few steps up to the ST3 bus stop to catch the shuttle bus back to the hotel; or continue up to the top of the lakes. For a short visit, I'd return to the P2 boat dock by foot. For a really short visit—or a lazy one—catch the bus. To get away from the crowds and feel like you've covered the lakes thoroughly, continue to the top of the park. From here on up, the scenery is less stunning, the waterfalls are fewer and farther between, and the crowds thin out. If you do continue up to the top of the Upper Lakes, you'll finish at shuttle bus stop ST4 (with food stalls and a WC), where you can easily get a short ride back to Entrance 2. Nice work.

SLEEPING

At the Park

The most convenient way to sleep at Plitvice is to use the park's lodges. Book any of these hotels through the same office (reservation tel. 053/751-015, fax 053/751-013, www.np-plitvice.com,

---

Sleep Code

(€1 = about $1.20, country code: 385, area code: 053)
English is spoken, credit cards are accepted, and breakfast is included at each place. The tourist tax (€1 per person, per day) is not included in these prices.

To help you sort easily through these listings, I've divided the rooms into three categories based on the price for a standard double room with bath in peak season:

$$$ **Higher Priced**—Most rooms €100 or more.
  $$ **Moderately Priced**—Most rooms between €50–100.
    $ **Lower Priced**—Most rooms €50 or less.

---

info@np-plitvicka-jezera.hr; reception numbers are listed below for each hotel).

$$$ Hotel Jezero is big and modern, with all the comfort—and charm—of a Holiday Inn. It's well-located right at the park entrance, and offers 200 rooms that feel newish, but generally have at least one thing that's broken. Parkside rooms have big glass doors and balconies (July–Aug: Sb-€82, Db-€116; May–June and Sept–Oct: Sb-€75, Db-€106; Nov–April: Sb-€60, Db-€84, elevator, reception tel. 053/751-400).

$$ Hotel Plitvice, a little less plush than Jezero, offers 50 rooms and mod, wide-open public spaces on two floors with no elevators (reception tel. 053/751-100). For rooms, choose from economy (fine, older-feeling; July–Aug: Sb-€59, Db-€84; May–June and Sept–Oct: Sb-€53, Db-€76; Nov–April: Sb-€45, Db-€64), standard (just a teeny bit bigger; July–Aug: Sb-€64, Db-€90; May–June and Sept–Oct: Sb-€58, Db-€82; Nov–April: Sb-€48, Db-€68), or superior (bigger still, with a sitting area; July–Aug: Sb-€71, Db-€100; May–June and Sept–Oct: Sb-€64, Db-€90; Nov–April: Sb-€56, Db-€78).

$$ Hotel Bellevue is simple and bare-bones (no TVs or elevator). It has an older feel to it, but the price is right and the 80 rooms are sleepable (July–Aug: Sb-€54, Db-€72; May–June and Sept–Oct: Sb-€49, Db-€66; Nov–April: Sb-€39, Db-€52, reception tel. 053/751-700).

Near the Park

While the park's lodges are the easiest choice for non-drivers, those with a car should consider these cheaper alternatives.

$ Knežević Guest House, with 11 bright, modern rooms, is a new family-run hotel a five-minute drive south of the park in the nondescript workers' town of Mukinje. The street is new, but the yard is peaceful, with an inviting hammock (Db-€35, breakfast-€5, family rooms; driving south from the park, take first right turn into Mukinje and you'll see #57; tel. 053/774-081, mobile 098-168-7576, nikola.knezevic@gs.t-com.hr, daughter Christina speaks English).

$ Sobe: Drivers looking for character and preferring to spend €40, rather than €80, should simply find a room in a private home, advertised with *sobe* signs for miles on either side of the park. For details, see "Dalmatian Accommodation," page 610.

EATING

The park runs all of the restaurants at Plitvice. These places are handy, and the food is tasty and affordable. If you're staying at the hotels, you have the option of paying for half-board with your room (lunch or dinner, €11 each May–Oct, €8 each Nov–April). This option is designed for the restaurants inside hotels Jezero and Plitvice, but you can also use the voucher at other park eateries (you'll pay the difference if the bill is more). The half-board option is worth doing if you're here for dinner, but don't lock yourself in for lunch—you'll want more flexibility as you explore Plitvice (excellent picnic spots and decent food stands abound inside the park).

Hotel Jezero and **Hotel Plitvice** both have big restaurants with good food and friendly, professional service (half-board for dinner, described above, is a good deal; or order à la carte: fish 50–60 kn, meat dishes 80–100 kn; both open daily until 23:00).

Lička Kuća, across the pedestrian overpass from Entrance 1, has a wonderfully dark and smoky atmosphere around a huge open-air wood-fired grill (grilled trout-50 kn, more elaborate dishes up to 100 kn, daily 11:00–24:00, tel. 053/751-024).

Restaurant Poljana, behind Hotel Bellevue, has the same boring, park-lodge atmosphere in both of its sections: cheap, self-service cafeteria (25–40 kn) and sit-down restaurant with open wood-fired grill (same choices and prices as the better-atmosphere Lička Kuća, above; both parts open daily but closed in winter, tel. 053/751-092).

For **picnic** fixings, there's a small supermarket across road D1 from Entrance 2. The boat docks come with a few eating options. At the P3 boat dock, locals sell homemade goodies, and at the P1 boat dock, you can buy grilled meat and drinks.

TRANSPORTATION CONNECTIONS

To reach the park, see "Getting to Plitvice," above. Moving on from Plitvice is trickier. Buses pass by the park in each direction—northbound (to **Zagreb,** 2–2.5 hrs) and southbound (to coastal destinations such as **Split,** 4–6 hrs, and **Dubrovnik,** 9–10 hrs).

There is no bus station—just a low-profile *Plitvice Center* bus stop shelter: To reach it from the park, go out to the main road from either Hotel Jezero or Hotel Plitvice, then turn right; the bus stops are just after the pedestrian overpass. The one on the hotel side of the road is for buses headed for the coast; the stop on the opposite side is for Zagreb. But here's the catch: Many buses that pass through Plitvice don't stop (either because they're full, or because they don't have anyone to drop off there). You can stand at the bus stop and try to flag one down, but it's safer to get help from the park's hotel staff. They can help you figure out which bus suits your schedule, then they'll call ahead to be sure the bus stops for you. If you don't want to make the 10-minute walk out to the bus stop, someone at the hotel can usually drive you out for a modest fee.

AUSTRIA

AUSTRIA
(Österreich)

Most people wouldn't consider Austria "Eastern Europe." The country barely slipped out of communism's clutches in 1955, when it became an independent country with the Soviet Union's blessing...provided it remained neutral (it never joined NATO).

Cold War blinders have forced us to separate the communist East from the capitalist West, but consider this part of Europe in the days before Hitler. A hundred years ago, Austria was the head of an enormous empire that encompassed virtually every single destination in this book. In the big picture, no other city had more of a cultural and political impact in Eastern Europe than Vienna. In fact, the German name for Austria—Österreich—literally means "the Kingdom of the East."

From a practical standpoint, Vienna serves as a prime "gateway" city. The location is central and convenient for most major Eastern European destinations. Actually farther east than Prague, Ljubljana, and Zagreb, and just upstream on the Danube from Budapest and Bratislava, Vienna is an ideal launchpad for a journey into the East.

In its 18th- and 19th-century glory days, the Austrian Empire (a.k.a. the Austro-Hungarian Empire, a.k.a. the Hapsburg Empire)

Key German Phrases

English	German	Pronounced*
Hello.	Guten Tag.	GOO-tehn tahg
Do you speak English?	Sprechen Sie Englisch?	SHPREHKH-ehn zee ENG-lish
yes / no	ja / nein	yah / nin
Please. / You're welcome. / Can I help you?	Bitte.	BIT-teh
Thank you.	Danke.	DAHNG-keh
I'm sorry.	Es tut mir leid.	ehs toot meer līd
Excuse me. (to pass or to get attention)	Entschuldigung.	ehnt-SHOOL-dig-oong
Good.	Gut.	goot
Goodbye.	Auf Wiedersehen.	owf VEE-der-zayn
one / two	eins / zwei	īns / tsvī
three / four	drei / vier	drī / feer
five / six	fünf / sechs	fewnf / zehks
seven / eight	sieben / acht	ZEE-behn / ahkht
nine / ten	neun / zehn	noyn / tsayn
hundred	hundert	HOON-dert
thousand	tausend	TOW-sehnd
How much?	Wie viel?	vee feel
local currency	euro (€)	OY-roh
Where is...?	Wo ist...?	voh ist
...the toilet	...die Toilette	dee toy-LEH-teh
men	Herren	HEHR-ehn
women	Damen	DAH-mehn
water / coffee	Wasser / Kaffee	VAH-ser / kah-FAY
beer / wine	Bier / Wein	beer / vīn
Cheers!	Prost!	prohst
the bill	die Rechnung	dee REHKH-noong

*When using the phonetics, pronounce ī as the long i sound in "light."

was arguably the most powerful European entity since Rome. The Hapsburg family built this giant kingdom of more than 60 million people by making love, not war—having lots of children and marrying them into the other royal houses of Europe.

Today, this small, landlocked country (with just 8 million people) does more to cling to its elegant past than any other nation in Europe. The waltz is still the rage. Austrians are very sociable; it's important to greet people in the breakfast room and those you pass on the streets or meet in shops. The Austrian version of "Hi" is a cheerful "*Grüss Gott*" ("May God greet you"). You'll get the correct pronunciation after the first volley—listen and copy.

While they speak German and talked about unity with Germany long before Hitler ever said *Anschluss,* the Austrians cherish their distinct cultural and historical traditions. They are not Germans. Austria is mellow and relaxed compared to Deutschland—but stiff and formal compared to most Eastern Europeans (except maybe the Hungarians). *Gemütlichkeit* is the local word for this special Austrian cozy-and-easy approach to life. It's good living—whether engulfed in mountain beauty or bathed in lavish high culture. The people stroll as if every day were Sunday, topping things off with a cheerful visit to a coffee or pastry shop.

It must be nice to be past your prime—no longer troubled by being powerful, able to kick back and celebrate life in the clean, untroubled mountain air. While the Austrians make more money than their Eastern European neighbors, they enjoy a short workweek and a long life span. And compared to much of Eastern Europe, which only recently joined the European Union, Austria is a long-established EU member that adopted the euro as its currency years ago.

Austrians eat on about the same schedule we do. Treats include Wiener schnitzel (breaded veal cutlet), *Knödel* (dumplings), *Apfelstrudel,* and fancy desserts like the *Sachertorte*, Vienna's famous chocolate cake.

In Austria, all cars must have a ***Vignette*** toll sticker stuck to the inside of their windshield to legally drive on the freeways. These are sold at all border crossings (24 hours a day), big gas stations near borders, and car-rental agencies. Stickers cost €8 for 10 days (€22 for 2 months). Not having one earns you a stiff fine.

VIENNA

(Wien)

Vienna is a head without a body. For 640 years the capital of the once-grand Hapsburg Empire, she started and lost World War I, and with it her far-flung holdings. Today, you'll find an elegant capital of 1.6 million people (one-fifth of Austria's population) ruling a small, relatively insignificant country. Culturally, historically, and from a sightseeing point of view, this city is the sum of its illustrious past. The city of Freud, Brahms, Maria Theresa's many children, a gaggle of Strausses, and a dynasty of Holy Roman Emperors ranks right up there with Paris, London, and Rome.

Vienna has always been the easternmost city of the West. In Roman times, it was Vindobona, on the Danube facing the Germanic barbarians. In the Middle Ages, Vienna was Europe's bastion against the Ottoman Turks—a Christian breakwater against the riding tide of Islam (hordes of up to 200,000 Turks were repelled in 1529 and 1683). During this period, as the Turks dreamed of conquering what they called "the big apple" for their sultan, Vienna lived with a constant fear of invasion (and the Hapsburg court ruled from safer Prague). You'll notice none of Vienna's great palaces were built until after 1683, when the Turkish threat was finally over. While Vienna's old walls held out the Turks, World War II bombs destroyed nearly a quarter of the city's buildings. In modern times, neutral Austria took a big bite out of the U.S.S.R.'s Warsaw Pact buffer zone. And today, Vienna is a springboard for newly popular destinations in Eastern Europe.

The truly Viennese person is not Austrian, but a second-generation Hapsburg cocktail, with grandparents from the distant corners of the old empire—Hungary, the Czech Republic,

Greater Vienna

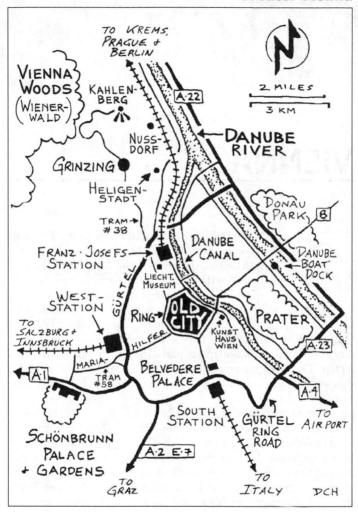

Slovakia, Poland, Slovenia, Croatia, Bosnia, Serbia, Romania, and Italy. Vienna is the melting-pot capital of a now-collapsed empire that, in its heyday, consisted of 60 million people—only eight million of whom were Austrian.

In 1900, Vienna's 2.2 million inhabitants made it the world's fifth-largest city (after New York, London, Paris, and Berlin). But these days—with dogs being the preferred "child" and the average Viennese mother having only 1.3 children—the population is down to about 1.6 million.

The Hapsburgs, who ruled the enormous Austrian Empire

from 1273 to 1918, shaped Vienna. Some ad agency has convinced Vienna to make Elisabeth, wife of Emperor Franz Josef—with her narcissism and struggles with royal life—the darling of the local tourist scene. You'll see "Sissy" all over town. But stay focused on the Hapsburgs who mattered: Maria Theresa (r. 1740–1780, see page 710) and Franz Josef (r. 1848–1916, see page 710).

After the defeat of Napoleon and the Congress of Vienna in 1815 (which shaped 19th-century Europe), Vienna enjoyed its violin-filled belle époque, which shaped our romantic image of the city: fine wine, chocolates, cafés, and waltzes.

Planning Your Time

For a big city, Vienna is pleasant and laid-back. Packed with sights, it's worth two days and two nights on the speediest trip. To be Grand Tour efficient, you could sleep in and sleep out on the train (Berlin, Kraków, Venice, Rome, the Swiss Alps, Paris, and the Rhine are each handy night trains away).

Day 1: 9:00–Circle the Ring by tram, following my self-guided tour (page 687); 10:00–Drop by the TI for any planning and ticket needs, then see the sights in Vienna's old center (using my self-guided commentary)—Monument Against War and Fascism, Kaisergruft crypt, Kärntner Strasse, St. Stephen's Cathedral, and Graben; 12:00–Finger sandwiches for lunch at Buffet Trzesniewski; 13:00–Tour the Hofburg and treasury; 16:00–Hit one more museum, or shop, browse, and people-watch; 19:30–Choose classical music (concert or opera), House of Music museum, or *Heurige* wine garden.

Day 2: Morning–Choose between Schönbrunn Palace (arrive at 9:00, return to central Vienna by noon) or Lipizzaner stallions' morning practice (10:00–12:00); 12:00–Have lunch at Naschmarkt or Rosenberger Markt, 13:00–Tour the Opera; 14:00–Kunsthistorisches Museum; 16:00–Your choice of the many sights left to see in Vienna; Evening–See Day 1 evening options.

The year 2006 is a good time to visit Vienna, as the city celebrates the 250th birthday of Wolfgang Amadeus Mozart. For details on all the festivities, see page 730.

ORIENTATION

(area code: 01)

Vienna—Wien in German (pronounced "veen")—sits between the Vienna Woods (Wienerwald) and the Danube (Donau). To the southeast is industrial sprawl. The Alps, which arc across Europe from Marseille, end at Vienna's wooded hills, providing a popular playground for walking and sipping new wine. This greenery's momentum carries on into the city. More than half of Vienna is parkland, filled with ponds, gardens, trees, and statue-maker memories of Austria's glory days.

Think of the city map as a target. The bull's-eye is St. Stephen's Cathedral, the first circle is the Ringstrasse, and the second is the Gürtel outerbelt. The old town—snuggling around towering cathedral south of the Danube—is bound tightly by the Ringstrasse, marking what used to be the city wall. The Gürtel, a broader ring road, contains the rest of downtown.

Addresses start with the district, or *Bezirk,* followed by street and building number. The Ring circles the first *Bezirk.* Any address higher than the ninth *Bezirk* is beyond the Gürtel, far from the center. The middle two digits of Vienna's postal codes show the *Bezirk.* The address "7, Lindengasse 4" is in the seventh district, #4 on Linden Street. Its postal code would be 1070.

Nearly all your sightseeing will be done in the core first district or along the Ringstrasse. As a tourist, concern yourself only with this compact old center. When you do, sprawling Vienna suddenly becomes manageable.

Tourist Information

Vienna's one real tourist office is a block behind the Opera House at Albertinaplatz (daily 9:00–19:00, tel. 01/24555, press 2 for English info, www.vienna.info). Confirm your sightseeing plans and pick up the free and essential city map with a list of museums and hours (also available at most hotels), the monthly program of concerts (called *Wien-Programm*—includes daily calendar and information on the contemporary cultural scene, including live music, jazz, walks, expositions, and evening museum options), the biannual city guide *(Vienna Journal)*, and the youth guide *(Vienna Hype)*. The TI also books rooms for a €2.90 fee. While hotel and ticket-booking agencies at the train stations and airport can answer questions and give out maps and brochures, I'd rely on the official TI if possible.

Consider the TI's handy €3.60 **Vienna from A to Z** booklet. Every important building sports a numbered flag banner that keys into this guidebook. *A to Z* numbers are keyed into the TI's city map. When lost, find one of the "famous-building flags" and match its number to your map. If you're at a famous building, check the map to see what other key numbers are nearby, then check the *A to Z* book description to see if you want to go in. This system is especially helpful for those just wandering aimlessly among Vienna's historic charms.

The much-promoted €17 **Vienna Card** might save the busy sightseer a few euros. It gives you a 72-hour transit pass (worth €12) and discounts of 10–50 percent at the city's museums. (Seniors and students will do better with their own discounts.)

Arrival in Vienna

By Train at the West Station (Westbahnhof): The *Reisebüro am Bahnhof* books hotels (for a €4.50 fee), has maps, answers questions, and has a train info desk (daily 7:30–21:00). The Westbahnhof also has a grocery store (daily 5:30–23:00), ATMs, Internet access, change offices, and storage facilities. Airport buses and taxis wait in front of the station.

To get to the city center (and most likely, your hotel), take the U-Bahn on the U-3 line (buy your ticket or transit pass—described under "Getting Around Vienna," below—from a *Tabak* shop in the station or from a machine). Blue *U-3* signs lead down to the tracks (direction Simmering for Mariahilfer Strasse hotels or the center). If your hotel is along Mariahilfer Strasse, your stop is on this line (see page 739). If you're sleeping in the center or just sightseeing, ride five stops to Stephansplatz, escalate in the exit direction Stephansplatz, and you'll hit the cathedral. The TI is a five-minute stroll down the busy Kärntner Strasse pedestrian street.

By Train at the South Station (Südbahnhof): Those arriving from Prague will likely land here. The Südbahnhof has all the services, left luggage, and a TI (daily 9:00–19:00). To reach Vienna's center, follow the S (Schnellbahn) signs to the right and down the stairs, and take any train in the direction Floridsdorf; transfer in two stops (at Landsstrasse/Wien Mitte) to the U-3 line, direction Ottakring, which goes directly to Stephansplatz and Mariahilfer Strasse hotels. Tram D also goes to the Ring, and bus #13A goes to Mariahilfer Strasse.

By Plane: Vienna's airport is 12 miles from the center (tel. 01/7007-22233, www.viennaairport.com). It's connected to the very central Wien-Mitte station by S-Bahn (S-7 yellow, €3, 2/hr, 24 min). A speedier new City Airport Train (CAT) connects the airport to Wien-Mitte (green signs, €9, 2/hr, 16 min, www.cityairporttrain .com). Express airport buses (parked immediately in front of the arrival hall, €6, 2/hr, 30 min, buy tickets from drivers) go conveniently to Schwedenplatz, Westbahnhof, and Südbahnhof, from which it's easy to continue by public transportation. Taxis into town cost about €35 (including €10 airport surcharge). Hotels arrange for fixed-rate car service to the airport (€30, 30-min ride).

The airport in Bratislava, Slovakia, is surprisingly close to downtown Vienna (see page 174).

Helpful Hints

Money: ATMs are everywhere. Banks are open weekdays roughly from 8:00 to 15:00 (until 17:30 on Thu). After hours, you can change money at train stations, the airport, post offices, or the American Express office (Mon–Fri 9:00–17:30, Sat 9:00–12:00, closed Sun, Kärntner Strasse 21–23, tel. 01/5124-0040).

Internet Access: The TI has a list of Internet cafés. **BigNet** is the dominant outfit (www.bignet.at), with lots of stations at Kärntner Strasse 61 (daily 10:00–24:00) and Hoher Markt 8–9 (daily 10:00–24:00). **Surfland Internet Café** is near the Opera (daily 10:00–23:00, Krugerstrasse 10, tel. 01/512-7701).

Post Offices: Choose from the main post office (Postgasse in center, open 24 hrs daily, handy metered phones), Westbahnhof (Mon–Fri 7:00–22:00, Sat–Sun 9:00–20:00), Südbahnhof (daily 7:00–22:00), or near the Opera (Mon–Fri 7:00–19:00, closed Sat–Sun, Krugerstrasse 13).

English Bookstores: Consider the **British Bookshop** (Mon–Fri 9:30–19:30, Sat 9:30–18:00, closed Sun, at corner of Weihburggasse and Seilerstätte, tel. 01/512-1945; same hours at branch at Mariahilfer Strasse 4, tel. 01/522-6730) or **Shakespeare & Co.** (Mon–Sat 9:00–19:00, closed Sun, north of Hoher Markt square, Sterngasse 2, tel. 01/535-5053).

Travel Agency: Intropa is convenient, with good service for flights and train tickets (Mon–Fri 9:00–18:00, Sat 10:00–13:00, closed Sun, Neuer Markt 8, tel. 01/513-4000). Train tickets come with a €2 service charge when purchased from an agency rather than at the station—but the convenience is worth this modest cost.

Getting Around Vienna

By Public Transportation: Take full advantage of Vienna's simple, cheap, and super-efficient transit system, which includes trams, buses, subway (U-Bahn), and faster suburban trains (S-Bahn). I use the tram mostly to zip around the Ring (tram #1 or #2) and take the U-Bahn to outlying sights or hotels. Numbered lines (such as #38) are trams, and numbers followed by an *A* (such as #38A) are buses. The smooth, modern trams are Porsche-designed, with "backpack technology" locating the engines and mechanical hardware on the roofs for a lower ride and easier entry. Lines that begin with U (e.g., U-3) are U-Bahn lines (designated by the end-of-the-line stops). Blue lines are the speedier S-Bahns. Take a moment to study the eye-friendly city-center map on station walls to internalize how the transit system can help you. The free tourist map has essentially all the lines marked, making the too-big €1.50 transit map unnecessary (information tel. 01/790-9105).

Trams, buses, the U-Bahn, and the S-Bahn all use the same tickets. Buy your tickets from *Tabak* shops, station machines, *Vorverkauf* offices in the station, or on board (just on trams, single tickets only, more expensive). You have lots of choices:

• Single tickets (€1.50, €2 if bought on tram, good for 1 journey with necessary transfers).

• 24-hour transit pass (€5).

• 72-hour transit pass (€12).

• 7-day transit pass (*Wochenkarte*, €12.50, pass always starts on Mon).

• 8-day card (*Acht Tage Karte*), covering eight full days of free transportation for €24 (can be shared—for example, 4 people for 2 days each). With a per-person cost of €3/day (compared to €5/day for a 24-hour pass), this can be a real saver for groups. Kids under 15 travel free on Sundays and holidays.

Stamp a time on your ticket as you enter the Metro system, tram, or bus (stamp it only the first time for a multiple-use pass). Cheaters pay a stiff €44 fine if caught—and then they make you buy a ticket. Rookies miss stops because they fail to open the door. Push buttons, pull latches—do whatever it takes. Study the excellent wall-mounted street map before you exit the U-Bahn station. Choosing the right exit—signposted from the moment you step off the train—saves lots of walking.

By Taxi: Vienna's comfortable, civilized, and easy-to-flag-down taxis start at €2.50. You'll pay about €8 to go from the Opera to the Westbahnhof. Pay only what's on the meter—any surcharges (other than the €2 fee added to fares when you telephone them, or €10 for the airport) are just crude cabbie rip-offs.

By Car with Driver: Consider the luxury of having your own car and driver. Johann (a.k.a. John) Lichtl is a kind, honest, English-speaking cabbie who can take up to four passengers in his car (€25/1 hr, €20/hr for 2 or more hours, mobile 0676-670-6750).

By Bike: Vienna is a great city for biking—*if* you own a bike. Bike rental is a hassle (get list at TI). There are no bike-rental options in the center; the nearest is out at Prater Park (see page 729). The bikes you'll see parked in public racks all over town are part of a loaner system that is only workable for locals with mobile phones. The bike path along the Ring is wonderfully entertaining.

By Buggy: Rich romantics get around by traditional horse and buggy. These buggies, called *Fiakers*, clip-clop visitors on tours lasting 20 minutes (€40—old town), 40 minutes (€65—old town and the Ring), or one hour (€95—all of the above, but more thorough). You can share the ride and cost with up to five people. Because it's a kind of guided tour, before settling on a carriage, talk to a few drivers and pick one who's fun and speaks English.

TOURS

Walking Tours—The TI's Walks in Vienna brochure describes Vienna's many guided walks. The basic 90-minute "Vienna First Glance" introductory walk is offered daily throughout the summer (€12, leaves at 14:00 from near the Opera, in English and German, tel. 01/894-5363, www.wienguide.at).

Vienna

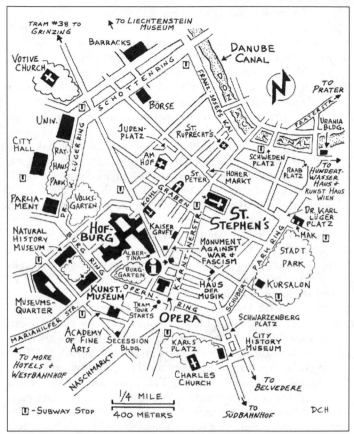

Bus Tours—**Vienna Sightseeing** operates hop-on, hop-off tours covering 13 predictable sightseeing stops (departures from Opera at top of each hour 10:00–17:00, recorded commentary). Given Vienna's excellent public transportation and this outfit's meager one-bus-per-hour frequency, I'd take this not to hop on and off, but only to get the narrated orientation drive through town (€20 for 24-hr ticket, or €12 if you stay on for the full 60-minute circular ride—skipping the hop-on, hop-off privileges). Their 3.5-hour Vienna city sights tour includes a visit to Schönbrunn Palace and a bus tour around town (€34; April–Oct 3/day—9:45, 10:30, and 14:45; Nov–March 2/day—9:45 and 14:00; call 01/7124-6830 to book this or get info on other tours). These leave from the Opera or, 30 minutes later, from the Südbahnhof.

Local Guides—The tourist board Web site (www.vienna.info) has a long list of local guides with specialties and contact information.

Lisa Zeiler is a good English-speaking guide (2-hr walks for €125—if she's booked up, she can set you up with another guide, tel. 01/402-3688, lisa.zeiler@gmx.at). **Ursula Klaus,** an art scholar specializing in turn-of-the-century Vienna, enjoys tailoring tours to specific interests (especially music, art, architecture). She does two-hour tours for €120 (tel. 01/522-8556, mobile 0676-421-4884, ursula.klaus@aon.at).

SELF-GUIDED TRAM TOUR

Around the Ringstrasse

In the 1860s, Emperor Franz Josef had the city's ingrown medieval wall torn down and replaced with a grand boulevard 190 feet wide. The road, arcing nearly three miles around the city's core, predates all the buildings that line it—so what you'll see is very "neo": neo-classical, neo-Gothic, and neo-Renaissance. One of Europe's great streets, the Ringstrasse is lined with many of the city's top sights. Trams #1 and #2 and a great bike path circle the whole route—and so should you.

This self-guided tram tour, rated ▲▲, gives you a fun orientation and a ridiculously quick glimpse of the major sights as you

glide by (€1.50, €2 if bought on tram, 30-min circular tour). Tram #1 goes clockwise; tram #2, counterclockwise. Most sights are on the outside, so use tram #2 (sit on the right, ideally in the front seat of the front car; or—for maximum view and minimum air—sit in the bubble-front seat of the second car). Start immediately across the street from the Opera House. You can

jump on and off as you go (trams come every 5 min). Read ahead and pay attention—these sights can fly by. Let's go:

● Immediately on the left: The city's main pedestrian drag, Kärntner Strasse, leads to the zigzag roof of **St. Stephen's Cathedral.** This tram tour makes a 360-degree circle around the cathedral, staying about this same distance from it.

● At first bend (before first stop): Look right, toward the tall fountain and the guy on a horse. Schwarzenberg Platz shows off its **equestrian statue** of Prince Charles Schwarzenberg, who fought Napoleon. Behind that is the Russian monument (behind the fountain), which was built in 1945 as a forced thanks to the Soviets for liberating Austria from the Nazis. Formerly a sore point, now it's just ignored. Beyond that (out of sight, on tram D route) is Belvedere Palace (see page 725).

● Going down Schubertring, you reach the huge **Stadtpark** (City Park) on the right, which honors many great Viennese musicians and composers with statues. At the beginning of the park, the gold-and-cream concert hall bchind the trees is the **Kursalon,** opened in 1867 by the Strauss brothers, who directed many waltzes here. The touristy Strauss concerts are held in this building (see "Music Scene," page 731).

● Immediately after the next stop, look right: In the same park, the gilded statue of "Waltz King" **Johann Strauss** holds a violin as he did when he conducted his orchestra, whipping his fans into a three-quarter-time frenzy.

● At the next stop at end of the park: On the left, a green statue of **Dr. Karl Lüger** honors the popular man who was mayor of Vienna until 1910.

● At the next bend: On the right, the quaint white building with military helmets decorating the windows was the **Austrian ministry of war**—back when that was a big operation. Field Marshal Radetzky, a military big shot in the 19th century under Franz Josef, still sits on his high horse. He's pointing toward the post office, the only Art Nouveau building facing the Ring. Locals call the architecture along the Ring "**historicism**" because it's all neo-this and neo-that—generally fitting the purpose of the particular building (for example, farther along the Ring, we'll see the neo-Gothic City Hall—recalling when medieval burghers ran the city government in Gothic days; a neoclassical parliament building--celebrating ancient Greek notions of democracy; and a neo-Renaissance opera house—venerating the high culture filling it).

● At the next corner: The white-domed building over your right shoulder as you turn is the Urania, Franz Josef's 1910 **observatory.** Lean forward and look behind it for a peek at the huge red cars of the giant 100-year-old Ferris wheel in Vienna's Prater Park (fun for families, described on page 729).

● Now you're rolling along the **Danube Canal.** This "Baby Danube" is one of the many small arms of the river that once made up the Danube at this location. The rest have been gathered together in a mightier modern-day Danube, farther away. This neighborhood was thoroughly bombed in World War II. The buildings across the canal are typical of postwar architecture (1960s). They were built on the cheap, and are now being replaced by sleek, futuristic buildings. This was the site of the original Roman town, Vindobona. In three long blocks, on the left (opposite the BP station, be ready—it passes fast), you'll see the ivy-covered walls and round Romanesque arches of St. Ruprecht's, the oldest church in Vienna (built in the 11th century on a bit of Roman ruins). Remember, medieval Vienna was defined by that long-gone wall that you're tracing on this tour. Across the river is an OPEC headquarters, where oil ministers often meet to set prices. Relax for a few stops until the corner.

● Leaving the canal, turning left up Schottenring, at first corner: A block down on the right, you can see a huge red-brick **castle**—actually a high-profile barracks built here at the command of a nervous Emperor Franz Josef (who found himself on the throne as an 18-year-old in 1848, the same year people's revolts against autocracy were sweeping across Europe).

● At the next stop: On the left, the orange-and-white, neo-Renaissance temple of money—the **Börse**—is Vienna's stock exchange.

● The next stop, at the corner: The huge, frilly, neo-Gothic church on the right is a "**votive church,**" built as a thanks to God when an 1853 assassination attempt on Emperor Franz Josef failed. Ahead on the right (in front of tram stop) is the **Vienna University** building (established in 1365, it has no real campus as the buildings are scattered around town). It faces (on the left, behind a gilded angel across the Ring) a chunk of the old **city wall.**

● At the next stop, on the right: The neo-Gothic **City Hall** (Rathaus), flying the flag of Europe, towers over Rathaus Platz. This square is a festive site in summer, with a huge screen showing outdoor movies, operas, and concerts and a thriving food circus (see page 735—if you're hungry and it's thriving, hop off now). In the winter, the City Hall becomes a huge Advent calendar, with 24 windows opening—one each day—as Christmas approaches. Immediately across the street (on left) is the **Burgtheater,** Austria's national theater.

● At the next stop, on the right: The neo-Greek temple of democracy houses the **Austrian Parliament.** The lady with the golden helmet is Athena, goddess of wisdom. The big construction mess is for the restoration of the building's grand ramp. Across the street (on left) is the imperial park called the **Volksgarten.**

● After the next stop on the right is the **Natural History Museum,** the first of Vienna's huge twin museums. It faces the **Kunsthistorisches Museum,** containing the city's greatest collection of paintings. The **MuseumsQuartier** behind them completes the ensemble with a collection of mostly modern-art museums. A hefty statue of Empress Maria Theresa squats between the museums, facing the grand gate to the **Hofburg,** the emperor's palace (on left, across the Ring). Of the five arches, only the center one was used by the emperor. (Your tour is essentially finished. If you want to jump out here, you're at many of Vienna's top sights.)

● Fifty yards after the next stop, on the left through a gate in the black-iron fence, is a statue of Mozart. It's one of many charms in the **Burggarten,** which until 1918 was the private garden of the emperor. Vienna had more than its share of intellectual and creative geniuses. A hundred yards farther (on left, just out of the park), the German philosopher Goethe sits in a big, thought-provoking chair playing trivia with the poet Schiller (across the street on your right). Behind the statue of Schiller is the **Academy of Fine Arts**.

● Hey, there's the **Opera** again. Jump off the tram and see the rest of the city.

SELF-GUIDED WALK

Welcome to Vienna

This walk connects the top three sights in Vienna's old center: the Opera, St. Stephen's Cathedral, and the Hofburg Palace. Along the way, you'll get a glimpse of Vienna past and present. The total trip takes about an hour, not counting sightseeing stops (which could be lengthy).

• *Begin by standing on the square in front of Vienna's landmark Opera.*

Opera: This is regarded by music-lovers as one of the planet's premier houses of music. If you're a fan, consider taking a guided tour of the Opera, or spring for a performance (standing-room tickets are surprisingly cheap; for information on all your Opera options, see page 696). The U-Bahn station in front of the Opera is actually a huge underground shopping mall with fast food, newsstands, lots of pickpockets, and even an Opera Toilet Vienna experience (€0.50, *mit Musik*).

• *Walk behind the Opera to find the famous...*

Sacher Café: This is the home of every chocoholic's fantasy, the *Sachertorte*. While locals complain that the cakes have gone downhill (and many tourists are surprised how dry they are), a coffee and slice of cake here can be €8 well invested. For maximum elegance, sit inside (daily 8:00–23:30, Philharmoniker Strasse 4, tel. 01/51456).

• *Near the Sacher Café (turn right as you exit) is a square called Albertinaplatz, where you'll find the TI, as well as the evocative...*

Monument Against War and Fascism: This powerful, thought-provoking four-part statue merits ▲. The split white monument, *The Gates of Violence*, remembers victims of all wars and violence, including the 1938–1945 Nazi rule of Austria. A montage of wartime images—clubs and WWI gas masks, a dying woman birthing a future soldier, chained slave laborers—sits on a pedestal of granite cut from the infamous quarry at Mauthausen Concentration Camp. The hunched-over figure on the ground behind is a Jew forced to wash anti-Nazi graffiti off a street with a toothbrush. The statue with its head buried in the stone (Orpheus entering the underworld) reminds Austrians of the consequences of not keeping their government on track. Behind that, the 1945 declaration of Austria's second republic—with human rights built into it—is cut into the stone. This monument stands on the spot where several hundred people were buried alive while hiding in the cellar of a building demolished in a WWII bombing attack (see photo to right of park).

Austria was pulled into World War II by Germany, which annexed the country in 1938, saying Austrians were wannabe Germans anyway. But Austrians are not Germans—never were, never will be. They're quick to tell you that while Austria was founded in the 10th century, Germany wasn't born until 1870. For seven years during World War II (1938–1945), there was no Austria. In 1955, after 10 years of joint occupation by the victorious Allies, Austria regained total independence on the condition that it would be forever neutral (and never join NATO or the Warsaw Pact). To this day, Austria is outside of NATO (and Germany).

• *Across the square from the TI is the...*

Albertina Museum: Overlooking Albertinaplatz is what looks like a big terrace. This was actually part of Vienna's original defensive rampart. Later, it was the home to Empress Maria Theresa's daughter Maria Christina. And today, it's topped by a sleek, controversial titanium canopy (called the "diving board" by critics) that welcomes visitors into a recently restored museum. For details on the Albertina Museum, see page 709.

• *Across Albertinaplatz from the Albertina Museum is the street called Tegetthoffstrasse. Walk down this street a block to the square called Neuer Markt. Fronting the square is the...*

Kaisergruft: This church houses the remains of the Hapsburgs (not as gruesome as it sounds—it's basically a bunch of fancy coffins labeled with names you might recognize). Before moving on, consider paying your respects here (described on page 709).

• *After visiting the Kaisergruft, cross Neuer Markt and turn left down...*

Kärntner Strasse: This grand, mall-like street (traffic-free since 1974) is the people-watching delight of this in-love-with-life city. While it's mostly a crass commercial pedestrian mall with its famed elegant shops now long gone, locals know it's the same road crusaders marched down as they headed off for the Holy Land in the 12th century. Its name indicates that it points south, in the direction of the region of Kärnten (Carinthia, today divided between Austria and Slovenia).

Along this drag, you'll find lots of action—shops, street music, the city casino (at #41), the venerable Lobmeyr Crystal shop (#26), American Express (#21), the Loos American bar (dark, plush, small, great €8 cocktails, no shorts, Kärntnerdurchgang 10, tel. 01/512-3283), and then, finally, the cathedral. Where Kärntner Strasse hits Stephansplatz (at #3), the Equitable Building (filled

> ## Adolf Loos
> ### (1870–1933)
>
> Adolf Loos—Vienna's answer to Frank Lloyd Wright—famously condemned needless ornamentation, declaring, "Decoration is a crime." You can see three good examples of his work (all c. 1900 and described in this chapter) as you stroll the old center. Just off Kärntner Strasse is the Loos American Bar (Kärntnerdurchgang 10). On the Graben, you can descend into the finest public toilets in town. And facing Michaelerplatz, in front of the Hofburg entrance, is the Loos House (a.k.a. the "house without eyebrows").

with lawyers, bankers, and insurance men) is a fine example of historicism from the turn of the century. Step in, climb the stairs, and imagine how slick the courtyard must have felt in 1900.

• *At the end of Kärntner Strasse, you'll wander into...*

Stephansplatz: Vienna's fun and colorful main square is also home to its cathedral, St. Stephen's. Now it's time to visit this massive church (see page 697).

• *When you're finished on Stephansplatz, head for the Hofburg. At the bottom of the square (near the start of Kärntner Strasse) is the street called...*

Graben: This was once a *Graben*, or ditch—originally the moat for the Roman military camp. In the middle of this pedestrian zone (at the intersection with Bräuner Strasse), top-notch

street entertainers dance around an extravagant **plague monument**. In the Middle Ages, people didn't understand the causes of plagues, and figured they were a punishment from God. It was common for survivors to bribe or thank God with a monument like this one (c. 1690). Find Emperor Leopold, who ruled during the plague and made this statue in gratitude. (Hint: The typical inbreeding of royal families left him with a gaping underbite.) Below Leopold, Faith (with the help of a disgusting little cupid) tosses old naked women—symbolizing the plague—into the abyss.

Just before the plague monument is Dorotheergasse, leading to the Dorotheum auction house (see page 720). Just beyond the monument, you'll pass a fine set of **public WCs.** In about 1900, a local chemical maker needed a publicity stunt. He purchased two wine cellars under the Graben and hired Adolf Loos to design classy WCs in the Modernist style (complete with chandeliers and finely crafted mahogany) to prove that his chemicals really got things clean. The restrooms remain clean to this day—in fact, they're so inviting that they're used for poetry readings. Locals and tourists happily pay €0.50 for a quick visit.

• *The Graben dead-ends at the aristocratic supermarket Julius Meinl am Graben (see "Eating," page 744). At the end of Graben, turn left onto...*

Kohlmarkt: This is Vienna's most elegant shopping street (except for "American Catalog Shopping" at #5, 2nd floor), with the emperor's palace at the end. Strolling Kohlmarkt, daydream about the edible window displays at **Demel** (#14, daily 10:00–19:00). Demel is the ultimate Viennese chocolate shop. During the summer, when the tables are moved outside, a room is filled with Art Nouveau boxes of Empress Sissy's choco-dreams come true: *Kandierte Veilchen* (candied violet petals), *Katzenzungen* (cats' tongues), and so on. The cakes here are moist (compared to the dry *Sachertortes*). The delectable window displays change about weekly, reflecting current happenings in Vienna. Inside, an impressive cancan of cakes is displayed to tempt visitors into springing for the €10 cake-and-coffee deal (point to the cake you want). You can sit inside, with a view of the cake-making, or outside, with the street action. Shops like this boast "K. u. K."—good enough for the *König und Kaiser* (king and emperor—same guy).

Just beyond Demel and across the street, at #1152, you can pop into a charming little Baroque **carriage courtyard,** with the surviving original carriage garages.

• *Kohlmarkt ends at...*

Michaelerplatz: In the center of this square, a scant bit of Roman Vienna lies exposed. On the left are the fancy Loden Plankl shop, with traditional formal wear, and the stables of the Spanish Riding School. Study the grand entry facade to the Hofburg Palace—it's neo-Baroque from around 1900. The four heroic giants illustrate Hercules wrestling with his great challenges (much like the Hapsburgs, I'm sure). Opposite the facade, notice the modern Loos House (now a bank), which was built at about the same time. It was nicknamed the "house without eyebrows" for the simplicity of its windows. An anti–Art Nouveau statement (inspired by Frank Lloyd Wright and considered Vienna's first "modern" building), this was actually shocking at the time. To quell some of the outrage, the architect added flower boxes.

• *You've made it to the Hofburg Palace. To get to the sights inside, simply walk through the gate, under the dome, and into the first square (In der Burg). For details on all the sights here, see page 699.*

Vienna at a Glance

▲▲▲**Opera** Dazzling, world-famous opera house. Hours: Visit by guided 45-min tour only, daily in English; July–Aug at 11:00, 13:00, 14:00, 15:00, and often at 10:00 and 16:00; Sept–June fewer tours, afternoon only; call ahead to confirm tour times.

▲▲▲**Hofburg Treasury** The Hapsburgs' collection of jewels, crowns, and other valuables—the best on the Continent. **Hours:** Wed–Mon 10:00–18:00, closed Tue.

▲▲▲**Kunsthistorisches Museum** World-class exhibit of the Hapsburgs' art collection, including Raphael, Titian, Caravaggio, Bosch, and Bruegel. **Hours:** Tue–Sun 10:00–18:00, Thu until 21:00, closed Mon.

▲▲▲**Schönbrunn Palace** Spectacular summer residence of the Hapsburgs, similar in grandeur to Versailles. **Hours:** Daily July–Aug 8:30–18:00, April–June and Sept–Oct 8:30–17:00, Nov–March 8:30–16:30, reservations recommended.

▲▲**St. Stephen's Cathedral** Enormous, historic Gothic cathedral in the center of Vienna. **Hours:** Church doors open Mon–Sat 6:00–22:00, Sun 7:00–22:00, officially only open for tourists Mon–Sat 8:30–11:30 & 13:00–16:30, Sun 13:00–16:30.

▲▲**Hofburg Imperial Apartments** Lavish main residence of the Hapsburgs. **Hours:** Daily 9:00–17:00.

▲▲**New Palace Museums** Uncrowded collection of armor, musical instruments, and ancient Greek statues, in the elegant halls of a Hapsburg palace. **Hours:** Wed–Mon 10:00–18:00, closed Tue.

▲▲**Albertina Museum** Hapsburg residence with decent apartments and world-class permanent and temporary exhibits. **Hours:** Daily 10:00–18:00, Wed until 21:00.

▲▲**Kaisergruft** Crypt for the Hapsburg royalty. **Hours:** Daily 9:30–16:00.

▲▲**Haus der Musik** Modern musuem with interactive exhibits on Vienna's favorite pastime. **Hours:** Daily 10:00–22:00.

▲▲**Belvedere Palace** Elegant palace of Prince Eugene of Savoy, with a collection of 19th- and 20th-century Austrian art (including Klimt). **Hours:** Tue–Sun 10:00–18:00, closed Mon.

▲**Monument Against War and Fascism** Powerful four-part statue remembering victims of the Nazis. **Hours:** Always open.

▲**Lipizzaner Museum** Displays dedicated to the regal Lipizzaner Stallions; horse-lovers should check out their practice sessions. **Hours:** Museum open daily 9:00–18:00; stallions practice across the street roughly Feb–June and Sept–Oct Tue–Sat 10:00–12:00 when the horses are in town— call to confirm.

▲**Augustinian Church** Hapsburg marriage church, now hosting an 11:00 Sunday Mass with wonderful music. **Hours:** Open long hours daily.

▲**Imperial Furniture Collection** Eclectic collection of Hapsburg furniture. **Hours:** Tue–Sun 10:00–18:00, closed Mon.

▲**Naschmarkt** Sprawling, lively, people-filled outdoor market. **Hours:** Mon–Fri 6:00–18:30, Sat 6:00–17:00, closed Sun, closes earlier in winter.

▲**Natural History Museum** Big building facing Kunsthistorisches Museum, featuring the ancient *Venus of Willendorf*. **Hours:** Wed–Mon 9:00–18:30, Wed until 21:00, closed Tue.

▲**Dorotheum** Vienna's highbrow auction house. **Hours:** Mon–Fri 10:00–18:00, Sat 9:00–17:00, closed Sun.

▲**Academy of Fine Arts** Small but exciting collection with works by Bosch, Botticelli, Rubens, Guardi, and Van Dyck. **Hours:** Tue–Sun 10:00–18:00, closed Mon.

▲**Liechtenstein Museum** Baroque art collection of the family that governs one of Europe's tiniest nations. **Hours:** Wed–Mon 9:00–20:00, closed Tue.

▲**KunstHausWien** Modern art museum dedicated to zany local artist/environmentalist Hundertwasser. **Hours:** Daily 10:00–19:00.

SIGHTS

For a self-guided walk connecting these first three landmark sights, see page 690.

Opera (Staatsoper)

The Opera, facing the Ring and near the TI, is a central point for any visitor—easily worth ▲▲▲. While the critical reception of the building 130 years ago led the architect to commit suicide, and though it's been rebuilt since being destroyed by WWII bombs, it's still a sumptuous place.

Tours: Unless you're attending a performance, you can enter the Opera only with a guided 45-minute tour (€4.50, daily in English; July–Aug at 11:00, 13:00, 14:00, 15:00, and often at 10:00 and 16:00; Sept–June fewer tours, afternoon only). Tours are often canceled for rehearsals and shows, so check the posted schedule or call 01/514-442-606.

Performances: The Vienna State Opera—with musicians provided by the Vienna Philharmonic Orchestra in the pit—is one of the world's top opera houses. There are 300 performances a year, but in July and August the singers rest their voices. Since there are different operas nearly nightly, you'll see big trucks out back and constant action backstage—all the sets need to be switched each day. Even though the expensive seats normally sell out long in advance, the opera is perpetually in the red and subsidized by the state.

To **buy tickets** in advance, call 01/513-1513 (phone answered daily 10:00–21:00, www.wiener-staatsoper.at). If seats aren't sold out, last-minute tickets (for pricey seats—up to €100) are sold for €40 from 9:00 to 14:00 only the day before the show.

Unless Placido Domingo is in town, it's easy to get one of 567 **standing-room tickets** (*Stehplätze*, €2 at the top or €3.50 downstairs). While the front doors open one hour before the show starts, a side door (on the Operngasse side, the door under the portico nearest the fountain) is open an hour and a half before curtain time, giving those in the know an early grab at standing-room tickets. Just walk in straight, then head right until you see the ticket booth marked *Stehplätze* (tel. 01/5144-42419). If fewer than 567 people are in line, there's no need to line up early. If you're one of the first 160 in line, try for the "Parterre" section and you'll end up directly under the Emperor's Box. You can even buy standing-room tickets after the show has started—in case you want only a little taste of opera. Dress is casual (but do your best) at the standing-room bar. Locals save their spot along the rail by tying a scarf to it.

Rick's Crude Tip: For me, three hours is a lot of opera. But just to see and hear the Opera House in action for half an hour is a treat. You can buy a standing-room spot and just drop in for part of the show. Ushers don't mind letting tourists with standing-room tickets in for a short look. Ending time is posted in the lobby—you could stop by for just the finale. If you go at the start or finish, you'll see Vienna dressed up.

St. Stephen's Cathedral (Stephansdom)

This massive church is the Gothic needle around which Vienna spins. Today worth ▲▲, it has survived Vienna's many wars and symbolizes the city's freedom.

Cost: Entering the church is free, but going up the towers costs €3 (by stairs, south tower) or €4 (by elevator, north tower). For more information, see "Towers" below.

Hours: The church doors are open Mon–Sat 6:00–22:00, Sun 7:00–22:00, but it's officially only open for tourists Mon–Sat 8:30–11:30 & 13:00–16:30, Sun 13:00–16:30. During services, you can't enter the main nave (unless you're attending Mass), but you can go into the back of the church to reach the north tower elevator (daily 8:30–17:30, Nov–March until 16:30). The stairs up to the south tower (enter from outside) are open daily 9:00–17:30.

Tours: The €4 tours in English are entertaining (daily April–Oct at 15:45, check information board inside entry to confirm schedule).

◗ **Self-Guided Tour:** This is the third church to stand on this spot. The church survived the bombs of World War II, but, in the last days of the war, fires from the street fighting between Russian and Nazi troops leapt to the rooftop. The original timbered Gothic rooftop burned, and the cathedral's huge bell crashed to the ground. With a financial outpouring of civic pride, the roof was rebuilt in its original splendor by 1952. The ceramic tiles are purely decorative (locals who contributed to the postwar reconstruction each "own" one for their donation).

The **grounds** around the church were a cemetery until Josef II emptied it as an "anti-plague" measure. (Inside, a few of the most important tombstones decorate the church walls.) You can still see the footprint of the old cemetery church in the pavement, today ignored by the human statues. Remains of the earlier Virgil Chapel (dating from the 13th century) are immediately under this (on display in the U-Bahn station).

Study the church's **main entrance** (west end). You can see the original Romanesque facade (c. 1240) with classical Roman statues embedded in it. Above are two stubby towers nicknamed "pagan towers" because they're built with Roman stones (flipped over to hide the inscriptions and expose the smooth sides). Two 30-foot-tall columns flank the main entry. If you stand back and look at the tops, you'll see that they symbolize creation (one's a penis, the other's a vagina).

Go inside. Find the dramatic photos of **WWII damage** (with bricks neatly stacked and ready) in glass cases 20 yards opposite the south entrance (on the wall near 3a).

The nave is ringed with **chapels.** The church once had more than a hundred. This was typical of Catholic churches, as each guild and leading family had their own chapel. The Tupperware-colored glass windows date from 1950. Before WWII, the entire church was lit with windows like the ones behind the altar. Those, along with the city's top art treasures, were hidden safely from the Nazis in salt mines. The altar painting of the stoning of St. Stephen is early Baroque, painted on copper.

St. Stephen's is proud to be Austria's national church. A **plaque** explains how each region contributed to the rebuilding after World War II: windows from Tirol, furniture from Vorarlberg, the floor from Lower Austria, and so on.

The Gothic sandstone **pulpit** in the middle of the nave (on left) is a realistic masterpiece carved from three separate blocks

(find the seams). A spiral stairway winds up to the lectern, surrounded and supported by the four Latin Church fathers: Saints Ambrose, Jerome, Gregory, and Augustine. The railing leading up swarms with symbolism: lizards (animals of light) and battle toads (animals of darkness). The "Dog of the Lord" stands at the top, making sure none of those toads pollutes the sermon. Below the toads, wheels with three parts (the Trinity) roll up, while wheels with four parts (the four seasons, symbolizing mortal life) roll down. This work, by Anton Pilgram, has all the elements of the Flamboyant Gothic style in miniature. Gothic art was done for the glory of God. Artists were anonymous. But this was circa 1500, and the Renaissance was going strong in Italy. While Gothic persisted in the North, the Renaissance spirit had already arrived. In the more humanist Renaissance, man was allowed to shine—and artists became famous. So Pilgram included a rare self-portrait bust in his work (the guy with sculptor's tools, in the classic "artist observing the world from his window" pose under the stairs).

Towers: You can ascend both towers, the south (outside right transept, by spiral staircase) and the north (via crowded elevator inside on the left). The 450-foot-high south tower, called St. Stephen's Tower, offers the far better view, but you'll earn it by hiking 343 tightly wound steps up the spiral staircase (€3, daily 9:00–17:30, this hike burns about 1 *Suchertorte* of calories). From the top, use your *Vienna from A to Z* to locate the famous sights. The north tower shows you a mediocre view and a big bell: the 21-ton Pummerin, cast from the cannon captured from the Turks in 1683, and supposedly the second biggest bell in the world that rings by swinging (locals know it as the bell that rings in the Austrian New Year; €4, daily 8:30–17:30, Nov–March until 16:30).

Cathedral Museum (Dom Museum): This forlorn museum (outside left transept past horses) gives a close-up look at piles of religious paintings, statues, and a treasury (€5, Tue–Sat 10:00–17:00, closed Sun–Mon, Stephansplatz 6, tel. 01/515-523-560).

Hofburg Palace

The complex, confusing, and imposing Imperial Palace, with 640 years of architecture, demands your attention. This first Hapsburg residence grew with the family empire from the 13th century until 1913, when the last "new wing" opened. The winter residence of the Hapsburg rulers until 1918, it's still the home of the Spanish Riding School, the Vienna Boys' Choir, the Austrian president's office, 5,000 government workers, and several important museums.

Rather than lose yourself in its myriad halls and courtyards, focus on three sections: the Imperial Apartments, Treasury, and Neue Burg (New Palace).

Orientation from In der Burg: Begin at the square called In der Burg (enter through the gate from Michaelerplatz). The statue is of Emperor Franz II, grandson of Maria Theresa, grandfather of Franz Josef, and father-in-law of Napoleon. Behind him is a tower with three kinds of clocks (the yellow disk shows the stage of the moon tonight). On the right, a door leads to the Imperial Apartments. Franz faces the oldest part of the palace. The colorful gate, which used to have a drawbridge, leads to the 13th-century Swiss Court (named for the Swiss mercenary guards once stationed here), the Treasury (Schatzkammer), and the Imperial Chapel (Hofburgkapelle, where the Boys' Choir sings the Mass—see page 730). For the Heroes' Square and the New Palace, continue opposite the way you entered In der Burg, passing through the left-most tunnel (with a tiny but handy sandwich bar—Hofburg Stüberl, Mon–Fri 7:00–18:00, Sat–Sun 10:00–16:00, your best bet if you

Sissy
(1837–1898)

Empress Elisabeth—Franz Josef's mysterious, narcissistic, and beautiful wife—is in vogue. Sissy was mostly silent. Her main goals in life seem to have been preserving her reputation as a beautiful empress, maintaining her Barbie Doll figure, and tending to her fairytale, ankle-length hair. In spite of severe dieting and fanatic exercise, age took its toll. After turning 30, she allowed no more portraits to be painted and was generally seen in public with a delicate fan covering her face (and bad teeth). Complex and influential, she was adored by Franz Josef, whom she respected. Her personal mission and political cause was promoting Hungary's bid for nationalism. Her personal tragedy was the death of her son Rudolf, the crown prince, by suicide. Disliking Vienna and the confines of the court, she traveled more and more frequently. Over the years, the restless Sissy and her hardworking husband became estranged. In 1898, while visiting Geneva, Switzerland, she was murdered by an Italian anarchist.

Sissy has been compared to Princess Diana because of her beauty, bittersweet life, and tragic death. Her story is wonderfully told in the new Sissy Museum, now part of the Hofburg Imperial Apartments tour.

need a bite or drink before touring the Imperial Apartments). Note that Hapsburg sights not actually inside the Hofburg (including the Lipizzaner Stallions, the Augustinian Church, and the Albertina Museum) are covered on page 707.

▲▲▲**Imperial Apartments (Kaiserappartements)**—These lavish, Versailles-type, "wish-I-were-God" royal rooms are the downtown version of the grander Schönbrunn Palace. If you're rushed and have time for only one palace, do this (€8.90, daily 9:00–17:00, last entry 16:30, from courtyard through St. Michael's Gate, just off Michaelerplatz, tel. 01/533-7570). Palace visits are a one-way romp through 20 rooms. You'll find some helpful posted English information, and, with that and the following description, you won't need the €7.50 *Imperial Apartments and Sissy* museum guidebook. The included audioguide brings the exhibit to life. Tickets also get you into the royal silver and porcelain collection *(Silberkammer)* near the turnstile. If touring the silver and porcelain, do it first to save walking.

→ **Self-Guided Tour:** Get your ticket, tour the silver and porcelain collection, climb the stairs, go through the turnstile, study the family tree tracing the Hapsburgs from 1273 to their messy WWI demise, and use the big model of the palace complex

Vienna's Hofburg Palace

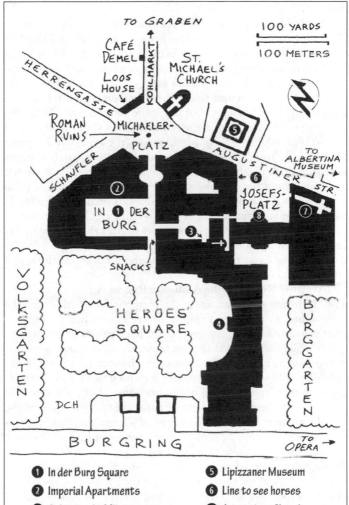

1. In der Burg Square
2. Imperial Apartments
3. Schweizerhof (Entrances to Treasury & Imperial Chapel)
4. Hofburg New Palace Museums
5. Lipizzaner Museum
6. Line to see horses
7. Augustiner Church
8. National Library

to understand the complex lay of the imperial land. Then head into the...

Sissy Museum: The first six rooms tell the life story of Empress Elisabeth's fancy world—her luxury homes and fairytale existence. While Sissy's life story is the perfect stuff of legends, the exhibit tries to keep things from getting too giddy, and doesn't add to the sugary, kitschy image that's been created. The exhibit starts with her assignation and traces the development of her legend, analyzing how her fabulous but tragic life could create a 19th-century Princes Diana from a rocky start (when she was disdained for abandoning Vienna and her husband, the venerable Emperor Franz Josef). You'll read bits of her poetic writing, catch snatches of movies made about her, see exact copies of her now-lost jewelry, and learn about her escapes, dieting mania, and chocolate bills. Admire Sissy's hard-earned thin waist (20 inches at age 16, 21 inches at age 50...after giving birth to 4 children). The black statue in the dark room represents the empress after the suicide of her son—aloof, thin, in black, with her back to the world.

After the Sissy rooms, a one-way route takes you through a series of royal rooms.

Waiting Room for the Audience Room: A map and mannequins from the many corners of the Hapsburg realm illustrate the multi-ethnicity of the vast empire. Every citizen had the right to meet privately with the emperor. Three huge paintings entertained guests while they waited. They were propaganda, showing crowds of commoners enthusiastic about their Hapsburg royalty. On the right: An 1809 scene of the emperor returning to Vienna, celebrating news that Napoleon had begun his retreat. Left: The return of the emperor from the 1814 Peace of Paris, the treaty that ended the Napoleonic wars. (The 1815 Congress of Vienna that followed was the greatest assembly of diplomats in European history. Its goal: to establish peace through a "balance of power" among nations. While rulers ignored nationalism in favor of continued dynastic rule, this worked for about 100 years, until a colossal war—World War I—wiped out the Hapsburgs and the rest of Europe's royal families.) Center: Less important, the emperor makes his first public appearance to adoring crowds after recovering from a life-threatening illness (1826). The chandelier--considered the best in the palace—is Baroque, made of Bohemian crystal.

Audience Room: Suddenly, you were face-to-face with the emperor. The portrait on the easel shows Franz Josef in 1915, when he was more than 80 years old. Famously energetic, he lived a spartan life dedicated to duty. He'd stand at the high table here to meet with commoners, who came to show gratitude or make a request. (Standing kept things moving.) On the table, you can read a partial list of 56 appointments he had on January 3, 1910

Emperor Franz Josef
(1830–1916)

Franz Josef I—who ruled for 68 years (1848–1916)—was the embodiment of the Hapsburg Empire as it finished its six-century-long ride. Born in 1830, Franz Josef had a stern upbringing that instilled in him a powerful sense of duty and—like so many men of power—a love of things military.

His uncle, Ferdinand I, was a dimwit, and, as the revolutions of 1848 were rattling royal families throughout Europe, the Hapsburgs replaced him, putting 18-year old Franz Josef on the throne. FJ put down the revolt with bloody harshness and spent the first part of his long reign understandably paranoid as social discontent simmered.

FJ was very conservative. But worse, he figured wrongly that he was a talented military tactician, leading Austria into disastrous battles against Italy (which was fighting for its unification and independence) in the 1860s. His army endured severe, avoidable casualties. It was clear: FJ was a disaster as a general.

Wearing his uniform to the end, he never saw what a dinosaur his monarchy was becoming, and never thought it strange that the majority of his subjects didn't even speak German. He had no interest in democracy and pointedly never set foot in Austria's parliament building. But, like his contemporary Queen Victoria, he was the embodiment of his empire—old-fashioned but sacrosanct. His passion for low-grade paperwork earned him the nickname "Joe Bureaucrat." Mired in these petty details, he missed the big picture. He helped start a Great War that ultimately ended the age of monarchs. The year 1918 marked the end of Europe's big royal families: Hohenzollerns (Prussia), Romanovs (Russia), and Hapsburgs (Austria).

(family name and topic of meeting).

Conference Room: The emperor presided here over the equivalent of cabinet meetings. After 1867, he ruled the Austro-Hungarian Empire, so Hungarians sat at these meetings. The paintings on the wall show the military defeat of a popular Hungarian uprising subtle.

Emperor Franz Josef's Study: The desk was originally between the windows. Franz Josef could look up from his work and see his lovely, long-haired, tiny-waisted Empress Elisabeth's reflection in the mirror. Notice the trompe l'oeil paintings above each door, giving the believable illusion of marble relief. Notice also all the family photos—the perfect gift for the dad/uncle/hubby who has it all.

The walls between the rooms are wide enough to hide servants' corridors (the door to his valet's room is in the back left corner). The emperor lived with a personal staff of 14: "three valets, four lackeys, two doormen, two manservants, and three chambermaids."

Emperor's Bedroom: This features his famous no-frills iron bed and portable washstand (necessary until 1880, when the palace got running water). While he had a typical emperor's share of mistresses, his dresser was always well-stocked with photos of Sissy. Franz Josef lived here after his estrangement from Sissy. An etching shows the empress—a fine rider and avid hunter—riding sidesaddle while jumping a hedge. The big, ornate stove in the corner was fed from behind. Through the 19th century, this was a standard form of heating.

Small Salon: This is dedicated to the memory of the assassinated Emperor Maximilian of Mexico (bearded portrait, Franz Josef's brother, killed in 1867). This was also a smoking room—necessary in the early 19th century, when smoking was newly fashionable (but only for men—never in the presence of women). Left of the door is a small button the emperor had to buzz before entering the quarters of his estranged wife. You can go right in.

Empress' Bedroom and Drawing Room: This was Sissy's, refurbished neo-rococo in 1854. She lived here—the bed was rolled in and out daily—until her death in 1898.

Sissy's Dressing/Exercise Room: Servants worked two hours a day on Sissy's famous hair here. She'd exercise on the wooden structure. While she had a tough time with people, she did fine with animals. Her favorite dogs hang adorably on the wall.

Sissy's Bathroom: Detour into the behind-the-scenes palace. In the narrow passageway, you'll walk by Sissy's hand-painted-porcelain, dolphin-head WC (on the right). In the main bathroom, you'll see her huge copper tub (with the original wall coverings behind it). Sissy was the first Hapsburg to have running water in her bathroom (notice the hot and cold faucets). You're walking on the first linoleum ever used in Vienna—from about 1880. Next, enter the servants' quarters, with tropical scenes painted by Bergl in 1766. As you leave these rooms and re-enter the imperial world, look back to the room on the left.

Empress' Great Salon: The room is painted with Mediterranean escapes, the 19th-century equivalent of travel posters. The statue is of Elisa, Napoleon's oldest sister (by the neoclassical master, Canova). Turn the corner and pass through the anterooms of Alexander's apartments.

Red Salon: The Gobelin wall hangings were a 1776 gift from Marie Antoinette and Louis XVI in Paris to their Viennese counterparts.

Dining Room: It's dinnertime, and Franz Josef has called his extended family together. The settings are modest...just silver. Gold was saved for formal state dinners. Next to each name card was a menu with the chef responsible for each dish. (Talk about pressure.) While the Hofburg had tableware for 4,000, feeding 3,000 was a typical day. The cellar was stocked with 60,000 bottles of wine. The kitchen was huge—50 birds could be roasted on the hand-driven spits at once.

Through the shop, you're back on the street. Two quick lefts take you back to the palace square (In der Burg), where you can pass through the black, red, and gold gate and to the treasury.

▲▲▲**Treasury (Weltliche und Geistliche Schatzkammer)**— This "Secular and Religious Treasure Room" contains the best jewels on the Continent. Slip through the vault doors and reflect on the glitter of 21 rooms filled with scepters, swords, crowns, orbs, weighty robes, double-headed eagles, gowns, gem-studded bangles, and an eight-foot-tall, 500-year-old unicorn horn (or maybe the tusk of a narwhal)—which was considered incredibly powerful in the old days, giving its owner the grace of God. These were owned by the Holy Roman Emperor—a divine monarch (€8, Wed–Mon 10:00–18:00, closed Tue, follow *Schatzkammer* signs to the Schweizerhof, tel. 01/52524).

◐ **Self-Guided Tour:** The well-produced, €2 audioguide provides a wealth of information. Here are the highlights.

Room 2: The personal crown of Rudolf II has survived since 1602—it was considered too well-crafted to cannibalize for other crowns. This crown is a big deal because it's the adopted crown of the Austrian Empire, established in 1806 after Napoleon dissolved the Holy Roman Empire (an alliance of Germanic kingdoms so named because it tried to be the grand continuation of the Roman Empire). Pressured by Napoleon, the Austrian Francis II—who had been Holy Roman Emperor—became Francis I, Emperor of Austria. Francis I/II (the stern guy on the wall, near where you entered) ruled from 1792 to 1835. Look at the crown. Its design symbolically merges the typical medieval king's crown and a bishop's miter.

Rooms 3 and 4: These contain some of the coronation vestments and regalia needed for the new Austrian emperor.

Room 5: Ponder the Throne Cradle. Napoleon's son was born in 1811 and made king of Rome. The little eagle at the foot is symbolically not yet able to fly, but glory-bound. Glory is symbolized by the star, with dad's big *N* raised high.

Room 11: The collection's highlight is the 10th-century crown of the Holy Roman Emperor. The imperial crown swirls with symbolism "proving" that the emperor was both holy and Roman. The jeweled arch over the top is reminiscent of the parade helmet of ancient Roman emperors whose successors the HRE claimed to be. The cross on top says the HRE ruled as Christ's representative on earth. King Solomon's portrait (on the crown, right of cross) is Old Testament proof that kings can be wise and good. King David (next panel) is similar proof that they can be just. The crown's eight sides represent the celestial city of Jerusalem's eight gates. The jewels on the front panel symbolize the 12 apostles.

The nearby 11th-century Imperial Cross preceded the emperor in ceremonies. Encrusted with jewels, it carried a substantial chunk of *the* cross and *the* holy lance (supposedly used to pierce the side of Jesus while on the cross; both items displayed in the same glass case). This must be the actual holy lance, as Holy Roman Emperors actually carried this into battle in the 10th century. Look behind the cross to see how it was actually a box that could be clipped open and shut. You can see bits of the "true cross" anywhere, but this is a prime piece—with the actual nail hole.

The other case has jewels from the reign of Karl der Grosse (Charlemagne), the greatest ruler of medieval Europe. Notice Charlemagne modeling the crown (which was made a hundred years after he died) in the tall painting adjacent.

Room 12: The painting shows the coronation of Maria Theresa's son Josef II in 1764. He's wearing the same crown and royal garb you've just seen.

Room 16: Most tourists walk right by perhaps the most exquisite workmanship in the entire treasury, the royal vestments (15th century). Look closely—they're painted with gold and silver threads.

▲Heroes' Square (Heldenplatz) and the New Palace (Neue Burg)

—This last grand addition to the palace, from the early 20th century, was built for the Hapsburg heir Franz Ferdinand (it was tradition for rulers not to move into their predecessor's quarters). But—while he was waiting politely for his long-lived uncle, Emperor Franz Josef, to die so he could move into his new  digs—Franz Ferdinand was murdered in Sarajevo in 1914, sparking the beginning of World War I. The rest, as they say, is...

The palace's grand facade arches around **Heroes' Square**. Notice statues of two great Austrian heroes on horseback: Prince Eugene of Savoy (who defeated the Turks that had earlier threatened Vienna) and Archduke Charles (first to beat Napoleon in a battle, breaking Nappy's image of invincibility and heralding the end of the Napoleonic age). The frilly spires of Vienna's neo-Gothic

City Hall break the horizon, and a line of horse-drawn carriages await their customers.

▲▲New Palace Museums: Armor, Music, and Ancient Greek Statues—The Neue Burg—technically part of the Kunsthistorisches Museum across the way—houses three fine museums (same ticket): an armory (with a killer collection of medieval weapons), historical musical instruments, and classical statuary from ancient Ephesus. The included audioguide brings the exhibits to life and lets you actually hear the fascinating old instruments in the collection being played. An added bonus is the chance to wander all alone among those royal Hapsburg halls, stairways, and painted ceilings (€8, Wed–Mon 10:00–18:00, closed Tue, almost no tourists, tel. 01/5252-4484). This place should be open throughout 2006 (after being renovated last fall); but if you're traveling early in the year, call to make sure it's open.

More Hapsburg Sights near the Hofburg

Central Vienna has plenty more sights associated with the Hapsburgs. With the exception of the last one (on Mariahilfer Strasse), these are all near the Hofburg. Remember that the biggest Hapsburg sight of all, Schönbrunn Palace, makes a great half-day trip (4 miles from the center—see page 726).

Palace Garden (Burggarten)—This greenbelt, once the back yard of the Hofburg and now a people's park, welcomes people to loiter on the grass. On nice days, it's lively with office workers enjoying a break. The statue of Mozart facing the Ringstrasse is popular. The iron-and-glass pavilion now houses the recommended Palmenhaus Restaurant (see page 747) and a small but fluttery butterfly exhibit

 (€5; April–Oct Mon–Fri 10:00–16:45, Sat–Sun 10:00–18:15; Nov–March daily 10:00–15:45). The butterfly zone is delightfully muggy on a brisk off-season day, but trippy any time of year. If you tour it, notice the butterflies hanging out on the trays with rotting slices of banana. They lick the fermented banana juice as it beads, and then just hang out there in a stupor...or fly in anything but a straight line.

▲Lipizzaner Museum—A must for horse-lovers, this tidy museum in the Renaissance Stallburg Palace shows (and tells in English) the 400-year history of the famous riding school. Lipizzaner fans have a warm spot in their hearts for General Patton, who, at the end of World War II—knowing that the Soviets were about to take control of Vienna—ordered a raid on the stable to save the horses and ensure the survival of their fine old bloodlines. Videos show the horses in action on TVs throughout the museum. The "dancing" originated as battle moves: *pirouette* (quick turns) and *courbette* (on hind legs to make a living shield for the knight). The 45-minute movie in the basement theater also has great horse footage (showings alternate between German and English). These are very special horses—you'll notice they actually have "surnames," as all can be traced to the original six 16th-century stallions (€5, daily 9:00–18:00, between Josefsplatz and Michaelerplatz at Reitschulgasse 2, tel. 01/5252-4583, www .lipizzaner.at). Any time of day, you can see the horses prance on video in the museum's window. Video cameras allow visitors to "peek in" on the horses live.

Seeing the Lipizzaner Stallions: Seats for performances by Vienna's prestigious Spanish Riding School book up months in advance, but standing room is often available the same day (tickets-€45–160, standing room-€28, March–June and Sept–Oct Sun at 11:00, sometimes also Fri at 18:00, tel. 01/533-9031, www.srs.at). Luckily for the masses, training sessions with music in a chandeliered Baroque hall are open to the public (€12 at the door, roughly Feb–June and Sept–Oct Tue–Sat 10:00–12:00—but only when the horses are in town). Tourists line up early at Josefsplatz, gate 2. Save money and avoid the wait by buying the €15 combo-ticket that covers both the museum and the training session (and lets you avoid that ticket line). Or, better yet, simply show up late. If you want to hang out with Japanese tour groups, get there early and wait for the doors to open at 10:00. But almost no one stays for the full two hours—except for the horses. As people leave, new tickets are printed continuously, so you can just waltz in with no wait at all. If you arrive at 10:45, you'll see the best action as one group of horses finishes and two more perform before they call it a day.

▲Augustinian Church (Augustinerkirche)—This is the Gothic and neo-Gothic church where the Hapsburgs latched, then buried, their hearts (weddings took place here, and the royal hearts are in the vault). Don't miss the exquisite, tomb-like Canova memorial (neoclassical, 1805) to Maria Theresa's favorite daughter, Maria Christina, with its incredibly sad white-marble procession. The church's 11:00 Sunday Mass is a hit with music-lovers—both a Mass and a concert, often with an orchestra accompany- ing the choir. To pay, contribute to the offering plate and buy a CD afterwards. Programs are available at the table by the entry all week (church open long hours daily, Augustinerstrasse 3).

The church faces Josefsplatz, with its statue of the great reform emperor Josef II. The **National Library** (€5, Tue–Sun 10:00–18:00, Thu until 21:00, closed Mon, next to the Augustinian Church) is worth a look.

▲▲**Albertina Museum**—This building, at the southern tip of the Hofburg complex (near the Opera), was the residence of Maria Teresa's favorite daughter: Maria Christina, who was the only one allowed to marry for love rather than political strategy. Her many sisters were jealous. (Marie Antoinette had to marry the French king...and lost her head over it.) Maria Christina's husband, Albert of Saxony, was a great collector of original drawings. He amassed an enormous assortment of works by Dürer, Rembrandt, Rubens, and others. Today the Albertina presents wonderful exhibitions of these fine works and allows visitors to tour its elegant state rooms and enjoy temporary exhibits of other artists (€9, price can vary based on special exhibits, €3.50 audioguide also available for both permanent and temporary exhibits, daily 10:00–18:00, Wed until 21:00, overlooking Albertinaplatz across from TI and Opera House, tel. 01/534-830, www.albertina.at).

The Albertina consists of three components. First, stroll through the Hapsburg state rooms (French classicism—lots of white marble). Top quality facsimiles of the collection's greatest pieces hang in these rooms. Then browse the modern gallery, featuring special exhibitions. From March 15 until August 27, 2006, the Albertina devotes this space to a specially designed Mozart installation, celebrating the composer's 250th birthday. (For more "Year of Mozart" events, see page 730.) Finally, the Albertina also displays selections from its own spectacular collection of works by Michelangelo, Rubens, Rembrandt, and Raphael, plus a huge sampling of precise drawings by Albrecht Dürer. Of Dürer's 400 original drawings that survived, Albert collected 300 of them. Most were sold or stolen over the ages, and today the collection is down to about 100. Since these fragile sketches and exquisite drawings are very sensitive to light, they're kept mostly in darkness and shown only rarely, in rotation. The collection is vast, so you'll always see exciting originals, thoughtfully described in English.

▲▲**Kaisergruft, the Remains of the Hapsburgs**—Visiting the imperial remains is not as easy as you might imagine. These original organ donors left their bodies—about 150 in all—in the unassuming Kaisergruft (Capuchin Crypt), their hearts in the Augustinian Church (described above; church open long hours daily, but to see the goods you'll have to talk to a priest), and their entrails in the crypt below St. Stephen's Cathedral. Don't tripe.

Upon entering the Kaisergruft (€4, daily 9:30–16:00, last entry 15:40, behind Opera on Neuer Markt), buy the €0.50 map with a Hapsburg family tree and a chart locating each coffin.

Empress Maria Theresa (1717–1780) and Her Son, Emperor Josef II (1741–1790)

Maria Theresa was the only woman to officially rule the Hapsburg Empire in that family's 700-year reign. She was a strong and effective empress (r. 1740–1780). People are quick to remember Maria Theresa as the mother of 16 children (10 survived). Imagine that the most powerful woman in Europe either was pregnant or had a newborn for most of her reign. Maria Theresa ruled after the Austrian defeat of the Turks, when Europe recognized Austria as a great power. (Her rival, the Prussian emperor, said, "When at last the Hapsburgs get a great man, it's a woman.")

The last of the Baroque imperial rulers, and the first of the modern rulers of the Age of Enlightenment, Maria Theresa marked the end of the feudal system and the beginning of the era of the grand state. She was a great social reformer. During her reign, she avoided wars and expanded her empire by skillfully marrying her children into the right families. For instance, after daughter Marie Antoinette's marriage into the French Bourbon family (to Louis XVI), a country that had been an enemy became an ally. (Unfortunately for Marie, her timing was off. Arriving in time for the Revolution, she lost her head.)

Maria Theresa was a great reformer and in tune with her age. She taxed the Church and the nobility, provided six years of obligatory education to all children, and granted free health care to all in her realm. Maria Theresa also welcomed the boy genius Mozart into her court.

The empress' legacy lived on in her son, **Josef II,** who ruled as emperor himself for a decade (1780–1790). He was an even more avid reformer, building on his mother's accomplishments. An enlightened monarch, Josef mothballed the too-extravagant Schönbrunn Palace, secularized the monasteries, established religious tolerance within his realm, freed the serfs, made possible the founding of Austria's first general hospital, and promoted relatively enlightened treatment of the mentally ill. Josef was a model of practicality (for example, reusable coffins à la *Amadeus,* and no more than 6 candles at funerals)—and very unpopular with other royals. But his policies succeeded in preempting the revolutionary anger of the age, enabling Austria to avoid the turmoil that shook so much of the rest of Europe.

The double coffin of **Maria Theresa** (1717–1780) and her husband, **Franz I** (1708–1765), is worth a close look for its artwork. Maria Theresa outlived her husband by 15 years—which she spent in mourning. Old and fat, she installed a special lift enabling her to get down into the crypt to be with her dear, departed Franz (even though he had been far from faithful). The couple recline—Etruscan style—atop their fancy lead coffin. At each corner are the crowns of the Hapsburgs—the Holy Roman Empire, Hungary, Bohemia, and Jerusalem. Notice the contrast between the rococo splendor of Maria Theresa's tomb and the simple box holding her more modest son, **Josef II** (at his parents' feet; for more on Maria Theresa and Joe II, see the sidebar on page 710).

Franz Josef (1830–1916) is nearby, in an appropriately austere military tomb. Flanking Franz Josef are the tombs of his son, the archduke **Rudolf**, and Empress Elizabeth. Rudolf and his teenage love committed suicide together in 1889 and—since the Church figured he forced her and was therefore a murderer—it took considerable legal hair-splitting to win Rudolf this spot (after examining his brain, it was determined that he was physically retarded and therefore incapable of knowingly killing himself and his girlfriend). *Kaiserin* Elisabeth (1837–1898), a.k.a. **Sissy**, always gets the "Most Flowers" award.

In front of those three is the most recent Hapsburg tomb. **Empress Zita** was buried in 1989. Her burial procession was probably the last such Old Regime event in European history. The monarchy died hard in Austria.

While it's fun to chase down all these body parts, remember that the real legacy of the Hapsburgs is the magnificence of this city. Step outside. Look up. Watch the clouds glide by the ornate gables of Vienna.

▲**Imperial Furniture Collection (Kaiserliches Hofmobiliendepot)**—Bizarre, sensuous, eccentric, or precious, this is your peek at the Hapsburgs' furniture—from grandma's wheelchair to the emperor's spittoon—all thoughtfully described in English. The Hapsburgs had many palaces, but only the Hofburg was permanently furnished. The rest were furnished on the fly—set up and taken down by a gang of royal roadies called the "Depot of Court Movables" (Hofmobiliendepot). When the monarchy was dissolved in 1918, the state of Austria took possession of the Hofmobiliendepot's inventory—165,000 items. Now this royal storehouse is open to the public in a fine, new, sprawling museum.

Don't go here for the *Jugendstil* furnishings. The older Baroque, rococo, and Biedermeier pieces are the most impressive and tied most intimately to the royals. Combine a visit to this museum with a stroll down the lively shopping boulevard, Mariahilfer Strasse (€7, Tue–Sun 10:00–18:00, closed Mon, Mariahilfer Strasse 88, tel. 01/5243-3570).

Kunsthistorisches Museum

This exciting museum, across the Ring from the Hofburg Palace, is worth ▲▲▲. It showcases the grandeur and opulence of the Hapsburgs' collected artwork in a grand building (built as a museum in 1888). There are European masterpieces galore, all well displayed on one glorious floor, plus fine examples of Egyptian, classical, and applied arts.

Cost, Hours, Location: €10, audio-guide–€2, Tue–Sun 10:00–18:00, Thu until 21:00, closed Mon, on the Ringstrasse at Maria Theresien-Platz, U-2 or U-3: Volkstheater/Museumsplatz, tel. 01/525-240, www.khm.at.

❂ **Self-Guided Tour:** Thanks to Gene Openshaw for writing the following tour.

The Kunsthistorwhateveritis Museum—let's just say "Koonst"—houses some of the most beautiful, sexy, and fun-loving art from two centuries (c. 1450–1650). The collection reflects the *joie de vivre* of Austria's luxury-loving Hapsburg rulers. At their peak of power in the 1500s, the Hapsburgs ruled Austria, Germany, northern Italy, the Netherlands, and Spain—and you'll see a wide variety of art from all these places and beyond.

Of the museum's many exhibits, we'll tour only the Painting Gallery (Gemäldegalerie) on the first floor. Climb the main staircase, featuring Antonio Canova's statue of *Theseus Clubbing the Centaur.* Italian Art is in the right half of the building (as you face Theseus), and Northern Art to the left. Notice that the museum labels the largest rooms with Roman numerals (Saal I, II, III), and the smaller rooms around the perimeter with Arabic (Rooms 1, 2, 3).

• *Enter Saal I and walk right into the High Renaissance.*

Venetian Renaissance (1500–1600)—Titian, Veronese, Tintoretto: Around the year 1500, Italy had a Renaissance, or "rebirth," of interest in the art and learning of ancient Greece and Rome. In painting, that meant that ordinary humans and Greek gods joined saints and angels as popular subjects.

Kunsthistorisches Museum—First Floor

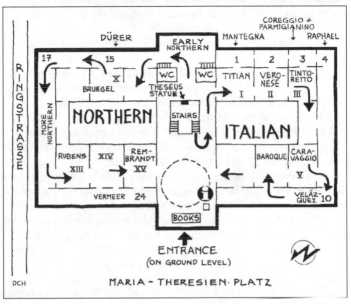

Saal I spans the long career of **Titian** the Venetian (that rhymes)—from creamy Madonnas to down-to-earth portraits to erotic Greek myths. *Nymph and Shepherd*, a late work, creates a misty landscape where a flute-playing shepherd ogles a naked nymph while fingering his instrument. In *Ecce Homo*, a crowd mills about, when suddenly there's a commotion. They nudge each other and start to point. Follow their gaze diagonally up the stairs to a battered figure entering way up in the corner. "Ecce Homo!" says Pilate. "Behold the man." And he presents Jesus to the mob. For us, as for the unsympathetic crowd, the humiliated Son of God is not the center of the scene, but almost an afterthought.

In the next large gallery (Saal II), the large, colorful works by **Paolo Veronese** reflect the wealth of Venice, the funnel where luxury goods from the exotic East flowed into Northern Europe. So, in the *Adoration of the Magi (Die Anbetung der Könige)*, these-Three-Kings-from-Orient-are dressed not in biblical costume, but in the imported silks of Venetian businessmen.

In Saal III, **Tinoretto**'s *Susanna and the Elders (Susanna im Bade)* is an often-painted Old Testament story that gave pious Christians a religious excuse to show some skin. Virtuous Susanna is spied on in her bath by dirty old men who then wrongly accuse her to hide their own hypocrisy. We're drawn into the story by Susanna's beauty—and by the wall of flowers that stretches almost straight back, making the painting an extension of where we stand.

At the far end, an old man leers at Susanna. Tintoretto places us at the near end, looking at Susanna through the picture frame... making us peeping Toms, as well.

• *Find the following paintings in Rooms 1–4, the smaller rooms that adjoin Saals I, II, and III.*

Italian Renaissance and Mannerism: Mantegna's *St. Sebastian (Der hl. Sebastian)*, shot through with arrows, was an early Christian martyr, but he stands like a Renaissance statue—on a pedestal, his weight on one foot, and displaying his Greek-god anatomy. Mantegna places the three-dimensional "statue" in a three-dimensional setting, using floor tiles and roads that recede into the distance to create the illusion of depth.

In **Correggio**'s *Jupiter and Io*, the king of the gods appears in a cloud—see his foggy face and hands?—to get a date with a beautiful nymph named Io. ("Io, Io, it's off to earth I go.") Correggio tips Renaissance "balance"—the enraptured Io may be perched vertically in the center of the canvas right now, but she won't be for long.

In his *Self-Portrait in a Convex Mirror*, 21-year-old **Parmigianino** (like the cheese) gazes into a convex mirror and perfectly reproduces the curved reflection on a convex piece of wood. Amazing.

The 22-year-old **Raphael** (roff-eye-EL) captured the spirit of the High Renaissance, combining symmetry, grace, beauty and emotion. His *Madonna of the Meadow (Die Madonna im Gruben)* is a mountain of motherly love—Mary's head is the summit and her flowing robe is the base—enfolding Baby Jesus and John the Baptist. The geometric perfection, serene landscape, and Mary's adorable face make this a masterpiece of sheer grace...but then you get smacked by an ironic fist: The cross the little tykes play with foreshadows their gruesome deaths.

• *Find Caravaggio in Saal V.*

Caravaggio: Caravaggio (karra-VAH-jee-oh) shocked the art world with brutally honest reality. Compared with Raphael's super-sweet *Madonna of the Meadow*, Caravaggio's *Virgin of the Rosary (Die Rosenkranzmadonna)* looks perfectly ordinary, and the saints kneeling around her have dirty feet.

In *David with the Head of Goliath (David mit dem Haupt des Goliath)*, Caravaggio turns a third-degree-interrogation light on a familiar Bible story. David shoves the dripping head of the slain giant right in our noses. The painting, bled of color, is virtually a black-and-white crime-scene photo, slightly over-exposed. Out of the deep darkness shine only a few crucial details. This David is not a heroic Renaissance Man like Michelangelo's famous statue, but a homeless teen that Caravaggio paid to portray God's servant. And the severed head of Goliath is none other than Caravaggio himself, an in-your-face self-portrait.

• *Find Room 10, in the corner of the museum.*

Velázquez: When the Hapsburgs ruled both Austria and Spain, cousins kept in touch through portraits of themselves and their kids. Diego Velázquez (vel-LOSS-kes) was the greatest of Spain's "photo-journalist" painters: heavily influenced by Caravaggio's realism, capturing his subjects without passing judgment, flattering, or glorifying them.

Watch little Margarita Hapsburg grow up in three different *Portraits of Margarita Theresa (Die Infantin Margarita Teresa)* from age two to age nine. Margarita was destined from birth to marry her Austrian cousin, the future Emperor Leopold I. Pictures like these, sent from Spain every few years, let her pen-pal/fiancé get to know her. Also see a portrait of Margarita's little brother, *Philip Prospero*, looking like a tiny priest. The kids' oh-so-serious faces, regal poses, and royal trappings are contradicted by their cuteness. No wonder Velázquez was so popular.

• *Complete the Italian Art wing by passing through several rooms of Baroque art, featuring large, colorful canvases showcasing over-the-top emotions and the surefire mark of Baroque art—pudgy winged babies. Northern Art is in the east wing, opposite the Titian room.*

Early Northern Art: The Northern "Renaissance," brought on by the economic boom of Dutch and Flemish trading, was more secular and Protestant than Catholic-funded Italian art. We'll see fewer Madonnas, saints, and Greek gods and more peasants, landscapes, and food. Paintings are smaller and darker, full of down-to-earth objects. Northern artists sweated the details, encouraging the patient viewer to appreciate the beauty in everyday things.

Rogier Van Der Weyden's *Triptych: The Crucifixion (Kreuzinungsaltar)* strips the crucifixion down to the essential characters, set in a sparse landscape. The agony is understated, seen in just a few solemn faces and dramatically creased robes. Hieronymous Bosch's *Christ Carrying the Cross (Kreutzragning)* is crammed with puny humans, not supermen. And in the painstakingly detailed *Portrait of Cardinal Niccolo Albergati*, Jan Van Eyck refuses to airbrush out the jowls and wrinkles, showcasing the quiet dignity of an ordinary man.

• *Room X contains the largest collection of Bruegels in captivity. Linger. If you like it, linger longer.*

Pieter Bruegel (c. 1525-1569)—Norman Rockwell of the 16th Century: The undisputed master of the slice-of-life village scene was Pieter Bruegel the Elder. (His name is pronounced BROY-gull, and is sometimes spelled Brueghel. Don't confuse Pieter Bruegel the Elder with his sons, Pieter Brueghel the Younger and Jan Brueghel, who added luster and an "h" to the family name.) Despite his many rural paintings, Bruegel was actually an urban metrosexual who liked to wear peasants' clothing to observe country folk at play (a trans-fest-ite?). He celebrated their simple life, but he also skewered their weaknesses—not to single them out as hicks, but as universal examples of human folly.

The Peasant Wedding (Bauernhochfest), Bruegel's most famous work, is less about the wedding than the food. It's a farmers' feeding frenzy as the barnful of wedding guests scramble to get their share of free eats. Two men bring in the next course, a tray of fresh pudding. The bagpiper pauses to check it out. A guy grabs bowls and passes them down the table, taking our attention with them. Everyone's going at it, including a kid in an oversized red cap who licks the bowl with his fingers. In the middle of it all, look who's been completely forgotten--the demure bride sitting in front of the blue-green cloth. (One thing: The guy carrying the front end of the food tray--is he stepping forward with his right leg, or with his left, or with...all three?)

Speaking of two left feet, Bruegel's *Country Dance (Bauerntanz)* shows peasants happily clogging to the tune of a lone bagpiper who wails away while his pit crew keeps him lubed with wine. The three Bruegel landscape paintings are part of an original series of six "calendar" paintings, depicting the seasons of the year. *The Gloomy Day* opens the cycle, as winter turns to spring...slowly. The snow has melted, flooding the distant river, the trees are still leafless, and the villagers stir, cutting wood and mending fences. We skip ahead to autumn *(The Return of the Herd)*—still sunny, but winter's storms are fast approaching. We see the scene from above, emphasizing the landscape as much as the people. Finally, in *The Hunters in Snow (Die Jäger im Schnee)* it's the dead of winter, and three dog-tired hunters with their tired dogs trudge along with only a single fox to show for their efforts. As they crest the hill, the grove of bare trees opens up to a breathtaking view—they're almost home, where they can join their mates playing hockey. Birds soar like the hunters' rising spirits—emerging from winter's work and looking ahead to a new year.

• *Linger among the Breugels, then exit into the adjoining Room 15.*

Albrecht Dürer: As the son of a goldsmith and having traveled to Italy, Dürer (DEW-rer) combined meticulous Northern detail with Renaissance symmetry. So his *Altarpiece of the Trinity (Die Anbetung der hl. Dreifaltigkeit)* may initially look like a complex pig-pile of saints and angels, but it's perfectly geometrical. The crucified Christ forms a triangle in the center, framed by triangular clouds and flanked by three-sided crowds of people--appropriate for a painting about the Trinity. Dürer practically invented the self-portrait as an art form, and he included himself, the lone earthling in this heavenly vision (bottom right), with a plaque announcing that he, Albrecht Dürer, painted this in 1511.

• *Locate these paintings scattered through Rooms 17–21.*

More Northern Art: Contrast Dürer's powerful Renaissance Christ with Lucas Cranach's all-too-human *Crucifixion (Die Kreuznigung)*—twisted, bleeding, scarred and vomiting blood, as the storm clouds roll in.

Albrecht Altdorfer's garish *Resurrection (Die Anferstehung Christi)* looks like a poster for a bad horror film—"EASTER SUNDAY III. He's back from the dead... and he's ticked!" A burning Christ ignites the dark cave, tingeing the dazed guards.

Hans Holbein painted *Jane Seymour*, wife number III of the VI wives of Henry VIII. The former lady in waiting—timid and modest—poses stiffly, trying very hard to look the part of Henry's queen. Next.

Giuseppe Arcimboldo's *Summer*—a.k.a "Fruit Face"—is one of four paintings the Hapsburg court painter did showing the seasons (and elements) as people. With a pickle nose, pear chin, and corn-husk ears, this guy literally is what he eats.

In *The Big Flower Bunch (Der Grosse Blumentraub)*, Jan Brueghel, the son of the famous Bruegel, puts meticulously painted flowers from different seasons together in one artfully arranged vase

• *Leaving the simplicity of Northern Art—small canvases, small themes, attention to detail—re-enter the big-canvased, bright-colored world of Baroque in Saals XIII and XIV.*

Peter Paul Rubens: Stand in front of Rubens' *Self-Portrait (Selbstbildnis)* and admire the darling of Catholic-dominated Flanders (Belgium) in his prime: famous, wealthy, well-traveled, the friend of kings and princes, an artist, diplomat, man about town, and—obviously—confident. Rubens' work runs the gamut, from realistic portraits to lounging nudes, Greek myths to altarpieces, from pious devotion to violent sex. But, can we be sure it's Baroque? Ah yes, I'm sure you'll find a pudgy winged baby somewhere.

The 53 year-old Rubens married *Helene Fourment ("The Little Fur")*, this dimpled girl of 16. She pulls the fur around her ample flesh, simultaneously covering herself and exalting her charms. Rubens called both this painting and his young bride "The Little Fur." Hmm. Helene's sweet cellulite was surely an inspiration to Rubens—many of his female figures have Helene's gentle face and dimpled proportions.

In the large *Ildefonso Altarpiece*, a glorious Mary appears (with her entourage of p.w.b.'s) to reward the grateful Spanish saint with a chasuble (priest's smock). How could Rubens paint all these enormous canvases—this one alone is 130 square feet—in one lifetime? He didn't. He kept a workshop of assistants busy painting backgrounds and minor figures, working from Rubens' small sketches (often displayed alongside). Then the master stepped in to add the finishing touches.

• *Continue into Saal XV.*

Rembrandt van Rijn: Rembrandt got wealthy painting portraits of Holland's upwardly-mobile businessmen, but his greatest subject was himself. In *The Large Self-Portrait (Das Grosse Selbstbildnis)* we see the hands-on-hips, defiant, open-stance determination of a man who will do what he wants, and if they don't like it, tough.

In typical Rembrandt style, most of the canvas is a dark, smudgy brown, with only the side of his face glowing from the darkness. (Remember Caravaggio? Rembrandt did.) Unfortunately, the year this was painted, Rembrandt's fortunes changed. Looking at the *Self-Portrait 1655 (Selfbildnis 1655)*, consider Rembrandt's last years. His wife died, his children died young, and commissions for paintings dried up as his style veered from the common path. He had to auction off paintings to pay debts and died a poor man. Rembrandt's numerous self-portraits painted from youth till old age show a man always changing—from wide-eyed youth, to successful portraitist to this disillusioned but still defiant old man.

• *Complete your Kunst visit in the adjoining Room 24.*

Jan Vermeer: In his small canvases, the Dutch painter Jan Vermeer quiets the world down to where we can hear our own heartbeat, letting us appreciate the beauty in common things.

The curtain opens and we see *The Artist in his Studio (Allegorie der Malerei)*, a behind-the-scenes look at Vermeer at work. He's painting a model dressed in blue, starting with her laurel-leaf headdress. The studio is its own little dollhouse world framed by a chair in the foreground and the wall in back. Then Vermeer fills this space with the few gems he wants us to focus on—the chandelier, the map, the painter's costume. Everything is lit by a crystal-clear light, letting us see these everyday items with fresh eyes.

The painting is subtitled *An Allegory of Painting*. The model has the laurel leaves, trumpet, and book that symbolize fame. The artist—his back to the public—earnestly tries to capture fleeting fame with a small sheet of canvas.

The Rest of the Kunst: We've seen only the "Kunst" (art) half of the Kunst-"Historisches" (history) Museum. The collections on the ground floor are among Europe's best, filled with ancient rubble and medieval curios. Highlights include a statue of the Egyptian pharaoh Thutmosis III and the Gemma Augustea, a Roman cameo. Sadly, one of the jewels in the museum's crown is now missing. Cellini's *Salt Cellar*, a divine golden salt bowl valued at €50 million, was stolen in 2003 by expert thieves—to the anguish of the Vienna art world.

Near the Kunsthistorisches Museum

▲**Natural History Museum**—In the twin building facing the Kunsthistorisches Museum, you'll find moon rocks, dinosaur stuff, and the fist-sized *Venus of Willendorf*—at 30,000 years old, the world's oldest sex symbol, found in the Danube Valley. This museum is a hit with children (€8, Wed–Mon 9:00–18:30, Wed until 21:00, closed Tue, tel. 01/521-770).

MuseumsQuartier—The vast grounds of the former imperial stables now corral several impressive, cutting-edge museums.

Walk into the complex from the Hofburg side, where the main entrance (with visitors center) leads to a big courtyard with cafés, fountains, and ever-changing "installation lounge furniture," all surrounded by the quarter's various museums (behind Kunsthistorisches Museum, U-2 or U-3: Volkstheater/Museumsplatz). Various combo-tickets are available for those interested in more than just the Leopold and Modern Art museums (visit www.mqw.at).

The **Leopold Museum** features modern Austrian art, including the largest collection of works by Egon Schiele (1890–1918) and a few drawings by Kokoschka and Klimt (€9, €2.50 audio-guide, Wed–Mon 10:00–19:00, Thu until 21:00, closed Tue, tel. 01/525-700, www.leopoldmuseum.org). Note that for these three artists, you'll do better in the Belvedere Palace (described below).

The **Museum of Modern Art** (Museum Moderner Kunst Stiftung Ludwig, a.k.a. "Mumok") is Austria's leading modern-art gallery. It's the striking lava-paneled building—three stories tall and four stories deep, offering seven floors of far-out art encased in very young stone. This huge, state-of-the-art museum displays revolving exhibits showing off art of the last generation—including Klee, Picasso, and Pop (€8, Tue–Sun 10:00–18:00, Thu until 21:00, closed Mon, tel. 01/525-001-440, www.mumok.at).

Rounding out the sprawling MuseumsQuartier are an architecture museum, Transeuropa, Electronic Avenue, children's museum, and the Kunsthalle Wien—an exhibition center for contemporary art (€7.50, Thu–Tue 10:00–19:00, Thu until 22:00, closed Wed).

Central Vienna, inside the Ring

▲▲**Haus der Musik**—Vienna's House of Music has a small first-floor exhibit on the Vienna Philharmonic, and upstairs you'll enjoy fine audiovisual exhibits on each of the famous hometown boys (Haydn, Mozart, Beethoven, Strauss, and Mahler). But the museum is unique for its effective use of interactive touch-screen computers and headphones to actually explore the physics of sound. You can twist, dissect, and bend sounds to make your own musical language, merging your voice with a duck's quack or a city's traffic roar. Wander through the "sonosphere" and marvel at the amazing acoustics—I could actually hear what I thought only a piano tuner could hear. Pick up a virtual baton to conduct the Vienna Philharmonic Orchestra (each time you screw up, the musicians put their instruments down and ridicule you). A computer will help you compose your own waltz by throwing dice. Really experiencing the place takes time. It's open late and makes a good evening activity (€10, daily 10:00–22:00, last entry 75 min before closing, 2 blocks from Opera at Seilerstatte 30, tel. 01/51648, www.hdm.at).

▲**Vienna's Auction House, the Dorotheum**—For an aristocrat's flea market, drop by Austria's answer to Sotheby's, the Dorotheum. Its five floors of antique furniture and fancy knickknacks have been put up either for immediate sale or auction, often by people who inherited old things they don't have room for (Mon–Fri 10:00–18:00, Sat 9:00–17:00, closed Sun, classy little café on 2nd floor, between Graben and Hofburg at Dorotheergasse 17, tel. 01/515-600, www.dorotheum.com). Fliers show schedules for actual auctions, which you are welcome to attend.

Judenplatz Memorial and Museum—The square called Judenplatz marks the location of Vienna's 15th-century Jewish community, one of Europe's largest at the time. The square, once filled with a long-gone synagogue, is now dominated by a blocky memorial to the 65,000 Austrian Jews killed by the Nazis. The memorial—a library turned inside out—symbolizes Jews as "people of the book" and causes one to ponder the huge loss of culture, knowledge, and humanity that took place between 1938 and 1945.

The Judenplatz Museum, while sparse, has displays on medieval Jewish life and a well-done video re-creating community scenes from five centuries ago. Wander the scant remains of the medieval synagogue below street level—discovered during the construction of the Holocaust memorial. This was the scene of a medieval massacre. Since Christians weren't allowed to lend money, Jews were Europe's moneylenders. As so often happened in Europe, when Christian locals fell too deeply into debt, they found a convenient excuse to wipe out the local ghetto—and their debts at the same time. In 1421, 200 of Vienna's Jews were burned at the stake. Others who refused a forced conversion committed mass suicide in the synagogue (€3, €7 combo-ticket includes a synagogue and Jewish Museum of the City of Vienna—see page 728, Sun–Thu 10:00–18:00, Fri 10:00–14:00, closed Sat, Judenplatz 8, tel. 01/535-0431).

Near Karlsplatz

These sights cluster around Karlsplatz, just southeast of the Ringstrasse (U-1, U-2, or U-4: Karlsplatz).

Karlsplatz—This fine and picnic-friendly square, with its Henry Moore sculpture in the pond, is ringed with sights. The Art Nouveau station pavilions—from the 19th-century municipal train system—are textbook *Jugendstil* by Otto Wagner (steel frame and decorative marble slabs with painted gold ornaments). One of Europe's first subway systems, it was built with a military purpose in mind: to move troops quickly in time of civil unrest—specifically, out to Schönbrunn Palace.

Charles Church (Karlskirche)—Charles Borromeo, a 16th-century bishop from Milan, was an inspiration during plague times. This "votive church" was dedicated to him in 1713, when an epidemic spared Vienna. The church offers the best Baroque in Vienna, with a unique combination of columns (showing scenes from the life of Charles Borromeo, à la Trajan's Column in Rome), a classic pediment, and an elliptical dome. But it's especially worthwhile for the chance (probably through 2006) to see restoration work in progress and up close (€6 includes a skippable 1-room museum, audioguide, and visit to renovation site; Mon–Sat 9:00–12:30 & 13:00–18:00, Sun 13:00–18:00, last entry 30 min before closing). The entry fee may seem steep, but remember that it funds the restoration.

Visitors ride the industrial lift to a platform at the base of the dome. (Consider that the church was built and decorated with a

scaffolding system essentially the same as this one.) Once up there, you'll climb stairs to the steamy lantern at the extreme top of the church. At that dizzying height, you're in the clouds with cupids and angels. Many details that appear smooth and beautiful from ground level—such as gold leaf, rudimentary paintings, and fake marble—look rough and sloppy up close. It's surreal to observe the 3-D figures from an unintended angle. Faith, Hope, Charity, and Borromeo triumph and inspire—while Protestants and their stinkin' books are trashed. Borromeo lobbies heaven for plague relief. At the very top, you'll see the tiny dove representing the Holy Ghost, surrounded by a cheering squad of nipple-lipped cupids.

Historical Museum of the City of Vienna (Wien Museum Karlsplatz)—This under-appreciated museum walks you through the history of Vienna with fine historic artifacts. You'll work your way up, chronologically: The ground floor exhibits Roman artifacts and original statues from St. Stephen's Cathedral (c. 1350), with various Hapsburgs showing off the slinky hip-hugging fashion of the day. The first floor features old city maps, booty from a Turkish siege, and an 1850 city model showing the town just before the wall was replaced by the Ring. Finally, the second floor displays a city model from 1898 (with the new Ringstrasse), sentimental Biedermeier paintings and objets d'art, and early-20th-century paintings (including some by Gustav Klimt). The museum is worth the €4 admission (free Sun and Fri morning, open Tue–Sun 9:00–18:00, closed Mon, www.wienmuseum.at).

▲Academy of Fine Arts (Akademie der Bildenden Künste)— This small but exciting collection includes works by Bosch, Botticelli, and Rubens (quick, sketchy cartoons used to create his giant canvases); a Venice series by Guardi; and a self-portrait by a 15-year-old Van Dyck. It's all magnificently lit and well-described by the €2 audioguide, and comes with comfy chairs (€5, Tue–Sun 10:00–18:00, closed Mon, 3 blocks from Opera at Schillerplatz 3, tel. 01/5881-6225, www.akademiegalerie.at). The fact that this is a working art academy gives it a certain realness. As you wander the halls of the academy, ponder how history might have been different if Hitler—who applied to study architecture here but was rejected—had been accepted as a student. Before leaving, peek into the ground floor's central hall—textbook historicism, the Ringstrasse style of the late 1800s.

The Secession—This little building, behind the Academy of Fine Arts, is nicknamed the "golden cabbage" today (and "a temple for bullfrogs" when it was first built around the turn of the 20th century). It was created by the Vienna Secession movement, a group of non-conformist artists led by Gustav Klimt, Otto Wagner, and friends. The Secession, whose slogan was "To each age its art, and to art its liberty," first exhibited their "liberty-style" art here in 1897. The young trees carved into the walls and its bushy "cabbage" rooftop are symbolic of renewal cycle. Today, the Secession continues to showcase cutting-edge art, as well as one of Gustav Klimt's most famous works, the *Beethoven Frieze* (€6, Tue–Sun 10:00–18:00, Thu until 20:00, closed Mon, Friedrichstrasse 12, tel. 01/587-5307, www.secession.at).

   While the staff hopes you take a look at the temporary exhibits (and the ticket includes this whether you like it or not), most tourists head directly for the basement, home to a small exhibit

about the history of the building and the museum's highlight: Klimt's classic *Beethoven Frieze* (a.k.a. the "Searching Souls"). One of the masterpieces of Viennese Art Nouveau, this 105-foot-long fresco was a centerpiece of a 1902 "homage to Beethoven" exhibition. Sit down and read the free flier, which explains Klimt's still-powerful work. The theme, inspired by Beethoven's *Ninth Symphony*, features floating female figures "yearning for happiness." They drift and weave and search—like most of us do—through internal and external temptations and forces, falling victim to base and ungodly temptations, and losing their faith. Then, finally, they become fulfilled by poetry, music, and art as they reach the "Ideal Kingdom" where "True Happiness, Pure Bliss and Absolute Love" are found in a climactic embrace.

▲**Naschmarkt**—In 1898, the city decided to cover up its Vienna River. The long, wide square they created was filled with a lively produce market that still bustles most days (closed Sun). From near the Opera, the Naschmarkt (roughly, "Munchies Market") stretches along Wienzeile Street. This "Belly of Vienna" comes with two parallel lanes—one lined with fun and reasonable eateries, and the other featuring the town's top-end produce and gourmet goodies. This is where top chefs like to get their ingredients. At the gourmet vinegar stall, you sample the vinegar like perfume—with a drop on your wrist. Farther from the center, the Naschmarkt becomes likeably seedy and surrounded by sausage stands, Turkish *döner kebab* stalls, cafés, and theaters. Each Saturday, it's infested by a huge flea market where, in olden days, locals would come to hire a monkey to pick little critters out of their hair (Mon–Fri 6:00–18:30, Sat 6:00–17:00, closed Sun, closes earlier in winter, U-4: Kettenbruckengasse). For a picnic park, pick up your grub here and walk over to Karlsplatz (described above).

Beyond the Ring

▲**Liechtenstein Museum**—The noble Liechtenstein family (who own only a tiny country, but whose friendship with the Hapsburgs goes back generations) amassed an incredible private art collection. Their palace was long a treasure for Vienna art lovers. Then, in 1938—knowing Hitler was intent on plundering artwork to create an immense "Führer Museum"—the family fled to their tiny homeland with their best art. Only in March of 2004 was the collection re-established in Vienna, and opened again to the adoring public. The Liechtensteins' "world of Baroque pleasures" includes the family's rare French rococo carriage (which was used for their

---

Art Nouveau Sights

Vienna gave birth to its own curvaceous brand of Art Nouveau around the early 1900s: *Jugendstil* ("youth style"). The TI has a brochure laying out Vienna's 20th-century architecture. The best of Vienna's scattered *Jugendstil* sights: the gilded, cabbage-domed Secession building at the Ring end of the Naschmarkt (see page 723); the Belvedere Palace collection; and the clock on Hoher Markt (which does a musical act at noon).

---

grand entry into Paris; it had to be carted to the edge of town and assembled, as nearly all such carriages were destroyed in the French Revolution), a plush Baroque library, an inviting English Garden, and an impressive collection of paintings including a complete cycle of early Rembrandts (€10, €4 audioguide, Wed–Mon 9:00–20:00, closed Tue, tram D to Bauernfeldplatz, Fürstengasse 1, tel. 01/319-5767-252, www.liechtensteinmuseum.at).

▲**KunstHausWien: Hundertwasser Museum**—This "make yourself at home" museum is a hit with lovers of modern art. It

mixes the work and philosophy of local painter/environmentalist Friedensreich Hundertwasser (1928–2000). Stand in front of the colorful checkerboard building and consider Hundertwasser's style. He was against "window racism": Neighboring houses allow only one kind of window, but 100H2O's windows are each different—and he encouraged residents to personalize them. He recognized "tree tenants" as well as human tenants. His buildings are spritzed with a forest and topped with dirt and grassy little parks—close to nature, good for the soul. Floors and sidewalks are irregular—to "stimulate the brain" (although current residents complain it just causes wobbly furniture and sprained ankles). Thus 100H2O waged a one-man fight—during the 1950s and 1960s, when concrete and glass ruled—to save the human soul from the city. (Hundertwasser claimed that "straight lines are godless.") Inside the museum, start with his interesting biography. His fun-loving paintings are half *Jugendstil* ("youth style") and half just kids' stuff. Notice the photographs from his 1950s days as part of Vienna's bohemian scene. Throughout the museum, notice the fun philosophical quotes from an artist who believed, "If man is creative, he comes nearer to his creator" (€9 for Hundertwasser Museum, €12 combo-ticket includes special exhibitions, half-price on Mon, open daily 10:00–19:00, extremely fragrant and colorful garden café, U-3: Landstrasse, Weissgerberstrasse 13, tel. 01/712-0491, www.kunsthauswien.com).

The KunstHausWien provides by far the best look at Hundertwasser. For an actual lived-in apartment complex by the green master, walk five minutes to the one-with-nature **Hundertwasserhaus** (free, at Löwengasse and Kegelgasse). This complex of 50 apartments, subsidized by the government to provide affordable housing, was built in the 1980s as a breath of architectural fresh air in a city of boring, blocky apartment complexes. While not open to visitors, it's worth visiting for its fun-loving and colorful patchwork exterior and the Hundertwasser festival of shops across the street. Don't miss the view from Kegelgasse to see the "tree tenants" and the internal winter garden residents enjoy.

Hundertwasser detractors—of which there are many—remind visitors that 100H2O was a painter, not an architect. They describe the Hundertwasserhaus as a "1950s house built in the 1980s," and colorfully painted with no real concern about the environment, communal living, or even practical comfort. Nearly all the original inhabitants got fed up with the novelty and moved out.

▲▲**Belvedere Palace**—This is the elegant palace of Prince Eugene of Savoy (1663–1736), the still-much-appreciated conqueror of the Turks. Eugene, a Frenchman considered too short and too ugly to be in the service of Louis XIV, offered his services to the Hapsburgs. While he was short and ugly indeed, he became the greatest military genius of his age. When you conquer cities, as Eugene did, you get really rich. He had no heirs, so the state got his property and Emperor Josef II established the Belvedere as Austria's first great public art gallery. Today, his palace boasts sweeping views and houses the Austrian gallery of 19th- and 20th-century art (€7.50, €2.50 audioguide, Tue–Sun 10:00–18:00, closed Mon, entrance at Prinz-Eugen-Strasse 27, tel. 01/7955-7134, www.belvedere.at). To get here from the center, catch tram D at the Opera (direction Südbahnhof, it stops at the palace gate).

Belvedere means "**beautiful view.**" Sit at the top palace and look over the Baroque gardens, the mysterious sphinxes (which symbolized solving riddles and the finely educated mind of your host, Eugene), the lower palace, and the city. The spire of St. Stephen's Cathedral is 400 feet tall, and no other tall buildings are allowed inside the Ringstrasse. The hills—covered with vineyards—are where locals love to go to sample the new wine. (You can see Kahlenberg, from where you can walk down to several recommended *Heurigen* beyond the spire—see page 733.) These are the first of the Alps, which stretch from here all the way to

Marseilles, France. The square you're overlooking was filled with people on May 15, 1955, as local leaders stood on the balcony of the Upper Palace (behind you) and proclaimed Austrian independence following a decade-long Allied occupation after World War II.

The **Upper Palace** was Eugene's party house. Today, like the Louvre in Paris (but much easier to enjoy), this palace contains a fine collection of paintings. The collection is arranged chronologically: on the first floor, you'll find historicism, Romanticism, Impressionism, Realism, tired tourism, expressionism, Art Nouveau, and early modernism. Each room tries to pair Austrian works from that period with much better-known European works. It's fun to see the work of artists like van Gogh, Munch, and Monet hung with their lesser-known Austrian contemporaries. As Austria becomes a leader in art around 1900, the collection gets stronger, with fine works by Gustav Klimt, Oskar Kokoschka, and Egon Schiele. The Klimt room shows how even in his early work, the face was vivid and the rest dissolved into decor. During his "golden period," this background became his trademark gold leaf studded with stones. The corner room shows a small exhibit on Prince Eugene, Archduke Franz Ferdinand, and the signing of the state treaty in 1955. Don't miss the poignant Schiele family portrait from 1918—his wife died while he was still working on it. (Schiele and his child were soon taken by the influenza epidemic that swept through Europe after WWI.)

The upper floor shows off early-19th-century Biedermeier paintings (hyper-sensitive, super-sweet, uniquely Viennese Romanticism—the poor are happy, things are lit impossibly well, and folk life is idealized). Your ticket also includes the Austrian Baroque and Gothic art in the Lower Palace. Prince Eugene lived in that palace, but he's long gone and I wouldn't bother to visit.

Schönbrunn Palace (Schloss Schönbrunn)

Among Europe's palaces, only Schönbrunn rivals Versailles. Worth ▲▲▲, this summer residence of the Hapsburgs is located four miles from the center. It's big (1,441 rooms), but don't worry—only 40 rooms are shown to the public. (Today the families of 260 civil servants rent simple apartments in the rest of the palace.)

Getting There: Take tram #58 from the Westbahnhof directly to the palace, or ride U-4 to Schönbrunn and walk 400 yards. The main entrance is in the left side of the palace as you face it.

Royal Apartments—While the exterior is Baroque, the interior was finished under Maria Theresa in let-them-eat-cake rococo. The chandeliers are either of hand-carved wood with gold-leaf gilding or of Bohemian crystal. Thick walls hid the servants as they ran around stoking the ceramic stoves from the back, and attending to other behind-the-scenes matters. Most of the public rooms are decorated in neo-Baroque, as they were under Franz Josef (r. 1848–1916). When WWII bombs rained on the city and the palace grounds, the palace itself took only one direct hit. Thankfully, that bomb, which crashed through three floors—including the sumptuous central ballroom—was a dud.

Cost: The admission price is based on which route you select (each one includes an audioguide): the **Imperial Tour** (22 rooms, €8.90, 35 min, Grand Palace rooms plus apartments of Franz Josef and Elisabeth—mostly 19th-century and therefore least interesting) or the **Grand Tour** (40 rooms, €11.50, 50 min, adds apartments of Maria Theresa—18th-century rococo). A combo-ticket called the **Schönbrunn Pass Classic** includes the Grand Tour, as well as other sights on the grounds: the Gloriette viewing terrace, maze, privy garden, and court bakery—complete with *Apfelstrudel* demo and tasting (€15, available April–Oct only). I'd go for the Grand Tour.

Hours: Daily July–Aug 8:30–18:00, April–June and Sept–Oct 8:30–17:00, Nov–March 8:30–16:30. Information: www .schoenbrunn.at.

Crowd-Beating Tips: Schönbrunn suffers from crowds. It's busiest from 9:30 to 11:30, especially on weekends and in July and August; it's least crowded from 12:00 to 14:00 and after 16:00. To avoid the long delays in summer, make a reservation by telephone (tel. 01/8111-3239, answered daily 8:00-17:00). You'll get an appointment time and a ticket number. Check in at least 30 minutes early. Upon arrival, go to the group desk, give your number, pick up your ticket, and jump in ahead of the masses. If you show up in peak season without calling first, you deserve the frustration. (In this case, you'll have to wait in line, buy your ticket, and wait until the listed time to enter—which could be tomorrow.) If you have any time to kill, spend it exploring the gardens or Coach Museum.

Palace Gardens—After strolling through all the Hapsburgs tucked neatly into their crypts, a stroll through the emperor's garden with countless commoners is a celebration of the natural evolution of civilization from autocracy into real democracy. As a civilization, we're doing well.

The park itself is free (daily sunrise to dusk, entrance on either side of the palace). Inside are several other sights, including a **palm house** (€3.50, daily May–Sept 9:30–18:00, Oct–April 9:30–17:00), Europe's oldest **zoo** (*Tiergarten*, built by Maria Theresa's husband for the entertainment and education of the court in 1752; €12, May–Sept daily 9:00–18:30, less off-season, tel. 01/877-9294), and—at the end of the gardens—the **Gloriette,** a purely decorative monument celebrating an obscure Austrian military victory and offering a fine city view (viewing terrace-€2, included in €15

Schönbrunn Pass Classic, daily April–Sept 9:00–18:00, July–Aug until 19:00, Oct until 17:00, closed Nov–March). A touristy choo-choo train makes the rounds all day, connecting Schönbrunn's many attractions.

Coach Museum Wagenburg—The Schönbrunn coach museum is a 19th-century traffic jam of 50 impressive royal carriages and sleighs. Highlights include silly sedan chairs, the death-black hearse carriage (used for Franz Josef in 1916, and most recently for Empress Zita in 1989), and an extravagantly gilded imperial carriage pulled by eight Cinderella horses. This was rarely used other than for the coronation of Holy Roman Emperors, when it was disassembled and taken to Frankfurt for the big event (€4.50; April–Oct daily 9:00–18:00; Nov–March Tue–Sun 10:00–16:00, closed Mon; last entry 30 min before closing, 200 yards from palace, walk through right arch as you face palace, tel. 01/877-3244).

"Honorable Mentions": More Vienna Museums

There's much, much more. The city map lists everything. If you're into Esperanto, undertakers, tobacco, clowns, firefighting, Freud, or the homes of dead composers, you'll find them all in Vienna.

These good museums try very hard but are submerged in the greatness of Vienna: **Jewish Museum of the City of Vienna** (€5, or €7 combo-ticket includes synagogue and Judenplatz Museum—described on page 720, Sun–Fri 10:00–18:00, Thu until 20:00, closed Sat, Dorotheergasse 11, tel. 01/535-0431, www .jmw.at), **Folkloric Museum of Austria** (Tue–Sun 10:00–17:00, closed Mon, Laudongasse 15, tel. 01/406-8905), and **Museum of Military History**, one of Europe's best if you like swords and shields (Heeresgeschichtliches Museum, €5.10, includes audioguide, Sat–Thu 9:00–17:00, closed Fri, Arsenal district, Objekt 18, tel. 01/795-610).

The vast **Austrian Museum of Applied Arts** (Österreichisches Museum für Angewandte Kunst, or "MAK") is Vienna's answer to London's Victoria and Albert collection. The museum shows off the fancies of local aristocratic society, including a fine *Jugendstil* collection (€8, free on Sat, open Tue–Sun 10:00–18:00, Tue until 24:00, closed Mon, Stubenring 5, tel. 01/711-360, www.mak.at).

ACTIVITIES

People-Watching and Strolling

These activities allow you to take it easy and enjoy the Viennese good life.

▲**City Park (Stadtpark)**—Vienna's City Park is a waltzing world of gardens, memorials to local musicians, ponds, peacocks, music in bandstands, and locals escaping the city. Notice the *Jugendstil* entrance at the Stadtpark U-Bahn station. The Kursalon, where Strauss was the violin-toting master of waltzing ceremonies, hosts daily touristy concerts in three-quarter time.

▲Prater—Since the 1780s, when the reformist Emperor Josef II gave his hunting grounds to the people of Vienna as a public park, this place has been Vienna's playground. While tired and a bit run-down these days, Vienna's sprawling amusement park still tempts visitors with its huge 220-foot-tall, famous, and lazy Ferris wheel *(Riesenrad)*, roller coaster, bumper cars, Lilliputian railroad, and endless eateries. Especially if you're traveling with kids, this is a fun, goofy place to share the evening with thousands of Viennese (daily 9:00–24:00 in summer, but quiet after 22:00, U-1: Praterstern). For a local-style family dinner, eat at Schweizerhaus (good food, great beer) or Wieselburger Bierinsel.

Sunbathing—Like most Europeans, the Austrians worship the sun. Their lavish swimming centers are as much for tanning as swimming. To find the scene, follow the locals to their "Danube Sea" and a 20-mile, skinny, man-made beach along Danube Island. It's traffic-free concrete and grass, packed with in-line skaters and bikers, with rocky river access and a fun park (easy U-Bahn access on U-1 to Donauinsel).

A Walk in the Vienna Woods (Wienerwald)—For a quick side-trip into the woods and out of the city, catch the U-4 to Heiligenstadt, then bus #38A to Kahlenberg, where you'll enjoy great views and a café overlooking the city. From there, it's a peaceful 45-minute downhill hike to the *Heurigen* of Nussdorf or Grinzing to enjoy some new wine (see "Vienna's Wine Gardens," page 733).

Naschmarkt—Vienna's busy produce market is a great place for people-watching (see page 723).

EXPERIENCES

Music Scene

As far back as the 12th century, Vienna was a mecca for musicians—both sacred and secular (troubadours). The Hapsburg emperors of the 17th and 18th centuries were not only generous supporters of music, but fine musicians and composers themselves. (Maria Theresa played a mean double bass.) Composers like Haydn, Mozart, Beethoven, Schubert, Brahms, and Mahler gravitated to this music-friendly environment. They taught each other, jammed together, and spent a lot of time in Hapsburg palaces. Beethoven was a famous figure, walking—lost in musical thought—through Vienna's woods. In the city's 19th-century belle époque, "Waltz King" Johann Strauss and his brothers kept Vienna's 300 ballrooms spinning.

2006: The Year of Mozart (Mozartjahr)

Mozart, born in 1756, would be 250 years old in 2006 if he had taken better care of himself. Everyone in Salzburg (where he was born, but largely ignored until the late 19th century—when someone figured out how well he could be marketed) and Vienna (where he spent the last 10 years of his life) is eager to lay claim to one of the world's most celebrated musicians. Starting with his birthday in January 27, you'll find a veritable Mozartpalooza: concerts, opera performances, exhibits about his life and work, and plenty of modern compositions inspired by his genius (www.wienmozart2006.at).

Everyone from the marionettes to the Vienna Boys' Choir is busy rehearsing Mozart-inspired programs. The **Vienna State Opera** will perform Mozart's most popular operas (his complete opera repertoire will be performed in Salzburg). From March 15 to August 27, the **Albertina Museum** hosts an installation on Mozart. The **Mozart Haus** (also known as the "Figaro Haus" because he wrote *The Marriage of Figaro* while living here) is planned to re-open in January after extensive restorations (just off of Stephansplatz, behind St. Stephen's Cathedral at Domgasse 5, www.mozarthausvienna.at).

This musical tradition continues into modern times, leaving some prestigious Viennese institutions for today's tourists to enjoy: the Opera (see page 696), the Boys' Choir, and the great Baroque halls and churches, all busy with classical and waltz concerts.

Vienna is Europe's music capital. It's music *con brio* from October through June, reaching a symphonic climax during the Vienna Festival each May and June. Sadly, in July and August, the Boys' Choir, the Opera, and many more music companies are—like you—on vacation. But Vienna hums year-round with live classical music. Except for the Boys' Choir, the musical events listed below are offered in summer.

Vienna Boys' Choir—The boys sing (from a high balcony, where they are heard but not seen) at the 9:15 **Sunday Mass** from September through March in the Hofburg's Imperial Chapel (Hofburgkapelle; entrance at Schweizerhof, from Josefsplatz go through tunnel). Reserved seats must be booked two months in advance (€5–29, reserve by fax, e-mail, or mail: fax from the U.S. 011-431-533-992-775, hmk@aon.at, or write Hofmusikkapelle, Hofburg-Schweizerhof, 1010 Wien; call 01/533-9927 for information only—they can't book tickets at this number). Much easier, standing room inside is free and open to the first 60 who line up. Even better, rather than line up early, you can simply swing by and stand in the narthex just outside, where you can hear the boys and see the Mass on a TV monitor. Boys' Choir **concerts** (on stage at the Musikverein) are also given Fridays at 16:00 in May, June, September, and October (€35–48, standing room goes on sale at 15:30 for €15, Karlsplatz 6, U-1, U-2, or U-4: Karlsplatz, tel. 01/5880-4141). They're nice kids, but, for my taste, not worth all the commotion. Remember, many churches have great music during Sunday Mass. Just 200 yards from the Boys' Choir chapel, Augustinian Church has a glorious 11:00 service each Sunday (see page 708).

Touristy Mozart and Strauss Concerts—If the music comes to you, it's touristy—designed for flash-in-the-pan Mozart fans.

Powdered-wig orchestra performances are given almost nightly in grand traditional settings (€25–50). Pesky wigged-and-powdered Mozarts peddle tickets in the streets. They rave about the quality of the musicians, but you'll get second-rate chamber orchestras, clad in historic costumes, performing the greatest hits of Mozart and Strauss. These are casual, easygoing concerts with lots of tour groups. While there's not a local person in the audience, the tourists generally enjoy the evening.

To sort through all your options, check with the ticket office in the TI (same price as on the street, but with all venues to choose from). Savvy locals suggest getting the cheapest tickets, as no one seems to care if cheapskates move up to fill unsold pricier seats. Critics explain that the musicians are actually very good (often Hungarians, Poles, and Russians working a season here to fund an entire year of music studies back home), but that they haven't performed much together so aren't "tight." The Mozarthaus is a small room richly decorated in Venetian Renaissance style with intimate chamber-music concerts (€29–35, almost nightly at 19:30, near St. Stephen's Cathedral at Singerstrasse 7, tel. 01-911-9077).

Strauss Concerts in the Kursalon—For years, Strauss concerts have been held in the Kursalon, where the "Waltz King" himself directed wildly popular concerts 100 years ago (€36–49, 4 concerts nightly April–Oct, 1 concert nightly other months, tel. 01/512-5790). Shows are a touristy mix of ballet, waltzes, and a 15-piece orchestra in wigs and old outfits. For the cheap option, enjoy a summer-afternoon coffee concert (free if you buy a drink, weekends and maybe also weekdays July–Aug 15:00–17:00).

Serious Concerts—These events, including the Opera, are listed in the monthly *Wien-Programm* (available at TI). Tickets run from €36 to €75 (plus a stiff 22 percent booking fee when booked in advance or through a box office like the one at the TI). While it's easy to book tickets online long in advance, spontaneity is also workable, as there are invariably people with tickets they don't need selling them at face value or less outside the door before concert time. If you call a concert hall directly, they can advise you on the availability of (cheaper) tickets at the door. Vienna takes care of its starving artists (and tourists) by offering cheap standing-room tickets to top-notch music and opera (1 hr before show time).

Summer of Music Festival (a.k.a. "KlangBogen")—This annual festival assures that even from June through September, you'll find lots of great concerts, choirs, and symphonies (special *KlangBogen* brochure at TI; get tickets at Wien Ticket pavilion off Kärntner Strasse next to Opera House, or go directly to location of particular event; Summer of Music tel. 01/42717, www.klangbogen.at).

Musicals—The Wien Ticket pavilion sells tickets to contemporary American and British musicals done in German language (€10–95 with €2.50 standing room), and offers these tickets at half price from 14:00 until 17:00 the day of the show. Or you can reserve (full-price) tickets for the musicals by calling up to one day ahead (call combined office of the 3 big theaters at tel. 01/58885).

Films of Concerts—To see free films of great concerts in a lively, outdoor setting near City Hall, check "Nightlife," page 735.

Classical Music to Go—To bring home Beethoven, Strauss, or the Wiener Philharmonic on a top-quality CD, shop at Gramola on the Graben, Emi on Kärntner Strasse, or Virgin Megastore on Mariahilfer Strasse.

Vienna's Cafés

In Vienna, the living room is down the street at the neighborhood coffeehouse. This tradition is just another example of Viennese expertise in good living. Each of Vienna's many long-established (and sometimes even legendary) coffeehouses has its individual character (and characters). These classic cafés are a bit tired, with a shabby patina and famously grumpy waiters who treat you like an uninvited guest invading their living room. Still, it's a welcoming place. They offer newspapers, pastries, sofas, quick and light workers' lunches, elegance, smoky ambience, and "take all the time you want" charm for the price of a cup of coffee. Order it *melange* (like a cappuccino), *brauner* (strong coffee with a little milk), or *schwarzer* (black). Americans who ask for a latte are mistaken for Italians and given a cup of hot milk. Rather than buy the *Herald Tribune* ahead of time, spend the money on a cup of coffee and read it for free, Vienna-style in a café.

These are my favorites:

Café Hawelka has a dark, "brooding Trotsky" atmosphere, paintings by struggling artists who couldn't pay for coffee, a saloon-wood flavor, chalkboard menu, smoked velvet couches, an international selection of newspapers, and a phone that rings for regulars (Wed–Mon 8:00–2:00, Sun from 16:00, closed Tue, just off Graben, Dorotheergasse 6).

Café Central features *Jugendstil* decor and great *Apfelstrudel* (high prices and stiff staff, Mon–Sat 8:00–22:00, Sun 10:00–18:00, Herrengasse 14, tel. 01/533-376-326).

Café Sperl dates from 1880, and is still furnished identically to the day it opened—from the coat tree to the chairs (Mon–Sat 7:00–23:00, Sun 15:00–20:00 except closed Sun July–Aug, just off Naschmarkt near Mariahilfer Strasse, Gumpendorfer 11, tel. 01/586-4158).

If **Starbucks** seems big in Vienna, it's because the Seattle-based coffee firm has decided to test the Euro-waters here. Apparently, they figured that Vienna—with its love of fine coffee—would be a tough market to crack...and if they could succeed here, they could take Europe. Locals report that Starbucks is popular with teenagers and tourists, but the coffee is overpriced, and "flavored" coffee is nonsense to Viennese connoisseurs. Even so, the "coffee to go" trend has been picked up by many bakeries and other joints.

Vienna's Wine Gardens *(Heurigen)*

The uniquely Viennese institution of *Heurige* is two things: a wine, and a place to drink it. When the Hapsburgs let Vienna's vintners sell their own new wine *(Heurige)* tax-free, several hundred families opened *Heurigen* (wine-garden restaurants clustered around the edge of town)—and a tradition was born. Today they do their best to maintain the old-village atmosphere, serving the homemade new wine (the last vintage, until November 11, when a new vintage year begins) with light meals and strolling musicians. Most *Heurigen* are decorated with enormous antique presses from their vineyards. Wine gardens might be closed on any given day; always call ahead to confirm, if you have your heart set on a particular place. (For a near-*Heurige* experience right downtown, drop by Gigerl Stadtheuriger—see "Eating," page 744.)

At any *Heurige,* fill your plate at a self-serve cold-cut buffet (€6–9 for dinner). Food is sold by the *"10 dag"* unit. (A *dag* is a decigram, so *10 dag* is 100 grams...about a quarter pound.) Dishes to look for...or look out for: *Stelze* (grilled knuckle of pork), *Fleischlaberln* (fried ground-meat patties), *Schinkenfleckerln* (pasta with cheese and ham), *Schmalz* (a spread made with pig fat), *Blunzen* (black pudding...sausage made from blood), *Presskopf* (jellied brains and innards), *Liptauer* (spicy cheese spread), *Kornspitz* (whole-meal bread roll), and *Kummelbraten* (crispy roast pork with caraway). Waitresses will then take your wine order (€2.20 per quarter liter, about 8 oz). Many locals claim it takes several years of practice to distinguish between *Heurige* and vinegar.

There are more than 1,700 acres of vineyards within Vienna's city limits, and countless *Heurige* taverns. For a *Heurige* evening, rather than go to a particular place, take a tram to the wine-garden district of your choice and wander around, choosing the place with the best ambience.

Getting to the *Heurigen*: You have three options: a 15-minute taxi ride, trams and buses, or a goofy tourist train.

Trams make a trip to the Vienna Woods quick and affordable. The fastest way is to ride U-4 to its last stop, Heiligenstadt, where trams and buses in front of the station fan out to the various neighborhoods. Ride tram D to its end point for Nussdorf. Ride bus #38A for Grinzing and on to the Kahlenberg viewpoint—#38A's end station. (Note that tram #38—different from bus #38A—starts at the Ring and finishes at Grinzing). To get to Neustift am Walde, ride U-6 to Nussdorfer Strasse and catch bus #35A. Connect Grinzing and Nussdorf with bus #38A and tram D (transfer at Grinzingerstrasse).

The **Heuriger Express** train is tacky but handy and relaxing, chugging you on a hop-on, hop-off circle from Nussdorf through Grinzing and around the Vienna Woods with a light narration (€7.30, buy ticket from driver, 60 min, daily April–Oct 12:00–19:00, departs from end station of tram D in Nussdorf at the top of every hr, tel. 01/479-2808).

Here are a couple of good *Heurige* neighborhoods:

Grinzing: Of the many *Heurige* suburbs, Grinzing is the most famous, lively...and touristy. Many people precede their visit to Grinzing by riding tram #38 from Schottentor (on the Ring) to its end (up to Kahlenberg for a grand Vienna view), and then ride 20 minutes back into the *Heurige* action. From the Grinzing tram stop, follow Himmelgasse uphill toward the onion-top dome. You'll pass plenty of wine gardens—and tour buses—on your way up. Just past the dome, you'll find the heart of the *Heurige*.

Heiligenstadt (Pfarrplatz): Between Grinzing and Nussdorf, this area features several decent spots, including the famous and touristy Mayer am Pfarrplatz (a.k.a **Beethovenhaus,** Mon–Sat 16:00–23:00, Sun 11:00–23:00, bus #38A stop: Fernsprechamt/Heiligenstadt, walk 5 min uphill on Dübling Nestelbachgasse to Pfarrplatz 2, tel. 01/370-1287). This place has a charming inner courtyard with an accordion player and a sprawling backyard with a big children's play zone. Beethoven lived—and composed his *Sixth Symphony*—here in 1817. He hoped the local spa would cure his worsening deafness. **Weingut and Heuriger Werner Welser,** a block uphill from Beethoven's place, is lots of fun, with music nightly from 19:00 (open daily 15:30–24:00, Probusgasse 12, tel. 01/318-9797).

Nussdorf: A less-touristy district—characteristic and popular with locals—Nussdorf has plenty of *Heurige* ambience. Right at the end station of tram D, you'll find three long and skinny places side by side: **Schübel-Auer Heuriger** (Tue–Sat 16:00–24:00, closed Sun–Mon, Kahlenbergerstrasse 22, tel. 01/370-2222) is my favorite. Also consider **Heuriger Kierlinger** (daily 15:30–24:00, Kahlenbergerstrasse 20, tel. 01/370-2264) and **Steinschaden** (daily 15:00–24:00, Kahlenbergerstrasse 18, tel. 01/370-1375). Walk through any of these and you pop out on Kahlenbergerstrasse, where a walk 20 yards uphill takes you to some more eating and drinking fun: **Bamkraxler** (literally, "Tree Jumper"), the only beer garden amid all these vineyards. It's a fun-loving, youthful place with fine keg beer and a regular menu—traditional, ribs, veggie, kids' menu—rather than the *Heurige* cafeteria line (€6–10 meals, kids' playground, Tue–Sat 16:00–24:00, Sun 11:00–24:00, closed Mon, Kahlenbergerstrasse 17, tel. 01/318-8800).

Sirbu Weinbau Heuriger is actually in the vineyards, high above Vienna with great city and countryside views, a top-notch buffet, a glass veranda, and a traditional interior for cool weather. This place is a bit more touristy, since it's more upmarket and famous as "the ultimate setting" (April—Oct from 15:00, closed Sun, big children's play zone, Kahlenbergerstrasse 210, tel. 01/320-5928). It's high above regular transit service, but fun to incorporate into a little walking. Ideally, ride bus #38A to the end at Kahlenberg, and ask directions to the Heuriger (a 20-min walk downhill).

NIGHTLIFE

If old music and new wine aren't your thing, Vienna has plenty of alternatives. For an up-to-date rundown on fun after dark, get the TI's free Vienna Hype booklet.

Open-Air Cinema and Food Circus at City Hall—A thriving people scene erupts each evening in July and August at the park in front of the City Hall (Rathaus) on the Ring. A huge screen is set up with top-end speakers to show films of great concerts. While it's not live, the quality is excellent and it's free. Classical, opera, or jazz—there's a different concert every night. Go early to enjoy dinner in the

park, as there are countless (mostly ethnic) stalls serving fun and cheap meals to the youthful gang (daily from 11:00 until late in July and Aug). Single locals know this is the best pick-up place in town. Film schedules are at the TI.

Bermuda Triangle (Bermuda Dreieck)—The area known as the "Bermuda Triangle"—north of St. Stephen's Cathedral, between Rotenturmstrasse and Judengasse—is the hot local nightspot. You'll find lots of music clubs and classy pubs, or *Beisl* (such as Krah Krah, Salzamt, Bermuda Bräu, and First Floor—for cocktails with live fish). The serious-looking guards have nothing to do with the bar scene—they're guarding the synagogue nearby.

Gürtel—The Gürtel is Vienna's outer ring road. The arches of a lumbering viaduct (which carries a train track) are now filled with trendy bars, dance clubs, antique shops, and restaurants. To experience—or simply see—the latest scene in town, head out here. The people-watching—the trendiest kids on the block—makes the trip fun even if you're looking for exercise rather than a drink. Ride U-6 to Nussdorfer Strasse or Thaliastrasse and hike along the viaduct.

English Cinema—Two great theaters offer three or four screens of English movies nightly (€6–9): **English Cinema Haydn,** by my recommended hotels on Mariahilfer Strasse (Mariahilfer Strasse 57, tel. 01/587-2262, www.haydnkino.at); and **Artis International Cinema,** right in the town center a few minutes from the cathedral (Schultergasse 5, tel. 01/535-6570).

SLEEPING

As you move out from the center, hotel prices drop. My listings are in the old center (figure at least €100 for a decent double), along the likeable Mariahilfer Strasse (about €80), and near the Westbahnhof (about €60). While few accommodations in Vienna are air-conditioned (they are troubled by the fact that, per person, Las Vegas expends more energy keeping people cool than arctic Norway does to keep people warm), you can generally get fans on request. Places with elevators often have a few stairs to climb, too.

These hotels lose big and you pay more if you find a room through Internet booking sites. Book direct by phone, fax, or e-mail and save.

Within the Ring, in the Old City Center

You'll pay extra to sleep in the atmospheric old center, but if you can afford it, staying here gives you the best classy Vienna experience.

$$$ **Pension Pertschy** circles an old courtyard and is bigger and more hotelesque than the others listed here. Its 50 rooms are huge, but well-worn and a bit musty. Those on the courtyard are quietest (Sb-€87, small Db-€119, large Db-€172, cheaper

Hotels and Restaurants in Central Vienna

1 Pension Pertschy

2 Pension Neuer Markt

3 Pension Aviano

4 To Hotel Schweizerhof
& Pension Dr. Geissler

5 Hotel zur Wiener Staatsoper

6 Pension Nossek

7 Pension Suzanne

8 To Schweizer Pension Solderer

9 Restaurant Rosenberger Markt

10 Restaurant Gigerl Stadtheuriger

11 To Restaurants Brezel-Gwölb,
Ofenloch & Beisl Zum Scherer

12 To Zu den Drei Hacken

13 Wrenkh Vegetarian Restaurant

14 Buffet Trzesniewski

15 Café Rest. Palmenhaus & BBQ

16 Julius Meinl am Graben Deli

17 Café Hawelka

18 Rest. Esterhazykeller

19 To Café Central &
Restaurant Molker Stiftskeller

20 Sacher Café

21 Zanoni & Zanoni Ice Cream

22 Plachutta Restaurant

23 Ferdinandt Zwickl-Beisl

24 Loos American Bar

Sleep Code

(€1 = about $1.20, country code: 43, area code: 01)
S = Single, **D** = Double/Twin, **T** = Triple, **Q** = Quad, **b** = bathroom, **s** = shower only. English is spoken at each place. Unless otherwise noted, credit cards are accepted and breakfast is included.

To help you sort easily through these listings, I've divided the rooms into three categories, based on the price for a standard double room with bath:

$$$ **Higher Priced**—Most rooms €115 or more.
$$ **Moderately Priced**—Most rooms between €75–115.
$ **Lower Priced**—Most rooms €75 or less.

off-season, extra bed-€32, non-smoking rooms, elevator, U-1 or U-3: Stephansplatz, Habsburgergasse 5, tel. 01/534-490, fax 01/534-4949, www.pertschy.com, pertschy@pertschy.com).

$$$ Pension Neuer Markt is family-run, with 37 quiet, comfy, old-feeling rooms in a perfectly central locale (Ss-€85, Sb-€90–110, smaller Ds-€96, Db-€100–130, prices vary with season and room size, extra bed-€20, elevator, Seilergasse 9, tel. 01/512-2316, fax 01/513-9105, www.hotelpension.at/neuermarkt, neuermarkt@hotelpension.at).

$$$ Pension Aviano is another peaceful place, with 17 comfortable rooms on the fourth floor above lots of old center action (Sb-€92, Db-€132–-152 depending on size, 15 percent cheaper Nov–March, extra bed-€30, elevator, non-smoking rooms, between Neuer Markt and Kärntner Strasse at Marco d'Avianogasse 1, tel. 01/512-8330, fax 01/5128-3306, www.pertschy .com, aviano@pertschy.com).

$$$ Hotel Schweizerhof is classy, with 55 big rooms, all the comforts, and a more formal ambience. It's centrally located midway between St. Stephen's Cathedral and the Danube canal (Sb-€84–95, Db-€109–140, Tb-€131–160, low prices are for July–Aug and slow times, with cash and this book get your best price and then claim a 10 percent discount in 2006, can be noisy on weekends, elevator, Bauernmarkt 22, U-1 or U-3: Stephansplatz, tel. 01/533-1931, fax 01/533-0214, www.schweizerhof.at, office@schweizerhof.at).

$$$ Hotel zur Wiener Staatsoper, the Schweizerhof's sister hotel, is quiet and rich. Its 22 tight rooms come with high ceilings, chandeliers, and fancy carpets on parquet floors—ideal for people whose hotel tastes are a cut above mine. The singles are tiny, with beds too short for anyone over six feet tall (Sb-€84–95,

Db-€109–140, Tb-€131–160, extra bed-€22, cheaper prices are for July–Aug and Dec–March, fans on request, elevator, U-1, U-2, or U-4: Karlsplatz, a block from Opera at Krugerstrasse 11, tel. 01/513-1274, fax 01/513-127-415, www.zurwienerstaatsoper.at, office@zurwienerstaatsoper.at, manager Claudia).

$$ At **Pension Nossek,** an elevator takes you above any street noise into Frau Bernad's and Frau Gundolf's world, where the children seem to be placed among the lace and flowers by an interior designer. With 30 rooms right on the wonderful Graben, this is a particularly good value (S-€46–54, Ss-€58, Sb-€69–73, Db-€110, €26 extra for sprawling suites, extra bed-€35, Internet in lobby, cash only, elevator, U-1 or U-3: Stephansplatz, Graben 17, tel. 01/5337-0410, fax 01/535-3646, www.pension-nossek.at, reservation@pension-nossek.at).

$$ **Pension Suzanne,** as Baroque and doily as you'll find in this price range, is wonderfully located a few yards from the Opera. It's small, but run with the class of a bigger hotel; the 25 rooms are packed with properly Viennese antique furnishings. Streetside rooms come with some noise (Sb-€76, Db-€94–115 depending on size, 4 percent discount with cash, extra bed-€30, spacious apartment for up to 6 also available, discounts in winter, fans on request, elevator, a block from Opera, U-1, U-2, or U-4: Karlsplatz and follow signs for Opera exit, Walfischgasse 4, tel. 01/513-2507, fax 01/513-2500, www.pension-suzanne.at, info@pension-suzanne.at, manager Michael).

$$ **Schweizer Pension Solderer** has been family-owned for three generations. The current owner, Anita, runs an extremely tight ship, offering 11 homey rooms, parquet floors, and lots of tourist info (S-€38–42, Sb-€55–65, D-€58–65, Db-€78–87, Tb-€102–109, Qb-€126–131, prices depend on season and room size, cash only, entirely non-smoking, elevator, laundry-€14/load, U-2 or U-4: Schottenring, Heinrichsgasse 2, tel. 01/533-8156, fax 01/535-6469, www.schweizerpension.com, schweizer.pension@chello.at).

$$ **Pension Dr. Geissler** has 23 comfortable rooms on the eighth floor of a modern building about 10 blocks northeast of St. Stephen's, near the canal (S-€48, Ss-€68, Sb-€76, D-€65, Ds-€77, Db-€95, 20 percent less in winter, elevator, U-1 or U-4: Schwedenplatz, Postgasse 14, tel. 01/533-2803, fax 01/533-2635, www.hotelpension.at/dr-geissler, dr.geissler@hotelpension.at).

Hotels and Pensions along Mariahilfer Strasse

Lively Mariahilfer Strasse connects the Westbahnhof (West Train Station) and the city center. The U-3 line, starting at the Westbahnhof, goes down Mariahilfer Strasse to the cathedral. This very Viennese street is a tourist-friendly and vibrant area filled with local shops and cafés. Most hotels are within a few steps of a

Hotels and Restaurants Outside the Ring

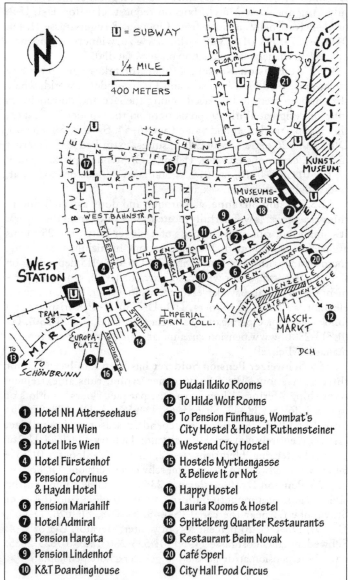

1 Hotel NH Atterseehaus
2 Hotel NH Wien
3 Hotel Ibis Wien
4 Hotel Fürstenhof
5 Pension Corvinus
    & Haydn Hotel
6 Pension Mariahilf
7 Hotel Admiral
8 Pension Hargita
9 Pension Lindenhof
10 K&T Boardinghouse

11 Budai Ildiko Rooms
12 To Hilde Wolf Rooms
13 To Pension Fünfhaus, Wombat's
    City Hostel & Hostel Ruthensteiner
14 Westend City Hostel
15 Hostels Myrthengasse
    & Believe It or Not
16 Happy Hostel
17 Lauria Rooms & Hostel
18 Spittelberg Quarter Restaurants
19 Restaurant Beim Novak
20 Café Sperl
21 City Hall Food Circus

U-Bahn stop, just one or two stops from the Westbahnhof (direction from the station: Simmering).

$$$ NH Hotels, a Spanish chain, runs two stern, passionless business hotels a few blocks apart on Mariahilfer Strasse. Both rent ideal-for-families suites, each with a living room, two TVs, bathroom, desk, and kitchenette (rack rate: Db suite-€155, going rate usually closer to €100, plus €14 per person for optional breakfast, apartments for 2–3 adults, kids under 12 free, non-smoking rooms, elevator). The 78-room **NH Atterseehaus** is at Mariahilfer Strasse 78 (U-3: Zieglergasse, tel. 01/5245-6000, fax 01/524-560-015, nhatterseehaus@nh-hotels.com), and the **NH Wien** has 106 rooms at Mariahilfer Strasse 32 (U-3: Neubaugasse, tel. 01/521-720, fax 01/521-7215, nhwien@nh-hotels.com). The Web site for both is www.nh-hotels.com.

$$ Pension Corvinus is bright, modern, and warmly run by a Hungarian family: Miklós, Judit, and Zoltan. Its eight comfortable rooms are spacious, with small, compact bathrooms (Sb-€58, Db-€91, Tb-€105, extra bed-€26, non-smoking rooms, portable air-con-€10/day, elevator, free Internet in lobby, parking garage-€11/day, on the 3rd floor at Mariahilfer Strasse 57–59, tel. 01/587-7239, fax 01/587-723-920, www.corvinus.at, hotel@corvinus.at).

$$ Pension Mariahilf offers a clean, aristocratic air in an affordable and cozy pension package. Its 12 rooms are spacious but outmoded, with an Art Deco flair (Sb-€59–66, Db-€95–102, Tb-€124, lower prices are for longer stays, may be under new management in 2006, elevator, U-3: Neubaugasse, Mariahilfer Strasse 49, tel. 01/586-1781, fax 01/586-178-122, www.mariahilf-hotel, penma@inode.at).

$$ Haydn Hotel, in the same building as the Pension Corvinus (listed above), is big, fancy, and dark, with 50 spacious rooms. Most rooms have been remodeled, but some have seen better days (Sb-€65–90, Db-€90–100, 10 percent discount with cash and this book in 2006, suites and family apartments, extra bed-€30, air-con, non-smoking rooms, elevator, free Internet in lobby, Mariahilfer Strasse 57–59, tel. 01/587-44140, fax 01/586-1950, www.haydn-hotel.at, info@haydn-hotel.at, Nouri).

$$ Hotel Admiral is huge, quiet, and practical, with 80 large, comfortable rooms (Sb-€66, Db-€91, extra bed-€23, manager Alexandra promises these prices through 2006 with this book and cash, cheaper in winter, breakfast-€5 per person, free Internet in lobby, free parking, U-2 or U-3: Volkstheater, a block off Mariahilfer Strasse at Karl Schweighofer Gasse 7, tel. 01/521-410, fax 01/521-4116, www.admiral.co.at, hotel@admiral.co.at).

$ Pension Hargita rents 24 generally small, bright, and tidy rooms (mostly twins) with Hungarian decor. This spick-and-span, well-run, well-located place is a fine value (S-€35, Ss-€40, Sb-€52,

D-€48, Ds-€55, Db-€63, Ts-€70, Tb-€76, Qb-€87, breakfast-€4, U-3: Zieglergasse, corner of Mariahilfer Strasse and Andreasgasse, Andreasgasse 1, tel. 01/526-1928, fax 01/526-0492, www.hargita .at, pension@hargita.at, classy Amalia). As the pension has street noise, request a room in the back.

$ Pension Lindenhof rents 19 worn but clean rooms and is filled with plants (S-€30, Sb-€37, D-€51, Db-€67, cash only, elevator, U-3: Neubaugasse, Lindengasse 4, tel. 01/523-0498, fax 01/523-7362, pensionlindenhof@yahoo.com, Gebrael family, Zara and Keram speak English).

$ K&T Boardinghouse rents four big, comfortable rooms facing the bustling Mariahilfer Strasse (Db-€65, Tb-€85, Qb-€105, 2-night minimum, no breakfast, air-con-€10/day, cash only, non-smoking, free Internet in lobby, 3 flights up, no elevator, Mariahilfer Strasse 72, tel. 01/523-2989, fax 01/522-0345, www.kaled .at, kaled@chello.at, Tina and Kaled).

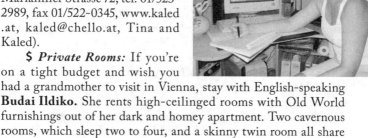

$ *Private Rooms:* If you're on a tight budget and wish you had a grandmother to visit in Vienna, stay with English-speaking **Budai Ildiko.** She rents high-ceilinged rooms with Old World furnishings out of her dark and homey apartment. Two cavernous rooms, which sleep two to four, and a skinny twin room all share one bathroom (S-€32, D-€45, T-€64, Q-€79, no breakfast but free coffee, lots of tourist information, cash only, laundry-€4, classic old elevator, Lindengasse 39, apartment #5, tel. 01/523-1058, tel. & fax 01/526-2595, www.wienwien.at, budai@hotmail.com).

$ Hilde Wolf, with the help of her grandson, Patrick, shares her apartment with travelers. Her four huge but stuffy rooms are like old libraries (S-€33, D-€50, T-€70, Q-€90, breakfast-€4, cash only, U-2: Karlsplatz, 3 blocks below Naschmarkt at Schleifmühlgasse 7, tel. 01/586-5103, fax 01/689-3505, www .schoolpool.at/bb). There's no sign or name at the street—she's on the first floor.

Near the Westbahnhof (West Station)

$$ Hotel Ibis Wien, a modern high-rise hotel with American charm, is ideal for anyone tired of quaint old Europe. Its 340 cookie-cutter rooms are bright, comfortable, and modern, with all the conveniences (Sb-€71, Db-€86, Tb-€101, €5 cheaper in July, breakfast-€9, non-smoking rooms, air-con, elevator, parking garage-€10/day, exit Westbahnhof to the right and walk 400 yards, Mariahilfer Gürtel 22–24, tel. 01/59998, fax 01/597-9090, h0796@accor.com).

$$ Hotel Fürstenhof, right across from the station, rents 58 spacious but borderline-musty rooms. This venerable hotel has an Old World maroon-velvet feel (S-€46, Sb-€69-94, D-€65, Db-€110, Tb-€120, Qb-€128, 10 percent cheaper if you book online, ask for quiet side—*ruhige Seite*, elevator, Internet in lobby, Europaplatz 4, tel. 01/523-3267, fax 01/523-326-726, www.hotel-fuerstenhof .com, reception@hotel-fuerstenhof.com).

$ Pension Fünfhaus is big, clean, stark, and quiet—almost institutional. Although the neighborhood is rundown and comes with a few ladies loitering late at night, this 47-room place is a good value (S-€32, Sb-€40, D-€44, Db-€52, T-€66, Tb-€78, 4-person apartment-€90, prices promised with this book in 2006, cash only, closed mid-Nov–Feb, Sperrgasse 12, tel. 01/892-3545 or 01/892-0286, fax 01/892-0460, www.pension5haus.at, pension5haus@tiscali.at, Frau Susi Tersch). Half the rooms are in the fine main building and half are in the annex, which has good rooms but is near the train tracks and a bit scary on the street at night. From the station, ride tram #52 or #58 two stops down Mariahilfer Strasse away from center to the Kranzgasse stop, then backtrack two blocks to Sperrgasse.

Cheap Dorms and Hostels near Mariahilfer Strasse

$ Believe It or Not is a tiny, basic hostel with about the cheapest bunk beds in town in two coed rooms for up to 10 travelers. Hardworking and friendly Heny requires a minimum two-night stay and warns that this place is appropriate only for the young at heart (bed-€13.50, €10.50 Nov–Easter, cash only, locked up 10:00–12:30, no curfew, kitchen facilities, Myrthengasse 10, ring apt. #14, tel. 01/526-4658, www.believe-it-or-not-vienna.at, believe_it_or_not _vienna@hotmail.com).

$ Jugendherberge Myrthengasse is a well-run youth hostel (260 beds, €15–19 each in 3- to 6-bed rooms, includes sheets and breakfast, non-members pay €3.50 extra, always open, no curfew, lockers and lots of facilities, Myrthengasse 7, tel. 01/523-6316, fax 01/523-5849, hostel@chello.at).

$ Westend City Hostel, just a block from the Westbahnhof and Mariahilfer Strasse, is well-run and well-located, with 180 beds in 4- to 12-bed dorms (€17–25 per person, depending on how many in the room; includes sheets, breakfast, and locker; cash only, laundry, Internet in lobby, Fügergasse 3, tel. 01/597-6729, fax 01/597-672-927, www.westendhostel.at, westendcityhostel@aon.at).

$ Happy Hostel rents five ramshackle yet homey apartments for two to five people beautifully located on a quiet street a couple blocks from the Westbahnhof and Mariahilfer Strasse (€25/person, S-€35, Sb-€40, Db-€50–70, no breakfast, Aegidigasse 19, tel.

01/208-2618, www.happyhostel.at, info@happyhostel.at).

$ Lauria Rooms and Hostel is a creative little place run by friendly Gosha, with two 10-bed dorms (boys and girls mixed, with lockers) and several other rooms sleeping two to six each (€13.50 dorm beds, about €24 per person in other rooms, Kaiserstrasse 77, tram #5 or a 10-minute walk from Westbahnhof, tel. 01/522-2555, www.panda-vienna.at, panda_vienna@hotmail.com).

$ More Hostels: Other hostels with €16 beds and €40 doubles near Mariahilfer Strasse are **Wombat's City Hostel** (Grangasse 6, tel. 01/897-2336, www.wombats-hostels.com, office@wombats -vienna.at) and **Hostel Ruthensteiner** (Robert-Hamerling-Gasse 24, tel. 01/893-4202, www.hostelruthensteiner.com, info @hostelruthensteiner.com).

EATING

The Viennese appreciate the fine points of life, and right up there with waltzing is eating. The city has many atmospheric restaurants. As you ponder the Eastern European specialties on menus, remember that Vienna's diverse empire may be gone, but its flavor lingers.

While cuisines are routinely named for countries, Vienna claims to be the only *city* with a cuisine of its own: Vienna soups come with fillings (semolina dumpling, liver dumpling, or pancake slices). *Gulasch* is a beef ragout of Hungarian origin (spiced with onion and paprika). Of course, Viennese schnitzel (Wiener Schnitzel) is traditionally a breaded and fried veal cutlet (though pork is more common these days). Another meat specialty is boiled beef *(Tafelspitz)*. While you're sure to have *Apfelstrudel,* try the sweet cheese strudel, too (*Topfenstrudel*—wafer-thin strudel pastry filled with sweet cheese and raisins).

On nearly every corner, you can find a colorful *Beisl*. These uniquely Viennese taverns are a characteristic cross between an English pub and a French brasserie—filled with poetry teachers and their students, couples loving without touching, housewives on their way home from cello lessons, and waiters who enjoy serving hearty food and good drink at an affordable price. Ask at your hotel for a good *Beisl*.

Wherever you're eating, some vocabulary helps. Try the *grüner Veltliner* (dry white wine), *Traubenmost* (a heavenly grape juice—alcohol-free but on the verge of wine), *Most* (the same thing but lightly alcoholic), and *Sturm* (stronger than *Most*, autumn only). The local red wine (called *Portugieser*) is pretty good. Since the Austrian wine is often sweet, remember the word *trocken* (dry). You can order your wine by the *Viertel* (quarter liter, 8 oz) or *Achtel* (eighth liter, 4 oz). Beer comes in a *Krügel* (half liter, 17 oz) or

Seidel (0.3 liter, 10 oz). The *dag* you see in some prices stands for "decigram" (10 grams). Therefore, *10 dag* is 100 grams, or about a quarter pound.

Near St. Stephen's Cathedral
All of these eateries are within a five-minute walk of the cathedral.

Gigerl Stadtheuriger offers a near-*Heurige* experience (à la Grinzing—see "Vienna's Wine Gardens," page 733), often with accordion or live music, without leaving the city center. Just point to what looks good. Food is sold by the weight; 100 grams *(10 dag)* is about a quarter pound (cheese and cold meats cost about €3 per 100 grams, salads are about €2 per 100 grams; price sheet is posted on the wall to right of buffet line). They also have menu entrées, along with spinach strudel, quiche, *Apfelstrudel,* and, of course, casks of new and local wines. Meals run €7–11 (daily 15:00–24:00, indoor/outdoor seating, behind cathedral, a block off Kärntner Strasse, a few cobbles off Rauhensteingasse on Blumenstock, tel. 01/513-4431).

Am Hof Eateries: The square called Am Hof (U-3: Herrengasse) is surrounded by a maze of atmospheric medieval lanes; the following places are all within a block of the square. **Restaurant Ofenloch** serves good, old-fashioned Viennese cuisine with friendly service, both indoors and out. This 300-year-old eatery, with great traditional ambience, is central but not overrun with tourists (€12–18 main dishes, Tue–Sat 11:30–24:00, Mon 18:00–24:00, closed Sun, Kurrentgasse 8, tel. 01/533-8844). **Brezel-Gwölb,** a wonderfully atmospheric wine cellar with outdoor dining on a quiet square, serves delicious light meals, fine *Krautsuppe* (cabbage soup), and old-fashioned local dishes. It's ideal for a romantic late-night glass of wine (daily 11:30–1:00, leave Am Hof on Drahtgasse, then take first left to Ledererhof 9, tel. 01/533-8811). Around the corner, **Beisl "Zum Scherer"** is just as untouristy and serves traditional plates for €10. Sitting outside, you'll face a stern Holocaust memorial. Inside comes with a soothing woody atmosphere and intriguing decor (Mon–Sat 11:30–24:00, food until 22:00, closed Sun, Judenplatz 7, tel. 01/533-5164). Just below Am Hof, the ancient and popular **Esterhazykeller** has traditional fare deep underground or outside on a delightful square (Mon–Fri 11:00–23:00, Sat–Sun 16:00–23:00, self-service buffet in lowest cellar or from menu, Haarhof 1, tel. 01/533-3482).

Wine Cellars: These wine cellars are fun and touristy but typical, in the old center, with reasonable prices and plenty of smoke: **Melker Stiftskeller,** less touristy, is a *Stadtheurige* in a deep and rustic cellar with hearty, inexpensive meals and new wine (Tue–Sat 17:00–24:00, closed Sun–Mon and most of July, between Am

Hof and Schottentor U-Bahn stop at Schottengasse 3, tel. 01/533-5530). **Zu den Drei Hacken** is famous for its local specialties (€10 plates, Mon–Sat 11:00–23:00, closed Sun, indoor/outdoor seating, Singerstrasse 28, tel. 01/512-5895).

Ferdinandt Zwickl-Beisl is an inviting little pub with a user-friendly menu featuring the classic traditional *Beisl* plates, plus salads and vegetarian dishes. Choose between Old World, woody indoor seating and pleasant streetside seating (€9–15 plates, daily 9:00–24:00, a block off the Kärntner Strasse mob scene at Neuer Markt 2, tel. 01/513-8991).

Wrenkh Vegetarian Restaurant and Bar is popular for its high vegetarian cuisine. Chef Wrenkh offers daily €8–10 lunch *menus* and €8–13 dinner plates in a bright, mod bar or in a dark, smoke-free, fancier restaurant (Mon–Sat 11:30–23:00, closed Sun, July–Aug also closed Sat, Bauernmarkt 10, tel. 01/533-1526).

Buffet Trzesniewski is an institution—justly famous for its elegant and cheap finger sandwiches and small beers (€0.80 each). Three different sandwiches and a *kleines Bier (Pfiff)* make a fun, light lunch. Point to whichever delights look tasty (or grab the English translation sheet and take time to study your options). Pay for your sandwiches and a drink. Take your drink tokens to the lady on the right. Sit on the bench and scoot over to a tiny table when a spot opens up (Mon–Fri 8:30–19:30, Sat 9:00–17:00, closed Sun, 50 yards off Graben, nearly across from brooding Café Hawelka, Dorotheergasse 2, tel. 01/512-3291). This is a good opportunity (in the fall) to try the fancy grape juices—*Most* or *Traubenmost* (described above).

Julius Meinl am Graben, a posh supermarket right on the Graben, has been famous since 1862 as a top-end delicatessen with all the gourmet fancies. Along with the picnic fixings on the shelves, there's a café with light meals and great outdoor seating, a stuffy and pricey restaurant upstairs, and a take-away counter (shop open Mon–Fri 8:30–19:30, Sat 9:00–18:00, closed Sun; restaurant open Mon–Sat until 24:00, closed Sun; Am Graben 19, tel. 01/532-3334).

Akakiko Sushi: If you're just schnitzeled out, this small chain of Japanese restaurants with an easy sushi menu may suit you. The bento box meals are tasty. Three locations have no charm but are fast, reasonable, and convenient (€7–10 meals, all open daily 10:30–23:30): Singerstrasse 4 (a block off Kärntner Strasse near the cathedral), Heidenschuss 3 (near other recommended eateries just off Am Hof), and Mariahilfer Strasse 42–48 (5th floor of Kaufhaus Gerngross, near many recommended hotels).

Plachutta Restaurant, with a stylish green-and-crème, elegant-but-comfy interior and breezy covered terrace, is famous for the best beef in town. You'll find an enticing menu with all the classic Viennese beef dishes, fine deserts, attentive service, and an enthusiastic local clientele. They've developed the art of beef to the point of producing popular cookbooks (€15–20 meals, daily 11:30–23:00, U-3: Stubentor, 10-min walk from St. Stephen's Cathedral, Wollzeile 38, tel. 01/512-1577).

Ice Cream!: **Zanoni & Zanoni** is a very Italian *gelateria* run by an Italian family. They're mobbed by happy Viennese hungry for their huge €2 cones to go. Or, to relax, lick your gelato at their fun outdoor seating (daily 7:00–24:00, 2 blocks up Rotenturmstrasse from cathedral at Lugeck 7, tel. 01/512-7979).

Near the Opera

Café Restaurant Palmenhaus, overlooking the Palace Garden (Burggarten—see page 707), tucked away in a green and peaceful corner two blocks behind the Opera in the Hofburg's back yard, is a world apart. If you want to eat modern Austrian cuisine with palm trees rather than tourists, this is it. And, since it's at the edge of a huge park, it's great for families (€8 2-course lunches available Mon–Fri, €15–18 entrees, open daily 10:00–2:00 in the morning, serious vegetarian dishes, fish, extensive wine list, indoors in greenhouse or outdoors, tel. 01/533-1033). While nobody goes to the Palmenhaus for good prices, the **Palmenhaus BBQ,** a cool parkside outdoor pub just below that uses the same kitchen, is a wonderful value with more casual service (summer Thu–Sat from 20:00, closed Sun–Wed, open in good weather only, informal with €8–10 BBQ and meals posted on chalkboard).

Rosenberger Markt Restaurant is my favorite for a fast, light, and central lunch. Just a block toward the cathedral from the Opera, this cafeteria—while not cheap—is brilliant. Friendly and efficient, with special theme rooms for dining, it offers a fresh, smoke-free, and healthy cornucopia of food and drink (daily 10:30–23:00, lots of fruits, veggies, fresh-squeezed juices, addictive banana milk, ride the glass elevator downstairs, Maysedergasse 2, tel. 01/512-3458). You can stack a small salad or veggie plate into a tower of gobble for €2.90.

City Hall (Rathaus) Food Circus: During the summer, scores of outdoor food stands and hundreds of picnic tables are set up in the park in front of the City Hall. Local mobs enjoy mostly ethnic meals on disposable plates for decent-but-not-cheap prices. The fun thing here is the energy of the crowd, and a feeling that you're truly eating as the locals do...not schnitzel and quaint traditions, but trendy "world food" with people out having pure and simple fun in a fine Vienna park setting (July–Aug daily from 11:00 until late, in front of City Hall on the Ringstrasse).

Spittelberg Quarter

A charming cobbled grid of traffic-free lanes and Biedermeier apartments has become a favorite neighborhood for Viennese wanting a little dining charm between the MuseumsQuartier and Mariahilfer Strasse (handy to many recommended hotels; take Stiftgasse from Mariahilfer Strasse, or wander over here after you close down the Kunsthistorisches or Leopold Museum). Tables tumble down sidewalks and into breezy courtyards filled with appreciative locals enjoying dinner or a relaxing drink. Stroll Spittelberggasse, Schrankgasse, and Gutenberggasse and pick your favorite place. Don't miss the vine-strewn wine garden at Schrankgasse 1. **Amerlingbeisl,** with a casual atmosphere both on the cobbled street and in its vine-covered courtyard, is a great value (€7 plates, €6–8 daily specials, salads, veggie dishes, traditional specialties, daily 9:00–24:00, Stiftgasse 8, tel. 01/526-1660). The neighboring **Plutzer Bräu** is also good (ribs, burgers, traditional dishes, Tirolean beer from the keg, daily 11:00–2:00, food until 22:30, Schrankgasse 4, tel. 01/526-1215). For traditional Viennese cuisine with tablecloths, consider the classier **Witwe Bolte** (daily 11:30–15:00 & 17:30–23:30, Gutenberggasse 13, tel. 01/523-1450).

Near Mariahilfer Strasse

Mariahilfer Strasse is filled with reasonable cafés serving all types of cuisine.

Restaurant Beim Novak serves tasty and well-presented Viennese cuisine away from the modern rush. While this small and intimate place, thoughtfully run by Maximilian, has no outdoor seating, the charming back room offers a relaxing atmosphere (€7 lunch specials, €10–15 plates, Mon–Fri 11:30–15:00 & 18:00–22:00, open Sat for dinner Sept–March, closed Sun and in Aug, a block down Andreasgasse from Mariahilfer Strasse at Richtergasse 12, tel. 01/523-3244).

Naschmarkt (described on page 723) is Vienna's best Old World market, with plenty of fresh produce, cheap local-style eateries, cafés, *döner kebab* and sausage stands, and the best-value sushi in town (Mon–Fri 6:00–18:30, Sat 6:00–17:00, closed Sun, closes earlier in winter, U-4: Kettenbrückengasse). Survey the lane of eateries at the end of the market nearest the Opera. The circa-1900 pub is inviting. Picnickers can buy their goodies at the market and eat on nearby Karlsplatz (plenty of chairs facing Charles Church).

TRANSPORTATION CONNECTIONS

Vienna has two main train stations: the Westbahnhof (West Station), serving Munich, Salzburg, Melk, and Budapest; and the Südbahnhof (South Station), serving Italy, Budapest, Prague, Poland, Slovenia, and Croatia. A third station, Franz Josefs, serves Krems and the Danube Valley (but Melk is served by the Westbahnhof). Metro line U-3 connects the Westbahnhof with the center, tram D takes you from the Südbahnhof and the Franz Josefs station to downtown, and tram #18 connects West and South stations. Train info: tel. 051-717 (to get an operator, dial 2, then 1).

From Vienna by Train to: **Bratislava** (about hrly, 1 hr), **Budapest** (6/day, 3 hrs), **Prague** (3/day, 5 hrs), **Český Krumlov** (4/day, 6–7 hrs, up to 3 changes), **Ljubljana** (7/day, 6–7 hrs, convenient early-morning direct train, others change in Villach, Maribor, or Graz), **Zagreb** (8/day, 6.5–10.5 hrs, 3 direct, others with up to 3 changes including Villach and Ljubljana), **Kraków** (2/day direct including a night train departing at about 22:00, arriving around 6:00, 6.5–8.25 hrs), **Warsaw** (1/day, with transfer in Břeclav, Czech Republic, 7.75 hrs; or 2 direct including a night train, 7.75–10 hrs), **Melk** (hrly, 75 min, sometimes change in St. Pölten), **Krems** (hrly, 1 hr), **Salzburg** (hrly, 3 hrs), **Innsbruck** (every 2 hrs, 5.5 hrs), **Munich** (hrly, 5.25 hrs, change in Salzburg, a few direct trains), **Berlin** (2/day, 10 hrs, longer on night train), **Zürich** (3/day, 9 hrs), **Rome** (1/day, 13.5 hrs), **Venice** (3/day, 7.5 hrs, longer on night train), **Frankfurt** (4/day, 7.5 hrs), **Amsterdam** (1/day, 14.5 hrs).

Excursions by Car with Driver: Those wishing they had wheels may consider hiring Johann (see page 685) for Danube excursions from Vienna or en route to Salzburg (particularly economic for groups of 3–4).

To Eastern Europe: Vienna is the springboard for a quick trip to Prague and Budapest—it's three hours by train from Budapest (€40 one way, €50 round-trip if you stay 4 days or less; covered by any railpass that includes both Austria and Hungary) and four hours from Prague (€42 one way, €84 round-trip, €53 round-trip with Eurailpass). Americans and Canadians do not need visas to enter the Czech Republic or Hungary. Purchase tickets at most travel agencies. Eurail passholders bound for Prague must pay to ride the rails in the Czech Republic.

UNDERSTANDING YUGOSLAVIA

Americans struggle to understand the complicated breakup of Yugoslavia (especially when visiting two of its former parts, Slovenia and Croatia). During the Yugoslav era, it was no less confusing. As the old joke went, Yugoslavia had eight distinct peoples in six republics, with five languages, three religions (Orthodox, Catholic, and Muslim), and two alphabets (Roman and Cyrillic), but only one Yugoslav—Tito.

Everyone you talk to in the former Yugoslavia will have a different version of events. A very wise Bosnian Muslim told me, "Listen to all three sides—Muslim, Serb, and Croat. Then decide for yourself what you think." That's the best advice I can offer. But since you likely won't have time for that on your brief visit, here's an oversimplified, as-impartial-as-possible history to get you started.

Who's Who

For starters, it helps to have a handle on the Balkans—the southeastern European peninsula between the Adriatic and the Black Sea, stretching from Hungary to Greece. The Balkan Peninsula has always been a crossroads of cultures. The Illyrians, Greeks, and Romans had settlements here before the Slavs moved into the region from the north around the seventh century. During the next millennium and a half, the western part of the peninsula—which would become Yugoslavia—was divided by a series of cultural, ethnic, and religious fault lines.

The most important influences were three religions: **Western Christianity** (i.e., Roman Catholicism, primarily brought to the western part of the region by Charlemagne, and later reinforced by the Austrian Hapsburgs), **Eastern Orthodox Christianity** (brought to the east from the Byzantine Empire), and **Islam** (in

Yugoslav Succession

the south, from the Ottoman Turks).

Two major historical factors made the Balkans what they are today: The first was the **split of the Roman Empire** in the fourth century A.D., dividing the Balkans down the middle into Roman Catholic (west) and Byzantine Orthodox (east)—roughly along today's Bosnian-Serbian border. The second was the **invasion of the Islamic Ottoman Turks** in the 14th century. The Turkish victory at the Battle of Kosovo (1389) began five centuries of Islamic influence in Bosnia-Herzegovina and Serbia, further dividing the Balkans into Christian (north) and Muslim (south).

Because of these and other events, several distinct ethnic identities emerged. Confusingly, the major "ethnicities" of Yugoslavia are all South Slavs—they're descended from the same ancestors, and speak essentially the same language, but they practice different religions. Catholic South Slavs are called **Croats** or **Slovenes**

Who's Who in Yugoslavia

Yugoslavia was made up of six republics, which were inhabited by eight different ethnicities (not counting small minorities such as Jews, Germans, and Roma). This chart shows each ethnicity, and in which republic they were most concentrated. Not coincidentally, the more ethnicities in a region, the more conflict took place.

	Serbia	Croatia	Bosnia-Herz.	Slovenia	Montenegro	Macedonia
Serbs (Orthodox)	x	x	x			
Croats (Catholic)		x	x			
Bosniaks (Muslims)			x			
Slovenes (Catholic)				x		
Macedonians (like Bulgarians)						x
Montenegrins (like Serbs)					x	
Hungarians	x*					
Albanians	x*		x			x

*Within Serbia were two "autonomous provinces," each of which was dominated by a non-Slavic ethnic group: Hungarians in Vojvodina and Albanians in Kosovo. Tito intentionally set up these two autonomous provinces to prevent Serbia from becoming too powerful. Tito was right: Slobodan Milošević's annexation of Kosovo is precisely what tipped the balance of power in Yugoslavia, sparking the Balkan wars of the 1990s.

(mostly west of the Dinaric Mountains: Croats along the Adriatic coast, and Slovenes farther north, towards Austria); Orthodox South Slavs are called **Serbs** (mostly east of the Dinaric range); and Muslim South Slavs are called **Bosniaks** (who converted to Islam under the Turks, mostly living in the Dinaric Mountains). To complicate matters, the region is also home to several non-Slavic groups, including **Hungarians** (in the northern province of Vojvodina) and **Albanians,** concentrated in the southern province of Kosovo (descended from the Illyrians, who lived here long before the Greeks and Romans).

Of course, these geographic divisions are extremely general. The groups overlapped a lot—which is exactly why the breakup of Yugoslavia was so contentious. One of the biggest causes of this ethnic mixing came in the 16th century. The Ottoman Turks were threatening to overrun Europe, and the Austrian Hapsburgs wanted a buffer zone—a "human shield." The Hapsburgs encouraged Serbs who were fleeing from Turkish invasions to settle along today's Croatian-Bosnian border (known as *Vojna Krajina*, or "Military Frontier"). The Serbs stayed after the Turks had left, establishing homes in predominantly Croat communities.

After the Turkish threat subsided in the late 17th century, some of the Balkans (basically today's Slovenia and Croatia) became part of the Austrian Hapsburg Empire. The Turks stayed longer in the south and east (today's Bosnia-Herzegovina and Serbia)—making the cultures in these regions even more different. Serbia finally gained its independence from the Ottomans in the mid-19th century, but it wasn't too long before World War I started...after a disgruntled Serbian nationalist killed the Austrian archduke.

South Slavs Unite

When the Austro-Hungarian Empire fell at the end of World War I, the European map was redrawn for the 20th century. After centuries of being governed by foreign powers, the South Slavs began to see their shared history as more important than their minor differences. A tiny country of a few million Croats or Slovenes couldn't have survived. Rather than be absorbed by a non-Slavic power, the South Slavs decided that there was safety in numbers, and banded together as a single state—first called the "Kingdom of the Serbs, Croats, and Slovenes" (1918), later known as Yugoslavia (literally, "Union of the South Slavs"—*yugo* means "south") "Yugoslav unity" was in the air, but this new union was artificial and ultimately bound to fail (not unlike the partnership between the Czechs and Slovaks, formed at the same time and for much the same reasons).

From the very beginning, the various ethnicities struggled for power within the new union. Croats in particular often felt they were treated as lesser partners under the Serbs. (For example, many Croats objected to naming the country's official language "Serbo-Croatian"—why not "Croato-Serbian?") Serbia already had a very strong king, Alexander Karađorđević, who immediately made attempts to give his nation a leading role in the federation. A nationalistic Croatian politician named Stjepan Radić, pushing for a more equitable division of powers, was shot by a Serb during a parliament session in 1928. Karađorđević abolished the parliament and became dictator. Six years later, infuriated Croatian separatists killed him.

Many Croat nationalists sided with the Nazis in World War II in the hopes that it would be their ticket to independence from Serbia. The Nazi puppet government in Croatia (called Ustaše) conducted an extermination campaign, murdering many Serbs (along with Jews and Roma) living in Croatia; other Serbs were forced to flee the country or convert to Catholicism. Most historians consider the Ustaše concentration camps to be the first instance of "ethnic cleansing" in the Balkans...and the Serbs' long memory of it may go far in explaining their own ethnic cleansing of the Croats in the 1990s.

At the end of World War II, the rest of Eastern Europe was "liberated" by the Soviets—but the Yugoslavs regained their independence on their own, as their communist partisan army forced out the Nazis. After the short but rocky Yugoslav union between the World Wars, it seemed that no one could hold the southern Slavs together in a single nation. But there was one man who could, and did: Tito.

Tito

Communist Party president and war hero Josip Broz—who dubbed himself with the simple nickname Tito—emerged as a political leader after World War II. With a Slovene for a mother, a Croat for a father, a Serb for a wife, and a home in Belgrade, Tito was a true Yugoslav. Tito had a compelling vision that this fractured union of the South Slavs could function. And it did. For the next three decades, Tito managed to keep Yugoslavia intact, essentially by the force of his own personality.

Tito's new incarnation of Yugoslavia aimed for a more equitable division of powers. It was made up of six republics, each with its own parliament and president: **Croatia** (mostly Catholic Croats), **Slovenia** (mostly Catholic Slovenes), **Serbia** (mostly Orthodox Serbs), **Bosnia-Herzegovina** (the most diverse—mostly Muslims, but with very large Croat and Serb populations), **Montenegro** (mostly Serb-like Montenegrins), and **Macedonia** (with about 25 percent Albanians and 75 percent Macedonians—who are claimed variously by Bulgarians and Serbs). There were also two autonomous provinces, each one dominated by an ethnicity that was a minority in greater Yugoslavia: Albanians in **Kosovo** (to the south) and Hungarians in **Vojvodina** (to the north). Tito hoped that by allowing these two provinces some degree of independence—including voting rights—they could balance the political clout of Serbia, preventing a single republic from dominating the union.

Each republic managed its own affairs...but always under the watchful eye of president-for-life Tito, who said that the borders between the republics should be "like white lines in a marble column."

Tito was unquestionably a political genius, carefully crafting a workable union. For example, every Yugoslav had to serve in the National Army, and Tito made sure that each unit was a microcosm of the complete Yugoslavia—with equal representation from each ethnic group. (Allowing an all-Slovene unit, stationed in Slovenia, would be begging for trouble.) There was also a dark side to Tito, who resorted to violent, strong-arming measures to assert his power, especially early in his reign. He staged brutal, Stalin-esque "show trials" to intimidate potential dissidents, and imprisoned church leaders, such as Alojzije Stepinac (see page 660). Nationalism was strongly discouraged, and this tight control—though sometimes oppressive—kept the country from unraveling. In retrospect, most former Yugoslavs forgive Tito for governing with an iron fist, believing that this was necessary for keeping the country strong and united. Today, most of them consider Tito more of a hero than a villain, and usually speak of him with reverence.

Tito's Yugoslavia was communist, but it wasn't Soviet communism; you'll find no statues of Lenin or Stalin here. Despite strong pressure from Moscow, Tito refused to ally himself with the Soviets—and therefore received good will (and $2 billion) from the United States. Tito's vision was for a "third way," where Yugoslavia could work with both East and West, without being dominated by either. Yugoslavia was the most free of the communist states: While large industry was nationalized, Tito's system allowed for small businesses. This experience with market economy benefited Yugoslavs when Eastern Europe's communist regimes eventually fell. And even during the communist era, Yugoslavia remained a popular tourist destination, keeping its standards more in line with the West than the Soviet states.

Things Fall Apart

With Tito's death in 1980, Yugoslavia's six constituent republics gained more autonomy, with a rotating presidency. But before long, the delicate union Tito had held together began to unravel. In the late 1980s, Serbian politician Slobodan Milošević took advantage of ethnic-motivated conflicts in the province of Kosovo to become president of Serbia and grab more centralized power. Other republics (especially Slovenia and Croatia) feared that he would gut their nation to create a "Greater Serbia," instead of a friendly coalition of diverse Yugoslav republics. During the next decade, Yugoslavia broke apart, with much bloodshed.

The Slovene Secession

Slovenia was the first Yugoslav republic to hold free elections, in the spring of 1990. The voters wanted the communists out—and their own independent nation. Along with being the most ethnically homogeneous of the Yugoslav nations, Slovenia was also the most Western-oriented, most prosperous, and most geographically isolated—so secession just made sense. But that didn't mean that there was no violence.

After months of stockpiling weapons, Slovenia closed its borders and declared independence from Yugoslavia on June 25, 1991. Belgrade sent in the Yugoslav National Army to take control of Slovenia's borders with Italy and Austria, figuring that whoever controlled the borders had a legitimate claim on sovereignty. Fighting broke out around these borders. Because the Yugoslav National Army was made up of soldiers from all republics, many Slovenian soldiers found themselves fighting their own countrymen. (The army had cut off communication between these conscripts and the home front, so they didn't know what was going on—and often didn't realize they were fighting their friends and neighbors until they were close enough to see them.)

Slovenian civilians bravely entered the fray, blockading the Yugoslav barracks with their own cars and trucks. Most of the Yugoslav soldiers—now trapped—were young and inexperienced, and were terrified of the ragtag (but relentless) Slovenian militia even though their own resources were far superior.

After 10 days of fighting and fewer than a hundred deaths, Belgrade relented. The Slovenes stepped aside and allowed the Yugoslav National Army to take all of the weapons with them back into Yugoslavia, and destroy all remaining military installations. When the Yugoslav National Army had cleared out, they left the Slovenes with their freedom.

The Croatian Conflict

In April of 1990, a historian named Franjo Tuđman—and his highly nationalistic, right-wing party, the HDZ (Croatian Democratic Union)—won Croatia's first free elections (for more on Tuđman, see page 576). Like the Slovenian reformers, Tuđman and the HDZ wanted more autonomy from Yugoslavia. But Tuđman's methods were more extreme than that of the gently progressive Slovenes. Tuđman immediately invoked the spirit of the last group that led an "independent" Croatia—the Ustaše, who had ruthlessly run Croatia's puppet government under the Nazis. Tuđman reintroduced the Ustaše's red-and-white checkerboard flag and their currency (the *kuna*). The 600,000 Serbs living in Croatia, mindful of their grandparents who had been massacred by the Ustaše, saw the writing on the wall and began to rise up.

The first conflicts were in the Serb-dominated Croatian city of Knin. Among Tuđman's reforms was the decree that all of Croatia's policemen wear the same uniform, which bore a striking resemblance to Nazi-era Ustaše uniforms. Infuriated by this slap in the face, and inspired by Slobodan Milošević's rhetoric, Serb police officers in Knin refused. Over the next few months, tense negotiations ensued. Serbs from Knin and elsewhere began the so-called "tree trunk revolution"—blocking important tourist roads to the coast with logs and other barriers. Meanwhile, the Croatian government—after being denied support from the United States—illegally purchased truckloads of guns from Hungary. Tensions escalated, and the first shots of the conflict were fired on Easter Sunday of 1991 at Plitvice Lakes National Park, between Croatian policemen and Serb irregulars from Knin.

By the time Croatia declared its independence (on June 25, 1991—the same day as Slovenia), it was already embroiled in the beginnings of a bloody war. Croatia's more than half-million Serb residents, nervous about their rights and backed by the Serbian-dominated Yugoslav Army, immediately declared their own independence from Croatia. The Yugoslav National Army swept in, supposedly to keep the peace between Serbs and Croats—but it soon became obvious that they were there to support the Serbs. The ill-prepared Croatian resistance, made up mostly of policemen and a few soldiers who defected from the Yugoslav National Army, were quickly overwhelmed. The Serbs gained control over a large swath of inland Croatia, mostly around the Bosnian border (including Plitvice) and in Croatia's inland panhandle (the region of Slavonia). They called this territory—about a quarter of Croatia—the **Republic of Serbian Krajina** (*krajina* means "border"). This new "country" (hardly recognized by any other nations) minted its own money and had its own army, much to the consternation of Croatia—which was now worried about the safety of Croats living in Krajina.

As the Serbs advanced, hundreds of thousands of Croats fled to the coast and lived as refugees in resort hotels. The Serbs began a campaign of ethnic cleansing, systematically removing Croats from their territory—often by murdering them. The bloodiest siege was at the town of **Vukovar,** which the Yugoslav army surrounded and shelled relentlessly for three months. At the end of the siege, thousands of Croat soldiers and civilians mysteriously disappeared. Many of these people were later discovered in mass graves; hundreds are still missing, and bodies are still continually being found. In a surprise move, Serbs also attacked the tourist capital of **Dubrovnik** (see page 596). By early 1992, both Croatia and the Republic of Serbian Krajina had established their borders, and a tense ceasefire fell over the region.

The standoff lasted until 1995, when the now well-equipped Croatian Army retook the Serbian-occupied areas in a series of two offensives—**"Lightning"** *(Blijesak),* in the northern part of the country, and **"Storm"** *(Oluja)*, farther south. Some Croats retaliated for earlier ethnic cleansing by doing much of the same to Serbs—torturing them, killing them, and dynamiting their homes. Croatia quickly established the borders that exist today, and the Erdut Agreement brought peace to the region—but most of the 600,000 Serbs who once lived in Croatia/Krajina were forced into Serbia or were killed. Today, only a few thousand Serbs remain in Croatia. While Serbs have long since been legally invited back to their ancestral Croatian homes, few have returned—afraid of the "welcome" they might receive from the Croat neighbors who killed their relatives or blew up their houses just a few years ago.

The War in Bosnia-Herzegovina

Bosnia-Herzegovina declared its independence from Yugoslavia four months after Croatia and Slovenia did. But Bosnia-Herzegovina was always at the crossroads of Balkan culture, and therefore even more diverse than Croatia—predominantly Muslim Bosniaks (mostly in the cities), but also with large Serb and Croat populations (often farmers), as well as Albanian Kosovars.

In the spring of 1992, Serbs within Bosnia-Herzegovina (with the support of Serbia) began a campaign of ethnic cleansing against the Bosniaks and Croats. Before long, the Croats did the same against the Serbs. A three-way war (between the Bosniaks, Serbs, and Croats) raged for years, as former neighbors turned their guns on each other, proud and beautiful cities like Sarajevo and Mostar were turned to rubble, and people throughout Bosnia-Herzegovina lived in a state of constant terror. Through it all, the United Nations Protection Force (UNPROFOR)—dubbed "Smurfs" both for their light-blue helmets and for their ineffectiveness—exercised their limited authority to try to prevent atrocities. This ugly situation was brilliantly parodied in the film *No Man's Land* (which won the Oscar for Best Foreign Film in 2002), a very dark comedy about the absurdity of the Bosnian war.

Finally, in 1995, the Dayton Peace Accords carefully divided Bosnia-Herzegovina among the different ethnicities. Today, Bosnia-Herzegovina continues to work on its tenuous peace, rebuild its devastated country, and bring its infrastructure up to its neighbors' standards.

Kosovo

The ongoing Yugoslav crisis finally reached its peak in the Serbian province of Kosovo. After years of poor treatment by the Serbs, Kosovars rebelled in 1998. The Yugoslav National Army moved in, and in March 1999, they began a campaign of ethnic cleansing. Thousands of Kosovars were murdered, and hundreds of thousands fled into Albania and Macedonia. NATO planes, under the command of U.S. General and Supreme Allied Commander Wesley Clark, bombed Serb positions for two months, forcing the Serb army to leave Kosovo in the summer of 1999.

The Fall of Milošević

After years of bloody conflicts, Serbian public opinion had decisively swung against their president. The transition began gradually in early 2000, spearheaded by Otpor and other nonviolent, grassroots, student-based opposition movements. These organizations used clever PR strategies to gain support and convince Serbians that real change was possible. As anti-Milošević sentiments gained momentum, opposing political parties banded together and got behind one candidate, Vojislav Koštunica. Public support for Koštunica mounted, and when the arrogant Milošević called an early election in September 2000, he was soundly defeated. Though Milošević tried to claim that the election results were invalid, determined Serbs streamed into their capital, marched on their parliament, and—like the Czechs and Slovaks a decade before—peacefully took back their nation.

The nation of "Yugoslavia" no longer exists, having been officially renamed "Serbia and Montenegro," which are the only two republics that remain in the union of South Slavs. Though the Montenegrins have wanted independence, Serbia has made concessions to keep the nations loosely united. While they share an army, each country has its own government and currency (Montenegro officially uses the euro, even though it's not in the EU).

Finding Their Way:
The Former Yugoslav Republics

Today, Slovenia and Croatia are as stable as Western Europe, Bosnia-Herzegovina is slowly putting itself back together, and an ailing Slobodan Milošević is on trial for war crimes in The Hague.

It's important to remember that there were no "good guys" and no "bad guys" in these wars—just a lot of ugliness on all sides. If there were any victims, they were the Muslim Bosniaks and the Kosovars—but even they were not blameless. When considering specifically the war between the Croats and the Serbs, it's tempting for Americans to take Croatia's "side"—because we saw them in the role of victims first; because they're Catholic, so they seem more "like us" than the Orthodox Serbs; and because we admire their striving for an independent nation. But in the streets and the trenches, it was never that clear-cut. When Croatians retook the Serb-occupied areas in 1995, they were every bit as brutal as the Serbs had been a few years before. Both sides resorted to ethnic cleansing, both sides had victims, and both sides had victimizers.

Perhaps the only "easy" villains in this conflict were Serbian President Slobodan Milošević and Croatian President Franjo Tuđman. As Milošević's trial in The Hague drags on (and on... and on...), information continually emerges that makes these two leaders out to be even more ruthless than once thought. It's increasingly clear that Tuđman and Milošević secretly orchestrated the whole brutal war in close association with each other, using their citizens as pawns in a giant war game. (It seems their ultimate plan was to partition Bosnia-Herzegovina between their newly independent countries, much as Hitler and Stalin secretly plotted to divide Poland.)

It's easy for us to simply blame these conflicts on some deep-seated, inevitable cultural hatred among the Yugoslav ethnic groups. This is an oversimplification, and ignores the fact that Serbs, Croats, Bosniaks, and Kosovars coexisted more or less peacefully and happily during the Tito era. While some long-standing tensions and misunderstandings did exist, it wasn't until Milošević and Tuđman expertly colluded to manipulate them that the country fell into war. By vigorously fanning the embers of ethnic grudges, and carefully controlling media coverage of the escalating violence, these two leaders turned a healthy political debate into a holocaust.

Tension still exists throughout the former Yugoslavia—especially areas that were most war-torn. When Serbs or Croats encounter other Yugoslavs in their travels, they immediately evaluate each other's accent to determine: Are they one of us, or one of them?

But, with time, these hard feelings are fading. The younger generations don't look back—teenaged Slovenes no longer learn Serbo-Croatian, can't imagine not living in an independent little country, and get bored (and a little irritated) when their old-fashioned parents wax nostalgic about the days of a united Yugoslavia. A middle-aged Slovene friend of mine thinks fondly of his months of compulsory service in the Yugoslav National Army, when his unit was made up of Slovenes, Croats, Serbs, Bosniaks, Macedonians, and Montenegrins—all of them countrymen, and all good friends. To these young Yugoslavs, minor ethnic differences didn't matter. He still often visits with his army buddy from Dubrovnik—600 miles away, not long ago part of the same nation—and wishes there had been a way to keep it all together. But he says, optimistically, "I look forward to the day when the other former Yugoslav republics also join the European Union. Then, in a way, we will all be united once again."

APPENDIX

Let's Talk Telephones

To make international calls, you need to break the codes: the international access codes and country codes (see below). For specifics on making local, long-distance, and international calls, please see the "European Calling Chart" in this Appendix. You'll find more information on telephones in the Introduction on page 34.

Country Codes

After you've dialed the international access code (011 if you're calling from the U.S. or Canada; 00 if you're calling from Europe), dial the code of the country you're calling.

Austria—43
Belgium—32
Britain—44
Canada—1
Croatia—385
Czech Rep.—420
Denmark—45
Estonia—372
Finland—358
France—33
Germany—49
Gibraltar—350
Greece—30
Ireland—353

Italy—39
Morocco—212
Netherlands—31
Norway—47
Poland—48
Portugal—351
Slovakia—421
Slovenia—386
Spain—34
Sweden—46
Switzerland—41
Turkey—90
U.S.A.—1

U.S. Embassies

Austria: Boltzmanngasse 16, Vienna, tel. 01/313-390, www.usembassy.at

European Calling Chart

Just smile and dial, using this key:
AC = Area Code, LN = Local Number.

European Country	Calling long distance within ...	Calling from the U.S.A./ Canada to ...	Calling from a European country to ...
Austria	AC + LN	011 + 43 + AC (without the initial zero) + LN	00 + 43 + AC (without the initial zero) + LN
Belgium	LN	011 + 32 + LN (without initial zero)	00 + 32 + LN (without initial zero)
Britain	AC + LN	011 + 44 + AC (without initial zero) + LN	00 + 44 + AC (without initial zero) + LN
Croatia	AC + LN	011 + 385 + AC (without initial zero) + LN	00 + 385 + AC (without initial zero) + LN
Czech Republic	LN	011 + 420 + LN	00 + 420 + LN
Denmark	LN	011 + 45 + LN	00 + 45 + LN
Finland	AC + LN	011 + 358 + AC (without initial zero) + LN	00 + 358 + AC (without initial zero) + LN
France	LN	011 + 33 + LN (without initial zero)	00 + 33 + LN (without initial zero)
Germany	AC + LN	011 + 49 + AC (without initial zero) + LN	00 + 49 + AC (without initial zero) + LN
Greece	LN	011 + 30 + LN	00 + 30 + LN
Hungary	06 + AC + LN	011 + 36 + AC + LN	00 + 36 + AC + LN
Ireland	AC + LN	011 + 353 + AC (without initial zero) + LN	00 + 353 + AC (without initial zero) + LN
Italy	LN	011 + 39 + LN	00 + 39 + LN

European Country	Calling long distance within ...	Calling from the U.S.A./ Canada to ...	Calling from a European country to ...
Netherlands	AC + LN	011 + 31 + AC (without initial zero) + LN	00 + 31 + AC (without initial zero) + LN
Norway	LN	011 + 47 + LN	00 + 47 + LN
Poland	AC + LN	011 + 48 + AC (without initial zero) + LN	00 + 48 + AC (without initial zero) + LN
Portugal	LN	011 + 351 + LN	00 + 351 + LN
Slovakia	AC + LN	011 + 421 + AC (without initial zero) + LN	00 + 421 + AC (without initial zero) + LN
Slovenia	AC + LN	011 + 386 + AC (without initial zero) + LN	00 + 386 + AC (without initial zero) + LN
Spain	LN	011 + 34 + LN	00 + 34 + LN
Sweden	AC + LN	011 + 46 + AC (without initial zero) + LN	00 + 46 + AC (without initial zero) + LN
Switzerland	LN	011 + 41 + LN (without initial zero)	00 + 41 + LN (without initial zero)
Turkey	AC (if no initial zero is included, add one) + LN	011 + 90 + AC (without initial zero) + LN	00 + 90 + AC (without initial zero) + LN

- The instructions above apply whether you're calling a fixed phone or mobile phone.
- The international access codes (the first numbers you dial when making an international call) are 011 if you're calling from the U.S.A./Canada, or 00 if you're calling from anywhere in Europe.
- To call the U.S.A. or Canada from Europe, dial 00, then 1 (the country code for the U.S.A. and Canada), then the area code and number. In short, 00 + 1 + AC + LN = Hi, Mom!

Croatia: Ulica Thomasa Jeffersona 2, Zagreb, tel. 01/661-2200, consular services tel. 01/661-2300, www.usembassy.hr
Czech Republic: Tržiště 15, Prague, tel. 257-530-663, www.usembassy.cz
Hungary: Szabadság tér 12, Budapest, tel. 1/475-4400, after hours tel. 1/475-4703 or 1/475-4924, www.usembassy.hu
Poland: Aleja Ujazdowskie 29/31, Warsaw, tel. 022/504-2000, www.usinfo.pl; also a U.S. Consulate in Kraków at ulica Stolarska 9, tel. 012/424-5100, fax 012/424-5103
Slovakia: Bratislava, tel. 02/5443-3338, www.usis.sk
Slovenia: Prešernova 31, Ljubljana, tel. 01/200-5500, fax 01/200-5555, www.usembassy.si

Eastern European Festivals and Holidays in 2006
Note that this isn't a complete list; holidays strike without warning.

Jan 1	New Year's Day, all countries
Jan 6	Epiphany, Poland and Croatia
Feb 8	National Day of Culture, Slovenia (celebrates Slovenian culture and national poet France Prešeren)
March 15	National Day, Hungary (celebrates 1848 Revolution)
March 17–April 2	Budapest Spring Festival, Budapest, Hungary (www.festivalcity.hu)
Mid-March	Ski Flying World Championships, Planica, Slovenia (www.fis-ski.com)
April 16	Easter Sunday, all countries
April 17	Easter Monday, all countries
April 27	National Resistance Day, Slovenia
May 1	Labor Day, all countries
May 3	Constitution Day, Poland (celebrates Europe's first constitution)
May 8	Liberation Day, Czech Republic
1 week in May	Juvenalia, Kraków, Poland (student festival, costumes, and parties)
Mid-May–early June	"Prague Spring" Music Festival, Prague, Czech Republic (www.festival.cz)
Late May	Dance Week Festival, Zagreb, Croatia (www.danceweekfestival.com)
Late May	Return to the Age of Marco Polo Festival, Korčula, Croatia (concerts, folk dancing, parades)
June 5	Whitmonday, Hungary
June 15	Corpus Christi, Poland and Croatia

2006

JANUARY						
S	M	T	W	T	F	S
1	2	3	4	5	6	7
8	9	10	11	12	13	14
15	16	17	18	19	20	21
22	23	24	25	26	27	28
29	30	31				

FEBRUARY						
S	M	T	W	T	F	S
			1	2	3	4
5	6	7	8	9	10	11
12	13	14	15	16	17	18
19	20	21	22	23	24	25
26	27	28				

MARCH						
S	M	T	W	T	F	S
			1	2	3	4
5	6	7	8	9	10	11
12	13	14	15	16	17	18
19	20	21	22	23	24	25
26	27	28	29	30	31	

APRIL						
S	M	T	W	T	F	S
						1
2	3	4	5	6	7	8
9	10	11	12	13	14	15
16	17	18	19	20	21	22
23/30	24	25	26	27	28	29

MAY						
S	M	T	W	T	F	S
	1	2	3	4	5	6
7	8	9	10	11	12	13
14	15	16	17	18	19	20
21	22	23	24	25	26	27
28	29	30	31			

JUNE						
S	M	T	W	T	F	S
				1	2	3
4	5	6	7	8	9	10
11	12	13	14	15	16	17
18	19	20	21	22	23	24
25	26	27	28	29	30	

JULY						
S	M	T	W	T	F	S
						1
2	3	4	5	6	7	8
9	10	11	12	13	14	15
16	17	18	19	20	21	22
23/30	24/31	25	26	27	28	29

AUGUST						
S	M	T	W	T	F	S
		1	2	3	4	5
6	7	8	9	10	11	12
13	14	15	16	17	18	19
20	21	22	23	24	25	26
27	28	29	30	31		

SEPTEMBER						
S	M	T	W	T	F	S
					1	2
3	4	5	6	7	8	9
10	11	12	13	14	15	16
17	18	19	20	21	22	23
24	25	26	27	28	29	30

OCTOBER						
S	M	T	W	T	F	S
1	2	3	4	5	6	7
8	9	10	11	12	13	14
15	16	17	18	19	20	21
22	23	24	25	26	27	28
29	30	31				

NOVEMBER						
S	M	T	W	T	F	S
			1	2	3	4
5	6	7	8	9	10	11
12	13	14	15	16	17	18
19	20	21	22	23	24	25
26	27	28	29	30		

DECEMBER						
S	M	T	W	T	F	S
					1	2
3	4	5	6	7	8	9
10	11	12	13	14	15	16
17	18	19	20	21	22	23
24/31	25	26	27	28	29	30

June	Dance Prague, Czech Republic (modern dance festival, www.tanecpha.cz)
Mid-June	Celebration of the Rose, Český Krumlov, Czech Republic (medieval festival, music, theater, dance, knights' tournament)
June 22	Antifascist Struggle Day, Croatia
June 25	National Day, Slovenia; Statehood Day, Croatia
Late June	Budapest Farewell, Budapest, Hungary (celebrates last Soviet soldier leaving; parades, costumes, music)
Late June–early July	Jewish Culture Festival, Kraków, Poland (www.jewishfestival.pl)
July 5	Sts. Cyril and Methodius Day, Czech Republic

July 6	Jan Hus Day, Czech Republic
July 10–Aug 25	Dubrovnik Summer Festival, Croatia (www.dubrovnik-festival.hr)
July	"Budafest" Summer Opera and Ballet Festival, Budapest, Hungary (www.viparts.hu)
Early July–late Aug	Ljubljana Summer Festival, Slovenia (www.festival-lj.si)
Mid-July	Visegrád International Palace Games, Visegrád, Hungary (archery, jousting, medieval arts; www.palotajatekok.hu)
Mid-July–mid-Aug	Summer Festival, Split, Croatia (music and theater; www.splitsko-ljeto.hr)
Mid-July–late Aug	International Music Festival, Český Krumlov, Czech Republic (www.czechmusicfestival.com)
Late July	International Folklore Festival, Zagreb, Croatia (costumes, songs, dances from all over Croatia; www.msf.hr)
Late July or early Aug	Formula 1 races, Budapest, Hungary (www.hungaroinfo.com/formel1)
Aug 5	National Thanksgiving Day, Croatia
Aug 15	Assumption of Mary, Poland, Slovenia, and Croatia
Mid-Aug	Sziget Festival, Budapest, Hungary (rock and pop music, www.sziget.hu)
Aug 20	Constitution Day and St. Stephen's Day, Hungary (fireworks, celebrations)
Late Aug	Jazz at Summer's End Festival, Český Krumlov, Czech Republic
Late Aug–early Sept	Jewish Summer Festival, Budapest, Hungary (www.jewishfestival.hu)
Early Sept	Marco Polo Naval Battle Reenactment, Korčula, Croatia
Mid-Sept–early Oct	Prague Autumn Music Festival, Czech Republic (www.pragueautumn.cz)
Sept 28	St. Wenceslas Day, Czech Republic (celebrates national patron saint and Czech statehood)
Late Sept	Warsaw Autumn, Poland (contemporary music festival, www.warsaw-autumn.art.pl)

Oct 23	Republic Day, Hungary (remembrances of 1956 Uprising)
Oct 28	Independence Day, Czech Republic
Oct 31	Reformation Day, Slovenia
Late Oct	Budapest Autumn Festival, Budapest, Hungary (music, www.festivalcity.hu)
Nov 1	All Saints' Day, Poland, Slovenia, and Croatia (religious festival, some closures)
Nov 11	Independence Day, Poland; St. Martin's Day (official first day of wine season), Slovenia and Croatia
Nov 17	Velvet Revolution Anniversary, Czech Republic
Dec 5	St. Nicholas Eve, Prague, Czech Republic (St. Nick gives gifts to children in town square)
Dec 25	Christmas Day, all countries
Dec 26	Boxing Day, Hungary; Independence Day, Slovenia; St. Stephen's Day, Croatia
Dec 31	St. Sylvester's Day, Prague, Czech Republic (fireworks)

Numbers and Stumblers

- Europeans write a few of their numbers differently than we do: 1 = 1, 4 = 4, 7 = 7. Learn the difference or miss your train.
- Europeans write dates as day/month/year (Christmas is 25/12/06).
- Commas are decimal points, and decimals are commas. A dollar and a half is 1,50. There are 5.280 feet in a mile.
- When counting with fingers, start with your thumb. If you hold up your first finger to request one item, you'll probably get two.
- What we Americans call the second floor of a building is the first floor in Europe.
- Europeans keep the left "lane" open for passing on escalators and moving sidewalks. Keep to the right.

Climate

Here is a list of average temperatures (1st line—average daily low; 2nd line—average daily high; 3rd line—days of rain). This can be helpful in planning your itinerary, but I have never found European weather to be particularly predictable, and these charts ignore humidity.

	J	F	M	A	M	J	J	A	S	O	N	D
AUSTRIA • Vienna
	25°	28°	30°	42°	50°	56°	60°	59°	53°	44°	37°	30°
	34°	38°	47°	58°	67°	73°	76°	75°	68°	56°	45°	37°
	15	14	13	13	13	14	13	13	10	13	14	15
CROATIA • Dubrovnik
	42°	43°	57°	52°	58°	65°	69°	69°	64°	57°	51°	46°
	53°	55°	58°	63°	70°	78°	83°	82°	77°	69°	62°	56°
	13	13	11	10	10	6	4	3	7	11	16	15
CZECH REPUBLIC • Prague
	23°	24°	30°	38°	46°	52°	55°	55°	49°	41°	33°	27°
	31°	34°	44°	54°	64°	70°	73°	72°	65°	53°	42°	34°
	13	11	10	11	13	12	13	12	10	13	12	13
HUNGARY • Budapest
	25°	28°	35°	44°	52°	58°	62°	60°	53°	44°	38°	30°
	34°	39°	50°	62°	71°	78°	82°	81°	74°	61°	47°	39°
	13	12	11	11	13	13	10	9	7	10	14	13
POLAND • Kraków
	22°	22°	30°	38°	48°	54°	58°	56°	49°	42°	33°	28°
	32°	34°	45°	55°	67°	72°	76°	73°	66°	56°	44°	37°
	16	15	12	15	12	15	16	15	12	14	15	16
SLOVENIA • Ljubljana
	25°	25°	32°	40°	48°	54°	57°	57°	51°	43°	36°	30°
	36°	41°	50°	60°	68°	75°	80°	78°	71°	59°	47°	39°
	13	11	11	13	16	16	12	12	10	14	15	15

Temperature Conversion: Fahrenheit and Celsius

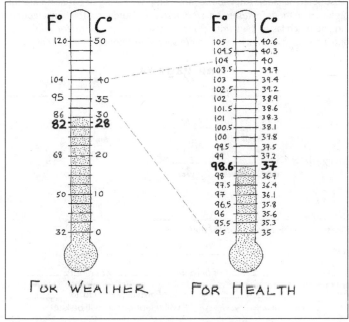

F°	C°
120	50
104	40
95	35
86	30
82	**28**
68	20
50	10
32	0

F°	C°
105	40.6
104.5	40.3
104	40
103.5	39.7
103	39.4
102.5	39.2
102	38.9
101.5	38.6
101	38.3
100.5	38.1
100	37.8
99.5	37.5
99	37.2
98.6	**37**
98	36.7
97.5	36.4
97	36.1
96.5	35.8
96	35.6
95.5	35.3
95	35

FOR WEATHER   FOR HEALTH

Europe takes its temperature using the Celsius scale, while we opt for Fahrenheit. For weather, remember that 28°C is 82°F—perfect. For health, 37°C is just right.

Metric Conversion (approximate)

1 inch = 25 millimeters	32° F = 0° C
1 foot = 0.3 meter	82° F = about 28° C
1 yard = 0.9 meter	1 ounce = 28 grams
1 mile = 1.6 kilometers	1 kilogram = 2.2 pounds
1 centimeter = 0.4 inch	1 quart = 0.95 liter
1 meter = 39.4 inches	1 square yard = 0.8 square meter
1 kilometer = 0.62 mile	1 acre = 0.4 hectare

Making Your Hotel Reservation

Most hotel managers know basic "hotel English." Faxing or e-mailing are the preferred methods for reserving a room. They're more accurate than telephoning and much faster than writing a letter. Use this handy form for your fax or find it online at www.ricksteves.com/reservation. Photocopy and fax away.

One-Page Fax

To: _____ @ _____
        hotel   *fax*

From: _____@ _____
           name   *fax*

Today's date: _____ / _____ / _____
                  day   *month*   *year*

Dear Hotel _____ ,
Please make this reservation for me:

Name: _____

Total # of people:_____ # of rooms: _____ # of nights: _____

Arriving: _____ / ____ / ____   My time of arrival (24-hr clock): _____
              day   *month* *year*   (I will telephone if I will be late)

Departing:____ / ____/____
               day *month* *year*

Room(s): Single _____Double ____Twin _____Triple ____ Quad_____

With: Toilet _____ Shower_____Bath _____ Sink only _____

Special needs: View____ Quiet ____ Cheapest ____ Ground Floor ____

Please fax, mail, or e-mail confirmation of my reservation, along with the type of room reserved and the price. Please also inform me of your cancellation policy. After I hear from you, I will quickly send my credit-card information as a deposit to hold the room. Thank you.

_____
Signature

_____
Name

_____
Address

_____
City   *State*   *Zip Code*   *Country*

_____
E-mail Address

INDEX

CREDITS

Contributor

Gene Openshaw

Gene is the co-author of eight Rick Steves books. For this book, he wrote material on Europe's art, history, and contemporary culture. When not traveling, Gene enjoys composing music, reco ering from his 1973 trip to Europe with Rick, and living everyday life with his wife and daughter.

Images

Front Matter

Title Page: Bled Island	Cameron Hewitt
1st Full-Page Color: Kraków, Poland— Wawel Cathedral	Cameron Hewitt
2nd Full-Page Color: Ljubljana, Slovenia	Cameron Hewitt
Czech Republic (full-page image): Prague— Charles Bridge	Cameron Hewitt
Prague: Vltava River, Charles Bridge, and Prague Castle	Cameron Hewitt
Český Krumlov: View of City	Dave Hoerlein
Slovakia (full-page image): Bratislava— St. Michael's Gate	Cameron Hewitt
Bratislava: Bratislava Castle	Cameron Hewitt
The Spiš Region: Spiš Castle	Cameron Hewitt
Poland (full-page image): Warsaw— Old Town Square	Cameron Hewitt
Kraków: Main Market Square	Cameron Hewitt
Auschwitz-Birkenau: Birkenau Guard Tower	Rick Steves
Warsaw: Castle Square and the Old Town	Rick Steves
Gdańsk: Artus Court on Ulica Długa	Cameron Hewitt
Pomerania, Malbork: Malbork Castle	Cameron Hewitt
Hungary (full-page image): Budapest— Széchenyi Baths	Cameron Hewitt
Budapest: Parliament	Rick Steves
The Danube Bend: View over the Danube Bend from Visegrád Citadel	Cameron Hewitt
Eger: Minorite Church and Eger Castle	Cameron Hewitt
Slovenia (full-page image): Soca River Valley near Kobarid	Cameron Hewitt
Ljubljana: Ljubljana Castle overlooking Prešeren Square	Cameron Hewitt
The Karst: Predjama Castle	Rick Steves
Piran: Breakwater	Rick Steves

continued next page

Images, *continued*

Start your trip at
www.ricksteves.com

Rick Steves' website is packed with over 3,000 pages of timely travel information. It's also your gateway to getting FREE monthly travel news from Rick— and more!

Free Monthly European Travel News

Fresh articles on Europe's most interesting destinations and happenings. Rick will even send you an e-mail every month (often direct from Europe) with his latest discoveries!

Timely Travel Tips

Rick Steves' best money-and-stress-saving tips on trip planning, packing, transportation, hotels, health, safety, finances, hurdling the language barrier…and more.

Travelers' Graffiti Wall

Candid advice and opinions from thousands of travelers on everything listed above, plus whatever topics are hot at the moment (discount flights, packing tips, scams…you name it).

Rick's Annual Guide to European Railpasses

The clearest, most comprehensive guide to the confusing array of railpass options out there, and how to choo-choose the railpass that best fits your itinerary and budget. Then you can order your railpass (and get a bunch of great freebies) online from us!

Great Gear at the Rick Steves Travel Store

Enjoy bargains on Rick's guidebooks, planning maps and TV series DVDs— and on his custom-designed carry-on bags, wheeled bags, day bags and light-packing accessories.

Rick Steves Tours

Every year more than 6,000 lucky travelers explore Europe on a Rick Steves tour. Learn more about our 30 different one-to-three-week itineraries, read uncensored feedback from our tour alums, and sign up for your dream trip online!

Rick on Radio and TV

Read the scripts and run clips from public television's "Rick Steves' Europe" and public radio's "Travel with Rick Steves."

Respect for Your Privacy

Ordering online from us is secure. When you buy something from us, join a tour, or subscribe to Rick's free monthly travel news e-mails, we promise to never share your name, information, or e-mail address with anyone else. You won't be spammed!

Have fun raising your Travel I.Q. at
www.ricksteves.com

Travel smart...carry on!

The latest generation of Rick Steves' carry-on travel bags is easily the best—benefiting from two decades of on-the-road attention to what really matters: maximum quality and strength; practical, flexible features; and no unnecessary frills. You won't find a better value anywhere!

Convertible, expandable, and carry-on-size:

Rick Steves' Back Door Bag $99

This is the same bag that Rick Steves lives out of for three months every summer. It's made of rugged water-resistant 1000 denier Cordura nylon, and best of all, it converts easily from a smart-looking suitcase to a handy backpack with comfortably-curved shoulder straps and a padded waistbelt.

This roomy, versatile 9" x 21" x 14" bag has a large 2600 cubic-inch main compartment, plus three outside pockets (small, medium and huge) that are perfect for often-used items. And the cinch-tight compression straps will keep your load compact and close to your back—not sagging like a sack of potatoes.

Wishing you had even more room to bring home souvenirs? Pull open the full-perimeter expando-zipper and its capacity jumps from 2600 to 3000 cubic inches. When you want to use it as a suitcase or check it as luggage (required when "expanded"), the straps and belt hide away in a zippered compartment in the back.

Attention travelers under 5'4" tall: This bag also comes in an inch-shorter version, for a compact-friendlier fit between the waistbelt and shoulder straps.

Convenient, expandable, and carry-on-size:

Rick Steves' Wheeled Bag $129

At 9" x 21" x 14" our sturdy Rick Steves' Wheeled Bag is rucksack-soft in front, but the rest is lined with a hard ABS-lexan shell to give maximum protection to your belongings. We've spared no expense on moving parts, splurging on an extra-long button-release handle and big, tough inline skate wheels for easy rolling on rough surfaces.

Wishing you had even more room to bring home souvenirs? Pull open the full-perimeter expando-zipper and its capacity jumps from 2600 to 3000 cubic inches.

Rick Steves' Wheeled Bag has exactly the same three-outside-pocket configuration as our Back Door Bag, plus a handy "add-a-bag" strap and full lining.

Our Back Door Bags and Wheeled Bags come in black, navy, blue spruce, evergreen and merlot.

For great deals on a wide selection of travel goodies, begin your next trip at the Rick Steves Travel Store!

Visit the Rick Steves Travel Store at
www.ricksteves.com

Rick Steves

More *Savvy*. More *Surprising*. More *Fun*.

COUNTRY GUIDES 2006

England
France
Germany & Austria
Great Britain
Ireland
Italy
Portugal
Scandinavia
Spain
Switzerland

CITY GUIDES 2006

Amsterdam, Bruges & Brussels
Florence & Tuscany
London
Paris
Prague & The Czech Republic
Provence & The French Riviera
Rome
Venice

BEST OF GUIDES

Best of Eastern Europe
Best of Europe

As the #1 authority on European travel, Rick gives you inside information on what to visit, where to stay, and how to get there—economically and hassle-free.

www.ricksteves.com

PHRASE BOOKS & DICTIONARIES

French
French, Italian & German
German
Italian
Portuguese
Spanish

MORE EUROPE FROM RICK STEVES

Easy Access Europe
Europe 101
Europe Through the Back Door
Postcards from Europe

RICK STEVES' EUROPE DVDs

All 43 Shows 2000-2005
Britain
Eastern Europe
France & Benelux
Germany, The Swiss Alps & Travel Skills
Ireland
Italy
Spain & Portugal

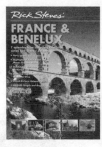

PLANNING MAPS

Britain & Ireland
Europe
France
Germany, Austria & Switzerland
Italy
Spain & Portugal

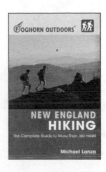
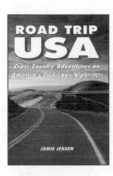